IRELAND

Rick Steves & Pat O'Connor

2013

CONTENTS

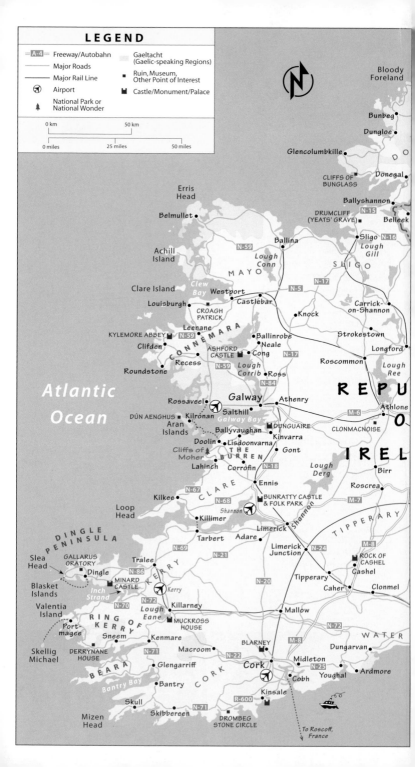

LEGEND

- ═ A-4 ═ Freeway/Autobahn
- Major Roads
- Major Rail Line
- ✈ Airport
- 🌲 National Park or National Wonder
- Gaeltacht (Gaelic-speaking Regions)
- ■ Ruin, Museum, Other Point of Interest
- 🏰 Castle/Monument/Palace

0 km — 50 km

0 miles — 25 miles — 50 miles

Bloody Foreland

Bunbeg

Dungloe

Glencolumbkille

CLIFFS OF BUNGLASS

Donegal

DO

Erris Head

Belmullet

Ballyshannon

Belleek

DRUMCLIFF (YEATS' GRAVE)

N-15

Ballina

N-59

Sligo N-16

Lough Gill

SLIGO

Lough Conn

MAYO

Achill Island

Clare Island

Clew Bay

Westport

Castlebar

Knock

Carrick-on-Shannon

N-5

N-17

Louisburgh

CROAGH PATRICK

Strokestown

Leenane

CONNEMARA

Ballinrobe

Neale

Cong

N-17

Longford

KYLEMORE ABBEY

N-59

ASHFORD CASTLE

Roscommon

Clifden

Recess

Lough Corrib

N-59

Ross

N-84

Lough Ree

Roundstone

REPU

Rossaveel ✈ Galway

Salthill

Athenry

Athlone

M-6

O

DÚN AENGHUS ■ Kilrónan

Galway Bay

DUNGUAIRE

CLONMACNOISE

IREL

Aran Islands

Ballyvaughan

Kinvarra

Doolin

Lisdoonvarna

Gont

THE BURREN

Cliffs of Moher 🌲

Lahinch

Corrofin

N-18

Lough Derg

Birr

Atlantic Ocean

Kilkee

CLARE

Ennis

Roscrea

N-67

N-68

BUNRATTY CASTLE & FOLK PARK

M-7

Loop Head

Killimer

Shannon ✈

Limerick

Shannon

TIPPERARY

Tarbert

Adare

Limerick Junction

M-8

DINGLE PENINSULA

N-69

Slea Head

GALLARUS ORATORY

Tralee

N-21

N-24

ROCK OF CASHEL

Cashel

Dingle

N-86

KERRY

N-20

Tipperary

Caher

Clonmel

Blasket Islands

MINARD CASTLE

Inch Strand

Kerry ✈

N-72

Valentia Island

N-70

Killarney

Lough Eane

Mallow

N-72

WATER

Port-magee

RING OF KERRY

MUCKROSS HOUSE

BLARNEY

Dungarvan

Skellig Michael

DERRYNANE HOUSE

Sneem

Kenmare

Macroom

N-22

M-8

Midleton

N-25

Ardmore

BEARA

Glengarriff

CORK

Cork ✈

Youghal

Bantry Bay

Bantry

Cobh

Kinsale

Skull

Skibbereen

R-600

DROMBEG STONE CIRCLE

Mizen Head

To Roscoff, France

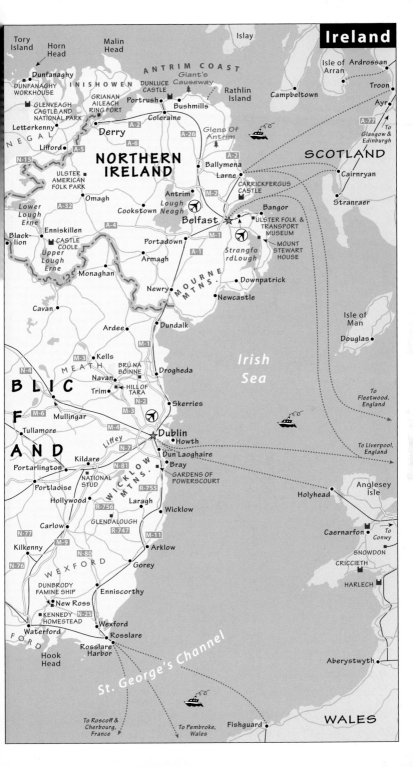

SIGHTS

1. Abbey Theatre
2. Book of Kells & Trinity Old Library
3. Chester Beatty Library
4. Christ Church Cathedral
5. Dublin Castle
6. Dublin City Hall
7. Dublin Writers' Museum
8. Dublinia
9. Duke Pub (Literary Pub Crawl)
10. Garden of Remembrance
11. General Post Office
12. Gogarty's Pub (Musical Pub Crawl)
13. To Guinness Storehouse & Kilmainham Gaol
14. Ha' Penny Bridge
15. Hugh Lane Gallery
16. James Joyce Cultural Centre
17. Little Museum of Dublin & City of a Thousand Welcomes
18. Merrion Square
19. National Gallery
20. National Leprechaun Museum
21. National Library
22. National Museum: Archaeology
23. To National Museum: Decorative Arts & History
24. National Museum: Natural History
25. Number 29 Georgian House
26. Old Jameson Distillery & Smithfield Village
27. St. Patrick's Cathedral
28. St. Stephen's Green

Transportation

29. To Airport & M-1 to Belfast
30. Busáras Central Bus Station
31. Connolly Station
32. To Heuston Station

LEGEND

- Pedestrian-Friendly Area
- Popular Shopping Area
- - - - DART Commuter Rail Line
- T - Red Line LUAS Tram with stops
- T - Green Line LUAS Tram with stops
- ■ Landmark or Point of Interest
- Tourist Information

0 _____ 250 m

0 _____ 250 yds

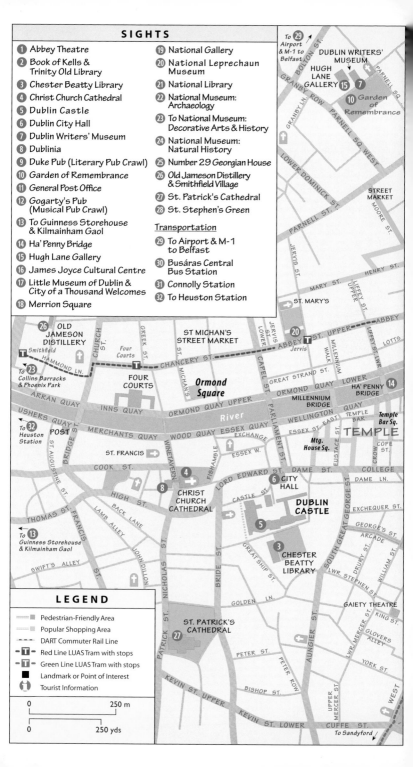

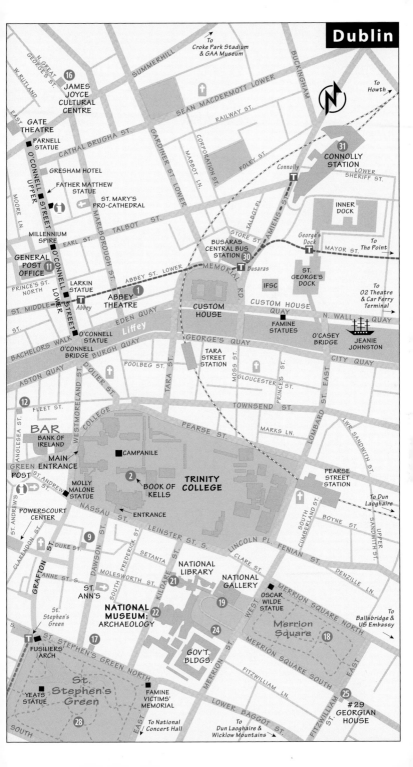

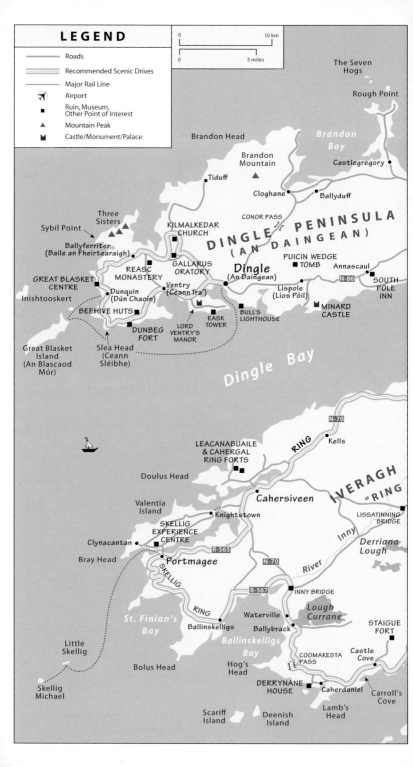

LEGEND

Roads	
Recommended Scenic Drives	
Major Rail Line	
✈	Airport
■	Ruin, Museum, Other Point of Interest
▲	Mountain Peak
⌂	Castle/Monument/Palace

0   10 km
0   5 miles

The Seven Hogs

Rough Point

Brandon Head

Brandon Bay

Castlegregory

Brandon Mountain ▲

Tiduff

Cloghane

Ballyduff

CONOR PASS

DINGLE PENINSULA (AN DAINGEAN)

Three Sisters

Sybil Point

Ballyferriter (Baile an Fheirtearaigh)

KILMALKEDAR CHURCH

PUICIN WEDGE TOMB

Annascaul

N-86

SOUTH POLE INN

REASC MONASTERY

GALLARUS ORATORY

Dingle (An Daingean)

GREAT BLASKET CENTRE

Inishtooskert

Dunquin (Dún Chaoin)

Ventry (Ceann Trá)

Lispole (Lios Póil)

MINARD CASTLE

BEEHIVE HUTS

LORD VENTRY'S MANOR

EASK TOWER

BULL'S LIGHTHOUSE

Great Blasket Island (An Blascaod Mór)

DUNBEG FORT

Slea Head (Ceann Sléibhe)

Dingle Bay

LEACANABUAILE & CAHERGAL RING FORTS

RING

N-70

Kells

Doulus Head

IVERAGH

Cahersiveen

"RING"

LISSATINNING BRIDGE

Valentia Island

SKELLIG EXPERIENCE CENTRE

Knightstown

R-565

Inny

Derriana Lough

Clynacantan

Bray Head

Portmagee

SKELLIG

RING

N-70

Inny River

Little Skellig

St. Finian's Bay

Ballinskelligs

RING

R-567

INNY BRIDGE

Waterville

Ballybrack

Lough Currane

STAIGUE FORT

Ballinskelligs Bay

COOMAKESTA PASS

Castle Cove

Bolus Head

Hog's Head

DERRYNANE HOUSE

Caherdaniel

Carroll's Cove

Skellig Michael

Scariff Island

Deenish Island

Lamb's Head

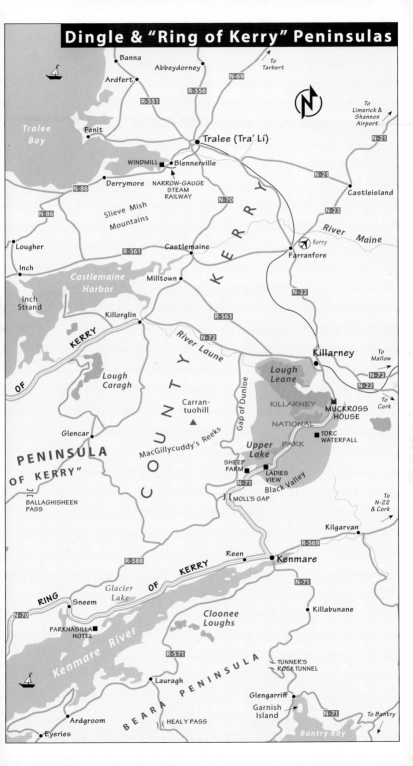

Dingle & "Ring of Kerry" Peninsulas

Ireland

You probably won't find the proverbial pot of gold in Ireland, but you will find plenty of treasure, starting with the engaging and feisty Irish people.

Belly up to the bar in a neighborhood pub and engage a local in conversation. Want to really get to know the Irish? Ask for directions. It's almost always a rich experience and a fast way to connect with locals. Nearby friends often chime in with additional tidbits that may or may not be useful, and soon it's a communal chitchat session.

That legendary Irish "gift of gab" has its roots in the  ancient Celtic culture. With no written language (until the arrival of Christianity), the ancient Celts passed their history, laws, and folklore verbally from generation to generation. Even today, most transactions come with an ample side-helping of friendly banter. As an Irishman once joked, "How can I know what I think until I hear what I say?"

The Irish love their proverbs and revere their past. According to an old Irish adage, "When God made time, he made a lot of it." Irish

history stretches back thousands of years, yet is as close as the mist-shrouded ruins around the next bend of a country road. Ireland is dusted with undisturbed prehistoric stone circles, burial mounds, standing stones, and table-like dolmens...some older than the pyramids, and all speckled with moss. While much of Europe has buried older cultures under new, Ireland still reveals its cultural bedrock, dating back to the time when our ancestors finally stopped hunting and gathering and began to build to last. It's a place to connect with your roots, even if you're not Irish.

Though a relatively small island (about the size of the state of Maine), Ireland has had a disproportionately large impact on the rest of the world. Geographically isolated in the damp attic of Dark Age Europe, Christian Irish monks

tended the flickering flame of literacy, then bravely reintroduced it to the barbaric Continent. Ireland later turned out some of modern literature's greatest authors. In the 1800s, great waves of Irish emigrants fled famine and colonial oppression, seeking new opportunities abroad and making their mark in the US, Canada, and Australia. And although peace now prevails in Northern Ireland, the conflict there long held the world's attention, with its volatile mix of religion and politics.

Politically, the Irish people are split between the Republic of Ireland to the south (with 4.5 million people and 80 percent of the land) and Northern Ireland (with 1.8 million people). Northern Ireland is a province of the United Kingdom—like Scotland or Wales—while the Republic is an independent nation with its own seat at the UN...stuck alphabetically between Iraq and Israel. The island is further quartered into four provinces (Leinster, Munster, Connaught, and Ulster) and 32 counties (26 in the Republic and 6 in the North), each with its own identity and regional pride.

This 300-mile-long, saucer-shaped island, ringed with some of Europe's most scenic coastal cliffs, is only 150 miles across at its wid-

est point—no matter where you go in Ireland, you're never more than 75 miles from the sea. Despite being as far north as Newfoundland, Ireland has a mild maritime climate, thanks to the Gulf Stream. Snowfall is rare and temporary here. Rainfall, on the other hand, ranges from more than 100 inches a year in soggy, boggy Connemara to about 30 inches a year in Dublin. Any time of year, bring rain gear. As Ireland's own Oscar Wilde once quipped, "There is no bad weather...only inappropriate clothing."

Republic of Ireland

Forget everything you learned from ads for Lucky Charms cereal or Irish Spring soap, and immerse yourself in authentic Ireland.

Passionate, poetic, and pugnacious...the Irish have confounded others throughout time. Queen Elizabeth I, as tough a British monarch as has ever graced the throne, once famously hissed in frustration that the Irish "were all Blarney" as she negotiated with the highly evasive Irish lord of Blarney Castle. An exasperated Sigmund Freud said, "The Irish are the only race whose insanities cannot be cured by psychoanalysis." And the Irish inspired the English poet G. K. Chesterton to write:

> *The great Gaels of Ireland*
> *The lord hath made them mad*
> *For all their wars are merry*
> *And all their songs are sad.*

The Irish seem born with a love of music. At social gatherings, everyone's ready to sing his or her "party piece." Performances are judged less by skill than by uninhibited sincerity or showmanship. Nearly every Irish household has some kind of musical instrument on a shelf or in a closet. And live music is a weekly (if not nightly) draw at any town pub worth its salt. Pub music ranges from traditional instrumentals (jigs and reels) to ballads (songs of tragic love lost or heroic deeds done) to contemporary sing-along

strummers. It's worth staying until the wee hours for the magical moment when a rare *sean nos* (Gaelic for "old style") lament is sung to

a hushed and attentive pub crowd.

Part of the fun of traveling in Ireland is getting an ear for how locals express themselves in English (sort of)— from the surprised distant relative who is "gobsmacked" (astounded) by your appearance, to the businessman in the pub who complains that the weak economy is utterly "banjaxed" (messed up).

You're most likely to hear the Irish Gaelic language (similar to but different from Scottish Gaelic, and—more distantly—Welsh) spoken in the Gaeltacht, the government-subsidized cultural preserve found mostly in far western

coastal regions. But less than 5 percent of the Irish are fluent in Gaelic, and school kids—who must pass rigorous exams to graduate—agonize over its complex grammar.

The Republic of Ireland tilts toward the US—both geographically and economically. Every Irish family seems to have a brother, niece, cousin, or uncle in America. About 50 million people claim Irish descent in North America alone. Irish immigrants brought with them to the US the first political organization for the downtrodden: the "green machine" grassroots voting blocks that came to dominate big-city politics in Boston, New York, and Chicago. To cozy up to these valuable votes, every politician wanted to be seen marching in the parade on St. Patrick's Day. Today, St. Patrick's Day is the most widely celebrated national feast day in the English-speaking world, and a particularly raucous four-day festival in Dublin.

During the "Celtic Tiger" boom years (1995-2007), American corporations saw big advantages in locating here, making Ireland an economic beachhead on European turf. Ireland's "Silicon Bog" is the European home to such big names as IBM, Intel, Microsoft, Apple, Facebook, and Google. Ireland's economic success (tarnished now due to the global recession and bank bailouts) was the model that Eastern European nations hoped to emulate when a number of them joined the European Union in 2004. The Irish are also big pharmaceutical producers: More Viagra is made in Ireland than in any other country...though the proudly virile Irish males claim it's all for export.

Other famous exports from the Republic of Ireland include rock and contemporary music (U2, Thin Lizzy, the Corrs, Sinéad O'Connor, Enya, The Swell Season—Glen Hansard and Markéta Irglová), traditional Irish music (the Chieftains, Dubliners), opera (The Irish Tenors and John McCormack), dance (Riverdance), trivia *(Guinness World Records*—see sidebar on page 85), crystal (Waterford), beer (Guinness), festivals (Halloween has Celtic roots), British military heroes (the Duke of Wellington), authors (Jonathan Swift, W. B. Yeats, James Joyce, George Bernard Shaw, Samuel Beckett, Oscar Wilde, and Frank McCourt), and actors (Colin Farrell, Jonathan Rhys Meyers, Richard Harris, Barry Fitzgerald, Gabriel Byrne, and Maureen O'Hara).

Until recently Ireland was one of the most ethnically homogenous nations on earth, but the Celtic Tiger economy changed all that, attracting thousands of Eastern Europeans (mostly Poles), Africans (mostly Nigerians), and South Americans (mostly Brazilians). The 2006 census found that 10 percent of Ireland's population had been born elsewhere.

That cultural exchange may have something to do with Ireland's appealing cuisine. At one time known only for its

poor imitation of bad British food, today's Irish cuisine has gone global. Expatriate chefs have come home with newly refined tastes, and immigrants have added a world of interesting flavors. Modern Irish cuisine is skillfully prepared with fresh local ingredients. Irish beef, lamb, and dairy products are among the EU's best. And there are streams full of trout and salmon and a rich ocean of fish and shellfish right offshore. While fish and potatoes remain staples, potatoes are often replaced with rice or pasta in many dishes.

Travelers on a budget will invariably encounter the Holy Trinity of pub grub: Irish stew, chicken curry, and fish-and-chips. Popular beer choices are Guinness (a dark stout), Smithwicks (an amber ale), and Harp (a golden lager). The most common spirit is triple-distilled Irish whiskey.

Sports in the Republic are dominated by the Gaelic Athletic Association (GAA; see sidebar on page 88), which operates Irish hurling and football (not to be confused with

soccer) leagues. Each county fields a team of skilled amateur players. The weekend sports heroes of each county are not professionals, they're talented athletes who are regular guys during the workweek—teachers, truck drivers, bakers, and the like. Horse racing and dog racing appeal to those who enjoy a wager. And it's hard to go 25 miles in Ireland without running into a golf course.

Most Irish claim to be Catholic, and shrines to the Virgin Mary still grace rural roadsides. But church atten-

dance has decreased dramatically over the past 30 years, due in part to child-abuse scandals at parochial schools. If not for the influx of newly arriving devout Catholic Poles, attendance would be even lower. Yet the

shamrock—used by St. Patrick to explain the concept of the Holy Trinity—remains the most recognizable symbol of Ireland. And the resilient Irish people maintain an unsinkable and optimistic belief in the future.

Northern Ireland

Northern Ireland is an underrated and often overlooked region that usually surprises visitors with its memorable scenery and friendly people.

An interesting hybrid of Irish and Scottish cultures, Northern Ireland is only 17 miles from Scotland at its closest point. The accents you'll hear in the North are distinctly different from their counterparts south of the border. When a Northern Irishman on a train asks to have a look at your "pepper," he means your "paper" (as in "newspaper").

Northern Ireland is part of the United Kingdom and occupies six of the nine counties of the ancient Irish province of Ulster. With a population just a bit larger than that of Phoenix, it's small enough to have one phone book for the entire province. Its coast boasts the alligator-skin volcanic geology of the Giant's Causeway and the lush Glens of Antrim, while its interior is dominated by rolling hills of pastoral serenity and Lough Neagh, the UK's biggest lake.

The people of the North generally fall into two categories: those who feel they're British (Unionists) and those who feel they're Irish (Nationalists). Those born in the North can choose which of the two passports they want. The Troubles—the decades-long conflict between Unionists and Nationalists, starting in the 1960s—were always more about nationality than religion. But the ugly ruptures of the past are healing. Both paramilitary camps have set aside their arms, and Northern Ireland is now statistically one of

the safest places in the western world.

The industrious people of Northern Ireland have a legendary work ethic. When they emigrated to the US, they became known as the Scotch-Irish and played a crucial role in our nation's founding. They were signers of our Declaration of Independence, a dozen of our presidents, and the ancestors of Davy Crockett and Mark Twain. They have a proclivity for making things that go. They've produced far-reaching inventions like Dunlop's first inflatable tire. The Shorts aircraft factory (in Belfast) built the Wright Brothers' first six aircraft for commercial sale and the world's first vertical take-off jet. The *Titanic* was the only flop of Northern Ireland's otherwise successful shipbuilding industry. The once-futuristic DeLorean sports car was made in Belfast.

Notable people from Northern Ireland include musicians Van Morrison and James Galway, and actors Liam Neeson and Kenneth Branagh. The North also produced Christian intellectual and writer C. S. Lewis, Victorian physicist Lord Kelvin, and soccer-star playboy George Best—who once famously remarked, "I spent most of my money on liquor and women...and the rest I wasted."

The Northern Irish have a good sense of humor and a long memory. Commercial pilots joke to their arriving passengers to set their watches to local time: 1690 (the date of the famous Battle of the Boyne).

About half of the people in Northern Ireland attend church weekly—significantly more than in the Republic (30 percent) or the rest of the UK (15 percent). Only in Northern Ireland can a union between a Christian man and woman of the same ethnicity and nationality be considered a "mixed marriage."

As in the Republic, sports are big in the North. In addition to football and hurling, you'll find some sports that are rare in the Republic—such as motorcycle racing and cricket. With close ties to Scotland, many Northern Irish fans follow the exploits of the soccer teams from

Glasgow—but which team you root for betrays which side of the tracks you come from. Those who cheer for Glasgow Celtic are Nationalist and Catholic; those waving banners for the Glasgow Rangers are Unionist and Protestant. In an effort to maintain peace, some pubs post signs on their doors banning patrons from wearing sports jerseys. Luckily, sports with no sectarian history are now being introduced, such as the Belfast Giants ice hockey team—a hit with both communities.

Northern Ireland has inextricable ties with the Republic. The town of Armagh, in central Northern Ireland, is the seat of both the Protestant and Catholic Archbishops of all Ireland (Republic and North). People from both countries cross the border on a daily basis to shop; there are no crossing restrictions along the 225-mile border. Dublin businessmen from the Republic have invested large sums in the rejuvenation of Belfast's once-derelict Titanic Quarter. And vacationers from the North often head over to the Republic's County Donegal for midsummer holidays. The former president of the Republic, Mary McAleese, was born in Belfast. The fact remains, however, that more citizens of the Republic have been to London than have visited the northern end of their own island.

No matter which side of the border you visit, today's Ireland is cosmopolitan, vibrant, business-savvy, and impressively globalized. The caricatures of tweed-clad bogtrotters and AK-47-armed terrorists have faded. But the seductive scenery and the culture as old as the stones remain. The Irish people have a worldwide reputation as talkative, athletic, musical, moody romantics with a quick laugh and a ready smile. Come join them.

INTRODUCTION

Flung onto the foggy fringe of the Atlantic pond like a mossy millstone, Ireland drips with mystery, drawing you in for a closer look and then surprising you. An old farmer cuts turf from the bog, while his son staffs the tech helpline for an international software firm. Buy them both a pint in a pub that's whirling with playful conversation and exhilarating traditional music. Pious, earthy, witty, brooding, proud, and unpretentious, Irish culture is an intoxicating potion to sip or slurp—as the mood strikes you.

This book breaks Ireland into its best big-city, small-town, and rural destinations. It gives you all the information and opinions necessary to wring the maximum value out of your limited time and money in each of these locations. Experiencing Irish culture, people, and natural wonders economically and hassle-free has been my goal for three decades of traveling, tour guiding, and travel writing. With this new edition, I pass on to you the lessons I've learned, updated for your trip in 2013.

The destinations covered in this book are balanced to include the most exciting big cities and great-to-be-alive-in small towns. Note that this book covers the highlights of the entire island, including Northern Ireland. While you'll find the predictable biggies—such as the Book of Kells, the Newgrange tomb (at Brú na Bóinne), and the Cliffs of Moher—I've also mixed in a healthy dose of Back Door intimacy (rope-bridge hikes, holy wells, and pubs with traditional Irish music). This book is selective. On a short trip, visiting both the monastic ruins of Glendalough and Clonmacnoise is redundant; I cover only the best—Glendalough. There are plenty of great manor-house gardens, but I recommend just the top one—the Gardens of Powerscourt.

The best is, of course, only my opinion. But after spending more than half of my adult life exploring and researching Europe,

INTRODUCTION

Map Legend

⅃	Viewpoint	✈	Airport	) ⟨	Tunnel
↟	Entrance	Ⓣ	Taxi Stand		Pedestrian Zone
🛈	Tourist Info	▣	Tram Stop	— — —	Railway
WC	Restroom	Ⓑ	Bus Stop	⋯⋯⋯	Ferry/Boat Route
◪	Castle	Ⓜ	Metro Stop	⊢—⊣	Tram
⛪	Church	Ⓟ	Parking	⟋⟋⟋⟋	Stairs
▪	Statue/Point of Interest	)(	Mtn. Pass	· · · · ·	Walk/Tour Route
		⬡	Park	- - - - -	Trail

Use this legend to help you navigate the maps in this book.

I've developed a sixth sense for what touches the traveler's imagination. The places featured in this book will give anyone the "gift of gab."

About This Book

Rick Steves' Ireland 2013 is a personal tour guide in your pocket. Better yet, it's actually two tour guides in your pocket: The co-author of this guidebook is Pat O'Connor. As you can tell from the lad's name, Pat has long had a travel passion for the Emerald Isle. He's the Ireland specialist and senior Ireland tour guide at my company, Rick Steves' Europe Through the Back Door. Together, Pat and I keep this book up-to-date and accurate (though for simplicity, from this point "we" will shed our respective egos and become "I").

This book is organized by destinations. Each destination is a mini-vacation on its own, filled with exciting sights, strollable towns, homey and affordable places to stay, and memorable places to eat. In the following chapters, you'll find these sections:

Planning Your Time suggests a schedule for how to best use your limited time.

Orientation includes specifics on public transportation, helpful hints, local tour options, easy-to-read maps, and tourist information.

Sights describes the top attractions and includes their cost and hours.

Self-Guided Walks take you through interesting neighborhoods, with a personal tour guide in hand.

Key to This Book

Updates
This book is updated every year, but things change. For the latest, visit www.ricksteves.com/update. For a valuable list of reports and experiences—good and bad—from fellow travelers, check www.ricksteves.com/feedback.

Abbreviations and Times
I use the following symbols and abbreviations in this book:
Sights are rated:

 Don't miss

▲▲ Try hard to see

▲ Worthwhile if you can make it

No rating Worth knowing about

Tourist information offices are abbreviated as **TI,** and bathrooms are **WC**s. To categorize accommodations, I use a **Sleep Code** (described on page 24).

Like Europe, this book uses the **24-hour clock.** It's the same through 12:00 noon, and then keeps going: 13:00, 14:00, and so on. For anything over 12, subtract 12 and add p.m. (14:00 is 2:00 p.m.).

When giving **opening times,** I include both peak season and off-season hours if they differ. So, if a museum is listed as "May-Oct daily 9:00-16:00," it should be open from 9 a.m. until 4 p.m. from the first day of May until the last day of October (but expect exceptions).

For **transit** or **tour departures,** I first list the frequency, then the duration. So, a train connection listed as "2/hour, 1.5 hours" departs twice each hour, and the journey lasts an hour and a half.

Sleeping describes my favorite hotels, from good-value deals to cushy splurges.

Eating serves up a range of options, from inexpensive pubs to fancy restaurants.

Connections outlines your options for traveling to destinations by train, bus, and plane, plus route tips for drivers.

Ireland: Past and Present, at the end of the book, gives you a quick overview of Irish history, a look at contemporary Ireland, a taste of the Irish language, and an Irish-Yankee vocabulary list.

The **appendix** is a traveler's tool kit, with telephone tips, useful phone numbers, transportation basics (on trains, buses, car rentals, driving, and flights), recommended books and films, a festival list, a climate chart, a handy packing checklist, and a hotel reservation form.

Browse through this book, choose your favorite destinations, and link them up. Then have a great trip! Traveling like a tempo-

INTRODUCTION

Top Destinations in Ireland

PORTRUSH &
ANTRIM COAST

DERRY
& COUNTY
DONEGAL

BELFAST

CONNEMARA
& COUNTY
MAYO

NEAR
DUBLIN

ARAN
ISLANDS

GALWAY

COUNTY CLARE
& THE BURREN

DUBLIN

DINGLE
PENINSULA

KILKENNY
& ROCK OF
CASHEL

WATERFORD
& COUNTY
WEXFORD

KENMARE &
"RING OF
KERRY"

KINSALE
& COBH

DCH

rary local, you'll get the absolute most out of every mile, minute, and dollar. As you visit places I know and love, I'm happy that you'll be meeting some of my favorite Irish people.

Planning

This section will help you get started on planning your trip—with advice on trip costs, when to go, and what you should know before you take off.

Travel Smart

Your trip to Ireland is like a complex play—easier to follow and really appreciate on a second viewing. While no one does the same trip twice to gain that advantage, reading this book in its entirety before your trip accomplishes much the same thing.

Design an itinerary that enables you to visit sights at the best possible times. Note holidays, specifics on sights, and days when sights are closed or most crowded (all topics covered in this book). To get between destinations smoothly, read the tips in this book's appendix on taking trains and buses, and renting a car and driving. A smart trip is a puzzle—a fun, doable, and worthwhile challenge.

Be sure to mix intense and relaxed periods in your itinerary. To maximize rootedness, minimize one-night stands. It's worth taking a long drive after dinner (or a train ride with a dinner picnic) to get settled in a town for two nights. Hotels are more likely to give a better price to someone staying more than one night. Every trip—and every traveler—needs slack time (laundry, picnics, people-watching, and so on). Pace yourself. Assume you will return.

Reread this book as you travel, and visit local TIs. Upon arrival in a new town, lay the groundwork for a smooth departure; write down (or print out from an online source) the schedule for the train or bus you'll take when you depart. Drivers can study the best route to their next destination.

Get online at Internet cafés or at your hotel, and carry a mobile phone (or use a phone card) to make travel plans: You can find tourist information, learn the latest on sights (special events, tour schedules, etc.), book tickets and tours, make reservations, reconfirm hotels, research transportation connections, check weather, and keep in touch with your loved ones.

Enjoy the friendliness of the Irish people. Connect with the culture. Set up your own quest for the best pub, traditional music, ruined castle, or ring fort. Slow down and be open to unexpected experiences. Ask questions—most locals are eager to point you in their idea of the right direction. Keep a notepad in your pocket for confirming prices, noting directions, and organizing your thoughts. Wear your money belt, learn the currency, and figure out how to estimate prices in dollars. Those who expect to travel smart, do.

Trip Costs

Five components make up your trip costs: airfare, surface transportation, room and board, sightseeing and entertainment, and shopping and miscellany.

Airfare: A basic round-trip flight from the US to Dublin can cost about $1,000-1,800 total, depending on where you fly from and when (it's cheaper in winter). Smaller budget airlines may provide bargain service from several European capitals to many cities in Ireland. Consider saving time and money in Europe by flying into one city and out of another—for instance, into Dublin and out of Paris.

Surface Transportation: For a three-week whirlwind trip of my recommended destinations, allow $300 per person for public transportation (trains and buses). For a three-week car rental, tolls, parking, gas, and full insurance, allow about $750 per person (based on two people sharing). Car rentals are cheapest if arranged from the US. Because Ireland's train system has gaps, you'll likely save money by simply buying train and bus tickets as you go, rather

Ireland at a Glance

These attractions are listed (as in this book) roughly clockwise around the island of Ireland.

Republic of Ireland

▲▲▲**Dublin** Bustling Irish capital, with fascinating tours (historical, musical, and literary), passionate rebel history (Kilmainham Gaol), treasured Dark Age gospels (Book of Kells), intricate Celtic artifacts (National Museum: Archaeology and History), and a rambunctious pub district (Temple Bar).

▲▲**Near Dublin** Great day-trip options: North to the Boyne Valley's ancient pre-Celtic burial mounds of Brú na Bóinne and majestic Norman castle of Trim, west to the green horse-racing pastures of the Irish National Stud, and south to the graceful Gardens of Powerscourt and evocative monastic ruins of Glendalough.

▲▲**Kilkenny and the Rock of Cashel** Best two destinations in Ireland's interior: the town of Kilkenny, with its narrow medieval lanes, cathedrals, and castle; and the Rock of Cashel, with its dramatic hilltop hodgepodge of church ruins overlooking the Plain of Tipperary.

▲**Waterford and County Wexford** Gritty historic port town with famous Waterford Crystal Visitor Centre, and the hinterland of early Norman invasions, with a huge lighthouse and the JFK ancestral farm.

▲▲**Kinsale and Cobh** County Cork's two quaint harbor towns: Gourmet capital Kinsale, guarded by squat Charles Fort, and emigration hub Cobh—the *Titanic*'s last stop.

▲▲**Kenmare and the Ring of Kerry** Colorful, tidy town and ideal base for side-stepping the throngs flocking to drive Ireland's most-famous scenic loop route.

▲▲▲**Dingle Peninsula** My favorite fishing village (a traditional Irish-music pub paradise), which serves as a launchpad for the gorgeous Slea Head loop drive (or bike ride), featuring a wealth of Celtic and early Christian sites.

▲▲**County Clare and the Burren** Ireland's rugged western fringe, with the take-your-breath-away Cliffs of Moher, stone landscape of the Burren, cozy trad music crossroads of Doolin, and handy Shannon Airport access from friendly Ennis.

▲**Galway** Energetic university city with thriving pedestrian street scene, great people-watching pubs, and the west coast's best base from which to reach the Burren, Aran Islands, and Connemara.

▲▲▲**Aran Islands** Three windswept, treeless limestone islands in the Atlantic, laced with a maze of angular rock walls, crowned by Iron Age ring forts, and inhabited by sparse villages of hardy fisher-folk.

▲▲**Connemara and County Mayo** Lushly green and hilly Irish outback of cottages, lakes, and holy peaks, dotted with photogenic settlements such as Cong, Kylemore Abbey, and leafy riverside Westport.

Northern Ireland
▲**Belfast** No-nonsense industrial revolution metropolis, with stirring sectarian political murals, grandly domed City Hall, sprawling Ulster Folk Park and Transport Museum, and the charming nearby Victorian seaside retreat of Bangor.

▲▲**Portrush and the Antrim Coast** Unpretentious beach resort of arcades and amusement park rides, a stone's throw from the geologic wonderland of the Giant's Causeway, dramatic cliff-edge ruins of Dunluce Castle, and exhilarating Carrick-a-Rede Rope Bridge.

▲**Derry and County Donegal** Seventeenth-century English settlement ringed by stout town walls—infamous as the powder keg that ignited Ireland's tragic modern "Troubles"—with an insightful city history museum and access to the rugged beauty of Donegal.

INTRODUCTION

than buying a railpass. For more on public transportation and car rental, see "Transportation" in the appendix.

Room and Board: You can thrive in Ireland in 2013 on $125 a day per person for room and board (more in big cities). This allows $20 for lunch, $30 for dinner, $5 for snacks or a Guinness, and $70 for lodging (based on two people splitting a $140 double room that includes breakfast). That's doable, particularly outside Dublin, and it's easy for many travelers to come in under budget. Students and tightwads can enjoy Ireland for as little as $75 a day ($35 for a bed, $40 for meals and snacks).

Sightseeing and Entertainment: In big cities, figure about $10-15 per major sight (for example, the Book of Kells at Dublin's Trinity College-$13), $5 for minor ones (climbing church towers), $15-20 for guided walks, $45-50 for day-trip bus tours, and up to $80 for splurge experiences (such as the Dunguaire Castle medieval banquet or a flight to the Aran Islands).

An overall average of $25 a day works for most people. Don't skimp here. After all, this category is the driving force behind your trip—you came to sightsee, enjoy, and experience Ireland. Two sightseeing passes—the Heritage Card and the Heritage Island Explorer Touring Guide—can help you economize and simplify your sightseeing (see "Sightseeing Passes," page 20).

Shopping and Miscellany: Figure roughly $2 per postcard, tea, or ice cream cone, and $5 per pint of beer. Shopping can vary in cost from nearly nothing to a small fortune, though good budget travelers find that this has little to do with assembling a trip full of lifelong and wonderful memories.

Sightseeing Priorities

Depending on the length of your trip, and taking geographic proximity into account, here are my recommended priorities:

3 days:	Dublin
5 days, add:	Dingle Peninsula
7 days, add:	Galway, County Clare/Burren
9 days, add:	Aran Islands, Kilkenny/Cashel
11 days, add:	Belfast, Antrim Coast
15 days, add:	Kinsale, Kenmare/Ring of Kerry
19 days, add:	Derry, Connemara, Wicklow Mountains/Valley of the Boyne
21 days, add:	Waterford, Donegal

(This includes almost everything on the "Ireland's Best Three-Week Trip by Car" map and itinerary on page 10.)

When to Go

July and August are my favorite times—with long days, the best weather, and the busiest schedule of tourist fun. Summer crowds don't go up as dramatically in Ireland as they do in much of Europe. Still, travel during "shoulder season" (May, early June, Sept, and early Oct) is easier and a bit less expensive. Shoulder-season travelers get minimal crowds, decent weather, the full range of sights and tourist fun spots, and the ability to grab a room almost whenever and wherever they like—often at a flexible price. Winter travelers find absolutely no crowds and soft room prices, but shorter sightseeing hours. Some attractions are open only on weekends or are closed entirely in the winter (Nov-Feb). The weather can be cold and dreary, and nightfall draws the shades on sightseeing well before dinnertime. While Ireland's rural charm falls with the leaves, city sightseeing is fine in the winter.

Plan for rain no matter when you go. Just keep traveling and take full advantage of "bright spells." The weather can change several times in a day, but rarely is it extreme. Bring a jacket and dress in layers. Daily averages throughout the year range between 42°F and 70°F. Temperatures below 32°F cause headlines, and days that break 80°F—while increasing in recent years—are still rare. For more information, see the climate chart in the appendix.

While sunshine may be rare, summer days are very long. Dublin is as far north as Edmonton, Canada, and Portrush is as far north as Ketchikan on the Alaskan panhandle. The midsummer sun is up from 4:30 until 22:30. It's not uncommon to have a gray day, eat dinner, and enjoy hours of sunshine afterward.

Know Before You Go

Your trip is more likely to go smoothly if you plan ahead. Check this list of things to arrange while you're still at home.

You need a **passport**—but no visa or shots—to travel in Ireland. You may be denied entry into certain European countries if your passport is due to expire within three to six months of your ticketed date of return. Get it renewed if you'll be cutting it close. It can take up to six weeks to get or renew a passport (for more on passports, see www.travel.state.gov). Pack a photocopy of your passport in your luggage in case the original is lost or stolen.

Book rooms well in advance if you'll be traveling during peak season (mid-June-Aug) or any major holidays, such as St. Patrick's Day (see page 503).

Call your **debit- and credit-card companies** to let them know the countries you'll be visiting, to ask about fees, request your PIN (it will be mailed to you), and more. See page 14 for details.

Do your homework if you want to buy **travel insurance.** Compare the cost of the insurance to the likelihood of your using it and your potential loss if something goes wrong. Also, check whether your existing insurance (health, homeowners, or renters) covers you

Ireland's Best Three-Week Trip by Car

Day	Plan	Sleep in
1	Fly into Dublin, rent car, Glendalough	Kilkenny
2	Kilkenny with side-trip to Cashel	Kilkenny
3	Waterford	Waterford
4	Explore Wexford	Waterford
5	Cobh	Kinsale
6	Kinsale	Kinsale
7	Muckross House and Farms	Kenmare
8	Ring of Kerry	Dingle
9	Dingle Peninsula loop	Dingle
10	Blaskets, Dingle town (laundry and rest)	Dingle
11	Cliffs of Moher, the Burren, Dunguaire Castle banquet	Galway
12	Aran Islands	Aran Islands
13	Drive through Connemara	Westport
14	Drive to Northern Ireland	Derry
15	Explore Derry, then drive to Portrush	Portrush
16	Explore Antrim Coast	Portrush
17	Belfast	Belfast
18	Drive to Valley of the Boyne sights, return car	Dublin
19	Dublin	Dublin
20	Dublin	Dublin
21	Fly home	

While this three-week itinerary is aggressive and designed to be done by car, most of it can be done by train and bus. For three weeks without a car, spend your first three nights in Dublin, using buses and taxis. Cut back on the recommended sights with the most frustrating public transportation (Ring of Kerry, the Burren, Valley of the Boyne, Connemara, and Coun-

and your possessions overseas. For more tips, see www.ricksteves.com/insurance.

If you're planning on **renting a car** in Ireland, bring your driver's license. If you're picking up a car at Dublin Airport, consider a gentler **small-town start** in Trim, and let Dublin be the finale, when you're rested and ready to tackle the city.

Popular guides can get booked up—if you plan to hire a **local guide,** reserve ahead by email.

ty Wexford). You can book day tours by bus for some of these areas at local tourist offices. For at least two people traveling together, taxis—though expensive—can work in a pinch if bus schedules don't fit your plans (i.e., Cork to Kinsale). If you have time for only one idyllic peninsula on your trip, I'd suggest the Dingle Peninsula over the Ring of Kerry (for specifics, see sidebar on page 213).

If you're bringing a **mobile device,** download any apps you might want to use on the road, such as maps and transit schedules. Check out **Rick Steves Audio Europe,** featuring hours of travel interviews and other audio content about Ireland (via www.ricksteves.com/audioeurope, iTunes, Google Play, or the Rick Steves Audio Europe free smartphone app; for details, see page 499).

Check the **Rick Steves guidebook updates** page for any recent changes to this book (www.ricksteves.com/update).

Because **airline carry-on restrictions** are always changing, visit the Transportation Security Administration's website (www.tsa.gov/travelers) for an up-to-date list of what you can bring on the plane with you...and what you must check. If you're flying into Dublin from London, note that some airlines may restrict you to only one carry-on (no extras like a purse or backpack); check with your airline or at Britain's transportation website for the latest (www.dft.gov.uk).

Practicalities

Emergency and Medical Help: In Ireland, dial 999 for police or a medical emergency. If you get sick, do as the Irish do and go to a pharmacist for advice. Or ask at your hotel for help—they'll know the nearest medical and emergency services.

Theft or Loss: To replace a passport, you'll need to go in person to an embassy (see page 482). If your credit and debit cards disappear, cancel and replace them (see "Damage Control for Lost Cards" on page 16). File a police report, either on the spot or within a day or two; it's required if you submit an insurance claim for lost or stolen railpasses or travel gear, and can help with replacing your passport or credit and debit cards. For more information, see www.ricksteves.com/help. Precautionary measures can minimize the effects of loss—back up your photos and other files frequently.

Time Zones: Ireland, which is one hour earlier than most of continental Europe, is five/eight hours ahead of the East/West coasts of the US. The exceptions are the beginning and end of Daylight Saving Time: Ireland and Europe "spring forward" the last Sunday in March (two weeks after most of North America) and "fall back" the last Sunday in October (one week before North America). For a handy online time converter, see www.timeanddate.com/worldclock.

Business Hours: In Ireland, most stores are open Monday through Saturday from roughly 10:00 to 17:30, with a late night on Wednesday or Thursday (until 19:00 or 20:00), depending on the neighborhood. Saturdays are virtually weekdays with earlier closing hours and no rush hour (though transportation connections can be less frequent than on weekdays). Sundays have the same pros and cons as they do for travelers in the US: special events, limited hours, banks and many shops closed, limited public transportation, no rush hours, street markets lively with shoppers.

Watt's Up? Europe's electrical system is 220 volts, instead of North America's 110 volts. Most newer electronics (such as laptops, battery chargers, and hair dryers) convert automatically, so you won't need a converter plug, but you will need an adapter plug with three square prongs, sold inexpensively at travel stores in the

US. Avoid bringing older appliances that don't automatically convert voltage; instead, buy a cheap replacement in Europe. Low-cost hair dryers and other small appliances are sold at Dunnes and Tesco stores in bigger cities; ask your hotelier for the closest branch.

Discounts: Discounts (called "concessions" in Ireland) aren't listed in this book. However, many Irish sights offer discounts for youths (up to age 18), students (with proper identification cards, www.isic.org), families, seniors (loosely defined as retirees or those willing to call themselves a senior), and groups of 10 or more. Always ask. Some discounts are available only for EU citizens.

Money

This section offers advice on paying for purchases on your trip (including getting cash from ATMs and paying with plastic), dealing with lost or stolen cards, VAT (sales tax) refunds, and tipping.

What to Bring

Bring both a credit card and a debit card. You'll use the debit card at cash machines (ATMs) to withdraw local currency for most purchases, and the credit card to pay for larger items. Some travelers carry a third card, in case one gets demagnetized or eaten by a temperamental machine.

For an emergency reserve, bring several hundred dollars in hard cash in easy-to-exchange $20 bills. Avoid using currency exchange booths because of their lousy rates and/or outrageous fees.

Cash

Cash is just as desirable in Ireland as it is at home. Small businesses (hotels, restaurants, shops, etc.) prefer that you pay your bills with cash. Some vendors will charge you extra for using a credit card, and some won't take credit cards at all. Cash is the best—and sometimes only—way to pay for bus fare, taxis, and local guides.

Throughout Europe, ATMs are the standard way for travelers to get cash. Stay away from "independent" ATMs such as Travelex,

Euronet, and Forex, which charge huge commissions and have terrible exchange rates.

To withdraw money from an ATM, you'll need a debit card (ideally with a Visa or MasterCard logo for maximum usability), plus a PIN code. Know your PIN code in numbers; there are only numbers—no letters—on European keypads. For security, it's best to shield the keypad when entering your PIN at an ATM. Although you can use a credit card for ATM transactions, it's generally more expensive (and only makes sense in an emergency), because it's considered a cash advance rather than a withdrawal. Try to withdraw large sums of money to reduce the number of per-transaction bank fees you'll pay.

Even in mist-kissed Ireland, you'll need to keep your cash safe. Pickpockets target tourists. To safeguard your cash, wear a money belt—a pouch with a strap that you buckle around your waist like a belt and tuck under your clothes. Keep your cash, credit cards, and passport secure in your money belt, and carry only a day's spending money in your front pocket.

Credit and Debit Cards

For purchases, Visa and MasterCard are more commonly accepted than American Express. Just like at home, credit and debit cards are accepted by larger hotels, restaurants, and shops. I typically use a debit card to withdraw cash to pay for most purchases. I use my credit card only in a few specific situations: to book hotel reservations by phone, to cover major expenses (such as car rentals, plane tickets, and hotel stays), and to pay for things near the end of my trip (to avoid another visit to the ATM). While you could use a debit card to make most large purchases, using a credit card offers a greater degree of fraud protection (because debit cards draw funds directly from your account).

Ask Your Credit- or Debit-Card Company: Before your trip, contact the company that issued your debit or credit cards.

• Confirm that your **card will work overseas,** and alert them that you'll be using it in Europe; otherwise, they may deny transactions if they perceive unusual spending patterns.

• Ask for the specifics on transaction **fees.** When you use your credit or debit card—either for purchases or ATM withdrawals—you'll often be charged additional "international transaction" fees of up to 3 percent (1 percent is normal) plus $5 per transaction. If your fees seem high, consider getting a different card just for your trip: Capital One (www.capitalone.com) and most credit unions have low-to-no international fees.

• If you plan to withdraw cash from ATMs, confirm your daily **withdrawal limit,** and if necessary, ask your bank to adjust it. Some travelers prefer a high limit that allows them to take out more

INTRODUCTION

Exchange Rates

I've priced things throughout this book in the local currencies. The Republic of Ireland uses the euro currency. Northern Ireland, which is part of the United Kingdom, has retained its traditional currency, the British pound sterling. Border towns in the North might take euros, but at a lousy exchange rate. (To get the latest rates and print a cheat sheet, see www. oanda.com).

1 euro (€1) = about $1.30
1 British pound (£1) = about $1.60

Republic of Ireland: To convert prices in euros to dollars, add about 30 percent: €20 = about $26, €50 = about $65. Just like the dollar, one euro (€) is broken down into 100 cents. You'll find coins ranging from €0.01 to €2, and bills ranging from €5 to €500.

Northern Ireland: To convert prices in pounds to dollars, add 60 percent: £20 = about $32, £50 = about $80. The British pound (£), also called a "quid," is broken into 100 pence (p). Pence means "cents." You'll find coins ranging from 1p to £2 and bills from £5 to £50. Fake pound coins are easy to spot (real coins have an inscription on their outside rims; the edges of fakes resemble tree bark).

Northern Ireland issues its own currency, which is worth the same as an English pound. If you're traveling on to Great Britain, note that English and Northern Ireland's Ulster pounds are technically interchangeable in both regions, although Ulster pounds are "undesirable" in Britain. Banks in either region will convert your Ulster pounds into English pounds at no charge. Don't worry about the coins, which are accepted throughout Great Britain and Northern Ireland.

cash at each ATM stop (saving on bank fees), while others prefer to set a lower limit in case their card is stolen. Note that foreign banks also set maximum withdrawal amounts for their ATMs.

• Get your bank's emergency **phone number** in the US (but not its 800 number, which isn't accessible from overseas) to call collect if you have a problem.

• Ask for your credit card's **PIN** in case you need to make an emergency cash withdrawal or encounter Europe's "chip-and-PIN" system; the bank won't tell you your PIN over the phone, so allow time for it to be mailed to you.

Chip and PIN: If your card is declined for a purchase in Europe, it may be because Europeans are increasingly using chip-and-PIN cards, which are embedded with an electronic chip (rather than the magnetic stripe used on our American-style cards). Much of Europe is adopting this system, and some merchants rely on it exclusively. You're most likely to encounter chip-and-PIN problems at automated payment machines, such as those at train and subway stations, toll roads, parking garages, luggage lockers, and self-serve gas pumps. If a machine won't take your card, look for a cashier nearby who can make your card work (they can print a receipt for you to sign), or see if there's a machine that takes cash.

But don't panic. Most travelers who are carrying only magnetic-stripe cards never encounter any problems. Still, it pays to carry plenty of euros (you can always use an ATM with your magnetic-stripe debit card). Memorizing the PIN lets you use it at some chip-and-PIN machines—just enter your PIN when prompted.

If you're still concerned, you can apply for a chip-and-PIN card in the US (though I think it's overkill). While big US banks offer these cards with high annual fees, a better option is the no-annual-fee GlobeTrek Visa, offered by Andrews Federal Credit Union in Maryland (open to all US residents; see www.andrewsfcu.org).

Dynamic Currency Conversion: If merchants offer to convert your purchase price into dollars (called dynamic currency conversion, or DCC), refuse this "service." You'll pay even more in fees for the expensive convenience of seeing your charge in dollars.

Damage Control for Lost Cards

If you lose your credit, debit, or ATM card, you can stop people from using it by reporting the loss immediately to the respective global customer-assistance centers. Call these 24-hour US numbers collect: Visa (tel. 303/967-1096), MasterCard (tel. 636/722-7111), and American Express (tel. 336/393-1111). In Ireland, to make a collect call to the US, dial 001, then the area code and phone number. European toll-free numbers (listed by country) can be found at the websites for Visa and MasterCard.

At a minimum, you'll need to know the name of the financial institution that issued you the card, along with the type of card (classic, platinum, or whatever). Providing the following information will allow for a quicker cancellation of your missing card: full card number, whether you are the primary or secondary cardholder, the cardholder's name exactly as printed on the card, billing address, home phone number, circumstances of the loss or theft, and identification verification (your birth date, your mother's maiden name, or your Social Security number—memorize this, don't carry a copy). If you are the secondary cardholder, you'll also need to provide the primary cardholder's identification-verification details.

You can generally receive a temporary card within two or three business days in Europe (see www.ricksteves.com/help for more).

If you report your loss within two days, you typically won't be responsible for any unauthorized transactions on your account, although many banks charge a liability fee of $50.

Tipping

Tipping in Ireland isn't as automatic and generous as it is in the US, but for special service, tips are appreciated, if not expected. As in the US, the proper amount depends on your resources, tipping philosophy, and the circumstance, but some general guidelines apply.

Restaurants: At a pub or restaurant with waitstaff, check the menu or your bill to see if the service is included; if not, tip about 10 percent. At pubs where you order at the counter, you don't have to tip.

Taxis: To tip the cabbie, round up. For a typical ride, round up your fare a bit (for instance, if the fare is €9, give €10). If the cabbie hauls your bags and zips you to the airport to help you catch your flight, you might want to toss in a little more. But if you feel as if you're being driven in circles or otherwise ripped off, skip the tip.

Services: In general, if someone in the service industry does a super job for you, a small tip (the equivalent of a euro or two) is appropriate...but not required. If you're not sure whether (or how much) to tip for a service, ask your hotelier or the TI.

Getting a VAT Refund

Wrapped into the purchase price of your Irish souvenirs is a Value-Added Tax (VAT); it's about 23 percent in the Republic and 20 percent in Northern Ireland. You're entitled to get most of that tax back if you purchase your goods at a store that participates in the VAT-refund scheme. In Ireland, you do not have to meet a minimum purchase amount in order to qualify for a refund.

Getting your refund is usually straightforward and, if you buy a substantial amount of souvenirs, well worth the hassle. If you're lucky, the merchant will subtract the tax when you make your purchase. (This is more likely to occur if the store ships the goods to your home.) Otherwise, you'll need to:

Get the paperwork. Have the merchant completely fill out the necessary refund document, called a "Tax-Free Shopping Cheque." You'll have to present your passport. Get the paperwork done before you leave the store to ensure you'll have everything you need (including your original sales receipt).

Get your stamp at the border or airport. Process your VAT document at your last stop in the EU (such as at the airport) with the customs agent who deals with VAT refunds. Before checking in for your flight, find the local customs office, and be prepared to stand in line. It's best to keep your purchases in your carry-on for viewing, but if they're too large or dangerous to carry on (such as knives), have your purchases easily accessible in the bag you're about to check, ready to show the customs agent. You're not supposed to use your purchased goods before you leave. If you show up at customs wearing your new Irish sweater, officials might look the other way—or deny you a refund.

Collect your refund. You'll need to return your stamped document to the retailer or its representative. Many merchants work with a service, such as Global Blue or Premier Tax Free, that has offices at major airports, ports, or border crossings (either before or after security, probably strategically located near a duty-free shop). These services, which extract a 4 percent fee, can refund your money immediately in cash or credit your card (within two billing cycles). If the retailer handles VAT refunds directly, it's up to you to contact the merchant for your refund. You can mail the documents from home, or more quickly, from your point of departure (using a stamped, self-addressed envelope you've prepared or one that has been provided by the merchant). You'll then have to wait—it can take months.

Customs for American Shoppers

You are allowed to take home $800 worth of items per person duty-free, once every 30 days. You can also bring in, duty-free, a liter of alcohol. As for food, you can take home many processed and packaged foods: vacuum-packed cheeses, dried herbs, jams, baked goods, candy, chocolate, oil, vinegar, mustard, and honey. However, fresh fruits and vegetables and most meats are not allowed. Any liquid-containing foods must be packed in checked luggage, a potential recipe for disaster. To check customs rules and duty rates, visit www.cbp.gov.

Sightseeing

Sightseeing can be hard work. Use these tips to make your visits to Ireland's finest sights meaningful, fun, efficient, and painless.

Plan Ahead

Set up an itinerary that allows you to fit in all your must-see sights. For a one-stop look at opening hours in Dublin, see the "At a Glance" sidebar on page 60. Most sights keep stable hours, but you can easily confirm the latest by checking their website or asking the local TI.

Don't put off visiting a must-see sight—you never know when a place will close unexpectedly for a holiday, strike, or restoration. On holidays (see list on page 503), expect reduced hours or closures. In summer, some sights may stay open late. Off-season, many museums have shorter hours.

Going at the right time helps avoid crowds. This book offers tips on specific sights. Try visiting popular sights very early or very late. Evening visits are usually peaceful, with fewer crowds.

Study up. To get the most out of the self-guided walks and sight descriptions in this book, read them before you visit.

At Sights

Here's what you can typically expect:

Some important sights may require you to check daypacks and coats. To avoid checking a small backpack, carry it under your arm like a purse as you enter. From a guard's point of view, a backpack is generally a problem while a purse is not.

Flash photography is often banned, but taking photos without a flash is usually allowed. Flashes damage oil paintings and distract others in the room. Even without a flash, a handheld camera will take a decent picture (or buy postcards or posters at the museum bookstore).

Museums may have special exhibits in addition to their permanent collection. Some exhibits are included in the entry price, while others come at an extra cost (which you may have to pay even if you don't want to see the exhibit).

Expect changes—artwork can be on tour, on loan, out sick, or shifted at the whim of the curator. To adapt, pick up any available free floor plans as you enter, and ask museum staff if you can't find a particular item.

Some sights rent audioguides, which generally offer dry-but-useful recorded descriptions in English (sometimes included with admission). If you bring along your earbuds, you can enjoy better sound and avoid holding the device to your ear. To save money, bring a Y-jack and share one audioguide with your travel partner.

Important sights may have an on-site café or cafeteria (usually a handy place to rejuvenate during a long visit). The WCs at many sights are free and nearly always clean.

Many sights sell postcards that highlight their attractions. Before you leave a sight, scan the postcards and thumb through the biggest guidebook (or skim its index) to be sure that you haven't overlooked something that you'd like to see.

Most sights stop admitting people 30-60 minutes before closing time, and some rooms may close early (often about 45 minutes before the actual closing time). Guards usher people out, so don't save the best for last.

Every sight or museum offers more than what is covered in this book. Use the information in this book as an introduction—not the final word.

Sightseeing Passes

Ireland offers two passes (each covering a different set of sights) that can save you money. The first is smart for anyone, and the second works best for two people traveling together. Twosomes who love to sightsee should get both passes.

Heritage Card: This pass gets you into 96 historical monuments, gardens, and parks maintained by the OPW (Office of Public Works) in the Republic of Ireland. It will pay off if you plan on visiting half a dozen or more included sights over the course of your trip (€21, seniors age 60 and older–€16, students–€8, families–€55, covers entry to all Heritage sights for one year, comes with handy map and list of sights' hours and prices, purchase at any Heritage sight or Dublin's  tourist information office on Suffolk Street, cash only, tel. 01/605-7700 or 01/647-6592, fax 01/661-6764, www.heritageireland.ie, heritagecard@opw.ie). People traveling by car are most likely to get their money's worth out of the card.

Without the Heritage Card, your costs will add up fast, and you'll waste time in line. An energetic sightseer with three weeks in Ireland will probably pay to see nearly all 20 of the following sights (covered in this book):

- Dublin Castle–€4.50
- Kilmainham Gaol–€6 (Dublin)
- Brú na Bóinne (Knowth and Newgrange tombs and Visitors Centre)–€11 (Valley of the Boyne)
- Battle of the Boyne–€4
- Hill of Tara–€3 (Valley of the Boyne)
- Old Mellifont Abbey–€3 (Valley of the Boyne)
- Trim Castle–€4 (Valley of the Boyne)
- Glendalough Visitors Centre–€3 (Wicklow Mountains)
- Kilkenny Castle–€6
- Rock of Cashel–€6
- Reginald's Tower–€3 (Waterford)
- Charles Fort–€4 (Kinsale)
- Desmond Castle–€3 (Kinsale)
- Muckross House–€7 (near Killarney)
- Derrynane House–€3 (Ring of Kerry)
- Garnish Island Gardens–€4 (near Kenmare)
- Great Blasket Centre–€4 (near Dingle)
- Ennis Friary–€3 (Ennis)
- Dún Aenghus–€3 (Inishmore, Aran Islands)
- Glenveagh Castle and National Park–€5 (Donegal)

Together these sights total nearly €90; a pass saves you almost

€70 (about $90) per person over paying individual entrance fees. It also moves you through ticket lines more quickly. Note that scheduled tours given by OPW guides at any of these sites are included in the price of admission—regardless of whether you have the Heritage Card—and that the card covers no sights in Northern Ireland.

Heritage Island Explorer Touring Guide: Ambitious travelers covering more ground should seriously consider this €7 pass, which does not overlap with the above Heritage sights and gives a

variety of discounts (usually 2-for-1 discounts, but occasionally 10-20 percent off) at 90 sights in both the Republic of Ireland and Northern Ireland. This is a great no-brainer deal for two people traveling together—you just need to buy one Touring Guide, so you'll save the cost of the guide after only a couple of stops. (Solo travelers might have to go to half a dozen sights before the discounts recoup the initial €7.) At some sites that already

have free admission, you may get 10 percent off on purchases at their shop or café. You can buy the guide at TIs and participating sights, but study the full list of sights first (tel. 01/775-3870, fax 01/284-4845, www.heritageisland.com).

Discounted sights mentioned in this guidebook include:
• Trinity College Library (Book of Kells, Dublin)
• Christ Church Cathedral (Dublin)
• St. Patrick's Cathedral (Dublin)
• Dublin City Hall
• Dublinia
• Hugh Lane Gallery (Dublin)
• Old Jameson Distillery (Dublin)
• Guinness Storehouse (Dublin)
• Number Twenty-Nine Georgian House (Dublin)
• Jeanie Johnston Famine Ship (Dublin)
• Little Museum of Dublin (Dublin)
• Power & Glory (Trim)
• Irish National Stud (Kildare)
• Gardens of Powerscourt (Enniskerry)
• Avondale House (Wicklow Mountains)
• Bru Boru Cultural Centre (Cashel)
• Rothe House (Kilkenny)
• Dunbrody Famine Ship (New Ross)
• Waterford Crystal Visitor Centre (Waterford)
• Old Midleton Distillery (Midleton)
• Blarney Castle (County Cork)

- Kerry County Museum (Tralee)
- Burren Centre (Kilfenora)
- Caherconnell Ring Fort (Burren)
- Aillwee Cave (Burren)
- Atlantic Edge exhibit (Cliffs of Moher)
- Clare Museum (Ennis)
- Kylemore Abbey (Letterfrack)
- Strokestown Park National Famine Museum (Strokestown)
- Mount Stewart House and Gardens
- Somme Heritage Centre (near Bangor)
- Titanic Belfast (Belfast)
- Tower Museum (Derry)
- Belleek Pottery Visitors Centre (Belleek)

Sleeping

I favor hotels and restaurants that are handy to your sightseeing activities. Rather than list hotels scattered throughout a city, I choose two or three favorite neighborhoods and recommend the best accommodations values in each, from dorm beds to fancy doubles with all the comforts. Outside of Dublin you can expect to find good doubles for $100-150, including tax and a cooked breakfast.

A major feature of this book is its extensive listing of good-value rooms. I like places that are clean, central, relatively quiet at night, reasonably priced, friendly, small enough to have a hands-on owner and stable staff, run with a respect for Irish traditions, and not listed in other guidebooks. (In Ireland, for me, six out of these eight criteria means it's a keeper.) I'm more impressed by a convenient location and a fun-loving philosophy than flat-screen TVs and shoeshine machines.

Book your accommodations well in advance if you'll be traveling during busy times. Also reserve in advance for Dublin for any weekend, for Galway during its many peak-season events, and for Dingle throughout July and August. See page 503 for a list of major holidays and festivals throughout Ireland; for tips on making reservations, see page 26.

The Republic of Ireland and Northern Ireland have banned smoking in the workplace (pubs, offices, taxicabs, etc.), but some hotels still have a floor or two of rooms where guests are allowed to smoke. If you don't want a room that a smoker might have occupied before you, let the hotelier know when you make your reservation. About 90 percent of my recommended B&Bs prohibit smoking. While some places allow smoking in the sleeping rooms, breakfast rooms are nearly always smoke-free.

Rates and Deals

I've described my recommended accommodations using a Sleep Code (see the sidebar on the next page). Prices listed are for one-night stays in peak season, include a hearty breakfast (unless otherwise noted), and assume you're booking directly (not through a TI or online hotel-booking engine). Using an online booking service costs the hotel about 20 percent and logically closes the door on special deals. Book direct.

These days, many hotels change prices from day to day according to demand. Given the economic downturn, hoteliers are often willing and eager to make a deal. I'd suggest emailing several hotels to ask for their best price. Comparison-shop and make your choice.

As you look over the listings, you'll notice that some accommodations promise special prices to my readers who book direct (without using a room-finding service or hotel-booking website, which take a commission). To get these rates, you must mention this book when you reserve and then show the book upon arrival. Rick Steves discounts apply to readers with ebooks as well as printed books. Discounts may not apply to promotional rates.

In general, prices can soften if you do any of the following: offer to pay cash, stay at least three nights, or mention this book. You can also try asking for a cheaper room or a discount, or offer to skip breakfast.

When establishing prices, confirm if the charge is per person or per room (if a price is too good to be true, it's probably per person). Because many places in Ireland charge per person, small groups often pay the same for a single and a double as they would for a triple. Note: In this book, room prices are listed per room, not per person.

Types of Accommodations

Ireland has a rating system for hotels and B&Bs. These stars and shamrocks are supposed to imply quality, but I find that they mean only that the place sporting symbols is paying dues to the tourist board. Rating systems often have little to do with value.

Hotels

Many of my recommended hotels have three floors of rooms and steep stairs; expect good exercise and be happy you packed light. Elevators are rare except in the larger hotels. If you're concerned about stairs, call and ask about ground-floor rooms or pay for a hotel with a lift (elevator).

Know the terminology: "Twin" means two single beds, and "double" means one double bed. If you'll take either one, let them know, or you might be needlessly turned away. An "en suite" room

Sleep Code

Price Rankings

To help you easily sort through my listings, I've divided the accommodations into three categories based on the price for a double room with bath during high season:

$$$	Higher Priced
$$	Moderately Priced
$	Lower Priced

I always rate hostels as $, whether or not they have double rooms, because they have the cheapest beds in town.

Prices can change without notice; verify the hotel's current rates online or by email.

Abbreviations

To pack maximum information into minimum space, I use the following code to describe accommodations in this book. Prices are listed per room, not per person. When a price range is given for a type of room (such as double rooms listing for €100-150), it means the price fluctuates with the season, size of room, or length of stay; expect to pay the upper end for peak-season stays.

S = Single room (or price for one person in a double).

D = Double or twin room. "Double beds" are often two twins sheeted together and are usually big enough for nonromantic couples.

T = Triple (generally a double bed with a single).

Q = Quad (usually two double beds; adding an extra child's bed to a T is usually cheaper).

b = Private bathroom with toilet and shower or tub.

s = Private shower or tub only (the toilet is down the hall).

According to this code, a couple staying at a "Db-€100" hotel would pay a total of €100 (about $130) for a double room with a private bathroom. Unless otherwise noted, breakfast is included and credit cards are accepted.

There's almost always Wi-Fi and/or Internet access available, either free or for a fee.

has a bathroom (toilet and shower/tub) inside the room; a room with a "private bathroom" can mean that the bathroom is all yours, but it's across the hall; and a "standard" room has access to a bathroom that's shared with other rooms and down the hall. Figuring there's little difference between "en suite" and "private" rooms, some places charge the same for both. If you want your own bathroom inside the room, request "en suite."

If money's tight, ask for a standard room. You'll almost always have a sink in your room, and as more rooms go "en suite," the hallway bathroom is shared with fewer standard rooms.

Most hotels offer family deals, which means that parents with young children can easily get a room with an extra child's bed or a discount for a larger room. Call to negotiate the price. Teenagers are generally charged as adults. Kids under five sleep almost free.

Note that to be called a "hotel," a place technically must have certain amenities, including a 24-hour reception (though this rule is loosely applied). TVs are standard in rooms.

If you're arriving early in the morning, your room probably won't be ready. You can drop your bag safely at the hotel and dive right into sightseeing.

Hoteliers can be a great help and source of advice. Most know their city well and can assist you with everything from public transit and airport connections to finding a good restaurant, the nearest launderette, or an Internet café. Even at the best places, mechanical breakdowns occur: Air-conditioning malfunctions, sinks leak, hot water turns cold, and toilets gurgle and smell. Report your concerns clearly and calmly at the front desk. For more complicated problems, don't expect instant results.

If you suspect night noise will be a problem (if, for instance, your room is over a pub), ask for a quieter room in the back or on an upper floor. Pubs are plentiful and packed with revelers on weekend nights. (James Joyce once said it would be a good puzzle to try to walk across Dublin without passing a pub.)

To guard against theft in your room, keep valuables out of sight. Some rooms come with a safe, and other hotels have safes at the front desk. I've never bothered using one.

Checkout can pose problems if surprise charges pop up on your bill. If you settle your bill the afternoon before you leave, you'll have time to discuss and address any points of contention (before 19:00, when the night shift usually arrives).

Above all, keep a positive attitude. Remember, you're on vacation. If your hotel or B&B is a disappointment, spend more time out enjoying the city you came to see.

Hotels Beyond this Book: If you're traveling beyond my recommended destinations, you'll find accommodations where you need them. Any town with tourists has a TI that books rooms or can give you a list and point you in the right direction. In the absence of a TI, ask people on the street or in pubs and restaurants for help. The Republic of Ireland also has a nationwide room-booking phone number; within Ireland, dial 1-800-363-626 (Mon-Sat 9:00-20:00, closed Sun).

Small Hotels and B&Bs

Compared to hotels, bed-and-breakfast places give you double the

Making Hotel Reservations

Given the good value of the accommodations I've found for this book, reserve your rooms several weeks in advance—or as soon as you've pinned down your travel dates—particularly if you'll be traveling during peak times. Note that some national holidays jam things up and merit your making reservations far in advance (see "Holidays and Festivals" on page 503).

Requesting a Reservation: It's usually easiest to book your room through the hotel's website; many have a reservation-request form built right in. (For the best rates, be sure to use the hotel's official site and not a booking agency's site.) Just type in your preferred dates and the website will automatically display a list of available rooms and prices. Simpler websites will generate an email to the hotelier with your request. If there's no reservation form, or for complicated requests, send an email from your personal address. Other options include calling (see "Phoning" below, and be mindful of time zones) or faxing.

The hotelier wants to know these key pieces of information (also included in the sample request form in the appendix):

- number and type of rooms
- number of nights
- date of arrival
- date of departure
- any special needs (such as bathroom in the room or down the hall, twin beds vs. double bed, air-conditioning, quiet, view, ground floor, etc.)

When you request a room, use the European style for writing dates: day/month/year. For example, for a two-night stay in July 2013, I would request "1 double room for 2 nights, arrive 16/07/13, depart 18/07/13." Consider carefully how long you'll stay; don't just assume that you can tack on extra days once you arrive. Make sure you mention any discounts—for Rick Steves readers or otherwise—when you make the reservation.

If you don't get a response to your email, it usually means the hotel is already fully booked. But, there may be another reason: Overly aggressive email spam filters used by Internet service providers in North America may block a hotel's correspondence from reaching you. If you don't get an email response from a hotel or B&B, don't assume they are ignoring you. Many innkeepers have shown me emails they sent to travelers—who later complained that they never got a response. To reduce the chance of this happening to you, include an alternate email address from a different provider (for example, if you're using a Comcast address, also include a Yahoo, Hotmail, Gmail, or other address). Phone the hotel or B&B directly if you haven't heard back from them within a week (see "Phoning," below, for international dialing instructions).

Confirming a Reservation: Most places will request your

credit-card number to hold the room. To confirm a room using a hotel's secure online reservation form, enter your contact information and credit-card number; the hotel will email a confirmation.

If you sent an email to request a reservation, the hotel will reply with its room availability and rates. This is not a confirmation. You must email back to say that you want the room at the given rate. While you can email your credit-card information (I do), it's safer to share that confidential info via phone call, two emails (splitting your number between them), or the hotel's secure online reservation form.

Canceling a Reservation: If you must cancel your reservation, it's courteous to do so with as much notice as possible—at least three days. Simply make a quick phone call or send an email. Family-run hotels lose money if they turn away customers while holding a room for someone who doesn't show up. Understandably, many hoteliers bill no-shows for one night.

Cancellation policies can be strict: For example, you might lose a deposit if you cancel within two weeks of your reserved stay, or you might be billed for the entire visit if you leave early. Internet deals may require prepayment, with no refunds for cancellations. Ask about cancellation policies before you book.

If canceling via email, request confirmation that your cancellation was received to avoid being accidentally billed.

Reconfirming a Reservation: Always call to reconfirm your room reservation a few days in advance. (Don't have a TI call for you; they may take a commission.) Smaller hotels and B&Bs appreciate knowing your estimated time of arrival. If you'll be arriving late (after 17:00), let them know. On the small chance that a hotel loses track of your reservation, bring along a hard copy of their confirmation.

Reserving Rooms as You Travel: You can make reservations as you travel, calling hotels or B&Bs a few days to a week before your arrival. If everything's full, don't despair. Call a day or two in advance and fill in a cancellation. If you'd rather travel without any reservations at all, you'll have greater success snaring rooms if you arrive at your destination early in the day. When you anticipate crowds (weekends are worst), call hotels at about 9:00 or 10:00 on the day you plan to arrive, when the receptionist knows who'll be checking out and which rooms will be available.

Phoning: The country code for the Republic of Ireland is 353, and for Northern Ireland, it's 044. To call from the US or Canada to the Republic of Ireland, dial 011-353 followed by the local number (drop the initial 0 from the local number). To call Northern Ireland, dial 011-44-28 (28 is Northern Ireland's area code without its initial 0), then the local number. For more tips on calling, see page 474.

cultural intimacy for half the price. While you may lose some of the conveniences of a hotel—such as lounges, in-room phones, frequent bed-sheet changes, and being able to pay with a credit card—I happily make the trade-off for the lower rates and personal touches. If you have a reasonable but limited budget, skip hotels and go the B&B way. In 2013, you'll generally pay €40-60 (about $50-80) per person for a double room in a B&B in Ireland. Prices include a big cooked breakfast. The amount of coziness, teddies, tea, and biscuits tossed in varies tremendously.

B&Bs range from large guesthouses with 15-20 rooms to small homes renting out a spare bedroom, but they typically have six rooms or fewer. A "townhouse" or "house" is like a big B&B or a small family-run hotel—with fewer amenities but more character than a hotel. The philosophy of the management determines the character of a place more than its size and facilities offered. Avoid places run as a business by absentee owners (their hired hands often don't provide the level of service that pride of ownership brings). My top listings are run by people who enjoy welcoming the world to their breakfast table.

Book direct. If you buy the lodging vouchers sold by many US travel agents (see sidebar), you'll pay more. If you have a local TI book a room for you, it'll take a 10 percent commission from the B&B and may charge you up to €5. But if you book direct, the B&B gets it all, and you'll have a better chance of getting a discount. I have negotiated special prices with this book (often for payment in cash).

Small hotels and B&Bs come with their own etiquette and quirks. Keep in mind that B&B owners are at the whim of their guests—if you're getting up early, so are they; and if you check in late, they'll wait up for you. It's polite to call ahead to confirm your reservation the day before and give them a rough estimate of your arrival time. This allows your hosts to plan their day and run errands before or after you arrive...and also allows them to give you specific directions for driving or walking to their place.

A few tips: B&B proprietors are selective as to whom they invite in for the night. At some B&Bs, children are not welcome. Risky-looking people (two or more single men are often assumed to be troublemakers) find many places

Lodging Vouchers

Many US travel agents sell vouchers for lodging in Ireland. In essence, you're paying ahead of time for your lodging, with the assurance that you'll be staying in B&Bs and guesthouses that live up to certain standards. I don't recommend buying into these, since your choices will be limited to only the places in Ireland that accept vouchers. Sure, there are hundreds in the program to choose from. But in this guidebook, I list any place that offers a good value—a useful location, nice hosts, and a comfortable and clean room—regardless of what club they do or don't belong to. Lots of great B&Bs choose not to participate in the voucher program because they have to pay to be part of it, slicing into their already thin profit. And many Irish B&B owners lament the long wait they endure between the date a traveler stays with them and the date the voucher company reimburses them. In short, skip it. The voucher program is just another middleman between you and the innkeeper.

suddenly full. If you'll be staying for more than one night, you are a "desirable." In popular weekend-getaway spots, you're unlikely to find a place to take you for Saturday night only. If my listings are full, ask for guidance. (Mentioning this book can help.) Owners usually work together and can call up an ally to land you a bed.

B&Bs serve a hearty "Irish fry" breakfast (for more about B&B breakfasts, see "Eating," later in this chapter). You'll quickly figure out which parts of the "fry" you do and don't like. B&B owners prefer to know this up front, rather than serve you the whole shebang and have to throw out uneaten food. Because your B&B owner is also the cook, there's usually a quite limited time span when breakfast is served (typically about an hour, starting at about 8:00—make sure you know the exact time before you turn in for the night). It's an unwritten rule that guests shouldn't show up at the very end of the breakfast period and expect a full cooked breakfast. If you do arrive at the last minute (or if you need to leave before breakfast is served), most B&B hosts are happy to let you help yourself to cereal, fruit or juice, and coffee; ask politely if it's possible.

B&Bs are not hotels. Think of your host as a friendly acquaintance who's invited you to stay in her home, rather than someone you're paying to wait on you.

Americans often assume they'll get new towels each day. The Irish don't, and neither will you. Hang them up to dry and reuse. And pack a washcloth (many Irish B&Bs don't provide them).

Some B&Bs stock rooms with an electric kettle, along with

cups, tea bags, and coffee packets (if you prefer decaf, buy a jar at a grocery, and dump the contents into a baggie for easy packing).

Electrical outlets sometimes have switches that turn the current on or off; if your electrical appliance isn't working, flip the switch at the outlet. When you unplug your appliance, don't forget your adapter—most B&Bs have boxes of various adapters and converters that guests have left behind (which is handy if you left yours at the last place).

Most B&Bs come with thin walls and doors. This can make for a noisy night, especially with people walking down the hall to use the bathroom. If you're a light sleeper, bring earplugs. And please be quiet in the halls and in your rooms (gently shut your door, talk softly, and keep the TV volume low)...those of us getting up early will thank you for it.

Virtually all rooms have sinks. You'll likely encounter unusual bathroom fixtures. The "pump toilet" has a flushing handle that doesn't kick in unless you push it just right: too hard or too soft, and it won't go. (Be decisive but not ruthless.) There's also the "dial-a-shower," an electronic box under the showerhead where you'll turn a dial to select the heat of the water, and (sometimes with a separate dial or button) turn on or shut off the flow of water. If you can't find the switch to turn on the shower, it may be just outside the bathroom.

Your B&B bedroom might not include a phone. In the mobile-phone age, street phone booths can be few and far between. Some B&B owners will allow you to use their phone, but understandably they don't want to pay for long-distance charges. If you must use their phone, show them your international calling card (see page 481) and keep the call short (5-10 minutes max). If you plan to stay in B&Bs and make frequent calls, consider buying an Irish mobile phone (see page 475). And if you're bringing your laptop, look for places with Wi-Fi (noted in my hotel listings). Ask your host about using this service, as some rooms might have better reception than others.

A few B&B owners are also pet owners. And, while pets are rarely allowed into guest rooms, and B&B proprietors are typically very tidy, those with pet allergies might be bothered. I've tried to list which B&Bs have pets, but if you're allergic, ask about pets when you reserve.

Remember that you'll likely need to pay cash for your room. Think ahead so you have enough cash to pay up when you check out.

Big, Cheap, Modern Hotels

Hotel chains—popular with budget tour groups—offer predictably comfortable, no-frills accommodations at reasonable prices. These

Laundry

If you're not planning to wash your clothes in the sink in your room, it's a good idea to plan ahead for when you'll need to do laundry. Figure on an average of about €10 per load (up to €12 for smaller towns with only one launderette).

Most launderettes in Ireland are drop-off rather than self-serve. Drop-off operations are a smarter use of your valuable travel time. The €5 you might save plugging coins into a self-serve washer/dryer is not worth the two or three hours you'll waste when you could be out enjoying a sight.

Drop your load off first thing in the morning, and pick it up late that afternoon (washed, dried, and kind-of folded). If you wait until too late in the morning to drop it off, they might not be able to get it done for you by closing time that day (be sure to confirm closing time when you drop it off). Note that most places are closed on Sunday; waiting to pick up your load until Monday morning may cramp your plans. When I know I might be distracted by sightseeing, I set my alarm watch to go off late in the afternoon to remind me to pick up my laundry.

If you've packed only basic, practical wash-and-wear clothes, you have nothing to fear from an Irish launderette. If you're traveling with your favorite silk kimono, don't tempt fate—it might come back leprechaun-size.

hotels are popping up in big cities in Ireland. They can be located near the train station, in the city center, on major arterials, and outside the city center. What you lose in charm, you gain in savings. I can't stress this enough: Check online for the cheapest deals. And be sure to go through the hotel's website rather than an online middleman.

These hotels are ideal for families, offering simple, clean, and modern rooms for up to four people (two adults/two children) for €100-150, depending on the location. Note that couples or families (up to four) pay the same price for a room. Most rooms have a double bed, single bed, five-foot trundle bed, private shower, WC, and TV. Hotels usually have an attached restaurant, good security, an elevator, and a 24-hour staffed reception desk. Of course, they're as cozy as a Motel 6, but many travelers love them. You can book online (be sure to check their websites for deals) or over the phone with a credit card, then pay when you check in. When you check out, just drop off the key, Lee.

The biggies are Jurys Inn (call their hotels directly or book online at www.jurysinns.com), Comfort/Quality Inns (Republic of Ireland tel. 1-800-500-600, Northern Ireland tel. 0800-444-444, US tel. 877-424-6423, www.choicehotels.com), and Travelodge (also has freeway locations for tired drivers, reservation center in Britain tel. 08700-850-950, www.travelodge.co.uk).

Hostels

Ireland has hundreds of hostels of all shapes and sizes. Choose yours selectively; hostels can be historic castles or depressing tenements, serene and comfy or overrun by noisy school groups.

You'll pay about €25 per bed to stay at a hostel. Travelers of any age are welcome, if they don't mind dorm-style accommodations and meeting other travelers. Most hostels offer kitchen facilities, Internet access, Wi-Fi, and a self-service laundry. Nowadays, concerned about bedbugs, hostels are likely to provide all bedding, including sheets. Family and private rooms may be available on request.

Independent hostels tend to be easygoing, colorful, and informal (no membership required); see www.hostelz.com, www.hostels europe.com, www.hostels.com, and www.hostelbookers.com. Ireland's Independent Holiday Hostels (www.hostels-ireland.com) is a network of independent hostels, requiring no membership and welcoming all ages. All IHH hostels are approved by the Irish Tourist Board.

Official hostels are part of Hostelling International (HI) and share an online booking site (www.hihostels.com). HI hostels typically require that you either have a membership card or pay extra per night.

Self-Catering Cottages and Apartments

Travelers wanting to slow down and base themselves in one place for extended periods can rent a cottage or an apartment (sometimes called a "flat" in Ireland). This type of lodging varies greatly, but almost always includes a kitchen and living room. The owners discourage short stays and usually require a minimum one-week rental, plus a deposit.

I focus on short-term-stay sleeping recommendations in this book (B&Bs, guesthouses, and hotels), rather than self-catering options. But if a B&B I've listed also offers a worthwhile self-catering option nearby, I'll mention it.

A variety of organizations specialize in this longer-term alternative. Your most reliable source for places that live up to certain standards is the Irish Tourist Board (www.discoverireland.ie).

Eating

Denis Leary once quipped, "Irish food isn't cuisine...it's penance." For years, Irish food was just something you ate to survive rather than to savor. In this country, long known as the "land of potatoes," the diet reflected the economic circumstances. But times have changed. A study in 2010 found that the average Irishman was eating half as many spuds as he had a decade before. You'll find modern-day Irish cuisine delicious and varied, from vegetables, meat, and dairy products to fresh- and saltwater fish. Try the local specialties wherever you happen to be eating.

The traditional breakfast, the "Irish Fry" (known in the North as the "Ulster Fry"), is a hearty way to start the day—with juice, tea or coffee, cereal, eggs, bacon, sausage, a grilled tomato, sautéed mushrooms, and optional black pudding (made from pigs' blood). Toast is served with butter and marmalade. This meal tides many travelers over until dinner. But there's nothing un-Irish about skipping the "fry"—few locals actually start their day with this heavy traditional breakfast. You can simply skip the heavier fare and enjoy the cereal, juice, toast, and tea (surprisingly, the Irish drink more tea per capita than the British).

When restaurant-hunting, choose a spot filled with locals, not tourists. Venturing even a block or two off the main drag leads to higher-quality food for less than half the price of the tourist-oriented places. Locals eat better at lower-rent locales. At classier restaurants, look for "early-bird specials," which allow you to eat well and affordably, but early (about 17:30-19:00, last order by 19:00). At a sit-down place with table service, tip about 10 percent—unless the service charge is already listed on the bill. If you order at a counter, there's no need to tip.

Picnicking saves time and money. Try boxes of orange juice (pure, by the liter), fresh bread (especially Irish soda bread), tasty Cashel blue cheese, meat, a tube of mustard, local-eatin' apples, bananas, small tomatoes, a small tub of yogurt (it's drinkable), rice crackers, gorp or nuts, plain digestive biscuits (the chocolate-covered ones melt), and any local specialties. At open-air markets and supermarkets, you can get produce in small quantities. Supermarkets often have good deli sections, packaged sandwiches, and sometimes salad bars. Hang on to the half-liter mineral-water bottles (sold everywhere for about €1). Buy juice in cheap liter boxes, then drink some and store the extra in your water bottle. I often munch a relaxed "meal on wheels" in a car, train, or bus to save 30 precious minutes for sightseeing.

Pub Grub and Beer

Pubs are a basic part of the Irish social scene, and whether you're a teetotaler or a beer-guzzler, they should be a part of your travel here. "Pub" is short for "public house." It's an extended living room where, if you don't mind the stickiness, you can feel the pulse of Ireland.

Smart travelers use pubs to eat, drink, get out of the rain, watch the latest sporting event, and make new friends. Unfortunately, many city pubs have been afflicted with an excess of brass, ferns, and video games. The most traditional atmospheric pubs are in the countryside and smaller towns.

Pub grub gets better every year—it's Ireland's best eating value. But don't expect high cuisine; it is, after all, comfort food. For about $15-20, you'll get a basic hot lunch or dinner in friendly surroundings. Pubs that are attached to restaurants, advertise their food, and are crowded with locals are more likely to have fresh food and a chef than to be the kind of pub that sells only lousy microwaved snacks.

Pub menus consist of a hearty assortment of traditional dishes, such as Irish stew (mutton with mashed potatoes, onions, carrots, and herbs), soups and chowders, coddle (bacon, pork sausages, potatoes, and onions stewed in layers), fish-and-chips, collar and cabbage (boiled bacon coated in bread crumbs and brown sugar, then baked and served with cabbage), boxty (potato pancake filled with fish, meat, or vegetables), and champ (potato mashed with milk and onions). Irish bread nicely rounds out a meal. In coastal areas, a lot of seafood is available, such as mackerel, mussels, and Atlantic salmon. There's seldom table service in Irish pubs. Order drinks and meals at the bar. Pay as you order, and only tip (by rounding up to avoid excess coinage) if you like the service.

I recommend certain pubs, and your B&B host is usually up-to-date on the best neighborhood pub grub. Ask for advice (but adjust for nepotism and cronyism, which run rampant).

When you say "a beer, please" in an Irish pub, you'll get a pint of Guinness (the black beauty with the blonde head). If you want a small beer, ask for a glass, which is a half-pint. Never rush your bartender when he's pouring a Guinness. It takes time—almost sacred time.

The Irish take great pride in their beer. At pubs, long hand

pulls are used to draw the traditional, rich-flavored "real ales" up from the cellar. These are the connoisseur's favorites: They're fermented naturally, vary from sweet to bitter, and often have a hoppy or nutty flavor. Experiment with obscure local microbrews. Short hand pulls at the bar mean colder, fizzier, mass-produced, and less interesting keg beers. Stout is dark and more bitter, like Guinness. If you think you don't like Guinness, try it in Ireland. It doesn't travel well and is better in its homeland. Murphy's is a very good Guinness-like stout, but a bit smoother and milder. For a cold, refreshing, basic, American-style beer, ask for a lager, such as Harp. Ale drinkers swear by Smithwick's (I know I do). Caffrey's is a satisfying cross between stout and ale. Try the draft cider (sweet or dry)...carefully. Teetotalers can order a soft drink.

Pubs are generally open daily from 11:00 to 23:30 and Sunday from noon to 22:30. Children are served food and soft drinks in pubs (sometimes in a courtyard or the restaurant section). You'll often see signs behind the bar asking that children vacate the premises by 20:00. You must be 18 to order a beer, and the Gardí (police) are cracking down hard on pubs that don't enforce this law.

You're a guest on your first night; after that, you're a regular. A wise Irishman once said, "It never rains in a pub." The relaxed, informal atmosphere feels like a refuge from daily cares. Women traveling alone need not worry—you'll become part of the pub family in no time.

Craic (crack), Irish for "fun" or "a good laugh," is the sport that accompanies drinking in a pub. People are there to talk. To encourage conversation, stand or sit at the bar, not at a table.

In 2004, the Irish government passed a law making all pubs in the Republic smoke-free. Smokers take their pints outside, turning alleys into covered smoking patios. An incredulous Irishman responded to the law by saying, "What will they do next? Ban drinking in pubs? We'll never get to heaven if we don't die."

It's a tradition to buy your table a round, and then for each person to reciprocate. If an Irishman buys you a drink, thank him by saying, "Go raibh maith agat" (guh rov mah UG-ut). Offer him a toast in Irish—"Slainte" (SLAWN-chuh), the equivalent of "cheers." A good excuse for a conversation is to ask to be taught a few words of Gaelic.

Traditional Irish Music

Traditional music is alive and popular in pubs throughout Ireland. "Sessions" (musical evenings) may be planned and advertised or impromptu. Traditionally, musicians just congregate and play for the love of it. There will generally be a fiddle, a flute or tin whistle, a guitar, a *bodhrán* (goatskin drum), and maybe an accordion or mandolin. Things usually get going at about 21:30 (but note that Irish punctuality is unpredictable). Last call for drinks is at about 23:30.

The music often comes in sets of three songs. The wind and string instruments embellish melody lines with lots of tight ornamentation. Whoever happens to be leading determines the next song only as the current tune is about to be finished. If he wants to pass on the decision, it's done with eye contact and a nod. A *ceilidh* (KAY-lee) is an evening of music and dance...an Irish hoedown.

Percussion generally stays in the background. The *bodhrán* (BO-run) is played with a small, two-headed club. The performer's hand stretches the skin to change the tone and pitch. You'll sometimes be lucky enough to hear a set of bones crisply played. These are two cow ribs (boiled and dried) that are rattled in one hand like spoons or castanets, substituting for the sound of dancing shoes in olden days.

Watch closely if a piper is playing. The Irish version of bagpipes, the *uilleann* (ILL-in) pipes are played by inflating the airbag (under the left elbow) with a bellows (under the right elbow) rather than with a mouthpiece like the Scottish Highland bagpipes. *Uilleann* is Gaelic for "elbow," and the sound is more melodic, with a wider range than the Highland pipes. The piper fingers his chanter like a flute to create individual notes and uses the heel of his right hand to play chords on one of three regulator pipes. It takes amazing coordination to play this instrument well, and the sound can be haunting.

Occasionally, the fast-paced music will stop and one person will sing a lament. Called *sean nos* (Gaelic for "old style"), this slightly nasal vocal style may be a remnant of the ancient storytelling tradition of the bards whose influence died out when Gaelic culture waned 400 years ago. This is the one time when the entire pub will stop to listen as sad lyrics fill the room. Stories—often of love lost, emigration to a faraway land, or a heroic rebel death struggling against English rule—are always heartfelt. Spend a lament studying the faces in the crowd.

A session can be magical or lifeless. If the chemistry is right, it's one of the great Irish experiences. The music churns intensely while members of the group casually enjoy exploring each other's musical style. The drummer dodges the fiddler's playful bow. Sipping their pints, they skillfully maintain a faint but steady buzz.

How Was Your Trip?

Were your travels fun, smooth, and meaningful? If you'd like to share your tips, concerns, and discoveries, please fill out the survey at www.ricksteves.com/feedback. I value your feedback. Thanks in advance—it helps a lot.

The floor on the musicians' platform is stomped paint-free, and barmaids scurry artfully through the commotion, gathering towers of empty, cream-crusted glasses. Make yourself right at home, "playing the boot" (tapping your foot) under the table in time with the music. Talk to your neighbor. Locals often have an almost evangelical interest in explaining the music.

Traveling as a Temporary Local

We travel all the way to Ireland to enjoy differences—to become temporary locals. You'll experience frustrations. Certain truths that we find "God-given" or "self-evident," such as cold beer, ice in drinks, bottomless cups of coffee, hot showers, and bigger being better, are suddenly not so true. One of the benefits of travel is the eye-opening realization that there are logical, civil, and even better alternatives. A willingness to go local ensures that you'll enjoy a full dose of Irish hospitality.

The Irish generally like Americans. But if there is a negative aspect to their image of us, it's that we are loud, wasteful, ethnocentric, too informal (which can seem disrespectful), and a bit naive.

While the Irish look bemusedly at some of our Yankee excesses—and worriedly at others—they nearly always afford us individual travelers all the warmth we deserve. Judging from all the happy feedback I receive from travelers who have used this book, it's safe to assume you'll enjoy a great, affordable vacation—with the finesse of an independent, experienced traveler.

Thanks, and have a grand holiday!

Back Door Travel Philosophy

From *Rick Steves' Europe Through the Back Door*

Travel is intensified living—maximum thrills per minute and one of the last great sources of legal adventure. Travel is freedom. It's recess, and we need it.

Experiencing the real Europe requires catching it by surprise, going casual..."Through the Back Door."

Affording travel is a matter of priorities. (Make do with the old car.) You can eat and sleep—simply, safely, and enjoyably—anywhere in Europe for $120 a day plus transportation costs. In many ways, spending more money only builds a thicker wall between you and what you traveled so far to see. Europe is a cultural carnival, and time after time, you'll find that its best acts are free and the best seats are the cheap ones.

A tight budget forces you to travel close to the ground, meeting and communicating with the people. Never sacrifice sleep, nutrition, safety, or cleanliness to save money. Simply enjoy the local-style alternatives to expensive hotels and restaurants.

Connecting with people carbonates your experience. Extroverts have more fun. If your trip is low on magic moments, kick yourself and make things happen. If you don't enjoy a place, maybe you don't know enough about it. Seek the truth. Recognize tourist traps. Give a culture the benefit of your open mind. See things as different, but not better or worse. Any culture has plenty to share.

Of course, travel, like the world, is a series of hills and valleys. Be fanatically positive and militantly optimistic. If something's not to your liking, change your liking.

Travel can make you a happier American, as well as a citizen of the world. Our Earth is home to seven billion equally precious people. It's humbling to travel and find that other people don't have the "American Dream"—they have their own dreams. Europeans like us, but with all due respect, they wouldn't trade passports.

Thoughtful travel engages us with the world. In tough economic times, it reminds us what is truly important. By broadening perspectives, travel teaches new ways to measure quality of life.

Globetrotting destroys ethnocentricity, helping us understand and appreciate other cultures. Rather than fear the diversity on this planet, celebrate it. Among your most prized souvenirs will be the strands of different cultures you choose to knit into your own character. The world is a cultural yarn shop, and Back Door travelers are weaving the ultimate tapestry. Join in!

REPUBLIC OF IRELAND

REPUBLIC OF IRELAND

 The Republic of Ireland has existed since 1922, but its inhabitants proudly claim their nation to be the only modern independent state to sprout from purely Celtic roots (sprinkled with a few Vikings and shipwrecked Spanish Armada sailors for good measure). The Romans never bothered to come over and organize the wild Irish. Through the persuasive and culturally enlightened approach of early missionaries such as St. Patrick, Ireland may also be the only country to have initially converted to Christianity without much bloodshed. The religious carnage came later with the Reformation. Irish culture absorbed the influences of Viking raiders and Norman soldiers of fortune, eventually enduring the 750-year shadow of English occupation.

Just a few decades ago, Ireland was an isolated agricultural economic backwater that had largely missed out on the Industrial Revolution. Things began to turn around when Ireland joined the European Community (precursor to the EU) in 1973. The Irish government instituted farsighted tax laws, including a corporate tax rate of only 12.5 percent (compared to 35 percent in the US) to entice foreign corporations to set up shop here. It proved so successful in attracting US business that by 2009, America had invested €158 billion in Ireland (more than its investments in Brazil, India, Russia, and China combined).

Today, the Republic attracts expatriates returning to Ireland and new foreign investment. As the only officially English-speaking country to have adopted the euro currency, Ireland makes an efficient base from which to access the European marketplace. More than 35 percent of the Irish population is under 25 years old, leading many high-tech and pharmaceutical firms to locate

Republic of Ireland

Atlantic Ocean

Dunfanaghy

Portrush

Derry

DONEGAL

NORTHERN IRELAND

Bangor

Belfast

Drumcliff

Belleek

MAYO

Knock

Strokestown

BRÚ NA BÓINNE

Westport

Irish Sea

REPUBLIC OF IRELAND

CONNEMARA

TRIM

Galway

Howth

Aran Islands

NATIONAL STUD

Dublin

Dun Laoghaire

The Burren

Cliffs of Moher

CLARE

Ennis

Shannon

Wicklow Mtns.

GLENDALOUGH

Limerick

Kilkenny

Dingle Peninsula

Tralee

ROCK OF CASHEL

Waterford

Dingle

Killarney

Rosslare Harbor

KERRY

BLARNEY

Ardmore

Kenmare

Cork

Beara Peninsula

Bantry

Cobh

Kinsale

50 Kilometers

50 Miles

here, taking advantage of this young, well-educated labor force. And for the first time, Ireland has become a destination for immigrants, who've come mostly from the Third World and the newer EU nations. Eastern Europeans (especially Poles) come in search of higher pay...a reversal from the days when many Irish fled to start new lives abroad.

As time passes, relations between Ireland and her former colonial master Britain are starting to heal. In May 2011, Queen Elizabeth II became the first British monarch to visit the Republic of Ireland since its 1921 split from the United Kingdom, which was under her grandfather's reign at the time. Her four-night visit (to Dublin, Cashel, and Cork) unexpectedly charmed the Irish people and did much to repair old wounds between the two countries, which are now, in the words of the Queen, "equal partners and good neighbors."

Just a couple of days after the Queen's visit, Barack Obama dropped in for a brief 12-hour stop, guided by American ambassador to Ireland (and Pittsburgh Steelers owner) Dan Rooney. Being

REPUBLIC OF IRELAND

Republic of Ireland Almanac

Official Name: The Republic of Ireland (aka just "Ireland" or, in Irish, Éire).

Population: Ireland's 4.5 million people (same as Kentucky) are of Celtic stock. They speak English, though Irish (Gaelic) is spoken in pockets along the country's west coast. Nearly nine in 10 are nominally Catholic, though only one in three attends church.

Latitude and Longitude: 53°N and 8°W. The latitude is equivalent to Alberta, Canada.

Area: With 27,000 square miles—half the size of New York State—it occupies the southern 80 percent of the island of Ireland. The country is small enough that radio broadcasts manage to cover traffic snarls nationwide.

Geography: The isle is mostly flat, ringed by a hilly coastline. The climate is moderate, with cloudy skies about every other day.

Biggest Cities: The capital of Dublin (1.2 million) is the only big city; more than one in four Irish live in the greater Dublin area. Cork has 190,000 people, while Limerick has about 91,000 and Galway about 76,000.

Economy: The Gross Domestic Product is $182 billion, and the GDP per capita is $39,500—one of Europe's highest and 10 percent more than Britain's. Major moneymakers include tourism and exports (especially to the US and UK) of machines, medicine, Guinness, glassware, crystalware, and software. Traditional agriculture (potatoes and other root vegetables) is fading fast, but dairy still does well.

Government: The elected president, Michael Higgins, appoints the prime minister (Enda Kenny), who is nominated by Parliament. The Parliament consists of the 60-seat Senate, chosen by an electoral college, and the House of Representatives, with 166 seats apportioned after the people vote for a party. Major parties include Fianna Fail, Fine Gael, and Sinn Fein, the political arm of the (fading) Irish Republican Army. Ireland is divided into 26 administrative counties—including Kerry, Clare, Cork, Limerick, and so on.

Flag: The Republic of Ireland's flag is made of three vertical bands of green, white, and orange.

The Average Irish: A typical Irish person is 5'6", 35 years old, has 1.85 kids, and will live to be 80. Every day, he or she drinks four cups of tea and spends $5 on alcohol.

one-sixteenth Irish, O'Bama made sure to helicopter into his ancestral home village of Moneygall in County Offaly and have a pint with Henry, his cousin eight times removed, whom he nicknamed "Henry VIII." Later that day, he delivered a speech to a huge crowd packed into Dublin's College Green, drawing cheers when he dusted off his Irish Gaelic and proclaimed, "Is féidir linn." ("Yes we can.")

Don't worry if your Irish Gaelic is rustier than the president's—the vast majority of Irish people speak English, though you'll still encounter Irish Gaelic if you venture to the western fringe of the country. The Irish love of conversation shines through wherever you go. All that conversation is helped along by the nebulous concept of Irish time, which never seems to be in short supply. Small shops post their hours as "9:00ish until 5:00ish." The local bus usually makes a stop at "10:30ish." A healthy disdain for being a slave to the clock seems to be part of being Ir-"ish." And the warm welcome you'll receive has its roots in ancient Celtic laws of hospitality toward stranded strangers.

Still, aspects of modern life continue to make inroads in traditional Ireland. In 2003, shops began charging customers for plastic sacks for carrying goods (the surcharge is currently €0.22), which has cut down on litter. In 2004, smoking was banned in all Irish pubs. Some pubkeepers initially grumbled about lost business, but the air has cleared. And you can't drive too far without running into road construction, as the recently affluent Irish (for a decade flush with Celtic Tiger money) try to cope with more cars crowding their streets. New motorways are making travel between bigger cities faster, but the country is still laced with plenty of humble country lanes perfect for getting scenically lost.

At first glance, Ireland's landscape seems unspectacular, with few mountains higher than 3,000 feet and an interior consisting of grazing pastures and peat bogs. But its seductive beauty slowly grows on you. The gentle rainfall, called "soft weather" by the locals, really does create 40 shades of green—and quite a few rainbows as well. Ancient, moss-covered ring forts crouch in lush valleys, while stone-strewn monastic ruins and lone castle turrets brave the wind on nearby hilltops. Charming fishing villages dot the coast near rugged, wave-battered cliffs. Slow down to contemplate the checkerboard patterns created by the rock walls outlining the many fields. Examine the colorful small-town shop fronts that proudly state the name of the proprietor.

The resilient Irish character was born of dark humor, historical reverence, and a scrappy, "we'll get 'em next time" rebel spirit.

Though the influence of the Catholic Church is less apparent these days, it still plays a major part in Irish life. The national radio and TV station, RTE, pauses for 30 seconds at noon and at 18:00 to broadcast the chimes of the Angelus bells. The Irish say that if you're phoning heaven, it's a long-distance call from the rest of the world, but a local call from Ireland.

DUBLIN

With reminders of its stirring history and rich culture on every corner, Ireland's capital and largest city is a sightseer's delight. Dublin holds its own above its weight class in arts, entertainment, food, and fun. Dublin's fair city will have you humming, "Cockles and mussels, alive, alive-O."

Founded as a Viking trading settlement in the ninth century, Dublin grew to be a center of wealth and commerce, second only to London in the British Empire. Dublin, the seat of English rule in Ireland for 750 years, was the heart of a "civilized" Anglo-Irish area (eastern Ireland) known as "the Pale." Anything "beyond the Pale" was considered uncultured and almost barbaric...purely Irish.

The Golden Age of English Dublin was the 18th century. The British Empire was on a roll, and the city was right there with it. Largely rebuilt during this Georgian era, Dublin—even with its tattered edges—became an elegant and cultured capital.

Those glory days left a lasting imprint on the city. Squares and boulevards built in the Georgian style give the city an air of grandeur (Georgian is British for Neoclassical...named for the period when four consecutive King Georges occupied the British throne from 1714 to 1830). The National Museum, the National Gallery, and many government buildings are in the Georgian section of town. Few buildings (notably Christ Church and St. Patrick's cathedrals) survive from before this Georgian period.

But nationalism—and a realization of the importance of human rights—would forever change Dublin. The American and French revolutions inspired Irish intellectuals to buck British rule, and life in Dublin was never quite the same after the Rebellion of 1798. In 1801, the Act of Union with Britain resulted in the loss of Ireland's parliament (no need for two with the dominant one in London). As the Irish members of parliament moved to Westminster, the movers and shakers of the Anglo-Irish aristocracy followed suit, and Dublin slowly began to decay.

Throughout the 19th century, as Ireland endured the Great Potato Famine and saw the beginnings of the modern struggle for independence, Dublin was treated—and felt—more like a British colony than a partner. The tension culminated in the Easter Uprising of 1916, soon followed by a successful guerilla war of independence against Britain and Ireland's tragic civil war. With many of its grand streets left in ruins, Dublin emerged as the capital of the British Empire's only former colony in Europe.

While bullet-pocked buildings and dramatic statues keep memories of Ireland's struggle for independence alive, the city is looking ahead to a brighter future. Dubliners are energetic and helpful, while visitors enjoy a big-town cultural scene wrapped in a small-town smile.

Planning Your Time

On a three-week trip through Ireland, Dublin deserves three nights and two days. Be aware that some important sights close on Mondays. Consider this ambitious sightseeing plan:

Day 1:

10:15	Take the Trinity College guided walk.
11:00	Visit the Book of Kells and Old Library ahead of midday crowds.
12:00	Browse Grafton Street, have lunch there or picnic on St. Stephen's Green.
13:30	See Number Twenty-Nine Georgian House (closed Mon).
15:00	Head to the National Museum: Archaeology branch (also closed Mon).
17:00	Return to hotel, rest, have dinner—eat well for less during early-bird specials.
19:30	Go for an evening guided pub tour (musical or literary).
22:00	Drop in on Irish music in the Temple Bar area.

Day 2:

10:00	Take the Dublin Castle tour.
11:30	Hop on one of the hop-on, hop-off buses, jumping off to see the Guinness Storehouse and Kilmainham Gaol (bring a sandwich to munch in transit on the open-top bus, or stop off to picnic in one of Dublin's green squares).

DUBLIN

15:00   Leave the bus at Parnell Square, visit the Garden of Remembrance, and stroll down to O'Connell Bridge, sightseeing and shopping as you like along the way.

Evening   Catch a play or concert—or try the story-telling dinner at The Brazen Head.

With More Time: Dublin, while relatively small, can keep you busily sightseeing for days without even leaving the center of town. And with all its music, theater, and after-hours tours—not to mention the lively pub scene—evenings are just as fun.

Orientation to Dublin

Greater Dublin sprawls with 1.2 million people—more than a quarter of the country's population. But the center of tourist interest is a tight triangle between O'Connell Bridge, St. Stephen's Green, and Christ Church Cathedral. Within this triangle you'll find Trinity College (Book of Kells), Grafton Street (top pedestrian shopping zone), Temple Bar (trendy and touristy nightlife center), Dublin Castle, and the hub of most city tours and buses. The only major sights outside this easy-to-walk triangle are the Kilmainham Gaol, the Guinness Storehouse, and the National Museum: Decorative Arts and History branch (all west of the center).

The River Liffey cuts the town in two. Focus on the southern half, where most of your sightseeing will take place. Dublin's wide main drag, O'Connell Street, starts north of the river at the Parnell monument and runs south, down to the central O'Connell Bridge. After crossing the bridge, it continues south as the major city axis past Trinity College and through pedestrian-only Grafton Street to St. Stephen's Green. Get used to the fact that many long Dublin streets change their names every few blocks. A prime example of this: the numerously named Quays (pronounced "keys") that run east-west along the River Liffey.

The suburban port of Dun Laoghaire (dun LEERY) lies south of Dublin, 25 minutes away by DART commuter train. Travelers looking for a mellow town to sleep in outside of urban Dublin can easily home-base here. Another option is the northern suburb of Howth, also 25 minutes away on the DART and closer to the airport. Room prices are about one-fourth cheaper in Dun Laoghaire or Howth than in downtown Dublin.

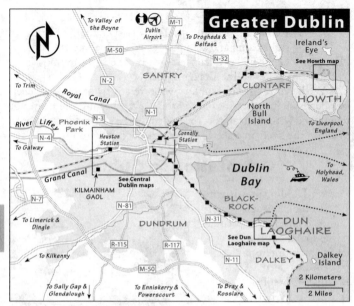

Tourist Information

Dublin's main tourist information office (TI) is a thriving hub of ticket and info desks filling an old church (June-Sept Mon-Sat 9:00-17:30, Oct-May Mon-Sat 9:30-17:30, Sun 10:30-15:00 year-round; a block off Grafton Street on Suffolk Street, tel. 01/850-230-330 or 01/605-7700, www.visitdublin.com). It has a bus-info desk, sandwich bar, more maps and books than you'll ever need, and racks advertising the busy entertainment scene. You can buy tickets to many theater and concert events here. It's also a good place to pick up brochures for destinations throughout Ireland. There's another TI at the airport (daily 8:00-20:00, Terminal 1). A smaller satellite TI is halfway down the east side of O'Connell Street (Mon-Sat 9:00-17:00, closed Sun).

Pick up the TI's *The Guide,* which includes a decent city map (free). Inside is a minimal schedule of happenings in town. The excellent *Collins Illustrated Discovering Dublin Map* (€6 at TIs and newsstands) is the ultimate city map, listing just about everything of interest, along with helpful opinions and tidbits of Dublin history.

Dublin Pass: This sightseeing pass is a good deal only if you like to visit lots of sights quickly (€35/1 day, €55/2 days, €65/3 days, €95/6 days, sold at TIs, www.dublinpass.ie). The pass saves a few minutes, when you'd otherwise need to wait in line to buy a ticket. It covers 34 museums, churches, literature-related sights, and expensive stops such as the Guinness Storehouse and the Old Jameson Distillery, plus the Aircoach airport bus—one-way from the airport to the city only (doesn't cover Airlink buses). However, the pass doesn't include the famous Book of Kells at Trinity College and gives only minor discounts on some bus tours and walking tours. Note that some of the sights it claims to "cover"—such as the National Gallery, the Chester Beatty Library, and the National Museum's Archaeology and Decorative Arts and History branches—are actually free (although passholders get other benefits that regular visitors won't, such as a free glossy guide at the National Gallery that normally costs €5). The booklet that comes with the pass can be a handy planning tool. But the bottom line is that most travelers won't get their money's worth out of this pass.

Arrival in Dublin

By Train

Dublin has two train stations. **Heuston Station,** on the west end of town, serves west and southwest Ireland (45-minute walk from O'Connell Bridge; take the LUAS light rail or bus #90—see below). **Connolly Station,** which serves the north, northwest, and Rosslare, is closer to the center (15-minute walk from O'Connell Bridge). Each station has ATMs, but only Heuston has lockers (small locker-€4/day, large-€6/day, 7-day maximum).

The two train stations are connected by the red line of the LUAS light rail system (see "Getting Around Dublin" on page 53) and by bus. Bus #90 runs along the river, linking both train stations, the bus station, and the city center (€1.40, 6/hour).

To reach Heuston Station from the city center, catch bus #90 on the south side of the river; to get to Connolly Station and Busáras Central Bus Station from the city center, catch #90 on the north side of the river.

By Bus

Bus Éireann, Ireland's national bus company, uses the **Busáras Central Bus Station** (pronounced Bu-SAUR-us...like a dinosaur). Located next to Connolly Station, it's a 10-minute walk or a short ride on bus #90 (described above) to the city center.

By Plane

Dublin Airport has two terminals. Terminal 2 serves American carriers (Delta, United, American, and US Airways), plus most Aer Lingus flights. Terminal 1 serves Ryanair, Aer Arann, Air Canada, Aer Lingus (some regional flights), and most European carriers, including British Airways, SAS, Lufthansa, Air France, Swiss Air, and Iberia (airport code: DUB, tel. 01/814-1111, www.dublinairport.ie).

Both terminals, located an easily walkable 150 yards apart, have ATMs, exchange bureaus, cafés, Wi-Fi, and luggage storage.

At Terminal 1, the left-luggage office (daily 6:00-23:00) is across the street in the Short-Term Car Park Atrium, along with a small supermarket. Terminal 1 also has a TI (daily 8:00-20:00), pharmacy, bus-and-rail info desk, and car-rental agencies (on ground/arrivals level).

Getting Downtown by Bus: You have two main choices—Airlink (double-decker green bus) or Aircoach (single-deck blue bus). Both pick up on the street directly in front of airport arrivals, at ground level at both terminals. Consider buying a **Rambler** city-bus pass at the airport TI (€6.50/1 day, €14.20/3 days, €23/5 days, see "Getting Around Dublin" on page 53), which covers the Airlink bus into town—but read the following description first to make sure Airlink is the best choice for your trip.

Airlink: Airlink bus #747 stops at both airport terminals, linking the airport to the city center along a strip a few blocks north and south of the river. The route includes the Busáras Central Bus Station, Connolly Station, O'Connell Street, Trinity College, Christ Church, and Heuston Station. Ask the driver which stop is closest to your hotel (€6, pay driver, 3/hour, 35-45 minutes, tel. 01/873-4222, www.dublinbus.ie).

Aircoach: To reach recommended hotels near St. Stephen's Green (south of the city center), the Aircoach bus is best (€7, covered by Dublin Pass, 3/hour, runs 5:00-23:30; pay driver and confirm best stop for your hotel, tel. 01/844-7118, www.aircoach.ie).

City Bus: The cheapest (and slowest) way from the airport to downtown Dublin is by city bus; buses marked #16A, #41, #41A, and #41B go to O'Connell Street (€2.40, exact change required, no change given, 4/hour, 55 minutes, tel. 01/873-4222, www.dublin-bus.ie).

Getting to Dun Laoghaire by Bus: The best way to get to Dun Laoghaire is to take the **Aircoach** bus (€9, hourly, 50 minutes, tel. 01/844-7118, www.aircoach.ie).

Taking a Taxi: Taxis from the airport into Dublin cost about €25; to Dun Laoghaire, about €45; to Howth, about €20 (see "Getting Around Dublin—By Taxi," page 53).

By Ferry

Coming from the UK, you have two choices. **Irish Ferries** has four sailings per day arriving at Dublin Port at the mouth of the River Liffey (two miles east of the town center). **Stena Line** also has four sailings per day, three arriving at Dublin Port and one at Dun Laoghaire (does not run off-season, easy DART train connections to and from Dublin—see page 105). For more information, see "Dublin Connections" on page 102.

By Car

Trust me: You don't want to drive in downtown Dublin. Cars are unnecessary for sightseeing in town, parking is expensive (about €25/day), and traffic will get your fighting Irish up. Save your car-rental days for cross-country travel between smaller towns and see this energetic city by taxi, bus, or on foot. If you have a car, sleep out in the suburbs (Dun Laoghaire or Howth), and ask your innkeeper about the best places to park.

Drivers renting a car at Dublin Airport but not staying in Dun Laoghaire or Howth can bypass the worst of the big-city traffic by taking the M-50 ring road south or west. The M-50 uses an automatic tolling system called eFlow. Your rented car should already come with an eFlow tag installed; however, confirm this when you pick up your car at the airport. The €3 toll per trip is automatically debited from the credit card that you used to rent the car (for pass details, see www.eflow.ie). Your rental car's eFlow tag will only work automatically for the M-50. On any other Irish toll roads (there aren't many), you'll have to pay with cash.

Helpful Hints

High Costs: Despite the demise of the Celtic Tiger economic boom (1995-2007—R.I.P.), Ireland is still one of the EU's more expensive countries. Restaurants and lodging—other than hostels—are more expensive the closer you get to the touristy Temple Bar district (see cheaper options under "Sleeping in Dublin" on page 91). A pint of beer in a Temple Bar pub costs €5 (a sobering thought).

Pickpockets: Irish destinations, especially Dublin, are not immune to this scourge. Wear a money belt or risk spending a couple of days of your cherished vacation in bureaucratic purgatory—on the phone canceling credit cards (see page 16) and at the embassy waiting for a replacement passport (see below). Wasting vacation time this way is like paying to wait in line at the DMV.

Tourist Victim Support Service: This service can be helpful if you run into any problems (Mon-Sat 10:00-18:00, Sun 12:00-18:00, tel. 01/478-5295, www.itas.ie).

Festivals: Book ahead during festivals and for any weekend. St. Patrick's Day is a four-day extravaganza in Dublin (March 15-18 in 2013, www.stpatricksday.ie). June 16 is Bloomsday, dedicated to the Irish author James Joyce and featuring the Messenger Bike Rally (www.jamesjoyce.ie). Hotels raise their prices and are packed on rugby weekends (about four per year), during the all-Ireland Gaelic football and hurling finals (Sundays in September), and during summer rock concerts.

Meet a Dubliner: The **City of a Thousand Welcomes** offers a free

DUBLIN

service that brings together volunteers and first-time visitors for a cup of tea or a pint. Visitors sign up online in advance, pick an available time slot, and meet their Dublin "ambassador" at the Little Museum of Dublin on St. Stephen's Green. You'll head for a nearby tearoom or pub and enjoy a short, informal conversation to get you oriented to the city (free, must be at least 21, 15 St. Stephens Green, tel. 01/661-1000, mobile 087-131-7129, www.cityofathousandwelcomes.com).

Internet Access: Internet cafés are plentiful. **Viva Internet** is close to Christ Church Cathedral (Mon-Thu 10:00-22:00, Fri-Sat 10:30-22:00, Sun 12:00-22:00, Lord Edward Street near City Hall, tel. 01/672-4725). **Central Internet Café** is aptly named (Mon-Fri 9:00-22:00, Sat 11:00-19:00, Sun 12:00-18:00, 6 Grafton Street, easy-to-miss door is directly opposite AIB Bank, tel. 01/677-8298, www.centralinternetcafe.com). **Global Internet Café** is north of the River Liffey (Mon-Fri 8:00-21:00, Sat 9:00-20:00, Sun 10:00-20:00, 8 Lower O'Connell Street, tel. 01/878-0295).

Bookstores: The giant granddaddy of them all is **Eason's**, five minutes north of the O'Connell Bridge (Mon-Sat 8:30-18:30, Sun 12:00-17:30, 40 Lower O'Connell Street, tel. 01/858-3800). South of the River Liffey, check out the intimate **Bookstore Upstairs,** 50 yards from the front gate of Trinity College (Mon-Fri 10:00-19:00, Sat 10:00-18:00, Sun 14:00-18:00, 36 College Green, tel. 01/679-6687).

Laundry: Patrick Street Launderette, a block southwest of Jurys Inn Christ Church on Patrick Street, is full-service only. Allow six hours and about €10 for a load (Mon-Sat 9:00-18:00, closed Sun, tel. 01/473-1779). The **All-American Launderette** offers self- and full-service options (Mon-Sat 8:30-19:00, Sun 10:00-18:00, 40 South Great George's Street, tel. 01/677-2779).

Bike Rental: Phoenix Park Bike Hire offers a stress-free ride option in huge, 1,750-acre Phoenix Park. It's located off Chesterfield Avenue, the main road bisecting the park, at the closest corner of the park to the city center, roughly across the river from Heuston Station (€5/hour, €20/day, daily 10:00-19:00 "weather depending," mobile 086-265-6258, www.phoenix-parkbikehire.com).

Car Rental: For Dublin car-rental information, see page 483.

Updates to this Book: For news about changes to this book's coverage since it was published, see www.ricksteves.com/update.

Getting Around Dublin

You'll do most of Dublin on foot, though when you need public transportation, you'll find it readily available and easy to use.

By Bus: Buses are cheap and cover the city thoroughly. Most lines start at the four quays, or piers, that are nearest to O'Connell Bridge. If you're away from the center, nearly any bus takes you back downtown. Some bus stops are "request only" stops: Be alert to the bus numbers (above the windshield) of approaching buses. When you see your bus coming, hold your arm out from your side with your palm extended into the street to flag it down. Tell the driver where you're going, and he'll ask for €1.40-2.65 depending on the number of stops. Bring change or lose any excess. Bus #90 connects the bus and train stations (see "Arrival in Dublin—By Train" on page 49).

The bus office at 59 Upper O'Connell Street has free bus-route maps and sells two different city-bus passes (Mon 8:30-17:30, Tue-Fri 9:00-17:30, Sat 9:00-14:00, Sun 9:30-14:00, tel. 01/873-4222, www.dublinbus.ie). The three-day **Rambler pass** is handiest for the average traveler's stay, costing €14.20 and covering the Airlink airport bus (but not Aircoach buses or DART trains). The one-day **Short Hop pass,** which costs €11.75, includes DART trains (but not Airlink or Aircoach buses). Passes are also sold at TIs, and at newsstands and markets citywide (mostly Centra, Mace, Spar, and Londis).

By DART (Train): Speedy commuter trains run along the coast, connecting Dublin with Dun Laoghaire's ferry terminal, Howth's harbor, and recommended B&Bs. Think of the DART line as a giant "C" that serves coastal suburbs from Bray in the south to Howth in the north (€2.50, €4.70 round-trips valid same day only, Eurail Pass valid but you'll use up a valuable flexi-day, tel. 01/703-3504, www.irishrail.ie/home). For more information, see "Getting to Dun Laoghaire" on page 105 and "Getting to Howth" on page 111.

By LUAS (Light Rail): The city's light-rail system has two main lines (red and green) that serve inland suburbs. The more useful line for tourists is the red line, connecting the Heuston and Connolly train stations (a 15-minute ride apart) at opposite edges of the Central 1 Zone. In between, the Busáras Central Bus Station, Smithfield, and Museum stops can be handy (€1.60, 6/hour, runs 5:30-24:45, tel. 1-800-300-604, www.luas.ie). Check the 15-foot-high pillars at each boarding platform that display the time and destination of the next LUAS train. Make sure you're on the right platform for the direction you want to go.

By Taxi: Taxis are everywhere and easy to hail (cheaper for 3-4 people). In recent years, Dublin has acquired a glut of new cabbies who are fiercely competing for fewer customers due to the downfall of the Celtic Tiger economy. Cabbies are generally honest, friendly, and good sources of information (€4.10 daytime minimum 8:00-20:00, €4.45 nighttime minimum 20:00-8:00, €1 for each additional adult, figure about €12 for most crosstown rides, €40/hour for guided joyride).

Tours in Dublin

While Dublin's physical treasures are lackluster by European standards, the gritty city has a fine story to tell and people with a natural knack for telling it. It's a good town for walking tours, and the competition is fierce. Dublin is noisy; if you can't hear the guide, move in closer. Pamphlets touting creative walks are posted all over town. Choices include medieval walks, literary walks, Georgian Dublin walks, traditional music pub crawls, and even a rock-and-stroll walk tracing the careers of contemporary Irish bands. Taking an evening walk is a great way to meet other travelers. The Dublin TI also offers series of free, good-quality "iWalks" for travelers with iPods or other portable media players (download with maps at www.visitdublin.com). There is also a Visit Dublin app for iPhones and Android smartphones.

For help finding the departure points of the following recommended tours, see the map on page 58.

By Foot

▲▲**Historical Walking Tour**—This is your best introductory walk. A group of hardworking history graduates—many of whom claim to have done more than just kiss the Blarney Stone—enliven Dublin's basic historic strip (Trinity College, Old Parliament House, Dublin Castle, and Christ Church Cathedral). You'll get the story of their city, from its Viking origins to the present. Guides speak at length about the roots of Ireland's struggle with Britain. As you listen to your guide, you'll stand in front of buildings that aren't much to look at, but are lots to talk about (May-Sept daily at 11:00 and 15:00, April and Oct daily at 11:00, Nov-March Fri-Sun only at 11:00). All walks last two hours and cost €12 (get the €10 "student" discount rate with this book in 2013, free for kids under 14, departs from front gate of Trinity College, private tours available, mobile 087-688-9412 or 087-830-3523, www.historicalinsights.ie).

▲▲▲**Traditional Irish Musical Pub Crawl**—This impressive and entertaining tour visits the upstairs rooms of three pubs; there, you'll listen to two musicians talk about, play, and sing traditional Irish music. While having only two musicians makes the music a bit thin (Irish music aficionados will say you're better off just finding a good session), the evening—though touristy—is not gimmicky.

It's an education in traditional Irish music. The musicians clearly enjoy introducing rookies to their art and are very good at it. Humor is their primary educational tool. In the summer, this popular tour frequently sells out—reserve ahead (€12, €1 discount with this book in 2013, beer extra, allow 2.5 hours, April-Oct daily at 19:30, Nov-March Thu-Sat only, maximum 50 tourists, meet upstairs at Gogarty's Pub at the corner of Fleet and Anglesea in the Temple Bar area, tel. 01/475-3313, www.musicalpubcrawl.com).

▲Dublin Literary Pub Crawl—Two actors take 40 or so tourists on a walk, stopping at four pubs. Their clever banter introduces the novice to the high *craic* of James Joyce, Seán O'Casey, and W. B. Yeats. The two-hour tour is punctuated with 20-minute pub breaks (free time). While the beer lubricates the social fun, it dilutes the content of the evening. (If you want straight lit and drama, find a real performance; there are many throughout the summer, such as the lunchtime hour on weekends at 13:00 at the Dublin Writers' Museum, described on page 77.) However, the pub crawl is an easygoing excuse to drink beer in busy pubs, hook up with other travelers, and get a dose of Irish witty lit (€12, April-Oct daily at 19:30, Nov-March Thu-Sun at 19:30; you can normally just show up, but call ahead in July-Aug when it can fill up; meet upstairs in the Duke Pub—off Grafton on Duke Street, tel. 01/670-5602, mobile 087-263-0270, www.dublinpubcrawl.com). Connoisseurs of Irish pubs will want to buy the excellent *Dublin Literary Pub Crawl* guidebook by pub-crawl founder Colm Quilligan.

1916 Rebellion Walking Tour—This two-hour walk breathes gritty life into the most turbulent year in modern Irish history, when idealistic Irish rebels launched the Easter Uprising—eventually leading to independence from Britain. Guide Lorcan Collins has written a guidebook called *The Easter Rising*—worth seeking out—and is passionate about his walks (€12, €2 discount with this book in 2013, daily March-Oct Mon-Sat at 11:30, Sun at 13:00, no tours Nov-March, departs from International Bar at 23 Wicklow Street, mobile 086-858-3847, www.1916rising.com).

Pat Liddy's Walking Tours—Pat Liddy is one of Dublin's top historians. He and his guides take groups on enthusiastic and informal 1.5-hour walks of hidden Dublin districts. Unlike most Dublin walks, this one does a good job of covering the often overlooked but historic north side of town. You'll start near the General Post Office building, wind down across the river to City Hall, through Temple Bar, and end at Trinity College (€10, April-Oct

DUBLIN

daily at 11:00, meet in front of the Dublin Bus Office at 59 Upper O'Connell Street, tel. 01/832-9406, mobile 087-905-2480, www. walkingtours.ie).

Rebel Tours of Dublin—These 1.5-hour walks focus on revolutionary events in Dublin from 1913 to 1923 as Ireland shed British rule. Strongly opinionated, these guides view history through the lens of Irish Republicanism (€10, departs Mon-Sat at 11:30 from Sinn Fein Bookshop at 58 Parnell Square, book ahead by phone, tel. 01/814-8542).

By Bike

Dublin City Bike Tours—You'll "get your *craic* on a saddle" with Dublin City Bike Tours as you pedal across this flat city on innovative urban bikes. Their fun tours visit 20 points of interest north and south of the River Liffey, covering more ground (five miles) than walking tours. Designed for riders of average fitness, they set a casual pace, and rarely let a little rain stop them (€24; includes bike, helmet, snack, and water; €4 discount with this book—show when you pay, cash only, reserve in advance, 2.5 hours, March-Nov daily at 10:00, additional tours Fri and Sat at 14:00, custom tours available for groups of 8 or more, departs Isaac's Hostel a half-block west of Busáras Central Bus Station at 2-5 Frenchman's Lane, mobile 087-134-1866, www.dublincitybiketours.com).

By Bus (on Land and Water)

▲Hop-on, Hop-off Bus Tours— Two companies (Dublin Bus Tour and City Sightseeing Dublin) offer hop-on, hop-off bus tours of Dublin, doing virtually identical 1.5-hour circuits. You can get on or off at your choice of about 20 stops (€18, 4/ hour, daily 9:00-17:00—Dublin Bus

Tour until 18:30, buy ticket on board, valid for 48 hours). Buses are double-deckers (roofless is fun on dry days), with live running commentaries. **Dublin Bus Tour** (green buses) drivers provide fun and quirky narration (tel. 01/703-1328, www.dublinsightseeing.ie). **City Sightseeing Dublin** (red buses) come with both a guide and a driver, rather than just a driver who guides (tel. 01/872-9010, www.irishcitytours.com).

This type of tour, which runs in many European cities but isn't always well executed, is made-to-order for Dublin, and buses run so frequently that they make your sightseeing super-efficient. Stops include the far-flung Guinness Storehouse and Kilmainham Gaol, although the Dublin Bus Tour stops a few blocks from the Gaol. Each company's map, free with your ticket, details various discounts that you'll get at Dublin's sights (such as the Guinness Storehouse, Viking Splash tour, Old Jameson Distillery, Dublin Writers' Museum, Dublinia, Christ Church Cathedral, and others). To take advantage of the discounts, take a bus tour before you do all of your sightseeing.

▲**Viking Splash Tours**—If you'd like to ride in a WWII amphibious vehicle—driven by a Viking-costumed guide who's as liable to spout history as he is to growl—this is for you. The tour starts with a group roar from the Viking within us all. At first, the guide talks as if he were a Viking ("When we came here in 841..."), but soon the patriot emerges as he tags Irish history onto the sights you pass. Near the end of the 1.25-hour tour (punctuated by occasional group roars at passersby), you don a life jacket for a slow spin up and down a boring canal. Although it's covered, the boat is breezy—dress appropriately. Kids who expect a Viking splash may feel like they've been trapped in a classroom, but historians will enjoy the talk more than the gimmick (€20, Feb-Nov daily 10:00-17:00, no tours Dec-Jan, departs about hourly from the north side of St. Stephen's Green opposite Dawson Street, ticket office at 64-65 Patrick Street, tel. 01/707-6000, www.vikingsplash.com).

Weekend Tour Packages for Students in Dublin

Andy Steves (Rick's son) runs Weekend Student Adventures, offering experiential three-day weekend tours for €299, designed for American students studying abroad (www.wsaeurope.com for details on tours of Dublin and other great cities).

Sights in Dublin

South of the River Liffey
Trinity College

Founded in 1592 by Queen Elizabeth I to establish a Protestant way of thinking about God, Trinity has long been Ireland's most prestigious college. Originally, the student body was limited to rich Protestant males. Women were admitted

in 1903, and Catholics—though allowed entrance by the school much earlier—were only given formal permission by the Catholic Church to study at Trinity in the 1970s. Today, half of Trinity's

DUBLIN

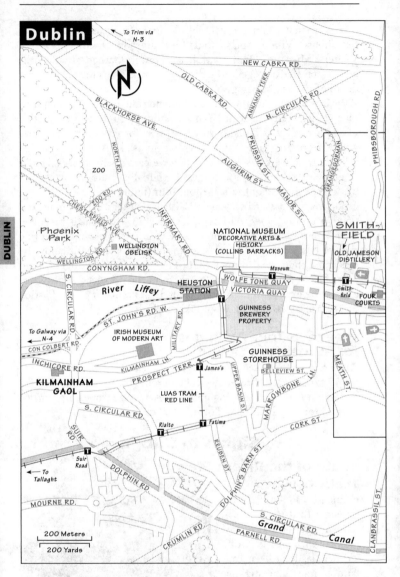

Dublin

To Trim via N-3

NEW CABRA RD.

OLD CABRA RD.

BLACKHORSE AVE.

ANNAMOE TERR.

N. CIRCULAR RD.

PHIBSBOROUGH RD.

NORTH RD.

PRUSSIA ST.

AUGHRIM ST.

MANOR ST.

GRANGEGORMAN

ZOO

ZOO RD.

CHESTERFIELD AVE.

INFIRMARY RD.

SMITH-FIELD

Phoenix Park

WELLINGTON OBELISK

NATIONAL MUSEUM
DECORATIVE ARTS &
HISTORY
(COLLINS BARRACKS)

OLD JAMESON DISTILLERY

WELLINGTON RD.

CONYNGHAM RD.

WOLFE TONE QUAY

Museum

River Liffey

HEUSTON STATION

VICTORIA QUAY

Smithfield

FOUR COURTS

S. CIRCULAR RD.

St. John's Rd. W.

GUINNESS BREWERY PROPERTY

MEATH ST.

To Galway via N-4

CON COLBERT RD.

IRISH MUSEUM OF MODERN ART

MILITARY RD.

GUINNESS STOREHOUSE

INCHICORE RD.

KILMAINHAM LN.

PROSPECT TERR.

James's

UPPER BASIN ST.

BELLEVIEW ST.

KILMAINHAM GAOL

LUAS TRAM RED LINE

MARROWBONE LN.

CORK ST.

S. CIRCULAR RD.

Rialto

Fatima

SUIR RD.

Suir Road

DOLPHIN RD.

REUBEN ST.

DOLPHIN'S BARN ST.

To Tallaght

MOURNE RD.

S. CIRCULAR RD.

CLANBRASSIL ST.

200 Meters
200 Yards

CRUMLIN RD.

PARNELL RD.

Grand Canal

DUBLIN

12,500 students are women, and 70 percent are culturally Catholic (although only about 20 percent of Irish youth are churchgoing).

▲▲Trinity College Tour—Trinity students organize and lead 30-minute **tours** of their campus (look just inside the gate for posted departure times and a ticket-seller on a stool). You'll get a rundown of the mostly Georgian architecture; a peek at student life past and present; and the enjoyable company of your guide, a witty Irish college kid.

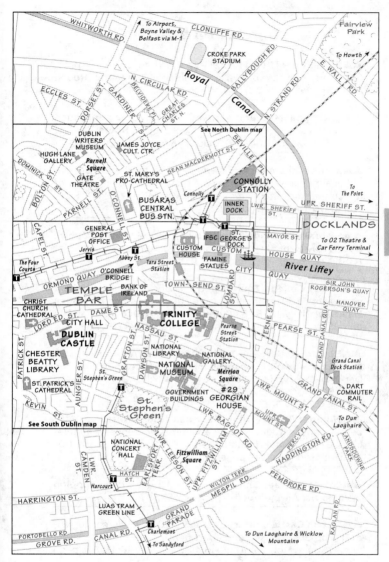

Cost and Hours: €10, includes €9 fee to see Book of Kells, where the tour leaves you; May-Sept daily 10:15-15:40, Feb-April and Oct-Nov Sat-Sun only, no tours Dec-Jan, departs roughly every 30 minutes, weather permitting.

▲▲**Book of Kells in the Trinity Old Library**—The only Trinity campus interior welcoming tourists is the Old Library (just follow the signs), with its precious Book of Kells. Written on vellum (calfskin) in the late eighth century—by Irish monks on the island

Dublin at a Glance

▲▲▲**Traditional Irish Musical Pub Crawl** A fascinating, practical, and enjoyable primer on traditional Irish music. **Hours:** April-Oct daily at 19:30, Nov-March Thu-Sat only. See page 54.

▲▲▲**National Museum: Archaeology** Interesting collection of Irish treasures from the Stone Age to today. **Hours:** Tue-Sat 10:00-17:00, Sun 14:00-17:00, closed Mon. See page 63.

▲▲▲**Kilmainham Gaol** Historic jail used by the British as a political prison—today a museum that tells a moving story of the suffering of the Irish people. **Hours:** Mon-Sat 9:30-16:30, Sun 10:00-16:30. See page 83.

▲▲**Historical Walking Tour** Your best introduction to Dublin. **Hours:** May-Sept daily at 11:00 and 15:00, April and Oct daily at 11:00, Nov-March Fri-Sun only at 11:00. See page 54.

▲▲**Trinity College Tour** Ireland's most famous school, best visited with a 30-minute tour led by one of its students. **Hours:** May-Sept daily 10:15-15:40, Feb-April and Oct-Nov Sat-Sun only, no tours Dec-Jan; weather permitting. See page 58.

▲▲**Book of Kells in the Trinity Old Library** An exquisite illuminated manuscript, the most important piece of art from the Dark Ages. **Hours:** May-Sept daily 9:30-17:00; Oct-April Mon-Sat 9:30-16:30, Sun 12:00-16:30. See page 59.

▲▲**Number Twenty-Nine Georgian House** Restored 18th-century house; tours provide an intimate glimpse of middle-class Georgian life. **Hours:** Tue-Sat 10:00-17:00, Sun 12:00-17:00, closed Mon. See page 65.

▲▲**Grafton Street** The city's liveliest pedestrian shopping mall. **Hours:** Always open. See page 65.

▲▲**Dublin Castle** The city's historic 700-year-old castle, featuring ornate English state apartments, tourable only with a guide. **Hours:** Mon-Sat 10:00-16:45, Sun 12:00-16:45. See page 68.

▲▲**Chester Beatty Library** American expatriate's eclectic yet sumptuous collection of literary and religious treasures from Islam, the Orient, and medieval Europe. **Hours:** May-Sept Mon-Fri 10:00-17:00, Sat 11:00-17:00, Sun 13:00-17:00; Oct-April Tue-Fri 10:00-17:00, Sat 11:00-17:00, Sun 13:00-17:00, closed Mon. See page 68.

▲▲**Temple Bar** Dublin's trendiest neighborhood, with shops, cafés, theaters, galleries, pubs, and restaurants—a great spot for live traditional music. **Hours:** Always open. See page 71.

▲▲**O'Connell Bridge** Landmark bridge spanning the River Liffey at the center of Dublin. **Hours:** Always open. See page 72.

▲▲**O'Connell Street** Dublin's grandest promenade and main drag, packed with history and ideal for a stroll. **Hours:** Always open. See page 73.

▲**National Gallery** Fine collection of top Irish painters and European masters. **Hours:** Mon-Sat 9:30-17:30, Thu until 20:30, Sun 12:00-17:30. See page 63.

▲**Merrion Square** Enjoyable and inviting park with a fun statue of Oscar Wilde. **Hours:** Always open. See page 65.

▲**St. Stephen's Green** Relaxing park surrounded by fine Georgian buildings. **Hours:** Always open. See page 66.

▲**Dublinia** A fun, kid-friendly look at Dublin's Viking and medieval past with a side order of archaeology and a cool town model. **Hours:** Daily March-Sept 10:00-17:00, Oct-Feb 11:00-16:30. See page 70.

▲**Guinness Storehouse** The home of Ireland's national beer, with a museum of beer-making, a gallery of clever ads, and the spectacular Gravity Bar with panoramic city views. **Hours:** Daily 9:30-17:00, July-Aug until 19:00. See page 84.

▲**National Museum: Decorative Arts and History** Shows off Irish dress, furniture, silver, and weaponry with a special focus on the 1916 rebellion, fight for independence, and civil war. **Hours:** Tue-Sat 10:00-17:00, Sun 14:00-17:00, closed Mon. See page 86.

▲**Gaelic Athletic Association Museum** High-tech museum of traditional Gaelic sports such as hurling and Irish football. **Hours:** June-Aug daily 9:30-18:00; Sept-May Mon-Sat 9:30-17:00, Sun 11:30-17:00. On game Sundays, it's open only to ticket-holders. See page 86.

DUBLIN

of Iona, Scotland—this enthusiastically decorated copy of the four Gospels was taken safely inland to the Irish monastery at Kells in A.D. 806 after a series of Viking raids. Arguably the finest piece of art from what is generally called the Dark Ages, the Book of Kells shows that monastic life in this far fringe of Europe was far from dark.

Cost and Hours: €9, included in €10 Trinity College tour—see earlier, audioguide-€5; May-Sept daily 9:30-17:00; Oct-April Mon-Sat 9:30-16:30, Sun 12:00-16:30; tel. 01/896-2320, www.tcd.ie/library/bookofkells. A long line often snakes out of the building. Minimize your wait by avoiding the midday crunch (roughly 11:00-14:30).

Visiting the Library: The first-class "Turning Darkness into Light" **exhibit,** with a one-way route, puts the 680-page illuminated manuscript in its historical and cultural context, preparing you to see the original book and other precious manuscripts in the treasury. Make a point to spend time in the exhibit (before reaching the actual Book of Kells). Especially interesting are the five-minute video clips showing the exacting care that went into transcribing the monk-uscripts and the ancient art of bookbinding. Two small TV screens (on opposite walls of the exhibition room) run continuously, silently demonstrating the monks' labors of love.

The manuscript has been bound into four separate volumes, and at any given time, two of the four gospels are on display in the **treasury.** The crowd around the one glass case that displays the treasures can be off-putting, but hold your own and get up close. You'll see four richly decorated, 1,200-year-old pages—two text and two decorated cover pages. The library treasury also displays two other books—likely the Book of Armagh (A.D. 807) and the Book of Durrow (A.D. 680)—neither of which can be checked out.

Next, a stairway leads upstairs to the 200-foot-long main chamber of the Old Library (from 1732), stacked to its towering ceiling with 200,000 of the library's oldest books. Here, you'll find one of a dozen surviving original copies of the **Proclamation of the Irish Republic.** Patrick Pearse read these words outside the General Post Office on April 24, 1916, starting the Easter Uprising that led to Irish independence. Read the entire thing...imagining it was yours. Notice the inclusive opening phrase and the seven signatories (each of whom was executed).

Another national icon is nearby: the 15th-century **Brian Boru harp,** the oldest surviving Irish harp (its name is misleading—the Irish High King Brian Boru died 400 years before the harp was created). The Irish love of music is so intense that Ireland is the only nation with a musical instrument as its national symbol. You'll see this harp's likeness everywhere, including on the back of all Irish euro coins and government documents. The harp's inspirational effect on Gaelic culture was so strong that Queen Elizabeth I, who tried to eradicate the Gaelic culture during her reign (1558-1603), ordered Irish harpists to be hung wherever found and their instruments smashed.

For more on the Book of Kells, see page 458 in the Ireland: Past and Present chapter.

National Museums South of Trinity College

▲▲▲National Museum: Archaeology—Showing off the treasures of Ireland from the Stone Age to modern times, this branch of the National Museum is itself a national treasure. Under one dome, it's wonderfully digestible. Ireland's Bronze Age gold fills the center. Up four steps, a prehistoric Ireland exhibit rings the gold. To the right, you'll find the treasury, with the museum's most famous pieces (brooches, chalices, and other examples of Celtic metalwork). To the left are three circular walls, which hide 2,000-year-old bog mummies. The collection's superstar is the gold, enamel, and amber eighth-century Tara Brooch.

The best Viking artifacts in town are upstairs with the medieval collection. If you'll be visiting Cong (in Connemara, near Galway—see page 327), seek out the original Cross of Cong.

Cost and Hours: Free entry, guided tour-€2, Tue-Sat 10:00-17:00, Sun 14:00-17:00, closed Mon, good café, between Trinity College and St. Stephen's Green on Kildare Street, tel. 01/677-7444—call in morning for sporadic tour schedule, www.museum.ie. For background information, read "Irish Art" on page 457.

Nearby: As you exit the museum, glance over at **Leinster House,** next door (guarded and safely distant from the street). It was once the Duke of Leinster's town residence. Today, it houses the Irish Dáil (parliament) and Seanad (senate), which meet here 90 days of each year.

▲National Gallery—This museum has Ireland's best collection of European masters: Vermeer, Caravaggio, Monet, and Picasso. It also features a hall that displays the work of top Irish painters, including Jack Yeats (the brother of the famous poet). Don't miss the wonderfully romantic *Meeting on the Turret Stairs* by Frederic Burton, voted Ireland's favorite painting in 2012. The works are

DUBLIN

all impressive—although the collection is not nearly as extensive as national galleries in London or Paris.

Study the floor-plan flier and take advantage of the free audioguide. Be sure to walk the series of rooms on the ground floor devoted to Irish painting and get to know artists you may never have heard of before. Visit the National Portrait Gallery on the mezzanine level for an insight into the great personalities of Ireland. You'll find Caravaggio and Vermeer on the top floor. In his *Taking of Christ*, Caravaggio, master of the chiaroscuro style, makes dramatic use of light and shadow for emphasis. Vermeer's *Lady Writing a Letter with her Maid*, one of only 30-some known works by the Dutch artist, shows his trademark focus on life's quiet moments.

Cost and Hours: Free, Mon-Sat 9:30-17:30, Thu until 20:30, Sun 12:00-17:30, Merrion Square West, tel. 01/661-5133, www. nationalgallery.ie.

Tours: The museum offers free audioguide tours (donations accepted) and free 45-minute guided tours (Sat at 14:00, Sun at 13:00 and 14:00).

National Museum of Natural History—Called "the dead zoo" by Dubliners, this cramped collection of stuffed exotic animals comes across like the locker room on Noah's Ark. But if you're into beaks, bones, bugs, and boars, this Victorian relic is for you. Standing tall above a sea of taxidermy is the regal skeleton of a giant Irish elk from the last Ice Age; this relic dwarfs a modern moose. The earnest displays need a new home, and a fund-raising effort is under way.

Cost and Hours: Free, Tue-Sat 10:00-17:00, Sun 14:00-17:00, closed Mon, Merrion Square West, tel. 01/677-7444, www. museum.ie.

National Library—Literature holds a lofty place in the Irish psyche. To feel the fire-and-ice pulse of Ireland's most influential poet, visit the W. B. Yeats exhibit in the library basement. This space was originally intended to host rotating exhibits, but the display on the life of Yeats proved so popular it became permanent. The artifacts flesh out the very human passions of this poet and playwright, with samples of his handwritten manuscripts and surprisingly interesting mini-documentaries of the times he lived in. Upstairs, you can get help making use of the library records to trace your genealogy.

Cost and Hours: Free; Mon-Wed 9:30-20:00, Thu-Fri 9:30-17:00, Sat 9:30-16:30, closed Sun; Yeats tours Wed at 13:00 and Sat at 11:00 and 15:00; café, tel. 01/603-0200, 2-3 Kildare Street, www.nli.ie.

Merrion Square and Nearby

▲**Merrion Square**—Laid out in 1762, this square is ringed by elegant Georgian houses decorated with fine doors—a Dublin trademark. (If you're inspired by the ornate knobs and knockers, there's a shop by that name on nearby Nassau Street.) The park, once the exclusive domain of the residents, is now a delightful public escape and ideal for a picnic. To learn what "snogging" is, walk through the park on a sunny day, when it's full of smooching lovers. Oscar Wilde, lounging wittily on a boulder on the corner nearest the town center and surrounded by his clever quotes, provides a fun photo op (see photo on page 80).

▲▲**Number Twenty-Nine Georgian House**—The carefully restored house at Number 29 Lower Fitzwilliam Street gives an intimate glimpse of middle-class Georgian life (which seems pretty high-class). From the sidewalk, descend the stairs to the basement-level entrance (corner of Lower Fitzwilliam and Lower Mount Streets, opposite southern corner of Merrion Square). Start with an interesting 15-minute video (you're welcome to bring in a cup of coffee from the café) before joining your guide, who takes you on a fascinating 35-minute walk through this 1790 Dublin home.

Cost and Hours: €6, tours leave regularly, Tue-Sat 10:00-17:00, Sun 12:00-17:00, closed Mon, tel. 01/702-6165.

Grafton Street and St. Stephen's Green Area

▲▲**Grafton Street**—Once filled with noisy traffic, today's Grafton Street is Dublin's liveliest pedestrian shopping mall and people-watching paradise. A 10-minute stroll past street musicians takes you from Trinity College to St. Stephen's Green (and makes you wonder why some American merchants are so terrified of a car-free street). Walking south from Trinity College, you'll pass a buxom statue of "sweet" Molly Malone (also known as "the tart with the cart"). Next, you'll pass two venerable department stores: the Irish Brown Thomas and the English Marks & Spencer. Johnson's Court alley leads to the Powerscourt Townhouse Shopping Centre, which tastefully fills a converted Georgian mansion. The huge, glass-covered St. Stephen's Green Shopping Centre and the peaceful green itself mark the top of Grafton Street. For fun, gather a pile of coins and walk the street, putting each human statue into action with a donation. Consider stopping at the recommended Bewley's Café for coffee with a second-floor view of the action.

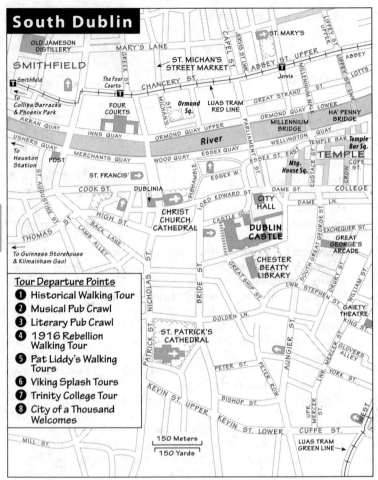

South Dublin

Tour Departure Points
1 Historical Walking Tour
2 Musical Pub Crawl
3 Literary Pub Crawl
4 1916 Rebellion Walking Tour
5 Pat Liddy's Walking Tours
6 Viking Splash Tours
7 Trinity College Tour
8 City of a Thousand Welcomes

150 Meters
150 Yards

DUBLIN

▲**St. Stephen's Green**—This city park was originally a medieval commons, complete with gory public executions. It was enclosed in 1664 and gradually surrounded with fine Georgian buildings. Today, it provides 22 acres of grassy refuge for Dubliners. At the northwest corner (near the end of Grafton Street) you'll be confronted by a looming marble arch erected to honor British officers killed during the Boer War. Locals nicknamed it "Traitor's Arch," as most Irish sympathized with the underdog Boers. On a sunny afternoon, this open space is a wonderful world apart from the big city. When marveling at the elegance of Georgian Dublin, remember that during the Georgian period, Dublin was the second-most important city in the British Empire. Area big shots knew that any money wrung from the local populace not spent in Dublin would

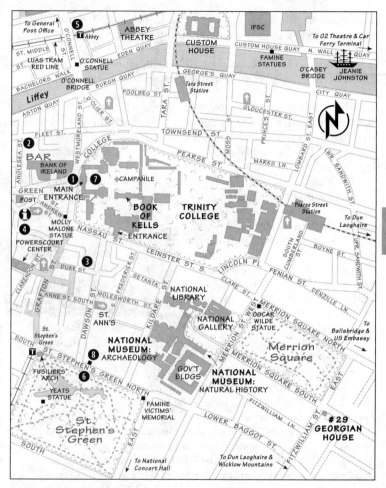

end up in London. Since it was "use it or lose it," they used it—with gusto—to beautify their city.

Little Museum of Dublin—A fun, two-room labor of love just north of St. Stephen's Green, this collection was donated by local Dubliners and focuses on life in the city since 1900. An engaging mix of history and pop culture, this museum also sponsors the City of a Thousand Welcomes Meet a Dubliner program (see page 51). Artifacts range from a first edition copy of James Joyce's *Ulysses* to a sticker proving that discount airline Ryanair once provided something unthinkable today—business class seating. Other displays cover local rock band U2 and Muhammad Ali's 1972 fight at Croke Park. History buffs linger at sly Eamon de Valera's five-part memo to his fellow Irish rebel Michael Collins. In part one, he gives Collins complete authority to negotiate with British officials over Irish independence—and then waters down this authority over the next four parts.

Cost and Hours: €5, daily 11:00-18:00, tours on request, 15 St. Stephen's Green, tel. 01/661-1000, www.littlemuseum.ie.

Dublin Castle and Nearby

▲▲**Dublin Castle**—Built on the spot of the first Viking fortress, this castle was the seat of English rule in Ireland for 700 years. Located where the Poddle and Liffey rivers came together, making a black pool (*dubh linn* in Irish), Dublin Castle was the official residence of the viceroy who implemented the will of the British

royalty. In this stirring setting, the Brits handed power over to Michael Collins and the Irish in 1922. Today, it's used for fancy state and charity functions.

Standing in the courtyard, you can imagine the ugliness of the British-Irish situation. Notice the statue of justice above the gate—pointedly without her blindfold and admiring her sword. As Dubliners say, "There she stands, above her station, with her face to the palace and her arse to the nation." The fancy interior is viewable only with a 45-minute tour, which offers a fairly boring room-by-room walk through the lavish state apartments of this most English of Irish palaces. The tour finishes with a look at the foundations of the Norman tower and the best remaining chunk of the 13th-century town wall.

Cost and Hours: €4.50, buy tickets in courtyard under portico opposite clock tower, required tours depart hourly, Mon-Sat 10:00-16:45, Sun 12:00-16:45, tel. 01/645-8813, www.dublincastle.ie.

▲▲**Chester Beatty Library**—Chester Beatty was a rich American mining engineer who retired to Ireland in 1950, later becoming its first honorary citizen. He left this priceless and eclectic collection to his adopted homeland as a public charitable trust. Today, Ireland has put a modern glass roof over the parade ground separating two old army barracks and filled it with Beatty's treasures. It's a small collection, but delightfully displayed and described. The top floor focuses on the world's great religions (strong on Islam and Christianity) with displays on dervish whirls, calligraphy in Islam, and early Asian Christian manuscripts. The bottom floor is all about the written word, with topics including etching, medieval bookbinding, and fine old manuscripts.

As you wander, you'll see books carved out of jade, ornate snuff bottles, rhino-horn cups, and even the oldest surviving copy of St. Paul's letter to the Romans (A.D. 180). Other highlights include a graceful Burmese book written on palm leaves—bound together to unfold like an accordion—and a densely ornamental sunburst motif from a 500-year-old Iranian Quran.

Cost and Hours: Free; May-Sept Mon-Fri 10:00-17:00, Sat 11:00-17:00, Sun 13:00-17:00; Oct-April Tue-Fri 10:00-17:00, Sat 11:00-17:00, Sun 13:00-17:00, closed Mon; coffee shop, tel. 01/407-0750, www.cbl.ie. You'll find the library behind Dublin Castle (follow the signs).

Dublin City Hall—The first Georgian building in this very Georgian city stands proudly overlooking Dame Street, in front of the gate to Dublin Castle. Built in 1779 as the Royal Exchange, it introduced the Georgian style (then very popular in Britain and on the Continent) to Ireland. Step inside (it's free) to feel the prosperity and confidence of Dublin in her 18th-century glory days. In 1852, this building became the City Hall. Under the grand rotunda, a cycle of heroic paintings tells the city's history. (The mosaics on the floor convey such homilies as "Obedience makes the happiest citizenry.")

Pay your respects to the 18-foot-tall statue of Daniel O'Connell, the great orator and liberator who, in 1829, won emancipation for Catholics in Ireland from the much-despised Protestants over in London. The body of modern Irish rebel leader Michael Collins lay in state here after his assassination in 1922. The greeter sits like the Maytag repairman at the information desk, eager to give you more information. Downstairs is the excellent *Story of the Capital* exhibition, which has storyboards and video clips of Dublin's history.

Cost and Hours: €4, free audioguide, coffee shop, Mon-Sat 10:00-17:00, closed Sun, tel. 01/222-2204, www.dublincity.ie.

Dublin's Cathedrals Area

Because of Dublin's English past (particularly Henry VIII's Reformation, which led to the dissolution of the Catholic monasteries in both Ireland and England in 1539), neither of its top two churches is Catholic. Christ Church Cathedral and nearby St. Patrick's Cathedral are both Church of Ireland (Anglican). In the late 19th century, the cathedrals underwent extensive restoration. The rich Guinness brewery family forked out the dough to try to make St. Patrick's Cathedral outshine Christ Church—whose patrons were the equally rich, rival Jameson family of distillery fame. However, in Catholic Ireland, these Anglican sights feel hollow, and they're more famous than visit-worthy.

Christ Church Cathedral—Occupying the same site as the first wooden church built on this spot by King Sitric in late Viking times (c. 1030), the present structure dates from a mix of periods: Norman and Gothic, but mostly Victorian Neo-Gothic (1870s restoration work). Inside you'll find the reputed tomb of the Norman warlord Strongbow, who led the thin edge of the English military wedge that eventually dominated Ireland for centuries. This oldest building in Dublin has an unusually large underground crypt, containing stocks, statues, the cathedral's silver, and an atmospheric café.

Cost and Hours: €6 donation to church includes downstairs crypt silver exhibition, €12.25 combo-ticket includes Dublinia (described next)—saving you €1.25; Mon-Sat 9:30-18:30, Sun 12:30-14:30; €4 guided tours Sat at 11:00, 12:00, 14:00, and 15:00; tel. 01/677-8099, http://cccdub.ie.

Evensong: A 45-minute evensong service is sung Sun at 15:30.

▲**Dublinia**—This exhibit, which highlights Dublin's Viking and medieval past, is a hit with youngsters. The exhibits are laid out on three floors. The ground floor focuses on Viking Dublin, explaining life aboard a Viking ship and inside a Viking house. Viking traders introduced urban life and commerce to Ireland—but kids will be most interested in gawking at their gory weaponry.

The next floor up reveals Dublin's day-to-day life in medieval times, from chivalrous knights and damsels in town fairs to the brutal ravages of the Plague. Like the rest of Europe at that time (1347-49), Ireland lost one-third of its population to the Black Death. The huge scale model of medieval Dublin is especially well done.

The top floor's "History Hunters" section is devoted to how the puzzles of modern archaeology and science shed light on Dublin's history. From this floor you can climb a couple of flights of stairs into the tower for so-so views of Dublin, or exit across an enclosed stone bridge to adjacent Christ Church Cathedral.

Cost and Hours: €7.50, €12.25 combo-ticket includes Christ Church Cathedral; daily March-Sept 10:00-17:00, Oct-Feb 11:00-16:30, last entry 45 minutes before closing, top-floor coffee shop open in summer, across from Christ Church Cathedral, tel. 01/679-4611, www.dublinia.ie.

St. Patrick's Cathedral—The first church here was built on the site where St. Patrick baptized local pagan converts. The core of the Gothic structure you see today was built in the 13th century. After the Reformation, it passed into the hands of the Anglican Church. A century later, Oliver Cromwell's puritanical Calvinist troops—who considered the Anglicans to be little more than Catholics without a pope—stabled their horses here as a sign of disrespect.

Jonathan Swift (author of *Gulliver's Travels*) was dean of the Cathedral for 32 years in the 18th century. His grave is located near the front door (on the right side of the nave), where his cutting, self-penned epitaph reads: "He lies where furious indignation can no longer rend his heart." Check out the large wooden Door of Reconciliation hanging in the north transept, with the rough hole in the middle. This was the Chapter House door through which two feuding, sword-bearing 15th-century nobles shook hands..."chancing their arms" and giving the Irish that expression of trust.

Cost and Hours: €5.50 donation to church; Mon-Fri 9:00-17:30, Sat 9:00-18:30, Sun 12:30-15:00, last entry one hour before closing.

Evensong: You'll get chills listening to the local "choir of angels" Mon-Fri at 17:45 and Sun at 15:15.

▲▲Temple Bar

This much-promoted area—with trendy shops, cafés, theaters, galleries, pubs with live music, and restaurants—feels like the heart of the city. It's Dublin's touristy "Left Bank," and as in Paris, it's on the south shore of the river, filling the cobbled streets between Dame Street and the River Liffey.

Three hundred years ago, this was the city waterfront, where tall sailing ships offloaded their goods (a "bar" was a loading dock along the river, and the Temples were a dominant merchant family). Eventually, the city grew eastward, filling in tidal mudflats, to create the docklands of modern Dublin. Once a thriving Georgian center of craftsmen and merchants, this neighborhood fell on hard times in the 19th century. Ensuing low rents attracted students and artists, giving the area a bohemian flair. With government tax incentives and lots of development money, the Temple Bar district has now become a thriving cultural (and beer-drinking) hot spot.

Temple Bar can be an absolute spectacle in the evening, when it bursts with revelers. The noise, pushy crowds, and inflated prices have driven most Dubliners away. But even if you're just gawking, don't miss the opportunity to wander through this human circus. It can be a real zoo on summer weekend nights, holidays, and nights after big sporting events let out. Women in funky hats, part of loud "hen" (bachelorette) parties, promenade down the main drag as drunken dudes shout from pub doorways to get their attention. Be aware that a pint of beer here is €5—about €1 more than at less-glitzy pubs just a couple of blocks away (north of the River Liffey or south of Dame Street).

Temple Bar Square, just off Temple Bar Street (near Ha' Penny Bridge), is the epicenter of activity. It hosts free street theater and a Saturday book market, and has handy ATMs. On busy weekends, people-watching here is a contact sport. You're bound to meet some characters.

Irish music fans find great CDs at **Claddagh Records** (Cecilia Street, just around the corner from Luigi Malone's, Mon and Wed-Sat 11:30-17:30, closed Sun and Tue, tel. 01/677-0262). Unlike big, glitzy chain stores, this is a little hole-in-the-wall shop staffed by informed folks who love turning visitors on to Irish tunes. Grab a couple of CDs for your drive through the Irish countryside. Farther west and somewhat hidden is **Meeting House Square,** with a lively organic-produce market (Sat 10:00-18:00). Bordering the square is the **Irish Film Institute** (main entry on Eustace Street), which shows a variety of art-house flicks. A bohemian crowd relaxes in its bar/café, awaiting the next film (6 Eustace Street, box office daily 13:30-21:00, tel. 01/679-5744, www.irishfilm.ie).

Rather than follow particular pub or restaurant recommendations (mine are listed later, under "Eating in Dublin"), venture down a few side lanes off the main drag to see what looks good. The pedestrian-only **Ha' Penny Bridge,** named for the half-pence toll people used to pay to cross it, leads from Temple Bar over the River Liffey to the opposite bank and more sights. If the rowdy Temple Bar scene gets to be too much, cross over to the north bank of the River Liffey on the Millennium Pedestrian Bridge (next bridge west of the Ha' Penny Bridge), where you'll find a mellower, more cosmopolitan choice of restaurants with outdoor seating in the Millennium Walk district (see page 89).

North of the River Liffey
▲▲O'Connell Bridge

This bridge spans the River Liffey, which has historically divided the wealthy, cultivated south side of town from the poorer, cruder north side. While there's plenty of culture north of the river, even today "the north" is considered rougher and less safe. Dubliners joke that north-side residents are known as "the accused," while residents on the south side are addressed as "your honor."

From the bridge, look upriver (west) as far upstream as you can see. On the left in the distance, the **big concrete building**—nicknamed "the bunker" and considered an eyesore by locals—houses the city planning commission. Ironically, it's in charge of new building permits. It squats on the still-buried precious artifacts of the first Viking settlement, established in Dublin in the ninth century. Archaeologists were given minimal time to study the dig

DUBLIN

before officials paved paradise and put up a parking lot (actually the Dublin City Council offices).

Across the river stands the **Four Courts**—the Supreme Court building. It was shelled and burned in 1922, during the tragic civil war that followed Irish independence. The national archives office burned, and irreplaceable birth records were lost, making it more difficult today for those with Irish roots to trace their ancestry. The closest bridge upstream—the elegant iron **Ha' Penny Bridge** (see photo on facing page)—leads left, into the Temple Bar nightlife district. Just beyond that old-fashioned, 19th-century bridge is Dublin's pedestrian **Millennium Bridge,** inaugurated in 2000. (Note that buses leave from O'Connell Bridge—specifically Aston Quay—for the Guinness Storehouse and Kilmainham Gaol.)

Turn 180 degrees and look downstream to see the tall **Liberty Hall** union headquarters (16 stories tall, some say in honor of the 1916 Easter Uprising). Modern Dublin is developing downstream. During the Celtic Tiger economy, the Irish (forever clever tax fiddlers) subsidized and revitalized this formerly dreary quarter. A short walk downstream along the north bank leads to a powerful series of gaunt statues memorializing the Great Potato Famine of 1845-1849. Beyond, you'll see the masts of the *Jeanie Johnston*, a replica transport ship (see page 81).

▲▲O'Connell Street Stroll

Dublin's grandest street leads from O'Connell Bridge through the heart of north Dublin. Since the 1740s, it has been a 45-yard-wide promenade, and ever since the first O'Connell Bridge connected it to the Trinity side of town in 1794, it's been Dublin's main drag. (However, it was only named O'Connell after independence was won in 1922.) These days, the city has made the street more pedestrian-friendly, and a new LUAS line extension will eventually run within the median. Though lined with fast-food and souvenir shops, O'Connell Street echoes with history.

• *Take the following stroll along the wide, tree-lined median strip, which is less crowded than either sidewalk, and closer to the statues I mention here. Start at the base of the street, near O'Connell Bridge.*

Statues and Monuments: The median running down the middle of O'Connell Street is lined with statues celebrating great figures from Ireland's past. At the base of the street stands **Daniel O'Connell** (1775-1847), known as "the Liberator" for founding the Catholic Association and demanding Irish Catholic rights in the British Parliament.

Walk a block east down Abbey Street to find the famous **Abbey Theatre**—rebuilt after a fire into a nondescript, modern building. It's still the much-loved home of the Irish National Theatre.

DUBLIN

1. Daniel O'Connell Statue
2. Abbey Theatre
3. James Larkin Statue
4. Millennium Spire
5. General Post Office
6. Moore Street Market
7. St. Mary's Pro-Cathedral
8. Father Matthew Statue
9. Gresham Hotel
10. Charles Stewart Parnell Monument
11. Gate Theatre
12. Garden of Remembrance
13. Dublin Writers' Museum
14. James Joyce Cultural Ctr.
15. The Hugh Lane Gallery & Francis Bacon Studio
16. National Leprechaun Museum

Accommodations & Services
17. Jurys Inn Custom House
18. The Townhouse
19. Jurys Inn Parnell Street
20. Belvedere Hotel
21. Charles Stewart Hotel
22. Internet Café
23. Bike Tours
24. Rebel Tours

The statue of **James Larkin** honors the founder of the Irish Transport Workers' Union. The one monument that didn't wave an Irish flag—a tall column crowned by a statue of the British hero of Trafalgar, Admiral Horatio Nelson—was blown up in 1966...the IRA's contribution to the local celebration of the Easter Uprising's 50th anniversary.

This spot is now occupied by the 390-foot-tall, stainless steel **Millennium Spire** that was finally completed in 2003. While it trumpets rejuvenation on that side of the river, it's a memorial to nothing and has no real meaning. Dubious Dubliners call it the tallest waste of €5 million in all of Europe. Its nickname? Take your pick: the Stiletto in the Ghetto, the Stiffy on the Liffey, the Pole in the Hole, the Poker near the Croker (after nearby Croke Park), or the Spike in the Dike.

• *On your left is the...*

North Dublin

JAMES JOYCE CULTURAL CENTRE

To Croke Park Stadium & GAA Museum

SUMMERHILL

W. RUTLAND SQ.

N. GREAT GEORGE'S ST.

14

GATE THEATRE

150 Meters
150 Yards

To Howth

11 **10**

CATHAL BRUGHA ST.

SEAN MACDERMOTT LOWER

RAILWAY ST.

CONNOLLY STATION

LOWER SHERIFF ST.

9

GARDINER ST. LOWER

MABBOT LN.

CORPORATION ST.

FOLEY ST.

Connolly

8

7 ST. MARY'S PRO-CATHEDRAL

MARLBOROUGH ST.

TALBOT ST.

TALBOT PL.

AMIENS ST.

INNER DOCK

O'CONNELL ST. UPPER

4 EARL ST.

18

23

STORE ST.

George's Dock

MOORE IN.

LUAS TRAM RED LINE

Busáras Central Bus Station

MAYOR ST.

GENERAL POST OFFICE

5

O'CONNELL ST. LWR.

ABBEY ST. LOWER

MEMORIAL RD.

Busáras

IFSC

ST. GEORGE'S DOCK

PRINCE'S ST. NORTH

3

2 ABBEY THEATRE

CUSTOM HOUSE

To O2 Theatre & Car Ferry Terminal

ST. MIDDLE

T Abbey

EDEN QUAY

CUSTOM HOUSE QUAY

17

N. WALL QUAY

22

ST.

1

Liffey

GEORGE'S QUAY

FAMINE STATUES

O'CASEY BRIDGE

JEANIE JOHNSTON

CITY QUAY

BACHELORS WALK

BURGH QUAY

O'CONNELL BRIDGE

WALK BEGINS

Tara Street Station

GLOUCESTER ST.

MOSS ST.

PRINCE'S ST.

LOMBARD ST. EAST

ASTON QUAY

WESTMORELAND ST.

D'OLIER ST.

TARA ST.

TOWNSEND ST.

N

ANGLESEA ST.

FLEET ST.

COLLEGE

BAR
BANK OF IRELAND

TRINITY COLLEGE

PEARSE ST.

To Dun Laoghaire

DUBLIN

General Post Office: This is not just any P.O. It was from here that Patrick Pearse read the Proclamation of Irish Independence in 1916, kicking off the Easter Uprising. The G.P.O. building itself—a kind of Irish Alamo—was the rebel headquarters and scene of a bloody five-day siege that followed the proclamation. The building was particularly strategic because it housed the main telegraph node for the entire country. Its pillars remain pockmarked with bullet holes (open for business and sightseers Mon-Sat 8:00-20:00, closed Sun).

Tucked in the ground floor of the building is the small **An Post Museum,** which stamp collectors and Irish rebels at heart will enjoy (€2, Mon-Fri 10:00-17:00, Sat 10:00-16:00, closed Sun, last entry 30 minutes before closing, on the right as you enter, www. anpost.ie/historyandheritage).

• *Turn left (west) past the post office, down people-filled Henry Street (residents' favorite shopping lane), then wander to the right into the nearby...*

Moore Street Market: Many of its merchants have staffed the same stalls for decades. Start a conversation. It's a great workaday scene. You'll see lots of mums with strollers—a reminder that Ireland is one of Europe's youngest countries, with more than 35 percent of the population under the age of 25 (Mon-Sat 8:00-18:00, closed Sun).

• *Back on O'Connell Street, return to the median strip and continue your walk. A block east (right) of O'Connell, down Cathedral Street, is...*

St. Mary's Pro-Cathedral: Although this is Dublin's leading Catholic church, it rather curiously isn't a "cathedral." The pope declared Christ Church to be a cathedral in the 12th century—and later, gave St. Patrick's the same designation. (The Vatican has chosen to stubbornly ignore the fact that Christ Church and St. Patrick's haven't been Catholic for centuries.) Completed in 1821, this church is done in the style of a Greek temple.

• *Continuing up O'Connell Street, you'll find a statue of...*

Father Matthew: A leader of the temperance movement of the 1830s, Father Matthew was responsible, some historians claim, for enough Irish peasants staying sober to enable Daniel O'Connell to organize them into a political force. (Perhaps studying this example, the USSR was careful to keep the price of vodka affordable.)

Nearby, the fancy **Gresham Hotel** is a good place for an elegant tea or beer. In an earlier era, this was where the beautiful people would alight during visits to Dublin. In the 1960s, Richard Burton and Liz Taylor stayed here while he was filming *The Spy Who Came in from the Cold*. (In those days, parts of Dublin were drab enough to pass for an inaccessible Eastern Bloc city.)

• *Standing boldly at the top of O'Connell Street is a monument to...*

Charles Stewart Parnell: The names of the four ancient provinces of Ireland and all 32 Irish counties (North *and* South, since this was erected before Irish independence) ring the monument, honoring Charles Stewart Parnell (1846-1891), the member of Parliament who nearly won Home Rule for Ireland in the late 1800s (and who served time at Kilmainham Gaol). A Cambridge-educated Protestant of landed-gentry stock and a member of Parliament, Parnell had a vision of a modern and free Irish nation filled mostly with Catholics but not set up as a religious state.  Despite his privileged birth, Parnell gained the love of the Irish people—who remembered their grandparents' harsh evictions during the famine—through his tireless work on land reforms to secure fair rents and land tenure. Momentum seemed to be on his side. With the British prime minister of the time, William Gladstone, in favor of a similar form of Home Rule, it looked as if all of Ireland was ripe for independence, as a Commonwealth nation similar to Canada or Australia. Then a sex scandal broke around Parnell and his mistress, the wife of another Parliament member. The press, egged on by the powerful Catholic bishops (who didn't want a secular, free Irish state), battered away at the scandal until finally Parnell was driven from office. Sadly, after that, Ireland became mired in the Troubles of the 20th century: an awkward independence (1921) featuring a divided island, a bloody civil war, and sectarian violence ever since. Wracked with exhaustion and only in his mid-40s, Parnell is thought to have died of a broken heart.

• *Continue straight up Parnell Square East. At the* **Gate Theatre** *(on the left), Orson Welles and James Mason had their professional acting debuts. One block up on the left is the...*

Garden of Remembrance: Honoring the victims of the 1916 Uprising, the park was dedicated in 1966 on the 50th anniversary of the revolt that ultimately led to Irish independence. The bottom of the cross-shaped pool is a mosaic of Celtic weapons, symbolic of how the early Irish would proclaim peace by breaking their weapons and throwing them into a lake or river. The Irish flag flies above the park: green for Catholics, orange for Protestants, and white for the hope that they can live together in peace.

One of modern Ireland's most stirring moments occurred here in May of 2011, when Queen Elizabeth II made this the first stop on her historic visit to Ireland. She laid a wreath at the Children of Lir sculpture under this flag and bowed her head for a moment of silence out of respect for the Irish rebels who had fought and died trying to gain freedom from her United Kingdom...a hugely cathartic moment for both nations. Until this visit, no British monarch had set foot in the Irish state since its founding 90 years earlier (free, daily 8:30-18:00).

• *On the uphill side, across the street, is a splendidly restored Georgian mansion, housing the...*

Dublin Writers' Museum: No other country so small has produced such a wealth of literature (see page 460). As interesting to those who are fans of Irish literature as it is boring to those who aren't, this three-room museum features the lives and works of Dublin's great writers (€7.50, includes helpful audioguide, ask

Modern Ireland's Turbulent Birth: A Timeline

Imagine if our American patriot ancestors had fought both our Revolutionary War and our Civil War over a span of seven chaotic years...and then appreciate the remarkable resilience of the Irish people. Here's a summary of what happened when.

1916: A nationalist militia called the Volunteers (led by **Patrick Pearse**) and the socialist Irish Citizen Army (led by **James Connolly**) join forces in the **Easter Uprising,** but they fail to end 750 years of British rule. The uprising is unpopular with most Irish, who are unhappy with the destruction in Dublin and preoccupied with the "Great War" on the Continent. But when 16 rebel leaders (including Pearse and Connolly) are executed, Irish

public opinion reverses as sympathy grows for the martyrs and the cause of Irish Independence.

Two important rebel leaders escape execution. New York-born **Eamon de Valera** is spared because of his American passport (the British don't want to anger their potential ally in World War I). **Michael Collins,** a low-ranking rebel officer who fought in the uprising at the General Post Office, refines urban guerrilla-warfare strategies in prison, and then blossoms after his release as the rebels' military and intelligence leader in the power vacuum that followed the executions.

1918: World War I ends and a general election is held in Ireland. Outside of Ulster, the nationalist **Sinn Fein** party wins 73 out of 79 seats in Parliament. Only 4 out of 32 counties vote to maintain the Union with Britain (all 4 are in Ulster, part of which would become Northern Ireland). Rather than take their seats in London, Sinn Fein representatives abstain from participating in a government they see as foreign occupiers.

1919: On January 19, the abstaining Sinn Fein members set up a rebel government in Dublin called Dail Eireann. On the same day, the first shots of the **Irish War of Independence**

---

about €11.50 combo-ticket with James Joyce Museum in Dun Laoghaire if that museum has reopened—see page 108; June-Aug Mon-Fri 10:00-18:00, Sat 10:00-17:00, Sun 11:00-17:00; Sept-May Mon-Sat 10:00-17:00, Sun 11:00-17:00; coffee shop, 18 Parnell Square North, tel. 01/872-2077, www.writersmuseum.com). The museum also offers walking tours highlighting nearby loca-

are fired as rebels begin ambushing police barracks, which are seen as an extension of British rule. De Valera is elected by the Dail to lead the rebels, with Collins as his deputy. Collins' web of spies infiltrates British intelligence at Dublin Castle. The Volunteers rename themselves the **Irish Republican Army;** meanwhile the British beef up their military presence in Ireland by sending in tough WWI vets, the Black and Tans. A bloody and very personal war ensues.

1921: Having lived through the slaughter of World War I, the British tire of the extended bloodshed in Ireland and begin negotiations with the rebels. De Valera leads rebel negotiations, but then entrusts them to Collins (a clever politician, De Valera sees that whoever signs a treaty will be blamed for its compromises). Understanding the tricky position he's been placed in, Collins signs the **Anglo-Irish Treaty** in December, lamenting that in doing so he has signed his "own death warrant."

The Dail narrowly ratifies the treaty (64 to 57), but Collins' followers are unable to convince De Valera's supporters that the compromises are a stepping stone to later full independence. De Valera and his anti-treaty disciples resign in protest. **Arthur Griffith,** founder of Sinn Fein, assumes the presidential post.

In June, the anti-treaty forces, holed up in the Four Courts building, are fired upon by Collins and his pro-treaty forces—thus igniting the **Irish Civil War.** The British want the treaty to stand and even supply Collins with cannons, meanwhile threatening to re-enter Ireland if the anti-treaty forces aren't put down.

1922: In August, Griffith dies of stress-induced illness, and Collins is assassinated 10 days later. Nevertheless, the pro-treaty forces prevail, as they are backed by popular opinion and better (British-supplied) military equipment.

1923: In April, the remaining IRA forces dump (or stash) their arms, ending the civil war...but many of their bitter vets vow to carry on the fight. De Valera distances himself from the IRA and becomes the dominant Irish political leader for the next 40 years.

tions that Joyce made famous (€10; Tue, Thu, and Sat at 11:00 and 14:00; 1.5 hours).

Aficionados of James Joyce's work may also want to visit the **James Joyce Cultural Centre,** two blocks east (€5; June-Aug Mon-Sat 10:00-17:00, Sun 12:00-16:00; Sept-May Tue-Sat 10:00-17:00, Sun 12:00-16:00, closed Mon; 35 North Great George's Street, tel. 01/878-8547).

DUBLIN

Dublin's Literary Life

Dublin in the 1700s, grown rich from a lucrative cloth trade, was one of Europe's most cultured and sophisticated cities.

The buildings were decorated in the Georgian style still visible today, and the city's Protestant elite shuttled between here and London, bridging the Anglo-Irish cultural gap. Jonathan Swift (1667-1745) was the era's greatest Anglo-Irish writer—a brilliant satirist and author of *Gulliver's Travels*. He was also dean of St. Patrick's Cathedral (1713-1745) and one of the city's eminent citizens.

Around the turn of the 20th century, Dublin produced some of the world's great modern writers. Bram Stoker (1847-1912) was creator of *Dracula*. Oscar Wilde (1854-1900) penned *The Picture of Dorian Gray* and a clutch of fine plays. George Bernard Shaw (1856-1950) wrote *Pygmalion, Major Barbara, Man and Superman*, and a host of other dramas. William Butler Yeats (1865-1939) was a prolific poet and playwright on Irish themes. And James Joyce (1882-1941) whipped up a masterpiece called *Ulysses*. For more on Irish literature (and to see which of these writers won the Nobel Prize), see page 460.

• *Next door to the Dublin Writers' Museum is...*

The Hugh Lane Gallery: In a grand Neoclassical building, this gallery has a fine, bite-size selection of Pre-Raphaelite, French Impressionist, and 19th- and 20th-century Irish paintings. Sir Hugh went down on the *Lusitania* in 1915; due to an unclear will, his collection is shared by this gallery and the National Gallery in London.

Tucked in the back of the gallery is the **Francis Bacon Studio,** reconstructed here in its original (messy) state from its London location at the time of the artist's death in 1992. Born in Dublin and inspired by Pablo Picasso, Bacon's shocking paintings reflected his belief that "chaos breeds energy." This compact space contains touch-screen terminals, display cases of personal items, and a few unfinished works. The 10-minute film interview of Bacon may fascinate like-minded viewers...and disquiet others (free, Tue-Thu 10:00-18:00, Fri-Sat 10:00-17:00, Sun 11:00-17:00, closed Mon, tel. 01/222-5564, www.hughlane.ie). Check out their free Sundays@Noon classical music concerts (Oct-June).

• *Your walk is over. Here on the north end of town, it's convenient to visit the Gaelic Athletic Association Museum at Croke Park Stadium (described on page 86, a 20-minute walk or short taxi ride away). Otherwise, hop on your skateboard and zip back to the river.*

More Sights North of the River Liffey

National Leprechaun Museum—This good-natured, low-tech attraction is fine for kids and lighthearted adults (but too corny for teens). An uninhibited guide leads the group on a 45-minute meander through Irish mythology. You'll visit a wishing well, a giant's living room, and a fairy fort listening to tales that will enchant your wee ones.

Cost and Hours: €10, Mon-Sat 10:00-18:30, Sun 10:30-18:30, last entry 45 minutes before closing, a block north of the River Liffey on Abbey Street across from Jervis LUAS stop, tel. 01/873-3899, www.leprechaunmuseum.ie.

The *Jeanie Johnston* (Tall Ship Famine Museum)—This modern, seaworthy replica of a transport ship, docked on the River Liffey, is modeled after its namesake. The original *Jeanie Johnston* embarked on 16 six- to eight- week transatlantic crossings, carrying more than 2,500 Irish emigrants to their new lives in America and Canada the decade after the Great Potato Famine. While many barely seaworthy hulks were known as "coffin ships," those who boarded the *Jeanie Johnston* were lucky: With a humanitarian captain and even a doctor, not one life was lost. Your tour guide will introduce you to the ship's main characters and help illuminate day-to-day life aboard a cramped tall ship 150 years ago. Because this ship makes goodwill voyages to Atlantic ports, it may be away during your visit.

Cost and Hours: €8.50, visits by 45-minute tour only, hourly April-Oct 11:00-16:00, Nov-March 11:00-15:00, on the north bank of the Liffey just east of Sean O'Casey Bridge, tel. 01/473-0111, www.jeaniejohnston.ie.

Dublin's Smithfield Village

This neighborhood is worth a look for the Old Jameson Distillery whiskey tour and Dublin's most authentic traditional-music pub. The two sights are on a long square, two blocks northwest of the Four Courts—the Supreme Court building. The modern square still fulfills its original function as a horse market (first Sat morning of the month, great for people-watching). The **Fresh Market,** near the top of the square, is a handy grocery stop for urban picnic fixings (Mon-Sat 7:00-22:00, Sun 8:00-22:00).

Old Jameson Distillery—Whiskey fans enjoy visiting the old distillery. You get a 10-minute video, a 20-minute tour, and a free shot in the pub. Unfortunately, the "distillery" feels fake and put together for tourists. The Bushmills tour in Northern Ireland (in a

DUBLIN

From Famine to Revolution

After the Great Potato Famine (1845-49), destitute rural Irish moved to the city in droves, seeking work and causing a housing shortage. Unscrupulous landlords came up with a solution: Subdivide the city's once-grand mansions into tiny rooms and cram poor renters into them. Dublin became one of the most densely populated cities in Europe—one out of every three Dubliners lived in a slum. On Henrietta Street, once a wealthy Dublin address, these new tenements bulged with humanity. According to the 1911 census, one district featured 835 people living in 15 houses (many with a single outhouse in back or a communal chamber pot in the room). In cramped, putrid quarters like this, tuberculosis was rampant, and infant mortality skyrocketed.

Those who could get work tenaciously clung to their precious jobs. The terrible working conditions prompted many to join trade unions. A 1913 strike and employer lockout, known as the "Dublin Lockout," lasted for seven months. The picket lines were brutally put down by police in the pocket of rich businessmen, led by newspaper owner and hotel magnate William Murphy. In response, James Larkin and James Connolly formed the Irish Citizen Army, a socialist militia to protect the poor trade unionists.

Murphy eventually broke the unions. Larkin headed for the US to organize workers there. During World War I, he praised the rise of the Soviet Union and later was persecuted during the post-war "Red Scare" (even doing time in Sing Sing for advocating "unlawful means" to overthrow the US government). Meanwhile, Connolly stayed in Ireland and brought the Irish Citizen Army into the 1916 Easter Uprising as an integral part of the rebel forces. During the uprising, he slyly had a rebel flag flown over Murphy's prized hotel on O'Connell Street. The uninformed British artillery battalions took the bait and pulverized it.

Connolly was the last of the rebel leaders executed in 1916. Unable to stand in front of the firing squad in Kilmainham Gaol (his ankle was shattered by a bullet while he was defending the General Post Office), Connolly was tied to a chair and shot sitting down. Of the 16 rebel executions, his was the one most credited with turning Irish public opinion in favor of the rebel martyrs.

Today you'll find heroic Dublin statues to honor them both. James Larkin, arms outstretched, is in front of the post office on O'Connell Street. James Connolly is on Beresford Place, behind the Customs House.

DUBLIN

working factory, see page 397) and the Midleton tour near Cork (in the huge original factory, page 192) are better experiences. If you do take this tour, volunteer energetically when offered the chance: This will get you a coveted seat at the whiskey taste-test table at the tour's end.

Cost and Hours: €13, daily 9:30-18:30, last tour at 17:15, Bow Street, tel. 01/807-2355, www.jamesonwhiskey.com.

Evening Events: Jameson offers "Irish Nights"—a splurge dinner-and-dance shindig with all the trimmings (€47.50, includes guided tour, cocktail, and four-course meal—book ahead; April-Oct Thu-Sat at 19:00).

Cobblestone Pub—Hiding in a derelict-looking building at the top of the square, this pub offers Dublin's least glitzy and most re-warding traditional-music venue. The candlelit walls, covered with photos of honored trad musicians, set the tone. Music is revered here, as reflected in the understated sign: "Listening area, please respect musicians."

Cost and Hours: Free, daily 17:00-23:45, trad-music sessions Mon-Tue at 21:00, Wed-Sat at 19:00, Sun at 13:30; at north end of square, 100 yards from Old Jameson Distillery's brick chimney tower; tel. 01/872-1799, www.cobblestonepub.ie.

Outer Dublin

The Kilmainham Gaol and the Guinness Storehouse are located to the west of the old center and can be combined in one visit, linked by a 20-minute walk, a five-minute taxi ride, or public bus #51B or #78A. (To ride the bus from the jail to the Guinness Storehouse, leave the prison and take three rights—crossing no streets—to the bus stop.) Another option is to take one of the hop-on, hop-off buses (see page 56): City Sightseeing Dublin stops right at Kilmainham Gaol, while Dublin Bus Tour stops 200 yards away, in front of the modern art museum in Kilmainham hospital. Both tours stop at the Guinness Storehouse.

▲▲▲**Kilmainham Gaol (Jail)**—Opened in 1796 as both the Dublin County Jail and a debtors' prison, it was considered a model

in its day. In reality, this jail was frequently used by the Brit-ish as a political prison. Many of those who fought for Irish independence were held or ex-ecuted here, including leaders of the rebellions of 1798, 1803, 1848, 1867, and 1916. National heroes Robert Emmett and Charles Stewart Parnell each did time here. The last prisoner to be held here was Eamon de Valera, who later became president of

Ireland. He was released on July 16, 1924, the day Kilmainham was finally shut down. The buildings, virtually in ruins, were restored in the 1960s. Today, it's a shrine to the Nathan Hales of Ireland.

Start your visit with a one-hour guided **tour** (2/hour, includes 15-minute prison-history slide show in the prison chapel—spend waiting time in museum). It's touching to tour the cells and places of execution—hearing tales of oppressive colonialism and heroic patriotism—alongside Irish schoolkids who know these names well. The museum is an excellent exhibit on Victorian prison life and Ireland's fight for independence. Don't miss the museum's dimly lit Last Words 1916 hall upstairs, which displays the stirring final letters that patriots sent to loved ones hours before facing the firing squad.

Cost and Hours: €6, Mon-Sat 9:30-16:30, Sun 10:00-16:30, last entry one hour before closing; bus #51B, #69, #78A, or #79 from Aston Quay—confirm with driver; tel. 01/453-5984. The humble cafeteria serves little more than sandwiches.

▲Guinness Storehouse—A visit to the Guinness Storehouse is, for many, a pilgrimage. Arthur Guinness began brewing the renowned stout here in 1759 and by 1868, it was the biggest brewery in the world. Today, the sprawling place fills several city blocks.

Cost and Hours: €14.50, includes a €5 pint; €1 off with your hop-on, hop-off bus ticket or 10 percent discount when you book online; daily 9:30-17:00, July-Aug until 19:00; enter on Bellevue Street, bus #78A from Aston Quay near O'Connell Bridge or bus #123 from Dame Street and O'Connell Street; tel. 01/408-4800, www.guinness-storehouse.com.

Visiting the Brewery: Around the world, Guinness brews more than 10 million pints a day (their biggest brewery is actually in Lagos, Nigeria). Although the home of Ireland's national beer welcomes visitors with a sprawling modern museum, there are no tours of the actual working brewery.

The museum fills the old fermentation plant used from 1902 through 1988, which reopened in 2000 as a huge shrine to the tradition. Step into the middle of the ground floor and look up. A tall, beer-glass-shaped glass atrium—14 million pints big—soars upward past four floors of exhibitions and cafés to the skylight. Then look down at Arthur's original 9,000-year lease, enshrined under Plexiglas in the floor...you realize that at £45 per year, it was quite a bargain. (The brewery eventually purchased the land, so the lease is no longer valid.)

The actual exhibit makes brewing seem more grandiose than

The Famous Record-Breaking Records Book

Look up "beer" in the *Guinness World Records* and you'll discover that the strongest one ever sold was a Scottish brew called *The End of History* (55 percent alcohol) and that a man set a record for removing beer bottle caps with his teeth (63 in one minute). But aside from listing records for amazing—or amazingly stupid—feats, this famous record book has a more subtle connection with beer.

In 1951, while hunting in Ireland's County Wexford, Sir Hugh Beaver, then the managing director at Guinness Breweries, got into a debate with his companions over which was the fastest game bird in Europe: the golden plover or the red grouse. That night at his estate, after scouring countless reference books, they were disappointed not to find a definitive answer.

Beaver realized that similar questions were likely being debated nightly across pubs in Ireland and Britain. So he hired twins Norris and Ross McWhirter, who ran a fact-finding agency in London, to compile a book of answers to various questions. They set up an office at 107 Fleet Street and began assembling the first edition of the book by contacting experts, such as astrophysicists, etymologists, virologists, and volcanologists. In 1955, the *Guinness Book of Records* (later renamed *Guinness World Records*) was published. By Christmas, it topped the British bestseller list.

In the beginning, entries mostly focused on facts about natural phenomena and animal oddities, but grew to include a wide variety of extreme human achievements. After more than a half-century of noting record-breaking traditions around the globe, the volume continues to answer a multitude of burning trivia questions, such as the wealthiest cat in the world, the largest burrito ever made, and the record time for peeling 50 pounds of onions (an event that likely caused a lot of tears).

The iconic books are now available in more than 100 countries and 26 languages, with more than 3.5 million copies sold annually. As the bestselling copyrighted book of all time, it even earns a record-breaking entry within its own pages.

it is and treats Arthur like the god of human happiness. His pints contain only 200 calories, but they pack a 4.2 percent alcohol content. Highlights are the cooperage (with 1954 film clips showing the master wood-keg-makers plying their now virtually extinct trade), a display of the brewery's clever ads, and a small exhibit about the beer's connection to the *Guinness World Records* (see sidebar on previous page).

Atop the building, the **Gravity Bar** provides visitors with a commanding 360-degree view of Dublin—with vistas all the way to the sea—and a free beer.

▲National Museum: Decorative Arts and History—This branch of the National Museum, which occupies the huge, 18th-century stone Collins Barracks in west Dublin, displays Irish dress, furniture, weapons, silver, and other domestic baubles from the past 700 years. History buffs will linger longest in the "Soldiers & Chiefs" exhibit, which covers the Irish at war both at home and abroad since 1500 (including the American Civil War). The sober finale is the "Understanding 1916" room, offering Ireland's best coverage of the painful birth of this nation, an event known as the "Terrible Beauty." Guns, personal letters, and death masks help illustrate the 1916 Easter Uprising, War of Independence against Britain, and Ireland's civil war. Croppies Acre, the large park between the museum and the river, was the site of Dublin's largest soup kitchen during the Great Potato Famine in 1845-1849.

Cost and Hours: Free, Tue-Sat 10:00-17:00, Sun 14:00-17:00, closed Mon, good café; on north side of the River Liffey in Collins Barracks on Benburb Street, roughly across the river from Guinness Storehouse, easy to reach by the LUAS red line—get off at Museum stop; tel. 01/648-6453, www.museum.ie. Call ahead for sporadic tour times.

▲Gaelic Athletic Association Museum—The GAA was founded in 1884 as an expression of an Irish cultural awakening (see sidebar on page 88). It was created to foster the development of Gaelic sports, specifically Gaelic football and hurling, and to exclude English sports such as cricket and rugby. The GAA played an important part in the fight for independence. This museum, at 82,000-seat Croke Park Stadium in east Dublin, offers a high-tech, interactive introduction to Ireland's favorite games. Relive the greatest moments in hurling and Irish-football history. Then get involved: Pick up a stick and try hurling, kick a football, and test your speed and balance. A 15-minute film (played on request) gives you a "Sunday at the stadium" experience.

Cost and Hours: €6; June-Aug daily 9:30-18:00; Sept-May Mon-Sat 9:30-17:00, Sun 11:30-17:00; on game Sundays the museum is open to ticket-holders only, café, located under the stands at Croke Park Stadium, a 20-minute walk northeast of Parnell Square—enter from St. Joseph's Avenue off Clonliffe Road, tel. 01/819-2323, www.crokepark.ie/gaa-museum.

Tours: The €12, one-hour museum-plus-stadium-tour option is worth it only for rabid fans who want a glimpse of the huge stadium and yearn to know which locker room is considered the unlucky one. The rooftop tour offers views 17 stories above the field from lofty catwalks (€25, daily at 10:30, 11:30, 12:30, 14:30, and 15:30).

Hurling or Gaelic Football at Croke Park Stadium—Actually seeing a match here, surrounded by incredibly spirited Irish fans, is a fun experience. Hurling is like airborne hockey with no injury time-outs. Gaelic football resembles a rugged form of soccer; you can carry the ball, but must bounce or kick it every three steps. Matches are held most Saturday or Sunday afternoons in summer (May-Aug), culminating in the hugely popular all-Ireland finals on Sunday afternoons in September. Tickets are available at the stadium except during the finals. Choose a county to support, buy their colors to wear or wave, scream yourself hoarse, and you'll be a temporary local.

DUBLIN

Cost and Hours: €15-55, box office open Mon-Fri 9:30-13:00 & 14:15-17:30, www.gaa.ie.

Greyhound Racing—For an interesting, lowbrow look at Dublin life, consider going to the dog races and doing a little gambling. Your best bets are Wednesday, Thursday, and Saturday at Shelbourne Park; and Monday, Tuesday, and Friday at Harold's Cross Racetrack.

Cost and Hours: €10, races start at 20:00, tel. 01/497-1081, www.igb.ie.

Shopping in Dublin

Shops are open roughly Monday-Saturday 9:00-18:00 and until 20:00 on Thursday. They have shorter hours on Sunday (if they're open at all). Good shopping areas include:

• **Grafton Street,** with its neighboring streets and arcades (such as the fun Great George's Arcade between Great George's and Drury Streets), and nearby shopping centers (Powerscourt Townhouse and St. Stephen's Green). Francis Street creaks with antiques.

• **Henry Street,** home to Dublin's top department stores (pedestrian-only, off O'Connell Street).

• **Nassau Street,** lining Trinity College, with the popular Kilkenny department store, the Irish Music store, and lots of touristy shops.

• **Temple Bar,** worth a browse any day for its art, jewelry, New Age paraphernalia, books, music (try Claddagh Records—see page 72), and gift shops. On Saturdays at Temple Bar's Meeting House Square, it's food in the morning (from 9:00) and books in the afternoon (until 18:00).

Ireland's Gaelic Athletic Association

The GAA has long been a powerhouse in Ireland. Ireland's national pastimes of Gaelic football and hurling pack stadiums all over the country. When you consider that 80,000 people—paying at least €20 to €30 each—stuff Dublin's Croke Park Stadium and that all the athletes are strictly amateur, you might wonder, "Where does all the money go?"

Ireland has a long tradition of using the revenue generated by these huge events to promote Gaelic athletics and Gaelic cultural events throughout the country in a grassroots and neighborhood way. So, while the players (many of whom are schoolteachers whose jobs allow for evenings and summers free) participate only for the glory of their various counties, the money generated is funding children's leagues, school coaches, small-town athletic facilities, and traditional arts, music, and dance—as well as the building and maintenance of giant stadiums such as Croke Park (which claims to be the third-largest stadium in Europe).

In America, sports are usually considered to be a form of entertainment. But in Ireland, sports have a deeper emotional connection. Gaelic sports are a heartfelt expression of Irish identity. There was a time when the Irish were not allowed to be members of the GAA if they also belonged to a cricket club (a British game).

In 1921, during the War of Independence, Michael Collins (leader of the early IRA, the man who practically invented urban guerrilla warfare) orchestrated the simultaneous assassination of a dozen British intelligence agents around Dublin in a single morning. The same day, the Black and Tans retaliated. These grizzled British WWI veterans, clad in black police coats and tan surplus army pants, had been sent to Ireland to stamp out the rebels. Knowing Croke Park would be full of Irish Nationalists, they entered the packed stadium during a Gaelic football match and fired into the stands, killing 13 spectators as well as a Tipperary player. It was Ireland's first Bloody Sunday, a tragedy that would be repeated 51 years later in Derry.

Today Croke Park's "Hill 16" grandstands are built on rubble dumped here after the 1916 Uprising...literally sacred ground. And the Hogan stands are named after the murdered player from Tipperary. Queen Elizabeth II made it a point to visit the stadium during her historic visit in 2011. Her warm interest in the stadium and in the institution of the GAA did much to heal old wounds.

• **Millennium Walk,** a trendy lane stretching two blocks north from the River Liffey to Abbey Street. It's filled with hip restaurants, shops, and coffee bars. It's easy to miss—look for the south entry at the pedestrian Millennium Bridge, or the north entry at Jervis Street LUAS stop.

• **Street markets,** such as Moore Street (produce, noise, and lots of local color, Mon-Sat 8:00-18:00, closed Sun, near General Post Office), and St. Michan Street (fish, Tue-Sat 7:00-15:00, closed Sun-Mon, behind Four Courts building).

Entertainment in Dublin

Ireland has produced some of the finest writers in both English and Irish, and Dublin houses some of Europe's best theaters. Though the city was the site of the first performance of Handel's *Messiah* (1742), these days Dublin is famous for its rock bands: U2, Thin Lizzy, Sinéad O'Connor, and Live Aid founder Bob Geldof's band the Boomtown Rats all started here.

Theater—**Abbey Theatre** is Ireland's national theater, founded by W. B. Yeats in 1904 to preserve Irish culture during British rule (€15-40, generally nightly at 19:30, Sat matinees at 14:00, 26 Lower Abbey Street, tel. 01/878-7222, www.abbeytheatre.ie). **Gate Theatre** does foreign plays as well as Irish classics (Cavendish Row, tel. 01/874-4045, www.gatetheatre.ie). The **Gaiety Theatre** offers a wide range of quality productions (King Street South, tel. 01/677-1717, www.gaietytheatre.com). Street theater takes the stage in Temple Bar on summer evenings. Browse the listings and fliers at the TI.

Concerts—**O2 Theatre,** once a railway terminus (easy LUAS access), is now sponsored by a hip phone company. Residents call it by its geographic nickname: The Point. It's considered the country's top live-music venue (East Link Bridge, tel. 01/676-6170 or 01/676-6154, www.theO2.ie).

At the **National Concert Hall,** the National Symphony Orchestra performs most Friday evenings (€20-40, off St. Stephen's Green at Earlsfort Terrace, tel. 01/417-0000, www.nch.ie).

The **Steeple Sessions** are traditional Irish music concerts in the Unitarian Church at the southwest corner of St. Stephen's Green. The intimate, candlelit setting has fine acoustics that attract Ireland's best trad musicians for 1.5-hour sessions (€15, May-Sept Tue and Thu at 20:00, 112 St. Stephen's Green West, tel. 01/678-8470, www.steeplesessions.com).

Pub Action—Folk music fills Dublin's pubs, and street entertainers ply their trade in the midst of the party people in Temple Bar and among shoppers on Grafton Street. The Temple Bar area in particular thrives with music—traditional, jazz, and pop. Although

DUBLIN

it's pricier than the rest of Dublin, it really is the best place for tourists and locals (who come here to watch the tourists). For locations, see the "Dublin Restaurants" map on page 100.

Gogarty's Pub has top-notch sessions downstairs daily at 14:00 and upstairs nightly from 21:00 (at corner of Fleet and Anglesea, tel. 01/671-1822). Use this pub as a kickoff for your Temple Bar evening. It's also where the Traditional Irish Musical Pub Crawl starts (see page 54).

A 10-minute hike up the river west of Temple Bar takes you to a twosome with a local and less-touristy ambience. **The Brazen Head,** which lays claim to being the oldest pub in Dublin, is a hit for an early dinner and late live music (nightly from 21:30), with atmospheric rooms and a courtyard perfect for balmy evenings. They also host "Food, Folk, and Fairies" evenings, even at €44 a great value. You get a hearty four-course meal punctuated between courses by soulful Irish history and fascinating Irish mythology (April-Nov Tue-Sun 19:00-22:00, Dec-March Wed and Sat; by south end of Father Matthew Bridge, 2 blocks west of Christ Church Cathedral at 20 Bridge Street; pub tel. 01/677-9549, show tel. 01/492-2543, www.irishfolktours.com). **O'Shea's Merchant Pub,** just across the street, is encrusted in memories of County Kerry football heroes. It's filled with locals taking a break from the grind. They have live traditional music nightly at 21:30 (the front half is a restaurant, the magic is in the back half—enter on Bridge Street, tel. 01/679-3797, www.themerchanttemplebar.com).

At **Palace Bar,** climb upstairs to a cozy room that is a favorite for traditional-music sessions (Thu-Sun at 21:00, east end of Temple Bar, where Fleet Street hits Westmoreland Street at 21 Fleet Street, tel. 01/671-7388, www.thepalacebardublin.com).

Porterhouse has an inviting and varied menu, Dublin's best selection of microbrews, and live music. You won't find Guinness here, just tasty homebrews. Try one of their fun sampler trays. You can check their music schedule online (€12-15 entrées, corner of Essex Street East and Parliament Street, tel. 01/671-5715, www. porterhousebrewco.com).

Pubs at two locations of the **Arlington Hotel** host Irish music and dinner shows. At either place, you'll be entertained by an Irish Rovers-type band singing ballads and a dance troupe scuffing up the floorboards to the delight of tour groups (€30, shows nightly 20:00, dinner reservations required, www.arlingtonhoteltemplebar.com). The Arlington Hotel O'Connell Bridge is north of the River Liffey at 23 Bachelors Walk, just off the north end of O'Connell Bridge

Sleep Code

(€1 = about $1.30, country code: 353, area code: 01)
S = Single, **D** = Double/Twin, **T** = Triple, **Q** = Quad, **b** = bath-room, **s** = shower only. Breakfast is included and credit cards are accepted unless otherwise noted.

To help you easily sort through these listings, I've divided the accommodations into three categories, based on the price for a standard double room with bath:

$$$ **Higher Priced**—Most rooms €150 or more.
$$ **Moderately Priced**—Most rooms between €85-150.
$ **Lower Priced**—Most rooms €85 or less.

Prices can change without notice; verify the hotel's current rates online or by email.

(tel. 01/804-9100). The Arlington Hotel Temple Bar is south of the river at the corner of Lord Edward Street and Exchange Street Upper, roughly opposite City Hall (tel. 01/670-8777). Make sure you know at which location you're booking reservations.

For guided **pub crawls** (focusing on either Irish literature or music), see page 54.

Sleeping in Dublin

Dublin is popular, loud, and expensive. Rooms can be tight. Book ahead for weekends any time of year, particularly in summer and during rugby weekends. In summer, occasional big rock concerts can make rooms hard to find. On Sundays in September, fans converge on Dublin from all over the country for the all-Ireland finals in Gaelic football and hurling. Prices are often discounted on weeknights (Mon-Thu) and from November through February. Check for specials on hotel websites.

Big and practical places (both cheap and moderate) are most central near Christ Church Cathedral, on the edge of Temple Bar. For classy, older Dublin accommodations, you'll stay a bit farther out (southeast of St. Stephen's Green). If you're a light sleeper or on a tight budget, get a room in quiet Dun Laoghaire (page 109) or small-town Howth (page 114), where rooms are roughly one-fourth cheaper. Both are an easy 25-minute DART train ride into the city.

South of the River Liffey
Near Christ Church Cathedral
These hotels cluster near Christ Church Cathedral, a five-minute

walk from the best evening scene (at Temple Bar), and 10 minutes from the sightseeing center (Trinity College and Grafton Street). The cheap hostels in this neighborhood have some double rooms. Full Irish breakfasts, which cost €8-10 at the hotels, are cheaper at the many small cafés nearby; try the **Queen of Tarts** or **Chorus Café** (see listings under "Eating in Dublin," later).

$$ Jurys Inn Christ Church, one of three Jurys Inns in downtown Dublin, is central and offers business-class comfort in all of its 182 identical rooms. This no-nonsense, American-style hotel chain has a winning keep-it-simple-and-affordable formula. If ye olde is getting old—and you don't mind big tour groups—these are a good option. Request a room far from the noisy elevator (Db-€79-119 Sun-Thu, €109-149 Fri-Sat, breakfast-€10, book long in advance for weekends, check website for discounts, pay Wi-Fi in lobby, parking-€15/day, Christ Church Place, tel. 01/454-0000, fax 01/454-0012, US tel. 800-423-6953, www.jurysinns.com, jurysinnchristchurch@jurysinns.com). The other Jurys Inns, described later, are near Connolly Station and Parnell Square.

$$ Harding Hotel is a hardworking, hardwood place with 55 earth-tone rooms that get stuffy on rare hot days (Sb-€55-70; Db-€70-97 Sun-Thu, €99-149 Fri-Sat; extra bed-€25, breakfast-€8; Rick Steves' readers get 10 percent discount in 2013 if booking by email, phone, or fax—but not online; on weekends, request a quiet upper-floor room away from the fun-but-noisy ground-floor pub; free Wi-Fi, on Fishamble Street across the street from Christ Church Cathedral, tel. 01/679-6500, fax 01/679-6504, www.harding hotel.ie, info@hardinghotel.ie).

$ Kinlay House, around the corner from Harding Hotel, is the backpackers' choice—definitely the place to go for cheap beds, a central location, and an all-ages-welcome atmosphere. This huge, red-brick, 19th-century Victorian building has 200 metal, prison-style beds in spartan rooms. There are singles, doubles, and four- to six-bed coed dorms (good for families), as well as a few giant dorms. It fills up most days—call well in advance, especially for singles, doubles, and summer weekends (S-€40-50, Sb-€45-60, D-€50-60, Db-€60-66, T-€72-87, Tb-€87-96, dorm beds-€12-18, includes continental breakfast, free Internet access and Wi-Fi, free 10-minute international phone call, kitchen access, launderette-€8, left luggage-€1/day, travel desk, TV lounge, small lockers-€1/day, lots of stairs, Christ Church, 2-12 Lord Edward Street, tel. 01/679-6644, fax 01/679-7437, www.kinlaydublin.ie, info@kinlaydublin.ie).

$ Four Courts Hostel is a 234-bed hostel beautifully located immediately across the river from the Four Courts. It's within a five-minute walk of Christ Church Cathedral and Temple Bar. Bare and institutional (as hostels typically are), it's also spacious and well-run, with a focus on security and efficiency (dorm beds-€12-18, S-€35, Sb-€38-45, bunk D-€40, bunk Db-€45-50, includes small breakfast, elevator, free Internet access and Wi-Fi, free 10-minute international phone call, game room, laundry service, some parking-€10/day, left-luggage room; 15-17 Merchant's Quay, bus #90 from Connolly Station or Busáras Central Bus Station; tel. 01/672-5839, www.fourcourtshostel.com, info@fourcourtshostel.com).

Trinity College Area

You can't get more central than Trinity College; these two listings offer a good value for what you're spending.

$$ Trinity Lodge offers fine, quiet lodging in 24 rooms split between two Georgian townhouses on either side of Frederick Street South, just south of Trinity College (Sb-€79-139, Db-€85-159, Tb-€149-209, Qb-€159-239, Wi-Fi, 12 South Frederick Street, tel. 01/617-0900, fax 01/617-0999, www.trinitylodge.com, trinitylodge@eircom.net).

$$ Trinity College turns its 800 student-housing rooms on campus into no-frills, affordable accommodations in the city center each summer. Look for the easy-to-miss Accommodations Office (open Mon-Fri 9:00-12:45 & 14:00-17:00) inside the huge courtyard, 50 yards down the wall on the left from the main entry arch (late-May-mid-Sept, S-€58, Sb-€71.50, D-€78, Db-€120, includes continental breakfast, cooked breakfast-€4 extra, tel. 01/896-1177, fax 01/671-1267, www.tcd.ie/accommodation/visitors, reservations@tcd.ie).

Near St. Stephen's Green

Dublin is filled with worn-yet-comfy townhouses. Albany House and Fitzwilliam Townhouse are dependable, basic lodgings, while the first two hotels are cushier.

$$ Buswells Hotel, one of the city's oldest, is a pleasant Georgian-style haven with 67 reasonably priced rooms in the heart of the city (Sb-€99-139, Db-€109-159, Tb-€139-169, breakfast-€10, free Wi-Fi, between Trinity College and St. Stephen's Green at 23-25 Molesworth Street, tel. 01/614-6500, fax 01/676-2090, www.buswells.ie, enquiries@buswells.ie).

$$ Grafton Capital Hotel has a good central location and fine rooms. The popular downstairs pub is noisy on weekend nights, so light sleepers should request a room facing the back (Sb-€69-109, Db-€79-129, Tb-€99-159, breakfast-€10, Wi-Fi in lobby, 2 blocks west of St. Stephen's Green on Lower Stephen's Street, tel. 01/648-1100, fax 01/648-1122, www.graftoncapital-hotel.com, info@graftoncapital-hotel.com).

$$ Albany House's 43 restful rooms come with high ceilings,

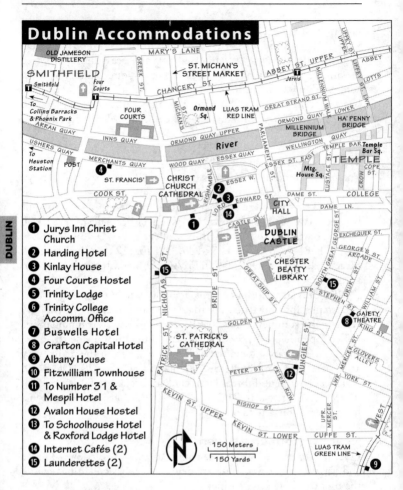

Dublin Accommodations

1. Jurys Inn Christ Church
2. Harding Hotel
3. Kinlay House
4. Four Courts Hostel
5. Trinity Lodge
6. Trinity College Accomm. Office
7. Buswells Hotel
8. Grafton Capital Hotel
9. Albany House
10. Fitzwilliam Townhouse
11. To Number 31 & Mespil Hotel
12. Avalon House Hostel
13. To Schoolhouse Hotel & Roxford Lodge Hotel
14. Internet Cafés (2)
15. Launderettes (2)

Georgian elegance, and some street noise—request a quieter room at the back (Sb-€60-110, Db-€120-140, Tb-€120-170, Una promises 10 percent off when booking direct by phone or email with this book in 2013, Wi-Fi, just one block south of St. Stephen's Green at 84 Harcourt Street, tel. 01/475-1092, fax 01/475-1093, www.albanyhousedublin.com, info@albanyhousedublin.com).

$$ Fitzwilliam Townhouse rents 14 basic rooms in a Georgian townhouse near St. Stephen's Green (Sb-€49-85, Db-€59-109, Tb-€75-119, Qb-€85-129, breakfast-€8-10, free Wi-Fi, 41 Upper Fitzwilliam Street, tel. 01/662-5155, fax 01/676-7488, www.fitzwilliamtownhouse.com, info@fitzwilliamtownhouse.com).

$ Avalon House Hostel, near Grafton Street, rents 282 simple, clean backpacker beds in refurbished rooms (dorm beds-€14-20, S-€25-30, Sb-€35-40, twin D-€50-60, twin Db-€60-70,

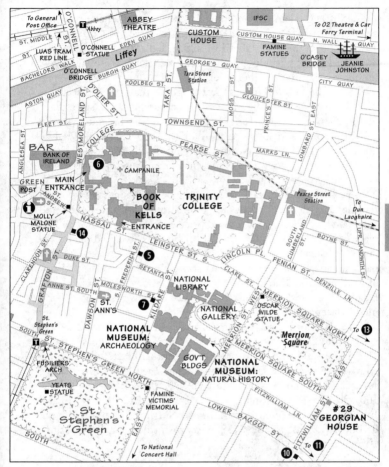

DUBLIN

includes continental breakfast, elevator, free Internet access and Wi-Fi, launderette, kitchen, lockers-€1/day, helpful staff, a few minutes off Grafton Street at 55 Aungier Street, tel. 01/475-0001, fax 01/475-0303, www.avalon-house.ie, info@avalon-house.ie).

Away from the Center, Southeast of St. Stephen's Green

The listings that follow are unique places (except for the business-class Mespil Hotel), and they charge accordingly. If you're going to break the bank, do it here.

$$$ Number 31 is a hidden gem reached via gritty little Lee-son Close (a lane off Lower Leeson Street). Its understated elegance is top-notch, with six rooms in a former coach house and 15 rooms in an adjacent Georgian house; the two buildings are connected by a quiet little garden. Guests appreciate the special touches (such as a sunken living room) and tasty breakfasts served in a classy glass atrium (Sb-€100-140, Db-€180-220, Tb-€240-280, Qb-€280-340, Wi-Fi, free parking, 31 Leeson Close, tel. 01/676-5011, www.number31.ie, info@number31.ie).

$$$ The Schoolhouse Hotel taught as many as 300 students in its heyday (1861-1969) and was in the middle of the street fight of the 1916 Easter Uprising. Now it's a serene hideout with 31 pristine rooms and a fine restaurant (Sb-€89-169, Db-€99-179, book early, Wi-Fi, 2-8 Northumberland Road, tel. 01/667-5014, fax 01/667-5015, www.schoolhousehotel.com, reservations@schoolhousehotel.com).

$$$ Mespil Hotel is a huge, modern, business-class hotel renting 255 identical three-star rooms (most with a double and single bed, phone, TV) at a good price with all the comforts. This place is a cut above Jurys Inn (Sb, Db, or Tb-€79-195, breakfast-€10, elevator, free Wi-Fi; small first-come, first-served free parking; apartments for weeklong stays; 10-minute walk southeast of St. Stephen's Green or take bus #37, #38, or #39, 50-60 Mespil Road; tel. 01/488-4600, fax 01/667-1244, www.mespilhotel.com, mespil@leehotels.com).

$$ Roxford Lodge Hotel is well-managed and the best value of my Dublin listings. In a quiet residential neighborhood a 25-minute walk from Trinity College, it has 20 tastefully decorated rooms awash with Jacuzzis and saunas. The €150-200 executive suite is honeymoon-worthy (Sb-€59-99, Db-€79-160, Tb-€85-160, Qb-€95-170, best rates online, breakfast-€12, free Wi-Fi and Internet access, secure free parking, 46 Northumberland Road, tel. 01/668-8572, fax 01/668-8158, www.roxfordlodge.ie, reservations@roxfordlodge.ie).

North of the River Liffey
Near Connolly Station
This once-tattered neighborhood (like much of the north side) is gradually becoming rejuvenated. To locate these hotels, see the map on page 74.

$$ Jurys Inn Custom House, on Custom House Quay, offers the same value as the other Jurys Inns in Dublin, but it's less central. Its 239 rooms border the financial district, a 10-minute riverside hike from O'Connell Bridge. Of the three Jurys Inns in town, this one is most likely to have rooms available (Db-€69-119 Sun-Thu, €109-149 Fri-Sat, breakfast-€10.50, pay Wi-Fi, parking-€15/day, tel. 01/854-1500, fax 01/829-0400, US tel. 800-423-6953, www.jurysinns.com, jurysinncustomhouse@jurysinns.com).

$$ The Townhouse, with 81 small, stylish rooms (some with pleasant views into a central garden courtyard), hides behind a brick Georgian facade one block north of the Customs House (Sb-€49-70, Db-€60-120, Tb-€75-144, Internet access and Wi-Fi; small first-come, first-served parking lot-€10/day; 47-48 Lower Gardiner Street, tel. 01/878-8808, fax 01/878-8787, www.town houseofdublin.com, info@townhouseofdublin.com).

Near Parnell Square

A swanky neighborhood 250 years ago, this is now workaday Dublin with a steady urban hum. To locate these hotels, see the map on page 74.

$$ Jurys Inn Parnell Street has 253 predictably soulless but good-value rooms. It's a block from the north end of O'Connell Street and the cluster of museums on Parnell Square (Db-€69-119 Sun-Thu, €129-149 Fri-Sat, breakfast-€10, pay Wi-Fi in lobby, tel. 01/878-4900, fax 01/878-4999, www.jurysinns.com, jurysinn parnellst@jurysinns.com).

$$ Belvedere Hotel has 92 plain-vanilla rooms that are short on character but long on dependable, modern comforts (Db-€69-99 Sun-Thu, €89-129 Fri-Sat, cheaper if you book online, free Wi-Fi, Great Denmark Street, tel. 01/873-7700, fax 01/873-7776, www.belvederehotel.ie, info@belvederehotel.ie).

$ Charles Stewart Guesthouse, big and basic, offers 60 forgettable rooms. But it's in a good location for a fair price (Sb-€45-59, Db-€59-79, Tb-€85-119, Qb-€85-139, breakfast-€7, frequent midweek discounts, ask for a quieter room in the back, free Wi-Fi, just beyond top end of O'Connell Street at 5-6 Parnell Square East, tel. 01/878-0350, fax 01/878-1387, www.charlesstewart.ie, sales@ charlesstewart.ie).

Eating in Dublin

It's easy to find fine, creative eateries all over town. While you can get decent pub grub for €10-15 on just about any corner, consider saving that for the countryside. There's just no pressing reason to eat Irish in cosmopolitan Dublin. In fact, going local these days is the same as going ethnic. The city's good restaurants are packed from 20:00 on, especially on weekends. Eating early (17:30-19:00) saves time and money, as many better places offer an early-bird special. Many restaurants serve free jugs of ice water with a smile.

Quick and Easy near Grafton Street

Cornucopia is a small, earth-mama-with-class, proudly vegetarian, self-serve place two blocks off Grafton. It's friendly and youthful, with hearty €12 lunches and €15 dinner specials (Mon-Wed 8:30-21:00, Thu-Sat 8:30-22:30, Sun 12:00-20:30, 19 Wicklow Street, tel. 01/677-7583).

The Farm, Dublin's healthiest dining option, shuns processed food and features fresh, organic, and free-range fare that's affordable and pretty darn tasty (€15-25 main courses, €20 two-course and €24 three-course early-bird specials, daily 11:00-23:00, a half-block south of Trinity College at 3 Dawson Street, tel. 01/671-8654).

O'Neill's Pub is a venerable, dark, and tangled retreat offering good grub, including dependable €10-15 carvery lunches. It's very central, located across from the main TI (daily 12:00-22:00, Suffolk Street, tel. 01/679-3656).

Two pubs on Duke Street—**The Duke** and **Davy Burns**—serve reliable pub lunches. (The nearby Cathach Rare Books shop, at 10 Duke Street, displays a rare edition of *Ulysses* inscribed by Joyce, among other treasures, in its window.)

Bewley's Café is an old-time favorite, offering light meals from €10 and full meals for €12-17. Sit on the ground floor among Art Deco lamps and windows by stained-glass artist Harry Clarke, or head upstairs to the bright atrium decorated by art students (self-service Mon-Sat 8:00-22:00, Sun 9:00-22:00, 78 Grafton Street, tel. 01/672-7720). For a taste of witty Irish lunch theater, check out **Bewley's Café Theatre** upstairs; you can catch a fun hour-long performance while having a lunch of soup and brown bread for €8-16 (Mon-Sat at 13:00 during a play's run—doors open at 12:45, closed Sun, booking info mobile 086-878-4001, www.bewleyscafe theatre.com).

Wagamama Noodle Bar, like its popular sisters in Britain, is a pan-Asian slurp-a-thon with great and healthy noodle and rice dishes (€12-17) served at long communal tables by energetic waiters (daily 12:00-23:00, no reservations, often a line but it moves quickly, South King Street underneath St. Stephen's Green Shopping Centre, tel. 01/478-2152).

Yamamori is a plain, mellow, and modern Japanese place serving seas of sushi and noodles (€10-15 lunches daily 12:00-17:30, €16-20 dinners nightly 17:30-23:00, 71 South Great George's Street, tel. 01/475-5001).

Supermarkets: **Dunnes,** on South Great George's Street, is your one-stop shop for assembling a picnic meal (Mon-Sat 8:30-19:00, Thu-Fri until 20:00, Sun 11:00-19:00, across from Yamamori). They have another outlet in the basement of the St. Stephen's Green Shopping Centre. **Marks & Spencer** department store has a fancy grocery store in the basement, with fine take-away sandwiches and salads (Mon-Fri 9:00-20:00, Thu until 21:00, Sat 8:30-20:00, Sun 11:00-19:00, Grafton Street).

Hip and Fun in North Dublin

The Church is a trendy café/bar/restaurant/nightclub/beer garden housed in the former St. Mary's Church. In its former life as a church, it hosted the baptism of Irish rebel Wolfe Tone and the marriage of brewing legend Arthur Guinness. The choir balcony has a huge pipe organ and a refined menu; the ground floor nave is dominated by a long bar and pub grub; and a disco thumps like hell in the bunker-like basement. On warm summer nights, the outdoor terrace is packed. Eating here is as much about the scene as the cuisine (pub grub daily 12:00-20:00, balcony restaurant open daily 17:00-22:30, €24 three-course early-bird special before 19:00, reservations a good idea Fri and Sat nights, corner of St. Mary's and Jervis Streets, tel. 01/828-0102).

The Epicurean Food Hall offers a fun selection of food stalls with big and splittable portions. Choices include Greek, Mexican, Chinese, Thai, Turkish, Italian, Brazilian, and good old Irish fish-and-chips. It's a hit with locals—and visitors—needing to eat cheaply (100 yards north of the Ha' Penny Bridge on Lower Liffey Street).

Fast and Cheap near Christ Church Cathedral

Many of Dublin's late-night grocery stores sell cheap salads, microwaved meat pies, and made-to-order sandwiches (such as **Spar** and **Centra** markets, open 24 hours a day in the city, spread all over Dublin). A €10 picnic dinner brought back to the hotel might be a good option after a busy day of sightseeing.

Queen of Tarts does yummy breakfasts, fruit salads, sandwiches, and wonderful pastries with quiet streetside seating. Get yours to go, and enjoy a picnic with a Georgian view in one of Dublin's grassy squares (€6-8 breakfasts, €8-12 lunches, Mon-Fri 8:00-19:00, Sat-Sun 9:00-19:00, hidden beside Kinlay House on Cow's Lane, tel. 01/670-7499).

Chorus Café is a friendly little hole-in-the-wall diner, perfect for breakfast, lunch, or dinner with a newspaper (€8 breakfasts, €10 lunches, €12-18 dinners, Mon-Fri 8:30-22:00, Sat 9:30-22:00, closed Sun, Fishamble Street, next door to the site of the first performance of Handel's *Messiah*, tel. 01/616-7088).

Dining at Classy Restaurants and Cafés

These two stylish restaurants serve well-presented food at fair prices. They're located within a block of each other, just south of Temple Bar and Dame Street, near the main TI.

Trocadero serves beefy European cuisine to Dubliners interested in a slow, romantic meal. The dressy, red-velvet interior is draped with photos of local actors. Come early or make a reservation—it's a favorite with theatergoers (€18-29 meals, Mon-Sat

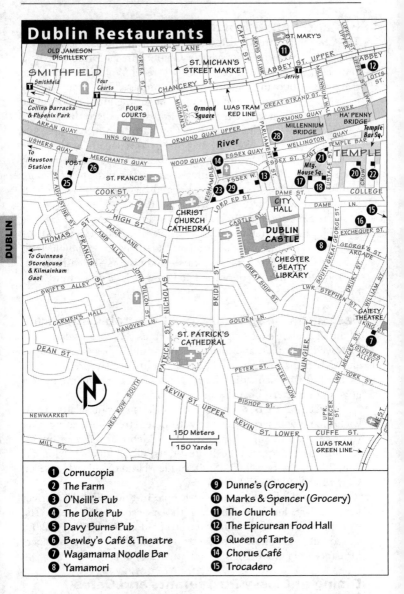

Dublin Restaurants

OLD JAMESON DISTILLERY

SMITHFIELD

Smithfield

To Collins Barracks & Phoenix Park

Four Courts

MARY'S LANE

ST. MICHAN'S STREET MARKET

ST. MARY'S

11

ABBEY ST. UPPER

Jervis

12

ABBEY ST. LWR.

LOTTS ST.

CHANCERY ST.

GREEK ST.

GREEN ST.

FOUR COURTS

Ormond Square

LUAS TRAM RED LINE

GREAT STRAND ST.

ORMOND QUAY LOWER

MILLENNIUM BRIDGE

HA' PENNY BRIDGE

Temple Bar Sq.

ARRAN QUAY

INNS QUAY

ORMOND QUAY UPPER

River

WELLINGTON

QUAY

TEMPLE

USHERS QUAY

MERCHANTS QUAY

POST **26**

WOOD QUAY

ESSEX QUAY

28

PARLIAMENT ST.

ESSEX ST. EAST

Mtg. House Sq.

21

20

CROW

22

To Heuston Station

25

ST. FRANCIS'

14

ESSEX W.

13

23 **29**

DAME ST.

17 **18**

EUSTACE ST.

COLLEGE

COOK ST.

LORD ED. ST.

CITY HALL

DAME

LN.

15

ST. AUGUSTINE ST.

HIGH ST.

CHRIST CHURCH CATHEDRAL

CASTLE ST.

DUBLIN CASTLE

16

EXCHEQUER ST.

THOMAS ST.

FRANCIS ST.

LAMB ALLEY

BACK LANE

JOHN DILLON ST.

GREAT SHIP ST.

8

SOUTH GREAT GEORGE'S ST.

GEORGE'S ST. ARCADE

GEORGE'S ST.

DRURY ST.

WILLIAM ST.

To Guinness Storehouse & Kilmainham Gaol

CHESTER BEATTY LIBRARY

LWR. STEPHEN ST.

GAIETY THEATRE

SWIFT'S ALLEY

NICHOLAS ST.

GOLDEN LN.

AUNGIER ST.

CARMEN'S HALL

HANOVER LN.

ST. PATRICK'S CATHEDRAL

BRIDE ST.

KING ST.

7

LWR. MERCER ST.

GLOVERS ALLEY

DEAN ST.

PATRICK ST.

PETER ST.

PETER ROW

LWR. YORK ST.

NEWMARKET

NEW ROW SOUTH

KEVIN ST. UPPER

BISHOP ST.

UPR. MERCER ST.

WEST

KEVIN ST. LOWER

CUFFE ST.

MILL ST.

150 Meters

150 Yards

LUAS TRAM GREEN LINE →

1 Cornucopia
2 The Farm
3 O'Neill's Pub
4 The Duke Pub
5 Davy Burns Pub
6 Bewley's Café & Theatre
7 Wagamama Noodle Bar
8 Yamamori

9 Dunne's (Grocery)
10 Marks & Spencer (Grocery)
11 The Church
12 The Epicurean Food Hall
13 Queen of Tarts
14 Chorus Café
15 Trocadero

17:00–24:00, closed Sun, 4 St. Andrew Street, tel. 01/677-5546). The three-course pre-theater special is a fine value at €25 (17:00–19:00, leave by 19:45).

Boulevard Café is mod, trendy, and likeable, dishing up Mediterranean cuisine that's heavy on the Italian. Their salads, pasta, and sandwiches cost roughly €9-15, and three-course lunch specials are €16 (Mon-Sat 10:00-18:00). It's smart to reserve for

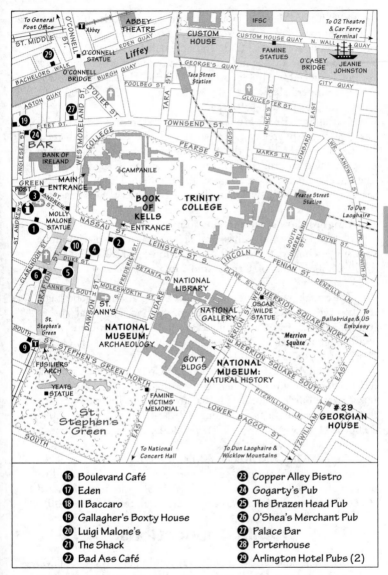

DUBLIN

⑯ Boulevard Café	㉓ Copper Alley Bistro
⑰ Eden	㉔ Gogarty's Pub
⑱ Il Baccaro	㉕ The Brazen Head Pub
⑲ Gallagher's Boxty House	㉖ O'Shea's Merchant Pub
⑳ Luigi Malone's	㉗ Palace Bar
㉑ The Shack	㉘ Porterhouse
㉒ Bad Ass Café	㉙ Arlington Hotel Pubs (2)

dinner, which runs about €17-24 (Mon-Sat 12:00-24:00, closed Sun, 27 Exchequer Street, tel. 01/679-2131).

In Temple Bar

Eden is a classy refuge serving a variety of contemporary Irish dishes in an airy space with a pleasant outdoor terrace (€18-27 meals, Mon-Sat 12:30-15:00 & 17:00-22:00, Sun 12:00-16:00 &

18:00-21:30; on Meeting House Square, a half-block off the busy tourist thoroughfare; tel. 01/670-5372). They offer a three-course pre-theater menu for €27 (Sun-Thu only before 19:00).

Il Baccaro, a cozy Italian wine tavern with an arched brick ceiling, is tucked in a quiet corner of Meeting House Square (€13-19 pasta dinners, daily 17:30-22:30, lunches Sat 12:00-16:00 only, closed Sun, tel. 01/671-4597).

Gallagher's Boxty House is touristy and traditional—a good, basic value with creaky floorboards and old Dublin ambience. Its specialty is the boxty, the generally bland-tasting Irish potato pancake filled and rolled with various meats, veggies, and sauces. The "Gaelic Boxty" is the liveliest (€15-21, daily 11:00-22:30, also serves stews and corned beef, 20 Temple Bar, reservations wise, tel. 01/677-2762).

Luigi Malone's, with its fun atmosphere and varied menu of pizza, ribs, pasta, sandwiches, and fajitas, is just the place to take your high-school date (€13-19 dishes, Mon-Sat 12:00-22:00, Sun 13:00-21:30, corner of Cecilia and Fownes streets, tel. 01/679-2723).

The Shack, while a bit touristy, has a reputation for good quality. It serves traditional Irish, chicken, seafood, and steak dishes (€16-25 entrées, €19 three-course early-bird special offered 17:00-19:00, open daily 12:00-22:00, in the center of Temple Bar, 24 East Essex Street, tel. 01/679-0043).

The Bad Ass Café, where Sinéad O'Connor once waitressed, has been spiffed up since her tenure. The fare is uncomplicated pizza, pasta, burgers, and salads that are cheap by Temple Bar standards. There's even a fun kids menu (€12-17 meals, daily 12:00-22:00, 9-11 Crown Alley, tel. 01/675-3005, live music or comedy most Fri and Sat evenings).

Copper Alley Bistro, a bit farther from the Temple Bar chaos and more reasonably priced, serves comfort-food lunches and dinners (daily 12:00-21:00, corner of Fishamble and Lord Edward streets, just opposite Christ Church Cathedral, tel. 01/679-6500).

Dublin Connections

Note that trains and buses generally run less frequently on Sundays.

By Train from Dublin's Heuston Station to: Tralee (every two hours, 6/day on Sun, most change in Mallow but one direct evening train, 4 hours), **Ennis** (4/day, 3.25-3.75 hours, change in Limerick), **Galway** (8/day, 2.5-3 hours). Train info: recorded time-table tel. 01/805-4222, www.irishrail.ie.

By Train from Dublin's Connolly Station to: Rosslare (3-4/day, 3 hours), **Portrush** (7/day, 2/day Sun, 5 hours, transfer in Belfast or Coleraine). The **Dublin-Belfast train** connects the two Irish capitals in two hours at 90 mph on one continuous, welded rail (8/day Mon-Sat, 5/day Sun, €40 "day return" tickets, €20 if you book online, can cost more Fri-Sun, tel. 01/836-3333). Train info: Tel. 01/836-6222. Northern Ireland train info: Tel. 048/9089-9400.

To Dun Laoghaire: See "Getting to Dun Laoghaire" on page 105.

By Bus to: Belfast (hourly, most via Dublin Airport, 2.75-3 hours), **Trim** (almost hourly, 1 hour), **Ennis** (almost hourly, 5-5.25 hours), **Galway** (hourly, 3.25 hours; faster on CityLink—hourly, 2.5 hours, tel. 890-280-808, www.citylink.ie), **Limerick** (hourly, 3.75 hours), **Tralee** (7/day, 6 hours), **Dingle** (4/day, 8-9 hours, transfer at Limerick and Tralee). Bus info: Tel. 01/836-6111, www.buseireann.ie.

Dublin Airport: The airport is well-connected to the city center seven miles away; for transportation options into the city, see "Arrival in Dublin" on page 49 (airport code: DUB, tel. 01/814-1111, www.dublinairport.ie). To sleep at Dublin Airport, a safe bet is the **$$ Radisson Blu Dublin Airport** (Db-€75-109, best prices if booked online, tel. 01/844-6000, www.radissonblu.ie).

Connecting Ireland and Britain

Spend a few minutes online researching your transportation options across the Irish Sea. Most airline and ferry companies routinely offer discounts for tickets purchased from their websites. And if you have to buy a ferry ticket in person or by phone, you'll be hit with an additional €3 fee. Before sorting out rail/ferry prices with individual companies, try www.arrivatrainswales.co.uk/sail-rail, which deals with several companies and has fares low enough to compete with cheap airlines.

Flights

If you're going directly to London, flying is your best bet. There's no need to waste a valuable day going by slower surface transportation.

Check **Ryanair** first, but keep in mind that they don't fly to Heathrow (1.5 hours, Irish tel. 081-830-3030, www.ryanair.com). Options to Heathrow include **British Airways** (Irish tel. 1-890-626-747, US tel. 800-247-9297, www.ba.com) and **Aer Lingus** (tel. 081-836-5000, www.aerlingus.com). To get the lowest fares, ask about round-trip ticket prices and book months in advance (though Ryanair offers deals nearly all the time).

Ferries

Discount airlines have cut into ferry business in a big way. But there are still seven daily crossings from Dublin Port (two miles east of O'Connell Bridge) and one daily seasonal crossing from Dun Laoghaire (seven miles south of city center) that all connect to Holyhead, Wales. The route is split between two competing companies, but both make you pay €5 more to take a fast, two-hour crossing compared to a slow, 3.5-hour sailing. Keep in mind that you must board at least 30 minutes before the scheduled sailing time or risk being denied boarding. Since these boats can fill  up in advance on summer weekends, try to book at least a week in advance during this peak period.

Dublin to Holyhead: Irish Ferries sails between Dublin Port and Holyhead four times daily, departing at 8:05, 8:45, 14:30, and 20:55. The first and last boats are the slower crossings (€40 one-way for fast boats taking 2 hours, €35 one-way for slow boats taking 3.5 hours; Dublin tel. 0818-300-400, UK tel. 08705-329-129, www.irishferries.com). **Stena Line** sails between Dublin Port and Holyhead three times daily, departing at 8:20, 16:00, and 21:15 (€35 one-way, 3.5 hours, Dublin tel. 01/204-7777, UK tel. 08447-707-070, www.stenaline.com).

Dun Laoghaire to Holyhead: Stena Line has one daily crossing on a fast, huge catamaran. It leaves April through September only at 13:15 (€40 one-way, 2 hours).

Ferries to France

With the glut of discount airlines that have sprung up over the past decade (see page 498), it makes little sense to waste your valuable time on a 20-hour ferry ride when you could fly to France in three hours. But if the nostalgia of a long, slow ferry ride and the risk of rough seas appeal to you, check **Irish Ferries,** which connects Ireland (Rosslare) with France (Cherbourg and Roscoff) a few days per month from May through September. Cherbourg has the quickest train connection to Paris, but your overall time between Ireland and Paris is about the same (20-hour ferry ride plus 2-hour train trip) regardless of which port is used. One-way fares cost €64-84 and are cheapest if booked online. In both directions, departures are generally between 15:30 and 17:30 and arrive late the next morning.

While passengers can nearly always get on, reservations are wise in summer and easy online. If you anticipate a crowded departure, you can reserve a seat for €15. Cabins (2 beds) go for €40-75. The easiest way to get a bed (except during summer) is, again, to book it online. The cafeteria serves bad food at reasonable prices. Upon arrival in France, buses and taxis connect you to your Paris-bound train (Irish Ferries: Dublin tel. 0818-300-400, www.irish-ferries.com).

Dun Laoghaire and Howth

Dun Laoghaire (dun LEERY) and Howth (rhymes with "growth") are two peas in a pod, dangling from opposite ends of Dublin Bay's crescent-shaped shoreline. They offer quieter, cheaper lodging alternatives to Dublin. Both offer easy DART light rail access to the city center, just a 25-minute ride away. Each houses its only worthwhile sightseeing options in pillbox martello (masonry) towers. And they were each once home to famous Irish writers: James Joyce in Dun Laoghaire and W. B. Yeats in Howth. The fundamental difference between the two is that Dun Laoghaire (south of Dublin) is a ferry port to Wales, while Howth (north of Dublin) is closer to the airport.

DUBLIN

Dun Laoghaire

Dun Laoghaire is seven miles south of Dublin. This snoozy suburb, with a ferry terminal for Wales and easy connections to downtown Dublin, is a convenient small-town base for exploring the big city. But as the majority of ferry crossings have moved to Dublin Port, this town has gotten even quieter in recent years. Its TI closed in 2012.

The Dun Laoghaire harbor was strategic enough to merit a line of martello towers, built to defend against an expected Napoleonic invasion (one tower now houses the James Joyce Museum, which may be closed during your visit). By the mid-19th century, its massive breakwaters were completed, protecting a huge harbor. Ships sailed regularly from here to Wales (75 miles away), and the first train line in Ireland connected the terminal with Dublin.

Getting to Dun Laoghaire

Buses run between Dublin and Dun Laoghaire, but the **DART** commuter train is much faster and not subject to Dublin traffic delays (4/hour, 25 minutes, runs Mon-Sat about 6:00-23:30, Sun from 9:00, €2.50 one-way, €4.70 round-trips are good same day only, 3-day pass-€12.50, Eurail Pass valid but uses a flexi-day, tel. 01/703-3504, www.irishrail.ie). If you're coming from Dublin, catch a DART train marked *Bray* or *Greystones* and get off at the Sandycove/Glasthule or Dun Laoghaire stop, depending on which B&B you choose. If you're leaving Dun Laoghaire, catch a train

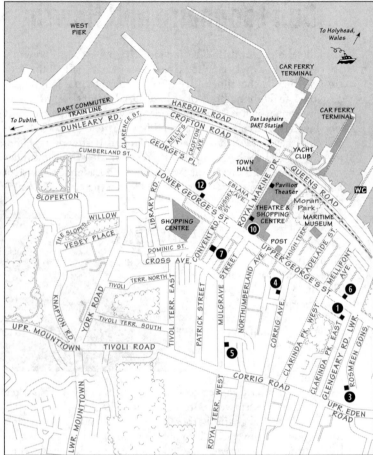

marked *Howth* to get to Dublin. Get off at the central Tara Street Station if you want to sightsee in Dublin; or, for train connections north, ride it one stop farther to Connolly Station.

The **Aircoach bus** makes it easy to connect Dublin Airport and Dun Laoghaire. You can catch it at either the front steps of the Marine Hotel in Dun Laoghaire or opposite St. Joseph's Church in nearby Glasthule (€9, departs Dun Laoghaire starting at 4:00 and runs from the airport 5:00-23:00, hourly, 50 minutes, tel. 01/844-7118, www.aircoach.ie).

The **taxi** fare from Dun Laoghaire to central Dublin is about €30; to the airport, about €45. With the options of the DART train to Dublin and the Aircoach bus to Dublin Airport, taking

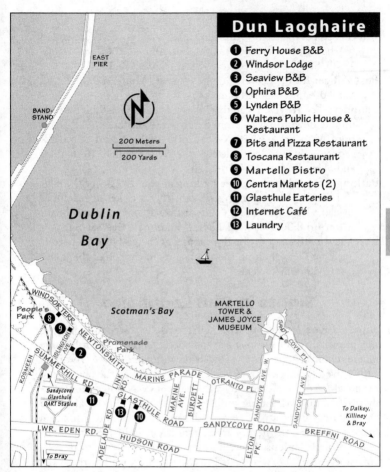

Dun Laoghaire

1. Ferry House B&B
2. Windsor Lodge
3. Seaview B&B
4. Ophira B&B
5. Lynden B&B
6. Walters Public House & Restaurant
7. Bits and Pizza Restaurant
8. Toscana Restaurant
9. Martello Bistro
10. Centra Markets (2)
11. Glasthule Eateries
12. Internet Café
13. Laundry

DUBLIN

a taxi is like throwing money away. But if you really need a taxi, try ABC Taxi service (tel. 01/285-5444). With DART access into Dublin, and cheap or sometimes free parking, Dun Laoghaire is ideal for those with **cars** (which can cost €25/day to park in Dublin).

Orientation to Dun Laoghaire

A busy transportation hub, Dun Laoghaire has a coastline defined by its nearly mile-long breakwaters—reaching like two muscular arms into the Irish Sea. The breakwaters are popular for strollers, bikers, bird-watchers, and fishermen.

DUBLIN

Helpful Hints

Internet Access: Central Internet Café provides a fast connection (€4/hour, Mon-Fri 9:00-22:00, Sat 10:00-20:00, Sun 11:00-19:00, 88B Lower George's Street, tel. 01/230-1811).

Post Office: It's on Lower George's Street (Mon-Fri 9:00-18:00, Sat 9:00-13:00, closed Sun).

Laundry: Try **Jeeves,** located in the village of Glasthule, a five-minute downhill walk from Sandycove/Glasthule DART station (Mon-Fri 8:30-18:00, Sat 9:00-18:00, closed Sun, full-service only, 34 Glasthule Road, next to Daniel's Restaurant and Wine Bar, tel. 01/230-1120).

Parking: If you don't have free parking at your B&B, try the pay-and-display street-parking system. Buy a ticket at machines spaced along the street, and display it on your dashboard (Mon-Fri 8:00-19:00, €2/hour, 3-hour max, free Sat-Sun).

Best Views: Hike out to the lighthouse, at the end of the interesting East Pier; or climb the tight stairs to the top of the James Joyce Museum/tower.

Sights in Dun Laoghaire

James Joyce Museum—This squat martello tower at Sandycove was originally built to repel a Napoleonic invasion, but it became famous chiefly because of its association with James Joyce. The great author lived here briefly and made it the setting for the opening of his novel *Ulysses*. Unfortunately, the museum was closed temporarily in 2012 due to funding problems; visitors should call ahead to check its current status. If open, the museum's round exhibition space is filled with literary memorabilia, including photographs and rare first editions. For a fine view, climb the claustrophobic, two-story spiral stairwell sealed inside the thick wall to reach the rooftop gun mount.

Cost and Hours: €6, €11.50 combo-ticket with Dublin Writers' Museum; March-Oct Tue-Sat 10:00-13:00 & 14:00-17:00, Sun 14:00-18:00, closed Mon, hours may change or museum may be closed in 2013—call to confirm; open by appointment only Nov-Feb, tel. 01/280-9265.

Plays and Concerts—The Pavilion Theatre offers performances in the center of town (€10-25, Marine Road, tel. 01/231-2929, www.paviliontheatre.ie).

Swimming—Kids of all ages enjoy swimming at the safe, sandy little cove bordered by rounded rocks beside the martello tower.

Sleeping in Dun Laoghaire

(€1 = about $1.30, country code: 353, area code: 01)

In Dun Laoghaire, near Sandycove DART Station

These listings are within a couple of blocks of the Sandycove/ Glasthule DART station and a 10-minute walk to the Dun Laoghaire DART station/ferry landing.

$ Ferry House B&B, with four high-ceilinged rooms, is a family-friendly place on a dead-end street (Sb-€40-50, Db-€65-75, Tb-€90, Qb-€110, €5 discount if you pay cash and book direct, Wi-Fi, 15 Clarinda Park North just off Clarinda Park West, tel. 01/280-8301, www.ferryhousedublin.com, ferry_house@hotmail. com, Eamon and Pauline Teehan).

$ Windsor Lodge rents four fresh, inviting rooms on a quiet street a block off the harbor and a block from the DART station (Db-€50-70, Tb-€70-90, cash only, Wi-Fi, 3 Islington Avenue, tel. 01/284-6952, mobile 086-844-6646, www.windsorlodge.ie, windsorlodgedublin@gmail.com, Mary O'Farrell).

$ Seaview B&B, a modern house run by Mrs. Kane, has three big, cheery rooms and a welcoming guests' lounge with a bright and friendly feeling (S-€35, Db-€70 with this book in 2013, cash only, just above Rosmeen Gardens at 2 Granite Hall, tel. & fax 01/280-9105, www.seaviewbedandbreakfast.com, seaviewbedand breakfast@hotmail.com).

Near the Dun Laoghaire DART Station

$ Ophira B&B is a historic house with four comfortably creaky rooms run by active diver-hiker-biker John O'Connor and his wife Cathy (Sb-€40-55, Db-€55-75, Tb-€75-100, Qb-€100-140, Wi-Fi, parking available, 10 Corrig Avenue, tel. 01/280-0997, www. ophira.ie, johnandcathy@ophira.ie).

$ Lynden B&B, with a classy 150-year-old interior hiding behind a somber front, rents four big rooms (S-€35-40, D-€55-60, Db-€60-70, Wi-Fi, go past Mulgrave Street to 2 Mulgrave Terrace, tel. 01/280-6404, www.lyndenbandb.com, lynden@iol.ie, Maria Gavin).

Eating in Dun Laoghaire

If staying in Dun Laoghaire, I'd definitely eat here rather than in Dublin.

George's Street, Dun Laoghaire's main drag three blocks inland, has plenty of eateries and pubs, many with live music. **Walters Public House and Restaurant** is a bright, modern place above

DUBLIN

a pub, offering good food to a dressy crowd. The multi-terraced back patio of the pub is great for a drink on a warm evening (€16-24 meals, €8-14 pub meals, daily 15:00-22:00, 68 Upper George's Street, tel. 01/280-7442). A good bet for families is the kid-friendly **Bits and Pizza** (daily 12:00-22:00, off George's Street at 15 Patrick Street, tel. 01/284-2411).

Toscana, on the seafront, is a popular little cubbyhole, serving hearty Italian dishes and pizza. Its prime location makes it easy to incorporate into your evening stroll. Reserve for dinner (€18 two-course and €21 three-course early-bird specials before 18:30, daily 12:00-22:00, 5 Windsor Terrace, tel. 01/230-0890).

Martello Bistro, also on the stroll-worthy waterfront, is a good bet for seafood or steak in a friendly atmosphere (€23 for two courses, €26 for three courses, daily 12:00-22:30, 1 Martello Terrace, tel. 01/280-9871).

Centra Market is centrally located for picnic shopping right on Marine Road (Mon-Sat 7:00-22:00, Sun 8:00-22:00).

Glasthule (called simply "the village" locally, just down the street from the Sandycove/Glasthule DART station) has an array of fun, hardworking little restaurants. The big **Eagle House pub** dishes up great Indian food and hearty €10-18 pub meals in a wonderful atmosphere; it's a super local joint for a late drink (Mon-Sat 12:30-21:30, Sun 12:30-19:30, 18-19 Glasthule Road, tel. 01/280-4740). The nearby **Daniel's Restaurant and Wine Bar** is less atmospheric, but it's also good (€18-24 meals, Tue-Sun 18:00-22:30, closed Mon, 34 Glasthule Road, tel. 01/284-1027). Another **Centra Market** is right next door and has your picnic makings (daily 7:00-23:00, Glasthule Road).

Howth

Eight miles north of Dublin, Howth rests on a teardrop-shaped peninsula that pokes the Irish Sea. Its active harbor teems with fishing boats bringing in the daily catch and seals trolling for their scraps. Weary Dubliners come here for refreshing coastal cliff walks near the city. Located at the north terminus of the DART light rail line, Howth makes a good place for travelers to settle in, with easy connections to Dublin for sightseeing.

Howth was once an important gateway to Dublin. Near the neck of the peninsula is the suburb of Clontarf, where Irish High King Brian Boru defeated the last concerted Viking attack in 1014. Eight hundred years later, a squat martello tower was built on a

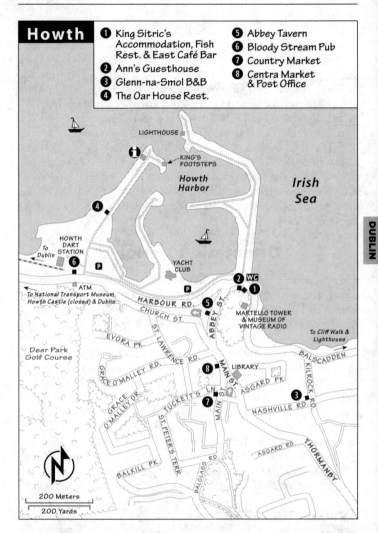

Howth

1. King Sitric's Accommodation, Fish Rest. & East Café Bar
2. Ann's Guesthouse
3. Glenn-na-Smol B&B
4. The Oar House Rest.
5. Abbey Tavern
6. Bloody Stream Pub
7. Country Market
8. Centra Market & Post Office

LIGHTHOUSE

KING'S FOOTSTEPS

Howth Harbor

Irish Sea

HOWTH DART STATION

To Dublin

YACHT CLUB

ATM
To National Transport Museum, Howth Castle (closed) & Dublin

HARBOUR RD.

CHURCH ST.

ABBEY ST.

MARTELLO TOWER & MUSEUM OF VINTAGE RADIO

To Cliff Walk & Lighthouse

EYORA PK.

ST. LAWRENCE RD.

Deer Park Golf Course

GRACE O'MALLEY RD.

GRACE O'MALLEY DR.

TUCKETT'S LN.

ST. PETER'S TERR.

LIBRARY

MAIN ST.

ASGARD PK.

NASHVILLE RD.

BALSCADDEN

KILROCK RD.

THORMANBY

ASGARD RD.

BALKILL PK.

BALGLASS RD.

200 Meters
200 Yards

DUBLIN

bluff above Howth's harbor to defend it from a Napoleonic invasion that never came. The harbor then grew as a port for shipping from Liverpool and Wales. It was eventually eclipsed by Dun Laoghaire, which was first to gain rail access. Irish rebels smuggled German-supplied guns into Ireland via Howth in 1914, making the 1916 Easter Uprising possible. These days this hamlet is so sleepy, it didn't open a TI until 2009.

Getting to Howth

The **DART** light rail system zaps travelers between Howth and the city twice as fast as the bus and sans traffic (4/hour, 25 minutes, runs Mon-Sat about 6:00-23:30, Sun from 9:00, €2.50 one-way, €4.70 round-trips good same day only, 3-day pass-€12.50, Eurail Pass valid but uses a flexi-day, tel. 01/703-3504, www.irishrail. ie). If you're coming from Dublin, catch a DART train marked "Howth" (not *Howth Junction, Malahide,* or *Drogheda*) and ride it to the end of the line—passing through Howth Junction en route. All trains departing Howth head straight to Dublin's Connolly Station, and then continue on to Tara and Pearse stations.

If you go by **bus,** #31 or #31B link Dublin's Eden Quay and the well-marked bus stop on Howth's harborfront (1 hour, €2.65). A **taxi** from the airport takes about 20 minutes and costs about €20. Try Executive Cabs (tel. 01/839-6020). With easy DART access into Dublin and plentiful parking, Howth is a good option for those with **cars.**

Orientation to Howth

Howth perches on the north shore of the peninsula, clustered along a quarter-mile harborfront promenade that stretches from the DART station (in the west) to the martello tower on the bluff (in the east). Its two stony piers clutch like crab claws at the Irish Sea. The West Pier has the fishing action and TI, while the East Pier extends to a stubby 200-year-old lighthouse and views of a rugged nearby island, Ireland's Eye. Abbey Street extends south, uphill from the harbor near the base of the martello tower bluff, becoming Main Street with most of the shops and pubs. Along the street you'll find the post office in the back of the Centra Market (Mon-Fri 9:00-13:00 & 14:15-18:00, Sat 9:00-13:00, closed Sun) and the library (free Internet access, only one terminal, Mon and Wed 14:00-20:30, Tue and Thu-Sat 10:00-13:00 & 14:00-17:00, closed Sun). Ulster Bank has the only ATM in town, across the street from the DART station and to the left of the Gem Market.

Tourist Information
The TI is at the far end of the West Pier, on the ground floor of the Aqua Building (May-Oct daily 9:00-17:00, shorter hours off-season, 1 West Pier, tel. 01/839-6955, www.howthismagic.com). If the TI is closed, another good info source is your innkeeper.

Sights in Howth

Other than coastal walks, sightseeing here pales in comparison to Dublin. Nearby Howth Castle is privately owned and cannot be toured.

Museum of Vintage Radio—The three-story martello tower on the bluff overlooking the East Pier is the only sight in Howth worth a glance. Curator Pat Herbert has spent almost 50 years acquiring his collection of lovingly preserved radios, phonographs, and even a hurdy-gurdy (a crank-action musical oddity)—all of which still work. Check out the WWII-era radio disguised as a picture frame, which was used by the resistance in occupied France during World War II.

Before leaving the compact bluff, catch the views of the harbor and the nearby island of Ireland's Eye. Spot the distant martello tower on the island's west end and the white guano coating its eastern side, courtesy of a colony of gannets.

Cost and Hours: €5, May-Oct daily 11:00-16:00, Nov-April Sat-Sun 11:00-16:00, entry up driveway off Abbey Street, mobile 086-815-4189.

National Transport Museum—Housed in a large shed on the castle grounds, this is a dusty waste of time unless you find rapture in old trams and buses.

Cost and Hours: €3.50, June-Aug Sat-Sun 14:00-17:00, otherwise by appointment only, tel. 01/848-0831.

St. Mary's Abbey—Looming above Abbey Street, the current ruins date from the early 1400s. Before that, a church built by Norse King Sitric in 1042 stood at this site. The entrance to the ruins is on Church Street, above the abbey grounds.

East and West Piers—The piers make for mellow strolls after a meal. Poke your head into the various fishmonger shops along the West Pier to see the day's catch. At the end of the pier (on the leeward side), you'll find the footsteps of King George IV carved into the stone after his 1821 visit. The East Pier is a quiet jetty barbed with a squat lighthouse and the closest views of Ireland's Eye. If you want to get even closer to the island, book a boat excursion (€15 round-trip, daily in summer on demand 10:00-18:00, call for  off-season trips, mobile 086-845-9154, www.islandferries.net).

Hiking Trails—Trails above the eastern cliffs of the peninsula offer enjoyable, breezy exercise. For a scenic three-hour round-trip, walk past the East Pier and martello tower, following Balscadden Road uphill. You'll soon pass Balscadden House, where writer W. B. Yeats spent part of his youth (watch for plaque on left). Where the road dead-ends, you'll find the well-marked trailhead. The trail is easy to follow, and soon you'll be walking south around the craggy coastline to grand views of the Bailey Lighthouse on the southeast rim of the peninsula. The gate to the lighthouse grounds is always locked, so enjoy the view from afar before retracing your steps back to Howth.

Sleeping in Howth

(€1 = about $1.30, country code: 353, area code: 01)

$$$ King Sitric's Accommodation is Howth's best lodging option and has a fine harborfront seafood restaurant (described later). It fills the old harbormaster's house with eight well-kept rooms and a friendly staff (Sb-€110-145, Db-€120-205, Tb-€190-245, discounts for 2-night stay with dinner, online deals, Wi-Fi, East Pier below martello tower, tel. 01/832-5235, www.kingsitric.ie, info@kingsitric.ie, Aidan and Joan MacManus).

$ Ann's Guesthouse, next door to King Sitric's, sports four bright, airy rooms on its top floor—two with skylight views of the harbor (Sb/Db-€80, 5 East Pier, tel. 01/832-3197, www.annsofhowth.com, info@annsofhowth.com).

$ Glenn-na-Smol B&B is a homey house with six unpretentious rooms in a quiet setting, a 15-minute walk uphill along the coast behind the martello tower (Sb-€40, Db-€70, Tb-€90, Qb-€100, cash only, Wi-Fi, parking, corner of Nashville Road & Kilrock Road, tel. 01/832-2936, mobile 085-716-1695, rickards@indigo.ie, Sean and Kitty Rickard).

Eating in Howth

King Sitric's Fish Restaurant, one of the area's most famous seafood experiences, serves Irish versions of French classics in a dining room (upstairs) with harbor views. Chef Aidan MacManus rises early each morning to select the best of the day's catch on the pier, to be enjoyed that evening by happy customers (€22-30 meals, Mon and Wed-Sat 18:30-22:00, Sun 13:00-19:00, closed Tue, reservations a good idea, tel. 01/832-5235). They also operate the more economical **East Café Bar,** on the ground floor with extra seating out front. Their soups, salads, steak sandwiches, and fish dishes are a good value (Wed-Mon 12:00-21:30, closed Tue).

The Oar House sits halfway down the West Pier, serving a variety of great €16-24 fish dishes in a bustling atmosphere (Mon-Sat 12:30-22:30, Sun 12:30-21:00, 8 West Pier, tel. 01/839-4562).

For pub grub, try the **Abbey Tavern** up the hill on Abbey Street (occasional trad music and dance, call for schedule, tel. 01/839-0307 or 01/832-2006). Another good choice is the **Bloody Stream Pub** in front of the DART station (tel. 01/839-5076). The **Country Market** sells picnic supplies, and its cheap and friendly upstairs tea room offers lunch (Mon-Sat 7:00-19:00, Sun 7:00-17:00, Main Street). The **Centra Market** is a block closer to the waterfront (daily 7:00-22:00, Main Street).

NEAR DUBLIN

Brú na Bóinne • Trim • Glendalough • Wicklow Mountains
• Irish National Stud

Not far from urban Dublin, the stony skeletons of evocative ruins sprout from the lush Irish countryside. The story of Irish history is told by ancient burial mounds, early Christian monastic settlements, huge Norman castles, and pampered estate gardens. In gentler inland terrain, the Irish love of equestrian sport is nurtured in grassy pastures ruled by spirited thoroughbreds. These sights are separated into three regions: north of Dublin (the Valley of the Boyne, including Brú na Bóinne and the town of Trim), south of Dublin (Powerscourt Gardens, Glendalough, and the Wicklow Mountains), and west of Dublin (the Irish National Stud).

North of Dublin:
The Valley of the Boyne

The peaceful, green Valley of the Boyne, just 30 miles north of Dublin, has an impressive concentration of historical and spiritual sights: The enigmatic burial mounds at Brú na Bóinne are older than the Egyptian pyramids. At the Hill of Tara (seat of the high kings of Celtic Ireland), St. Patrick preached his most persuasive sermon. The valley also contains the first monastery in Ireland built in the style used on the Continent, and several of the country's finest high crosses. You'll see Trim's 13th-century castle—Ireland's biggest—built by Norman invaders, and you can wander the site

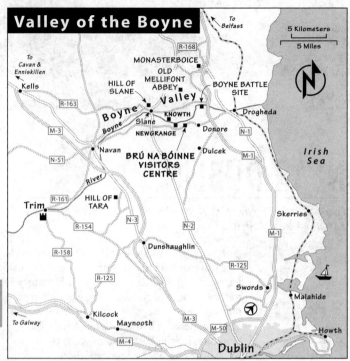

of the historic Battle of the Boyne (1690), in which the Protestants turned the tide against the Catholics and imposed British rule until the 20th century.

Planning Your Time

Of these sights, only Brú na Bóinne is worth ▲▲▲ (and deserves a good three hours). The others, while relatively meager physically, are powerfully evocative to anyone interested in Irish history and culture. Without a car, I'd visit only Brú na Bóinne, taking the shuttle bus from Dublin (see "Getting There" on page 118).

The region is a joy by car, because all of the described sights are within a 30-minute drive of one another. If you eat your Weetabix and get an early start, you could see the entire region in a day. Though the sights are on tiny roads, they're well-marked with brown, tourist-friendly road signs. You'll navigate best using an Ordnance Survey atlas.

As you plan your Ireland itinerary, if you're flying into or out of Dublin but want to avoid the intensity and expense of that big city, consider using Trim as an overnight base (45-minute drive from airport; accommodations listed on page 127) and tour these North of Dublin sights from there.

Tours of the Valley of the Boyne

If you lack a car and like tours, consider a round-trip excursion from Dublin. **Mary Gibbon's Tours** visits Brú na Bóinne (including inside the Newgrange tomb), the Hill of Tara, and the Hill of Slane in a seven-hour trip (€35, Mon-Fri only, 9:30 pickup at Mespil Hotel at 50-60 Mespil Road, 10:15 pickup at Dublin TI on Suffolk Street, 10:25 pickup at AIB Bank at 37-38 Upper O'Connell Street, home by 16:30, book direct rather than through TI, mobile 086-355-1355, www.newgrangetours.com, info@new grangetours.com).

Brú na Bóinne

The famous archaeological site properly known as Brú na Bóinne—"dwelling place of the Boyne"—is also commonly referred to as "Newgrange" (although that's actually the name of one of the tombs). The well-organized site, worth ▲▲▲, centers on a state-of-the-art museum and visitors center. You'll receive an appointment for a shuttle bus that ferries small groups five minutes away to one of two 5,000-year-old passage tombs, where a guide gives a 30-minute tour.

The **Newgrange** tomb is more famous and allows you inside. **Knowth** (rhymes with "south") opened more recently and is more extensive, but you can't go inside the tomb. At the visitors center, you'll buy a ticket to one or both sights and be given bus departure times (if you plan to see both sights, note that buses depart 1.5 hours apart). Newgrange sells out first, and has a longer wait. If you opt for Knowth, be sure to see the museum's replica of the Newgrange passage entrance (where a short tour and winter solstice light-show demo occur upon request); the replica is connected to the video room. Each site is different enough and worthwhile, but for many, seeing just one is adequate. For information on the prehistoric art, see page 457.

Orientation to Brú na Bóinne

Cost: The museum in the Brú na Bóinne Visitors Centre is included in the prices for the tombs: Newgrange-€6, Knowth-€5.

Hours: The site is open May-Sept daily 9:00-18:30, slightly shorter hours off-season, last entry to visitors center is 45 minutes before closing. Newgrange is open year-round, while Knowth is open May-Oct only. Allow an hour for the excellent museum and an hour for each of the tombs. Tel. 041/988-0300, www. heritageireland.ie.

Crowd-Beating Tips: Visits are limited, and on busy summer days those arriving in the afternoon may not get a spot on a shuttle

bus (no reservations possible). In peak season, try to arrive before 10:00 to avoid a wait caused by the big, tour-bus day-trip
crowds from Dublin. Upon arrival you'll generally get a bus
departure time for one or both of the passage-tomb sites (the
last bus leaves 1.75 hours before closing). Spend your wait-
time visiting the museum, watching the great seven-minute
video, and munching lunch in the cheery cafeteria. You can't
drive directly to the actual passage tombs.

Getting There: To reach Brú na Bóinne from Dublin by **car,** drive
north on N-1 to Drogheda, where signs direct you to the visitors center. To better understand the layout of this site and
shuttle-bus route, spend a moment studying the helpful aerial-
view panels by the stone pathway that leads from the parking
lot to the visitors center. Warning: If you're using a GPS, input
"Brú na Bóinne" into your system rather than "Newgrange"
or you'll end up at the actual Newgrange burial mound—two
miles (3.2 km) away, with no ticket booths or access into the
site.

    If you don't have a car and you're not taking a day tour,
hop on the **Newgrange shuttle bus,** a handy service that runs
from Dublin directly to the visitors center (€17 round-trip, 45
minutes, must book in advance, departs at 8:45 and 11:15 from
Gresham Hotel on Upper O'Connell Street, and at 9:00 and
11:30 from Dublin TI on Suffolk Street, return trips depart at
13:30 and 16:30 from the visitors center, run by Over the Top
Tours, book by calling 01/838-6128 or 1-800-424-252, www.
overthetoptours.com).

Visiting Brú na Bóinne

Newgrange is one single mound and is the
more restored of the Brú na Bóinne sites. Dating from 3200 B.C., it's 500 years older than
the pyramids at Giza. While we know nothing
of the builders, it most certainly was a sacred
spot devoted to some kind of Sun God ritual.
During the tour, you'll squeeze down a narrow
passageway to a cross-shaped central chamber
located under a 20-foot-high igloo-type stone
dome. Bones and ashes were placed here under
200,000 tons of stone and dirt to wait for a
special moment. As the sun rose on the shortest day of the year (winter solstice, Dec 21), a
ray of light crept slowly down the 60-foot-long passageway. For 17
minutes, it lit the center of the sacred chamber. Perhaps this was

the moment when the souls of the dead were transported to the afterlife, via that mysterious ray of life-giving and life-taking light.

Knowth (the second Brú na Bóinne site) is a necropolis of several grassy mounds around one 85-yard-wide grand tomb. The big mound, covering 1.5 acres, has two passages aligned so that on the spring and fall equinoxes, rays from the rising and setting sun shine down the passageways to the center chamber. Neither of the passages is open to the public, but when you visit a room cut into the mound—designed to expose the interior construction layers—you get a glimpse down one of the passages.

The Knowth site thrived from 3000 to 2000 B.C., with mysterious burial rituals and sun-tracking ceremonies to please the gods and ensure the regular progression of seasons for crops. The site then evolved into the domain of fairies and myths for the next 2,000 years, and became an Iron Age fortress in the early centuries after Christ. Around A.D. 1000, it was an all-Ireland political center, and later, a Norman fortress was built atop the mound. You'll see plenty of mysteriously carved stones and new-feeling grassy mounds that you can look down on from atop the grand tomb.

NEAR DUBLIN

More Sights in the Valley of the Boyne

▲▲Battle of the Boyne Site

One of Europe's lesser-known battlegrounds (but huge in Irish and British history), this is the pastoral riverside site of the pivotal battle in which the Protestant British broke Catholic resistance, establishing Protestant rule over all Ireland and Britain.

Cost and Hours: €4, daily May-Sept 10:00-18:00, March-April 9:30-17:30, Oct-Feb 9:00-17:00, last admission one hour before closing, tea room/cafeteria, tel. 041/980-9950, www.battleoftheboyne.ie.

Background: It was here in 1690 that Protestant King William III, with his English/Irish/Dutch/Danish/French Huguenot army, defeated his father-in-law—who was also his uncle—Catholic King James II and his Irish/French army. King William's forces, on the north side of the Boyne, managed to fight their way across the river, and by the end of the day, King James was fleeing south in full retreat. He soon left Ireland, but his forces fought on until their final defeat a year later. James the Second (called "James da Turd" by those who scorn his lack of courage and leadership) never returned, and he died a bitter ex-monarch in France. King William of Orange's victory, on the other hand, is still celebrated in Northern Ireland every July 12, with controversial marches by Unionist "Orangemen."

The 50,000 soldiers who fought here made this the largest battle ever to take place in the British Isles. Yet it was only a side skirmish in an even larger continental confrontation pitting France's King Louis XIV against the "Grand Alliance" of nations threatened by France's dominant military and frequent incursions into neighboring lands.

Louis ruled by divine right, answerable only to God—and James modeled himself after Louis. Even the Pope (who could control neither Louis nor James and was equally disturbed by Catholic France's aggressions) backed Protestant King William against Catholic King James—just one example of the pretzel logic that was the European mind-set at the time.

The site of the Battle of the Boyne was bought in 1997 by the Irish Office of Public Works, part of the Republic's governmental efforts to respect a place sacred to Unionists in Northern Ireland—despite the fact that the battle's outcome ensured Catholic subordination to the Protestant minority for the next 230 years.

Visiting the Site: The **Visitors Centre** is housed in a mansion built on the battlefield 50 years after the conflict. The exhibits do a good job illustrating the international nature of the battle and its place in the wider context of European political power struggles. The highlight is a huge battleground model with laser lights that move troops around the terrain, showing the battle's ebb and flow on that bloody day. A separate 15-minute film (shown in the former stable house) runs continuously and does a fine job of fleshing out the battle.

The Sunday afternoon **"Living History" demonstrations** (June-Aug) are a treat for history buffs and photographers, with guides clad in 17th-century garb. You'll get a bang out of the musket loading and firing demo (at 11:00, 13:00, 15:00, and 17:00), see cavalry combat in full gallop (at 12:00, 14:00, and 16:00), and learn that to be an Irish watermelon is to fear the sword.

▲Hill of Tara

This site was the most important center of political and religious power in pre-Christian Ireland. While aerial views show plenty of mysterious circles and lines, wandering with the sheep among the well-worn ditches and hills leaves you with more to feel than to see. Visits are made meaningful by an excellent 20-minute video presentation and the caring 20-minute guided walk that follows (always available upon request and entirely worthwhile). Wear good walking shoes—the ground is uneven and often wet.

Cost and Hours: €3, includes video and guided walk, June-mid-Sept daily 10:00-18:00, last tour at 17:00; during off-season access is free but visitors center is closed; tel. 046/902-5903.

Visiting the Site: You'll see the Mound of Hostages (a Bronze Age passage grave, c. 2500 B.C.), a couple of ancient sacred stones, a war memorial, and vast views over the Emerald Isle. While ancient Ireland was a pig pile of minor chieftain-kings scrambling for power, the high king of Tara was king of the mountain. It was at this ancient stockade that St. Patrick directly challenged the king's authority. When confronted by the high king, Patrick convincingly explained the Holy Trinity using a shamrock: three petals with one stem. He won the right to preach Christianity throughout Ireland, and the country had a new national symbol.

This now-desolate hill was also the scene of great modern events. In 1798, passionate young Irish rebels chose Tara for its defensible position, but were routed by better organized (and more sober) British troops. (The cunning British commander had sent three cartloads of whiskey along the nearby road earlier in the day, knowing the rebels would intercept it.) In 1843, the great orator and champion of Irish liberty Daniel O'Connell gathered 500,000 Irish peasants on this hill for his greatest "monster meeting"—a peaceful show of force demanding the repeal of the Act of Union with Britain (kind of the Woodstock of its day). In a bizarre final twist, a small group of British Israelites—who believed they were one of the lost tribes of Israel, who had ended up in Britain—spent 1899 to 1901 recklessly digging up parts of the hill in a misguided search for the Ark of the Covenant.

Stand on the Hill of Tara. Think of the history it's seen, and survey Ireland. It's understandable why this "meeting place of heroes" continues to hold a powerful place in the Irish psyche.

Old Mellifont Abbey

This Cistercian abbey (the first in Ireland) was established by French monks who came to the country in 1142 to bring the Irish monks more in line with Rome. (Even the abbey's architecture was unusual, marking the first time in Ireland that a formal, European-style monastic layout was used.) Cistercians lived isolated rural lives; lay monks worked the land, allowing the more educated monks to devote all their energy to prayer. After Henry VIII dissolved the abbey in 1539, centuries of locals used it as a handy quarry. Consequently, little survives beyond the octagonal lavabo, where the monks would ceremonially wash their hands before entering the refectory to eat. The lavabo gives a sense of the abbey's former grandeur.

The excellent 45-minute tours, available upon request and included in your admission, give meaning to what you're seeing. To get a better idea of the extent of the site, be sure to check out the model of the monastery in its heyday, located at the back of the small museum next to the ticket desk.

Cost and Hours: €3, May-Sept daily 10:00-18:00, last tour at 16:30, last entry 45 minutes before closing, no tours Oct-April when site is free and you can explore on your own, tel. 041/982-6459, www.heritageireland.ie.

Monasterboice

This ruined monastery is visit-worthy for its round tower and its or-nately carved high crosses—two of the best such crosses in Ireland. In the Dark Ages, these crosses, illustrated from top to bottom with Bible stories, gave monks a teaching tool as they preached to the illiterate masses. Imagine the crosses in their prime, when they were brightly painted (before years of wind and rain weathered the paint away). Today, Monasterboice is basically an old graveyard.

Cost and Hours: Free and always open.

Visiting the Site: The 18-foot-tall **Cross of Murdock** (Muire-dach's Cross, c. 923, named after an abbot) is considered the best high cross in Ireland. The circle—which characterizes the Irish high cross—could represent the perfection of God. Or, to help ease pagans into Christianity, it may represent the sun, which was worshipped in pre-Christian Celtic society. Whatever its symbolic purpose, its practical function was to support the weight of the crossbeam.

Face the cross (with the round tower in the background) and study the carved sandstone. The center panel shows the Last Judgment, with Christ under a dove, symbolizing the Holy Spirit. Those going to heaven are on Christ's right, and the damned are being ushered away by a pitchfork-wielding devil on his left. Working down, you'll see the Archangel Michael weighing souls, as the Devil tugs demonically at the scales; the adoration of the three—or four—Magi; Moses striking the rock to bring forth water; scenes from the life of David; and, finally, Adam, Eve, and the apple next to Cain slaying Abel. Imagine these carvings with their original, colorful paint jobs. Check out the plaque at the base of the nearby tree, which further explains the carvings on the cross.

Find the even-taller cross nearest the tower. It seems the top section was broken off and buried for a period, which protected it from weathering. The bottom part remained standing, enduring the erosive effect of Irish weather, which smeared the once-crisp features.

The door to the round tower was originally 15-20 feet above the ground (accessible by ladder). After centuries of burials, the ground level has risen.

Trim

The sleepy, workaday town of Trim, straddling the River Boyne, is marked by the towering ruins of Trim Castle. Trim feels littered with mighty ruins that seem to say, "This little town was big-time...750 years ago." The tall Yellow Steeple (over the river from the castle) is all that remains of the 14th-century Augustinian Abbey of St. Mary. Not far away, the Sheep's Gate is a humble remnant of the once-grand medieval town walls. Near the town center, the modest, 30-foot-tall Wellington Column honors native son Arthur Wellesley, the First Duke of Wellington (1769-1852), who spent his childhood in Trim, defeated Napoleon at Waterloo, and twice became prime minister.

Trim makes a great landing pad into—or launching pad out of—Ireland. If you're flying into or out of Dublin Airport and don't want to deal with big-city Dublin, this is a perfect alternative—an easy 45-minute, 30-mile drive away. You can rent a car at the airport and make Trim your first overnight base (getting used to driving on the other side of the road in easier country traffic), or spend your last night here before returning your car at the airport. Weather permitting, my evening stroll (described later) makes for a fine first or last night in the Emerald Isle.

Orientation to Trim

Trim's main square is a traffic roundabout, and everything's within a block or two. Most of the shops and eateries are on or near Market Street, along with banks and a supermarket.

Tourist Information

The TI is right next to the castle entrance and includes a handy coffee shop. Drop in to pick up a free map and check out the collage of photos in the entryway, showing the castle dolled up for the filming of *Braveheart* (June-Aug Mon-Fri 9:30-17:30, Sat-Sun 12:00-17:30, shorter hours Sept-May, Castle Street, tel. 046/943-7227).

The TI organizes historical walking tours of the town, led by enthusiastic volunteers (€5, pay at TI, daily at 14:30 and 19:00, one hour; tours depart from the bog oak sculpture—facing the TI, go 100 feet down sidewalk to right; tel. 046/943-7227).

NEAR DUBLIN

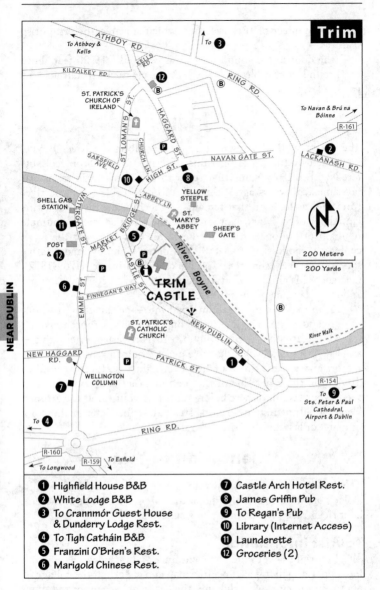

Trim

To Athboy & Kells
ATHBOY RD.
To 3
KILDALKEY RD.
KELLS RD.
RING RD.
St. Patrick's Church of Ireland
ST. LOMAN'S ST.
CHURCH LN.
HAGGARD ST.
To Navan & Brú na Bóinne
R-161
SARSFIELD AVE.
NAVAN GATE ST.
LACKANASH RD.
HIGH ST.
ABBEY LN.
MARKET ST.
WATERGATE ST.
BRIDGE ST.
CASTLE ST.
Yellow Steeple
St. Mary's Abbey
Sheep's Gate
River Boyne
200 Meters
200 Yards
SHELL GAS STATION
POST &
EMMET ST.
FINNEGAN'S WAY
TRIM CASTLE
River Walk
St. Patrick's Catholic Church
NEW DUBLIN RD.
NEW HAGGARD RD.
PATRICK ST.
Wellington Column
R-154
To Sts. Peter & Paul Cathedral, Airport & Dublin
RING RD.
R-160
To Longwood
R-159
To Enfield

NEAR DUBLIN

1 Highfield House B&B
2 White Lodge B&B
3 To Crannmór Guest House & Dunderry Lodge Rest.
4 To Tigh Catháin B&B
5 Franzini O'Brien's Rest.
6 Marigold Chinese Rest.
7 Castle Arch Hotel Rest.
8 James Griffin Pub
9 To Regan's Pub
10 Library (Internet Access)
11 Launderette
12 Groceries (2)

Helpful Hints

Internet Access: The **library** offers 30 minutes of free Internet access (Tue and Thu 10:00-20:30, Wed and Fri-Sat 10:00-13:00 & 14:00-17:00, closed Sun-Mon, High Street).

Post Office: It's tucked in the back of the **Spar Market** (Mon-Fri 9:00-17:30, Sat 9:00-13:00, closed Sun, Emmett Street).

Laundry: The launderette is located close to Market Street (€8/

load, Mon-Sat 9:00-13:00 & 14:00-17:30, closed Sun, Water-gate Street, tel. 046/943-7176).

Parking: To park on the street or in a public lot, use the pay-and-display parking system. Buy a ticket at one of the machines spaced along the street, and display it on your dashboard (Mon-Sat 9:00-18:00, €1/hour, 2-hour max, free Sun).

Fishing Tours: Marc O'Regan leads backcountry trout and pike fishing trips, making a splash with anglers who want to experience Ireland's bountiful lakes and rivers (tel. 046/943-1635, www.crannmor.com). O'Regan and his wife also run the recommended Crannmór Guest House.

Sights in Trim

▲▲**Trim Castle**—This is the biggest Norman castle in Ireland. Set in a grassy riverside park at the edge of this sleepy town, its mighty keep towers above a very ruined outer wall. It replaced a wooden fortification that was destroyed  in 1173 by Irish High King Rory O'Connor, who led a raid against the invading Normans. The current castle was completed in the 1220s and served as a powerful Norman statement to the restless Irish natives. It remained a sharp barb at the fringe of "the Pale" (English-controlled territory), when English rule shrank to just the area around Dublin in the 1400s. By that time, any lands further west were "beyond the Pale."

Cost and Hours: €3 for castle grounds, €4 for entrance to keep and required tour; roughly April-Oct daily 10:00-18:00; Nov-March Sat-Sun 10:00-17:00, closed Mon-Fri; last entry one hour before closing; 45-minute tours run 2/hour but spots are limited so arrive early in peak season as tours can fill up; tel. 046/943-8619, www.heritageireland.ie.

Visiting the Castle: Today the castle remains an impressive sight—so impressive that it was used in the 1994 filming of *Braveheart* (which was actually about Scotland's—not Ireland's—fight for freedom from the English). The best-preserved walls ring the castle's southern perimeter and sport a barbican gate that contained two drawbridges.

At the base of the castle walls, notice the cleverly angled "batter" wall—used by defenders who hurled down stones that banked off at great velocity into the attacking army. Notice also that the castle is built directly on bedrock, visible along the base of the

NEAR DUBLIN

walls. During sieges, while defenders of other castles feared that attackers would tunnel underground to weaken the defensive walls, that was not an issue here.

The massive 70-foot-high central keep, which is mostly a hollow shell, has 20 sides. This experimental design was not implemented elsewhere because it increased the number of defenders needed to cover all the angles. You can go inside the keep only with the included tour, where you'll start by checking out the cool ground-floor models showing the evolution of the castle. Then you'll climb a series of tightly winding original staircases and modern, high catwalks, learn about life in the castle, and end at the top with great views of the walls and the countryside.

Make time to take a 15-minute walk outside, circling the castle walls and stopping at the informative plaques that show the castle from each viewpoint during its gory glory days. Night strollers are treated to views of the castle hauntingly lit in blue-green hues.

Trim Evening Stroll—Given good weather, here's my blueprint for a fine night in Trim. Start the evening by taking the pleasant **River Walk** stroll along the River Boyne from Trim Castle. Cross the wooden footbridge behind the castle and turn right (east). The paved, level trail leads under a highway and extends a mile along fields that serfs farmed 750 years ago. During the filming of *Braveheart*, Mel Gibson's character met the French princess in her tent in these fields, with the castle looming in the background.

The trail ends in the medieval ruins of **Newtown.** This was indeed once the "new town" (mid-1200s) that sprouted as a religious satellite community to support political power housed in the castle. Wander the sprawling, ragtag ruins of **Saints Peter and Paul Cathedral** (1206), once the largest Gothic church in Ireland.

Just beyond the ruins, cross the old Norman bridge to the 13th-century scraps of the **Hospital of St. John the Baptist.** Medieval medicine couldn't have been fun, but this hospital was the best you could hope for back when life was nasty, brutish, and short. Many a knight was spent here.

Cross back over the bridge and stop for a pint at tiny, atmospheric **Regan's,** one of the oldest pubs in Ireland, set beside one of the oldest bridges in Ireland. Drink a toast to Rock Hudson, who filmed a pivotal scene from *Captain Lightfoot* (1955) on the bridge.

Then walk back along the river the way you came and have dinner at the recommended **Franzini O'Brien's** restaurant beside the castle. After dinner, assist your digestion by walking a lap around the castle (beautifully lit up at night). End the evening a few blocks away with a pint at the **James Griffin** pub (described later). A fine night, tis...or twas.

The Power & Glory—This grade-schoolish, 30-minute slideshow

Sleep Code

(€1 = about $1.30, country code: 353, area code: 046)
S = Single, **D** = Double/Twin, **T** = Triple, **Q** = Quad, **b** = bathroom, **s** = shower only. Credit cards are accepted and breakfast is included unless otherwise noted.

To help you easily sort through these listings, I've divided the accommodations into two categories, based on the price for a standard double room with bath:

$$ **Higher Priced**—Most rooms more than €70.
$ **Lower Priced**—Most rooms €70 or less.

Prices can change without notice; verify the hotel's current rates online or by email.

overview of the personalities and history of the castle is followed by an exhibit on life here in Norman times. The show and a cup of coffee help to pass the time as you wait for your castle tour.

Cost and Hours: €3, Mon-Sat 9:30-17:30, Sun 12:00-17:00, shorter hours off-season, show runs on demand, in visitors center with TI next to castle, Castle Street, tel. 046/943-7227.

Sleeping in Trim

$$ Highfield House B&B, across the street from the castle and a five-minute walk from town, is a stately 180-year-old former maternity hospital, with hardwood floors and nine spacious, high-ceilinged rooms (Sb-€50-55, Db-€78-84, Tb-€99-110, family-friendly, free Internet access and Wi-Fi; overlooks roundabout where Dublin Road hits Trim, just before castle at Castle Street; tel. 046/943-6386, www.highfieldguesthouse.com, info@highfield guesthouse.com, Geraldine and Edward Duignan).

$ White Lodge B&B, a 10-minute walk northwest of the castle, has six comfortably unpretentious rooms with an oak-and-granite lounge (Sb-€45, Db-€70, Tb-€78, Qb-€90, 10 percent discount for active-duty members of the US and Canadian armed forces with this book, free Internet access and Wi-Fi, parking, New Road, tel. 046/943-6549, www.whitelodgetrim.com, white lodgetrim@eircom.net, Todd O'Loughlin). They also offer a family-friendly self-catering house next door.

Countryside B&Bs

These two B&Bs are in the quiet countryside about a mile outside Trim (phone ahead for driving directions).

NEAR DUBLIN

$$ At **Crannmór Guest House,** north of town, Anne O'Regan decorates five rooms with cheery color schemes (Sb-€45-55, Db-€76-80, Tb-€90, Qb-€110, Wi-Fi, Dunderry Road, tel. 046/943-1635, mobile 087-288-7390, www.crannmor.com, cranmor@eircom.net). Her professional-guide husband Marc knows all the best fishing holes (see "Fishing Tours" on page 125).

$$ Mrs. Keane's **Tigh Catháin B&B,** southwest of town, has four large, bright, lacy rooms with a comfy, rural feel (Db-€70-75, Tb-€85-95, cash only, Wi-Fi, on R160/Longwood Road, tel. 046/943-1996, mobile 086-257-7313, www.tighcathain-bnb.com, tighcathain.bnb@gmail.com).

Eating in Trim

A country-market town, Trim offers basic meat-and-potatoes lunch and dinner options. Don't waste time searching here for gourmet food. The restaurants and cafés along Market Street are friendly, wholesome, and unassuming (soup-and-sandwich delis close at 17:30).

Franzini O'Brien's is the only place in town with a fun dinner menu and enough business to make it work. They serve pasta, steak, fish, and good salads in a modern, candlelit ambience. Nothing's Irish except the waiters (€15-24 dishes, €20 two-course or €25 three-course early-bird dinners before 19:30, Mon-Sat 17:00-22:00, Sun 13:00-21:00, French's Lane across from the castle parking lot, tel. 046/943-1002).

If you feel like having Chinese food, **Marigold** fits the bill (Mon-Sat 17:00-23:00, Sun 16:00-23:00, Emmett Street, tel. 046/943-8788).

For a tasty splurge of gourmet cooking out in the country, get driving directions to **Dunderry Lodge,** four miles (6.4 km) north of Trim off the Dunderry Road (€20 early-bird dinner Mon-Fri 17:30-19:00, Mon-Sat 19:30-21:30, Sun 12:30-14:30 & 18:30-21:00, tel. 046/943-1671).

The **Castle Arch Hotel,** popular with locals, serves hearty pub grub at reasonable prices in its bistro (€11-14 meals, daily 12:30-21:30, tel. 046/943-1516).

For a fun pub experience, check out Trim's two best watering holes. The **James Griffin** (on High Street) is full of local characters and old-fashioned atmosphere, with traditional Irish music sessions on Monday and Wednesday nights. Tiny, low-ceilinged **Regan's** is a fun, unpretentious pub next to the old Norman bridge over the River Boyne. You'll find it at the north end of the bridge, a half-mile stroll outside of town next to the ruins of Newtown.

Supermarkets: **Spar Market** has everything you need to create a picnic (daily 8:00-21:00, Emmett Street). The same goes for

Super Valu, a larger store on Haggard Street that's a bit farther from the town center (daily 8:00-22:00).

Trim Connections

Trim has no train station; the nearest is in Drogheda 25 miles away on the coast. Buses from Trim to **Dublin** (almost hourly, 1 hour) pick you up at the bus shelter next to the TI and castle entrance on Castle Street. For details, see www.buseireann.ie.

South of Dublin: Glendalough and the Wicklow Mountains

The Wicklow Mountains, while only 10 miles south of Dublin, feel remote—enough so to have provided a handy refuge for opponents to English rule. Rebels who took part in the 1798 Irish uprising hid out here for years. When the frustrated British built a military road in 1800 to help flush out the rebels, the area became more accessible. Today, this same road—now R-115—takes you through the Wicklow area to Glendalough at its south end. While the valley is the darling of the Dublin day-trip tour organizers, it doesn't live up to the hype. But two blockbuster sights—Glendalough and the Gardens of Powerscourt—make a visit worth considering.

Getting Around

By car or tour, it's easy. If you lack wheels, take a tour. It's not worth the trouble on public transport.

By Car: It's a delight. Take N-11 south from Dublin toward Bray, then R-117 to Enniskerry (accommodation listed on page 131), the gateway to the Wicklow Mountains. Signs direct you to the gardens and on to Glendalough. From Glendalough, if you're heading west, you can leave the valley (and pick up the highway to the west) over the famous but dull mountain pass called the Wicklow Gap.

By Tour from Dublin: Wild Wicklow Tours covers the region with an entertaining guide who packs every minute with information and *craic* (interesting, fun conversation). With a gang of 40 packed into tight but comfortable, mountain-gripping buses, the guide kicks into gear from the first pickup in Dublin. Tours cover Dublin's embassy row, Dun Laoghaire, the Bay of Dublin (with the mansions of Ireland's rich and famous), the windy military road over scenic Sally Gap, and the Glendalough monasteries (€28, €25

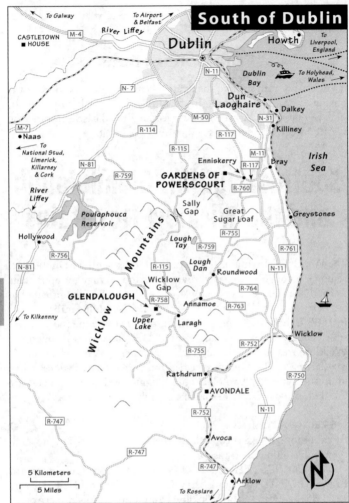

South of Dublin

for students and readers with this book in 2013, daily year-round, 9:10 pickup at Dublin TI on Suffolk Street, 10:00 pickup at Dun Laoghaire ferry terminal, stop for lunch at a pub—cost not included, return through Dun Laoghaire and on to Dublin by 17:30, Dun Laoghaire-ites could stay on the bus to continue into Dublin for the evening, advance booking required, tel. 01/280-1899, www.wildwicklow.ie).

Over the Top Tours bypasses mansions and gardens to focus on Wicklow rural scenery. Stops include Glendalough, Sally Gap, the Glenmacnass waterfall, and Blessington lakes (€28, 9:20 pickup at Gresham Hotel on Upper O'Connell Street, 9:45 pickup at

Dublin TI on Suffolk Street, return by 17:30, 14-seat minibus, reservations required, hold seat by leaving credit-card number, Ireland toll-free tel. 1-800-424-252, Dublin tel. 01/860-0404, mobile 087-259-3467, www.overthetoptours.com, info@overthetoptours.com).

Sights in the Wicklow Area

▲▲Gardens of Powerscourt

A mile above the village of Enniskerry, the Gardens of Powerscourt cover several thousand acres within the 16,000-acre estate. The dreamy driveway alone is a mile long. While the mansion's interior, only partially restored after a 1974 fire, isn't much, its meticulously kept aristocratic gardens are Ireland's best. The house was commissioned in the 1730s by Richard Wingfield, first viscount of Powerscourt. The gardens, created during the Victorian era (1858-1875), are called "the grand finale of Europe's formal gardening tradition...probably the last garden of its size and quality ever to be created." I'll buy that.

Upon entry, you'll get a flier laying out 40-minute and one-hour walks. The "one-hour" walk takes 30 minutes at a slow amble. With the impressive summit of the Great Sugar Loaf Mountain as a backdrop, and a fine Japanese garden, Italian garden, and goofy pet cemetery along the way, this attraction provides the scenic greenery I hoped to find in the rest of the Wicklow area. The lush movies *Barry Lyndon* and *The Count of Monte Cristo* were filmed in this well-watered aristocratic fantasy.

Cost and Hours: €8.50, daily 9:30-17:30, great cafeteria, tel. 01/204-6000, www.powerscourt.ie.

Nearby: Skip the Powerscourt Waterfall (€5.50, 4 miles/6.5 km away). Kids may enjoy a peek at the antique dollhouses of the upstairs Museum of Childhood (€3, Mon-Sat 10:00-17:00, Sun 12:00-17:00).

Sleeping in Enniskerry: Drivers coming straight from Dublin Airport can stay overnight in Enniskerry at **$$ Brook Cottage B&B,** a quiet guesthouse that's popular with hikers. It has a rambling floor plan and sports six rooms, one friendly greyhound, comfortable beds, and traditional breakfasts in a country setting (Sb-€50-55, Db-€80, Tb-€100-105, Qb-€120, cash only, 10 percent discount for multiple-night stays, Wi-Fi, tel. 01/276-6039, mobile 086-824-1687, www.enniskerry.org, brookcottagebb@eircom.net, Mary Moran). From the Enniskerry clock tower go 1.8 miles (3 km) up Kilgarron Hill toward Glencree, look for the B&B sign on the right, follow the arrow sign on the right side of the road to the end of the narrow lane on the left side of the road, and pass through the green gates.

▲Military Road over Sally Gap

This trip is only for those with a car. From the Gardens of Powerscourt and Enniskerry, go to Glencree, where you drive the tiny military road over Sally Gap and through the best scenery of the Wicklow Mountains (on Sundays, watch for dozens of bicycle racers). Look for the German military cemetery, built for U-boat sailors who washed ashore in World War II. Near Sally Gap, notice the peat bogs and the freshly cut peat bricks drying in the wind. Many locals are nostalgic for the "good old days," when homes were always peat-fire heated. At the Sally Gap junction, turn left, where a road winds through the vast Guinness estate. Look down on the glacial lake (Lough Tay) and the Guinness mansion (famous for jet-set parties). Nicknamed "Guinness Lake," the water looks like Ireland's favorite dark-brown stout, and the sand of the beach actually looks like the head of a Guinness beer. From here, the road meanders scenically down into the village of Roundwood and on to Glendalough.

▲▲Glendalough

The steep wooded slopes of Glendalough (GLEN-da-lock, "Valley of the Two Lakes"), at the south end of Wicklow's military road, hide Ireland's most impressive monastic settlement. Founded by St. Kevin in the sixth century, the monastery flourished (despite repeated Viking raids) throughout the Age of Saints and Scholars until the English destroyed it in 1398. Though it was finally abandoned during the Dissolution of the Monasteries in 1539, pilgrims kept coming, especially on St. Kevin's Day, June 3. (This might have something to do with the fact that a pope said seven visits to Glendalough had the same indulgence—or forgiveness from sins—value as one visit to Rome.) While much restoration was done in the 1870s, most of the buildings date from the 10th-12th centuries.

The valley sights are split between the two lakes. The lower lake has the visitors center and the best buildings. The upper lake has scant ruins and feels like a state park, with a grassy lakeside picnic area and school groups. Walkers and hikers will enjoy a choice of nine different trails of varying lengths through the lush Wicklow countryside (longest loop takes four hours, hiking-trail maps available at visitors center).

Planning Your Time: Park for free at the Glendalough Visitors Centre. Visit the center, wander the ruins (free) around the round tower, walk the traffic-free Green Road one mile to the upper lake, and then walk back to your car. Or you can drive to the upper lake (more free parking—except July-Aug, when it's €4). If you're rushed, skip the upper lake. Summer tour-bus crowds are terrible all day on weekends and 11:00-14:00 on weekdays.

Cost and Hours: Visitor center-€3, daily mid-March-mid-Oct 9:30-18:00, mid-Oct-mid-March 9:30-17:00, last entry 45 minutes before closing, tel. 0404/45352.

Visiting Glendalough: Start out at the **Glendalough Visitor Centre,** where a 20-minute video provides a good thumbnail background on monastic society in medieval Ireland. While the video is more general than specific to Glendalough, the adjacent museum room does feature this particular monastic settlement. The model in the center of the room re-creates the fortified village of the year 1050. A browse through the interactive exhibits here shows the contribution these monks made to intellectual life in Dark Age Europe (such as illuminated manuscripts and Irish minuscule, a more compact alphabet developed in the seventh century).

From the visitors center, a short and scenic walk along the Green Road takes you to the round tower of the **monastic village.** Easily the best ruins of Glendalough gather around this famous 110-foot-tall round tower. Towers like this (usually 60-110 feet tall) were standard features in such settlements, functioning as bell towers, storage lofts, beacons for pilgrims, and last-resort refuges during Viking raids (though given enough warning, monks were safer hiding in the surrounding forest). The towers had a high door with a pull-up ladder—both for safety and because a door at ground level would have weakened the tower's foundation. Several ruined churches (10th-12th centuries) and a sea of grave markers complete this evocative scene. Markers give short descriptions of the ruined buildings.

In an Ireland without cities, these monastic communities were mainstays of civilization. They were remote outposts where ascetics (with a taste for scenic settings) gathered to commune with God. In the 12th century, with the arrival of grander monastic orders such as the Franciscans and the Dominicans and with the growth of cities, these monastic communities were eclipsed. Today, Ireland is dotted with the reminders of this age: illuminated manuscripts, simple churches, carved crosses, and about 100 round towers.

The Green Road continues one mile farther up the valley to the **Upper Lake.** The oldest ruins—scant and hard to find—lie near this lake. If you want a scenic Wicklow walk, begin here.

▲Avondale House

Located in south County Wicklow (known as the Garden County), this mansion is the birthplace and lifelong home of Charles Stewart Parnell, the Nationalist politician and dynamo often called the "uncrowned King of Ireland" (see page 76).

Upon entering the opulent Georgian "big house" (built in 1777), you'll first view an informative 20-minute video on Parnell's life. Then you're set free to roam with a handout outlining each room's highlights. A fine portrait of Parnell graces the grand, high-ceilinged entry hall, and a painting of his American grandfather, who manned the USS *Constitution* in the War of 1812, hangs in one room. The dining room is all class, with fine plasterwork and hardwood floors. Original furniture such as Parnell's sturdy canopied bed graces the remaining rooms, and many come with cozy fireplaces and views. The lush surrounding estate of over 500 acres, laced with pleasant walking trails, was used by the Irish Forestry Service (Coillte) to try out forestry methods.

Cost and Hours: €7.50; June-Aug daily 11:00-17:00; Sept-Oct Sat-Sun 12:00-16:00, closed Mon-Fri; shorter hours off-season; café, tel. 0404/46111, www.coillte.ie.

Getting There: It's best to visit by car, as Avondale House is too far for the Dublin day-tour buses (45 miles south of Dublin). Trains depart Dublin's Connolly station (4/day, 1.5 hours) to Rathdrum; Avondale is a short taxi ride away (1.5 miles south of town).

West of Dublin: The Irish National Stud

Ireland's famed County Kildare has long been known to offer the perfect conditions for breeding horses. Its reputation dates all the way back to the 1300s, when Norman war horses were bred here. Kildare's grasslands lie on a bedrock table of limestone, infusing the soil with just the right mix of nutrients for grazing horses. And the nearby River Tully sparkles with high levels of calcium carbonate, essential for building strong bones in the expensive thoroughbreds (some owned by Arab sheikhs) raised and raced here.

In 1900, Colonel William Hall-Walker (Scottish heir to the Johnny Walker distilling fortune) bought a farm on the River Tully and began breeding a line of champion thoroughbreds. His amazing successes and bizarre methods were the talk of the sport. In 1916, the colonel donated his land and horse farm to the British government, which continued breeding horses here. The farm was eventually handed over to the Irish government, which in 1945 created the Irish National Stud Company to promote the thoroughbred industry.

Today, a tour of the grounds at the Irish National Stud gives you a fuller appreciation for the amazing horses that call this place home. Animal lovers and horse-racing fans driving between Dublin and Galway will enjoy a couple of hours here, combining the tour with lunch (inside the decent cafeteria or at a picnic table by the parking lot) and a stroll through the gardens.

Orientation to the Irish National Stud

Cost: €12.50 includes guided tour of the Irish National Stud, plus entry to Japanese Gardens, St. Fiachra's Garden, and Horse Museum.

Hours: Daily early Feb-mid-Dec 9:30-18:00, closed mid-Dec-early Feb, last entry one hour before closing, 30-minute tours run 3/day at 12:00, 14:30, and 16:00, tel. 045/522-963, www.irish-national-stud.ie.

Getting There: From M-7, **drivers** take exit #13 and follow the signs five minutes south (don't take exit #12 for the Curragh Racecourse). **Trains** departing Dublin's Heuston Station stop at Kildare town (1-3/hour, 45 minutes, www.irishrail.ie). A shuttle bus runs from Kildare's train station to the National Stud (2/hour), or you can take a taxi (about €12-15). One **bus** departs Dublin's Busáras Station Monday through Saturday at 9:30 and returns from the National Stud at 15:45. On Sunday, two buses run, departing Busáras at 10:00 and 12:00, with returns at 15:00 and 17:30. Confirm this schedule at the bus station in Dublin.

NEAR DUBLIN

Visiting the Irish National Stud

The guided tour begins in the **Sun Chariot Yard** (named for the winner of the 1942 Fillies Triple Crown), surrounded by stables housing pregnant mares. A 15-minute film of a foal's birth runs continuously in a stall in the corner of the yard.

The adjacent **Foaling Unit** is where births take place. The gestation period for horses is 11 months, with 90 percent of foals born at night. (In the wild, a mare and her foal born during the day would have been vulnerable to predators as the herd moved on. Instead, horses have adapted so that foals are born at night—and are able to keep up with the herd within a few hours.) Eccentric Colonel Hall-Walker noted the position of the moon and stars at the time of each foal's birth, and sold those born under inauspicious astrological signs (regardless of their parents' stellar racing records).

When Irish Horses Are Running

Every Irish town seems to have a betting shop for passionate locals who love to closely follow (and wager on) their favorite horses. A quick glance at the weekend sports sections of any Irish newspaper gives you an idea of this sport's high profile. Towns from Galway to Dingle host annual horse races that draw rabid fans from all over.

The five most prestigious Irish races take place at the **Curragh Racecourse,** just south of Kildare town (March-Oct, 1 hour west of Dublin, 10 minutes from the National Stud, www.curragh.ie). Horses have been raced here since 1741. The broad, open fields nearby are where the battle scenes in *Braveheart* were filmed (the neighboring Irish army base provided the blue-face-painted extras).

From here, you'll pass a working saddle-making shop and a forge where horseshoes are still hammered out on an anvil.

At the **Stallion Boxes,** you'll learn how stargazing Colonel Hall-Walker installed skylights in the stables—allowing the heavens maximum influence over the destiny of his prized animals. A brass plaque on the door of each stall proudly states the horse's name and its racing credentials. One stall bears the simple word, "Teaser." The unlucky occupant's job is to identify mares in heat...but rarely is the frustrated stallion given the opportunity to breed. Bummer.

After the tour, meander down the pleasant tree-lined **Tully Walk,** with paddocks on each side. You'll see mares and foals running free, with the occasional cow thrown in for good measure (cattle have a calming effect on rowdy horses). To ensure you come home with all your fingers, take full note of the *Horses Bite and Kick* signs. These superstar animals are bred for high spirits—and are far too feisty to pet.

Other Sights: Visitors with extra time can explore three more attractions (all included in your entry ticket). The tranquil and photogenic **Japanese Gardens** were created by the colonel to depict the trials of life (beware the Tunnel of Ignorance). A wander through the more extensive and natural **St. Fiachra's Garden** (the patron saint of gardening) demands more time. Equestrian buffs may want to linger among the memorabilia in the small **Horse Museum,** where you can get a grip on how many hands it takes to measure a horse.

KILKENNY and the ROCK OF CASHEL

If you're driving from Dublin (on Ireland's east coast) to Dingle (on Ireland's west coast), the best two stops to break the long journey across the Irish interior are Kilkenny, often called Ireland's finest medieval town, and the Rock of Cashel, a thought-provoking early Christian site crowning the Plain of Tipperary. With a few extra days, consider additional worthwhile destinations along the southeast coast, such as Waterford and County Wexford (described in the next chapter). Folks with more time can continue on the scenic southern coastal route west via Cobh, Kinsale, Kenmare, and the Ring of Kerry (covered in the Kinsale/Cobh and Kenmare/Ring of Kerry chapters).

Kilkenny

Famous as "Ireland's loveliest inland city," Kilkenny gives you a feel for salt-of-the-earth Ireland. Its castle and cathedral stand like historic bookends on either end of a higgledy-piggledy High Street of colorful shops and medieval facades. It's nicknamed the "Marble City" for its nearby quarry (actually black limestone, not marble), and you can see the white seashells fossilized within the black stone steps around town. While a small town today (fewer than 10,000 residents), Kilkenny has a big history. It used to be an important center—occasionally even the capital of Ireland in the Middle Ages. And of vital interest to contemporary women is the fact that actor George Clooney traces his roots to Kilkenny.

Kilkenny is a good overnight for drivers wanting to break the

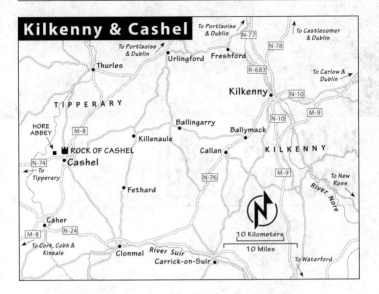

journey from Dublin to Dingle (necessary if you want to spend more time in the Wicklow area and at the Rock of Cashel). A night in Kilkenny comes with plenty of traditional folk music in its pubs.

Orientation to Kilkenny

Tourist Information

The TI is a block off the bridge in the 16th-century Shee Alms poorhouse (Mon-Sat 9:30-17:00, Sun 11:00-17:00 in summer, closed Sun Sept-May, Rose Inn Street, tel. 056/775-1500).

Arrival in Kilkenny

The train/bus station is four blocks from John's Bridge, which marks the center of town.

If you're arriving by car, the Market Yard Car Park behind Kyteler's Inn is handy for a few hours (€1.20/hour, daily 8:00-18:00, entry off Bateman's Quay). The multistory parking garage on Ormonde Street is the best long-term bet (€2/hour, or get the 3-day pass for €10 if staying overnight—it allows you to come and go; Sun-Thu 7:00-23:00, Fri-Sat 7:00-24:00). If parking overnight, wait until you depart to pay since some hotels will validate parking. Otherwise, you can use the pay-and-display meters on the street (€2/hour, enforced Mon-Sat 8:00-19:00).

Helpful Hints

Post Office: It's on High Street (Mon-Fri 9:00-17:30, Sat 9:00-13:00, closed Sun).

Laundry: Hennessy's is at 18 Parliament Street (Mon-Sat 9:00-17:30, closed Sun, mobile 086-071-1837).

Bookstore: The Book Centre, with a cheap and cheery café upstairs, is a great place to linger on a rainy day (Mon-Sat 9:00-18:00, Fri until 21:00, Sun 9:00-14:00, 10 High Street, tel. 056/776-2117).

Bike Rentals and Tours: Kilkenny Cycling rents bikes for €15 a day. They provide safety gear, deliver bikes to your hotel on request, and have route maps for exploring the pastoral charms of County Kilkenny. Their two-hour "easy paced" tour for €17 takes in a half-dozen of the town's best sights, including Kilkenny Castle, Rothe House, and St. Canice's Cathedral. Their €20, four-hour "bike-and-hike" tour includes a five-mile ride to Bennettsbridge (leave bikes there and visit pottery-making shop) followed by a pretty hike back along the river (10 percent discount with 2013 edition of this book, cash only, can arrange for tour to leave from your hotel, call for details—mobile 086-895-4961, www.kilkennycyclingtours.com).

Walking Tour: Local guide **Pat Tynan** and his staff offer hour-long town walks that depart from the TI (€6; mid-March-Oct Mon-Sat at 10:30, 12:15, and 15:00, Sun at 11:15 and 12:30; Nov-mid-March Sat only at 10:30, 12:15, and 15:00; mobile 087-265-1745).

Sights in Kilkenny

▲**Kilkenny Castle**—Dominating the town, this castle is a stony reminder that the Anglo-Norman Butler family controlled Kilkenny for 500 years. The castle once had four sides, but Oliver Cromwell's army knocked down one wall when it took the castle, leaving it as the roughly "U" shape we see today.

Enter the castle gate, turn right in the court-yard, and head into the base of the turret. Here you'll find the continuously running 12-minute video explaining how the wooden fort built here by Strongbow in 1172 evolved into a 17th-century château. Then go into the main castle entrance across the courtyard from the turret to buy your entry ticket. You'll be free to walk through the castle. A pamphlet explains the exhibits, and you can also talk to stewards in the important rooms.

Now restored to its Victorian splendor, the castle's highlight

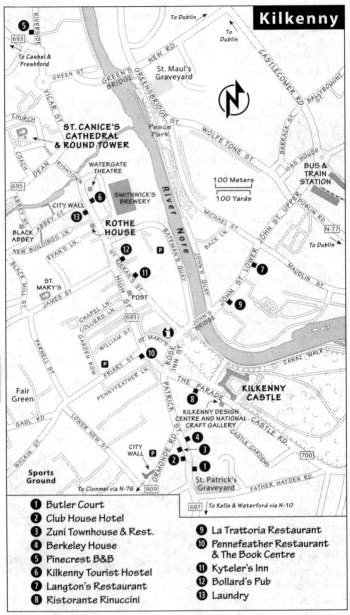

Kilkenny

To Dublin

To Dublin

RIVERSIDE

693

To Cashel & Freshford

GREEN ST.

NEW RD.

St. Maul's Graveyard

GREEN'S BRIDGE

GREENSBRIDGE ST.

WOLFE TONE ST.

CASTLECOMER RD.

BALLYBOUGHT ST.

BARRACK ST.

GAS HOUSE LN.

CHURCH

VICAR ST.

COACH RD.

ST. CANICE'S CATHEDRAL & ROUND TOWER

Peace Park

River Nore

BUS & TRAIN STATION

DEAN ST.

IRISHTOWN

695

WATERGATE THEATRE

SMITHWICK'S BREWERY

MICHAEL ST.

JOHN ST. UPPER

DUBLIN RD.

To Dublin

N-77

ABBEY ST.

CITY WALL

ROTHE HOUSE

BATEMAN'S QUAY

BACK LN.

MAUDLIN ST.

BLACK ABBEY

NEW BUILDINGS LN.

EVAN'S LN.

BLACK MILL ST.

ST. KIERAN'S ST.

HIGH ST.

P

JOHN'S QUAY

JOHN ST. LOWER

7

ST. MARY'S

JAMES ST.

CHAPEL LN.

COLLIERS LN.

GARDEN ROW

693

POST

JOHN'S BRIDGE

9

PARNELL ST.

WILLIAM ST.

FRIARY ST.

10

ST. MARY'S LN.

ROSE INN ST.

CANAL WALK

Fair Green

PENNYFEATHER LN.

P

THE PARADE

KILKENNY CASTLE

GAOL RD.

LOWER NEW ST.

PATRICK ST.

8

CASTLE GARDENS

CASTLE RD.

WALKIN ST.

CITY WALL

P

ORMONDE RD.

4

3

KILKENNY DESIGN CENTRE AND NATIONAL CRAFT GALLERY

700

Sports Ground

To Clonmel via N-76

909

1

St. Patrick's Graveyard

FATHER HAYDEN RD.

697

To Kells & Waterford via N-10

100 Meters

100 Yards

KILKENNY & CASHEL

1 Butler Court
2 Club House Hotel
3 Zuni Townhouse & Rest.
4 Berkeley House
5 Pinecrest B&B
6 Kilkenny Tourist Hostel
7 Langton's Restaurant
8 Ristorante Rinuccini

9 La Trattoria Restaurant
10 Pennefeather Restaurant & The Book Centre
11 Kyteler's Inn
12 Bollard's Pub
13 Laundry

is the beautiful family-portrait gallery, which puts you face-to-face with the wealthy Butler family ghosts.

Cost and Hours: €6, daily June-Aug 9:00-17:30, April-May and Sept 9:30-17:30, Oct-March 9:30-16:30, tel. 056/770-4100.

Nearby: The **Kilkenny Design Centre,** across the street from the castle in grand old stables, is full of local crafts and offers handy cafeteria lunches upstairs (April-Dec Mon-Sat 10:00-17:30, Sun 11:00-17:30; Jan-March Mon-Sat 10:00-17:30, closed Sun; tel. 056/772-2118, www.kilkennydesign.com).

St. Canice's Cathedral—This 13th-century cathedral is early-English Gothic, rich with stained glass, medieval carvings, and floors paved in history. Check out the model of the old walled town in its 1641 heyday. The 100-foot-tall **round tower,** built as part of a long-gone pre-Norman church, recalls the need for a watchtower and refuge. The fun ladder-climb to the top affords a grand view of the countryside.

Cost and Hours: Cathedral-€4, tower-€3, combo-ticket for both-€6; June-Aug Mon-Sat 9:00-18:00, Sun 14:00-18:00; April-May and Sept Mon-Sat 10:00-13:00 & 14:00-17:00, Sun 14:00-17:00; Oct-March Mon-Sat 10:00-13:00 & 14:00-16:00, Sun 14:00-16:00; tel. 056/776-4971, www.cashel.anglican.org.

Rothe House—This well-preserved Tudor merchant's house expanded around interior courtyards as the prosperous family grew. The museum, which also serves as the County Kilkenny genealogy center, gives a glimpse of life here in Elizabethan times. The gardens at the far back were a real luxury in their time.

Cost and Hours: €5; April-Oct Mon-Sat 10:30-17:00, Sun 14:00-18:00; Nov-March Mon-Sat 10:30-16:30, closed Sun; Parliament Street, tel. 056/772-2893, www.rothehouse.com.

Smithwick's Brewery—Smithwick's reddish ale has been my favorite Irish beer since my first visit to Ireland. Older than Guinness (but now owned by the same parent company), Smithwick's marked its tercentennial (300th anniversary) in 2010. To celebrate, the company offered extended tours of their working brewery—which were such a hit that the brewery has made them a tradition. Tours last 1.5 hours and include a good look at the ancient St. Francis Abbey on the brewery grounds, as well as a free pint in the Cellar Bar.

Cost and Hours: €10; tours Tue-Sat at 12:00, 13:00, 15:00, and 15:30; no tours Sun-Mon, enter on Parliament Street opposite Rothe House, tel. 056/779-6498, www.smithwicks.ie.

KILKENNY & CASHEL

Nightlife in Kilkenny

Bollard's Pub—Visitors seeking a cozy local watering hole may want to try this unpretentious pub at the north end of St. Kieran's Street, near the intersection with Parliament Street. Bollard's is a good bet for lively traditional music sessions (Tue and Thu-Fri at 21:00), good pub grub, and friendly conversation. Or sit out front under the awning and enjoy a pint as Kilkenny's humanity flows past you.

Theater—The Watergate Theatre houses live plays and other performances in its 300-seat space (€12-25, Parliament Street, tel. 056/776-1674, www.watergatetheatre.com).

Sleeping in Kilkenny

(area code: 056)
The first four listings are more central, clustered within a block of each other along Lower Patrick Street. The last two are at the north end of town, but still just a short walk from the action.

$$$ Butler Court, across the street and uphill from the Club House Hotel, is Kilkenny's best lodging value. Ever-helpful Yvonne and John offer 10 modern rooms behind cheery yellow walls that ensure a quiet night (Sb-€60-110, Db-€90-130, Tb-€100-160, wheelchair-accessible, continental breakfast in room, Wi-Fi, no parking but will validate overnight parking in nearby multistory garage on Ormonde Street, 14 Lower Patrick Street, tel. 056/776-1178, fax 056/779-0767, www.butlercourt.com, info@butlercourt.com).

$$$ Club House Hotel, originally a gentlemen's sporting club, comes with old-time Georgian elegance; a palatial, well-antlered breakfast room; and 35 large, comfy bedrooms (Sb-€50-75, Db-€100-130; for best rates, book direct from the hotel website; secure parking, Lower Patrick Street, tel. 056/772-1994, fax 056/777-1920, www.clubhousehotel.com, info@clubhousehotel.com).

$$ Zuni Townhouse, above a fashionable restaurant, has 13 boutique-chic rooms sporting colorfully angular furnishings. Ask about two-night weekend breaks and midweek specials that include a four-course dinner (Sb-€60-90, Db-€80-120, Tb-€120-160, parking in back, 26 Lower Patrick Street, tel. 056/772-3999, fax 056/775-6400, www.zuni.ie, info@zuni.ie).

$$ Berkeley House, with 10 rooms across the street and downhill from the Club House Hotel, is small, affordable, and comfortable (Db-€70-100, Tb-€110-140, 5 Lower Patrick Street, tel. 056/776-4848, fax 056/776-4829, www.berkeleyhousekilkenny.com, info@berkeleyhousekilkenny.com).

Sleep Code

(€1 = about $1.30, country code: 353)
S = Single, **D** = Double/Twin, **T** = Triple, **Q** = Quad, **b** = bath-room, **s** = shower only. All of these places include breakfast; credit cards are accepted unless otherwise noted.

To help you easily sort through these listings, I've divided the accommodations into three categories, based on the price for a standard double room with bath:

$$$ Higher Priced—Most rooms €110 or more.
$$ Moderately Priced—Most rooms between €80-110.
$ Lower Priced—Most rooms €80 or less.

Prices can change without notice; verify the hotel's cur-rent rates online or by email.

$ Pinecrest B&B has four nice rooms in a modern house on a quiet homey street, just a 10-minute walk from the center of town (Sb-€45-50, Db-€70-80, Tb-€90-120, cash only, parking, Bishop Meadows, just off the Freshford Road about 100 yards north of the roundabout to the New Bridge, tel. 056/776-3567, mobile 087-934-4579, pinecrestbnb@eircom.net, friendly Helen Heffernan).

$ Kilkenny Tourist Hostel, filling a fine Georgian town-house in the town center, offers 60 cheap beds, a friendly family room, a well-equipped members' kitchen, and a wealth of local information (dorm bed-€15-17, D-€36-42, T-€53-60, Q-€68-76, cash only, Wi-Fi, laundry service-€5, 2 blocks from cathedral at 35 Parliament Street, tel. 056/776-3541, www.kilkennyhostel.ie, info@kilkennyhostel.ie).

Eating in Kilkenny

Langton's is every local's first choice, serving quality Irish dishes under a Tiffany-skylight expanse (€12-15 lunches, €16-25 dinners, daily 8:00-22:30, 69 John Street, tel. 056/776-5133).

Ristorante Rinuccini serves classy, romantic, candlelit Italian meals (€11-18 lunches, €19-28 dinners, €28 three-course early-bird special before 19:00, open daily 12:00-15:00 & 17:30-22:00, 1 The Parade, tel. 056/776-1575).

La Trattoria is the friendly, informal Italian option in town, presided over by charming Giacomo (€13-19 dinners, €14 two-course early-bird special before 19:00, open daily 12:00-22:00, 84 John Street, tel. 056/777-0907).

Zuni is a stylish splurge, offering international cuisine (€23.50 two-course and €28.50 three-course early-bird specials before

KILKENNY & CASHEL

19:30 every night but Sat, open daily 12:30-14:30 & 18:00-21:00, weekend reservations a good idea, 26 Lower Patrick Street, tel. 056/772-3999).

Pennefeather Restaurant, above the Kilkenny Book Centre, is good for a quick, cheap, light lunch (Mon-Fri 9:00-17:30, Sat 9:00-17:00, closed Sun, 10 High Street, tel. 056/776-4063).

Kyteler's Inn serves basic pub grub in a timber-and-stone atmosphere with a heated and covered beer garden out back. Visit their fun 14th-century cellar and ask about their witch. Watch your head or risk leaving some of your DNA embedded in the low stone arches (Mon-Sat 12:00-21:00, Sun 12:00-20:00, 27 St. Kieran's Street, tel. 056/772-1064).

Kilkenny Connections

From Kilkenny by Train to: Dublin (5/day, 2 hours), **Waterford** (6/day, 45 minutes). For details, see www.irishrail.ie.

By Bus to: Dublin (7/day, 2.5 hours), **Waterford** (2/day, 1 hour), **Tralee** (3/day, 5.5 hours, change in Cork), **Galway** (3/day, 5 hours). For details, see www.buseireann.ie.

KILKENNY & CASHEL

Rock of Cashel

Rising high above the fertile Plain of Tipperary, the Rock of Cashel—worth ▲▲▲—is one of Ireland's most historic and evocative sights. Seat of the ancient kings of Munster (c. A.D. 300-1100), this is where St. Patrick baptized King Aengus in about A.D. 450. Strategically located and perfect for fortification, the Rock was fought over by local clans for hundreds of years. Finally, in 1101, clever Murtagh O'Brien gave the Rock to the Church. His seemingly benevolent donation increased his influence with the Church, while preventing his rivals, the powerful McCarthy clan, from regaining possession of the Rock. As Cashel evolved into an ecclesiastical center, Iron Age ring forts and thatch dwellings gave way to the majestic stone church buildings enjoyed by visitors today. Queen Elizabeth II's history-making, four-day visit to Ireland in 2011 included a visit to the Rock.

If you have time, start your visit at the Bru Boru Cultural Centre (at the base of the Rock; see page 151) to learn more about the Rock before you ascend. From there, it's a steep 100-yard walk up to the Rock itself. On this 200-foot-high outcrop of limestone, the first building you'll encounter is the 15th-century Hall of the Vicars Choral, housing the ticket desk, a tiny museum (with an original 12th-century high cross dedicated to St. Patrick and a few replica artifacts), and a 20-minute video (2/hour, shown in the hall's former dormitory). You'll also find a round tower, an early Christian cross, a delightful Romanesque chapel, and a ruined Gothic cathedral, all surrounded by my favorite Celtic-cross grave-yard.

Orientation to the Rock of Cashel

Cost and Hours: €6, families-€14, daily early June-mid-Sept 9:00-19:00, mid-March-early June and mid-Sept-mid-Oct 9:00-17:30, mid-Oct-mid-March 9:00-16:30, last entry 45 minutes before closing. Parking costs €4.50 (visit pay machine station by exit before you get in your car to drive out).

Renovations: An extensive and essential restoration project is under way. It's likely that sections of the ruins will be under scaffolding during your visit (especially Cormac's Chapel).

Crowd-Beating Tips: Summer crowds flock to the Rock (worst June-Aug 11:00-15:00). Try to plan your visit for early or late in the day. If you're here at a peak time, tour the Rock first and save the movie, museum, and Hall of the Vicars Choral for the end of your visit, when the tourist tide has receded. Otherwise, see the movie and museum first.

Dress Warmly: Bring a coat—deceptively sheltered conditions in the parking lot may not reflect those on the high, windy, exposed Rock.

Tours: Call ahead for the tour schedule (included in entry price, 45 minutes, tel. 062/61437). Otherwise, set your own pace with my self-guided tour.

WCs: Use the ones at the base of the Rock next to the parking lot (there are none up on the Rock).

Self-Guided Tour

In a sense, architecture is the marriage of art (what can be imagined) and science (what's possible). When this union is blended to serve God, it's a potent mix. Nowhere else in Ireland can you better see the evolution of Irish devotion expressed in stone. This large lump of rock is a pedestal supporting a compact tangle of three dramatic architectural styles: early Christian (round tower and St. Patrick's high cross), Romanesque (Cormac's Chapel), and Gothic (the main cathedral).

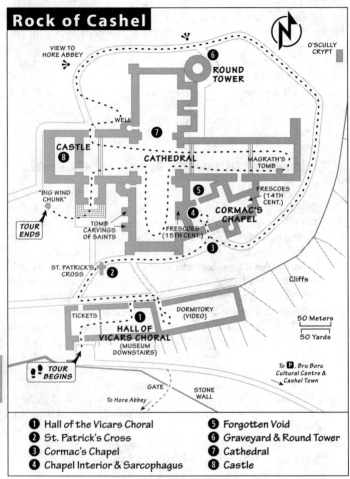

Rock of Cashel

VIEW TO
HORE ABBEY

O'SCULLY
CRYPT

6 ROUND
TOWER

WELL

7

CASTLE
8

CATHEDRAL

MAGRATH'S
TOMB

"BIG WIND
CHUNK"

5

FRESCOES
(14TH
CENT.)

TOUR
ENDS

TOMB
CARVINGS
OF SAINTS

4

FRESCOES
(15TH CENT.)

3

CORMAC'S
CHAPEL

ST. PATRICK'S
CROSS

2

Cliffs

DORMITORY
(VIDEO)

TICKETS

1

50 Meters

50 Yards

HALL OF
VICARS CHORAL
(MUSEUM
DOWNSTAIRS)

To **P**, Bru Boru
Cultural Centre &
Cashel Town

TOUR
BEGINS

GATE

STONE
WALL

To Hore Abbey

1 Hall of the Vicars Choral	**5** Forgotten Void
2 St. Patrick's Cross	**6** Graveyard & Round Tower
3 Cormac's Chapel	**7** Cathedral
4 Chapel Interior & Sarcophagus	**8** Castle

KILKENNY & CASHEL

• *Follow this tour counterclockwise around the Rock. To start the tour, climb the indoor stairs opposite the ticket desk.*

1 Hall of the Vicars Choral: This is the youngest building on the Rock (early 1400s). It housed the minor clerics appointed to sing during cathedral services. These vicars—who were granted nearby lands by the archbishop—lived comfortably here, with a large fireplace and white, lime-washed walls (to reflect light and act as a natural disinfectant that discouraged bugs as well). Window seats gave the blessedly literate vicars the best light to read by. The furniture is original, but the oak timber roof is a reconstruction, built to medieval specifications using wooden dowels instead of nails. The large wall tapestry, showing King Solomon with the Queen of Sheba, contains intentional errors—to remind viewers that only God can create perfection. The vicars, who formed a sort of corporate body to assist the bishop with local administration, used a special seal to authorize documents such as land leases. You can see an enlarged wooden copy of the seal (hanging above the fireplace), depicting eight vicars surrounding a seated organist. It was a good system—until some of the greedier vicars duplicated the seal for their own purposes, forcing the archbishop to curtail its use.

• *Go outside the hall and find...*

❷ **St. Patrick's Cross:** St. Patrick baptized King Aengus at the Rock of Cashel in about A.D. 450. Legend has it that St. Patrick, intensely preoccupied with the holy ceremony, accidentally speared the foot of the king with his crosier staff while administering the baptismal sacrament. But the pagan king stoically held his tongue until the end of the ceremony, thinking this was part of the painful process of becoming a Christian. Probably not that many other converts stepped forward that day.

This 12th-century cross, a stub of its former glory, was carved to celebrate the handing over of the Rock to the Church 650 years after St. Patrick's visit. Typical Irish high crosses use a ring around the cross' head to support its arms and to symbolize the sun (making Christianity more appealing to the sun-worshipping Celts). But instead, this cross uses the Latin design: The weight of the arms is supported by two vertical beams on each side of the main shaft, representing the two criminals who were crucified beside Christ (today only one of these supports remains).

On my first visit, more than 30 years ago, the original cross still stood here. But centuries of wind and rain were slowly eroding away important detail, so the cross was moved into the adjacent museum (opposite the ticket desk) and replaced by this replica.

• *Turn your back on St. Patrick's Cross, and walk about 100 feet slightly uphill along the gravel path beside the cathedral. Roughly opposite the far end of the Hall of the Vicars Choral is the entry to...*

❸ **Cormac's Chapel:** As the wild Celtic Christian church was reined in and reorganized by Rome 850 years ago, new architectural influences from continental Europe began to emerge on the remote Irish landscape. This small chapel—Ireland's first and finest Romanesque church, consecrated in 1134 by King Cormac MacCarthy—reflects this evolution. Travel in your imagination back to the 12th century, when this chapel and the tall round tower were the only stone structures on the Rock.

The "new" Romanesque style reflected the ancient Roman basilica floor plan. Its columns and rounded arches created an overall effect of massiveness and strength. Romanesque churches were like dark fortresses, with thick walls, squat towers, few windows, and minimal decoration. Irish stone churches of this period (like the one at Glendalough in the Wicklow Mountains) were simple rectangular buildings with no ornate stone carving at all.

Tradition says that the chapel's easy-to-cut sandstone was quarried 12 miles away, and the blocks were passed from hand to hand back to the Rock. (It's unlikely that they had the manpower to form a conga line that long—they probably used oxen-pulled carts.) The two square towers resemble those in Regensburg, Germany, further suggesting that well-traveled medieval Irish monks brought back new ideas from the Continent.

• *The modern, dark-glass chapel door (always unlocked) is a recent addition to keep out nesting birds. Enter the chapel (remembering to close the door behind you) and let your eyes adjust to the low light.*

❹ **Chapel Interior:** Just inside the chapel is an empty stone **sarcophagus.** Nobody knows for sure whose body once lay here (possibly the brother of King Cormac MacCarthy). The damaged front relief is carved in the Scandinavian Urnes style. Vikings raided Ireland, intermarried with the Irish, and were melting into Irish society by the time this chapel was built. Some scholars interpret the relief design (a tangle of snakes and beasts) as a figure-eight lying on its side, looping back and forth forever, symbolizing the eternity of the afterlife.

With your back to the sarcophagus, let your eyes wander around the chapel interior. You're standing in the **nave,** lit by the three windows (partially blocked by the later cathedral, which is outside to the left) in the wall behind you. Overhead is a round vaulted ceiling with support ribs. The strong round arches support not only the heavy stone roof, but also the (unseen) second-story scriptorium chamber, where monks once carefully copied manuscripts.

The **chancel arch,** studded with fist-size heads, framed the altar (now gone). The lower heads are more grotesque, while those nearing the top become serene as they climb closer to God. The arch is off-center in relation to the nave, symbolic of Christ's head drooping to the side as he died on the cross.

Walk into the chancel and look up at the ceiling, examining the faint **frescoes,** a labor of love from 850 years ago. Frescoes are rare in Ireland because of the perpetually moist climate. (Mixing pigments into wet plaster worked better in dry climates like Italy's.) Once vividly colorful, then fading over time, these frescoes were further damaged during the Reformation. Such ornamentation was considered vain by Protestants, who piously whitewashed over them. These surviving frescoes were discovered under multiple layers of whitewash during painstaking modern restoration. The rich blue color came from lapis lazuli, an expensive gemstone imported from Asia.

• *Walk through the other modern, dark-glass doorway (don't let the birds in), opposite the door you used to enter the chapel. You'll find yourself in a...*

❺ Forgotten Void: This enclosed space (roughly 30 feet square) was created when the newer cathedral was wedged between the older chapel and the round tower. Once the main entrance into the chapel, this forgotten doorway is crowned by a finely carved tympanum that decorates the arch above it. It's perfectly preserved because the huge cathedral shielded it from the wind and rain. The large lion (symbol of St. Mark's gospel) is being hunted by a centaur (half-man, half-horse) archer wearing a Norman helmet (essential conehead attire in the late Middle Ages).

As you exit the chapel (turning left), take a look at the more exposed and weathered tympanum outside, above the south entrance. The carved, bloated "hippo" is actually an ox, representing Gospel author St. Luke.

• *Tiptoe through the tombstones around the east end of the cathedral to the base of the round tower.*

❻ Graveyard and Round Tower: This graveyard still takes permanent guests—but only those put on a waiting list by their ancestors in 1930. A handful of these chosen few are still alive, and once they're gone, the graveyard will be considered full. The 20-foot-tall stone shaft at the edge of the graveyard, marking the O'Scully family crypt, was once crowned by an elaborately carved Irish high cross—destroyed during a lightning storm in 1976.

Look out over the **Plain of Tipperary.** Called the "Golden Vale," its rich soil makes it Ireland's most prosperous farmland. In St. Patrick's time, it was covered with oak forests (Ireland is now the most deforested nation in the EU). A path leads  to the ruined 13th-century **Hore Abbey** in the fields below (free, always open and peaceful). The abbey is named for the Cistercian monks who wore simple gray robes, roughly the same color as hoarfrost (the ice crystals that form on morning grass).

Gaze up at the **round tower,** the first stone structure built on the Rock after the Church took over in 1101. The shape of these towers is unique to Ireland. Though you might think towers like

KILKENNY & CASHEL

this were chiefly intended as a place to hide in case of invasion, they were instead used primarily as bell towers and lookout posts. (Enemies could smoke out anyone inside the tower, and with enough warning, monks were better off concealing themselves in the countryside.) The tower stands 92 feet tall, with walls over 3 feet thick. The doorway, which once had a rope ladder, was built high up not only for security, but also because having it at ground level would have weakened the foundation of the top-heavy structure. The interior once contained wooden floors connected by ladders, and served as safe storage for the monks' precious sacramental treasures. The tower's stability is impressive when you consider its age, the winds it has endured, and the shallowness of its foundation (only five feet under present ground level).

Continue walking around the cathedral's north transept, noticing the square holes in the exterior walls. During construction, wooden scaffolding was anchored into these holes. On your way to the cathedral entrance, in the corner where the north transept joins the nave, you'll pass a small, easy-to-miss **well.** Without this essential water source, the Rock could never have withstood a siege and would not have been as valuable to clans and clergy. In 1848, a chalice was dredged from the well, likely thrown there by fleeing medieval monks intending to survive a raid. They didn't make it. (If they had, they would have retrieved the chalice.)

• *Now enter the...*

❼ **Cathedral:** Traditionally, the choir of a church (where the clergy celebrate Mass) faces east, while the nave stretches off to the west. Because this cathedral was squeezed between the preexisting chapel, round tower, and drinking well, the builders were forced to improvise—giving it an extra-long choir and a cramped nave.

Built between 1230 and 1290, the church's pointed arches and high, narrow windows proclaim the Gothic style of the period (and let in more light than earlier Romanesque churches). Walk under the central bell tower and look up at the rib-vaulted **ceiling.** The hole in the middle was for a rope used to ring the church bells. The wooden roof is long gone. When the Protestant Lord Inchiquin (who became one of Oliver Cromwell's generals) attacked the Catholic town of Cashel in 1647, hundreds of townsfolk fled to the sanctuary of this cathedral. Inchiquin packed turf around the exterior and burned the cathedral down, massacring those inside.

Ascend the terraces at the choir end of the cathedral, where the main altar once stood. Stand on the gravestones (of the 16th-century rich and famous) with your back to the east wall (where the narrow windows have crumbled away) and look back down toward the nave. The right wall of the choir is filled with graceful Gothic windows, while the solid left wall hides Cormac's Chapel (which would have blocked any sunlight). The line of stone supports on the left wall once held the long, wooden balcony where the vicars sang. Closer to the altar, high on the same wall, is a small, rectangular window called the "leper's squint"—which allowed unsightly lepers to view the altar during Mass without offending the congregation.

The grand **wall tomb** on the left contains the remains of archbishop Miler Magrath, the "scoundrel of Cashel," who lived to be 100. From 1570 to 1622, Magrath was the Protestant archbishop of Cashel who simultaneously profited from his previous position as Catholic bishop of Down. He married twice, had lots of kids, confiscated the ornate tomb lid here from another bishop's grave, and converted back to Catholicism on his deathbed.

• *Walk back down the nave and turn left into the south transept.*

Take a peek into the modern-roofed wooden structure against the wall on your left. It's protecting 15th-century **frescoes** of the crucifixion of Christ that were rediscovered during renovations in 2005. They're as patchy and hard to make out (and just as rare for Ireland) as the century-older frescoes in the ceiling of Cormac's Chapel. On the opposite side of this transept, in alcoves built into the wall, wonderful **carvings** of early Christian saints line the outside walls of tombs (look down at shin level).

• *Return to the nave and continue down to the far end. Exit the cathedral on the left, through the porch entrance.*

❽ **Castle:** Back outside, stand beside the huge chunk of wall debris and try to picture where it might have fit in the ruins above. This end of the cathedral was converted into an archbishop's castle in the 1400s (shortening the nave even more). Looking high into the castle's damaged top floors, you can see the bishop's residence chamber and the secret passageways that were once hidden in the thick walls. Lord Inchiquin's cannons weakened the structure during the 1647 massacre, and in 1848, a massive storm (known as "Night of the Big Wind" in Irish lore) flung the huge chunk next to you from the ruins above.

In the mid-1700s, the Anglican Church transferred cathedral status to St. John's in town, and the archbishop abandoned the drafty Rock for a more comfortable residence, leaving the ruins that you see today.

Sights near the Rock of Cashel

Bru Boru Cultural Centre—Nestled below the Rock of Cashel parking lot, next to the statue of the three blissed-out dancers, this center adds to your understanding of the Rock in its wider histori-

KILKENNY & CASHEL

cal and cultural context. The highlight of the **Sounds of History Museum** downstairs is the exhibit showing the Rock's gradual evolution from ancient ring fort to grand church ruins—projected down onto a large disc that visitors gather around.

Those interested in Ireland's traditional music scene will enjoy the surprisingly good 15-minute film introduction to Irish trad music in the small museum theater.

Cost and Hours: Cultural Centre-free, Sounds of History Museum-€5; June-Aug Mon-Sat 9:00-18:00, closed Sun; Sept-May Mon-Fri 9:00-17:00, closed Sat-Sun; cafeteria, tel. 062/61122, www.bruboru.ie.

Performances: If you stay overnight in Cashel, consider taking in a performance of the Bru Boru musical dance troupe in the center's large theater (€20, €50 with dinner, mid-June-mid-Aug Tue-Sat at 21:00).

Town of Cashel—The huggable town at the base of the Rock affords a good break on the long drive from Dublin to Dingle (**TI** open mid-March-Oct daily 9:30-17:30, Nov-mid-March closed Sat-Sun, tel. 062/62511). The Heritage Centre, next door to the TI, presents a modest six-minute audio explanation of Cashel's history around a walled town model.

Sleeping in Cashel

(€1 = about $1.30, country code: 353, area code: 062)
If you spend the night in Cashel, you'll be treated to beautifully illuminated views of the ruins. The following listings are cozy, old-fashioned, and a five-minute walk from the Rock.

$$ Joy's Rockside House B&B is closest to the Rock, resting on its lower slopes. With four large, fresh rooms (all with views of the Rock), it's the best lodging value in Cashel (Db-€80-90, Tb-€120-140, Qb-€160, cash only, Wi-Fi, Rock Villas Street, parking, tel. 062/63813, www.joyrockside.com, joyrocksidehouse@eircom.net, Joan and Rem Joy). Families may want to ask about their self-catering house in town.

$ Rockville House, 100 yards from the Rock, is a traditional place run by gentleman owner Patrick Hayes. The house itself has six fine rooms, and its old stablehouse, lovingly converted by Patrick, has five more (Sb-€39, Db-€58-60, Tb-€80-85, Qb-€90, cash only, Wi-Fi, 10 Dominic Street, tel. 062/61760, pat@rockville house.com).

$ Wattie's B&B has three rooms that feel lived-in and comfy (Db-€60-75, Tb-€90-100, cash only, Wi-Fi, one wheelchair-accessible room, parking, 14 Dominic Street, tel. 062/61923, www. wattiesbandb.ie, wattiesbandb@eircom.net, Maria Dunne).

$ Cashel Lodge is a well-kept rural oasis housed in an old stone grain warehouse behind the Rock near the Hore Abbey ruins. Its seven comfortable rooms (one a dorm with three bunks) combine unpretentious practicality with Irish country charm (dorm beds-€20-23, Db-€65, Tb-€75, camping spots-€10/person, breakfast-€7.50, laundry service-€10, Wi-Fi, Dundrum Road R-505, tel. 062/61003, www.cashel-lodge.com, info@cashel-lodge.com, Tom and Brid O'Brien).

Eating in Cashel

Grab a soup-and-sandwich lunch at tiny, violet-colored **Granny's Kitchen** (next to the parking lot at the base of the Rock). Popular **Chez Hans Café,** with the best lunch selection and biggest crowds, is 75 yards down the road from the parking lot (€10-17 meals, Tue-Sat 12:00-17:30, closed Sun-Mon). And 50 yards farther down that same road, you'll find the **Rock House,** a cafeteria-style restaurant that's upstairs above the pharmacy (daily 9:00-16:00, tel. 062/62299). In town, next door to the TI, **Feehan's Bar** is a convenient stop for pub grub (tel. 062/61929).

For a splurge dinner, consider **Chez Hans,** the classy cousin of Chez Hans Café, listed above (€27 two-course early-bird meal before 20:00 Tue-Thu or before 19:00 Fri, otherwise €25-35 entrées, Tue-Sat 18:00-22:00, closed Sun-Mon, in an old church a block below the Rock, tel. 062/61177).

Cashel Connections

Cashel has no train station; the closest one is 13 miles away in the town of Thurles.

From Cashel by Bus to: Dublin (4/day, 3 hours), **Kilkenny** (3/day, 2.5 hours), **Waterford** (6/day, 2 hours). For details, see www. buseireann.ie.

KILKENNY & CASHEL

WATERFORD and COUNTY WEXFORD

The best overnight stop in southeast Ireland is the historic Viking port and Norman beachhead town of Waterford. From here, you can explore the varied sights of County Wexford.

This region has a pastoral serenity and a strong history of trading from its sheltered ports facing England. The Vikings built the ports and developed the trade routes. Their cousin Normans came along 200 years later with more efficient farming techniques than the Irish they displaced.

But the Irish made them fight to hang on to it. Like medieval Fort Apaches, Norman-fortified tower house castles dot the landscape in this area more so than in most other parts of Ireland. And throughout your travels here, you'll see evidence of the region's Norman (French) roots in its high concentration of family names with old Norman prefixes: De Berg, De Lacy, Devereux, Fitzgilbert, Fitzsimmons, Fitzgerald, and so on.

Waterford

The oldest city in Ireland, Waterford was once more important than Dublin. Its three fine history museums reflect this. But today, while tourists associate the town's name with its famous crystal, the 45,000 residents are quick to remind you that the crystal is named after the town, not vice versa (come for the crystal, stay for the history). That said, Waterford is a plain, gray, workaday town. Pubs outnumber cafés, and freighters offload cargo at the dock. It's a dose of gritty Ireland, with fewer leprechauns per capita than other Irish destinations. Wandering the back streets, you're reminded that until a couple of generations ago, Ireland was one of the poorest countries in Western Europe.

Planning Your Time

A day is enough time for Waterford's compact historic core. Visit the Waterford Crystal Visitor Centre early or late to avoid the big-bus-tour crowds at midday. Beyond that, your best activity is the historic walk (at 11:45 or 13:45 in peak season), followed by a visit to the branch of the Waterford Museum of Treasures housed in Reginald's Tower. History buffs may want to dig deeper with visits to the other two, less essential (but nearby) branches of this three-museum complex: Chorister's Hall (medieval life) and Bishop's Palace (Georgian to modern age). To feel the pulse of contemporary Waterford, hang out on the town's pedestrian square and stroll through its big, modern shopping mall. All of these sights are within a triangular six-block area clustered behind Reginald's Tower, facing the harborfront.

Orientation to Waterford

Waterford's main drag runs along its ugly harbor, where you'll find the bus station and easy parking lots (€1.80/hour, best overnight lot costs €5 for a stay from 17:00-11:00; entry next to bus station opposite TI; pay at automated station before driving out of gate, must have exact change in coins). All recommended accommodations and sights are within a 10-minute walk of the harbor. Both museums and the TI are on the harborfront. The stubby two-story Victorian clock tower marks the middle of the harbor. It's also the start of the pedestrian Barronstrand Street, which runs a block inland to the town square.

Tourist Information

The TI sits on the harborfront, where Greyfriars Street meets Merchant's and Meagher's Quays, facing a modern, white, tent-like sculpture (July-Aug Mon-Fri 9:00-18:00, Sat 10:00-18:00, Sun 11:00-17:00; April-June and Sept-Oct Mon-Fri 9:00-18:00, Sat 10:00-18:00, closed Sun; Nov-March Mon-Sat 9:15-17:00, closed Sun; tel. 051/875-823, www.discoverwaterfordcity.ie). As with all Irish TIs, it's basically a shop with a counter where clerks tell you about places that they "endorse" (that is, get money from).

Helpful Hints

Post Office: It's on Parade Quay (Mon-Fri 9:00-17:30, Sat 9:00-13:00, closed Sun).

Laundry: Snow White launderette is at 61 Mayor's Walk (Mon-Sat 9:30-13:30 & 14:30-17:30, closed Sun, tel. 051/858-905).

Bookstore: The multilevel **Book Centre** is a fun browse, right off the main square (Mon-Sat 9:00-18:00, Fri until 21:00, Sun 9:00-14:00, 25 John Roberts Square, tel. 051/873-823).

Shopping: The Kite Studios unites under one roof five artisans who work in different mediums right in front of you. Crystal-maker Sean Egan leads the way, fashioning his own unique crystal creations after decades honing his skills at the old Waterford factory. Other craftsmen include an engraver, an art printer, a silversmith, and a fashion designer (Mon-Sat 9:00-17:00, closed Sun, 11 Henrietta Street, tel. 051/858-914).

Taxis: Consider **Street Cabs Ltd.** (117 Parade Quay, tel. 051/877-778). **Rapid Cabs** operates local taxis (tel. 051/858-585), and **Rapid Express** offers coaches to Dublin's airport (tel. 051/872-149).

Tours of Waterford

▲▲**Waterford Historic Walking Tour**—Jack Burtchaell and his partners lead informative, hour-long, historical town walks that meet at the TI every day at 11:45 and 13:45—or join the tour as it swings by the Granville Hotel at 12:00 and 14:00 (just show up, pay €7 at the end, mid-March-mid-Oct only, tel. 051/873-711, www.jackswalkingtours.com). The tour—really the most enjoyable thing to do in Waterford—is an entertaining walk from the TI to the Waterford Crystal Visitor Centre, giving you a good handle on the story of Waterford.

Sights in Waterford

▲▲**Waterford Crystal Visitor Centre**

With a tradition dating back to 1783, Waterford was, until recently, the largest and most respected glassworks in the world. But the economic downturn of 2008 shattered the market for luxury items like crystal, and sadly, the huge Waterford Crystal factory outside town closed in January 2009.

The good news for crystal enthusiasts is that the company was bought by American investors, who opened a new, scaled-down factory in the town center in 2010. While 70 percent of Waterford Crystal is now manufactured by cheaper labor in Poland, Slovenia, and the Czech Republic, the finest glass craftsmen still reside here, where they create "prestige pieces" for special-order custom-

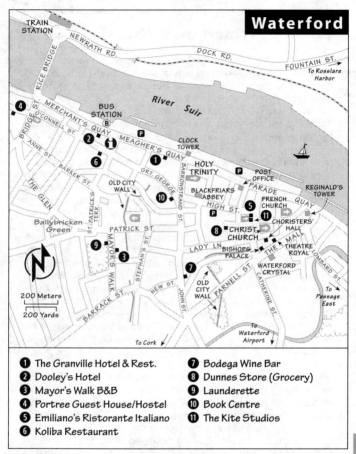

Waterford

TRAIN STATION

NEWRATH RD.

DOCK RD.

FOUNTAIN ST.

To Rosslare Harbor

River Suir

BUS STATION

MERCHANT'S QUAY

RICE BRIDGE

BRIDGE ST.

O'CONNELL ST.

ANNE ST.

BARKER ST.

THE GLEN

MEAGHER'S QUAY

CLOCK TOWER

HOLY TRINITY

GRT. GEORGE

BARRONSTRAND ST.

OLD CITY WALL

ST. PATRICK'S TERR.

PATRICK ST.

Ballybricken Green

MAYOR'S WALK

STEPHEN'S ST.

BLACKFRIARS ABBEY

HIGH ST.

PARADE QUAY

POST OFFICE

REGINALD'S TOWER

FRENCH CHURCH

CHRIST CHURCH

CHORISTERS' HALL

LADY LN.

BISHOPS PALACE

THE MALL

THEATRE ROYAL

WATERFORD CRYSTAL

PARNELL ST.

CATHERINE ST.

LOMBARD ST.

NEW ST.

JOHN ST.

OLD CITY WALL

BARRACK ST.

To Cork

To Waterford Airport

To Passage East

200 Meters

200 Yards

❶ The Granville Hotel & Rest.
❷ Dooley's Hotel
❸ Mayor's Walk B&B
❹ Portree Guest House/Hostel
❺ Emiliano's Ristorante Italiano
❻ Koliba Restaurant
❼ Bodega Wine Bar
❽ Dunnes Store (Grocery)
❾ Launderette
❿ Book Centre
⓫ The Kite Studios

ers. The one-hour tour of this hardworking little factory is a joy; it's more intimate than the old, larger factory. You're encouraged to ask questions.

Cost and Hours: Tours-€12, depart every 30 minutes, April-Oct Mon-Sat 9:00-16:15, Sun 10:00-16:15, shorter hours off-season, call to confirm; shop free and open longer hours; tel. 051/317-000, www.waterfordvisitorcentre.com.

Getting There: The Waterford Crystal Visitor Centre is conveniently located on a street called The Mall, an easy one-block walk south of Reginald's Tower.

Visiting the Factory: The tour begins with a bit of history and a look at an impressive six-foot-tall crystal grandfather clock. It then loses momentum as you're ushered into a glitzy and pointless five-minute fireworks film montage set to a techno beat. But things pick up as your guide takes you into the factory to meet the craftsmen in

Waterford's History

Arriving in 819, Vikings first established Waterford as their base for piracy. Waterford was a perfect spot for launching their ships, since it's located at the gateway to the most extensive river network in Ireland. From here, raiders could sail 50 miles into Ireland, an island with no towns, just scattered monastic settlements and small gatherings of clans—perfect for the Vikings' plan of rape, pillage, and plunder.

Later, the Vikings decided to "go legal." They turned to profiteering, setting up shop in an established trading base they named Vandrafjord, or "safe harbor"—eventually called Waterford—Ireland's first permanent town. It was from this base that the Norsemen invaded northern England.

In the 12th century, a deposed Irish king named Diarmuid MacMurrough opened the Irish version of Pandora's box by inviting the Normans over from England, hoping to use their advanced military technology to regain his land from a rival clan. The great warrior knight Strongbow came...and never left, beginning Ireland's long and troublesome relationship with the English. In 1170, Strongbow married the Gaelic princess Aoife in the Gothic church that once stood where Waterford's Christ Church Cathedral stands today. With this marriage, Strongbow was next in line for the title of King of Leinster, which he was named after the death of his father-in-law, MacMurrough, a year later.

Strongbow's success was so rapid that King Henry II got worried about a rival kingdom blossoming on his flank. He quickly gathered his navy and sailed over from England to make sure Strongbow knew who was boss—and to intimidate Irish clan leaders into swearing loyalty to the crown. England's first roots in Ireland had been planted.

For the English, Waterford has often proved to be a tough nut to crack. During Oliver Cromwell's brutal scorched-earth campaign of 1649-1650, he destroyed any town still loyal to King Charles I, whom he had beheaded (see "The Curse of Cromwell" sidebar, later). His forces decimated Ireland. But Waterford was the only Irish city to withstand his siege.

their element. Glassblowers magically spin glowing blobs of molten crystal into exquisite and recognizable shapes in minutes. If you get dizzy blowing up balloons for a kid's party, consider the lung stamina that these craftsmen display (hot crystal is a lot heavier to heave with a breath than thin rubber balloons). Watch closely as the glassblower puts his thumb over the opening between breaths to keep the heat and pressure inside the blob constant.

Heavy molten crystal has an intentionally high lead content (it's what distinguishes fine crystal from common glassware). A cooling-off stage allows the crystal to set. Then glass cutters deftly cradle the fragile creations against diamond-edged cutting wheels, applying exactly enough pressure to ensure that the grooves are replicated with surgical skill. Interestingly, the craftsmen are not at risk of slicing themselves on the wheels, which cut hard crystal but not soft flesh (I still can't figure that one out). The glasscutters will be glad to demonstrate if you ask.

Watch closely as the skilled cutters muscle rough unfinished pieces—weighing as much as bowling balls—and cut intricate patterns. The crystal vases and bowls may look light and delicate, but hold an unfinished piece (with its lead-enhanced heft) and you'll gain a new appreciation for the strength, touch, and hand-eye coordination of the glass cutters.

Afterward, visit the glittering salesroom, surrounded by hard-to-pack but easy-to-ship temptations. Take a look at the copies of famous sports trophies (they make backups of their most important commissions, just in case).

Museum of Treasures

In 2012, Waterford closed its original Museum of Treasures and split up the impressive collection. The artifacts are now found in three historic locations, just a damsel's handkerchief drop from each other. This museum complex is named the "Viking Triangle," and all three branches are located in the original triangular-shaped Viking fort section of town. Each branch is connected to the other by a two-minute walk (the museum's tagline is "1,000 years of history in under 1,000 paces"). To see the branches in historical sequence, first visit Reginald's Tower on the harborfront to understand the Viking roots of the city. Then stroll up The Mall to find Chorister's Hall, a modern structure tucked behind the Theatre Royal. This branch houses medieval artifacts in an original 13th-century vaulted cellar. Finally, right next door, you can visit the imposing Bishop's Palace, a fine mansion full of everything Waterford from 1700 to the present. Few Irish towns can claim a meatier bite of Irish history than Waterford.

▲**Reginald's Tower**— This oldest part of the oldest town in Ireland is named after Regnall, the first (Norwegian) Viking leader of Waterford, who built a fortified oaken tower here in A.D. 914 and later invaded Jorvik (York, England). Dating from  the late 1100s, the stone Norman tower you see today replaced the wooden one and was once the most important corner of the town

WATERFORD

wall. The tower is Ireland's oldest intact building and the first made with mortar. Today, its four floors are full of Viking artifacts.

Cost and Hours: €3, includes guided tour any time upon request—ask for the one-hour version, which adds a historic walk around the block to French Church; daily Easter-Oct 10:00-18:00, Nov-Easter 10:00-17:30, last entry 30 minutes before closing, tel. 051/304-220, www.waterfordtreasures.com.

Visiting the Museum: Before you enter, look for the cannonball embedded high above the entrance, courtesy of Cromwell's siege cannons.

Once inside, you'll find an interesting Viking town **model** opposite the ticket counter. Upstairs a display of early coins explains how the Vikings introduced the concept of coinage to the Irish after they eventually settled down and set up trade posts. Look for the tiny **Kite Brooch** that delicately blends both Scandinavian and Irish styles. In their day, brooches were considered badges of status, and this one's owner must have been at the top of the heap. As you climb the narrow stone stairways, watch your head (people were shorter 800 years ago). And be sure to go all the way to the top floor, where an informative 10-minute animated **video** traces the evolution of the town from muddy fort to modern city.

The **statue** outside (in the middle of the street) is of Thomas Francis Meagher (see sidebar), whose short, hell-bent-for-leather life took him on precarious adventures from Waterford to Tasmania to Nicaragua to Montana and finally, to an unknown watery grave.

Chorister's Hall—This middle branch of the museum triumvirate should be open to visitors by spring of 2013. The focus here is medieval life in Waterford, from the Norman invasion of the late 1100s to the Williamite English triumph of the late 1600s. The modern building sits on top of an original wine vault cellar complex from the 1200s, where much of the collection is on display.

Cost and Hours: €5, likely same hours as Bishop's Palace—described next, tel. 051/304-500, www.waterfordtreasures.com.

▲**Bishop's Palace**—Housed in the former mansion (built 1743) of the local Protestant bishop (with his Christ Church Cathedral looming right behind it), this museum presents a grand sweep through the history of Waterford since 1700. The refined interior hints of the privileged lifestyle of the holy resident and contains the world's largest collection of old Waterford glass. The bishop would meet you at the top of the grand stairway if you were an upper-class visitor, greet you at his office doorway if you were a middle-class merchant, and not budge from the chair behind his desk if you were lower-class. Under no circumstances would he come downstairs to greet anyone.

You'll work your way through three floors spiced with characters like Waterford-born action hero Thomas Francis Meagher

Thomas Francis Meagher (1823-1867)

Waterford's favorite son had a short but amazing life. The son of the town's conservative mayor, Meagher joined Daniel O'Connell's nonviolent movement to repeal the Act of Union with Britain. Impatient with the slow-moving political process of constant compromise, Meagher joined the radical Young Irelander movement, becoming an inspiring speaker. He went to France in 1848 and returned with the first Irish tricolor flag—a gift from the French that represented the Catholics (green), the Protestants (orange), and peaceful coexistence between the two (white).

Involved in a failed uprising, Meagher was sentenced to hang, but his sentence was commuted to life in prison in Tasmania. In 1852, Meagher escaped Tasmania via an American whaling ship and sailed to New York, where he eventually became a lawyer and started an Irish newspaper. After a trip to Nicaragua (to study the feasibility of building a canal or railway across the isthmus), he returned to New York to fight in the American Civil War. Meagher was made a Union general, raised a regiment of Irish immigrants, and famously led them into battle at Antietam and Fredericksburg. After the war, he became the first governor of the Montana territory. At age 44, Thomas Francis Meagher fell off a riverboat one night and drowned in the Missouri River. Sheer accident, foul play, or careless drunkenness? Nobody knows—but his body was never found.

WATERFORD

(see sidebar). You'll learn why the province of Newfoundland in Canada owes over 50 percent of its population to immigrants from Waterford. And if you've ever wondered what bull baiting is, you'll be filled in on this equally cruel Irish version of a bullfight.

Cost and Hours: €5; June-Aug Mon-Sat 9:30-18:00, Sun 11:00-18:00; Sept-May Mon-Sat 10:00-17:00, Sun 11:00-17:00; last entry one hour before closing, tel. 051/304-500, www.water fordtreasures.com.

Other Sights in Waterford

Cathedral of the Holy Trinity—In 1793, the English king granted Ireland the Irish Relief Act, which, among other things, allowed the Irish to build Catholic churches and worship publicly. With Catholic France (30 million) threatening Britain (8 million) on one side, and Ireland (6 million) stirring things up on the other, the king needed to take action to lessen Irish resentment. Allowed new freedom, the Irish built this interesting cathedral in 1796. It's Ireland's first Catholic post-Reformation church and its only Baroque church. The building was funded by wealthy Irish wine merchants from Cádiz, Spain. Among its treasures are 10 Waterford Crystal chandeliers.

Cost and Hours: Free, daily 8:00-19:00.

Nearby: The cathedral faces **Barronstrand Street,** which leads from the clock tower on the harborfront to the pedestrian-friendly **town square.** The street separates the medieval town (on your left when the river is behind you) from the 18th-century city (on your right). A river once flowed here—part of the town's natural defenses just outside the old wall. The huge **shopping center** that dominates the old town was built right on top of the Viking town. In fact, the center is built over a church dating from 1150, which you can see at the bottom of the escalator (next to the kiddie rides).

Christ Church Cathedral—The Protestant cathedral, with 18th-century Georgian architecture, is the fourth church to stand here. Look for the exposed Gothic column six feet below today's floor level, a remnant from an earlier church where the Norman conqueror Strongbow was married (see sidebar on page 158).

Wander over to the macabre tomb of 15th-century mayor James Rice, which bears a famous epitaph: "I am what you will be, I was what you are, pray for me." To emphasize the point, he requested that his body be dug up one year after his death (1482) and his partially decomposed remains be used to model his likeness, now seen on the tomb's lid...complete with worms and frogs.

Cost and Hours: Free though a €1 donation is requested, daily 10:00-17:00, tours available on request.

Nightlife in Waterford

Waterford's small but lively **Theatre Royal** claims a 220-year tradition. Given the dearth of other nighttime options in Waterford beyond pubs, it's worth checking out their schedule of plays, concerts, and light opera during your stay (located on The Mall across from the Waterford Crystal Visitor Centre, tel. 051/874-402, www.theatreroyal.ie).

Sleeping in Waterford

Waterford is a working-class city. Cheap accommodations are fairly rough; fancy accommodations are venerable old places that face the water. I recommend two cheap options and two elegant options below (little else in town splits the difference). Many find sleepy

Sleep Code

(€1 = about $1.30, country code: 353, area code: 051)
S = Single, **D** = Double/Twin, **T** = Triple, **Q** = Quad, **b** = bathroom, **s** = shower only. Unless otherwise noted, breakfast is included and credit cards are accepted.

   To help you easily sort through these listings, I've divided the accommodations into two categories, based on the price for a standard double room with bath:

   $$ Higher Priced—Most rooms €75 or more.
   $ Lower Priced—Most rooms €75 or less.

   Prices can change without notice; verify the hotel's current rates online or by email.

Ardmore, an hour southwest down the coast, a smaller and more scenic home base (see page 192).

$$ The Granville Hotel is Waterford's best and most historic hotel, grandly overlooking the center of the harborfront. The place is plush, from its Old World lounges to its extravagant rooms (Sb-€80-100, Db-€90-160, Tb-€120-200, ask about corporate discounts, Meagher's Quay, tel. 051/305-555, fax 051/305-566, www.granville-hotel.ie, stay@granville-hotel.ie).

$$ Dooley's Hotel, a more modern, family-run place on the harbor with 113 big rooms, is less expensive than the Granville but still high quality (Sb-€69-119, Db-€89-169, Tb-€109-199, even lower prices possible if you book direct from hotel's website, Merchant's Quay, tel. 051/873-531, fax 051/870-262, www.dooleys-hotel.ie, hotel@dooleys-hotel.ie).

$ Mayor's Walk B&B is a well-worn, grandmotherly place that takes you right back to the 1950s. Bob and Jane Hovenden rent four economical yet pleasant rooms with sincere humbleness (S-€28, D-€50, T-€75, cash only, Wi-Fi, 12 Mayor's Walk, tel. 051/855-427, www.mayorswalk.com, mayorswalk@gmail.com).

$ Portree Guest House, just across the bridge from the train station, combines 24 basic budget rooms upstairs with 14 dorm beds in its basement hostel (bed in dorm-€20, Sb-€32-40, Db-€59-69, Tb-€79-89, Qb-€119-130, breakfast-€7, Wi-Fi, guest kitchen in hostel section, parking behind, 10-11 Mary Street, tel. 051/874-574, fax 051/841-940, www.portreeguesthouse.ie, info@portreeguesthouse.ie).

WATERFORD

Eating in Waterford

For something livelier than tired pub grub, consider these good restaurants found on less-frequented back streets. They're small and popular with locals.

Emiliano's Ristorante Italiano is the most romantic place in town, hidden on a tiny lane behind Reginald's Tower. They serve a great selection of tasty pasta dishes and fine wines (€17-23 two- or three-course early-bird specials before 19:00, Tue-Sun 12:30-14:30 & 17:00-22:00, closed Mon, 21 High Street, tel. 051/820-333).

Koliba, a friendly Polish place with a B.Y.O.B. liquor policy, serves hearty Eastern European fare, including potato pancakes stuffed with pork goulash and topped with sour cream (€14 two-course early-bird special before 19:00, Tue-Sun 12:00-20:30, closed Mon, 11a O'Connell Street, tel. 087/171-8688).

The relaxed **Bodega** is my favorite wine bar, run by laid-back Cormac in a warm-glow Mediterranean atmosphere (Mon-Sat 12:00-22:00, closed Sun, 54 John Street, tel. 051/844-177).

On the Harborfront: The **Granville Hotel**'s carvery is your best €10 lunch option if you're looking for a central waterfront location (daily 12:30-14:30, otherwise good bar food daily 10:30-21:00, Meagher's Quay).

Pub Grub and Music: Waterford's staple food seems to be pub grub. Several typical pubs serve dinner in the city center. For your musical entertainment, hum a medley of your favorite show tunes. For some reason, not much live music exists in town. Ask at your hotel, or just wander around, read the notices, and follow your ears. Anything with a pulse will be found on George Street, Barron-strand Street, and Broad Street.

Supermarket: **Dunnes Store** in the shopping center is your best grocery option (Mon-Sat 9:00-19:00, Thu-Fri until 21:00, Sun 12:00-18:00).

Waterford Connections

From Waterford by Train to: Dublin (6/day, 2.5 hours), **Kilkenny** (6/day, 45 minutes). For details, see www.irishrail.ie.

By Bus to: Cork (almost hourly, 2.25 hours), **Kilkenny** (2/day, 1 hour), **Rosslare** (4/day, 1.5 hours), **Wexford** (5/day, 1 hour). Waterford bus station info: Tel. 051/879-000. For details, see www.buseireann.ie.

County Wexford

The southeast corner of Ireland, peppered with pretty views and historic sites, is easily accessible to drivers as a day trip from Waterford. While most of the sights are mediocre, five worth considering are within an hour's drive of Waterford.

The dramatic Hook Head Lighthouse—capping an intriguing and remote peninsula—comes with lots of history and a great tour. The Kennedy Homestead is a pilgrimage site for Kennedy fans. The *Dunbrody* Famine Ship in New Ross gives a sense of what 50 days on a "coffin ship" with dreams of "Americay" must have been like. The Irish National Heritage Park in Wexford is like a Knott's Berry Farm...circa the Stone Age. And the National 1798 Centre at Enniscorthy explains the roots of the Irish struggle for liberty.

Planning Your Time

New Ross, Enniscorthy, and Wexford are each less than 30 minutes apart, connected by fast roads. The Kennedy Homestead is a 10-minute drive from New Ross, and the lighthouse is a 45-minute trip to the end of the Hook Peninsula. All are well-signposted and easy to find. Connecting Dublin with Waterford, you could visit many of these sights in a best-of-County Wexford day en route. On a quick trip, the sights are not worth the trouble by public transit. If you'll be spending the night, Enniscorthy is a blue-collar town (with decent hotels and B&Bs) that provides a good glimpse of workaday Ireland.

If connecting Waterford to Hook Head, use the car-ferry shortcut from Passage East to Ballyhack (€8, 5-minute crossing, runs continuously April-Sept Mon-Sat 7:00-22:00, Sun 9:30-22:00; Oct-March Mon-Sat 7:00-20:00, Sun 9:30-20:00). To reach the ferry from Waterford, take Lombard Street (near Reginald's Tower) south, and follow it all the way to Passage East (it becomes R-683).

Sights in County Wexford

▲Hook Head Lighthouse

This is the oldest operating lighthouse in northern Europe. According to legend, St. Dubhan arrived in the fifth century and discovered the bodies of shipwrecked sailors. Dismayed, he and his followers began tending a fire on the headland to warn future mariners. What you see today is essentially a structure from the 12th century, built by the Normans, who first landed five miles up the east coast (at Baginbun Head, in 1169). They established Waterford

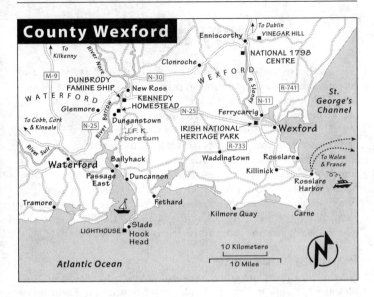

Harbor—a commercial beachhead for the rich Irish countryside they intended to conquer. This beacon assured them safe access.

Today's lighthouse is 110 feet tall and looks modern on the outside. (It was automated in 1996, and its light can be seen for 23 miles out to sea.) But it's actually 800 years old, built on a plan inspired by the lighthouse of Alexandria in Egypt—one of the seven wonders of the ancient world.

Cost and Hours: €6, daily June-Aug 9:30-18:00, May and Sept 9:30- 17:30, Oct-April 9:30-17:00, last tour usually at 16:00, call to check tour times before driving out, tel. 051/397-055, www. hookheritage.ie.

Visiting the Lighthouse: Since it's a working lighthouse, it can be toured only with a guide or escort. Fine 30-minute tours leave about hourly. When you're inside—seeing the lighthouse's black-stained, ribbed, vaulted ceilings and stout, 10-foot-thick walls—you can almost feel the presence of

the Cistercian monks who tended this coal-burning beacon for the Normans. Climbing 115 steps through four levels rewards you with a breezy, salt-air view from the top.

Oliver Cromwell arrived here to secure the English claim to this area. He considered his two options, and declared he'd take strategic Waterford "by Hook or by Crooke." Hook is the long

The Curse of Cromwell

The scariest bogeyman in all of Irish history was Oliver Cromwell. In 1649 he led Parliamentary forces to victory in the English Civil War and had King Charles I beheaded. Assuming the title of Lord Protector, he created a commonwealth (instead of a kingdom) and initiated one of the longest periods in the past 1,000 years in which England functioned without a monarch. Cromwell then turned his attention to Ireland, determined to root out the last royalists loyal to the English monarchy and to punish the Irish for the 1641 massacre of Protestant settlers.

Driven by his Puritan Calvinist beliefs, Cromwell claimed a divine right to carry out God's work as he saw it. To him, all Catholics were complicit in the Protestant deaths by virtue of their misguided faith. He saw priests as little more than witch doctors. Even Protestant Anglicans (the faith founded by Henry VIII a century before) were looked on with suspicion as "Catholics without a pope." Cromwell's self-righteous army of 12,000 soldiers had God on their side and Ireland in their musket-sights.

Cromwell and his tough New Model Army landed in Dublin on August 15, 1649 and marched north to the town of Drogheda. In a bloody siege lasting three days, his soldiers massacred all 3,000 inhabitants. Cromwell then turned south to Wexford, where his army again massacred 3,000-some civilians and Irish troops. Few garrison towns resisted after that. Cromwell's merciless efficiency brought almost the entire island under English control in less than a year.

Catholic landowners were forced to give up their land or face execution...a deal with the devil known as "to hell or to Connaught." About 11 million acres of productive land was handed over to Cromwell's soldiers, in "exchange" for unfertile ground west of the River Shannon. This forced mass migration essentially destroyed Ireland's Catholic land-owning class. (In 1641, Catholics owned 59 percent of Ireland—by 1714 they owned 7 percent.) Some Catholics were allowed to stay on as tenants, providing labor for their new English masters.

Upon Cromwell's death in 1658, his less-dynamic son took over, and the English began to miss their monarchy. In 1660, Charles I's son, Charles II, was invited back from exile in France and the monarchy was restored. Soon after, Cromwell's body was dug up, hung, and beheaded—his head was stuck on a pike and displayed in front of London's Parliament for 20 years (curiously, a heroic statue of him stands there today). But most of Ireland's Catholics never regained their land, and for the next two centuries Ireland continued its slow downward cultural spiral at the hands of English government.

WATERFORD

peninsula with the lighthouse. Crooke is a little village on the other side, just south of Passage East (see "The Curse of Cromwell" sidebar).

There's a decent cafeteria and a shop with fliers explaining other sights on the peninsula. Kids-at-heart can't resist climbing out on the rugged rocky tip of the windy Hook Head.

▲Kennedy Homestead

Patrick Kennedy, President John F. Kennedy's great-grandfather,

left Ireland in 1858. Distant relatives have turned his property into a little museum/shrine for Kennedy pilgrims. Physically, it's not much: A barn and a wing of the modern house survive from 1858. JFK dropped in by helicopter in June 1963, a few months before he was assassinated. You'll view two short videos: 5 minutes of Kennedy's visit to the farm and a 16-minute newsreel tracing the events of his 1963 trip through Ireland (both fascinating if you like Kennedy stuff).

After the videos, you're led on a 15-minute tour by Patrick Grennan, a distant Kennedy relative whose grandmother hosted the tea here for JFK. You're then free to peruse the barn, lined with Kennedy-in-Ireland memorabilia that details the history of the dynasty. While it's just a private home, anyone interested in the Kennedys will find it worth driving the long narrow lane to see.

Closure Alert: Closed in spring of 2012, this site is being refurbished and is scheduled to reopen with government assistance and funding in 2013. Call ahead to reconfirm prices and hours.

Cost and Hours: Likely €5; July-Aug daily 10:00-17:00; May-June and Sept Mon-Fri 11:30-16:30, closed Sat-Sun; by appointment after hours, in slow times, and Oct-April (no big deal, as it's their home); tel. 051/388-264, www.kennedyhomestead.com.

Getting There: It's four miles (6 km) south of New Ross near Dunganstown (look for sign off R-733, long one-lane road). Don't confuse the Kennedy Homestead with the nearby JFK Arboretum—a huge park with 4,500 species of trees and a grand six-county view. It's lovely if you like trees and plants, but there's no Kennedy history there.

▲▲Dunbrody Famine Ship

Permanently moored on a river in the tiny port of New Ross, this ship was built as a re-creation of similar vessels that sailed to America full of countless hungry Irish emigrants. The *Dunbrody* is a full-scale reconstruction of a 19th-century three-masted bark built in Quebec in 1845. It's typical of the trading vessels that originally sailed empty to America to pick up goods; during the famine, ship owners found that they could make a little money on the westward voyage. On board, extended families camped out for 50 days on bunk beds no bigger than a king-size mattress. Commonly, boats like this would arrive in America with only 80 percent of their original human  cargo (in worst cases, only 50 percent). Those who succumbed to "famine fever" (often typhus or cholera), were dumped overboard, and the ships gained their morbid moniker: "coffin ships."

Cost and Hours: €8.50, daily April-Oct 9:00-18:00, Nov-March 10:00-17:00, 45-minute tours go 2/hour, last tour starts one hour before closing, tel. 051/425-239, www.dunbrody.com.

Getting There: The *Dunbrody* is in New Ross, near the Kennedy Homestead. During work hours, you'll need to feed the parking meters in the lot (€1/hour, free on Sun).

Visiting the Ship: Your visit starts with an audiovisual presentation on the life Irish emigrants were leaving behind, followed by coverage about the building of the vessel. Then you'll follow an excellent guide on board the ship, encountering a couple of grumpy passengers who tell vivid tales about life aboard. At the end, you'll get a glimpse of the new life Irish immigrants would encounter in New York. Most arrived filthy (try skipping a shower for six weeks), illiterate, and often penniless.

Roots-seekers are welcome to peruse the computerized file of the names of the million immigrants who sailed on these ships from 1846 through 1865. Before you leave, check out the Irish America Hall of Fame, commemorating the contributions Irish men and women have made to US history (with short videos on Henry Ford and JFK, whose roots lie in this part of Ireland).

▲Irish National Heritage Park

This 35-acre wooded park, which contains an 1857 tower commemorating local boys killed in the Crimean War, features replicas of buildings from each era of Irish history. Ireland's countless ancient sights are generally unrecognizable ruins—hard to re-create in your mind. This park is intended to help out. You'll find buildings and settlements illustrating life in Ireland from the Stone Age through the 12th-century Norman Age. As a bonus, you'll see animal-skin-clad characters doing their prehistoric thing—gnawing on meat, weaving, making arrowheads, and so on.

WATERFORD

Your visit begins with a 12-minute video, followed by a 1.5-hour tour. During 13 stops, the guide explains various stages of Irish civilization. The highlight is a monastic settlement from the age when Europe was dark, and Ireland was "the island of saints and scholars." While you can wander around on your own, the place is a bit childish

(there's nothing actually old here), and only worthwhile if you take the included tour.

Cost and Hours: €8, daily 9:30-18:30, until 17:30 in winter, last entry 1.5 hours before closing, tel. 053/912-0733, www.inhp. com.

Getting There: It's clearly signposted on the west end of Wexford—you'll hit it before entering town on the N-11 Enniscorthy road.

National 1798 Centre

Located in Enniscorthy, this museum creatively tells the story of the rise of revolutionary thinking in Ireland, which led to the ill-fated rebellion of 1798. Enniscorthy was the crucial Irish battle-ground of a populist revolution (inspired by the American and French revolutions). The town witnessed the bloodiest days of the doomed uprising. The material is compelling for anyone intrigued by the struggles for liberty, but there's little more here than video clips of reenactments and storyboards on the walls.

Leaving the center, look east across the River Slaney, which divides Enniscorthy, and you'll see a hill with a stumpy tower on it. This is Vinegar Hill. The tower is the old windmill that once flew the green rebel flag. Drive to the top for the views that the rebels had of the surrounding British forces. The doomed rebels tried desperately to hold the high ground, with no shelter from the merciless British artillery fire.

Cost and Hours: €6; April-Oct Mon-Fri 9:30-17:00, Sat-Sun 12:00-17:00; Nov-March Mon-Fri 9:30-16:00, closed Sat-Sun; last entry one hour before closing, tel. 053/923-7596, www.1798centre.ie.

Getting There: Enniscorthy is 12 miles (19 km) north of Wexford town. The National 1798 Centre is the town's major sight and is well-signposted (follow the brown *Aras 98 Centre* signs).

KINSALE and COBH

County Cork, on Ireland's south coast, is fringed with historic port towns and scenic peninsulas. The typical tour-bus route here includes Blarney Castle and Killarney—places where most tourists wear nametags. A major mistake many travelers make is allowing destinations into their itineraries simply because they're famous from a song or as part of a relative's big-bus-tour memory. If you have the misfortune to spend the night in Killarney town (next door in County Kerry), you'll understand what I mean. The town is a sprawling line of green Holiday Inns and outlet malls littered with pushy shoppers looking for plastic shamrocks.

Rather than kissing the spit-slathered Blarney Stone, spend your time in County Cork, enjoying the bustling, historic maritime towns of Kinsale and Cobh.

Planning Your Time

Kinsale makes a great home base for a visit to the County Cork coast. From Kinsale, you can wade through the salty history of Cobh. Travelers approaching this region from Waterford can easily visit Ardmore and the Old Midleton Whiskey Distillery en route. If you're departing this region for the Ring of Kerry or Dingle, you can easily stop by Blarney Castle and Macroom en route.

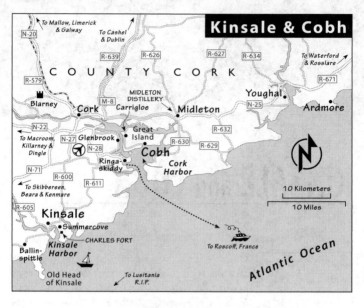

Kinsale

While nearby Cork is the biggest town in southern Ireland, Kinsale (15 miles south) is actually more historic and certainly cuter. It's delightful to visit. Thanks to the naturally sheltered bay barbed by a massive 17th-century star fort, you can submerge yourself in maritime history, from the Spanish Armada to the sailor who inspired Defoe's *Robinson Crusoe* to the *Lusitania*. Apart from all the history, Kinsale has a laid-back, Sausalito-like feel with a touch of wine-sipping class. Or, as a local told me with a wry smile, "Welcome to Happy Valley" (Eli Lilly manufactures much of its Prozac antidepressant just outside town).

Planning Your Time

Kinsale is worth two nights and a day. Spend the morning checking out one or two of the town's sights, and make sure to take Don and Barry's excellent Kinsale walking tour (at 11:15; some days also at 9:15). After lunch at the Fishy Fishy Café, head out to Charles Fort for great bay views and insights into British military life in colonial Ireland. On the way back, stop for a pint at the Bulman Bar. Finish the day with a good dinner and live music in a pub. Those on the blitz tour can give Kinsale four hours—see the fort, wander the town, and have a nice lunch—before driving on.

Orientation to Kinsale

Kinsale, because of its great natural harbor, is older than Cobh (Cork's harbor town). While the town is prettier than the actual harbor, the harbor was its reason for being. Today, Kinsale is a vibrant bustle of 2,200 residents. The town's long and skinny old center is part modern marina (attracting wealthy yachters) and part pedestrian-friendly medieval town (attracting scalawags like us). It's an easy 20-minute stroll from end to end.

Tourist Information

The TI is as central as can be, at the head of the harbor across from the bus stop (July-Aug Mon-Sat 9:15-18:00, Sun 10:00-17:00; March-June and Sept-Nov Mon-Sat 9:30-17:00, closed Sun; shorter hours Dec-Feb; tel. 021/477-2234, www.kinsale.ie). It has a free town map and brochures outlining a world of activities in the vicinity.

Arrival in Kinsale

Kinsale doesn't have a train station. The **bus** stop is on Pier Road, 100 yards behind the TI, by the gray swooping modern sculptures at the south end of town. Drivers should park the **car** and enjoy the town on foot. While Kinsale's windy medieval lanes are narrow and congested, parking is fairly easy. The most central lot is at the head of the harbor behind the TI (€2.60/2 hours, use pay-and-display machine, exact coins required, Mon-Sat 10:30-18:00, free on Sun and after 18:00). But there's a big, safe, free parking lot across the street from St. Multose Church at the top of town, a five-minute walk from most recommended hotels and restaurants. An even larger free lot is farther away, a 10-minute walk east of town by the fire station. Parking on the street is by pay-and-display machine (€1.20/hour, 2 hours maximum), except when it's free: before 10:30, after 18:00, or on Sundays. Outlying streets, a five-minute stroll from the action, have wide-open parking.

Helpful Hints

Rugby Crowds: The Kinsale Rugby Sevens Tournament draws dozens of teams and hundreds of loud and proud rowdy rugby fans on the first weekend in May (with its associated Bank Holiday Monday). If you're not up for the scrum, then scram.

Banking: The two banks in town are **Allied Irish Bank** on Pearse Street and **Bank of Ireland** on Emmett Street (both open Mon 10:00-17:00, Tue-Fri 10:00-16:00, closed Sat-Sun).

Internet Access: Your best bet is **Elasnik** (Kinsale spelled backwards), on Market Square across from the town museum

(€1.50/15 minutes, €5/hour, Mon-Sat 9:00-20:00, closed Sun, tel. 021/477-7356).

Post Office: It's on Pearse Street (Mon-Fri 9:00-13:00 & 14:00-17:30, Sat 9:00-13:00, closed Sun).

Laundry: Take your dirty duds to **Elite Laundry.** They'll do an average-sized load for about €12 (Mon-Fri 9:00-17:30, Sat 10:00-17:00, closed Sun, The Glen, tel. 021/477-7345).

Market: Check out the lively open-air market on Wednesdays from June through September (7:00-14:00) in the parking lot across from St. Multose Church. This location may change on short notice—ask at the TI.

Bike Rental: Mylie Murphy's rents bikes from a handy spot near the SuperValu (€10/day, Mon-Sat 9:30-18:00, closed Sun but arrangements can be made for pickup or drop-off, shorter hours in winter, tel. 021/477-2703). Paths good for biking or walking stretch around the harbor. For the best short-and-scenic route, bike past Charles Fort and two miles along the harbor to its mouth. Get other suggestions from the bike-rental shop.

Taxi: Kinsale Cabs has regular cab service and minibuses available (Market Square, tel. 021/477-2642 or 021/470-0100).

Tours in Kinsale

▲▲**Don & Barry's Kinsale Historic Stroll**—To understand the important role Kinsale played in Irish, English, and Spanish history,

join Don Herlihy or Barry Moloney on a fascinating 1.5-hour walking tour (€6, daily April-mid-Oct at 11:15, additional early-bird tour May-Sept Mon-Sat at 9:15, no reservation necessary, meet outside the TI, private tours possible, tel. 021/477-2873, www.historicstrollkinsale.com). Both guides are a joy to hear as they creatively bring to life Kinsale's past, place its story in the wider sweep of history, and make the stony sights more than just buildings. They collect payment at the end, giving anyone disappointed in the talk an easy escape midway through. Don't get hijacked by imitation tours that pretend to be "recommended by Rick Steves"—ask for Don or Barry. This walk is Kinsale's single best attraction.

Ghost Walk Tour—This is not just any ghost tour; it's more Monty Python-style slapstick comedy than horror. Two actors (Brian and David) weave funny stunts and stories into a loose history of the town, offering an entertaining 1.25 hours of fun on Kinsale's after-dark streets (€10, May-Oct daily at 21:00, leaves from Tap Tavern, call ahead to confirm, mobile 087-948-0910). You'll spend the first 15 minutes in the back of the Tap Tavern— time to finish your drink and get to know some of the group. This tour doesn't overlap with the more serious historic town walk described above.

Kinsale Harbour Cruise—Enjoy a 45-minute voyage around the historic harbor aboard the nimble little 50-passenger *Spirit of Kinsale*. The voyage offers sea-level views of both Charles and James forts, as well as seal and seafowl sightings with informative commentary from captain/historian/naturalist Jerome (€12.50, July-Aug daily at 11:00, 12:00, 14:00, and 15:00; June and Sept at 14:00 and 15:00; one sailing per day April-May and Oct, check website for schedule, departs from Pier Road in front of Acton's Hotel roughly 200 yards south of the TI, not necessary to book ahead but be at dock 30 minutes before departure, tel. 086/250-5456, www.kinsaleharbourcruises.com).

Sights in Kinsale

Remember that Kinsale's top sight is the town walking tour with Don and Barry (listed earlier, under "Tours in Kinsale.") But with extra time, there's much more to explore.

Kinsale Town Wander—Stroll the old part of town. The medieval walled town's economy was fueled by the harbor, where ships came to be stocked. The old walls defined the original town and created a small fortified zone following what is now O'Connell Street and Main Street. The windy Main Street traces the original coastline. Walking this street, you'll see tiny lanes leading to today's harbor. These originated as piers—just wide enough to roll a barrel down to an awaiting ship. The wall detoured inland to protect St. Multose Church, which dates from Norman times (back when worshippers sharpened their swords on the doorway of the church—check it out). After the James and Charles forts were built in the 1600s, the wall became obsolete—and also boxed in the town, preventing further expansion. The townspeople later disassembled the wall and used its ready-cut stones to build out the piers in the harbor.

What seems like part of the old center was actually built later on land reclaimed from the harbor. The town sits on the floor of a natural quarry, with easy-to-cut shale hills ideal for a ready supply of fill. Notice the mudflats in the harbor at low tide. Clear-cutting of the once-plentiful oak forest upriver (for shipbuilding and barrel-making) hastened erosion and silted up the harbor. By the early 1800s—when British ships needed lots of restocking for the Napoleonic Wars—Kinsale's port was slowly dying, and nearby Cobh's deepwater port took over the lion's share of shipping.

Kinsale

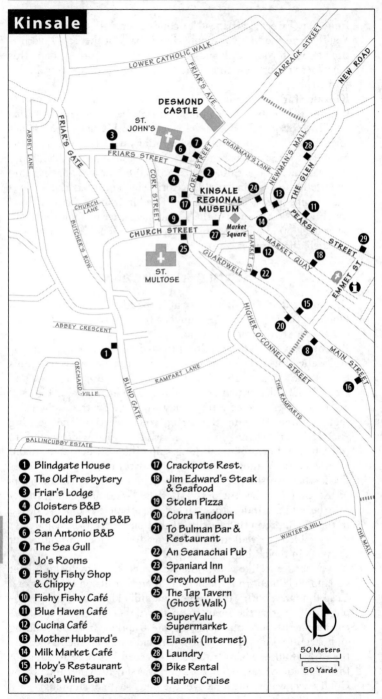

1 Blindgate House
2 The Old Presbytery
3 Friar's Lodge
4 Cloisters B&B
5 The Olde Bakery B&B
6 San Antonio B&B
7 The Sea Gull
8 Jo's Rooms
9 Fishy Fishy Shop & Chippy
10 Fishy Fishy Café
11 Blue Haven Café
12 Cucina Café
13 Mother Hubbard's
14 Milk Market Café
15 Hoby's Restaurant
16 Max's Wine Bar
17 Crackpots Rest.
18 Jim Edward's Steak & Seafood
19 Stolen Pizza
20 Cobra Tandoori
21 To Bulman Bar & Restaurant
22 An Seanachai Pub
23 Spaniard Inn
24 Greyhound Pub
25 The Tap Tavern (Ghost Walk)
26 SuperValu Supermarket
27 Elasnik (Internet)
28 Laundry
29 Bike Rental
30 Harbor Cruise

50 Meters
50 Yards

KINSALE & COBH

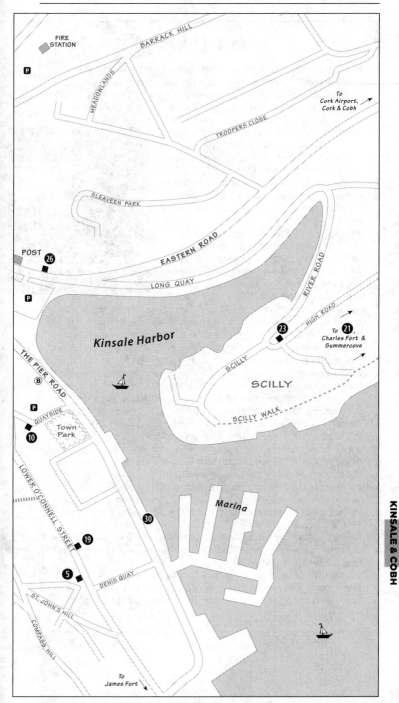

FIRE
STATION

BARRACK HILL

P

MEADOWLANDS

TROOPERS CLOSE

To
Cork Airport,
Cork & Cobh

SLEAVEEN PARK

EASTERN ROAD

POST
26

P

LONG QUAY

RIVER ROAD

Kinsale Harbor

23

HIGH ROAD

21

To
Charles Fort &
Summercove

THE PIER ROAD

B

SCILLY

SCILLY

P

QUAYSIDE

Town
Park

SCILLY WALK

10

LOWER O'CONNELL STREET

Marina

30

19

5

DENIS QUAY

ST. JOHN'S HILL

COMPASS HILL

To
James Fort

KINSALE & COBH

Kinsale's History

Kinsale's remarkable harbor has made this an important port since prehistoric times. The bay's 10-foot tide provided a natural shuttle service for Stone Age hunter-gatherers: They could ride it, at two miles per hour twice a day, for the eight miles up and down the River Bandon. In the Bronze Age, when people discovered that it takes tin and copper to make bronze, tin came from Cornwall (in southwest England) and copper came from this part of Ireland. From 500 B.C. to A.D. 500, Kinsale was a rich trading center. The result: Lots of Stonehenge-type monuments are nearby. The best is Drombeg Stone Circle (a one-hour drive west, just off R-597/Glandore Road).

Kinsale's importance peaked during the 16th, 17th, and 18th centuries, when sailing ships ruled the waves, turning maritime countries into global powers. Kinsale was Ireland's most perfect natural harbor and the gateway to both Spain and France—potentially providing a base for either of these two powers in cutting off English shipping. Because of this, two pivotal battles were fought here in the 17th century: in 1601 against the Spanish, and in 1690 against the French. Two great forts were built to combat these threats from the Continent. England couldn't rule the waves without ruling Kinsale.

To understand the small town of Kinsale, you need to understand the big picture: In about 1500, the pope divided newly discovered lands outside Europe between Spain and Portugal. With the Reformation breaking Rome's lock on Europe, maritime powers such as England were ignoring the pope's grant. This was important because trade with the New World and Asia brought huge wealth in spices (necessary for curing meat), gold, and silver. England threatened Spain's New World piñata, and Ireland was Catholic. Spain had an economic and a religious reason to defend the pope and Catholicism. The showdown between Spain and England for mastery of the seas (and control of all that trade) was in Ireland. The excuse: to rescue the dear Catholics of Ireland from the terrible treachery of Protestant England.

So the Irish disaster unfolded. The powerful Ulster chieftains Hugh O'Neill and Red Hugh O'Donnell and their clans had been on a roll in their battle against the English. With

Spanish aid, they figured they could actually drive the English out of Ireland. In 1601, a Spanish fleet dropped off 3,000 soldiers, who established a beachhead in Kinsale. After the ships left, the Spaniards were pinned down in Kinsale by the English commander (who, breaking with martial etiquette, actually fought in the winter). In harsh winter conditions, virtually the entire Irish clan fighting force left the north and marched to the south coast, thinking they could liberate their Spanish allies and win freedom from England.

The numbers seemed reasonable (8,000 Englishmen versus 3,000 Spaniards with 7,000 Irish clansmen approaching). The Irish attacked on Christmas Eve in 1601. But, holding the high ground around fortified and Spanish-occupied Kinsale, a relatively small English force kept the Spaniards hemmed in, leaving the bulk of the English troops to rout the fighting Irish, who were adept at guerilla ambushes but not at open-field warfare. (Today's visitors will be reminded of this crucial battle as they wander past pubs with names like "The 1601" and "The Spaniard"—see pub sign above.)

The Irish resistance was broken, and its leaders fled to Europe (the "flight of the Earls"). England made peace with Spain and began the "plantation" of mostly Scottish Protestants in Ireland (the seeds of today's Troubles in Ulster). England ruled the waves, and it ruled Ireland. The lesson: Kinsale is key. England eventually built two huge, star-shaped fortresses to ensure control of the narrow waterway, a strategy it would further develop in later fortifications built at Gibraltar and Singapore.

Kinsale's maritime history continued. Daniel Defoe used the real-life experience of Scottish privateer Alexander Selkirk, who departed from Kinsale in 1703 and was later marooned alone on a desert island, as the basis for his book *Robinson Crusoe.* (Selkirk was lucky to have been marooned when he was—his ship and all aboard later perished in a hurricane off Costa Rica.)

It was just 10 miles offshore from Old Kinsale Head that the passenger liner *Lusitania* was torpedoed by a German submarine in 1915. At the time, the liner was the fastest vessel on the seas (with a top speed of 25 knots). The primitive U-boats of the day were much slower (8 knots), giving *Lusitania*'s crew a false sense of security. Because World War I was the first conflict to employ submarine warfare, evasion tactics were largely untested. As the *Lusitania* sank, nearly 1,200 people were killed, sparking America's eventual entry into the war.

KINSALE & COBH

▲▲**Charles Fort**—Kinsale is protected by what was Britain's biggest star-shaped fort—a state-of-the-art defense when artillery made the traditional castle obsolete (low, thick walls were tougher for cannons to breach than the tall, thin curtain walls of a castle). The British occupied it until Irish independence in 1922. Its interior buildings were torched in 1923 by anti-treaty IRA forces to keep it from being used by Free State troops during the Irish Civil War. Guided 45-minute tours (which depart

on the hour—confirm at entry) engross you in the harsh daily life of the 18th-century British soldier. Before or after your tour, peruse the exhibits in the barracks and walk the walls.

Cost and Hours: €4, daily mid-March-Oct 10:00-18:00, Nov-mid-March 10:00-17:00, last entry 45 minutes before closing, a half-mile south of town in Summercove, tel. 021/477-2263.

After Your Visit: For a coffee, beer, or meal nearby, try the recommended Bulman Bar in Summercove, where the road runs low near the water on the way back to town (with small parking lot). And to see how easily the forts could bottle up this key harbor, stop for the grand harbor view at the high point on the road back into town (above Scilly, just uphill from The Spaniard pub). Or, from the fort, take the popular, scenic 45-minute Scilly Walk along the waterside back into town (see page 185).

James Fort—Older, overgrown, and filling a peaceful park, James Fort is Kinsale's other star fort, guarding the bay opposite Charles Fort. Built in the years just after the famous 1601 battle of Kinsale (when a Spanish force disembarked here—see the "Kinsale's History" sidebar), this fort is more ruined, less interesting, and less visited than Charles Fort. Its satellite blockhouse, which sits below the fort at the water's edge opposite Summercove, controlled a strong chain that could be raised to block ships from reaching Kinsale's docks (free, always open).

Getting There: Easily accessible by car or bike, it's two miles (3 km) south of town along Pier Road on the west shore of the bay (cross the bridge and turn left; you'll dead-end at Castle Park Marina, where you can park or leave your bike). It's up the hill behind the Dock pub.

▲**Desmond Castle**—This 15th-century fortified urban customs house has had a long and varied history. It was the Spanish armory during Spain's 1601 occupation of Kinsale. Nicknamed "Frenchman's Prison," it served as a British prison and once housed 600 prisoners of the Napoleonic Wars (not to mention earlier American

Revolutionary War prisoners captured at sea—who were treated as rebels, not prisoners, and chained to the outside of the building as a warning to any rebellion-minded Irish). In the late 1840s, it was a famine-relief center.

Today, the evocative little ruin comes with a scant display of its colorful history, as well as the modest two-room Museum of Wine, highlighting Ireland's little-known connection to the international wine trade. In the Middle Ages, Kinsale was renowned for its top-quality wooden casks. Developing strong trade links with Bordeaux, local merchants traded their dependable empty casks for casks full of wine. Later, Kinsale became a "designated wine port" for tax-collection purposes.

Cost and Hours: €3, Easter-Sept daily 10:00-18:00, closed Oct-Easter, last entry at 17:15, Cork Street, tel. 021/477-4855.

▲**Kinsale Regional Museum**—In the center of the old town, traffic circles the market, which later became a courthouse and is now the Regional Museum. Drop by at least to read the fun 1788 tax code for all Kinsale commercial transactions (outside at the front door). The modest museum is worth a quick visit for its fun mishmash of domestic and maritime bygones. It also gives a good perspective on the controversial *Lusitania* tragedy. Kinsale had maritime jurisdiction over the waters 10 miles offshore, where the luxury liner was torpedoed in 1915. Hearings were held here in the courthouse shortly afterward to investigate the causes of the disaster—which helped propel America into World War I—and to paint the German Hun as a bloodthirsty villain. Claims by Germany that the *Lusitania* was illegally carrying munitions seem to have been borne out by the huge explosion and rapid sinking of the vessel. But perhaps even more interesting, in the side room is the boot of the 8-foot-3-inch Kinsale giant, who lived here in the late 1700s.

Cost and Hours: Free, Wed-Sat 10:30-13:30, closed Sun-Tue, staffed by volunteers—hours can be erratic, Market Square, tel. 021/477-7930.

Sleeping in Kinsale

Kinsale is a popular place in summer for yachters and golfers (who don't flinch at paying $200 for 18 holes out on the exotic Old Head of Kinsale Golf Course). It's wise to book your room in advance. I've listed peak-season prices. These places are all within a five-minute walk of the town center.

$$$ Blindgate House, high up on the fringe of town behind St. Multose Church, offers 11 pristine rooms in fine modern comfort (Db-€100-140, Wi-Fi, tel. 021/477-7858, www.blindgate house.com, info@blindgatehouse.com, Maeve Coakley).

Sleep Code

(€1 = about $1.30, country code: 353, area code: 021)
S = Single, **D** = Double/Twin, **T** = Triple, **Q** = Quad, **b** = bathroom, **s** = shower only. Unless otherwise noted, breakfast is included and credit cards are accepted.

To help you easily sort through these listings, I've divided the accommodations into three categories, based on the price for a standard double room with bath:

$$$ Higher Priced—Most rooms €120 or more.
$$ Moderately Priced—Most rooms between €85-120.
$ Lower Priced—Most rooms €85 or less.

Prices can change without notice; verify the hotel's current rates online or by email.

$$ The Old Presbytery is a fine, quiet house a block outside the commercial district, with a goofy floor plan, plush lounge, and 10 pleasant rooms. Listed in most guidebooks, it has lots of American guests. The breakfasts are a delight, the rooms are stocking-feet cozy, and Noreen McEvoy runs the place with a passion for excellence (Db-€90-125, bigger Db-€115-140, biggest Db-€130-160, family Qb-€140-180, 2 Qb self-catering suites with no breakfast-€140-180, 10 percent discount with cash and this book in 2013, free Internet access and Wi-Fi, private parking, 43 Cork Street, tel. 021/477-2027, www.oldpres.com, info@oldpres.com).

$$ Friar's Lodge is a modern, shingled hotel, perched up the hill past St. John's Catholic Church. What its 18 spacious rooms lack in Old World character, they make up for in dependable quality. Three pleasant, self-catering cottages located up the slope behind their parking lot are great for families wanting their own space (Sb-€50-80, Db-€80-130, Tb-€100-160, Qb-€150, Wi-Fi, private parking, Friar Street, tel. 021/477-7384, www.friars-lodge.com, mtierney@indigo.ie).

$$ Cloisters B&B has four snug but bright and inviting rooms with a friendly atmosphere fostered by Orla Kenneally and Aileen Healy (Sb-€40-50, Db-€70-100, Tb-€110-125, Wi-Fi, 2 Friars Street, tel. 021/470-0680, www.cloisterskinsale.com, info@cloisterskinsale.com).

$ The Olde Bakery B&B makes you feel at home, with six quilt-bedded rooms, two friendly but mute mutts, and a jovial breakfast at the kitchen table cooked up by chatty Chrissie and beekeeper Tom Quigley. Their lovely self-catering house across the street is perfect for families (D-€75-80, Db-€80-85, cash only,

Wi-Fi, laundry service, 56 Lower O'Connell Street, tel. 021/477-3012, www.theoldebakerykinsale.com, oldebakery@gmail.com).

$ San Antonio B&B is a 200-year-old house with five rooms and a funky budget feel, lovingly looked after by owner Jimmie Conron. He occasionally joins other musicians to play at local pubs (Sb-€50-55, Db-€75-80, Tb-€100-110, cash only, tel. 021/477-2341, mobile 086/878-9800, jimmiesan@yahoo.ie).

$ The Sea Gull, perched up the hill right next to Desmond Castle, offers six retro-homey rooms. It's run by Mrs. Mary O'Neill, who also runs the Tap Tavern down the hill (S-€45, Db-€75-80, Tb-€110, 10 percent discount with this book in 2013, cash only, Cork Street, tel. 021/477-2240, marytap@iol.ie).

$ Jo's Rooms is a friendly place offering six cheap, spartan rooms in the center of town (Sb-€30-35, Db-€45-50, breakfast-€5-8 extra, cash only, Wi-Fi, small rooms with smaller double beds, 55 Main Street, mobile 087-948-1026, www.joskinsale.com, joskinsale@gmail.com).

Eating in Kinsale

Back in the 1990s, when Ireland was just getting its cuisine act together, Kinsale was the island's self-proclaimed gourmet capital. While good restaurants are commonplace in Irish towns today, Kinsale still has an edge at mealtime. Local competition is fierce, and restaurants offer creative and tempting menus. Seafood is king. With so many options in the ever-changing scene, it's worth a short stroll to assess your options. Reservations are smart, especially if eating late or on a weekend. Restaurant connoisseurs can check the menu details of Kinsale's most famous restaurants online (www.kinsalerestaurants.com).

Lunch

The following places are good for lunch; a few offer dinner as well.

Cafés: Meals at the **Fishy Fishy Shop & Chippy** are like eating in a fish market, surrounded by the day's catch and a pristine stainless-steel kitchen. The white-aproned staff hustle wonderful steaming plates of beautifully presented seafood to eager customers (€10-15 meals, Tue-Sat 12:00-16:00 for lunch only, closed Sun-Mon, across from St. Multose Church on Guardwell Street, tel. 021/477-4453). Look at the lobsters on death row in the tank and ponder this: Several years ago, a soft-hearted, deep-pocketed

Buddhist tourist bought up the entire day's supply of live lobster (worth more than €500) and set them free in the bay. They've re-filled the tank since.

Fishy Fishy Café is bigger, with more spacious seating (in-door, balcony, and terrace). It offers a wonderful menu (though a bit overpriced) with slightly longer hours, making it a good early-dinner option. Owner Martin Shanahan's cooking prowess has led him to host a weekly cooking show on Irish TV (daily 12:00-21:00, reservations recommended, Pier Road, tel. 021/470-0415).

Other inviting cafés are **Blue Haven Cafe** (daily, at Blue Haven Hotel on Pearse Street, with lots of old-time town photos) and **Cucina Café** (closed Sun, on Market Street).

Cheap and Cheery Lunches: Tiny **Mother Hubbard's,** packed with happy locals near Market Square, serves sandwiches or sal-ads with coffee for under €10 (daily 8:30-14:00). The **Milk Market Cafe**—right next door—offers burgers, pizza, and fish-and-chips. Or, gather picnic supplies at the **SuperValu** supermarket (Mon-Sat 8:00-21:00, Sun 8:30-21:00, Pearse Street).

Good Dinners in the Old Center

Hoby's Restaurant, a well-established favorite for seafood and duck, offers modern cuisine in a quiet, candlelit room. It's popular with people from Cork who've come down for a romantic night out (€25 three-course dinners, Mon-Sat 18:00-22:00, closed Sun, Main Street, tel. 021/477-2200).

Several other atmospheric wine-bar restaurants vie for your attention along the gently curving Main Street. **Max's Wine Bar** leads the pack, with subdued lighting and a menu that's big on quality seafood (€25 early-bird fixed-price meal before 19:30, open for lunch Wed-Sun 12:30-15:00, dinner Wed-Mon 18:30-22:30, closed Mon lunch and all day Tue, 48 Main Street, tel. 021/477-2443).

Crackpots sprouts distinctive ceramics created by owner Car-ole Norman in her romantically lit restaurant. Locally caught fish and organically grown veggies are menu staples, but don't over-look the duck, which gets rave reviews (great €25 three-course early-bird meal before 19:00, daily 18:00-22:00, 3 Cork Street, tel. 021/477-2847).

Jim Edward's Steak & Seafood keeps eaters happy in both the bar and the restaurant. Choose between the restaurant's mari-time setting (€18-25 meals, dinner only) or simpler food in the no-nonsense bar (€12-20 meals). Arrive early or wait. While cheaper and less gourmet than other Kinsale eateries, it's a high-energy place that's clearly a local family favorite for its decent steaks, sea-food, and vegetables (bar daily 12:30-22:00, restaurant daily 18:00-22:00, Market Quay, tel. 021/477-2541).

Stolen Pizza is classier than it sounds. With candlelit ambience and friendly service, it serves surprisingly good and reasonably priced (€13-18) pasta dinners and great pizzas (daily 18:00-21:00, 19 O'Connell Street, tel. 021/470-0488).

Ethnic Food: Walk around the old-town block for a full array of inviting international eateries (Thai, Chinese, and Indian). **Cobra Tandoori** is good for tasty Punjabi/Indian cuisine (€11-14 plates, daily 16:00-23:30, 69 Main Street, tel. 021/477-7911).

Fine Food near Charles Fort

Bulman Bar and Restaurant serves seafood with seasonal produce. The mussels are especially tasty; on a balmy day or evening, diners take a bucket and a beer out to the seawall. This is the only way to eat on the water in Kinsale. The pub, strewn with fun decor and sporting a big fireplace, is also good for a coffee or beer after your visit to the fort (€14 lunches, €20-25 meals upstairs in fancy restaurant, daily 12:30-21:30, 200 yards toward Kinsale from Charles Fort in hamlet of Summercove, tel. 021/477-2131).

Nearby: Without a car (and weather permitting), enjoy Kinsale's best 45-minute stroll back into town—with great harbor views—on the Scilly Walk pedestrian trail (trailhead on left after climbing 200 yards up the steep road from Bulman Bar; look for *Scilly Walk* sign and large cement slabs that block confused cars from entering the trail).

Pubs: Musical or Mellow

Kinsale's pubs are packed with atmosphere and live music (though not always traditional Irish). Rather than target a certain place, simply walk the area between Guardwell, Pearse Street, and the Market Square. Pop into each pub that has live music, and then settle in to your favorite. Several of the pubs wind deep into buildings. **An Seanachai** (SHAN-ah-key), meaning "storyteller" in Gaelic, is known for its ballad music (Main Street).

Irish music purists will be rewarded if they take the five-minute taxi ride (€7 one-way) out to the **Bulman Bar** near the base of Charles Fort. This is one of Kinsale's two best pubs for traditional Irish music sessions (Thu-Sat at 21:30, Sun at 17:00, get there early to ensure a seat, see listing above, tel. 021/477-2131). Otherwise, get your trad fix at the charmingly claustrophobic **Spaniard Inn,** a 10-minute walk out to the Scilly peninsula across the harbor from town. It fills the center of a hairpin turn on the crest of the peninsula. The darkly atmospheric interior is about the size of a rail car, with the long bar taking up half the space, so only about 10 seats get an actual view of the musicians (most nights at 21:30, you'll stand all night unless you arrive by 20:30, tel. 021/477-2436).

For conversation or an introspective pint with a newspaper,

I like the **Greyhound** (off Newman's Mall, behind the Milk Market Cafe)—no live music, just a scruffy, multichambered throwback with no pretenses. Another joint filled with characters who haven't changed in decades is the **Tap Tavern** (corner of Church Street and Guardwell). It's presided over by Mary O'Neill, the unofficial godmother of Kinsale, and her slyly humorous son Brian, who runs the town's recommended Ghost Tours. Check out the ancient holy well that came to light when they built their appealing back patio.

Kinsale Connections

Like many worthwhile corners of Ireland, Kinsale is not accessible by train. The closest train station is in Cork, 15 miles north. But buses run frequently between Kinsale (stop is on Pier Road, 100 yards behind TI, at south end of town) and Cork's bus station (14/day Mon-Sat, 4/day Sun, 50 minutes, €8 one-way, €11 round-trip).

In **Cork,** the bus station and train station are a 10-minute walk apart. The bus station (corner of Merchant's Quay and Parnell Place) is on the south bank of the River Lee, just over the nearest bridge from the train station (north of the river on Lower Glanmire Road).

From Cork by Train to: Dublin (hourly, 2.75 hours, www.irishrail.ie).

From Cork by Bus to: Dublin (every 2 hours, 4.5 hours), **Galway** (hourly, 4.25 hours), **Tralee** (hourly, 2.25 hours), **Kilkenny** (4-5/day, 2 direct, 3.5 hours). Bus info: Tel. 021/450-8188 or www.buseireann.ie.

Cobh

If your ancestry is Irish, there's a good chance that this was the last Irish soil your ancestors had under their feet. Cobh (pronounced "cove") was the major port of Irish emigration in the 19th century. Of the six million Irish who have emigrated to America, Canada, and Australia since 1815, nearly half left from Cobh.

The first steam-powered ship to make a transatlantic crossing departed from Cobh in 1838—cutting the journey time from 50 days to 18. When Queen Victoria came to Ireland for the first time in 1849, Cobh was the first Irish ground she set foot on. Giddy, the town renamed itself "Queenstown" in her honor. It was still going by that name in 1912,

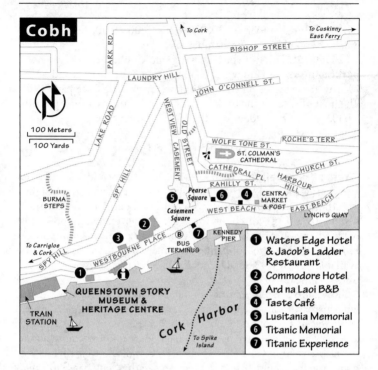

Cobh

To Cork

To Cuskinny →
East Ferry

BISHOP STREET

PARK RD.

LAUNDRY HILL

JOHN O'CONNELL ST.

WEST VIEW STREET

OLD STREET

CASEMENT

100 Meters

100 Yards

WOLFE TONE ST.   ROCHE'S TERR.

ST. COLMAN'S
CATHEDRAL

CATHEDRAL PL.   CHURCH ST.

HARBOUR HILL

RAHILLY ST.

LAKE ROAD

SPY HILL

BURMA
STEPS

To Carrigloe
& Cork

Pearse
Square

⑤   ⑥   ④   CENTRA
MARKET
& POST

WEST BEACH   EAST BEACH

Casement
Square

LYNCH'S QUAY

SPY HILL

WESTBOURNE PLACE

③   ②

B
BUS
TERMINUS

⑦   KENNEDY
PIER

① Waters Edge Hotel
& Jacob's Ladder
Restaurant

② Commodore Hotel

③ Ard na Laoi B&B

④ Taste Café

⑤ Lusitania Memorial

⑥ Titanic Memorial

⑦ Titanic Experience

①   ⓘ

QUEENSTOWN STORY
MUSEUM &
HERITAGE CENTRE

TRAIN
STATION

Cork Harbor

To Spike
Island

when the *Titanic* made its final fateful stop here before heading out on its maiden (and only) voyage...just over 100 years ago. To celebrate their new independence from British royalty in 1922, locals changed the town's name back to its original Irish moniker: Cobh.

Orientation to Cobh

Cobh sits on a large island in Cork harbor. The town's inviting waterfront is colorful yet salty, with a playful promenade. The butcher's advertisement reads, "Always pleased to meet you and always with meat to please you." Stroll past the shops along the water. Ponder the *Lusitania* memorial on Casement Square and the modest *Titanic* memorial nearby on Pearse Square.

A hike up the hill to the towering Neo-Gothic St. Colman's Cathedral rewards you with a fine view of the port. To get to the cathedral, walk behind the *Lusitania* memorial, go under the stone arch, and strut up steep Westview Street, passing the photogenic row of colorful houses on your right (nicknamed the "deck of cards" by locals). After panting your way to the top, turn right—you can't miss the cathedral steeple.

Tourist Information: The TI is in the Old Yacht Club on the harbor (Mon-Fri 9:30-17:30, Sat-Sun 13:00-17:00, tel. 021/481-3301, www.cobhharbourchamber.ie).

Helpful Hints: If you're driving into Cobh, there's a two-hour **parking** maximum anywhere in town (first hour free, second hour-€1, pay at machines on street; for more driving tips, see page 190). The **post office** is at the back of the Centra Market (Mon-Fri 9:00-17:30, Sat 9:00-13:00, closed Sun, West Beach Street).

Tours in Cobh

Titanic Trail Walking Tours—Michael Martin and his staff lead one-hour walking tours of Cobh that give you unexpected insights into the tragic *Titanic* voyage, Spike Island, and Cobh's maritime history (€9.50, €1 discount for Rick Steves readers—show this book when you pay, daily at 11:00, meet in lobby of Commodore Hotel, call ahead to confirm tour times in winter, private tours available, tel. 021/481-5211, mobile 087-276-7218, www.titanic.ie, info@titanic.ie.

Spike Island Boat Tours—Ireland's version of Alcatraz drips with history. It has been the site of a monastery, a smugglers' hide-away, the staging point for convicts being transported to Australia, a prison, and a military post. Michael Martin knows more about the island than anyone else; his boat-and-walking tour spends 1.5 hours on the island (€14.50, June-Aug daily, Sept Sat-Sun only, 14:00 sailing from Kennedy Pier subject to tides and 14-passenger minimum, allow 2.5 hours round-trip, must prebook—look for booth on waterfront opposite Taste café, same contact info as Titanic Trail tours, above). He also offers a 45-minute Titanic Trail harbor tour by boat, which points out important landmarks but does not stop on Spike Island (€9.50, June-Aug daily at 13:00).

Sights in Cobh

▲▲The Titanic Experience—It's stirring to think that this modest little port town was the ship's final anchorage—and the last chance to get off. Occupying the former White Star Line building where the *Titanic*'s final passengers boarded, this compact museum packs a decent punch as it recounts the story of the ship and its final moments.

Cost and Hours: €9.50, daily 9:00-18:00, Casement Square, tel. 021/481-4412, www.titanicexperiencecobh.ie.

Visiting the Museum: As you look off the back balcony into the harbor, note the decayed pilings in front of you. These once supported the old pier and represent the passengers' last chance to turn back. One lucky surviving crewman with a premonition did.

Inside the museum, you travel room to room with your host,

the ship's fourth mate, in audiovisual form. He meets you at the boarding dock, full of pride in the new vessel. He joins you in replicas of a posh first-class cabin and a no-frills third-class cabin before his commentary is interrupted by the sound of ice tearing at the hull. You then enter a small theater to view an animation that silently depicts the ship sinking in its steel-twisting, slow-motion ballet to the bottom (settling as two crunched hulls 70 yards apart and 12,000 feet deep).

The last stop is a room highlighting the luxurious ship's innovative firsts. It was one of the first equipped with a wireless "Marconi room" to send messages from sea to shore—or to other ships. *Titanic* was the first ever to issue an SOS message by Morse code. Another wall explains in grim detail the effects of hypothermia on the human body.

Before you leave, check out the list of 123 passengers who boarded the *Titanic* in Cobh. Your entry ticket has one of these passenger's names on it. See if you survived (you've got a 30 percent chance). A passenger with the same name as one of this book's co-authors is listed among the third-class passengers lost.

▲**The Queenstown Story**—Filling a harborside Victorian train station, this museum is an earnest attempt to make the city's history come to life. The topics—the famine, Irish emigration, Australia-bound prison ships, the sinking of the *Lusitania,* and the ill-fated voyage of the *Titanic*—are interesting enough to make it a worthwhile stop.

Coverage of the famous luxury liner was beefed up for the 100th anniversary year of the *Titanic*'s sinking. You'll learn about one priest who got off at Cobh. His photos of the early leg of the voyage are a priceless historical reference. But in general, the museum itself, while kid-friendly and engaging, is weak on actual historical artifacts. It reminds me of a big, interesting history picture book with the pages expanded and tacked on the wall.

Before departing, walk over to the Annie Moore statue next to the water, 25 yards from the front door. She emigrated from Cobh and was the first person to be processed through Ellis Island when it opened on January 1, 1892.

Cost and Hours: €7.50, May-Oct Mon-Sat 9:30-18:00, Sun 11:00-18:00; Nov-April Mon-Sat 9:30-17:00, Sun 11:00-17:00; last entry one hour before closing, Cobh Heritage Centre, handy café, tel. 021/481-3591, www.cobhheritage.com, info@cobhheritage.com.

Nearby: Those with Irish roots to trace can use the Heritage Centre's **genealogy search service,** located right across from the Queenstown Story ticket booth (€10 for 30 minutes of research assistance, email ahead to genealogy@cobhheritage.com).

KINSALE & COBH

Sleeping in Cobh

(€1 = about $1.30, country code: 353, area code: 021)
These hotels are all centrally located near the harbor, less than a
five-minute walk from the Queenstown Story.

$$$ **Waters Edge Hotel,** located 50 yards from the Queen-
stown Story, has 19 bright, modern rooms and a pleasant harbor-
view restaurant (Sb-€70-100, Db-€80-150, Tb-€100-160, Wi-Fi,
Yacht Club Quay, tel. 021/481-5566, fax 021/481-2011, www.
watersedgehotel.ie, info@watersedgehotel.ie).

$$$ **Commodore Hotel** is a grand 150-year-old historic land-
mark with 42 rooms. This place was once owned by the Humbert
family, wealthy Germans who opened it up to *Lusitania* refugees
after the 1915 sinking. Its high-ceilinged rooms creak with Victorian character (Sb-€57-65, Db-€114-130, Tb-€170-190, Westbourne Place, tel. 021/481-1277, fax 021/481-1672, www.commo
dorehotel.ie, commodorehotel@eircom.net).

$ **Ard na Laoi B&B** is a friendly place with five modest rooms
in a great central location (Sb-€50, Db-€60-70, Tb-€90-105, cash
only, 15 Westbourne Place, tel. 021/481-2742, www.ardnalaoi.ie,
info@ardnalaoi.ie, Michael O'Shea).

Eating in Cobh

I like the **Jacob's Ladder** restaurant in the Waters Edge Hotel.
Along the waterfront, you'll find a variety of pubs serving decent
grub. **Taste** is a hip little sandwich joint, a couple of doors down
from the *Titanic* Memorial. For picnic fixings, there's the **Centra
Market** (Mon-Sat 8:00-22:00, Sun 9:00-20:00, facing the water
on West Beach Street).

Cobh Connections

By Car: Driving to Cobh from Cork or Waterford, leave N-25
about eight miles (13 km) east of Cork, following little R-624 over
a bridge, onto the Great Island, and directly into Cobh.

Kinsale to Cobh is 25 miles (40 km), takes an hour, and involves catching a small ferry. Leave Kinsale north on R-600 toward
Cork. Just south of Cork and its airport, go east on R-613. You'll
follow little *car-ferry* signs, but they ultimately take you to the
wrong ferry (Ringaskiddy—to France). Instead, after you hit N-28,
take R-610 to Monkstown and then Glenbrook, where a (poorly
signposted) shuttle ferry takes you to Carrigloe on the Great Island
(€5, 5 minutes, daily 7:00-22:00). Once on the island, turn right
and drive two miles (3 km) into Cobh. In Cobh, follow the *Heritage Centre* signs to The Queenstown Story, where you'll find easy

parking at the museum (first hour free, second hour–€1, 2-hour maximum).

By Train: Cork's **Kent Station** has frequent short-hop service to both Cobh and Midleton, which are on separate lines (€6.50 round-trip, 25 minutes, usually depart on the hour, return on the half-hour, www.irishrail.ie).

By Plane: Cork Airport is a handy entry point into (or exit point from) Ireland. Located four miles south of Cork city (on N-27/R-600 to Kinsale, a 30-minute drive away), it offers connecting flights from London Heathrow on Aer Lingus, London Stansted on Ryanair, and Belfast on Aer Arann. More distant connections can be made from Munich, Amsterdam, Paris, Warsaw, and Málaga (tel. 021/431-3131, www.corkairport.com). Citylink airport buses run hourly to Kinsale (only 4/day on Sunday) and less frequently to other destinations, including Galway (6/day, 3.75 hours).

To sleep near Cork Airport, consider **$$ Radisson Blu Cork Airport** (Db–€89-109 Mon-Thu, €79-99 Fri-Sun, book online for best prices, tel. 021/494-7500, www.radissonblu.com).

More Sights in and near County Cork

These sights are convenient stops when connecting Kinsale and Cobh to Waterford (to the east) or the Ring of Kerry (to the west).

Between Waterford and Kinsale

If you're driving from Waterford (see previous chapter) to Cobh and Kinsale, you can easily visit these sights just off N-25 (listed roughly from east to west).

Ardmore

This funky little beach resort, with a famous ruined church and round tower, is a handy stop (just east of Youghal, 3 miles/5 km south of N-25 between Waterford and Cobh). A couple of buses run daily from Ardmore to Cork and to Waterford.

This humble little port town is just a line of pastel houses that appear frightened by the sea. Its beach claims (very modestly) to be "the most swimmable in Ireland."

The town's historic claim to fame: Christianity came to Ireland here first (thanks to St. Declan, who arrived in A.D. 416—15 years before St. Patrick...but with a weaker public-relations team). As if to proclaim that feat with an 800-year-old exclamation mark, one of Ireland's finest examples of a round tower stands perfectly intact, 97 feet above an evocative graveyard and a ruined church (noted for the faint remains of some early Christian carvings on its west facade). You can't get into the tower—the entrance is 14 feet off the ground.

An easy, scenic coastal loop hike (3 miles, 1 hour) leads from the parking lot of the ritzy Cliff House Hotel along the coast, eventually cutting inland and back into town (simple to follow, ask for free rudimentary map in newsstand at end of Main Street).

Sleeping in Ardmore: **$$$ Cliff House Hotel** is a died-and-gone-to-heaven splurge with 39 impeccably modern rooms, all with ocean views (Db-€195-225, Wi-Fi, tel. 024/87800, fax 024/87820, www.thecliffhousehotel.com, info@thecliffhousehotel.com).

$ Duncrone B&B, run by Jeanette Dunne, has four vividly colorful rooms (Sb-€40, Db-€60, Tb-€90, Qb-€120, cash only, Wi-Fi, half-mile outside town, up past the round tower, tel. 024/94860, www.duncronebandb.com, info@duncronebandb.com).

$ Roseville House is covered in ivy, with three pleasant rooms tended to by Pat Power (Sb-€35, Db-€60, cash only, in town 200 yards below the round tower, tel. 024/94430, mobile 087-248-7164).

Eating in Ardmore: The local favorite is **White Horses Restaurant** (Tue-Sun 11:00-22:00, closed Mon, Main Street, tel. 024/94040). For a fine lunch or dinner with cliff-perch views, check out the restaurant in the luxurious **Cliff House Hotel** (turn right at the coastal end of Main Street and drive up narrow lane to dead end, tel. 024/87800). **An Tobar,** the only pub in town, is down near the water.

▲Old Midleton Distillery

Sometime during your Ireland trip, even if you're a teetotaler, you'll want to tour a whiskey distillery. Of the three major distillery tours (this one, Jameson in Dublin, and Bushmills in Northern Ireland), the Midleton experience is the most interesting. After a 10-minute video, you'll walk with a guide through  a great old 18th-century plant on a 45-minute tour; see waterwheel-powered crankshafts and a 31,000-gallon copper still—the largest of its kind in the world; and learn the story of whiskey. Predictably, you finish in a tasting room and enjoy a free, not-so-wee glass. The finale is a Scotch vs. Irish whiskey taste test. Your guide will take two volunteers for this. Don't be shy—raise your hand like an eager little student and enjoy an opportunity to taste the different brands.

Cost and Hours: Tour-€13, daily 10:00-18:00, last tour at 16:00, 2/hour in summer, 3/day in winter, on-site cafeteria, tel. 021/461-3594, www.jamesonwhiskey.com.

Getting There: It's 12 miles (19 km) east of Cork in Midleton, about a mile off N-25, the main Cork-Waterford road. There's easy parking—just drive right into the distillery lot.

Between Kinsale and Killarney

If you're driving between Kinsale and the Ring of Kerry (see next chapter), you can easily visit these sights (listed from east to west).

Blarney Stone and Castle

The town of Blarney is of no importance, and the 15th-century Blarney Castle is an empty hulk (with little effort put forth to make it meaningful or interesting). It's only famous as the place of tourist pilgrimage, where busloads line up to kiss a stone on its top rampart and get "the gift of gab." The stone's origin is shrouded in myth (it was either brought back from the Holy Land by crusaders, or perhaps was part of Scotland's royal Stone of Scone). The best thing about this lame sight is the opportunity to watch a cranky man lower lemming tourists over the edge, belly up and head back, to kiss the stone while an automated camera snaps a photo—which will be available for purchase back in the parking lot. After a day of tour groups mindlessly climbing up here to perform this ritual, the stone is literally slathered with spit and lipstick.

The tradition goes back to the late 16th century, when Queen Elizabeth I was trying to plant loyal English settlers in Ireland to tighten her grip on the rebellious island. She demanded that the Irish clan chiefs recognize the crown, rather than the clan chiefs, as the legitimate titleholder of all lands. One of those chiefs was Cormac MacCarthy, Lord of Blarney Castle (who was supposedly loyal to the Queen). He was smart enough never to disagree with the Queen—instead, he would cleverly avoid acquiescing to her demands by sending a never-ending stream of lengthy and deceptive excuses, disguised with liberal doses of flattery (while subtly maintaining his native Gaelic loyalties). In her frustration, the Queen declared his endless words nothing but "blarney." Walking

KINSALE & COBH

back, you'll cross a stream littered with American pennies—as if the good-luck fairy can change them into euros.

While the castle is unimpressive, the gardens are beautiful, well kept, and picnic-worthy (if you're already there anyway). There are even some hints of Ireland's pre-Christian past on the grounds; you can see dolmens beside the trail in the forested Rock Close.

Cost and Hours: €12, Mon-Sat 9:00-18:30, Sun 9:30-17:30, later in peak season, shorter hours in winter, free parking lot, helpful TI, tel. 021/438-5252, www.blarney castle.ie.

Getting There: It's five miles (8 km) northwest of Cork, the major city in south Ireland. Looking for shopping galore? Adjacent Blarney Woolen Mills has it all (right next to the castle parking lot).

Macroom

This colorful, inviting market town is a handy stop between Cork and Killarney. The romanticized gateway where its ruined castle once stood was owned by the father of the William Penn who founded Pennsylvania. It overlooks an entertaining main square, where you'll find plenty of parking. The 2006 Irish Civil War saga *The Wind That Shakes the Barley* was filmed in this area. Macroom makes a good coffee or lunch stop midway between Cork and Killarney. The Next Door Café, in the Castle Hotel, serves a good, fast lunch.

Beal na Blath: Michael Collins Ambush Site

Irish history fans may want to make a brief detour en route from Kinsale to Macroom to visit nearby Beal na Blath (BALE-nuh-BLAH), where dynamic Irish rebel leader Michael Collins was assassinated on August 22, 1922, during the Irish Civil War. The site is not much more than a bend in a country road, with an Irish high cross on a raised platform to mark the spot. But it's Ireland's equivalent of Dallas' infamous "grassy knoll."

Take a moment to step out of the car and climb the steps onto the fenced platform. Next to the high cross, a plaque with a photo shows the road in 1922, with arrows approximating the position of the Collins convoy and the spots from which the ambushers fired.

Dusk was falling as the convoy carrying Collins to Cork came under attack. Collins could have ordered his driver to speed off, but chose instead to stand and fight. The identity of the anti-treaty IRA guerilla who fired the fatal shot (thought to have been an errant ricochet) is disputed. Following his death, Collins' body lay in state for three days at Dublin City Hall, drawing massive crowds. Although his pro-treaty Free State army later won the civil war, it's likely that modern Irish history would have been much different had Collins lived.

Getting There: Beal na Blath is just off N-22, the road that runs west from Cork to Macroom, and is easiest to find if you have a detailed Ordnance Survey atlas (it covers all tiny rural lanes). About halfway between Cork and Macroom, take R-585 south off N-22 through the tiny village of Crookstown. From Crookstown, follow *Beal na Blath* signs south for about a mile to the ambush site (well-marked, but be alert in case foliage on leafy rural lanes obscures a sign at a crossroads).

KENMARE and the RING OF KERRY

It's no wonder that, since Victorian times, visitors have been attracted to this dramatic chunk of Ireland. Mysterious ancient ring forts stand sentinel on mossy hillsides. A beloved Irish statesman maintained his ancestral estate here, far from 19th-century power politics. And early Christian hermit-monks left a lonely imprint of their devotion, in the form of simple stone dwellings atop an isolated rock crag far from shore...a holy retreat on the edge of the then-known world.

Today, it seems like every tour bus in Ireland makes the ritual loop around the scenic Ring of Kerry, using the bustling and famous tourist town of Killarney as a springboard. Killarney National Park is gorgeous and well worth driving through. But I prefer to skip Killarney town (useful only for its transportation connections). Instead, make the tidy town of Kenmare your home base, and use my suggestions to cleverly circle the much-loved peninsula—entirely missing the convoy of tour buses.

Kenmare

Cradled in a lush valley, this charming little town (known as Neidín, or "Little Nest," in Gaelic) hooks you right away with its rows of vividly colored shop fronts and go-for-a-stroll atmosphere. Its fresh appearance won it Ireland's "Tidy Town" award in 2000, and the nearby finger of the gentle sea feels more like a large lake (called the Kenmare River, just to confuse things). Far from the assembly-line tourism of Killarney town, Kenmare (rhymes with "chair") also makes a great launchpad for enjoying the sights along the road around the Iveragh (eev-er-AH) Peninsula—known to shamrock-lovers everywhere as the Ring of Kerry.

Planning Your Time

All you need in compact Kenmare is one night and a couple of hours to wander the town. Check out the Heritage Centre (in the back rooms of the TI) to get an overview of the region's history. Visit the Kenmare Lace and Design Centre (above TI, entry next door) to get a close look at its famously delicate lace. Hands-on access to an ancient stone circle is just a five-minute walk from the edge of town. Finish up by taking a peek inside Holy Cross Church to see the fine ceiling woodwork. Don't stay out too late in the pubs if you'd like to get an early start on the Ring of Kerry in the morning.

Orientation to Kenmare

Carefully planned Kenmare is shaped like an "X," forming two triangles. The upper (northern) triangle contains the town square (colorful markets Wed and Fri in summer), the adjacent TI and Heritage Centre, and a cozy park. The lower (southern) triangle contains three one-way streets busy with shops, lodgings, and restaurants. Use the tall Holy Cross Church spire to get your bearings (next to the northeast parking lot). Public WCs across the street are vile...if possible, wait to use one wherever you settle for lunch.

Tourist Information

The helpful TI is on the town square (July-Aug daily 9:00-19:00; May-June and Sept Mon-Sat 9:00-17:00, closed Sun; closed Oct-April; tel. 064/664-1233).

Helpful Hints

Banking: Bank of Ireland faces the town square, and **Allied Irish Bank** takes up the corner of Henry and Main streets (both open Mon 10:00-17:00, Tue-Fri 10:00-16:00, closed Sat-Sun).

Internet Access: You'll find three terminals inside the front window of **Murphy's Daybreak Supermarket** on Main Street (€1.50/30 minutes), and another three in the post office (€2/30 minutes).

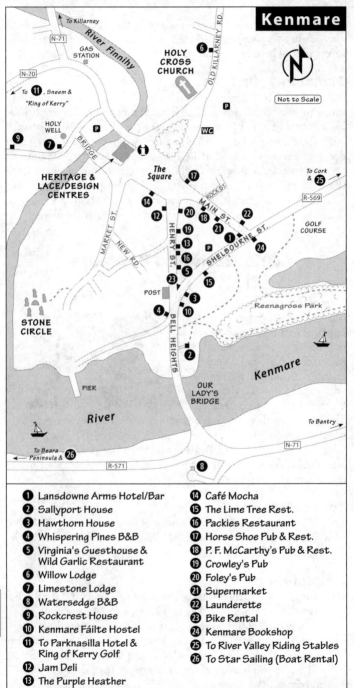

Post Office: It's located on Henry Street, at the intersection with Shelbourne Street (Mon-Fri 9:00-17:30, Sat 10:00-13:00, closed Sun).

Laundry: O'Shea's Cleaners and Launderette is across from the Lansdowne Arms Hotel, hidden in the back recesses of O'Shea's photography shop (Mon-Sat 9:00-18:00, Sun 14:00-18:00, tel. 064/664-0808).

Bookstore: Kenmare Bookshop is a cozy one-room cottage run by friendly John O'Connor (Mon-Sat 10:00-13:00 & 14:00-17:30, Sun 12:00-17:00, Shelbourne Street at roundabout across from Lansdowne Arms Hotel, tel. 064/664-1578).

Cultural Events: Carnegie Arts Center is a small-town venue offering a mixed bag of quality local concerts (€10-20), art exhibitions, and films. In summer (June-Aug), Thursday is movie night at 20:00 for €6 (www.carnegieartskenmare.ie, across Shelbourne Street from Lansdowne Arms Hotel, tel. 064/664-8701).

Bike Rental: Finnegan's Corner rents bikes and has route maps and advice on maximizing scenery and minimizing traffic (€15/day, €20/24 hours; Mon-Sat 9:30-18:30, July-Aug until 19:00; Sun 12:00-18:00, leave ID for deposit, office in gift shop at 37 Henry Street, across from post office, tel. 064/664-1083).

Parking: The town's two largest public parking lots (free overnight) cling to the two main roads departing town to the north (otherwise free street parking is allowed for 2 hours).

Taxi: Try **Murnane Cabs** (mobile 087-236-4353) or **Kenmare Coach and Cab** (mobile 087-248-0800).

Tours in Kenmare

Finnegan's Tours—This company runs a variety of local day tours, departing June through August from the TI at 10:00 and returning by 17:00. While this is little more than a scenic joyride, the tour guide gives a fun, anecdotal narration and generally makes three rest stops and one sightseeing stop (route depends on day: Ring of Kerry on Mon, Wed, and Fri; Ring of Beara on Tue; Glengarriff and Garnish Island on Thu; €30 for any tour, reserve a day in advance, can book private tours for small groups with enough notice, tel. 064/664-1491, mobile 087-248-0800, www.kenmarecoach andcab.com).

Sights in Kenmare

Heritage Centre—This museum, in the back rooms of the TI, consists of a series of storyboards and a model of the planned town. A 20-minute visit here explains the nearby ancient stone circle, the history of Kenmare's lacemaking fame, and the story of a feisty troublemaking nun (see the sidebar on Kenmare's history).

Cost and Hours: Free, May-Oct Mon-Sat 9:00-18:00, Sun 10:00-18:00, closed Nov-April, tel. 064/664-1233.

Kenmare Lace and Design Centre—A single large room (above the TI) displays the delicate lacework that put Kenmare on the modern map. From the 1860s until World War I, the Poor Clare convent at Kenmare was the center of excellence for Irish lacemaking. Inspired by antique Venetian lace, but creating their own unique designs, nuns taught needlepoint lacemaking as a trade to girls in a region struggling to get back on its feet in the wake of the catastrophic famine. Queen Victoria commissioned five pieces of lace in 1885, and by the end of the century tourists began visiting

Kenmare on their way to Killarney just for a peek at the lace. Nora Finnegan, who runs the center, usually has a work in progress to demonstrate the complexity of fine lacemaking to visitors.

Cost and Hours: Free, May-mid-Oct Mon-Sat 10:00-13:00 & 14:15-17:00, closed Sun and mid-Oct-April, tel. 064/664-2978, mobile 087-234-6998, www.kenmarelace.ie.

Ancient Stone Circle—Of the 100 stone circles that dot southwest Ireland (Counties Cork and Kerry), this is one of the biggest and most accessible. More than 3,000 years old, it may have been used both as a primitive calendar and as a focal point for rituals. The circle has a diameter of 50 feet and consists of 15 stones ringing a large center boulder (possibly a burial monument). Experts think this stone circle (like most) functioned as a celestial calendar—it tracked the position of the setting sun to determine the two solstices (in June and December), which mark the longest and shortest days of the year.

Cost and Hours: €2, drop coins into honor box in hut by entry when attendant is away, always open.

Getting There: It's a five-minute walk from the TI. From the city center, face the TI, turn left, and walk 200 yards down Market Street, passing a row of cute 18th-century houses on your right. Beyond the row of houses, veer right through an unmarked modern gate mounted in stone columns, and continue 50 yards down the

Kenmare's History:
Axes, Xs, Nuns, and Lace

Bronze Age people (2000 B.C.), attracted to this valley for its abundant game and fishing, stashed their prized axe heads and daggers in hidden hoards. Almost 4,000 years later (in 1930), a local farmer from the O'Sullivan clan pried a bothersome boulder from one of his fields and discovered it to be a lid for a collection of rare artifacts that are now on display in the National Museum in Dublin (the "Killaha hoard"). The O'Sullivans (Gaelic for "descendants of the one-eyed") were for generations the dominant local clan, and you'll still see their name on many Kenmare shop fronts.

Oliver Cromwell's bloody Irish campaign (1649), which subdued most of Ireland, never reached Kenmare. However, Cromwell's chief surveyor, William Petty, knew good land when he saw it and took a quarter of what is now County Kerry as payment for his valuable services, marking the "lands down" on maps. His heirs, the Lansdownes, created Kenmare as a model 18th-century estate town and developed its distinctive "X" street plan. William Petty-Fitzmaurice, the first Marquis of Lansdowne and landlord of Kenmare, became the British prime minister who negotiated the peace that ended the American War of Independence in 1783.

Sister Margaret Cusack, a.k.a. Sister Mary Francis Clare, lived in the town from 1862 to 1881, becoming the famous Nun of Kenmare. Her controversial religious life began when she decided to become an Anglican nun after her fiancé's sudden death. Five years later, she converted to Catholicism, joined the Poor Clare order as Sister Mary Francis Clare, and moved with the order to Kenmare. She became an outspoken writer who favored women's rights and lambasted the tyranny of the landlords during the Great Potato Famine (1845-1849). She eventually took church funds and attempted to set herself up as abbess of a convent in Knock. Her renegade behavior led to her leaving the Catholic faith, converting back to Protestantism, writing an autobiography, and lecturing about the "sinister influence of the Roman Church."

After the devastation of the famine, an industrial school was founded in Kenmare to teach trades to destitute youngsters. The school, run by the Poor Clare sisters, excelled in teaching young girls the art of lacemaking. Inspired by lace created earlier in Italy, Kenmare lace caught the eye of Queen Victoria and became much coveted by Victorian society. Examples of it are now on display in the Victoria and Albert Museum (London), the Irish National Museum (Dublin), and the US National Gallery (Washington, DC).

Beara: The Other Peninsula

This sleepy yet scenic wedge of land (just south of Kenmare) deserves honorable mention as a distant third choice after the Dingle and Ring of Kerry peninsulas. But locals rave about it like we would our home sports team. If you have the luxury of two nights in Kenmare, Beara is worth considering. If you don't have a full day to spare, you can spend a memorable half-day enjoying Garnish Island and Healy Pass, skipping the rest of the peninsula.

Garnish Island is a rocky island refuge, cloaked in garden splendor, plopped down in the corner of Bantry Bay. Crowned by a stout martello tower (a bunker built to repel feared Napoleonic invasions, free to climb for views), the gardens were the creation of a rich landlord, who turned the barren 37 acres into a lushly vegetated fantasy in the early 1900s. You'll meander past Italian reflecting pools, a Grecian temple framing views of a placid bay, and a walled garden nursery clad in roses. Pine-forested trails, punctuated with rhododendrons, connect it all. Boats depart from the well-marked pier in Glengarriff, about 18 miles (30 km) south of Kenmare, for the scenic 15-minute cruise past seals sunning on rocks to the island (boat-€12 round-trip, 2/hour; gardens-€4, March-Oct daily 9:30-17:00; tearoom, snacks, and WCs at island's pier; tel. 027/63116, www.harbourqueenferry.com).

A narrow, eight-mile mountain road (R-574) feels like a toboggan run as it squiggles over the peninsula's lumpy spine at **Healy Pass.** The views from the 1,000-foot summit make you marvel at the road-building skills of the famine-era workmen. The road linked the north coast (County Kerry) to the south coast (County Cork) to facilitate food-relief deliveries nearly 170 years ago. The barren, rocky landscape makes it easy to spot approaching cars (remember to look up on hairpin turns). Be cooperative by pulling over at wide spots to allow safe passage, and honk to alert other cars as you approach blind, rocky curves.

paved road. You'll pass the entry hut on your right. The stone circle is behind the adjacent hedge.

Holy Cross Church—Finished in 1864, this is Kenmare's grand Catholic church. It's worth visiting to see the ornate wooden ceiling with 10 larger-than-life angels (carved in Germany's Black Forest), which support the roof beams.

Horseback Riding—River Valley Riding Stables offers day treks for all levels of experience through beautiful hill scenery in the Roughty River Valley.

Cost and Hours: Adult-€20/hour, child-€15/hour, discounts for groups, open long hours, located about 7 miles east of Kenmare

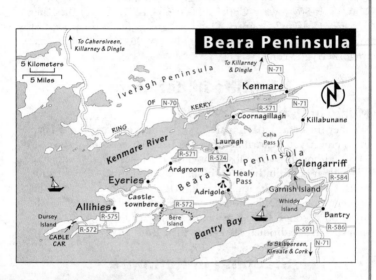

The rest of the peninsula is pastoral in the middle and edged with scenic cliffs near the tip. Ireland's only cable car connects the headland with mellow Dursey Island. Cattle can be transported on it (one at a time). The floor is slatted so water can be sloshed over the boards to wash out the dung. Castletownbere (on the south coast) is a fishing port with plenty of pubs for lunch. Allihies and Eyeries (on the north coast) are two of the most colorfully painted towns in Ireland, splattered with pastels and vivid hues.

off R-569 near Kilgarvan, tel. 064/668-5360, rivervalleystables@hotmail.com.

Boating and Hiking—Star Sailing rents boats, gives sailing lessons, and organizes hill walks. Hop on a small two-person sailboat (€45/hour) or canoe (€32/hour), or kick around in a kayak (€30/hour). Phone ahead to reserve boats or ask about hikes (daily 10:00-17:00, located 5 miles southwest of Kenmare on R-571 on Beara Peninsula, courtesy shuttle can pick you up in Kenmare, tel. 064/664-1222, www.staroutdoors.ie; adjacent Con's Restaurant is open daily 12:00-21:00).

Golfing—Another way to experience Ireland's 40 shades of green is to splurge on a scenic day on the links. The Kenmare Golf Club is right on the edge of town (€35 greens fee June-Aug, €25 Sept-May, on R-569 toward Cork, tel. 064/664-1291). Or try the Ring of Kerry Golf and Country Club (€40 greens fee, 4 miles west of town on N-70, prebook on weekends, tel. 064/664-2000, www. ringofkerrygolf.com).

Nightlife in Kenmare

Music in Pubs

Wander the compact Kenmare town triangle and stick your head in wherever you hear something you like. Music usually starts at 21:30 (although some pubs have early 18:30 sessions—ask at the TI) and ranges from Irish traditional sessions to sing-along strummers. **Crowley's** is an atmospheric little shoebox of a pub with an unpretentious clientele. **Foley's** jug-stacked window invites you in for a folksy songfest. The recommended Lansdowne Arms Hotel sponsors live traditional sessions in their **Bold Thady Quill Bar.**

Sleeping in Kenmare

$$$ Lansdowne Arms Hotel is the town's venerable grand hotel, with generous public spaces. This centrally located, 200-year-old historic landmark rents 26 large, crisp rooms (Sb-€50-85, Db-€80-150, Tb-€165-225; online discounts, music in pub until late on Fri-Sat, Wi-Fi, parking, corner of Main and Shelbourne Streets, tel. 064/664-1368, fax 064/664-1114, www.lansdownearms.com, info@lansdownearms.com).

$$$ Sallyport House, an elegant, quiet house with five rooms filled with antique furniture, has been in Helen Arthur's family for generations. Ask her to point out the foot-worn doorstep that was salvaged from the local workhouse and built into her stone chimney (Sb-€70-110, Db-€100-140, Tb-€130-160, closed Nov-mid-March, cash only, no kids, parking, 5-minute walk south of town before crossing Our Lady's Bridge, tel. 064/664-2066, www. sallyporthouse.com, port@iol.ie).

$$ Hawthorn House is a fine, modern, freestanding house with a lounge, a warm and classy hostess, and 10 comfy rooms sporting fine woodwork courtesy of Mr. O'Brien, who's also a carpenter. Its quiet residential location is just a block from all the pub and restaurant action (Db-€90-100, Tb-€120-140, Qb-€140, may be cheaper when slow, Wi-Fi, ample parking, Shelbourne Street, tel. 064/664-1035, www.hawthornhousekenmare.com, hawthorn@eircom.net, Mary and Noel O'Brien). Their two modern, self-catering apartments next door work well for those wanting to linger (weekly rentals).

$$ Whispering Pines B&B offers five rooms with sincere,

Sleep Code

(€1 = about $1.30, country code: 353, area code: 064)
S = Single, **D** = Double/Twin, **T** = Triple, **Q** = Quad, **b** = bathroom, **s** = shower only. Breakfast is included; credit cards are accepted unless otherwise noted.

To help you easily sort through these listings, I've divided the accommodations into three categories, based on the price for a standard double room with bath:

$$$ **Higher Priced**—Most rooms €100 or more.
$$ **Moderately Priced**—Most rooms between €75-100.
$ **Lower Priced**—Most rooms €75 or less.

Prices can change without notice; verify the hotel's current rates online or by email.

traditional Irish hospitality in a spacious house warmed by the presence of hostesses Mary Fitzgerald and daughter Kathleen (Sb-€60, Db-€76-84, Tb-€110, cash only, Wi-Fi, at the edge of town on Bell Height, tel. 064/664-1194, www.whisperingpineskenmare. com, wpines@eircom.net).

$$ Virginia's Guesthouse, ideally located near the best restaurants, is well kept by Neil and Noreen. Its eight rooms, in an older building, are freshly renovated, roomy, and appealing (Sb-€40-70, Db-€65-90, Tb-€90-130, Wi-Fi, upstairs above Wild Garlic Restaurant at 36 Henry Street, tel. 064/664-1021, www. virginias-kenmare.com, virginias@eircom.net).

$$ Willow Lodge, on the main road at the edge of town, feels American-suburban, with friendly hosts and seven comfortable rooms (Sb-€60-90, Db-€80-100, Tb-€120-150, Qb-€135-150, cash only, Wi-Fi, parking, 100 yards beyond Holy Cross Church, tel. 064/664-2301, www.willowlodgekenmare.com, willowlodge kenmare@yahoo.com, jovial Paul and talkative Gretta Gleeson-O'Byrne).

$ Limestone Lodge stands rock-solid beside a holy well, with four comfy rooms in a quiet location. Friendly hosts Maria and Siobhan Thomas are experts on Kenmare's famous lace (Sb-€35-45, Db-€60-70, Tb-€80-99, Qb-€100-132, cash only, Wi-Fi, tel. 064/664-2231, mobile 087-635-4503, www.limestonelodge kenmare.com, info@limestonelodgekenmare.com).

$ Watersedge B&B is a mile south of town, serenely isolated on a forested hillside and overlooking the estuary. The modern house has four clean, colorful rooms and a kid-pleasing backyard (Sb-€40-50, Db-€62-70, Tb-€75-85, cash only, Wi-Fi, parking, tel. 064/664-1707, mobile 087-413-4235, www.watersedge

kenmare.com, watersedgekenmare@gmail.com, Noreen and Vincent O'Shea). To get here, drive south over Our Lady's Bridge, bear left, immediately look for the B&B sign, and take the first right onto the road heading uphill. Go a couple of hundred yards up the bumpy paved road, then—at the end of the white cinder-block wall (on left)—turn right onto the gravel lane and drive a hundred yards to the dead-end. It's worth it.

$ Rockcrest House is secluded down a quiet, leafy lane, with six large rooms and a fine front-porch view (Sb-€35-50, Db-€60-80, Tb-€90-110, cash only, Wi-Fi; as you pass the TI heading north out of town, take the first left after crossing the bridge; tel. 064/664-1248, mobile 087-635-4503, www.visit-kenmare.com, info@visit-kenmare.com, Marian and David O'Dwyer). Ask about their two self-catering cottage rentals.

$ Kenmare Fáilte Hostel (fawl-chuh) maintains 40 budget beds in a well-kept, centrally located building with more charm than most hostels (dorm beds-€18 in rooms without bath, D-€44, Db-€52, T-€60, Tb-€69, Q-€76, Qb-€88, closed mid-Oct-April, Shelbourne Street, tel. 064/664-2333, mobile 087-753-197, run by Finnegan's Corner bike rental folks directly across street, www.kenmare.eu/failtehostel, failtefinn@eircom.net).

Sleeping in Luxury on the Ring of Kerry

$$$ Parknasilla Hotel is a 19th-century luxury hotel lost in 500 plush acres of a subtropical park overlooking the wild Atlantic Ocean. The tranquility, combined with old-fashioned service and Victorian elegance, makes this a good stop for anyone interested in luxuriating on the Ring of Kerry. Originally an old railroad hotel for Romantic Age tourists, in recent decades it has been a ritual splurge for Irish families and wedding groups (Db-€129-159 with breakfast, higher July-Aug, croquet, 19th-century diversions, park walks, see website for details and complex pricing scheme, tel. 064/667-5600, www.parknasillahotel.ie, info@parknasillahotel.ie).

Eating in Kenmare

This friendly little town offers plenty of quality choices. If dining, make a reservation or get a table early, as many finer places book up later in the evening during the summer. Pub dinners are a good value and easier on the budget, but pub kitchens close earlier than restaurants.

Lunch

Soup-and-sandwich lunch options abound. **Jam** is a handy deli that can make sandwiches or wraps to go for picnics (Mon-Sat 8:00-17:00, Sun 10:00-17:00, Henry Street). **The Purple Heather** has great salads and omelets (€9-15 meals, Mon-Sat 11:00-17:00, closed Sun, Henry Street, tel. 064/664-1016). **Café Mocha** is a basic €5 sandwich shop (Mon-Fri 9:00-17:30, Sat-Sun 10:00-17:00, on the town square, tel. 064/664-2133). **Murphy's Daybreak** supermarket is a good place to stock up for a Ring of Kerry picnic (Mon-Sat 8:00-22:00, Sun 9:00-21:00, Main Street).

Dinner

The Lime Tree Restaurant occupies the former Lansdowne Estate office, which gave more than 4,000 people free passage to America in the 1840s. These days, it serves delicious, locally caught seafood dishes in a modern yet cozy dining hall. It's wise to reserve ahead (€18-27 meals, April-Oct daily 18:30-21:30, closed Nov-March, Shelbourne Street, tel. 064/664-1225).

Packies is a popular bistro that has a leafy, low-light interior and cottage ambience and serves traditional cuisine with French influence. Their seafood gets rave reviews (€23-32 meals, Mon-Sat 18:00-22:00, closed Sun, reservations wise, Henry Street, tel. 064/664-1508).

Wild Garlic Restaurant has a jazz-mellowed, elegant ambience and creatively presented gourmet dishes. Given the Indian, Japanese, and American influences, there's always a good vegetarian entrée (€16-26 meals, daily 18:00-22:00, reservations a good idea, 36 Henry Street, tel. 064/664-2383).

Horse Shoe Pub and Restaurant, specializing in steak and spareribs, somehow turns rustic farm-tool decor into a romantic candlelit sanctuary (€17-25 meals, Mon-Fri 12:00-15:00 & 17:00-22:00, Sat-Sun 17:00-22:00, Main Street, tel. 064/664-1553).

P. F. McCarthy's Pub and Restaurant, which feels like a sloppy saloon, serves reasonable salad or sandwich lunches and filling dinner fare. Their €15 barbecued-ribs meal is a fine value (€14-22 meals, Mon-Sat 10:30-21:00, closed Sun, 14 Main Street, tel. 064/664-1516).

Kenmare Connections

Kenmare has no train station (the nearest is in Killarney, 20 miles away) and only a few bus connections (www.buseireann.ie). Most buses transfer in Killarney.

From Kenmare by Bus to: Killarney (3/day, 45 minutes), **Tralee** (3/day, 2 hours), **Dingle** (3/day, 3 hours, change in Killarney), **Kinsale** (4/day, 4-5 hours, 2 changes), **Dublin** (3/day, 7.5 hours, change in Killarney and Limerick).

Near Kenmare

These attractions are near Kenmare, at the eastern (inland) end of the Ring of Kerry. If you're approaching the region from Kinsale and Cobh, drive through Killarney and visit Muckross House and Muckross Traditional Farms (near the lakes), as well as Kissane Sheep Farm (in the mountains), the day before you make the big Ring of Kerry loop. This plan allows you to get an early start from Kenmare and helps you avoid all the bus traffic on the Ring.

Killarney

Killarney is a household word among American tourists, and it seems to be on every big-bus tour itinerary. Springing from the bus and train station of this thriving regional center are a few colorful streets lined with tourist-friendly shops and restaurants. Killarney's suburbs sprawl with vast hotels that, except for the weather, feel more like Nebraska than Ireland. Killarney's elegant Neo-Gothic church stands tall, as if to say the town existed and mattered long before tourism. But then you realize it dates from 1880...just about when Romantic Age tourism here peaked. For non-shoppers, Killarney's charm is its location at the doorstep of lush Killarney National Park. And for most tour organizers, it's the logical jumping-off point for excursions around the famous Ring of Kerry peninsula.

If you're traveling in the region without a car, you'll have to stop here. The Killarney bus and train stations flank the big, modern Killarney Outlet Centre mall. (In some touristy parts of Ireland, like this one, every other shopping center is called an "outlet"—implying factory-direct values.) If you have a layover between connections, walk five minutes straight out from the front of the mall, and check out Killarney's shop-lined High Street and New Street. The **TI** is a 15-minute walk from the train station, on Beech Street.

Killarney Connections

From Killarney Around the Ring of Kerry: Bus Éireann drives the loop around the Ring of Kerry from Killarney—suitable for a quick peek. While it generally stops only long enough to pick up and drop off travelers en route, there is a 50-minute stop in Sneem (€23, daily July-mid-Sept, departs the Killarney bus station at 12:45 and returns to Killarney at 17:45, no reservation needed, www.buseireann.ie). You can catch this same bus from Tralee at 11:50, returning to Tralee by 18:45 (€25).

By Bus to: Kenmare (3/day, 45 minutes), **Tralee** (hourly, 40 minutes), **Dingle** (5/day, 1.5-2 hours, 2 direct, 3 with change in

Tralee), **Shannon Airport** (6/day, 3.5 hours), **Dublin** (every 2 hours, 6 hours, change in Limerick). The bus station has a left-luggage desk. For bus schedules, call 01/836-6111 or visit www.buseireann.ie.

By Train to: Tralee (8/day, 30 minutes), **Cork** (every 2 hours, 1.5 hours, most with change in Mallow), **Waterford** (2/day, 3 hours), **Dublin** (every 2 hours, 6/day on Sun, 3.5 hours, 1 direct in morning, rest with change in Mallow). For train schedules, call 01/836-6222 or visit www.irishrail.ie.

To Muckross House: There's no bus service. You can hike 30 minutes (get directions from TI), rent a bike, hire a horse buggy, or catch a cab (€12).

Muckross House and Farms

Perhaps the best stately Victorian home you'll see in the Republic of Ireland, Muckross House (built in 1843 and worth ▲▲) is magnificently set at the edge of Killarney National Park. It's adjacent to Muckross Farms, a fascinating open-air farm museum that shows rural life in the 1930s (worth ▲). Besides the mansion and farms, this regular stop on the tour-bus circuit also includes a fine garden idyllically set on a lake and an information center for the national park. The poignant juxtaposition of the magnificent mansion and the humble farmhouses illustrates in a thought-provoking way the vast gap that once separated rich and poor in Ireland.

Cost and Hours: House-€7, farms-€7.50, €12 combo-ticket includes both (Heritage Cards not accepted for farms). House open daily 9:00-17:30, July-Aug until 19:00, shorter hours in winter, last entry one hour before closing. Farms open daily June-Aug 10:00-19:00, May and Sept daily 13:00-18:00, mid-March-April and Oct Sat-Sun only 13:00-18:00, closed Nov-Feb. Tel. 064/667-0144.

Tours: The only way to see the interior of the house is with the 45-minute guided tour, which gives more meaning to your visit (included with admission, offered frequently throughout the day). Book your tour as soon as you arrive (they can fill up). Then enjoy a walk in the gardens until your tour begins.

Getting There: Muckross House is conveniently located for a break on the long ride from Kinsale or Cashel to Dingle or Kenmare. From Killarney, follow signs to Kenmare, where you'll find Muckross House three miles (5 km) south of town. As you approach from Killarney, you'll see a small parking lot two miles before the actual parking lot. This is used by horse-and-buggy bandits to hoodwink tourists into thinking they have to pay to clip-clop to the house. Giddy-up on by to find a big, safe, and free parking lot right at the mansion.

Visiting the House and Farms: A visit to **Muckross House** takes you back to the Victorian period—the 19th-century boom

time, when the sun never set on the British Empire and the Industrial Revolution (born in England) was chugging the world into the modern age. Of course, Ireland was a colony back then, with big-shot English landlords. During the Great Potato Famine of 1845-1849, most English gentry lived very well—profiting off the export of their handsome crops to lands with greater buying power—while a third of Ireland's population starved.

Muckross House feels lived-in (and it was, until 1933). Its fine Victorian furniture is cluttered around the fireplace under Waterford crystal chandeliers and lots of antlers. You'll see Queen Victoria's bedroom (ground floor, since she was afraid of house fires). Though the owners of the house spent a couple of years preparing for the royal visit in 1861, nearly bankrupting themselves in the process, the queen stayed only three nights.

The house exit takes you through an **information center** for Killarney National Park, with a relaxing 15-minute video on "Ireland's premier national park," featuring lots of geology, flora, and fauna (free, shown on request).

The **garden** is a hit for those with a green thumb, and a €1.50 guide booklet makes the nature trails interesting. A bright, modern cafeteria (with indoor/outdoor seating) faces the garden. The adjacent crafts shop shows weaving and pottery-making in action.

Muckross Traditional Farms consists of six different vintage farmhouses. The farms are strung along a mile-long road, with an old bus shuttling those who don't want to hike (free, 4/hour).

For those interested in Irish farm life from the 1920s until electricity arrived in 1955, this is a great experience—but only if you engage the attendants in conversation. Each farm is staffed by a Kerry local who enjoys telling tales of life on the farm in the old days. When they first got electricity in 1955, they'd pull on their rubber Wellington boots for safety and nervously "switch it on." Poor farmers could afford electricity only with the help of money from relatives in America. They'd have one bulb hanging from the ceiling and, later, one plug for a hot pot. Every table had a Sacred Heart of Jesus shrine above it. The plug went directly below it. No one dreamed of actually heating the house with electricity. Children slept six to a bed, "three up and three down...feet in your face." You'll learn what happened when you had the only radio in the area, and how one flagstone on the mud floor was enough for the fiddler and dancer to set the beat. Probe with your questions...get personal.

From Muckross House to Kissane Sheep Farm: As you drive south on N-71, Torc Waterfall is a couple of miles past Muckross House (a 10-minute walk from the parking lot, through one of the oldest oak forests in Ireland). Driving farther, you pass the Black Valley, which separates you from a ridge with the highest point in Ireland (3,600 feet). This remote valley was the last chunk of Ireland to get electricity, in 1978. The scenic pullout called Ladies View is worth a stop.

▲▲Kissane Sheep Farm

Animal lovers will enjoy an hour's visit to this hardworking 2,500-acre Irish farm, perched on a scenic slope above the Black Valley. John Kissane, whose family has raised sheep here for five generations, gives hands-on demonstrations of sheep shearing. His Dutch wife Anne explains the process and invites you to touch the pile of fresh wool afterward. You can feel the lanolin, which acts as natural waterproofing for the sheep and is extracted from the wool to sell to pharmaceutical firms (synthetic manufacturing has driven the price of wool so low, it's not worth selling otherwise). But the highlight of any visit is the demonstration of sheepherding by the highly alert family dogs (Border collies trained here since puppyhood). John commands the dogs from afar using an array of verbal calls and hand signals.

Note that this is a working farm. Call ahead for demo times (often around 11:00 and 14:00), or check the website for the current schedule, which may change depending on necessary farm work.

Cost and Hours: €7, most afternoons June-Aug, April-May and Sept by appointment only, closed Oct-March, on N-71 between Ladies View and Moll's Gap, tel. 064/663-4791, www.kissanesheepfarm.com.

From Kissane Sheep Farm to Kenmare: Continue driving south on N-71. Going over Moll's Gap (WCs and Avoca Café beside parking lot), you'll descend into Kenmare. The rugged, bare rock on either side of the road was rounded and smoothed by the grinding action of thousands of years of glaciers. In the distance to the north (on your right) you can see the Gap of Dunloe, a perfect example of a U-shaped glacial valley notch.

Ring of Kerry

The Ring of Kerry (the Iveragh Peninsula) has been the perennial breadwinner of Irish tourism for decades now. Lassoed by a winding coastal road (the Ring), this mountainous, lake-splattered region comes with breathtaking scenery and the highest peak in Ireland. While a veritable fleet of big, tourist-laden buses circles it each day, they generally stay together and seem to stop at the same handful of attractions. Therefore, if you avoid those places at rush hour, the Ring feels remarkably unspoiled and dramatically isolated. Clever motorists, armed with a good map and a reliable alarm clock, can sidestep the crowds and enjoy one of the most rewarding days in Ireland.

Planning Your Time

More than twice the size of the Dingle Peninsula (see next chapter) and backed by a muscular tourism budget that promotes every sight as a "must-see," the Iveragh Peninsula can seem overwhelming. Be selective, and don't let them pull the turf over your eyes.

By Car: You can explore the Ring (primarily on N-70) in one satisfying day. Travelers linking overnights in Kinsale and Dingle can insert a night between them in Kenmare (a good base for enjoying the best of the Ring of Kerry). If visiting Muckross House and Kissane Sheep Farm (on the mountainous section of the Ring of Kerry), do so in the afternoon before arriving in Kenmare, to save all of the following day for the rest of the Ring.

Tackling the Kinsale-to-Dingle drive plus the Ring of Kerry all in the same day is doable with an early start (no later than 8:30)—but you add about two hours of driving just to reach the actual Ring, meaning you have little time to stop and enjoy what you came here to see. You also run the risk of meeting the big-bus convoy head on (see "Driving the Ring of Kerry," below).

If you're considering a boat trip out to the desperately remote and evocative island of Skellig Michael, you'll need to add another day to allow for an overnight in the Portmagee area...and hope for good weather.

By Public Transportation: You have three options for seeing the Ring of Kerry without a car, none of which is as enjoyable as driving the loop yourself: minibus tour from Kenmare (see page 199); big-bus tour from Killarney (TI tel. 064/663-1633); or public bus from Killarney (see page 208).

The Ring of Kerry vs. the Dingle Peninsula

If I had to choose one spot to enjoy the small-town charm of traditional Ireland, it would be Dingle and its history-laden scenic peninsula. But the Ring of Kerry—a much bigger, more famous, and more touristed peninsula just to its south—is also great to visit. If you go to Ireland and don't see the famous Ring of Kerry, your uncle Pat will never forgive you. Here's a comparison to help with your itinerary planning.

Both peninsulas come with a scenic loop drive. Dingle's is 30 miles. The Ring of Kerry is 120 miles. Both loops come with lots of megalithic wonder. Dingle's prehistory is more intimate, with numerous little evocative stony structures. The Ring of Kerry's prehistory shows itself in three massive ring forts—far bigger than anything on Dingle.

Dingle town is the perfect little Irish burg—alive with traditional music pubs, an active fishing harbor, and the sturdy cultural atmosphere of an Irish-speaking Gaeltacht region. You can easily spend three fun nights here. In comparison, Kenmare (the best base for the Ring of Kerry loop) is pleasant but forgettable. Those spending a night on the west end of the Ring of Kerry find a rustic atmosphere in Portmagee (the base for a cruise to magical Skellig Michael).

Near Dingle, the heather-and-moss-covered Great Blasket Island and the excellent Great Blasket Centre offer insights into the storytelling traditions and simple lives of hardy fisherfolk who—until 60 years ago—lived just off the tip of the Dingle Peninsula. Skellig Michael is a brutally rugged and remote chunk of rock in the Atlantic off the tip of the Ring of Kerry, with evocative medieval stone ruins of its long-gone hermit-monks. It's a world-class sight, but the Skellig Experience Centre near Portmagee on the mainland is less impressive compared to Dingle's Great Blasket Centre.

Muckross House, with its fascinating open-air farmhouse museum and beautiful lake views of Killarney National Park, is on the eastern side of the Ring of Kerry. It's also an efficient and natural stop for those driving between Kinsale and Dingle—so you can see it regardless of which scenic peninsula drive you take.

Both regions are beyond the reach of the Irish train system and require a car or spotty bus service to access. Both offer memorable scenery, great restaurants, warm B&B hospitality, and similar prices. The bottom line: With limited time, choose Dingle. If you have a day or two to spare, the Ring of Kerry is also a delight.

Driving the Ring of Kerry (Made Less Scary)

On a one-day visit to the Ring, I'd leave Kenmare by 8:30 and head clockwise (against the prevailing tour-bus traffic). Allow time for stops at Staigue Ring Fort (45 minutes) and Derrynane House (1 hour), and get to Waterville before noon. To entirely miss the chain of tour buses, which slithers (like a python swallowing a pig) counterclockwise around the Ring, get to Waterville by 11:00; shortly after that, leave the main drag for the Skellig Ring (with a road that's too narrow for big buses). Plan to have lunch out on the Skellig Ring, either at St. Finian's Bay, with an ideal picnic beach, or in the fun café at the Skelligs Chocolate Factory (200 yards from St. Finian's Bay). By the time you rejoin the main route, the python has slunk by. On the last half of the route, there are two more hour-long stops: the Skellig Experience Centre (near Portmagee) and two additional big ring forts (near Cahersiveen). For a stop-by-stop description of this route, see my self-guided driving tour, later.

The only downside of going against all the bus traffic is that, on the narrow parts of the Ring road, buses always have the right-of-way. It's up to you to back up to the nearest wide spot in the road to let a less-nimble bus get through a tight curve. But every year I notice that the road has been improved and bottlenecks widened. There are also lots of scenic-view pullouts. With an early start, you can avoid these hassles: On my last circuit, I got to  Waterville by 11:00, from where I slipped happily into the bus-free Skellig Ring...and didn't have to pass a single bus all day.

Smart drivers equip themselves with a good map before driving the Ring of Kerry loop. If you don't have one already, pick up the *Complete Road Atlas of Ireland* by Ordnance Survey (€10, sold in most TIs and bookstores in Ireland). The *Fir Tree Aerial* series provides a useful map that covers both the Iveragh (Ring of Kerry) and Dingle Peninsulas, giving you a bird's-eye feel for the terrain (€7, sold in many TIs and bookstores in County Kerry).

The flat, inland, northeastern section of the Ring, from Killorglin to Killarney on N-72, is entirely skippable. Tank up before leaving, as gas in Kenmare is cheaper than out on the Ring.

Self-Guided Driving Tour

The Ring of Kerry

Here's a sightseeing tip sheet for my preferred clockwise route, kilometer by kilometer. If you do any exploring, you'll likely get hopelessly off pace, but the kilometer references still help—just do the arithmetic to figure out how far various stops are from each other. Several of these stops are explained in far greater detail later in this chapter, in the same order in which they're listed here. To understand your options, read the rest of this chapter before you start on your tour.

0 km: Leave Kenmare.

17.6 km: On the right is Glacier Lake, with a long, smooth limestone "banister" carved by a glacier 10,000 years ago.

22.8 km: The recommended Parknasilla Hotel—a posh 19th-century hotel—is a great stop for tea and scones.

26 km: Visit the town of Sneem.

40.4 km: Turn off for the Staigue Ring Fort.

41.5 km: On the left, enjoy great views of the Beara Peninsula beyond a ruined hospital with IRA ties (it was funded about 1910 by a local Englishwoman sympathetic to the Irish Republican cause). No one wants to touch these ruins today, out of fear of "kicking up a beehive."

43.5 km: Carroll's Cove has a fine beach with some of the warmest water in Ireland, grand views of Kenmare Bay, a local trailer park, and "Ireland's only beachside bar."

46.4 km: Take the turnoff for Derrynane House (home of Daniel O'Connell).

50.4 km: Enjoy brilliant views for the next two kilometers to Coomakesta Pass.

52.4 km: The Coomakesta Pass lookout point (700-foot altitude) offers grand vistas in both directions.

54.5 km: Watch for fine views of the Skellig Islands.

56.4 km: Notice the ruins of famine villages on both sides of the road.

59.6 km: In the town of Waterville, you'll see a sculpture of Charlie Chaplin on the left. Waterville is also home to the Butler Arms Hotel—a fine stop for tea and scones in its Charlie Chaplin room (with lots of photos of the silent-film icon and his young wife frolicking as they lived well in Ireland).

65 km: After rejoining the main road and turning left, cross the small bridge that's locally famous for salmon fly-fishing. Take the first left (R-567) for the Skellig Ring loop (follow brown *Skellig Ring* signs through Ballinskelligs, and then scenically to Portmagee). At this point, you've left the big-bus route.

75 km: St. Finian's Bay lies about halfway around, with a pleasant little picnic-friendly beach that's recently been discovered by surfers (no WCs). Just before the bay is the small, modern Skelligs Chocolate Factory, with the handiest café on the Skellig Ring (Mon-Fri 10:00-17:00, Sat-Sun 12:00-17:00, free yummy samples and a fun visit for kids, tel. 066/947-9119, www.skelligschocolate.com).

80 km: Photographers and walkers will want to turn left into

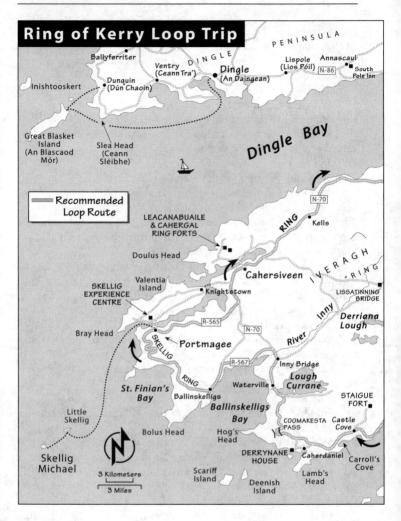

Ring of Kerry Loop Trip

PENINSULA

Ballyferriter

Ventry (Ceann Trá')

DINGLE

Dingle (An Daingean)

Lispole (Lios Póil)   Annascaul

N-86   South Pole Inn

Inishtooskert

Dunquin (Dún Chaoin)

Great Blasket Island (An Blascaod Mór)

Slea Head (Ceann Sléibhe)

Dingle Bay

Recommended Loop Route

LEACANABUAILE & CAHERGAL RING FORTS

Doulus Head

RING   N-70   Kells

IVERAGH

Cahersiveen

"RING"

LISSATINNING BRIDGE

Valentia Island

SKELLIG EXPERIENCE CENTRE

Knightstown

Bray Head

SKELLIG   R-565   N-70

Inny River

Derriana Lough

Portmagee

RING   R-567   Inny Bridge

St. Finian's Bay

Ballinskelligs   Waterville

Lough Currane

STAIGUE FORT

Little Skellig

Bolus Head

Ballinskelligs Bay

Hog's Head

COOMAKESTA PASS   Castle Cove

Caherdaniel   Carroll's Cove

Skellig Michael

N

3 Kilometers

3 Miles

DERRYNANE HOUSE

Scariff Island

Deenish Island

Lamb's Head

the driveway that advertises "Best View in County Kerry." Park and pay the €4 fee at the B&B reception. Then walk 10 minutes straight up the gravel road, where you'll be confronted by a dramatic coastal cliff that opens up onto what may indeed be the best view in County Kerry. The beehive huts nearby are replicas but true to the originals.

83 km: You reach Portmagee, a small port town and jumping-off point for boats to the Skellig Islands.

83.2 km: Cross the bridge to the Skellig Experience Centre. You're now on Valentia Island, its name hinting at medieval trading connections with nearby Spain—which lies due south. Dinosaur hunters may want to detour and follow the signs to the modest but

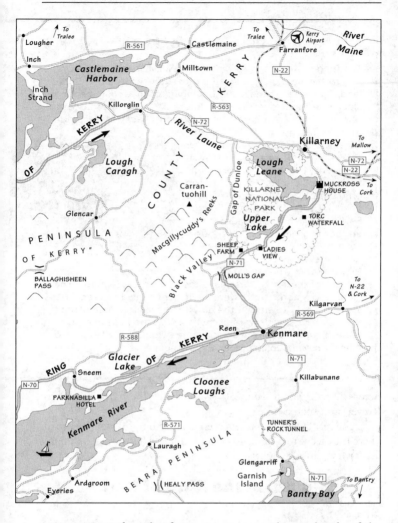

ancient tetrapod tracks, frozen in stone, on the north side of the island.

91.2 km: At the church in Knightstown, turn left for the Knightstown Heritage Museum.

93 km: Return to the main road and go through Knightstown to the tiny ferry (€6/car, runs constantly 8:00-21:00, 2-km trip).

95 km: Leaving the ferry, rejoin N-70 (the main Ring of Kerry route), turning left for the town of Cahersiveen. From here, you can detour a few kilometers to two impressive stone ring forts, Cahergal and Leacanabuaile.

100 km: Return to N-70 at Cahersiveen and follow signs for *Glenbeigh* and *Killorglin*. Enjoy views of the Dingle Peninsula

The Ring Forts of Kerry

The Ring of Kerry comes with three awe-inspiring prehistoric ring forts—among the largest and best preserved in all of Ireland. Staigue Fort (near the beginning of my recommended clockwise Ring route) is most impressive and in a desolate setting. The two others—Cahergal and Leacanabuaile, side by side just north of Cahersiveen (closer to the end of the Ring, after Valentia Island)—are easier to visit and plenty evocative. Each ring fort is about a 2.5-mile (4-km) side-trip off the main drag. If you're trying to beat the tour-bus convoy, Staigue Fort is problematic because it eats up morning time before the buses have passed you. The Cahersiveen ring forts are your last stop in the Ring of Kerry, when bus traffic is of no concern.

All of these ring forts have the same basic features. The circular drystone walls were built sometime between 500 B.C. and A.D. 300 without the aid of mortar or cement. About 80 feet across, with walls 12 feet thick at the base and up to 25 feet high, these brutish structures would have taken 100 men six months to complete. Expert opinion is divided on the

across Dingle Bay to your left (you can see the harbor and Ersk Tower) and Inch Beach.

The rest of the loop is less scenic. At Killorglin, you've seen all there is to see. From here, go either to Dingle (left) or to Kenmare/Killarney/Kinsale (right).

Sights on the Ring of Kerry

Sneem

Sneem is inundated by tour buses daily from 14:00 to 16:00. The rest of the day, Sneem is peaceful and laid-back. This humble town has two entertaining squares. The Irish joke, "As we're in Kerry, the square on the east side is called South Square and the one on the west is called North Square." On the first (South) square, you'll see a statue of Steve "Crusher" Casey, the local boy who reigned as world champion heavyweight wrestler (1938-1947). A sweet little peat-toned waterfall gurgles under the one-lane bridge connecting the two Sneem squares. The North Square features a memorial to former French president Charles de Gaulle's visit (Irish on his mother's side, de Gaulle came here for two weeks of R&R after his final retirement from office in 1969). Locals call it "da gallstone."

reason they were built, but most believe that the people who built them would have retreated here at times of tribal war. As this was an era when civilization was morphing from nomadic hunter-gatherers to settled farmers, herders used these forts. They likely brought their valuable cattle inside to protect them  from ancient rustlers. Other experts see the round design as a kind of amphitheater, where local clan chieftains would have gathered for important meetings or rituals. However, the ditch surrounding the outer walls of Staigue Fort suggests a defensive, rather than ceremonial, function. Without written records, we can only imagine the part these magnificent piles of finely stacked stones played in ancient dramas.

Because this region had copper mines, southwest Ireland has a wealth of prehistoric sights. The Bronze Age wouldn't have been the Bronze Age without copper, which was melted together with tin to make bronze for better weapons and tools (2000 to 500 B.C.). The many ring forts and stone circles reflect the affluence that the abundance of copper brought to the region.

▲Staigue Fort

This ring fort is worth a stop on your way around the Ring (always open, drop €2 in the little gray donation box beside the gate). While viewing the imposing pile of stone, read "The Ring Forts of Kerry" sidebar, earlier.

Getting There: The fort is 2.5 miles (4 km) off the main N-70 road up a narrow rural access lane (look for signs just after the hamlet of Castle Cove). Honk on blind corners to warn oncoming traffic as you drive up the hedge-lined lane.

▲Derrynane House

This is the home of Daniel O'Connell, Ireland's most influential pre-independence politician, whose tireless nonviolent agitation gained equality for Catholics 185 years ago. The coastal lands of the O'Connell estate that surround Derrynane House are now a national historic park. A visit here is a window into the life of a man who not only liberated Ireland from the last oppressive anti-Catholic penal laws, but also first developed the idea of a grassroots movement—organizing on a massive scale to achieve political ends without bloodshed (see sidebar).

Cost and Hours: €3; May-Sept daily 10:30-18:00; April and

Daniel O'Connell (1775-1847)

Born in Cahersiveen and elected from Ennis as the first Catholic member of the British Parliament, O'Connell was the hero of Catholic emancipation in Ireland.  Educated in France at a time when punitive anti-Catholic laws limited schooling for Irish Catholics at home, he witnessed the carnage of the French Revolution. Upon his return to Ireland, he saw more bloodshed during the futile Rebellion of 1798. He chose law as his profession and reluctantly killed a man who challenged him to a duel.

Abhorring all this violence, O'Connell dedicated himself to peacefully gaining equal rights for Catholics in an Ireland dominated by a wealthy Protestant minority. He formed the Catholic Association with a one-penny-per-month membership fee and quickly gained a huge following (especially among the poor) with his persuasive speaking skills. Although Catholics weren't allowed to hold office, he ran for election to Parliament anyway and won a seat in 1828. His unwillingness to take the anti-Catholic Oath of Supremacy initially kept him out of Westminster, but the moral force of his victory caused the government to give in and concede Catholic emancipation the following year.

Known as "the Liberator," O'Connell was working toward his next goal—repealing the Act of Union with Britain—when he was imprisoned in 1844 for seditious conspiracy. His massive "Monster Meeting" rallies had attracted thousands of peaceful poor, and his popularity spooked the British authorities, so they threw him in jail on trumped-up charges. But when the Great Potato Famine hit in 1845, some in the Irish ranks began to advocate for more violent action against the British, something O'Connell had long opposed. He died two years later in Genoa on his way to Rome, but his ideals lived on: His Catholic Association was the model of grassroots organization for the Irish, who later emigrated and rose within American big-city political "green machines."

Oct Wed-Sun 10:30-17:00, closed Mon-Tue; closed in winter, last entry 45 minutes before closing, tel. 066/947-5113.

Getting There: Just outside the town of Derrynane, pick up a handy free map of the area from the little TI inside the brown Wave Crest market (private TI open mid-May-mid-Sept daily 9:00-18:00, closed mid-Sept-mid-May, tel. 066/947-5188; market is a great place to buy picnic food). One mile after the market, take a left and follow the signs into Derrynane National Historic Park.

Visiting the House: Navigate the house's quirky floor plan with the €0.50 guide available at the front desk. Ask about the next scheduled 20-minute audiovisual show, which fleshes out the highlights of O'Connell's turbulent life and makes the contents of the house more interesting.

In the exhibition room downstairs is a glass case containing the pistols used in O'Connell's famous duel. Beside them are his black gloves, one of which he always wore on his right hand when he went to Mass (out of remorse for the part it played in taking a man's life). The drawing room upstairs is lined with family portraits and contains his ornately carved chair with tiny harp strings and wolfhound collars made of gold. On a wall in the upstairs bedroom is a copy of O'Connell's celebrated speech imploring the Irish not to riot when he was arrested.

The coach house (out back) shows off the enormous grand chariot that carried O'Connell through throngs of joyous Dubliners after his release from prison in 1844. He added the small chapel wing to the house in gratitude to God for his prison release.

Portmagee

Just a short row of snoozy buildings lining the bay, Portmagee is the best harbor for boat excursions out to the Skellig Islands (see "Getting to Skellig Michael" on page 225). It's a quiet village with a handful of B&Bs, two pubs, a bakery, a market, and no ATMs—the closest ATM is 6 miles (10 km) east in Cahersiveen. On the rough harborfront, a slate memorial to sailors lost at sea from here reads, "In the nets of God may we be gathered."

A 100-yard-long bridge connects Portmagee to gentle Valentia Island, where you'll find the Skellig Experience Centre (on the left at the Valentia end of the bridge). A public parking lot is at the Portmagee end of the bridge, with award-winning WCs (no kidding: the Irish Toilet of the Year 2002 runner-up plaque is proudly displayed). The first permanent transatlantic cable (for telegraph communication) was laid from Valentia Island in 1866. The tiny post office hides inside O'Connell's Market (both open Mon-Fri 9:00-17:30, Sat 9:00-13:00, closed Sun).

Sleeping in Portmagee: The first two listings are in town. The last listing is south of Portmagee, on St. Finian's Bay.

$$$ Moorings Guest House feels like a small hotel, with 17 rooms, a pub and a fine restaurant downstairs, and the most convenient location in town, 50 yards from the end of the pier (Sb-€70-90, Db-€90-130, Tb-€130-190, Qb-€170-240, tel. 066/947-7108, fax 066/947-7220, www.moorings.ie, moorings@iol.ie, Gerard and Patricia Kennedy).

$$ Portmagee Heights B&B is a modern, solid slate home at the edge of town, renting eight hotel-like rooms (Db-€70-80, Tb-€105-120, Wi-Fi, on the road into town, tel. 066/947-7251, www.

portmageeheights.com, portmageeheights@gmail.com, hostess Monica Hussey can arrange Skellig boat trips). They also have a cool self-catering cottage across the road—great for families who want some space to themselves.

$ Beach Cove B&B offers three comfortable, fresh, and lovingly decorated rooms in splendid isolation four miles south of Portmagee, over lofty Coomanaspic ridge, beside the pretty beach at St. Finian's Bay (200 yards past the Skelligs Chocolate Factory). Charming Bridie O'Connor will arrange a boat trip out to the Skelligs for you. Her adjacent cottage out back has two double rooms, making it ideal for families (Sb-€45-50, Db-€60-70, Tb-€95, family room-€100, tel. 066/947-9301, mobile 087-139-0224, www.stayatbeachcove.com, beachcove@eircom.net). Bridie's husband, Jack, is the head coach of the Kerry football team...a very important person in this part of Ireland (Kerry has won more football titles than any other Irish county).

Eating in Portmagee: These options all line the waterfront (between the pier and the bridge to Valentia Island). **The Moorings** is a nice restaurant with great seafood caught literally just outside its front door (€16-22 dinners, Tue-Sun 18:00-22:00, closed Mon, reservations a good idea, tel. 066/947-7108). The **Bridge Bar,** next door, does traditional pub grub but stops serving food a bit early. Call ahead to check on their traditional music and dance schedule (€10-18 meals, daily 10:00-20:30, live music Fri and Sun nights, tel. 066/947-7108). The **Fisherman's Bar** is less flashy, with more locals and cheaper prices (€10-19 meals, daily 10:00-21:00, tel. 066/947-7103).

For picnic supplies, **O'Connell's Market** is the only grocery (Mon-Sat 9:00-20:00, Sun 9:30-15:30). **Skellig Mist Bakery** can make basic lunch sandwiches to take on Skellig boat excursions (daily 9:30-17:30, tel. 066/947-7250).

Valentia Island

These two sights are on Valentia Island, across the bridge from Portmagee.

Skellig Experience Centre—Whether or not you're actually sailing to Skellig Michael (described later), this little center (with basic exhibits and a fine 20-minute film) explains it well—both the story of the monks and the natural environment.

Cost and Hours: €5, daily July-Aug 10:00-19:00, until 18:00 in spring and fall, closed mid-Nov-mid-March, last entry one hour before closing, call ahead outside of peak season as hours may vary, on Valentia Island beside bridge linking it to Portmagee, tel. 066/947-6306, www.skelligexperience.com.

Boat Trips: The Skellig Experience Centre arranges two-hour boat trips, circling both Skellig Michael and Little Skellig (without

Communication in Ireland: Tetrapods to Marconi

Many Irish paleontologists believe the first fish slithered out of the water here on four stubby legs 385 million years ago, onto what would become the Isle of Saints and Scholars. Over time, those tetrapods evolved. Irish scribes—living in remote outposts like the Skellig Islands just off this coast—kept literate life alive in Europe through the darkest depths of the so-called Dark Ages. In fact, in about the year 800, Charlemagne imported monks from this part of Ireland to be his scribes. Evolution, literacy, communication. Just more than a thousand years later, in the mid-19th century, Paul Julius Reuter—who provided a financial news service in Europe—knew his pigeons couldn't fly across the Atlantic. So he relied on ships coming from America to drop a news capsule overboard as they rounded this southwest corner of Ireland. His boys would wait in their little boats with nets to "get the scoop." They say Europe learned of Lincoln's assassination (1865) from a capsule tossed over a boat here. The first permanent cables were laid across the Atlantic from here to Newfoundland, giving the two hemispheres telegraphic communication. Queen Victoria got to be the first to send a message—greeting American president James Buchanan in 1858. The cable broke more than once, but it was finally permanently secured in 1866. Marconi achieved the first wireless transatlantic communication from this corner of Ireland to America in 1901. Today, driving under the 21st-century mobile-phone and satellite tower crowning a hilltop above Valentia Island while gazing out at the Skellig Islands, a traveler marvels at the progress in communication—and the part this remote corner of Ireland played in it.

actually bringing people ashore)—ideal for those who want a close look without the stair climb and vertigo that go with a visit to the island (€27.50, sailing daily about 14:45 and returning by 17:00, weather permitting, depart from Valentia Island pier 50 yards below the Skellig Experience Centre).

Valentia Heritage Museum—The humble Knightstown schoolhouse, built in 1861, houses an equally humble but interesting little museum highlighting the quirky things of historic interest on Valentia Island. You'll see a 19th-century schoolroom and learn about tetrapods (those first fish to climb onto land—which locals claim happened here). You'll also follow the long story of the expensive, frustrating, and heroic battle to lay telegraph cable across the Atlantic, which—after some false starts—finally succeeded in 1866, when the largest ship in the world connected this tiny island of Valentia with Newfoundland. This project was the initiative of the Atlantic Telegraph Company, which later became Western Union. These stories and more are told with intimate black-and-white photos and typewritten pages.

Cost and Hours: €3.50, daily April-Sept 10:30-17:00, closed Oct-March, tel. 066/947-6411, www.vhc.cablehistory.org.

Nearby: If you are interested in those tetrapods, the actual "first footprints" are a 15-minute drive from the museum, on a rugged bit of rocky shoreline, a 10-minute hike below a parking lot (free, always viewable, get details locally).

Cahergal and Leacanabuaile Ring Forts

Crowning bluffs in farm country, 2.5 miles (4 km) off the main road at Cahersiveen, these two windy and desolate forts are each different and worth a look. You'll hike a few hundred yards from the tiny parking lot (free, always open, no museum). Just beyond the Cahersiveen town church at the tourist office, turn left, cross the narrow bridge, turn left again, and follow signs for ancient forts—you'll see the huge stone structures in the distance. For details, see "The Ring Forts of Kerry" sidebar, earlier.

Skellig Michael

A trip to this jagged, isolated pyramid—the Holy Grail of Irish monastic island settlements—rates as a truly memorable ▲▲▲ experience. After visiting Skellig Michael a hundred years ago, Nobel Prize-winning Irish playwright George Bernard Shaw called it "the most fantastic and impossible rock in the world."

Rising seven miles offshore, the Skelligs (Gaelic for "splinter") are two gigantic slate-and-sandstone rocks crouched aggressively on the ocean horizon. The larger of the two, Skellig Michael, is more than 700 feet tall and a mile around, with a tiny cluster of abandoned beehive huts clinging near its summit like stubborn barnacles. The smaller island, Little Skellig, is home to a huge colony of gannet birds (like large, graceful seagulls with six-foot wingspans), protected by law from visitors setting foot onshore.

Skellig Michael (dedicated to the archangel) was first inhabited by sixth-century Christian monks. Inspired by earlier hermit-monks in the Egyptian desert, they sought the purity

of isolation to get closer to God. Neither Viking raids nor winter storms could dislodge them, as they patiently built a half-dozen small, stone, igloo-like dwellings and a couple of tiny oratories. Their remote cliff-terrace perch is still connected to the sea 600 feet below by an amazing series of rock stairs. Viking Olav Trygvasson, who later became king of Norway and introduced Christianity to his country, was baptized here in 956.

Chiseling the most rudimentary life from solid rock, the monks lived a harsh, lonely, disciplined existence here, their colony surviving for more than 500 years. They collected rainwater in cisterns and lived off fish and birds. To supplement their meager existence, they traded bird eggs and feathers with passing boats for cereals, candles, and animal hides (used for clothing and for copying scripture). They finally moved their holy community ashore to Ballinskelligs in the early 1100s.

Getting There

To book a boat trip from Portmagee, contact **Murphy Sea Cruise** (€45, April-Oct, mobile 087-676-2983, 087-234-2168, or 087-645-1909, www.esatclear.ie/~skelligsrock, murphyseacruise@esatclear.ie), **Joe Roddy** (mobile 087-284-4460, www.skelligstrips.com), **Brendan Casey** (tel. 066/947-2437, mobile 087-228-7519), or **Des Lavelle** (tel. 066/947-6124, mobile 087-237-1017).

Boat trips normally depart Portmagee at 10:00 (depending on tides), sail for an hour, leave you on the island from roughly 11:00 until 13:30, and get you back into Portmagee by 14:30 (with plenty of time to drive on to Dingle). Fifteen small boats (from Portmagee, Ballinskelligs, Waterville, and Valentia Island) have permits to land on Skellig Michael. Each boat can carry a dozen passengers. This limits the number of daily visitors and minimizes the impact on the sensitive island ecosystem.

Bring your camera, a sandwich lunch (easy to buy at the recommended Skellig Mist Bakery in Portmagee), water, sunscreen, rain gear, hiking shoes, and your sense of wonder.

Weather Warning: Landing on Skellig Michael is highly weather-dependent. If the seas are too choppy, the boats cannot safely drop people at the concrete island pier (it's a bit like jumping off a trampoline onto an ice rink). Excursions are scheduled to run daily from Easter to late September, but experienced boat captains say they are able to bring visitors ashore roughly five days out of seven in an average summer week.

Your best bet is to reserve a room near Portmagee or St. Finian's Bay—whichever best fits your itinerary. (It's possible to sleep in Kenmare and get up early to drive two hours straight to Portmagee—but you'll be frustrated by not having time to enjoy the Ring's attractions along the way). Then call a few days in advance to make a boat reservation. Keep your fingers crossed for good weather. Contact the boat operator on the morning of departure to get the final word. If the seas are too rough, he can tell from Portmagee and will make a decision that morning whether or not to go (rather than taking passengers halfway out, then aborting).

Visiting Skellig Michael

Since you'll have only 2.5 hours to explore the island, begin by climbing the seemingly un-ending series of stone stairs to the monastic ruins (600 vertical feet of uneven steps with no handrails). Save most of your photographing for the way down. Those who linger too long below risk missing the enlightening 20-min-ute free talk among the beehive huts, given by guides who camp on the island from April through October. Afterward, poke your head into some of the huts and try to imagine the

dark, damp, and devoted life of a monk here more than 1,000 years ago. After rambling through the ruins, you can give in to photo frenzy as you wander back down the stairs.

The two lighthouses on the far side of the island are now automated, and access to them has been blocked off. There are no WCs or modern shelters of any kind on Skel-lig Michael.

If you visit between late April and early August, you'll be sur-rounded by fearless rainbow-beaked puffins, which nest here in un-derground burrows. Their bizarre swallowed cooing sounds like a distant chainsaw. These portly little birds live off fish, and divers have reported seeing them 20 feet underwater in pursuit of their prey.

Your return boat journey usually includes a pass near Little Skellig, which looms like an iceberg with a white coat of guano—courtesy of the 20,000 gannets that circle overhead like feathered confetti. These large birds suddenly morph into sleek darts when pursuing a fish, piercing the water from more than 100 feet above. You're also likely to get a glimpse of gray seals lazing on rocks near the water's edge.

DINGLE PENINSULA

Dingle Town • Dingle Peninsula Loop Trip
• Blasket Islands • Tralee

The Dingle Peninsula, the westernmost tip of Ireland (and Europe, for that matter), offers just the right mix of far-and-away beauty, isolated walks and bike rides, and ancient archaeological wonders—all within convenient reach of its main town. Dingle town is just large enough to have all the necessary tourist services and a steady nocturnal beat of Irish traditional music.

Although Dingle is crowded in summer, it still feels like the fish and the farm really matter. Twenty fishing boats sail from here, tractor tracks dirty the main drag, and a faint whiff of peat fills the nighttime streets.

For over 30 years, my Irish dreams have been set here on this sparse but lush peninsula, where locals are fond of saying, "The next parish over is Boston." There's a feeling of closeness to the land in Dingle. When I asked a local if he was born here, he thought for a second and said, "No, it was about six miles down the road." When I told him where I was from, a faraway smile filled his eyes, and he looked out to sea and sighed, "Ah, the shores of Americay." I asked his friend if he'd lived here all his life. He said, "Not yet."

Dingle feels so traditionally Irish because it's part of the Gaeltacht, a region where the government subsidizes the survival of the Irish language and culture. While English is always there, the signs, chitchat, and songs come in Gaelic. Children carry hurling sticks to class, and even the local preschool brags "ALL Gaelic."

Dingle Town

Of the peninsula's 10,000 residents, 1,500 live in Dingle town (An Daingean). Its few streets, lined with ramshackle but gaily painted shops and pubs, run up from a rain-stung harbor always busy with fishing boats and leisure sailboats. Traditionally, the buildings were drab gray or whitewashed, but four decades ago, Ireland's "tidy town" competition prompted everyone to paint their buildings in playful pastels.

It's a peaceful town. The courthouse (1832) is open one hour a month. The judge does his best to wrap up business within a half hour. During the day, you'll see teenagers—already working on ruddy beer-glow cheeks—roll kegs up the streets and into the pubs in preparation for another night of music and *craic* (fun conversation and atmosphere).

Planning Your Time

For the shortest visit, give Dingle two nights and a day. It takes six hours to get here from Dublin, Galway, or the boat dock in Rosslare. By spending two nights, you'll feel more like a local on your second evening in the pubs. You'll need the better part of a day to explore the 30-mile loop around the peninsula by bike or car (following my "Dingle Peninsula Loop Trip" in this chapter). To do any serious walking or relaxing, you'll need three nights and two days. It's not uncommon to find Americans slowing way, way down in Dingle.

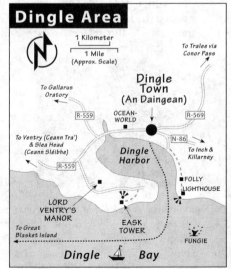

Dingle's season peaks in July and August and really dies off-season. If you're traveling during the summer months, it's wise to reserve your B&B in advance. I've generally listed hours for the tourist season (April-Sept). Hours may be longer in July and August, and most places cut back or shut down entirely from October to March.

Orientation to Dingle

Dingle—extremely comfortable on foot—hangs on a medieval grid of streets between the harborfront (where the bus to Tralee stops) and Main Street (three blocks inland). Nothing in town is more than a 15-minute walk away. Street numbers are used only when more than one place is run by a family of the same name. Most locals know most locals, and people on the street are fine sources of information. Remember, locals love their soda bread, and tourism provides the butter. You'll find a warm and sincere welcome.

Tourist Information

The TI has a great town map (free) and a staff who know the town, but not so much about the rest of the peninsula (July-Aug Mon-Sat 9:00-18:00, Sun 10:00-17:00, less off-season, on Strand Street by the water, tel. 066/915-1188). For additional advice on outdoor activities, drop by the Mountain Man shop on Strand Street (see "Helpful Hints," later), or talk to your B&B host.

Arrival in Dingle

By Bus: Dingle has no bus station and only one bus stop, on the waterfront behind the SuperValu supermarket (look for the bus shelter with the roof made from an overturned black *currach* boat). Bus Éireann does day trips to Dingle from Tralee (see "Day Trips from Tralee" on page 267).

    By Car: Drivers choose two roads into town: the easy southern route on N-86 or the much more dramatic, scenic, and treacherous Conor Pass on R-569 (see "Route Tips for Drivers," at the end of this chapter). It's 30 miles (48 km) from Tralee either way. If you're not staying overnight (i.e., parking at your B&B), use the waterfront parking lot extending west from the TI (€1/hour, pay at meter in lot and display on dashboard, daily 8:00-18:00).

    By Plane: Kerry Airport, halfway between Tralee and Killarney, is a one-hour drive from Dingle. For more on this airport and information on how to connect to Dingle, see the end of this chapter.

Helpful Hints

Before You Go: Check the local website for a list of festivals and events (www.dingle-peninsula.ie).

Crowds: Crowds trample Dingle's charm throughout July and August. The absolute craziest times are during the Dingle Races (early Aug), Dingle Regatta (early to mid-Aug), and

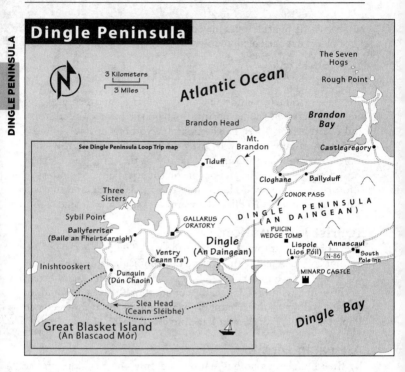

Dingle Peninsula

Atlantic Ocean

The Seven Hogs

Rough Point

Brandon Head

Brandon Bay

Mt. Brandon

Castlegregory

See Dingle Peninsula Loop Trip map

Tiduff

Cloghane   Ballyduff

CONOR PASS

Three Sisters

Sybil Point

Ballyferriter
(Baile an Fheirtearaigh)

GALLARUS ORATORY

D I N G L E   P E N I N S U L A
(A N   D A I N G E A N)

Dingle
(An Daingean)

PUICIN WEDGE TOMB

Lispole
(Lios Póil)

Annascaul

N-86

South Pole Inn

Ventry
(Ceann Tra')

Inishtooskert

Dunquin
(Dún Chaoin)

MINARD CASTLE

Slea Head
(Ceann Sléibhe)

Great Blasket Island
(An Blascaod Mór)

Dingle Bay

3 Kilometers
3 Miles

the Blessing of the Boats (end of Aug or beginning of Sept). The first Mondays in May, June, and August are Bank Holidays, giving Ireland's workers three-day weekends—and ample time to fill up Dingle. The town's metabolism (prices, schedules, activities) rises and falls with the tourist crowds, so October through April is sleepy, windy, and chilly.

Money: Two banks in town, both on Main Street, offer the same rates (Mon 10:00-17:00, Tue-Fri 10:00-16:00, closed Sat-Sun) and have cash machines. The TI happily changes cash and traveler's checks at mediocre rates. Expect to use cash (rather than credit cards) to pay for most peninsula activities.

Internet Access: The **Old Forge Internet Café** is friendly and central (€4/hour, daily 10:00-21:00, Holyground). The old **library** is free, but its three terminals are often busy. You can drop by and reserve a 30-minute slot anytime (Mon-Sat 10:00-17:00, Thu until 20:00, closed Sun, Green Street).

Post Office: It's off Main Street, down the lane behind the Centra grocery (Mon-Fri 9:00-17:30, Sat 9:00-13:00, closed Sun).

Laundry: There is no self-service laundry in Dingle. **Dingle Cleaners** is convenient (€12/up to 14 pounds, Mon-Sat 9:00-18:00, closed Sun, beside Moran's Market and gas station, tel. 066/915-0680, run by Ciaran—pronounced KEER-un).

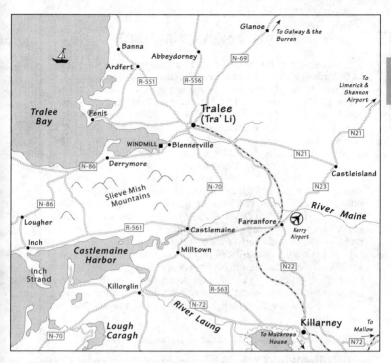

Bike Rental: Bike-rental shops abound, renting 21-speed hybrids. Try **Paddy's Bike Hire** (€10/day or €15/24 hours, includes helmet, daily 9:00-19:00, directly across Dykegate from An Café Liteartha, tel. 066/915-2311) or the **Mountain Man** (€10/day; for contact info, see "Dingle Activities," below). If you're biking the peninsula, get a bike with skinny street tires, not slow and fat mountain-bike tires. Plan on leaving €20, plus a driver's license or passport, as a security deposit.

Taxi: Try **Colm Bambury** (mobile 087-222-2248), **Diarmuid Begley** (mobile 087-250-4767), Sean with **S.O.L. Cabs** in Dingle (mobile 087-660-2323), or **Tom Kearney** out in Dunquin (mobile 087-933-2264).

Dingle Activities: The **Mountain Man,** a hiking shop run by local guide Adrian Curran, is a clearinghouse for information on hiking, biking, horseback riding, sea kayaking, climbing, peninsula tours, and trips to the Blasket Islands (the shop is the Dingle town contact for the Dunquin-Blasket Islands boats—see "Blasket Islands" on page 264). Give them a call a few days ahead to see which guided, scenic, mountain day-hikes are scheduled (daily June-mid-Sept 9:00-21:00, mid-Sept-May 9:00-18:00, just off harbor at Strand Street, tel. 066/915-2400, www.themountainmanshop.com).

Dingle or An Daingean?

Linguistic politics have stirred up a controversy over the name of this town and peninsula. Being a Gaeltacht, the entire region gets subsidies from the government (which supports the survival of the traditional Irish culture and language). A precondition of this financial support is that towns use their Irish (Gaelic) name. But Dingle, a.k.a. An Daingean ("on DANG-un") in Irish, has voted down this dictate from Dublin. Dingle has become so wealthy from the tourist trade that it sees its famous name as a trademark, and doesn't want to become "the cute tourist town with the unpronounceable name, formerly known as Dingle." While official road signs identify the town only as *An Daingean,* you'll notice that many have been modified by a crude, white *DINGLE* stenciled by stubborn locals. In town, most businesses, all tourist information, and nearly all people—locals and tourists alike—refer to it as Dingle.

For the sake of clarity, in this book I follow the local convention: Dingle instead of "An Daingean," Great Blasket Island instead of "An Blascoad Mór," and so on. But for ease of navigation, I've also included the place's Irish name in parentheses. For a list of these bilingual place names, see the sidebar on page 254.

Dingle Hillwalking Club: This informal, visitor-friendly hiking group is a great way to connect with fun, active locals (free, Sun at 10:00, meets in front of SuperValu, www.dinglehill walkingclub.com).

Travel Agency: Maurice O'Connor at **Galvin's Travel Agency** can book plane tickets, as well as ferry rides to Britain (Mon-Fri 9:30-18:00, Sat 9:30-14:00, closed Sun, John Street, tel. 066/915-1409).

Farmers Market: From mid-April to mid-October on Fridays from 9:00 to 15:00, farmers gather to sell their fresh produce, homemade marmalade, and homespun crafts (across the street from SuperValu grocery store).

Tours in Dingle

Here are several options for touring the peninsula.

▲▲**Sciuird Archaeology Tours**—Sciuird (SCEW-erd, Irish for "excursion") tours are offered by a father-son team with Dingle history—and a knack for sharing it—in their blood. Tim Collins, a retired Dingle police officer, and son Michael give serious 2.5-hour minibus tours (€20, departing at 10:30 and 14:00, depending upon demand). Drop by the recommended Eileen Collins Kir-rary B&B (at Dykegate and Grey's Lane), or call 066/915-1606 to put your name on the list. Call early; tours fill quickly in summer. Off-season (Oct-April), you may have to call back to see if the necessary five people have signed up to make a 14-seat bus

worth taking out. Skipping the folk legends, your guide will show you the highlights while driving down tiny farm roads (the Gaelic word for road literally means "cow path"), over hedges, and up ridges to hidden Celtic forts, mysterious stone tombs, and forgotten castles with sweeping seaside views. The running commentary gives an intimate peek into the history of Dingle, and their sound system allows you to hear clearly, no matter where you sit. Dress for the weather. In a gale storm with horizontal winds, Tim kept telling me, "You'll survive it."

More Minibus Tours—Moran's Tour, which does a quickie minibus tour around the peninsula, offers meager narration and a short stop at the Gallarus Oratory (€20 to Slea Head, normally May-Sept at 10:00 and 14:00 from Dingle TI, 2.5 hours; Moran's is at Esso station at roundabout, tel. 066/915-1155, mobile 087-275-3333). There are usually enough seats, though it's best to book a day ahead. But if no one shows up, consider a private Moran taxi trip around the peninsula (€90 for 4 people, cabbie narrates 2.5-hour ride).

Dingle Marine Activity Centre Cruises—Dingle Marine Eco Tours offers a two-hour birds-and-rocks boat tour of the peninsula. The guided tour sails either east toward Minard Castle or west toward the Blasket Islands (€35, runs April-Sept only, departs at 16:00 weather permitting, office around corner from TI, mobile 086-285-8802).

Self-Guided Walk

▲Dingle Introductory Historical Walk

This quick 10-stop circle through town gives you a once-over-lightly overview and good orientation.

Start at the **"old roundabout"** (next to O'Flaherty's Pub, not the "new roundabout" by the hospital), which replaced the big bridge over the town river in the 1980s. Step out on the tiny pedestrian bridge (toward the bay) with the black wrought-iron railing. This was the original train line coming into Dingle (the westernmost train station in all of Europe from 1891 to 1953). The train once picked up fish here; its operators boasted that the cargo would be in London markets within 24 hours. The narrow-gauge tracks ran right along the harborfront. All the land beyond the old buildings you see today has been reclaimed from the sea. Look inland and find the building on the left with the slate siding—this was the typical design for 19th-century weather-proofing. The radio tower marks the salmon-pink police station.

Cross the roundabout and walk 20 yards along the river up "The Mall" to the two stubby redbrick **pillars** that mark the entry to the police station. These pillars are all that remain of the 19th-century British Constabulary, which afforded a kind of Green Zone for British troops when they tried to subdue the local insurgents here. It was burned down in 1922, during the Civil War; the present building dates from 1938.

The big white **crucifix** across the street is a memorial to heroes who died in the 1916 Uprising. Note that it says in the people's language, "For honor and glory of Ireland, 1916 to 19   ." The date is unfinished until Ireland is united and free. The names listed are of patriots executed by the English, and one who died while on a hunger strike.

At the *Russels B&B* sign, take 15 paces up the driveway to see an old stone etched with a cross sitting atop the fence (on the right). This marks the place of a **Celtic holy well,** indicating this was a sacred spot for people here 2,000 years ago. Across the street, enjoy the fine landscaping work of Jim from the recommended Captain's House B&B.

Just beyond Jim's riverside garden (opposite the monastery) is another much-honored spot: the distribution center for **Guinness.** From this warehouse, pubs throughout the peninsula are stocked with beer. The wooden kegs have been replaced by what locals fondly call "iron lungs."

Farther up and across the street is the 19th-century **courthouse.** Once a symbol of British oppression, today it's a laid-back place where, on the last Friday of each month, the roving County Kerry judge drops by to adjudicate cases (mostly domestic disputes and drunken disorderliness). Next door, with the blue walls, is the popular and recommended **Court House Pub.**

The next intersection is the "Small Bridge" (a little stream runs under the road). Continuing straight would take you up the road a few miles to the ruggedly scenic Conor Pass. Instead, turn left into the commercial heart of the town, up **Main Street.** The old stagecoach from Tralee ended at Dingle's first hotel, the recommended Benners (half-way up on the left), with its Georgian facade and door surviving. Across the street, up a short gravel alley, is St. James' Church. Since the 13th century, a church has stood here (just inside the medieval wall). Today, it's Anglican on Sundays and filled with great traditional music several nights a week (schedule on gate; also see "Nightlife in Dingle," later).

Dingle's History

The wet sod of Dingle is soaked with medieval history. In the dimmest depths of the Dark Ages, peace-loving, bookish monks fled the chaos of the Continent and its barbarian raids. They sailed to the drizzly fringe of the known world—to places like Dingle. These monks kept literacy alive in Europe. Charlemagne, who ruled much of Europe in the year 800, imported Irish monks to be his scribes.

It was from this peninsula that the semi-mythical explorer-monk St. Brendan is said to have set sail in the sixth century in search of a legendary western paradise. Some think he beat Columbus to North America by almost a thousand years (see sidebar on page 279).

Dingle was a busy seaport in the late Middle Ages. Dingle and Tralee (covered later in this chapter) were the only walled towns in Kerry. Castles stood at the low and high ends of Dingle's Main Street, protecting the Normans from the angry and dispossessed Irish outside. Dingle was a gateway to northern Spain—a three-day sail due south. Many 14th- and 15th-century pilgrims left from Dingle for the revered Spanish church in Santiago de Compostela, thought to house the bones of St. James.

In Dingle's medieval heyday, locals traded cowhides for wine. When Dingle's position as a trading center waned, the town faded in importance. In the 19th century, it was a linen-weaving center. Until 1970, fishing dominated, and the only visitors were scholars and students of old Irish ways. In 1970, the movie *Ryan's Daughter* introduced the world to Dingle. The trickle of Dingle fans has grown to a flood as word of its musical, historical, gastronomical, and scenic charms—not to mention its friendly dolphin—has spread.

Continue uphill and poke your head into two of Dingle's most unapologetically traditional drinking holes, which face each other across Main Street: **Ó Curráin's** (on the right) and **Foxy John's** (on the left, both recommended). These two throwbacks are shops by day and pubs by night, as many Irish pubs once were. In years past, small-town pubs often also served as the town morgue (because they had the only large refrigerated space in town)—where you could literally drink until you dropped.

At the first intersection, take a left on Green Street. Pop into the beautiful, modern St. Mary's Church. The convent behind it shows off its delightful **Díseart windows** (described later, under "Sights in Dingle"). Wander in the backyard to check out the tranquil nuns' cemetery, with its white-painted iron crosses huddling peacefully together under a big copper beech tree. Across from St. Mary's is the recommended **Dick Mack's Pub,** another traditional pub well worth a peek, even for non-drinkers.

Green Street leads past lots of inviting boutiques, estate agents (showing the current price of houses here), and the library. The **library,** a gift from the Carnegie Foundation, has a shelf of tourist-information books and a small exhibit (in the foyer and upstairs) about local patriot Thomas Ashe and the Blasket Island writers. The best historic photos you'll find in town decorate the library's walls with images of 19th-century Dingle. Green Street continues to the Strand, where a right turn takes you to the harbor.

The **harbor** was built on land reclaimed (with imported Dutch expertise) in 1992. The string of old stone shops facing the harbor was the loading station for the railway that hauled the fish from Dingle until 1953. Walk out to the end of the breakwater—recently paved and illuminated at night. The Eask Tower, on the distant hill, helped ships locate Dingle's hidden harbor in pre-radar days (though it was built primarily as a famine-era make-work project). The fancy manor house (now a school) across the harbor was built in the 18th century by Lord Ventry, a big-shot landlord. Near the dolphin statue, you'll find an office that serves as a clearinghouse for the various boat excursions.

Sights in Dingle

▲▲**The Harry Clark Windows of Díseart**—Just behind Dingle's St. Mary's Church stands St. Joseph's Convent and Díseart (dee-SHIRT, rhymes with "T-shirt"), containing a beautiful Neo-Gothic chapel built in 1884. The sisters of this order, who came to Dingle in 1829 to educate local girls, worked heroically during the famine. During Mass in the chapel, the Mother Superior would sit in the covered stall in the rear, while the sisters—filling the carved

stalls—chanted in response.

The chapel was graced in 1922 with 12 windows—the work of Ireland's top stained-glass man, Harry Clark. Long appreciated only by the sisters, these special windows—showing six scenes from the life of Christ—are now open to the public. The convent has become a center for sharing Christian Celtic culture and spirituality.

Enjoy a quick orientation by the attendant, followed by a 15-minute recorded narration explaining the chapel and its windows. The scenes (clockwise from the back entrance) are: the visit of the Magi, the Baptism of Jesus, "Let the little children come to me," the Sermon on the Mount, the Agony in the Garden, and Jesus appearing to Mary Magdalene. Each face is lively and animated in the imaginative, devout, medieval, and fun-loving style of Harry Clark, whom locals talk about as if he's the kid next door.

Cost and Hours: €3, May-Sept Mon-Fri 9:30-13:00 & 14:00-17:00, closed Sat-Sun but may be open Sat July-Aug, shorter hours off-season, tel. 066/915-2476, www.diseart.ie.

▲**Fungie**—In 1983, a dolphin moved into Dingle Harbor and became a local celebrity. Fungie (FOON-ghee, with a hard *g*) is now the darling of the town's tourist trade and one reason you'll

find so many tour buses parked along the harbor. Hardy little tour boats thrive by baiting passengers with the chance of an up-close Fungie encounter, then motoring out to the mouth of the harbor, where they troll around looking for him. You're virtually assured of seeing the dolphin, but you don't pay unless you do (€16, kids-€8, one-hour trips depart 11:00-17:00 depending on demand, behind TI at Dolphin Trips office, tel. 066/915-2626). To actually swim with Fungie, rent wetsuits at Brosnan's B&B (Cooleen Street, tel. 066/915-1146 or 087-273-4970) and catch the early-morning 8:00-10:00 trip (€45 includes boat trip and wetsuit—unless you've packed your own—minimum 6 people or they won't go). As Fungie is getting on in years, locals admit that he doesn't come up as often as he used to.

▲**Oceanworld**—This aquarium offers a little peninsula history, 300 different species of fish in thoughtfully described tanks, and the easiest way to see Fungie the dolphin: on video. Walk through the tunnel while fish swim overhead. You'll see local fish as well as a colorful Amazon collection. The penguin exhibit has a dozen of the little tuxedo torpedoes darting underwater and splashing up onto their fake Arctic ice block. The aquarium's mission is to teach, and you're welcome to ask questions. The petting pool is fun. Splashing attracts the rays, which are unplugged.

Cost and Hours: €13, families-€38, daily 10:00-18:00, July-Aug Sat-Sun until 19:00, shorter hours off-season, cafeteria, just past harbor on west edge of town, tel. 066/915-2111, www.dingle-oceanworld.ie.

Dingle Brewing Company—This brewery opened in 2012 in the site of the old creamery building, which happens to sit atop a spring providing "the purest water in Kerry." They brew Tom Crean's Premium Irish Lager, named for the local Antarctic explorer-hero (see sidebar, later), and they also offer informal tours on request.

Cost and Hours: €6 includes sample pint, daily 12:00-18:00, 200 yards up Spa Road on way to Conor Pass, tel. 066/915-0743, www.dinglebrewingcompany.com.

▲Short Harbor Walk from Dingle—For an easy stroll along the harbor out of town (and a chance to see Fungie, 1.5 hours round-trip), head east from the old roundabout and walk uphill past the Esso station. Just after Bambury's B&B, take a right, then immediately bear left (toward the cell-phone tower). You'll soon spot an Irish Coast Guard station down beside the bay. Turn left at the station, climbing the steps over the low wall and following the seashore path to the mouth of Dingle Harbor (marked by an empty shell of a tower—some 19th-century fat cat's folly). Ten minutes beyond that is a two-story lighthouse. This is Fungie's neighborhood. If you see tourist boats out, you're likely to see the dolphin. The trail continues to a dramatic cliff.

▲Bike and Hike to Eask Tower—Here's a good compromise for those wanting more exercise than the mellow harbor walk (above), but less sweat than biking the entire 30-mile Slea Head Loop (described on page 255). Lazybones can always drive to the trailhead. Rent a bike in town and pedal west past the aquarium, going left at the roundabout that takes you over the bridge onto R-559 toward Slea Head. After about two miles, turn left at the brown sign to *Holden's Leather Workshop*. A narrow lane leads another two miles to a hut on the right marked *Eask Tower* (the tower looms on the bare hill above). Pay the €2 trail fee at the hut (if unattended, feed the honor box) and hike straight up the hill. Pace yourself on this steep trail. You'll zigzag around sheep and tiptoe over their droppings. You'll also need to climb a couple of waist-high metal-rung gates. After 45 minutes, you'll have huffed and puffed up to the stone signal tower on the crown of the hill. Enjoy fantastic views of Dingle town (to the north) and Dingle Bay with the Iveragh Peninsula (to the south). Try to spot the two distant jagged Skellig Islands off the tip of the Iveragh Peninsula. The tip of the right one (farthest from the mainland) was home to a monastic hermitage for five centuries (see previous chapter).

Horseback Riding—**Dingle Horse Riding** takes out beginners (€35/hour for a trail ride) and experienced riders on two-hour (€65), half-day (€100), and full-day (€150) excursions (call ahead to book, follow Main Street out of Dingle, turn right at sign, tel. 066/915-2199, www. dinglehorseriding.com). **Long's**

Horseriding Centre is farther out on the peninsula just past Ventry (look for sign on right)—an easy stop for bikers or drivers doing the Slea Head Loop (€30/hour, variety of rides for all levels, short rides often depart at 9:00, call to book, tel. 066/915-9034, mobile 087-225-0286, www.longsriding.com). In either case, beach rides are only for advanced riders, and all horses come with English-style saddles (no horns to hang on to).

Dingle Pitch & Putt—This course's 18 holes (ranging from 30 to 70 yards in length) offer a relaxing diversion on a lush green point overlooking the harbor.

Cost and Hours: €8 includes gear, April-Oct daily 10:00-19:00, closed Nov-March, 10-minute walk out of town—over bridge take first left and follow signs, Milltown, tel. 066/915-2020.

Golf—Located out west, near the wildly scenic tip of the Dingle Peninsula and the town of Ballyferriter, Ceann Sibéal/Dingle Links offers a round of golf in a hard-to-beat setting.

Cost and Hours: €50 greens fees 9:00-16:00, €35 outside those hours, open daily till dusk, Baile an Fheirtearaigh, 9 miles west of Dingle town, tel. 066/915-6255, www.dinglelinks.com.

East of Dingle Town

▲**Minard Castle**—Three miles southwest of the town of Annascaul (Abhainn an Scáil), off the Lispole (Lios Póil) Road, is the largest fortress on the peninsula. Built by the Knights of Kerry in 1551, Minard Castle was destroyed by Cromwell's troops in about 1650. With its corners undermined by Cromwellian explosives, it looks ready to split—it's no longer safe to enter this teetering ruin.

From the outside, look for the faint scallop in the doorway, the symbol of St. James. Medieval pilgrims would stop here before making a seafaring pilgrimage from Dingle to St. James' tomb at Santiago de Compostela in northern Spain. Imagine the floor plan of the castle: ground floor for animals and storage, main-floor living room with fireplace, then a floor with sleeping quarters; and, on top, the defensive level.

The setting is dramatic, with the Ring of Kerry across the way and Storm Beach below. The beach is notable for its sandstone boulders that fell from the nearby cliffs. Grinding against each other in the wave and tidal action, the boulders eroded into cigar-shaped rocks. Pre-Christian Celts would carry them off and

Tom Crean, Unsung Antarctic Explorer

Kerrymen are known as a hardy lot, and probably none more so than Antarctic explorer and Annascaul native Thomas Crean. As a 15-year-old lad looking for steady employment and a chance to see the world, Crean left these shores in 1893 to join the British Royal Navy, and in 1901 volunteered to join the crew of the RSS *Discovery*. Onboard were Captain Robert Falcon Scott and other soon-to-be famous explorers, including Ernest Shackleton. Their mission: to be the first men to reach the South Pole.

It was the world's first serious attempt to reach the pole, an effort that required pulling sleds laden with tons of supplies across miles and miles of ice in extreme conditions. One of the team's most able man-haulers, Crean quickly gained his mates' trust and respect for his hard work, calm presence, and cheerful (if tuneless) singing. The *Discovery* Expedition pushed the boundaries of Antarctic exploration, but didn't reach the pole (Britain's second attempt, in 1909 under Shackleton, got much closer before also turning back).

Determined to try again, Scott chose Crean among the first of his handpicked crew for the *Terra Nova* Expedition (1910-1913). Early on, Crean saved some expedition members stranded on a drifting ice floe—encircled by orcas (who can tip ice to make vulnerable seals slide off)—by leaping between floating chunks of ice, then scaling an ice wall, to get help. Later, Crean and two others were the last support team ordered to turn back as Scott made the final push to the pole (having come so close, the unshakable Crean wept at the news). Near the end of the 730-mile return trip, Crean's two

carve them into ogham stones to mark clan boundaries (for more on ogham stones, see page 264).

Next to the fortress, look for the "fairy fort," an Iron Age fort from about 500 B.C. Locals thought it unlucky to pluck stones from these ring forts, so they remain undisturbed, overgrown with greenery, all across Ireland.

▲**Puicin Wedge Tomb**—While pretty obscure, this is worth the trouble for its evocative setting. Above the hamlet of Lispole (Lios Póil) in Doonties, park your car and hike 10 minutes up a ridge. At the summit is a pile of rocks made into a little room with one of the finest views on the peninsula. Beyond the Ring of Kerry you

mates, sick and freezing, could go no farther. Exhausted and provisioned with only three cookies and two sticks of chocolate, Crean made a non-stop, solo, 35-mile march through a blizzard to reach help, saving his mates' lives. (Though Scott's party did reach the pole, a Norwegian team, under Amundsen, beat them to it by a month; Scott and his men didn't survive the trip back.)

Crean's most famous act of heroism took place on his third and final polar expedition (1914-1917), led by Shackleton. Their ship, the *Endurance*, was crushed by ice, marooning the crew on Elephant Island. Hoping to find help at a whaling station, Shackleton, Crean, and four others sailed a modified open lifeboat 800 miles in 17 days to South Georgia Island. There they were forced to hike across the rugged, unexplored interior to reach the station on the other side. A ship was sent to rescue the exhausted and malnourished crew, all of whom had miraculously survived the 18-month ordeal.

Crean never did reach the South Pole himself, turning down Shackleton's request to join him on his next (and last) trek. But Crean distinguished himself as a hero among explorers—who named both a mountain and a glacier after him in Antarctica—and was honored by King George V. In 1920, he retired from the navy, returned to County Kerry, and stashed his medals away, never again speaking of his experiences—partly out of modesty, and partly because his service in the (British) navy could have made him a target for Irish nationalists. An uneducated farmer's son, Crean left few records of his exploits and didn't achieve the fame of his lauded (and more well-to-do) contemporaries. Crean married, bought a pub (South Pole Inn—see listing), and raised three daughters. After bravely escaping many near-deaths in the Antarctic, he finally died in 1938 of a burst appendix.

may just make out the jagged Skellig Michael, noted for its sixth-century monastic settlement (see previous chapter).

South Pole Inn—This pub, once owned by Antarctic explorer Tom Crean, is still open for business. As you pass through Annascaul on N-86, consider dropping in. On its walls you can peruse the loving photo gallery devoted to Crean's incredible adventures (see sidebar).

Inch Strand—This four-mile sandy beach, shaped like a half-moon, was made famous by the movie *Ryan's Daughter*. It's rated a "Blue Flag" beach for its clean water and safe swimming (usually has a lifeguard in summer).

Shopping in Dingle

Dingle is a petri dish of capitalism, with boutiques and charming shops popping up all the time to meet the rising demand of all the tourists and its newly affluent residents. Shoppers enjoy plenty of options.

Local Crafts—Many fine Dingle shops show off work by local artisans. The **West Kerry Craft Guild**—a co-op selling the work of 14 area artists—is a delight, even if you're just browsing. The prices here are good, since you're buying directly from the artists (daily June-Aug 10:00-18:00; Sept-May Wed-Mon 11:00-17:00, closed Tue; 18 Main Street, tel. 066/915-2976). **Dingle Crystal,** on Green Street with a cozy little café, features Sean Daly and his Waterford-trained crystal-cutting skills. Sean prides himself on his deeper, sharper design cuts (daily 10:00-19:00 in summer, shorter hours off-season; ask about crystal-cutting demonstrations in their workshop just outside town; tel. 066/915-1550, www.dinglecrystal. ie). **Lisbeth Mulcahy Weaver,** filled with traditional but stylish woven wear, is also the Dingle sales outlet of the well-known potter from out on Slea Head (Mon-Fri 9:30-18:00, Sat 10:00-18:00, Sun 12:00-17:00, Green Street, tel. 066/915-1688). **John Weldon Jewellers** features fine, handcrafted workmanship of Celtic designs by the local Dingle goldsmith (Mon-Sat 10:00-17:00, Sun 12:00-17:00, Green Street, tel. 066/915-2522, www.johnweldonjewellers. com).

Music Shops—**Danlann Gallery** sells musical instruments and woodcrafts (daily 10:00-18:00 in summer, "flexible" on weekends, shorter hours off-season, owner makes violins, Green Street). **Siopa Ceoil** is a grand little music shop and coffee bar worth seeking out. It's enthusiastically run by Michael Herlihy, who offers free quick-and-dirty *bodhrán* (traditional drum) lessons and sells advance tickets to the St. James Church concert (see "Folk Concerts," later). Michael and his omni-pleasant partner Katrina are virtual encyclopedias of Irish music knowledge (Mon-Sat 9:30-20:00, Sun 14:00-19:00, shorter hours off-season, near the waterfront and the recommended Mountain Man shop on a short dead-end lane called The Colony, tel. 066/915-2618, mobile 087-914-5826, www.siopa ceoil.ie).

Nightlife in Dingle

▲▲▲Music in Dingle Pubs

Traditional pub music is Dingle town's best experience. Even if you're not into pubs, take a nap and then give these a whirl. Dingle is renowned among traditional musicians as a place to get work ("€40 a day, tax-free, plus drink"). The town has piles of pubs that feature music most nights, and with nary a cover charge. The scene is a decent mix of locals, Americans, and Germans. Music normally starts at 21:30-ish, and the last call for drinks is at "half eleven" (23:30), sometimes later on weekends. For a seat near the

music, arrive early. If the place is chockablock with people, power in and find breathing room in the back. By midnight, the door is usually closed and the chairs are stacked. For some background, see "Traditional Irish Music" on page 35. For locations of the following pubs, see the map on page 251.

While two pubs, the **Small Bridge Bar** (An Droichead Beag) and **O'Flaherty's,** are the most famous for their atmosphere and devotion to traditional Irish music, make a point to wander the town and follow your ear. Smaller pubs may feel a bit foreboding to a tourist, but rest assured that people—locals as well as travelers—are out for the *craic.* Irish culture is very accessible in the pubs; they're like highly interactive museums waiting to be explored. If you sit at a table, you'll be left alone. But stand or sit at the bar and you'll be engulfed in conversation with new friends. Have a glass in an empty, no-name pub and chat up the publican. Pubs are no longer smoky, but can be stuffy and hot, so leave your coat at home. I know it's going to be a great trad music session when my eyeglasses steam up as I enter.

Pub Crawl: The best place to start a pub crawl is along Holyground Street at **O'Flaherty's.** Quietly intense owner Fergus O'Flaherty, a fixture since my first visit to Dingle, joins a varying lineup of loyal local musicians as he sings and plays a half-dozen different instruments during nightly traditional-music sessions. His domain has a high ceiling and is dripping in old-time photos and town memorabilia—it's touristy but lots of fun. Moving up Strand Street, find **John Benny Moriarty's.** Its dependably good traditional-music sessions come with John himself joining in on accordion when he's not pouring pints.

Then head up Green Street. **Dick Mack,** across from the church, is nicknamed "the last pew." This was once a tiny leather shop that expanded into a pub at night. Today, Dick Mack keeps the old leather-shop ambience but sells only drinks, with several rooms, a fine snug (private booth, originally designed to allow women to drink discreetly), ample beer choices, and a strangely fascinating ambience. Notice the Hollywood-type stars on the sidewalk outside, recalling famous visitors. The pub was established in 1899 by Dick Mack (master of the westernmost train station in

Europe), whose mission was to provide "liquid replenishment" to travelers. The grandson of the original Dick Mack runs the place today. A painting in the window shows Dick Mack II with the local gang.

Green Street climbs to Main Street, where two more Dick Mack-type places are filled with locals deep in conversation (but no music): **Foxy John's** (a hardware shop by day) and **Ó Curráin's** (across the street, a small clothing shop by day).

A bit higher up Main Street is **McCarthy's Pub,** a smoke-stained relic. It's less touristy and has occasional traditional-music sessions on its little stage. Wander down Main Street. The **Dingle Pub** is well established as *the* place for jaunty, shanty-type folk-ballad singing rather than the churning traditional beat of an Irish folk session. At the bottom of Main Street, **Small Bridge Bar** offers live music nightly. Its dimly lit confines are popular for good reason: Eoin Duignan, an accomplished local piper, often plays here (a painting of him decorates the front of the pub). While the tourists gather around the music, poke around the back and do an end run around the wall, which leads to a window nook with great views that is actually closest to the musicians. And the **Court House Pub** (on The Mall, next to the old gray courthouse) is a steamy little hideaway with low ceilings and high-caliber musicians. Owner Tommy O'Sullivan is a guitar-strumming fixture on the trad music scene.

After Hours: The pubs close at about midnight. That's when people who are just warming up head up the Conor Pass road to the **Hillgrove Lounge** (€5 cover, only place open after pub hours). Some like to hang out at **Rob Roy's,** munching a bag of greasy curry-cheese fries and watching the late-night migration. It's quite a scene.

Off-Season: From October through April, the music semi-hibernates. But on weekends, your best bets are the Small Bridge Bar, O'Flaherty's, and John Benny Moriarty's.

Other Nightlife

▲▲**Folk Concerts**—Top local musicians offer a quality evening of live, acoustic, traditional Irish music in the fine little **St. James' Church,** just off Main Street. These concerts are organized by local piper Eoin Duignan, whose command of the melodic Uileann bag-pipes is a highlight most nights (€12 advance purchase, €15 at the door; Mon, Wed, and Fri at 19:30, May-Sept only; mobile 087-284-9656; see sign on church gate or, for more details or to book a ticket, drop by the TI, Murphy's Ice Cream shop, Court House Pub, or Siopa Ceoil music shop). If you're not a night owl or prefer not to be packed into a pub with the distractions of conversation, then this is your best opportunity to hear Irish traditional music in a more controlled environment. Keep in mind that in this setting, many of the musicians find flash photography to be an irritating distraction.

Blue Zone Jazz and Pizza Bar—Climb the stairs to enter a totally different nightlife zone—the only real mellow ambience in town, where Patrick Juillet brings a splash of French attitude to Dingle. A wonderful gourmet chef, he applies his cooking genius to pizzas (Tue-Sun 17:30-24:00, Fri-Sat until 1:00 in the morning, closed Mon, no cover, lots of live music, Green Street, tel. 066/915-0303). Warning: Patrick is very political.

Cinema—Dingle's great little theater is The Phoenix on Dykegate. Its film club (50-60 locals) meets here Tuesdays year-round at 20:30 for coffee and cookies, followed by a film at 21:00 (€8 for film, anyone is welcome). The leader runs it almost like a religion, with a sermon on the film before he rolls it. The regular film schedule for the week is posted on the door.

Sleeping in Dingle

In or near the Town Center

$$$ Greenmount House sits among chilly palm trees in the countryside at the top of town. A five-minute hike up from the town center, this guest house commands a fine view of the bay and mountains. John and Mary Curran run one of Ireland's best B&Bs, with two fine rooms (Db-€70-110), three superb rooms (Db-€100-140), and seven sprawling suites (Db-€120-170) in a modern building with lavish public areas and breakfast in a solarium (reserve in advance, most rooms at ground level, Wi-Fi, parking, top of John Street, tel. 066/915-1414, fax 066/915-1974, www.greenmount house.ie, info@greenmounthouse.ie). Seek out the hot tub in their back garden cabin.

$$$ Bambury's Guesthouse, big and modern with views of grazing sheep and the harbor, rents 12 airy, comfy rooms (Sb-€80, Db-€100-120, Tb-€150, less off-season, family deals, Wi-Fi; coming in from Tralee it's on your left on Mail Road, 2 blocks before Esso station; tel. 066/915-1244, fax 066/915-1786, www. bamburysguesthouse.com, info@bamburysguesthouse.com).

$$$ Benners Hotel was the only hotel in town a hundred years ago. It stands bewildered by the modern world on Main Street, with sprawling public spaces and 52 abundant, overpriced rooms (Db-€170-205 July-Aug, €140-165 May-June and Sept, €110-135 Oct-April, discounts on website, tel. 066/915-1638, fax 066/915-1412, www.dinglebenners.com, info@dinglebenners.com).

$$ Alpine Guest House looks like a Monopoly hotel, and is fittingly comfortable and efficient. Its 14 spacious, bright, and fresh rooms come with wonderful views of sheep and the harbor, a cozy lounge, a great breakfast, and friendly owners (Sb-€45-65,

Sleep Code

(€1 = about $1.30, country code: 353, area code: 066)
S = Single, **D** = Double/Twin, **T** = Triple, **Q** = Quad, **b** = bathroom, **s** = shower only. Prices vary with the season, with winter cheap and August tops. Breakfast is included unless otherwise noted. Many places only accept cash.

To help you easily sort through these listings, I've divided the accommodations into three categories, based on the price for a standard double room with bath:

$$$ Higher Priced—Most rooms €100 or more.
$$ Moderately Priced—Most rooms between €60-100.
$ Lower Priced—Most rooms €60 or less.

Prices can change without notice; verify the hotel's current rates online or by email.

Db-€70-110, Tb-€90-120, Qb-€100-130, less off-season, 10 percent discount with this book through 2013, Wi-Fi, easy parking, Mail Road, tel. 066/915-1250, www.alpineguesthouse.com, alpine dingle@eircom.net, Paul). Driving into town from Tralee, this will be the first lodging on your right, next to the sports field and a block uphill from the Dingle Esso station.

$$ O'Neill's B&B is homey and friendly, with six decent rooms on a quiet street at the top of town (Db-€65-70, family deals, Wi-Fi, parking, John Street, tel. 066/915-1639, www.oneillsbedandbreakfast.com, info@oneillsbedandbreakfast.com, Mary and Stephen O'Neill).

$$ Eileen Collins Kirrary B&B, which takes up a quiet corner in the town center, is run by the same Collins family that does archaeological tours of the peninsula (see page 232). They offer five fine rooms, great prices, a large garden, and a homey friendliness (Db-€70-76, cash only, Wi-Fi, tel. 066/915-1606, Kirrary House, just off The Mall on Avondale Road, collinskirrary@eircom.net, Eileen Collins). They also rent a cozy, family-friendly, self-catering cottage that sleeps five people (minimum 3-night stay). A couple hundred yards high up behind town, it has Dingle's best views.

$$ Sraíd Eoin House offers five pleasant, top-floor rooms above Galvin's Travel Agency (Db-€70-80, Tb-€90-110, Qb-€100-120, 10 percent discount with cash and this book in 2013, Wi-Fi, John Street, tel. 066/915-1409, www.sraideoinbnb.com, sraideoin house@hotmail.com, friendly Kathleen and Maurice O'Connor).

$$ Barr Na Sráide Inn, central and hotel-like, has 26 basic rooms (Sb-€35-55, Db-€70-110, Tb-€100-150, family deals, Wi-Fi, self-service laundry, bar, parking, past McCarthy's pub on

DINGLE PENINSULA

Upper Main Street, tel. 066/915-1331, fax 066/915-1446, www. barrnasraide.com, info@barrnasraide.ie).

$$ Captain's House B&B rents two suites in the town center, and Mary, whose mother ran a guest house before Dingle was discovered, provides a continental breakfast for her guests (two great suites-€100-120, 10 percent discount with cash and 3-night stay, Wi-Fi, The Mall, tel. 066/915-1531, captigh@eircom.net, Jim and Mary Milhench).

$$ Kelliher's Ballyegan House is a big, plain building on the edge of town, with six modest rooms and great harbor views (Db-€60-70, Tb-€90, cash only, parking, Upper John Street, tel. 066/915-1702, ballyeganhousedingle@gmail.com, James Kelliher).

Beyond the Pier

These accommodations are a 10-15-minute walk from Dingle's town center. They tend to be quieter, since they are farther from the late-night pub scene.

$$$ Heaton's Guesthouse, big, peaceful, and comfortable, is on the water just west of town at the end of Dingle Bay—a five-minute walk past Oceanworld on The Wood. The 16 thoughtfully appointed rooms come with all the amenities (Db-€78-130, suite Db-€118-170, less off-season, creative breakfasts, parking, The Wood, tel. 066/915-2288, www.heatonsdingle.com, heatons@iol. ie, Cameron and Nuala Heaton).

$$$ Castlewood House is a palatial refuge with 12 tasteful rooms, classy furnishings, and delicious breakfasts. The breakfast room and patio have a wonderful view of Dingle Harbor (Sb-€65-110, Db-€85-170, Tb-€120-195, parking, The Wood, tel. 066/915-2788, www.castlewooddingle.com, info@castlewooddingle.com, Brian and Helen Heaton).

$$ Milestone House, a 15-minute walk out of town, has six warmly decorated rooms, great views of Dingle Harbor, an ancient boundary stone in the front yard, and wonderful breakfasts. Friendly Barbara and Michael Carroll are brimming with sightseeing tips (Sb-€50-55, Db-€70-80, Tb-€110-120, Qb-€130-150, cash only, Wi-Fi, parking, tel. 066/915-1831, www.milestone dingle.com, milestonedingle@eircom.net).

$$ Tower View B&B is a big, bright-yellow modern home just outside of town on a lovely wooded lot. This kid-friendly mini-farm, with pettable animals, rents eight fine rooms (Sb-€50-60, Db-€70-80, Tb-€100-120, Qb-€120-140, cash only, Wi-Fi, just past the roundabout on the west side of town on High Road, tel. 066/915-2990, www.towerviewdingle.com, info@towerviewdingle. com, Mary and Robbie Griffin).

$$ Harbour Nights B&B weaves together a line of old row houses to create a 14-room guest house facing the harbor (Sb-€50,

DINGLE PENINSULA

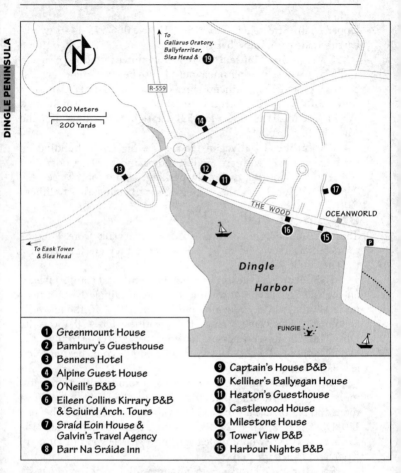

To Gallarus Oratory, Ballyferriter, Slea Head & ⑲

R-559

200 Meters
200 Yards

⑭

⑬

⑫

⑪

THE WOOD

⑰

OCEANWORLD

⑯

⑮

P

To Eask Tower
& Slea Head

Dingle

Harbor

FUNGIE

❶ Greenmount House
❷ Bambury's Guesthouse
❸ Benners Hotel
❹ Alpine Guest House
❺ O'Neill's B&B
❻ Eileen Collins Kirrary B&B
   & Sciuird Arch. Tours
❼ Sraíd Eoin House &
   Galvin's Travel Agency
❽ Barr Na Sráide Inn

❾ Captain's House B&B
❿ Kelliher's Ballyegan House
⑪ Heaton's Guesthouse
⑫ Castlewood House
⑬ Milestone House
⑭ Tower View B&B
⑮ Harbour Nights B&B

Db-€60-80, Tb-€90-105, free Internet access in guest lounge, Wi-Fi, just past the aquarium on The Wood, tel. 066/915-2499, mobile 087-686-8190, www.harbournightsguesthouse.com, info@dingle bandb.com, Seán and Kathleen Lynch).

$ The Last Cottage B&B is a good budget bet, with three old-fashioned rooms in a 1909 Council House on the harbor at the far edge of town. This time warp—almost like a museum—is modest, unpretentious, and comfortably cluttered (D-€60-65, closed Oct-April, The Wood, tel. 066/915-1469, www.dinglelast cottage.page.tl, dinglelastcottage@gmail.com, Elvis fan Margaret Holderied).

Hostels and Dorms
$ Dingle Harbour Lodge is a big and modern place on the edge

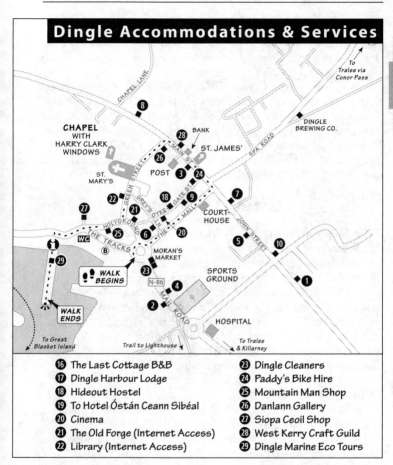

Dingle Accommodations & Services

16 The Last Cottage B&B
17 Dingle Harbour Lodge
18 Hideout Hostel
19 To Hotel Óstán Ceann Sibéal
20 Cinema
21 The Old Forge (Internet Access)
22 Library (Internet Access)
23 Dingle Cleaners
24 Paddy's Bike Hire
25 Mountain Man Shop
26 Danlann Gallery
27 Siopa Ceoil Shop
28 West Kerry Craft Guild
29 Dingle Marine Eco Tours

of town. You have the feeling of being a guest in a comfy hotel—a hotel-style breakfast is included—without the fancy prices (€25-30/person in 8-bed dorm room, Db-€60-90, Tb-€90-120, family rooms, Wi-Fi, up a long driveway off The Wood past the aquarium, tel. 066/915-1577, www.dingleharbourlodge.com, info@dingle harbourlodge.com, Trish Coogan).

$ Hideout Hostel is friendly and central, just across the lane from the movie theater. Michael (MEE-hall) grew up on this street and manages a relaxed, fun atmosphere while screening out loud stag/hen-party gangs (€18/person in 4-bed dorm room, additional nights-€15/person, Db-€50; these rates good only with 2013 edition of this book; family room available, includes continental breakfast, Wi-Fi, Dykegate Street, tel. 066/915-0559, www.the hideouthostel.com, info@thehideouthostel.com).

Near Dingle Town

If Dingle is too much of an urban metropolis for you, get away from it all in the quiet village of Ballyferriter, 10 miles (16 km) northwest of town on the Slea Head Loop.

$$ Hotel Óstán Ceann Sibéal is a modern and elegant hotel with all the comforts. Its 26 rooms are large, and half of the top-floor rooms face the countryside with grand skylight views. The downstairs pub serves good grub and has trad music sessions on Saturday and Sunday nights (Sb-€60-75, Db-€80-109, Tb-€109-139, tel. 066/915-6433, fax 066/915-6577, www.ceannsibealhotel.com, info@ceannsibealhotel.com).

Eating in Dingle

The Only Cheap Meal in Dingle: Picnic

The **SuperValu** supermarket/department store, at the base of town, has everything and stays open late (Mon-Sat 8:00-21:00, Sun 8:00-19:00, daily until 22:00 in July-Aug). Smaller groceries, such as **Centra** on Main Street (Mon-Sat 8:00-21:00, Sun 8:00-18:00), are scattered throughout the town. Consider a grand-view picnic out on the end of the newer pier (as you face the harbor, it's the pleasure-boat pier on your right). You'll find picnic tables on the harbor side of the roundabout and benches along the busy harborfront. The Chinese eatery on Green Street does take-away.

Dining in Dingle

All of these restaurants are good, but I've listed them in the order of my personal preference.

Chart House Restaurant serves contemporary cuisine in a sleek, well-varnished dining room. Settle back into the shipshape, lantern-lit, harborside ambience. The menu is shaped by what's fresh and seasonal. The chef, who has a Tuscan connection and a passion for South African wines, is committed to always offering a good vegetarian entrée (€20-30 dinners, June-Sept daily 18:00-22:00, Oct-May closed Mon, at roundabout at base of town, reservations wise, tel. 066/915-2255, Jim McCarthy).

Out of the Blue Seafood-Only Restaurant is the locals' choice for just plain great fresh fish. The interior is bright and elegantly simple. The menu—not printed, but on a chalkboard—is dictated by what the fishermen caught that morning. If they're closed, you know there's been a storm and the fishermen couldn't go out. The €12-17 lunches and heartier €21-30 dinners are artfully presented, with a touch of nouvelle cuisine and certainly no chips (daily 12:30-15:00 & 17:00-21:30, closed Wed and after a storm, some outdoor picnic-table seating, reservations smart, just past the TI, facing the harbor on The Waterside, tel. 066/915-0811).

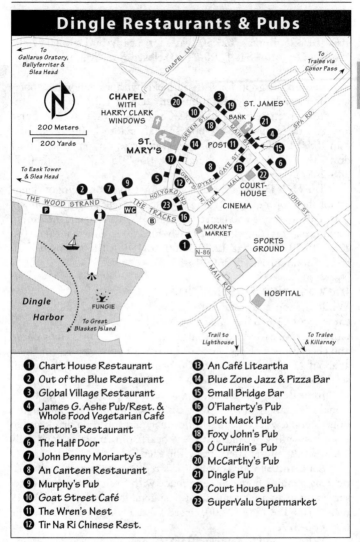

Dingle Restaurants & Pubs

To Gallarus Oratory, Ballyferriter & Slea Head

To Tralee via Conor Pass

CHAPEL LN.

200 Meters
200 Yards

CHAPEL
WITH
HARRY CLARK
WINDOWS

ST.
MARY'S

ST. JAMES'

GREEN ST.
MAIN ST.
SPA RD.
POST
BANK
MALL
GREY'S LN.
DYKE LN.
GATE ST.
HOLYGROUND
THE MALL
COURT-
HOUSE
JOHN ST.

To Eask Tower
& Slea Head

THE WOOD STRAND
THE TRACKS
P
WC
i
B

CINEMA

MORAN'S
MARKET

SPORTS
GROUND

N-86

Dingle
Harbor

FUNGIE

To Great
Blasket Island

MAIL RD.

HOSPITAL

Trail to
Lighthouse

To Tralee
& Killarney

- ❶ Chart House Restaurant
- ❷ Out of the Blue Restaurant
- ❸ Global Village Restaurant
- ❹ James G. Ashe Pub/Rest. & Whole Food Vegetarian Café
- ❺ Fenton's Restaurant
- ❻ The Half Door
- ❼ John Benny Moriarty's
- ❽ An Canteen Restaurant
- ❾ Murphy's Pub
- ❿ Goat Street Café
- ⓫ The Wren's Nest
- ⓬ Tir Na Ri Chinese Rest.
- ⓭ An Café Liteartha
- ⓮ Blue Zone Jazz & Pizza Bar
- ⓯ Small Bridge Bar
- ⓰ O'Flaherty's Pub
- ⓱ Dick Mack Pub
- ⓲ Foxy John's Pub
- ⓳ Ó Curráin's Pub
- ⓴ McCarthy's Pub
- ㉑ Dingle Pub
- ㉒ Court House Pub
- ㉓ SuperValu Supermarket

At the **Global Village Restaurant,** Martin Bealin concocts his favorite dishes with inspiration gleaned from his travels around the world. He has a passion for making things from scratch and giving dishes a creative twist. No chips, no deep-fat-fried anything. It's an eclectic, healthy, fresh seafood-eaters' place (€25-30 dinners, good salads, early-bird special 17:30-19:00, open June-Sept Wed-Mon 17:30-22:00, closed Tue and through the winter, top of Main Street, tel. 066/915-2325, mobile 087-917-5920).

James G. Ashe Pub and Restaurant, an old-fashioned joint, is popular with locals for its nicely presented, top-quality, traditional

Irish food and seafood at good prices. Try their beef-and-Guinness stew (€15-25 dinners, €21.50 two-course early-bird special 17:30-19:00, open Mon-Sat 17:00-21:30, closed Sun, Main Street, tel. 066/915-0989).

Fenton's is good for seafood meals with a memorable apple-and-berry-crumble dessert. On sunny days, I enjoy their delightful garden section out back (€23-30 main courses, €26 two-course and €30 three-course early-bird specials before 19:00, open Tue-Sun 18:00-21:30, closed Mon, reservations smart, on Green Street down the hill below the church, tel. 066/915-2172, mobile 087-248-2487).

The Half Door, at the top of the town, is one of Dingle's long-established top-notch restaurants (on John Street), satisfying diners with €30-40 meals and hearty portions. While elegant, the dining room feels a bit congested (€29 early-bird three-course meal served 17:30-18:30, Mon-Sat 12:30-14:00 & 18:00-21:30, closed Sun, reservations smart, tel. 066/915-2543).

Inexpensive Dingle Dinners

While the top-end restaurants charge on average €20-30, you can eat well for €12-16 in Dingle's pubs and ethnic eateries. Fancy restaurants serve early-bird specials from 17:30 to 19:00. Many cheap and cheery lunch places close at 18:00. Most pubs stop serving food at about 21:00 (to make room for their beer drinkers). Anyone will serve tap water for free. Here are some ideas:

John Benny Moriarty's is a waterfront pub dishing up traditional Irish fare with a relatively cozy interior. John, the proprietor, hopes people will come here for dinner, and stay for a drink and to enjoy his nightly live music (€12-16 hearty dinner plates, food daily 12:30-21:30, music after 21:30, The Pier).

An Canteen hides out up the street, across from the cinema, offering genuine home cooking made with fresh seasonal produce, served up in an unpretentious atmosphere, for great prices (€12-19 meals, Thu-Tue 12:00-21:00, closed Wed, Dykegate Street, mobile 086-660-3778).

Whole Food Vegetarian Café is a peaceful little place serving healthy soups, salads, pancakes, fruit smoothies, and home-baked cakes. Its serene back garden is perfect for enjoying a light lunch (Wed-Sat 12:00-17:00, closed Sun-Tue, Lower Main Street, mobile 087-741-6947).

Murphy's Pub is a favorite for good, sloppy pub grub with an extensive and kid-friendly menu and lots of fries (€12-15 plates, daily 12:00-21:00, at 21:00 the restaurant makes way for beer and music, The Strand, tel. 066/915-1450).

Goat Street Café is a good-natured, lunch-only cubbyhole away from the action, with dependable pasta and fish plates (€11-

16 lunches, Mon-Sat 10:00-16:00, closed Sun, at top of town where Main Street becomes Goat Street, tel. 066/915-2770, mobile 086-826-4118).

The Wren's Nest is a mellow coffeehouse, reflecting musician-owner John Ryan's philosophical demeanor. This lunch-only refuge, with an ultra-appealing back garden, serves wholesome omelets, sandwiches, cakes, and tea. A small corner stage hosts open-mic acoustic music gigs (June-Aug Thu and Sat at 20:00); you can also check out the schedule of dance and music lessons (daily 11:00-17:00, Dykegate Street, mobile 086-177-3119).

Tir Na Ri Chinese Restaurant serves what you'd expect in a relatively plush ambience (€12-19 plates, Mon-Fri 12:30-14:30 & 17:00-23:00, Sat-Sun 17:00-23:00, also take-away, Green Street, tel. 066/915-0823).

An Café Liteartha, a likeable and simple cubbyhole hidden behind a wonderfully cluttered bookstore, serves soup and sandwiches to a good-natured crowd of Gaelic speakers (June-Aug daily 10:00-18:00, Sept-May Mon-Sat 10:00-17:00, closed Sun, Dykegate Street, tel. 066/915-2204).

Meals on Slea Head Loop

The Stonehouse is an appealing lunch or dinner option about seven miles (12 km) west of Dingle on the Slea Head Loop road. Serving local specialties, from scones to fresh seafood and steak dishes, David and Michelle Foran nurture a cozy atmosphere. Their front porch outdoor tables are popular seaview perches on warm summer evenings (€11-15 meals, daily 11:00-21:30, reservations smart on weekends, tel. 066/915-9970).

Dingle Connections

Tralee (Tra' Li), 30 miles from Dingle, is the region's transportation hub (with the nearest train station to Dingle). All bus trips make connections in Tralee.

From Dingle by Bus to: Galway (5/day, 6.5 hours), **Dublin** (4/day, 8-9 hours, transfer in Tralee and Limerick), **Rosslare** (2/day, 9 hours), **Tralee** (5/day, 1.25 hours, €12.30 one-way, €20 round-trip); fewer departures on Sundays. Most bus trips out of Dingle require at least one or two (easy) transfers. Remember, buses stop on the waterfront behind the SuperValu (bus info tel. 01/836-6111 or Tralee station at 066/712-3566, Tralee train info tel. 066/712-3522). For more information, see "Tralee Connections" at the end of this chapter.

All Roads Lead to An Daingean

The western half of the Dingle Peninsula is part of the Gaeltacht, where locals speak the Irish (Gaelic) language. In an effort to ward off English-language encroachment, all place names on road signs were controversially changed to Irish-only in 2005 (see "Dingle or An Daingean?" sidebar, earlier). As you travel along Slea Head Drive (known as Ceann Sléibhe in Irish), you can refer to this cheat sheet of the most useful destination names. Remember that a complete translation of all Irish place names is included in the Gazetteer section at the back of the *Complete Road Atlas of Ireland* by Ordnance Survey.

English Name	Irish (Gaelic) Name	Pronounced
Dingle	*An Daingean*	on DANG-un
Ventry	*Ceann Tra'*	k'yown (rhymes with crown) thraw
Slea Head	*Ceann Sléibhe*	k'yown SHLAY-veh
Dunquin	*Dún Chaoin*	doon qween
Blasket Islands	*Na Blascaodai*	nuh BLAS-kud-ee
Great Blasket Island	*An Blascaod Mór*	on BLAS-kade moor
Ballyferriter	*Baile an Fheirtearaigh*	BALL-yuh on ERR-ter-ig
Reasc Monastery	*Mainistir Riaisc*	MON-ish-ter REE-isk
Gallarus	*Gallaras*	GAHL-russ
Kilmalkedar	*Cill Mhaoil-cheadair*	kill moyle-KAY-dir
Annascaul	*Abhainn an Scáil*	ow'en on skahl
Lispole	*Lios Póil*	leesh pohl
Tralee	*Tra' Li*	traw lee

Dingle Peninsula Loop Trip

A sight worth ▲▲▲, the Dingle Peninsula loop trip is about 30 miles (47 km) long and must be driven in a clockwise direction. It's easy by car, or it's a demanding four hours by bike—if you don't stop to catch your breath. Cyclists should plan on an early start

(preferably by 9:00) to allow for enough sightseeing and lunch/rest time.

While you can take the basic guided tour of the peninsula (see "Tours in Dingle" on page 232), the self-guided tour that follows makes it unnecessary. A fancy map is also not necessary with my instructions. I've provided distances to help locate points of interest. I've given distances below in kilometers so you can follow along with your rental-car odometer.

If you're driving, check your odometer at Oceanworld, as you leave Dingle (ideally, reset your odometer to zero—most likely you can do this by holding down the button next to it). Even if you get off track or are biking, you can subtract the kilometers listed below to figure out distances between points. To get the most out of your trip, read through this entire section before departing. Then go step-by-step (staying on R-559 and following the brown *Ceann Sléibhe/Slea Head Drive* signs). Roads are very congested mid-July to late August.

The Dingle Peninsula is 10 miles wide and runs 40 miles from Tralee to Slea Head. The top of its mountainous spine is Mount Brandon—at 3,130 feet, it's the second-tallest mountain in Ireland (after a nearby peak above Killarney that's almost 500 feet higher). While only a few tiny villages lie west of Dingle town, the peninsula is home to 500,000 sheep.

Self-Guided Tour

Leave Dingle town west along the waterfront (0.0 km at Oceanworld). Driving out of town, on the left you'll see a row of humble "two up and two down" flats from a 1908 affordable housing government initiative. Today, even these little places cost more than €250,000.

0.5 km: There's an eight-foot tide here. The seaweed was used to make formerly worthless land arable. (Seaweed is a natural source of potash—it's organic farming, before it was trendy.) Across the Milltown River estuary, the fancy Milltown House B&B (with flags) was Robert Mitchum's home for a year during

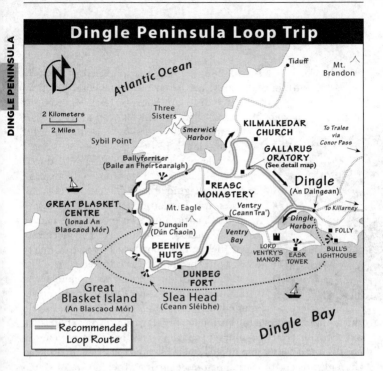

Dingle Peninsula Loop Trip

Atlantic Ocean

Tiduff
Mt. Brandon

Three Sisters

Smerwick Harbor

KILMALKEDAR CHURCH

To Tralee via Conor Pass

2 Kilometers

2 Miles

Sybil Point

Ballyferriter
(Baile an Fheirtearaigh)

GALLARUS ORATORY
(See detail map)

Dingle
(An Daingean)

REASC MONASTERY

GREAT BLASKET CENTRE
(Ionad An Blascaod Mór)

Mt. Eagle

Ventry
(Ceann Tra')

To Killarney

Dunquin
(Dún Chaoin)

Ventry Bay

Dingle Harbor

FOLLY

BEEHIVE HUTS

LORD VENTRY'S MANOR

EASK TOWER

BULL'S LIGHTHOUSE

Great Blasket Island
(An Blascaod Mór)

DUNBEG FORT

Slea Head
(Ceann Sléibhe)

Dingle Bay

Recommended Loop Route

the filming of *Ryan's Daughter*. (Behind that is a scenic pitch & putt range—described on page 239.) Look for the narrow mouth of this blind harbor (where Fungie the dolphin frolics) and the Ring of Kerry beyond that. Dingle Bay is so hidden that ships needed the Eask Tower to find its mouth.

0.7 km: At the roundabout, turn left over the bridge. The hardware-store building on the right was a corn-grinding mill in the 18th century. You'll pass the junction where you'll complete this loop trip later.

1.3 km: The Milestone B&B is named for the stone pillar (*gallaun* in Gaelic) in its front yard. This pillar may have been a prehistoric grave or a boundary marker between two tribes. The stone goes down as far as it sticks up. The peninsula, literally an open-air museum, is dotted with more than 2,000 such monuments dating from the Neolithic Age (4000 B.C.) through early-Christian times. Another stone pillar stands in the field across the street, in the direction of the yellow manor house of Lord Ventry (in the distance). Its function today: cow scratcher.

Lord Ventry, whose family came to Dingle as post-Cromwellian War landlords in 1666, built this mansion in about 1750. Today it houses an all-Irish-language boarding school for 140 high-school girls.

Currach Boats

A *currach* is the traditional fishing boat of the west coast of Ireland—lightweight and easy to haul. In your Dingle travels, you'll see a few actual *currach* boats—generally retired and stacked where visitors can finger them and ponder the simpler age when they were a key part of the economy. They were easy to make: Cover a wooden frame with canvas (originally cowhide) and paint with tar—presto. When transporting sheep, farmers would lash each sheep's pointy little hooves together and place it carefully upside-down in the *currach*—so it wouldn't puncture the frail little craft's canvas skin.

As you drive past the Ventry estate, you'll pass palms, magnolias, and exotic flora, which were introduced to Dingle by Lord Ventry. The Gulf Stream is the source of the mild climate (it rarely snows here), which supports subtropical plants. Consequently, fuchsias—imported from Chile and spreading like weeds—line the roads all over the peninsula and redden the countryside from June through September. More than 100 inches of rain a year gives this area its "40 shades of green."

The old red-sandstone and slate-roof cottages along the roadside housed Ventry estate workers in the 1840s.

3 km: A brown sign reading *Holden's Leather Workshop* leads up a road to the left. This is the narrow lane that connects to the trail up to Eask Tower (see page 238 for details on this active hiking/biking option).

4.6 km: Stay off the "soft margin" as you enjoy views of Ventry Bay, its four-mile-long beach (to your right as you face the water), and distant Skellig Michael, which you'll see all along this part of the route. Skellig Michael—an island jutting up like France's Mont St. Michel—contains the rocky remains of a sixth-century monastic settlement (described in previous chapter). Next to it is a smaller island, Little Skellig—a breeding ground for gannets (seagull-like birds with six-foot wingspans). In 1866, the first transatlantic cable was laid from nearby Valentia Island to Canada's Newfoundland (see sidebar on page 223). It was in use until 1965. Mount Eagle (1,660 feet), rising across the bay, marks the end of Ireland.

In the town of **Ventry**—a.k.a. Ceann Tra'—Gaelic is the first language. Ventry is little more than a bungalow holiday village today. Urban Irish families love to come here in the summer to immerse their kids in the traditional culture and wild nature. A large hall at the edge of the village is used as a classroom where big-city students come on field trips to learn the Gaelic language.

Just past the town, a lane leads left to a fine beach and mobile-home vacation community. An information board explains the history, geology, and bird life of this bay. The humble trailer park has no running water or electricity. Locals like it for its economy and proximity to the beach. From here, a lane also leads inland to **Long's Horseriding Centre** (described earlier, under "Sights in Dingle"). During World War II, a German U-boat churned into this bay and put 28 Greek sailors ashore on this beach (and therefore onto neutral Irish soil). They were survivors from a merchant ship that the sub had sunk...not the kind of humanitarian gesture that German U-boat captains were known for making.

5.2 km: The bamboo-like rushes on either side of the road are the kind used to make the local thatched roofs. Thatching, which nearly died out because of the fire danger, is more popular now that anti-flame treatments are available. It's not the cheap roofing alternative, however, as it's expensive to pay the few qualified craftsman thatchers who remain in Ireland. Black-and-white magpies fly overhead.

8.6 km: The Irish football (GAA) star Páidí Ó Sé (Paddy O'Shea) is a household name in Ireland. He won eight all-Ireland football titles for Kerry as a player. He then trained the Kerry team for many years, and he now runs the pub on the left (also notice the tiny grocery on the right; easy beach access from here).

9.2 km: The plain blue cottage hiding in the trees 100 yards off the road on the left (view through the white gate, harder to see in summer when foliage is thickest) was kept cozy by Tom Cruise and Nicole Kidman during the filming of *Far and Away*. Just beyond are fine views of the harbor and Dingle's stone tower.

10.7 km: *Taisteal go Mall* means "go slowly"; there's a red-colored, two-room **schoolhouse** on the right (20 students, two teachers). During the summer, it's used for Gaelic courses for kids from the big cities. On the left is the small Celtic and Prehistoric Museum, a quirky private collection of prehistoric artifacts collected by a retired busker named Harris (€4, family-€12, daily 10:00-17:30).

11.1 km: The circular mound (which looks like an elevated hedge) on the right is a late-Stone Age ring fort. In 500 B.C., it was a petty Celtic chieftain's headquarters, a stone-and-earth stockade filled with little thatched dwellings. These survived untouched through the centuries because of superstitious beliefs that they were "fairy forts." While this site is unexcavated, recent digging has shown that people have lived on this peninsula since well before 4000 B.C.

11.7 km: Look ahead up Mount Eagle at the patchwork of stone-fenced fields.

12.5 km: Dunbeg Fort, a series of defensive ramparts and ditches around a central *clochan,* is open to tourists—though it's ready to fall into the sea. There are no carvings to be seen, but the small *(beg)* fort *(dun)* is dramatic (€3, daily 9:00-19:00, May-Aug until 20:00, descriptive handout, includes 10-minute video shown in the modern stone house across the street, giving a bigger picture of the prehistory of the peninsula). Forts like this are the most important relics left from Ireland's Iron Age (500 B.C.-A.D. 500).

Along the road, you'll see a newer stone-roofed house built to blend in with the landscape and the region's ancient rock-slab architecture (A.D. 2000). It's the Stone House, a friendly restaurant with an adjacent visitors center where you can see the film mentioned above. A traditional *currach* boat is permanently dry-docked in the parking lot.

12.6 km: Roughly 50 yards up the hill is a thatched cottage abandoned by a family named Kavanaugh 150 years ago, during the famine. With a few rusty and chipped old artifacts and good descriptions, it offers an evocative peek into the simple lifestyles of the area in the 19th century (€3, family-€10, May-Oct daily 10:00-17:00, closed Nov-April, tel. 066/915-6241, mobile 087-762-2617).

13.4 km: A group of beehive huts *(clochans),* is a short walk up-

hill (€2, daily 9:30-19:00, WC). These mysterious stone igloos, which cluster together within a circular wall, are a better sight than the similar group of beehive huts a mile down the road. Look over the water for more Skellig views.

Farther on, you'll ford a stream. There has never been a bridge here; this bit of road—nicknamed the "upside-down bridge"—was designed as a ford.

14.9 km: Pull off to the left at this second group of beehive huts. Look downhill at the rocky field—in the movie *Far and Away,* that's where Lord Ventry evicted (read: torched) peasants from their cottages. Even without Hollywood, this is a bleak and godforsaken land. Look above at the patches of land slowly made into farmland by the inhabitants of this westernmost piece of Europe. Rocks were cleared and piled into fences. Sand and seaweed were laid on the clay, and in time it was good for grass. The created land, if at all tillable, was generally used for growing potatoes; otherwise, it was only good for grazing. Much of it has fallen out of use now. Look across the bay at the Ring of Kerry in the distance and ahead at the Blasket Islands (Na Blascaodai).

16.1 km: At Slea Head (Ceann Sléibhe)—marked by a crucifix, a pullout, and great views of the Blasket Islands (described later)—you turn the corner on this tour. On stormy days, the waves are "racing in like white horses."

16.9 km: Pull into the little parking lot (at *Dún Chaoin* sign) to

view the Blasket Islands and Dunmore Head (the westernmost point in Europe) and to review the roadside map (which traces your route) posted in the parking lot. The scattered village of Dunquin (Dún Chaoin) has many ruined rock homes abandoned during the famine. Some are fixed up, as this is a popular place these days for summer homes. You can see more good examples of land reclamation, patch by patch, climbing up the hillside. Mount Eagle was the first bit of land that Charles Lindbergh saw after crossing the Atlantic on his way to

Paris in 1927. Villagers here were as excited as he was—they had never seen anything so big in the air. About a kilometer down a road on the left, a plaque celebrates the 30th anniversary of the filming of *Ryan's Daughter*. From here, a trail leads down to a wild beach.

19.3 km: The Blasket Islands' residents had no church or cemetery on the island. This was their cemetery. The famous Blascaod

storyteller Peig Sayers (1873-1958) is buried in the center. At the next intersection, drive down the little lane that leads left (100 yards) to a small stone marker (hiding in the grass on the left) commemorating the 1588 shipwreck of the *Santa María de la Rosa* of the Spanish Armada. Below that is the often-tempestuous Dun-

quin Harbor, from where the Blasket Islands ferry departs. Island farmers—who on a calm day could row across in 30 minutes—would dock here and hike 12 miles into Dingle to sell their produce.

19.4 km: Back on the main road, follow signs to the *Ionad An Blascaod Mór* (Great Blasket Centre). You'll pass a village school from 1914 (its two teachers still teach 18 students, grades one through six).

22.3 km: Leave the Slea Head Road, turning left for the Great Blasket Centre (provides a worthwhile introduction to Blasket Islands—see page 266; also has a good cafeteria).

23.1 km: Back at the turnoff, head left (sign to *Louis Mulcahy Pottery*).

23.2 km: *Ryan's Daughter* film buffs will take a left turn here (a gravel lane) to visit the schoolhouse built for crucial scenes in that movie. Drive down the lane a few hundred yards and park at the dead end. Walk the trail another hundred yards (through a couple of kissing gates) and you'll see the schoolhouse below, ringed by a low stone wall. Never intended to be a permanent structure, it's the only building still standing from that outdoor movie set of some 40 years ago—and it's falling apart, too. But the lonely setting is memorable.

24.5 km: Passing land that was never reclaimed, think of the work it took to pick out the stones, pile them into fences, and bring up sand and seaweed to nourish the clay and make soil for growing potatoes. Look over the water to the island aptly named the "Sleeping Giant"—see his hand resting happily on his beer belly.

24.9 km: Grab the scenic pull-out. The view is spectacular. Ahead, on the right, study the top fields, untouched since the planting of 1845, when the potatoes didn't grow, but rotted in the ground. The faint vertical ridges of the potato beds can still be seen—a reminder of the famine (easier to see a bit later). Before the famine, 40,000 people lived on this peninsula. After the famine, the population was so small that there was never again a need to farm so high up. Today, only 10,000 live on the peninsula.

The lousy farmland on both sides of the straight stretch of road was stripped of seven feet of peat (turf) in the 19th century. The land may have provided a lot of warmth back then...but it provides no food today.

30 km: The town of **Ballyferriter** (Baile an Fheirtearaigh), established by a Norman family in the 12th century, is the largest on this side of Dingle. The pubs serve grub, and the old schoolhouse is a museum. Its modest exhibits provide the best coverage of this very historic peninsula (€2.50, June-Sept usually daily 10:00-17:00 but hours vary, closed Oct-May, tel. 066/915-6333, www.west kerrymuseum.com). The early-Christian cross in front of the schoolhouse looks real. Tap it...it's fiberglass—a prop from the *Ryan's Daughter* bus-stop scenes.

31.4 km: At the T-junction, signs direct you left to *An Daingean* (Dingle, 11 km). Go left, via *Gallaras* (and still following *Ceann Sléibhe/Slea Head Drive* signs). Take a right over the bridge, following signs to *Gallaras*.

32 km: Just beyond the bridge, you'll pass the Tigh Bhric market, pub, and microbrewery (good pub-grub lunches, tel. 066/915-6325). Five yards before the sign to *Mainistir Riaise* (Reasc Monastery), detour right up the lane. After 0.3 km (up the unsigned turnout on your right), you'll find the scant remains of the walled **Reasc Monastery** (dating from the 6th to 12th centuries, free, always open). The inner wall divided the community into sections for prayer and business (cottage industries helped support the monastery). In 1975, only the stone pillar was visible, as the entire site was buried. The layer of black tar paper (near the base of the walls) marks where the original rocks stop and the excavators' reconstruction begins. The stone pillar is Celtic (c. 500 B.C.). When the Christians arrived in the fifth century, they didn't throw out the Celtic society. Instead, they carved a Maltese-type cross over the Celtic scrollwork. The square building was an oratory (church—you'll see an intact oratory at the next stop). The round buildings would have been *clochan*s—those stone igloo-type dwellings. One of the cottage industries operated by the monastery was a double-duty kiln. Just outside the wall (opposite the oratory, past the duplex *clochan*, at the bottom end), find a stone hole with a passage facing the southwest wind. This was the kiln—fanned by the wind, it was used for cooking and drying grain. Locals would bring their grain to be dried and ground, and the monks would keep a 10 percent tithe. With the arrival of the Normans in the 12th century, these small religious communities were replaced by relatively big-time state and church governments.

32.8 km: Return to the main road, and continue to the right.

34.6 km: At the big hotel (Smerwick Harbor), turn left following the sign to *Gallaras* (Gallarus Oratory; rhymes with walrus).

35.6 km: At the big building (with *camping* sign), make a hard right up the long lane bordered by hedges. To park for free near the **Gallarus Oratory,** continue along this lane for a quarter-mile, where you'll find a five-car parking lot—which occasionally fills up (be prepared to cooperate with other drivers exiting this small lot). From the

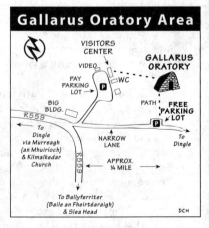

free parking lot, a sign points you up the fuchsia-hedge-lined path leading you to the oratory (about 100 yards away).

If, however, you don't mind paying €3 to park, veer left just

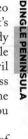

at the start of the hedge-lined lane into a large paved parking lot. Nearby is a small visitors center with a coffee shop, WC, and video theater. I prefer to park for free in the small lot (especially since it's closer to the oratory), but many will appreciate the large lot, handy WC, and informative 17-minute video overview of the Dingle Peninsula's historic sights (daily May-Sept 9:00-20:00, Oct-April 9:00-19:00, tel. 066/915-5333). This visitors center is the business initiative of a man who simply owns the adjacent land—not the oratory. If you park in his lot, you'll have to pay the fee, even if you skip the facilities and walk up the public lane.

The Gallarus Oratory, built about 1,300 years ago, is one of Ireland's best-preserved early-Christian churches. Shaped like an upturned boat, its finely fitted drystone walls are still waterproof. Lower your head (notice how thick the walls are), walk inside, and

give your eyes a moment to adjust to the low light. A simple, small arched window offers scant daylight to the opposite wall, where the altar would have stood. Picture the interior lit by candles during medieval monastic services. It would have been tough to fit more than about a dozen monks inside (especially if they decided to do jumping jacks). Notice the holes once used to secure covering at the door, and the fine alternating stonework on the corners.

From the oratory, return to the main road and continue, following the brown *Ceann Sléibhe/Slea Head Drive* signs. If instead you continue up the narrow lane from the free parking lot, you'll end up on R-559 (a shortcut to Dingle that misses the Kilmalkedar Church ruins).

37.7 km: Bear right at the fork and immediately take a right at the next fork. Here you leave the Slea Head Drive and head for Dingle (10 km away).

39.5 km: The **ruined church of Kilmalkedar** (Cill Mhaoil-cheadair, on the left) was the Norman center of worship for this

end of the peninsula. It was built when England replaced the old monastic settlements in an attempt to centralize their rule. The 12th-century Irish Romanesque church is surrounded by a densely populated graveyard (which has risen noticeably above the surrounding fields over the centuries). In front of the church, you'll find the oldest medieval tombs, a stately early-Christian cross (substantially buried by the rising graveyard and therefore oddly proportioned), and a much older ogham stone. This stone, which had already stood here 900 years when the church was built, is notched with the mysterious Morse code-type ogham script used from the third to seventh centuries. It marked a grave, indicating this was a pre-Christian holy spot. The hole was drilled through the top of the stone centuries ago as a place where people would come to seal a deal—standing on the graves of their ancestors and in front of the house of God, they'd "swear to God" by touching thumbs through this stone. You can still use this to renew your marriage vows (free, B.Y.O. spouse). The church fell into ruin during the Reformation. As Catholic worship went underground until the early 19th century, Kilmalkedar was never rebuilt.

40.2 km: Continue uphill, overlooking the water. You'll pass another "fairy fort" (Ciher Dorgan) on the right dating back to 1000 B.C. (free, go through the rusty kissing gate). The bay stretched out below you is Smerwick Harbor. In 1580 a force of 600 Italian and Spanish troops (sent by the pope to aid a rebellion against the Protestant English) surrendered at this bay to the English. All 600 were massacred by the English forces, which included Sir Walter Raleigh.

41.7 km: At the crest of the hill, enjoy a three-mile-long coast back into Dingle town (sighting, as old-time mariners did, on the Eask Tower).

46.3 km: *Tog Bog E* means "take it easy." At the T-junction, turn left. Then turn right at the roundabout.

47.5 km: You're back in Dingle town. Well done.

Blasket Islands

This rugged group of six islands (Na Blascaodai) off the tip of Dingle Peninsula seems particularly close to the soul of Ireland. The population of Great Blasket Island (An Blascaod Mór), once home to as many as 160 people, dwindled until the government moved the last handful of residents to the mainland in 1953. Life here was hard, but the sea provided for all, and no one went hungry. Each family had a cow, a few sheep, and a plot of potatoes. They cut their peat from the high ridge and harvested fish from the sea. To these folk, World War I provided a bonus, as occasional valuable cargo washed ashore from merchant ships sunk by U-boats. There was no priest, pub, or doctor. (No phones, no lights, no motor cars, not a single luxury.) Because they were not entirely dependent upon the potato, island inhabitants survived the famine relatively unscathed.

These people formed the most traditional Irish community of the 20th century—the symbol of ancient Gaelic culture.

A special closeness to an island—combined with a knack for vivid storytelling—is inspirational. From this simple but proud  fishing/farming community came three writers of international repute whose Gaelic works—basically tales of life on Great Blasket Island—have been translated into many languages. You'll find *Peig* (by Peig Sayers) and *The Islandman* (Thomas O'Crohan) in shops everywhere. But the most readable and upbeat is *Twenty Years A-Growing* (Maurice O'Sullivan), a somewhat-true, Huck Finn-esque account of the author's childhood and adolescence and of island life as it was a hundred years ago.

The island's café and hostel have closed down, and today Great Blasket is little more than a ghost town overrun with rabbits on a peaceful, grassy, three-mile-long poem.

Getting to the Blasket Islands

From Dunquin (Dún Chaoin): The 40-passenger Blasket Islands ferry runs hourly from Dunquin, at the tip of Dingle Peninsula. In summer, it goes every hour between 10:30 and 16:30, depending on weather and demand (€25 round-trip, Easter-Sept, no boats Oct-Easter, ferry tel. 066/915-6422 or 066/915-1344, mobile 087-231-6131, www.blasketisland.com). There are also scenic two-hour Blasket Island Eco Tour circuit cruises from Dunquin Harbor, which depart at 12:30 and 14:30 (€35, April-Sept only, same phone numbers). Or you can combine the Eco Tour with a stop for time on the island (€40, call for schedule). Dunquin has a fine hostel (tel. 066/915-6121).

From Dingle Town (An Daingean): In summer, two boats run between Dingle town and the Blasket Islands. The ride (which may include a quick look at Fungie the dolphin) traces the spectacular coastline all the way to Slea Head. The boats (*Lady Breda* and *Grievous Angel*) offer similar services from Dingle town and operate when there's enough demand. These boats also do three-hour eco-tours for those interested in puffins, dolphins, and seals. The tricky landing at Great Blasket Island's primitive little boat ramp makes getting off a challenge and landing virtually impossible in a storm (€30 same-day round-trip; departs from the marina pier in Dingle at 12:30 and 14:30; includes 45-minute ride with 3 hours to explore island, call Mary to confirm sailing times of either boat—or for more details on the eco-tours—at tel. 066/915-1344 or mobile 087-672-6100).

▲▲Great Blasket Centre (Ionad An Blascaod Mór)

Note that this sight isn't on the Blasket Islands, but on the mainland facing the islands. It's an essential stop before visiting the islands—or a good place to learn about them without making the crossing (fits neatly with my recommended "Dingle Peninsula Loop Trip," earlier).

This state-of-the-art Blascaod and Gaelic heritage center gives visitors the best look possible at the language, literature, and way of life of Blasket Islanders. The building's award-winning design mixes interpretation and the surrounding countryside. Its spine, a sloping village lane, leads to an almost sacred view of the actual island. Don't miss the exceptional 20-minute video (shows on the half hour), then hear the sounds, read the poems, browse through old photos, and gaze out the big windows at those rugged islands... and imagine. Even if you never got past limericks, the poetry of these people—so pure and close to each other and nature—will have you dipping your pen into the cry of the birds.

Cost and Hours: €4, Easter-Oct Mon-Sat 10:00-18:00, Sun 11:00-18:00, closed Nov-Easter, fine cafeteria, well-signposted on the Slea Head Drive near Dunquin/Dún Chaoin, tel. 066/915-6444.

Tralee

While Killarney is the tour-bus capital of County Kerry, Tralee (Tra' Li) is its true leading city. Except for the tourist complex around the TI and during a few festivals, Tralee feels like a bustling Irish town. A little outdoor market combusts on The Square (Thu-Sat).

The famous Rose of Tralee International Festival, usually held in mid-August, is a celebration of arts and music, culminating in the election of the Rose of Tralee—the most beautiful woman at the festival (no matter which country she was born in, as long as she has Irish heritage). While the rose garden in the Castle Gardens surrounding the TI is in bloom from summer through October, Tralee's finest roses are going about their lives year-round in the busy streets of this workaday town.

Orientation to Tralee

For the tourist, the heart of Tralee is Ashe Memorial Hall, housing the TI and the Kerry County Museum, located near the rose garden and surrounded by the city park. Beyond the park is the Aqua Dome, looking like a flying saucer that landed on earth.

Tourist Information

The TI is hidden under the east end of Ashe Memorial Hall. If you face the front entry, it's around to your left on the ground floor (TI open July-Aug Mon-Sat 9:00-18:00, Sun 10:00-18:00; May-June and Sept Mon-Sat 9:15-17:00, closed Sun; Oct-April Mon-Sat 9:15-17:00, closed Sun; also closed Sat in Jan-Feb, tel. 066/712-1288).

Arrival in Tralee

From the train and bus stations (located across the small parking lot from each other), Ashe Memorial Hall is a 10-minute walk through the center of town. Exit the station right, take a near-immediate left on Edward Street, and then turn right on Castle Street and left on Denny. The hall is at the south end of Denny, Tralee's grand, wide boulevard. Drivers should knock around the town center until they find a sign to the TI. Parking on the street is by pay-and-display machine (€1.20/hour, exact change required, display paid slip on dashboard, monitored Mon-Sat 8:30-18:30).

Helpful Hints

Post Office: It's on Edward Street (Mon-Fri 9:00-17:30, Sat 9:00-13:00, closed Sun).

Laundry: Kerin's launderette charges €12 for an average load (Mon-Sat 9:00-18:00, closed Sun, 103 Strand Street, tel. 066/711-9444).

Taxis: Try **Speedy Cab** (tel. 066/712-7411) or **Behan Cab** (tel. 066/712-6296).

Day Trips from Tralee: For those without their own wheels, **Dingle** town is a rushed day trip from Tralee in summer. Bus Éireann departs from the Tralee bus and train station at 11:30 (unfortunately nothing earlier), putting you in Dingle at 12:45; the last bus returns from Dingle at 17:30, getting you back to Tralee at 18:45 (June-mid-Sept only). You can also take a blitz bus tour of the **Ring of Kerry:** Bus Éireann departs the Tralee bus station at 11:50, drives the N-70 ring route, and gets you back to Tralee at 18:45 (runs late June-early Sept, stops only to pick up and drop off, also with connections from Killarney).

Sights in Tralee

▲▲**Kerry County Museum**—This is easily the best place to learn about life in Kerry. The museum has three parts: Kerry slide show, museum, and medieval-town walk. Get in the mood by relaxing for 10 minutes through the Enya-style continuous slide show of Kerry's spectacular scenery, then wander through 7,000 years of Kerry history in the museum (well-described, no need for free headphones). The Irish joke that when a particularly stupid guy moved from Cork to Kerry, he raised the average IQ in both counties—but this museum is pretty well done. It starts with good background info on the archaeological sites of Dingle, progresses through Viking artifacts found in the area, and goes right up to a video showing highlights of the Kerry football team (a fun look at Irish football, which is more like rugby than soccer). Good coverage is given to adventurous Kerryman Tom Crean, who survived three Antarctic expeditions with Scott and Shackleton (see sidebar on page 240). The lame finale is a stroll back in time on a re-creation of Tralee's circa-1450 Main Street. Before leaving, horticulture enthusiasts will want to ramble through the rose garden in the adjacent park.

Cost and Hours: €5; June-Sept daily 9:30-17:30; Oct-May Tue-Sat 9:30-17:00, closed Sun-Mon; tel. 066/712-7777, www.kerrymuseum.ie.

Blennerville Windmill—On the edge of Tralee, just off the Dingle road, spins a restored mill originally built in 1780. Its eight-minute video tells the story of the windmill, which ground grain to feed Britain as that country steamed into the Industrial Age.

In the 19th century, Blennerville was a major port for America-bound emigrants. It was also the home port where the *Jeannie Johnston* was built. This modern-day replica of a 19th-century ship tours Atlantic ports, explaining the Irish emigrant experience. Most of the time, it's docked and available to tour in Dublin, on the north shore of the River Liffey (see page 81).

Cost and Hours: €4 gets you a one-room emigration exhibit, the video, and a peek at the spartan interior of the working windmill; April-Oct daily 10:00-18:00, closed Nov-March, tel. 066/712-1064.

Siamsa Tíre Theatre—The National Folk Theatre of Ireland, Siamsa Tíre (shee-EM-sah TEE-rah), stages two-hour dance and theater performances based on Gaelic folk traditions. The songs are in Irish.

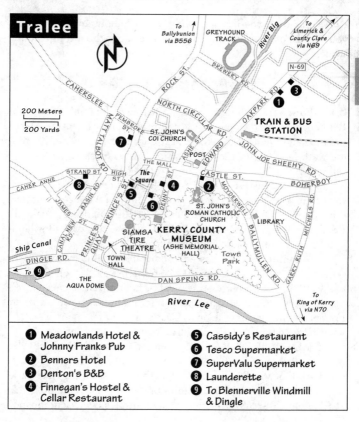

Tralee

200 Meters
200 Yards

To Ballybunion via B556

GREYHOUND TRACK

River Big

To Limerick & County Clare via N69

N-69

BREWERY RD.

CAHERSLEE

ROCK ST.

NORTH CIRCULAR RD.

OAKPARK RD.

TRAIN & BUS STATION

MATT TALBOT RD.

PEMBROKE ST.

ST. JOHN'S COI CHURCH

ASHE ST.

POST

EDWARD

JOHN JOE SHEEHY RD.

THE MALL

CASTLE ST.

BOHERBOY

STRAND RD.

HIGH ST.

The Square

CAHER ANNE

BASIN RD.

PRINCE'S ST.

DENNY ST.

ST. JOHN'S ROMAN CATHOLIC CHURCH

MOYDERWELL

BALLYMULLEN RD.

LIBRARY

GARRY RUTH

MITCHELS RD.

JAMES ST.

NEW ST.

CANAL

PRINCE'S QUAY

SIAMSA TIRE THEATRE

KERRY COUNTY MUSEUM (ASHE MEMORIAL HALL)

Town Park

Ship Canal

DINGLE RD.

To 9

TOWN HALL

THE AQUA DOME

DAN SPRING RD.

To Ring of Kerry via N70

River Lee

① Meadowlands Hotel & Johnny Franks Pub
② Benners Hotel
③ Denton's B&B
④ Finnegan's Hostel & Cellar Restaurant
⑤ Cassidy's Restaurant
⑥ Tesco Supermarket
⑦ SuperValu Supermarket
⑧ Launderette
⑨ To Blennerville Windmill & Dingle

Cost and Hours: €25; June-Aug Mon-Sat at 20:30, no shows Sun; April-May and Sept Mon-Thu and Sat at 20:30, no shows Fri or Sun; closed Oct-March; next to Kerry County Museum building in park, tel. 066/712-3055, www.siamsatire.com, boxoffice@ siamsatire.com.

Swimming—The Aqua Dome is a modern-yet-fortified swim-center—the largest indoor water world in Ireland—at the Dingle end of town, near Ashe Memorial Hall. Families enjoy the huge slide, wave pool, and other wet amusements.

Cost and Hours: Adults-€15, kids-€12, locker-€1, bring your own towels, July-Aug Mon-Fri 10:00-22:00, Sat-Sun 11:00-20:00, shorter hours off-season, tel. 066/712-8899.

Music and Other Distractions—Tralee has several fine pubs within a few blocks of each other (on Castle Street and Rock Street) offering live traditional music most evenings. There's greyhound racing (Fri-Sat year-round plus Tue in summer, 19:30-22:00, ten 30-second races, one every 15 minutes, 10-minute walk from station or town center, tel. 066/718-0008). Entry to the track costs

€10—plus what you lose gambling. At just about any time of day, you can drop into a betting office to check out the local gambling scene.

Sleeping in Tralee

(€1 = about $1.30, country code: 353, area code: 066)

Benners Hotel and Finnegan's accommodations are central. Meadowlands and Denton's B&B are next door to each other, a 10-minute walk north from the train station on Oakpark Road (or a €4 cab ride).

$$$ Meadowlands is a big 58-room hotel with a bar that serves great pub meals. If you want to splurge in Tralee, do it here (Sb-€60-85, Db-€90-130, suites-€150-200, parking, Oakpark Road, tel. 066/718-0444, fax 066/718-0964, www.meadowlands hotel.com, info@meadowlandshotel.com).

$$ Benners Hotel has 45 predictable-quality rooms in the center of town (April-Sept Sb-€49-69, Db-€59-89, Tb-€89-149, Qb-€110-150, a bit more on festival or holiday dates, cheaper off-season rates, breakfast-€10, downstairs nightclub noise until late Fri-Sat, some parking, Upper Castle Street, tel. 066/712-1877, www.bennershoteltralee.com, info@bennershoteltralee.com).

$$ Denton's B&B is a tidy, modern house and the best value in town, with four comfy rooms hosted by cheerful Eileen Doherty (Sb-€40, Db-€60-70, Tb-€80-90, cash only, Wi-Fi, private parking, on busy Oakpark Road before it becomes N-69, tel. 066/712-7637, mobile 087-687-7341, www.dentontralee.com, dentonbandb @gmail.com).

$ Finnegan's Hostel, in a stately Georgian house, is a block from the TI at 17 Denny Street (€17 beds in 4-, 6-, 8-, or 10-bed dorms, Sb-€25-30, Db-€50, tel. 066/712-7610, www.finnegans hostel.com, finneganshostel@eircom.net).

Eating in Tralee

Cassidy's is consistently good (€18-24 dinners, €22.50 early-bird deal before 19:00, open daily 17:00-22:00, a block off The Square, corner of Abbey and Mary Streets, tel. 066/712-8833). Or try candlelit **Finnegan's Cellar** (€15-25 dinners, daily 17:30-22:30, 17 Denny Street, tel. 066/718-1400). **Johnny Franks Pub** at the Meadowlands Hotel serves the best pub grub in town (daily 12:30-21:00, Oakpark Road, tel. 066/718-0444). Shop for a picnic at **Tesco,** the big grocery south of The Square (Mon-Sat 8:00-21:00, Sun 10:00-19:00), or at **SuperValu** on Rock Street (Mon-Sat 8:00-21:00, Sun 8:00-19:00).

Tralee Connections

Day-trippers can store bags for €2.50 per day, but not overnight, at the train station (ask at ticket window, hours vary depending on staffing and train schedule).

From Tralee by Train to: Dublin (every 2 hours, 6/day on Sun, 1 direct in morning, otherwise change in Mallow, 4 hours). Train info: Tel. 066/712-3522.

By Bus to: Dingle (4/day, less off-season and on Sun, 1.25 hours, €12.30 one-way, €20 round-trip), **Galway** (8/day, 4.5 hours), **Limerick** (9/day, 2 hours), **Doolin/Cliffs of Moher** (2/day, 5 hours), **Ennis** (9/day, 3.25 hours, change in Limerick), **Rosslare** (3/day, 6 hours), **Shannon** (9/day, 2.5 hours), **Dublin** (7/day, 6 hours). Tralee's bus station is across the parking lot from the train station. Bus info: Tel. 066/716-4700.

Car Rental: Duggan's Garage Practical Car Hire rents Fiat Puntos (around €90/48 hours, includes everything but gas, must be at least 23 years old, 2 blocks from train station on Ashe Street, tel. 066/712-1124, fax 066/712-7527).

Kerry Airport

Kerry Airport is a 20-minute drive from Tralee and a one-hour drive from Dingle (airport code: KIR, tel. 066/976-4644, www.kerryairport.ie). It's located just off the main N-22 road, halfway between Killarney and Tralee. It has a  half-dozen handy rental-car outlets and an ATM. Dingle Shuttle Bus is your best connection to Dingle town, but you must reserve in advance (€20/person one-way, minimum 2 passengers, mobile 087-250-4767, www.dingleshuttlebus.com). You can also connect to the airport via taxi (€25 from Tralee, €75 from Dingle) or bus (4/day to Dingle via Tralee). The Kerry Airport offers connecting flights from **Dublin** on Aer Lingus (3/day, www.aerlingus.com). It also has Ryanair (www.ryanair.com) flights to **London Stansted** or **Luton; Alicante, Spain; Faro, Portugal;** and **Hahn, Germany** (near Frankfurt).

Route Tips for Drivers

From Tralee to Dingle: Drivers choose between the narrow, but very exciting, Conor Pass road; or the faster, easier, but still narrow N-86 through Lougher and Annascaul (Abhainn an Scáil). On a clear day, Conor Pass comes with incredible views over Tralee Bay and Brandon Bay. On the north slope, pull out at the waterfall.

From here, there's a fun five-minute scramble to a dramatic little glacier-created lake. Pause also at the summit viewpoint to look down on Dingle town and harbor. While in Kerry, listen to Radio Kerry FM 97. To practice your Gaelic, tune in to FM 94.4.

Between Tralee and Galway/Burren/Doolin: The Killimer-Tarbert ferry connection allows those heading north for the Cliffs of Moher (or south for Dingle) to avoid the 80-mile detour around the Shannon River. If you're going straight to Galway, the inland Limerick route is faster. But the ferry route is more scenic and direct to the Cliffs of Moher and the Burren (hourly, 20 minutes, €18/carload, April-Sept departs Mon-Sat on the half hour 7:30-21:30 going north and on the hour 7:00-21:00 going south, on Sun the first departures are 9:30 going north and 9:00 going south, Oct-March last departures at 19:00, no need to reserve, tel. 065/905-3124, www.shannonferries.com).

COUNTY CLARE
and the BURREN

Ennis • Cliffs of Moher • Doolin • Lisdoonvarna •
The Burren • Ballyvaughan • Kinvarra

Those connecting Dingle in the south with Galway in the north can entertain themselves along the way by joyriding through the fascinating landscape and tidy villages of County Clare. Ennis, the county's major city, is a workaday Irish place with a medieval history and a market bustle—ideal for anyone tired of the tourist crowds. Overlooking the Atlantic, the dramatic Cliffs of Moher offer tenderfeet a thrilling hike. The Burren is a unique, windblown limestone wasteland that hides an abundance of flora, fauna, caves, and history. For your evening entertainment, you can join a tour-bus group in a castle for a medieval banquet in Kinvarra or meet up with traditional Irish music enthusiasts from around Europe for tin-whistling in Doolin.

Planning Your Time

A **car** is the best way to experience County Clare and the Burren. The region can be an enjoyable daylong drive-through or a destination in itself. None of the sights has to take much time. But do get out and walk a bit.

If you're driving from Dingle to Galway, I'd recommend the following day plan. Rather than the main road via Limerick, drive north from Tralee via Listowel to catch the Tarbert-Killimer car ferry (avoiding Limerick traffic and the 80-mile/1.5-hour end-run drive around the Shannon estuary; see "Dingle Route Tips for

COUNTY CLARE

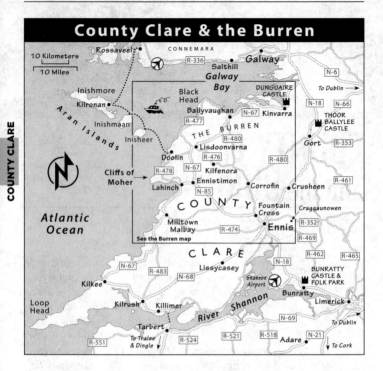

County Clare & the Burren

Drivers" at the end of the previous chapter). From Killimer, drive north on N-67 via Kilkee and Milltown Malbay. The little surfer-and-golfer village of Lahinch makes a good lunch stop. Then drive the coastal route to the Cliffs of Moher for an hour break. The scenic drive from the cliffs through the Burren, with a couple of stops and a tour of the caves, takes about two hours. Consider partaking in the 17:30 medieval banquet at Dunguaire Castle, near Kinvarra (just 30 minutes south of Galway).

By **train** or **bus,** your gateways to this region are Ennis from the south and Galway from the north. In 2010, a new rail line was finished, connecting Limerick (via Ennis) and Galway for the first time in decades—a big plus for those staying in Ennis and relying on public transport. But linking the smaller sights within County Clare and the Burren by bus is still difficult: Book a tour instead (see "Bus Tours of the Burren," next page).

Tips: Visit an ATM in Ennis, Galway, or Lahinch before you enter this region (there are no ATMs in Doolin, Lisdoonvarna, Kilfenora, or Ballyvaughan). Skip the **Bunratty Castle and Folk Park**—I'd leave this most commercial and least lively of all European open-air folk museums to the jet-lagged, big-bus American tour groups (located just a potty stop from the Shannon Airport, past Limerick on the road to Ennis).

Bus Tours of the Burren

From Galway: The **Burren Wild Tour** departs from Galway and combines an interactive walking tour of the Burren with a visit to the Cliffs of Moher. Their motto, "Don't be nuts, get off the bus," distinguishes their active hiking focus from other, more sedate tour outfits (€25, departs Galway private coach station across from TI at 10:00, returns by 17:30, mobile 087-877-9565, www. burrenwalks.com). They also offer "gentle" 1.5-hour nature walks from the Connolly family farm near the village of Oughtmama, roughly halfway between Ballyvaughan and Kinvarra, inland from Bellharbour (€10, daily at 10:30, call ahead for directions, same contact info as above).

Three other Galway-based companies—**Lally Tours, O'Neachtain Tours,** and **Galway Tour Company**—run standard all-day tours of nearby regions (€20-25, up to 25 percent discount if you book online). Their tours of the Burren do a loop south of Galway, covering Kinvarra, Aillwee Cave, Poulnabrone Dolmen, and the Cliffs of Moher (on a 2-hour lunch stop). Tours go most days from about 9:45 to 17:30 (departing from Galway private coach station across from TI; call to confirm exact itinerary: Lally tel. 091/562-905, www.lallytours.com; O'Neachtain tel. 091/553-188, mobile 087-166-5060, www.ontours.biz; Galway Tour Company tel. 091/566-566, www.galwaytourcompany.com). All three companies also offer day tours of Connemara, with discounts if you book two separate day tours. Drivers take cash only; to pay with a credit card, book at Galway's TI.

From Ennis: Barratt Tours runs tours of the Burren and Cliffs of Moher (see page 277).

County Clare

Ennis

This bustling market town (pop. 24,000), the main town of County Clare, provides those relying on public transit with a handy transportation hub (good connections to Limerick, Dublin, and Galway). Ennis is less than 15 miles from Shannon Airport and makes a good first- or last-night base in Ireland for travelers not locked into Dublin flights. It also offers a chance to wander around an Irish town that is not reliant upon the tourist dollar (though not shunning it either). Muhammad Ali visited the town in 2008 after discovering that one of his great-grandfathers had been born in Ennis. Locals credit his success to his fightin' Irish side.

COUNTY CLARE

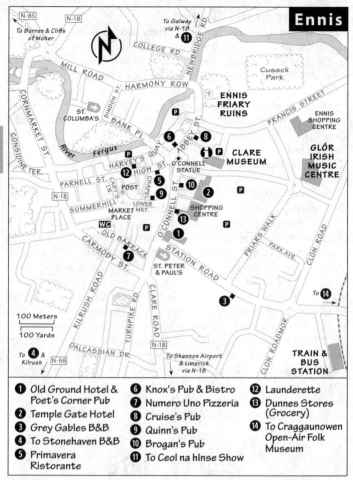

❶ Old Ground Hotel & Poet's Corner Pub	❻ Knox's Pub & Bistro
❷ Temple Gate Hotel	❼ Numero Uno Pizzeria
❸ Grey Gables B&B	❽ Cruise's Pub
❹ To Stonehaven B&B	❾ Quinn's Pub
❺ Primavera Ristorante	❿ Brogan's Pub
	⓫ To Ceol na hInse Show
⓬ Launderette	
⓭ Dunnes Stores (Grocery)	
⓮ To Craggaunowen Open-Air Folk Museum	

The center of Ennis is a tangle of contorted streets. Use the steeple of Saints Peter and Paul Cathedral and the Daniel O'Connell monument column (at either end of the main shopping drag, O'Connell Street) as landmarks.

Orientation to Ennis

Tourist Information

The TI is just off O'Connell Street Square (July-Aug daily 9:30-17:30; March-June and Sept-Dec Mon-Sat 9:30-17:00, closed Sun; Jan-Feb Mon-Fri 9:30-17:00, closed Sat-Sun; tel. 065/682-8366).

Arrival in Ennis

By Car: If you're not spending the night (i.e., stowing your car at your B&B), parking is best in one of several pay-and-display lots (€1.30/hour, Mon-Sat 9:30-17:30, free at night and on Sun, pay at meter in lot and display ticket on dashboard, usually 2-hour maximum). The centrally located multistory lot on Market Place Square charges €5 per day (Mon-Sat 7:30-19:30, closed Sun).

By Train or Bus: The train and bus station is located southeast of town, a 15-minute walk from the town center. To reach town, exit the station parking lot and turn left on Station Road, passing through a roundabout and past the recommended Grey Gables B&B. Turn right after the recommended Old Ground Hotel onto O'Connell Street.

By Plane: Shannon Airport is about 13 miles south of Ennis. For information, see "Shannon Airport" on page 281.

Helpful Hints

Post Office: It's on Bank Place (Mon-Fri 9:00-13:00 & 14:00-17:30, Sat 9:00-13:00, closed Sun).

Laundry: Fergus launderette is opposite the Parnell Street parking lot (Mon-Sat 8:30-18:00, closed Sun, tel. 065/682-3122).

Supermarket: Dunnes Stores has a location in the shopping center on O'Connell Street (daily 8:30-22:00, Thu-Fri until 23:00).

Walking Tours: June O'Brien leads 1.5-hour walking tours of Ennis departing from the TI (€8, May-Oct Mon-Tue and Thu-Sat at 11:00; no tours Wed, Sun, or off-season; mobile 087-648-3714, www.enniswalkingtours.com).

Bus Tours: Barratt Tours runs bus tours of the Cliffs of Moher and the Burren (€27, May-Sept daily, Oct-April Sat only, departing from the TI at 10:45 and returning by 18:15, call to confirm schedule, tel. 061/384-7000, mobile 087-237-5986, www.4tours.biz).

Sights in Ennis

Clare Museum—This worthwhile museum, housed in the large TI building, has eclectic displays about ancient ax heads, submarine development, and local boys who made good—from 10th-century High King Brian Boru to 20th-century statesman Eamon de Valera. Coverage includes the Battle of Dysert O'Dea in 1318. One of the few Irish victories over the invading Normans, it delayed English domination of most of County Clare for another 200 years.

Cost and Hours: Free, June-Sept Tue-Sat 9:30-12:30 & 14:00-17:30, closed Sun-Mon, tel. 065/682-3382, www.clarelibrary.ie.

Ennis Friary—The Franciscan monks arrived here in the 13th century, and the town grew up around their friary (like a monastery). Today, it's still worth a look, with some fine limestone carvings in its ruined walls. Ask the guide to fully explain the crucifixion symbolism in the 15th-century *Ecce Homo* carving.

Cost and Hours: €3, sometimes includes tour—depends on staffing, April-Sept daily 10:00-17:30, closed Oct-March, tel. 065/682-9100.

Near Ennis

▲Craggaunowen—This open-air folk museum nestles in a pretty forest, an easy 20-minute drive east of Ennis. All the structures are replicas, except for the small 16th-century castle (Tower House), which the park was built around. A friendly weaver, spinning her wool on the castle's ground floor, is glad to tell you the tricks of her fuzzy trade. A highlight is the Crannog, a fortified Iron Age thatch-roofed dwelling built on a small man-made island, which gives you a grubby idea of how clans lived 2,000 years ago. A modern surprise hides in a corner of the park under a large glass teepee: the *Brendan,* the original humble boat that scholar Tim Severin sailed from Ireland to North America in 1976 (via frosty stepping stones like Iceland and Greenland). He built this boat out of tanned hides, sewn together using primitive methods, to prove that Ireland's St. Brendan may indeed have been the first to discover America on his legendary voyage, 900 years before Columbus and 500 years before the Vikings.

Cost and Hours: €9, daily 10:00-17:00, shorter hours off-season, tel. 061/367-178, www.shannonheritage.com.

Getting There: The park is well-signposted nine miles (15 km) east of Ennis off R-469, which leads out of town past the train station.

Nightlife in Ennis

Glór Irish Music Centre—The town's modern theater center (*glór* is Irish for "sound") connects you with Irish culture. It's worth considering for traditional music, dance, or storytelling performances.

Cost and Hours: €12-25, year-round usually at 20:00, 5-minute walk behind TI, Friar's Walk, ticket office open Mon-Sat 10:00-16:00, closed Sun, tel. 065/684-3103, www.glor.ie.

Ceol na hInse—This original stage show, housed in the local Cois na hAbhna Hall, is a fine way to spend an evening. Like other ongoing Comhaltas-sponsored cultural productions, it's a celebration of Irish performing arts. The show is split in two parts. The first features great Irish music, song, and dance. After the break, you're invited to kick up your heels and take the floor as the dancers

The Voyage of St. Brendan

It has long been part of Irish lore that St. Brendan the Navigator (A.D. 484-577) and 12 followers sailed from the southwest of Ireland to the "Land of Promise" (what is now North America) in a *currach*—a wood-frame boat covered with ox hide and tar. According to a 10th-century monk who poetically wrote of the journey, St. Brendan and his crew encountered a paradise of birds, were attacked by a whale, and suffered the smoke of a smelly island in the north before finally reaching their Land of Promise.

The legend and its precisely described locations still fascinate modern readers. A British scholar of navigation, Tim Severin, re-created the entire journey in 1976-1977. He and his crew set out from Brendan Creek in County Kerry in a *currach.* The prevailing winds blew them to the Hebrides, the Faeroe Islands, Iceland, and finally to Newfoundland. While this didn't successfully prove that St. Brendan sailed to North America, it did prove that he could have. (You can visit Tim Severin's boat at the Craggaunowen open-air folk museum.)

According to his 10th-century biographer, "St. Brendan sailed from the Land of Promise home to Ireland. And from that time on, Brendan acted as if he did not belong to this world at all. His mind and his joy were in the delight of heaven."

teach some famous Irish set dances. Phone ahead to see if a *ceilidh* is scheduled on off nights.

Cost and Hours: €10, generally July-mid-August Wed and Fri at 20:30, on N-18 Galway road on edge of town, tel. 065/682-4276, www.coisnahabhna.ie.

Traditional Music—Live music begins in the pubs at about 21:30. The best is **Cruise's** on Abbey Street, with music nightly year-round and good food (bar is cheaper than restaurant, tel. 065/682-8963). Other pubs offering weekly traditional music nights (generally on weekends, but schedules vary) are **Quinn's** on Lower Market Street (tel. 065/682-8148) and **Brogan's** on O'Connell Street (tel. 065/682-9480). The **Old Ground Hotel** hosts live music year-round in its pub (Thu-Sun, open to anyone); although tour groups stay at the hotel, the pub is low-key and feels real, not staged.

Sleeping in Ennis

The first two listings are fancy hotels that you'll share with tour groups; the last two are B&Bs.

$$$ Old Ground Hotel is a stately, ivy-covered 18th-century manse with 105 rooms and a family feel. Pan Am clipper pilots stayed here during the early days of transatlantic seaplane flights

COUNTY CLARE

Sleep Code

(€1 = about $1.30, country code: 353, area code: 065)
S = Single, **D** = Double/Twin, **T** = Triple, **Q** = Quad, **b** = bathroom, **s** = shower only. Breakfast is included and credit cards are accepted unless otherwise noted.

To help you easily sort through these listings, I've divided the accommodations into three categories, based on the price for a standard double room with bath:

$$$ Higher Priced—Most rooms €75 or more.
  $$ Moderately Priced—Most rooms between €50-75.
    $ Lower Priced—Most rooms €50 or less.

Prices can change without notice; verify the hotel's current rates online or by email.

(Sb-€80-105, Db-€100-170, suite-€160-210, best rates online, 2-night weekend stays include a dinner, Wi-Fi, a few blocks from station at intersection of Station Road and O'Connell Street, tel. 065/682-8127, fax 065/682-8112, www.flynnhotels.com/Old_Ground_Hotel, reservations@oldgroundhotel.ie).

$$$ Temple Gate Hotel's 70 rooms are more modern and less personal (Db-€70-140, suites-€150-190, rates lower off-season, Wi-Fi, just off O'Connell Street, in courtyard with TI, tel. 065/682-3300, fax 065/682-3322, www.templegatehotel.com, info@templegatehotel.com).

$$ Grey Gables B&B has 12 tastefully decorated rooms (Sb-€35-40, Db-€70-75, Tb-€99, Qb-€125, cash only, Wi-Fi, wheelchair access, parking, on Station Road a block toward town center from train station, tel. 065/682-4487, www.bed-n-breakfast-ireland.com, marykeane.ennis@eircom.net, Mary Keane).

$$ Stonehaven B&B is a kid-friendly place with three comfortable rooms (Sb-€50-55, Db-€60-75, Tb-€85-90, cash only, Wi-Fi, 10-minute walk from town on N-68 Kilrush Road, tel. 065/684-1775, www.stonehavenclare.com, keatingem@gmail.com, Marie Keatinge).

Eating in Ennis

Primavera Ristorante is my pick for a satisfying Italian dinner, cheerful atmosphere, and central location (€18-22 meals, €16.50 two-course early-bird special 17:00-19:00, Mon-Thu 12:00-21:30, Fri-Sat 12:00-22:30, Sun 13:00-21:30, 7 High Street, tel. 65/684-5323).

The **Old Ground Hotel** serves up hearty meals in its Poet's Corner pub (€10-15 lunches, €15-22 dinners, daily 12:00-21:00).

For better than average pub grub, I like **Knox's Pub & Bistro** on Abbey Street (daily 12:00-21:00, tel. 065/682-287). Or try one of the places mentioned earlier, under "Nightlife in Ennis."

For an easy pub-free dinner, try the simple **Numero Uno Pizzeria** (Mon-Sat 12:00-23:00, Sun 15:00-23:00, on Old Barrack Street off Market Place, tel. 065/684-1740).

Ennis Connections

From Ennis by Train to: Galway (5/day, 1.25 hours), **Limerick** (9/day, 40 minutes), **Dublin** (6/day, 3.25-4 hours, change in Limerick and Limerick Junction). Train info: Tel. 065/684-0444, www.irishrail.ie.

By Bus to: Galway (hourly, 1.25 hours), **Dublin** (almost hourly, 4.5-5.5 hours), **Rosslare** (5/day, 5.5-9 hours), **Limerick** (hourly, 1 hour), **Lisdoonvarna** (2/day, 1.25-2.75 hours), **Ballyvaughan** (1/day, 1.75-2.75 hours), **Tralee** (9/day, 3.25 hours, change in Limerick), **Doolin** (5/day, 1.5-2.5 hours). Bus info: Tel. 065/682-4177, www.buseireann.ie.

Shannon Airport

This is the major airport in western Ireland and comes with far less stress than Dublin's overcrowded counterpart. The airport has a **TI** (daily June-Sept 6:30-19:30, Oct-May 6:30-17:30, tel. 061/471-664), ATMs, Wi-Fi, a change bureau, and a baggage storage desk. Direct flights leave to New York, Boston, Toronto, London, Edinburgh, and various destinations on the European Continent (airport code: SNN, airport tel. 061/712-000, www.shannonairport.ie).

From Shannon Airport by Bus to: Ennis (bus #51 runs between the airport and the Ennis train station hourly, 20 minutes after the hour starting at 8:20, 30 minutes), **Galway** (hourly, 1.75 hours), **Limerick** (hourly, 30-50 minutes, can continue to Tralee—2 hours more, and Dingle—4/day, another 2 hours; bus tel. 061/313-333, www.buseireann.ie).

Sleeping near Shannon Airport: If you want to stay at the airport, consider **$$$ Park Inn by Radisson Shannon Airport** (Db-€79-129, less off-season, best prices if you book online, tel. 061/471-122, www.parkinn.com).

Cliffs of Moher

A visit to the Cliffs of Moher (pronounced "more"...because who would visit the Cliffs of Less)—a ▲▲▲ sight—is one of Ireland's great natural thrills. For five miles, the dramatic cliffs soar as high as 650 feet above the Atlantic.

Getting There

The Cliffs of Moher are located on R-478, south of Doolin. The parking lot across the road from the visitors center is for the general public; pay the attendant as you drive in. The lot next to the visitors center is for tour buses and handicapped visitors. If you're without wheels, you can get here by bus from Galway (2/day in summer, some with change in Ennis, 2 hours, €15 round-trip, www.buseireann.ie). Or—to see (but not visit) the cliffs—you can take a boat from Doolin (described later).

Orientation to the Cliffs of Moher

Cost: €6/person, includes parking and admission to the visitors center and its Atlantic Edge exhibit (buy tickets online for a 10 percent discount). It costs €2 to climb O'Brien's Tower.

Hours: Daily May-Sept 9:00-19:30, gradually later closing times toward mid-summer—as late as 21:00 July-Aug; Oct-April 9:00-17:00.

Information: You'll find a TI in the visitors center—the stonework hobbit-hole building tucked into the grassy knoll across the street from the parking lot; tel. 065/708-6141, www.cliffsof moher.ie.

Self-Guided Tour

Start in the **visitors center,** built in a concentric-circle layout with local stone. Upstairs is the Long Dock restaurant (which serves coffee and substantial cafeteria-style meals until 19:00); a photo diorama showing aerial views of the cliffs and underwater photos of local marine life; and the toilets, where you can enjoy a huge panoramic photo of the cliffs on the stall doors as you wait in line. Downstairs is a small café, a gift shop, and the Atlantic Edge exhibit.

The **Atlantic Edge exhibit** focuses mainly on natural and geological history, native bird and marine life, and virtual interactive exhibits aimed at children (often occupied by adults). You may even learn why the cliffs are always windy. A small theater with an IMAX-style screen shows *The Ledge,* a film following a gannet who's a Jonathan Livingston Seagull wannabe, as he flies along the cliffs and then dives underwater, encountering puffins, seals, and even a humpback whale along the way.

After leaving the visitors center, walk 200 yards to the **cliff** edge and along the wall of the local Liscannor slate. Notice the squiggles made by worms, eels, and snails long ago when the slate was still mud on the seafloor.

For years, anyone could walk right up to the cliffs, until numerous fatal accidents prompted the hiring of "rangers"—ostensibly there to answer your questions and lead guided tours, but mainly there to keep you from getting too close to the edge (wind gusts can be sudden, strong, and deadly).

As you gaze down at the waves crashing far, far below you, consider this: Surfing in wet suits is becoming popular in Ireland. Most sane Irish surfers stick to the predictable waves at Lahinch (5 miles south of here). But the monster waves that rear up beneath the Cliffs of Moher on stormy days are coveted by extreme surfers, who work in tandem with tow/rescue helpers skimming the waves on Jet Skis. Don't strain your eyes looking for them...there aren't too many surfers crazy enough to attempt this.

O'Brien's Tower, built in 1835, marks the highest point of the cliffs (but isn't worth the fee to climb...30 feet up doesn't improve the views much). Hike five minutes up to the tower and look to the north (your right). In the distance, on windy days, you can see the Aran Islands wearing their white necklace of surf.

St BRIDGET'S WELL

Nearby: Before leaving the area, drivers can take 10 minutes to check out the **Holy Well of St. Bridget,** located beside the tall column about a half-mile (1 km) south of the cliffs on the main road to Liscannor. In the short hall leading into the hillside spring, you'll find a treasure of personal and religious memorabilia left behind by devoted visitors seeking cures and blessings. The simple gray column outside was a folly erected over 150 years ago by a local landlord with money and ego to burn.

Cruises from Doolin

To get a different perspective of the cliffs (looking up instead of down), you can cruise along their base. Try for an afternoon cruise, when the sun is coming from the west, illuminating the detail on the dramatic cliffs. Two companies—**Doolin2Aran Ferries**

(tel. 065/707-5949, mobile 087/245-3239, www.doolin2aranfer
ries.com) and **O'Brien Line** (tel. 065/707-5555, www.obrienline.
com)—offer almost identical cruise options. Both make the one-
hour voyage past sea stacks and crag-perching birds. Boats depart
from the pier in Doolin (same dock as Aran Islands boat, €15, runs
daily April-Oct, 3/day, weather and tides permitting, call or go
online for sailing schedule and to reserve). They also operate day-
trip cruises from Doolin to Inisheer (the closest Aran Island—described in the Aran Islands chapter), then along the base of the
Cliffs of Moher and back to Doolin (for details, see page 324).

Doolin

This town was once a strange phenomenon. Many music lovers
would go directly from Paris or Munich to Doolin, which was on
the tourist map for its traditional music. A few years ago, this was
a mecca for Irish musicians, who came together here to jam before
a few lucky aficionados. But now the crowds and the foreigners
have overwhelmed the musicians, and the quality of music is not
as reliable. I prefer Dingle's richer music scene. Still, as Irish and
European fans crowd the pubs, the *bodhrán* beat goes on.

Doolin has plenty of accommodations and a Greek-island-
without-the-sun ambience. The "town" is just a few homes and
shops strung out along a valley road from the tiny harbor. Residents
generally divide the town into an Upper Village and Lower Village. The Lower Village is the closest thing to a commercial center
(meaning it has a couple of pubs and a couple of music CD shops).
The Upper Village has a TI at Hotel Doolin that generally exists
to book lodging and Aran Islands boat trips (mid-March-Oct daily
9:00-19:00, tel. 065/707-5642).

Doolin Activity Lodge offers a handy grab-bag of services,
including recommended accommodations, an Internet café (€3/30
minutes, daily 8:00-21:00, 4 terminals), and a launderette (drop-off
only, pick up clothes in 6 hours, no self-service, same hours as café).
The staff can also recommend local horseback riding, hiking, and
fishing options.

Sights in Doolin

Traditional Music—Doolin is famous for three pubs, all featuring
Irish folk music: Nearest the harbor, in the Lower Village, is **Gus
O'Connor's Pub** (tel. 065/707-4168). A mile farther up the road,
the Upper Village—straddling a bridge—is home to two other destination pubs: **McGann's** (tel. 065/707-4133) and **McDermott's**
(tel. 065/707-4328). Music starts in the pubs between 21:30 and
22:00, finishing at about midnight. Get there before 21:00 if you

want a place to sit, or pop in later and plan on standing. The *craic* is fine regardless. Pubs serve decent dinners before the music starts. (**Dial-A-Cab** is a handy service for folks without wheels wanting to link a night of fun in Doolin with a bed in Lisdoonvarna; mobile 086-812-7049 or 087-290-2060.)

Hike or Cruise to the Cliffs of Moher—From Doolin, you can hike up the Burren Way for three miles to the Cliffs of Moher. (Get advice locally on the trail condition and safety.) Doolin also offers boat cruises along the Cliffs of Moher (see page 283).

Sleeping in Doolin

(€1 = about $1.30, country code: 353, area code: 065)

$$ Harbour View B&B is a fine modern house with six rooms, overlooking the valley a mile from the Doolin fiddles. Kathy Normoyle keeps the place immaculate, and serves home-baked bread from her mom's house out back (Sb-€45-55, Db-€60-76, Tb-€75-90, includes fine breakfast, Wi-Fi, on main road halfway between Lisdoonvarna and Cliffs of Moher, next to Mac's Daybreak Market and gas station, tel. 065/707-4154, www.harbourviewdoolin.com, clarebb@eircom.net).

$$ Doolin Activity Lodge is a modern compound of four stone buildings with 21 bright, airy, good-value rooms (Sb-€40, Db-€70, Tb-€100-110, Qb-€140, located halfway between Upper and Lower Villages, tel. 065/707-4888, mobile 087/223-9638, fax 065/707-4877, www.doolinlodge.com, info@doolinlodge.com). The lodge offers handy amenities (details listed earlier).

$$ Half Door B&B is the coziest place around, with five woody rooms and a pleasant sun porch. It's just a short walk from the best pubs in the Upper Village (Sb-€45-55, Db-€65-80, Tb-€100-105, cash only, Wi-Fi, a keg's roll from McDermott's pub, tel. 065/707-5959, www.halfdoordoolin.com, ann@halfdoordoolin.com).

$ Doolin Hostel, right in Doolin's Lower Village, caters creatively to the needs of backpackers in town for the music. Friendly Anthony and his wife Dierdre are on top of the local scene (dorm bed-€14-18, Db-€40-60, Tb-€49-69, Qb-€59-79, these prices guaranteed for Rick Steves readers in 2013, continental breakfast-€3, Lower Village, tel. 087/282-0587, www.doolinhostel.com, anthony@doolinhostel.com).

Eating in Doolin

Restaurants in this village have a habit of opening and then closing in less than two years (too fly-by-night to list in a guidebook). It's tough to make a go of it. But Doolin's reputation for pub grub is consistently good. In the Lower Village, try **Gus O'Connor's Pub,** and in the Upper Village, give **McGann's** a spin. **Mac's Daybreak** is the town market (Mon-Sat 7:30-21:00, Sun 8:30-20:30, on R-478 above town next to the Harbour View B&B).

Doolin Connections

From Doolin by Bus to: Galway (2/day, 1.5-2 hours), **Ennis** (5/day, 1.5-2.5 hours). Buses depart from the recommended Doolin Hostel.

By Ferry to the Aran Islands: For the full rundown on ferries from Doolin, see page 324. In short, if you want to day-trip from Doolin, go with either Doolin2Aran Ferries (tel. 065/707-5949, mobile 087-245-3239, www.doolin2aranferries.com) or O'Brien Line (tel. 065/707-5555, www.obrienline.com), both of which take you to the closest island, Inisheer (with time to explore), then back along the Cliffs of Moher. If you want to visit either or both of the farther islands—Inishmaan and Inishmore—plan on an overnight stop, due to the time involved.

Lisdoonvarna

This town of 1,000 was known for centuries for its spa, its matchmakers, and its traditional folk music festivals. Today, it's pretty sleepy, except for a few weeks in September and sometimes early October, during its Matchmaking Festival (www.matchmakerireland.com), which partially inspired the 1997 film *The Matchmaker.* The bank is open only one day a week. Still, it's more of a town than Doolin and, apart from festival time, less touristy.

Sleeping in Lisdoonvarna: **$$ Ballinsheen House** is the best value in town. It's perched on a hill with five tastefully decorated rooms and a pleasant, glassed-in breakfast terrace (Sb-€45-55, Db-€60-80, Tb-€90-118, Qb-€120, Wi-Fi, parking, 5-minute walk north of town on N-67 Galway Road, tel. 065/707-4806, mobile 087-124-1872, www.ballinsheen.com, ballinsheenhouse@hotmail.com, Mary Gardiner).

Eating in Lisdoonvarna: The **Roadside Tavern** is a favorite local hangout with filling pub grub, great atmosphere, and occasional traditional-music sessions (daily, tel. 065/707-4084, on N-67 in town behind the Spa Hotel, hard-to-miss bright red).

The Burren

Literally the "rocky place," the Burren is just that. This 10-square-mile limestone plateau, a ▲▲ sight, is so barren that a disappointed Cromwellian surveyor of the 1650s described it as "a savage land, yielding neither water enough to drown a man, nor a tree to hang him, nor soil enough to bury him." But he wasn't much of a botanist, because the Burren is a unique ecosystem, with flora that has managed to adapt since the last Ice Age, 10,000 years ago. It's also rich in prehistoric and early Christian sites. This limestone land is littered with hundreds of historic stone structures, including dozens of Iron Age stone forts. When the first human inhabitants of the Burren came about 6,000 years ago, they cut down its trees with shortsighted slash-and-burn methods, which accelerated erosion of the topsoil (already scoured to a thin layer by glaciers)—making those ancient people partially responsible for the stark landscape we see today.

COUNTY CLARE

Self-Guided Driving Tour

Exploring the Burren
The drive from Kilfenora to Ballyvaughan offers the best quick swing through the historic Burren.
• *Begin in the town of Kilfenora, eight kilometers (5 miles) southeast of Lisdoonvarna, at the T-intersection where R-476 meets R-481.*

Kilfenora
This town's hardworking, community-run **Burren Centre** shows an informative 10-minute video explaining the geology and botany of the region, and then ushers you into its enlightening museum exhibits (€6, daily June-Aug 9:30-17:30, mid-March-May and Sept-Oct 10:00-17:00, closed Nov-mid-March, tel. 065/708-8030, www.theburrencentre.ie). You'll also see copies of a fine eighth-century golden collar and ninth-century silver brooch (now in Dublin's National Museum).

The ruined **church** next door has a couple of 12th-century crosses, but isn't much to see. Mass is still held in the church, which claims the pope as its bishop. As the smallest and poorest diocese in Ireland, Kilfenora was almost unable to function after the Great Potato Famine, so in 1866 Pope Pius IX supported the town as best he could—by personally declaring himself its bishop.

COUNTY CLARE

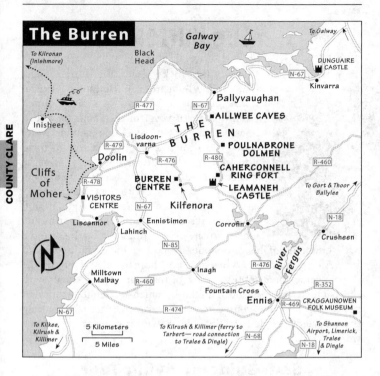

The Burren

To Galway

To Kilronan (Inishmore)

Galway Bay

Black Head

DUNGUAIRE CASTLE

Kinvarra

N-67

Inisheer

R-477

N-67

Ballyvaughan

AILLWEE CAVES

T H E

Lisdoon-varna

B U R R E N

R-479

POULNABRONE DOLMEN

Doolin

R-476

R-480

R-460

Cliffs of Moher

R-478

CAHERCONNELL RING FORT

BURREN CENTRE

LEAMANEH CASTLE

To Gort & Thoor Ballylee

VISITORS CENTRE

N-67

Kilfenora

Liscannor

Ennistimon

Corrofin

N-18

Lahinch

Crusheen

N-85

Milltown Malbay

Inagh

R-476

River Fergus

R-460

Fountain Cross

R-352

R-474

Ennis

R-469

CRAGGAUNOWEN FOLK MUSEUM

N-67

To Kilkee, Kilrush & Killimer

5 Kilometers

5 Miles

To Kilrush & Killimer (ferry to Tarbert— road connection to Tralee & Dingle)

N-68

To Shannon Airport, Limerick, Tralee & Dingle

N-18

For lunch in Kilfenora, consider the cheap and cheery **Burren Centre Tea Room** (daily 9:30-17:30, located at far back of building) or the more atmospheric **Vaughan's Pub.** If you're spending the night in County Clare, make a real effort to join the locals at the fun set-dancing get-togethers run by the Vaughans in the **Barn Pub,** adjacent to their regular pub (€5, Thu and Sun at 21:30, call ahead to confirm schedule, tel. 065/708-8004).

• *To continue from Kilfenora into the heart of the Burren, head east out of town on R-476. After about five kilometers (3 miles), you'll come to the junction with northbound R-480. Take the sharp left turn onto R-480, and slow down to gaze up (on the left) at the ruins of...*

Leamaneh Castle

This ruined shell of a fortified house is not open to anyone these days. From the outside, you can see how the 15th-century fortified tower house (the right quarter of the remaining ruin) was expanded 150 years later (the left three-quarters of the ruin). The castle evolved from a refuge into a manor, and windows were widened to allow for better views as defense became less of a priority.

• *From the castle, turn north on R-480 (direction: Ballyvaughan). After about eight kilometers (5 miles), you'll hit the start of the real barren Burren. Keep an eye out for the next stop.*

Caherconnell (Cahercommaun) Ring Fort

One of many ring forts in the area, you can see Caherconnell to the left on the crest of a hill just off the road. You can park in the gravel lot and walk up to the modest visitors center for a 15-minute film (a high-tech virtual tour) followed by a quick wander through the small fort. The fort sometimes features a sheep-herding demo with dogs (generally at 12:00 and 15:00—call to confirm).

Cost and Hours: €7, €9 includes sheep-herding demo, daily July-Aug 10:30-18:00, Easter-June and Sept-Oct 10:30-17:00, closed Nov-Easter, tel. 065/708-9999, www.burrenforts.ie.

• *The stretch from the ring fort north to Ballyvaughan offers the starkest scenery. Soon you'll see a 10-foot-high stone structure a hundred yards off the road to the right (east, toward an ugly gray metal barn). Pull over for a closer look.*

Poulnabrone Dolmen

While it looks like a stone table, this is a portal tomb. Two hundred years ago, locals called this a "druids' altar." Four thousand years ago, it was a grave chamber in a cairn of stacked stones. Amble over for a look. (It's crowded with tour buses at midday, but it's all yours early or late.)

Wander about for some quiet time with the wildflowers and try to think like a geologist. You're walking across a former seabed, dating from 250 million years ago when Ireland was at the equator (before continental drift nudged it north). Look for fossils—the white smudges were coral. Stones embedded in the belly of an advancing glacier ground the scratches you see in the rocks. The rounded boulders came south from Connemara, carried on a giant conveyor belt of ice, then left behind when the melting glaciers retreated north.

• *As you drive away from the dolmen (continuing north), look for the 30-foot-deep sinkhole beside the road on the right (a collapsed cave). From here, R-480 winds slowly downhill for about six kilometers (4 miles), eventually leaving the rocky landscape behind and entering a*

Botany of the Burren in Brief

The Burren is a story of water, rock, geological force, and time. It supports the greatest diversity of plants in Ireland. Like nowhere else, Mediterranean and Arctic wildflowers bloom side by side in the Burren. It's an orgy of cross-pollination that attracts more insects than Doolin does music-lovers—even beetles help out. Limestone, created from layers of coral, seashells, and mud, is the bedrock of the Burren. (The same formation resurfaces 10 miles or so out to sea to form the Aran Islands.)

Geologic forces in the earth's crust heaved up the land, and the glaciers swept it bare—dropping boulders as they receded. Rain, reacting naturally with the limestone to create a mild but determined acid, slowly drilled potholes into the surface. Rainwater cut through weak zones in the limestone, leaving crevices on the surface and Europe's most extensive system of caves below. Algae grew in the puddles, dried into a powder, and combined with bug parts and rabbit turds (bunnies abound in the Burren) to create a very special soil. Plants and flowers fill the cracks in the limestone. Grasses and shrubs don't do well here, and wild goats eat any trees that try to grow, giving tender little flowers a chance to enjoy the sun. Different flowers appear throughout the months, sharing space rather than competing. The flowers are best in June and July.

comparatively lush green valley. A little before Ballyvaughan, you'll see a sign pointing up a road to your right to...

Aillwee Caves

As these are touted as "Ireland's premier show caves," I couldn't resist a look. While fairly touristy and not worth the time or money if you've seen a lot of caves, they offer your easiest look at the massive system of caves that underlie the Burren. Your guide walks you 300 yards into the plain but impressive cave, giving a serious 40-minute geology lesson. During the Ice Age, underground rivers carved countless caves such as this one. Brown bears, which became extinct in Ireland a thousand years ago, found them great for hibernating. If you take the tour, you'll need a sweater: The caves are a constant 50°F.

Just below the caves (and on the same property) is the **Burren**

Birds of Prey Centre, with caged owls, eagles, hawks, and falcons (bird demonstrations likely at 12:00, 14:00, and 16:00 but call for daily schedule).

Adjacent to the caves, the **Hawk Walk** gets visitors face-to-beak with a Harris hawk, "the world's only social raptor." After a brief training session, an instructor leads a small group on a 45-minute hike up a nearby mountain trail. Each person gets his or her own bird to launch and call back.

Cost and Hours: Caves-€12, bird center-€8, €17 combo-ticket includes both sights, €70 for caves, bird center, and Halk Walk; open daily at 10:00, last tour at 18:30 July-Aug, otherwise 17:30, Dec-Feb call ahead for limited tours; clearly signposted just south of Ballyvaughan, tel. 065/707-7036, www.aillweecave.ie.

• *Continuing on, our final destination is...*

COUNTY CLARE

Ballyvaughan

Really just a crossroads, Bally-vaughan is the closest town to the Burren and an ideal rural base for those intending to really explore the region.

Shane Connolly leads in-depth, three-hour guided **walking tours** through the Burren, explaining the region's diverse flora, its geology and history, and the role humans have played in shaping this landscape. Wear comfortable shoes for the wet, rocky fields, and prepare to meet a proud farmer who really knows his stuff (€15, daily at 10:00 and 15:00, call to book and confirm meeting place in Ballyvaughan, tel. 065/707-7168, http://homepage.eircom.net/~burrenhillwalks).

Sleeping in Ballyvaughan: **$$$ Rusheen Lodge** feels like an oasis on the fringe of the Burren, with six luxurious rooms and three spotless suites, as well as a great breakfast (Sb-€60-70, Db-€80-100, suites-€100-140, Wi-Fi, tel. 065/707-7092, www.rusheenlodge.com, rusheen@iol.ie, Karen McGann).

Eating in Ballyvaughan: The local favorite is **Logues Lodge** (across from the Spar market). They specialize in roasts as well as the usual pub-grub fare (€11-20 meals, daily 12:30-21:30, tel. 065/707-7003).

Kinvarra

This tiny town, between Ballyvaughan and Galway (30 minutes from each), is waiting for something to happen in its minuscule harbor. It faces Dunguaire Castle, a four-story tower house from 1520 that stands a few yards out in the bay.

The touristy but fun **Dunguaire Castle medieval banquet** is Kinvarra's most worthy attraction (€56, cheaper if you book online, mid-April–mid-Oct Fri-Tue at 17:30 and sometimes at 20:45, closed Wed-Thu and mid-Oct–mid-April, reservations tel. 061/360-788, castle tel. 091/637-108, www.shannon heritage.com). Warning: The company also operates banquets

at Bunratty Castle (30 miles south), so be sure that you make your reservation for the correct castle.

The evening is as intimate as 55 tourists gathered under one time-stained, barrel-vaulted ceiling can be. You get a decent four-course meal with wine (or mead if you ask sweetly), served amid an entertaining evening of Irish tales and folk songs. Remember that in medieval times, it was considered polite to flirt with wenches. It's a small and multitalented cast: one harpist and three singer/actors who serve the "lords and ladies" between tunes. The highlight is the 40-minute stage show, which features songs and poems by local writers, and comes with dessert.

You can visit the castle itself by day without taking in an evening banquet (€6, daily 10:00-16:30).

Sleeping in Kinvarra: **$$ Cois Cuain B&B** is a small but stately house with a garden, overlooking the square and harbor of the most charming village setting you'll find. Mary Walsh rents three super-homey rooms for non-smokers (Db-€60-75, cash only, The Quay, tel. 091/637-119).

GALWAY

Galway feels like a boomtown—rare in Western Ireland. Until the recession hit in 2008, it was the fastest growing city in Ireland. And it's still its most international city, as one out of every four residents were born outside of Ireland. With 76,000 people, Galway is the county's main city, a lively university town, and the region's industrial and administrative center. As it's near the traditional regions of Connemara and the Aran Islands, it's also a gateway to these Gaelic cultural preserves.

While Galway has a long and interesting history, its British overlords (who ruled until 1921) had little use for anything important to the Irish heritage. Consequently, precious little from old Galway survives. What does remain has the interesting disadvantage of being built in the local limestone, which, even if medieval, looks like modern stone construction. The city's quincentennial celebration in 1984 awakened a spirit of preservation.

What Galway lacks in sights it makes up for in ambience. Spend an afternoon just wandering its medieval streets, with their delightful mix of colorful facades, labyrinthine pubs, weather-resistant street musicians, and steamy eateries. Galway also offers tourists plenty of traditional music, easy train connections to Dublin, and a convenient jumping-off point for a visit to the Aran Islands. After dark, blustery Galway heats up, with fine theaters and a pub scene that attracts even Dubliners. Visitors mix with old-timers and students as the traditional music goes round and round.

If you hear a strange language on the streets and wonder where those people are from, it's Irish, and so are they.

Galway's History

In 1234, the medieval fishing village of Galway went big time, when the Normans captured the territory from the O'Flaherty family. Making the town a base, the Normans invited in their Angle friends, built a wall (1270), and kicked out the Irish. Galway's Celtic name (Gaillimh) comes from an old Irish word, *gall,* which means "foreigner." Except for a small section in the Eyre Square Shopping Centre and a chunk at the Spanish Arch, that Norman wall is gone.

In the 14th century, 14 merchant families, or tribes, controlled Galway's commercial traffic, including the lucrative wine trade with Spain and France. These English families constantly clashed with the local Irish. Although the wall was built to "keep out the O's and the Macs," it didn't always work. A common prayer at the time was, "From the fury of the O'Flahertys, good Lord deliver us."

Galway's support of the English king helped it prosper. But with the rise of Oliver Cromwell in the 1640s (see sidebar on page 167), Galway paid for that prosperity. After sieges by Cromwell's troops (in 1651) and the Protestant King William of Orange (in 1691), Galway declined. It wasn't until the last half of the 20th century that it regained some of its importance and wealth.

Planning Your Time

Galway's sights are little more than pins on which to hang the old town. The joy of Galway is its street scene. You can see its sights in three hours, but without an evening in town, you've missed the best. Many spend three nights and two days: one for the town and another for a side-trip to the Burren (see previous chapter), the Aran Islands, or the Connemara region (see following chapters). Tour companies make day trips to all three regions cheap and easy.

Orientation to Galway

The center of Galway is Eyre Square. Within two blocks of the square, you'll find the TI, Aran boat offices, a tour pickup point, accommodations (from the best cheap hostel beds to fancy hotels), and the train station. The train and public bus station butt up against the Hotel Meyrick, a huge gray railroad hotel that overlooks and dominates Eyre Square. The lively old town lies between Eyre Square and the river. From Eyre Square, Williams Gate leads a pedestrian parade right through the old town (changing street names several times) to Wolfe Tone Bridge. Nearly everything you'll see and do is within a few minutes' walk of this spine.

Tourist Information

The TI, located a block from the bus/train station in the ground floor of the Forster Court Hotel, has a bookshop and many booking services (daily 9:00-17:00, Sun off-season until 11:45, Forster Street, tel. 091/537-700, www.discoverireland.ie). A tiny seasonal satellite TI is in a kiosk in the middle of Eyre Square (May-Sept only, Mon-Sat 9:00-17:00, closed Sun). Pick up the TI's free city guide with its simplified town map.

Arrival in Galway

Trains and most buses share the same station, virtually on Eyre Square (which has the nearest ATMs). The train station can store your bag (€2.50/day, Mon-Fri 8:00-18:00, closed Sat-Sun). To get from the station to the TI, go left on Station Road as you exit the station (toward Eyre Square), and then turn right on Forster Street.

Don't confuse the public bus station (in same building as the train station) with the coach station (a block away, across the street from the TI), which handles only privately owned coaches. City-link buses from Dublin and Dublin's airport, as well as regional day-tour buses, use the coach station.

Drivers staying overnight at a College Road B&B can park there for free (each has a small lot in front). For daytime parking, the most central and handiest parking garage is under the recommended Jurys Inn Galway in the town center (€2.20/hour, €20/24 hours, Mon-Sat 8:00-1:00 in the morning, Sun 9:00-18:00). To park nearby for free, try across the bridge along the Claddagh Quay. Otherwise, you'll have to buy a pay-and-display ticket and put it on your dashboard (€2.60, 2-hour maximum, buy from machines on street).

Helpful Hints

Crowd Control: Expect huge crowds—and much higher prices—during the Galway Arts Festival (mid-to-late-July, www.galwayartsfestival.com) and Galway Oyster Festival (late Sept, www.galwayoysterfest.com). The Galway Races are heaven for lovers of horse racing and hell for everyone else (summer races in late July-early Aug, fall races in mid-Sept and late Oct, www.galwayraces.com); prices double for food and lodging, and simple evening strolls feel like punt returns.

Markets: On Saturdays year-round and Sundays in summer, a fun market clusters around St. Nicholas' Church (all day, but best 9:00-14:00).

Internet Access: There are several good places along High Street near Jurys Inn.

Bookstore: Dubray Books is directly across the pedestrian drag

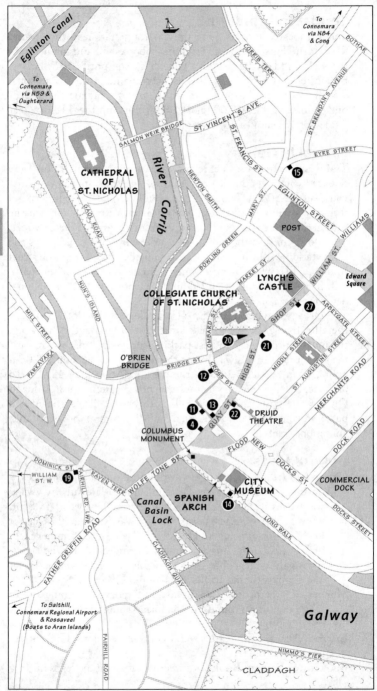

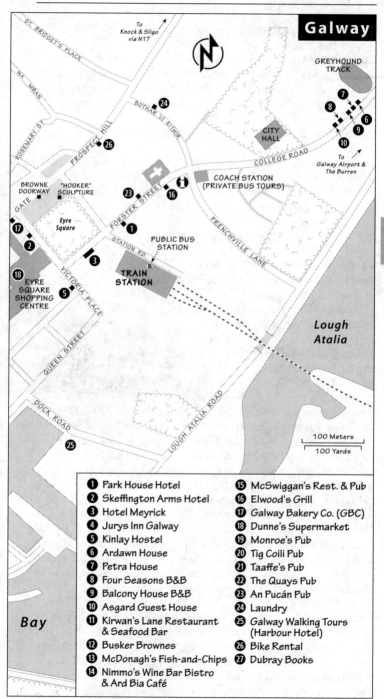

Galway

- **1** Park House Hotel
- **2** Skeffington Arms Hotel
- **3** Hotel Meyrick
- **4** Jurys Inn Galway
- **5** Kinlay Hostel
- **6** Ardawn House
- **7** Petra House
- **8** Four Seasons B&B
- **9** Balcony House B&B
- **10** Asgard Guest House
- **11** Kirwan's Lane Restaurant & Seafood Bar
- **12** Busker Brownes
- **13** McDonagh's Fish-and-Chips
- **14** Nimmo's Wine Bar Bistro & Ard Bia Café
- **15** McSwiggan's Rest. & Pub
- **16** Elwood's Grill
- **17** Galway Bakery Co. (GBC)
- **18** Dunne's Supermarket
- **19** Monroe's Pub
- **20** Tig Coili Pub
- **21** Taaffe's Pub
- **22** The Quays Pub
- **23** An Pucán Pub
- **24** Laundry
- **25** Galway Walking Tours (Harbour Hotel)
- **26** Bike Rental
- **27** Dubray Books

GALWAY

from Lynch's Castle (Mon-Sat 9:00-18:00, Sun 12:00-18:00, 4 Shop Street, tel. 091/569-070).

Bike Rental: On Yer Bike rents good bikes to tool around flat Galway town. Consider a pleasant ride out to the end of Salthill's beachfront promenade and back (€10/day, 42 Prospect Hill, tel. 091/563-393, mobile 087/942-5479, www.onyourbike cycles.com).

Post Office: It squats on Eglinton Street (Mon-Sat 9:00-17:30, closed Sun).

Laundry: Galway Dry Cleaners is close to the recommended B&Bs on College Road (€10 drop-off, Mon-Fri 8:00-18:30, Sat 9:00-18:00, Sun 12:00-16:00, on Bothar Ui Eithir, 2-minute walk uphill from TI, tel. 091/568-393).

GALWAY

Tours in Galway

▲**Hop-on, Hop-off City Bus Tours**—Guided one-hour double-decker bus tours depart from the TI and Eyre Square, making nine stops, including the cathedral, Salthill, and the Spanish Arch. You can get off and explore, and hop back on later (€10, April-Sept daily 10:30-16:30, 4/day, buses usually depart every 1.5 hours from  TI on Forster Street, tel. 091/524-728, mobile 087-679-8525).

Walking Tours—There are many walking tours in this town full of stories waiting to be told. **Galway Walking Tours** are led by Fiona Brennan, who takes her guests on leisurely 1.5-hour explorations of the city (€12, departs from beside the docks at the Harbour Hotel, call to arrange start time, mobile 087-290-3499, www. galwaywalkingtours.com, fiona@galwaywalkingtours.com). **Liam Silke** comes from one of Galway's oldest families and still serves as Galway's town crier as he leads 1.5-hour tours twice daily (€10, departs from Brown's Doorway in Eyre Square, call to arrange start time, tel. 091/588-897, mobile 086/348-0958, www.walkingtours galway.com, info@walkingtoursgalway.com). **Gore of Galway Walks** focus on the hidden history, folklore, murder, and mayhem of the "City of the Tribes" (€8, 1.5 hours, departs from TI Mon, Wed, and Fri at 17:00, mobile 086-727-4888). **Galway City Walk & Talk** tours discuss architecture, culture, and historic characters of Galway's past (€10, 2 hours, daily at 10:30, departs May-Sept from TI kiosk in middle of Eyre Square, mobile 087-690-1452).

Bus Tours—Several Galway-based companies offer bus tours to the Burren (see page 275) and Connemara (see page 326).

Sights in Galway

Medieval Galway's "Latin Quarter"

From the top of Eyre Square, Williams Gate—named for the old main gate of the Norman town wall that once stood here—is the spine of medieval Galway. While the road changes names several times (William, Shop, High, and Quay Streets), it leads generally downhill to the River Corrib, straight past the following sights.

Lynch's Castle—Now the Allied Irish Bank, Galway's best late-15th-century fortified townhouse was the home of the Lynch family—the most powerful of the town's 14 tribes—and the only one of their mansions to survive. More than 80 Lynch mayors ruled Galway in the 16th and 17th centuries.

Collegiate Church of St. Nicholas—This church, located a half-block off the main street on the right, is the finest medieval building in town (1320), and is dedicated to St. Nicholas of Myra, the patron saint of sailors. Columbus is said to have worshipped here in 1477, undoubtedly while contemplating a scary voyage. Its interior is littered with obscure town history (free entry but €3 suggested donation). Consider attending an evening concert of traditional Irish music in this atmospheric venue (see "Nightlife in Galway," later).

A wonderful **open-air market** surrounds the church most Saturdays year-round and also on Sundays in summer.

The Quays—This pub was once owned by "Humanity Dick," an 18th-century Member of Parliament who was the original animal-rights activist. It's worth a peek inside for its lively interior. The lane just before it leads to the...

Druid Theatre—This 100-seat theater offers top-notch contemporary Irish theater. While the theater company is often away on tour, it's worth checking their schedule online or dropping by to see if anything's playing tonight (€16-25 tickets, Chapel Lane, tel. 091/568-660, www.druid.ie).

Directly across the alley from the theater door (under the glass Revenue Building) are the foundations of Galway's oldest building. It was once the 13th-century hall of the Norman lord Richard DeBurgo.

Spanish Arch—Overlooking the River Corrib, this makes up the best remaining chunk of the old city wall. A reminder of Galway's former importance in trade, the Arch (c. 1584) is the place where Spanish ships would unload their cargo (primarily wine).

Galway Legends and Factoids

Because of the dearth of physical old stuff, the town milks its legends. Here are a few that you'll encounter repeatedly:

- In the 15th century, the mayor, one of the Lynch tribe, condemned his son to death for the murder of a Spaniard. When no one in town could be found to hang the popular boy, the dad—who loved justice more than he loved his son—did it himself.
- Columbus is said to have stopped in Galway in 1477. He may have been inspired by tales of the voyage of St. Brendan, the Irish monk who is thought by some (mostly Irish) to have beaten Columbus to the New World by almost a thousand years.
- On the main drag, you'll find a pub called The King's Head. It was originally given to the man who chopped off the head of King Charles I in 1649. For his safety, he settled in Galway—about as far from London as an Englishman could get back then.
- William Joyce, born in America, spent most of his childhood in Galway and later was seduced by fascist ideology in the 1930s. He moved to Germany and became "Lord Haw-Haw," infamous as the radio voice of Nazi propaganda during World War II. After the war, he was hanged in London for treason. His daughter had him buried in Galway.

City Museum—Fragments of old Galway are kept in this modern museum, located just behind the Spanish Arch. Enjoy temporary art exhibitions by local artists and occasional live music performances. Highlights include coverage of John F. Kennedy's 1963 visit and an intact Galway "hooker" boat hanging from the ceiling. The museum also houses prehistoric and medieval Galway-related treasures on loan from Dublin's National Museum.

Cost and Hours: Free, Tue-Sat 10:00-17:00, closed Sun-Mon; handy café with cheap lunches, tel. 091/532-460, www.galway citymuseum.ie.

River Corrib Sights—At the River Corrib, you'll find a riverside park that's perfect for a picnic (or get takeout from the recommended McDonagh's, the town's best chipper, across the street). Over the river (southeast of the bridge) is the modern housing project that replaced the original Claddagh in the 1930s. **Claddagh** (CLA-dah, like the "cla" in clatter) was a picturesque, Gaelic-speaking fishing village with a strong tradition of independence—and open sewers. This gaggle of thatched cottages functioned as an independent community with its own "king" until the early 1900s, when it was torn down for health reasons.

The old Claddagh village is gone, but the tradition of its popular ring (sold all over town) lives on. The Claddagh ring shows two hands holding a heart that wears a crown. The heart represents love, the crown is loyalty, and the hands are friendship. If the ring is worn with the tip of the heart pointing toward the wrist, it signifies that the wearer is married or otherwise taken. However, if the tip of the heart points toward the fingertip, it means the wearer is available.

Look at the **monument** (just before the bridge) given to Galway by the people of Genoa, Italy, to celebrate Columbus' visit here in 1477. (That acknowledgment, from an Italian town known for its stinginess, helps to substantiate the famous explorer's legendary visit.) From the middle of the bridge, look up the river. The green copper dome marks the city's Cathedral of St. Nicholas (described on the next page). Down the river is a tiny swan-infested harbor with a few of Galway's famous square-rigged "hooker" fishing ships tied up and on display. Called "hookers" for their hook-and-line fishing, these sturdy yet graceful boats were later used to transport turf from Connemara, until improved roads and electric heat made them obsolete. Beyond that, a huge park of reclaimed land is popular with the local kids for Irish football and hurling. From there, the promenade leads to the resort town of Salthill.

More Sights in Galway

▲**Eyre Square**—On a sunny day, grassy Eyre Square is a popular hangout. In the Middle Ages, it was a field just outside the town wall. The square is named for the mayor who gave the land to the city in 1710. While still called Eyre Square, it now contains John F. Kennedy Park—established in memory of the Irish-American president's visit in 1963, a few months before he was assassinated. Though Kennedy is celebrated as America's first Irish-Catholic president, several US presidents were descended from Protestant Ulster stock (even Barack Obama is part Irish, with roots in County Offaly). Take a look at the JFK bust near the kids' play area, which commemorates his visit.

Walk to the rust-colored "Hooker Sculpture," built in 1984 to celebrate the 500th anniversary of the incorporation of the city. The sails represent Galway's square-rigged fishing ships ("hookers") and the vessels that made Galway a trading center so long ago. The Browne Doorway, from a 1627 fortified townhouse, is a reminder of the 14 family tribes that once ruled the town (see Lynch's Castle, listed earlier, to get a feel for an intact townhouse). Each had a town castle—much like the towers that characterize the towns of Tuscany, with their feuding noble families. So little survives of medieval Galway that the town makes a huge deal of any remaining window or crest. Check out the 14 colorful flags lin-

GALWAY

ing the western edge of the square, each one with a different tribe name.

The Eyre Square Shopping Centre—a busy, modern shopping mall (see the arcaded entry from the square)—leads to a piece of the old town wall that includes two reconstructed towers (and an antiques market).

▲**Cathedral of St. Nicholas**—
Opened by American Cardinal
Cushing in 1965, this is one of
the last great stone churches
built in Europe. The interior is
a treat—mahogany pews set on
green Connemara marble floors
under a Canadian cedar ceiling.
The acoustically correct cedar

enhances the church's fine pipe organ. Two thousand worshippers sit in the round facing the central altar. A Dublin woman carved the 14 larger-than-life Stations of the Cross. The carving above the chapel (left of entry) is from the old St. Nicholas church. Explore the modern stained glass. Find the Irish Holy Family—with Mary knitting and Jesus offering Joseph a cup of tea. The window depicting the Last Supper is particularly creative—find the 12 apostles.

Next, poke your head into the side chapel with a mosaic of

Christ's resurrection (if you're standing in the nave facing the main altar, it's on the left and closest to the front). Take a closer look at the profiled face in a circular frame, below and to the right of Christ—the one looking up while praying with clasped hands. It's JFK, nearly a saint in Irish eyes at the time this cathedral was built.

Cost and Hours: Free, church bulletins at the doorway tell of upcoming Masses and concerts, located across Salmon Weir Bridge on outskirts of town, tel. 091/563-577.

Salmon Weir Bridge—This bridge was the local "bridge of sighs." It led from the courthouse (opposite the church) to the prison (torn down to build the cathedral—unlikely in the US). Today, the bridge provides a fun view of the fishing action. Salmon run up this river most of the summer (look for them). Fishermen, who wear waders and carry walking sticks to withstand the strong current, book long in advance to get half-day appointments for a casting spot.

Canals multiplied in this city (sometimes called the "Venice of Ireland") to power more water mills.

Outer Galway

▲**Salthill**—This small resort town packs pubs, discos, a splashy water park, amusement centers, and a fairground up against a fine, mile-long beach promenade (Ireland's longest). Watch for locals "kicking the wall" when they reach the western end of this mile-long promenade to emphasize that they've walked the entire distance.

At the **Atlantaquaria Aquarium,** which features native Irish aquatic life and some Amazonian species, kids can help feed the fish at 13:00 (fresh water), 15:00 (big fish), and 16:00 (small fish). They can cuddle the crustaceans anytime (€10.25, Mon-Fri 10:00-17:00, Sat-Sun 10:00-18:00, touch tanks, The Promenade, tel. 091/585-100, www.nationalaquarium.ie).

For beach time, a relaxing sunset stroll, late-night traditional music, or later-night disco action, Salthill hops. For accommodations in Salthill, see page 307.

Getting There: To get to Salthill, catch bus #1 from Eyre Square in front of the AIB bank, next to Meyrick Hotel (€1.50, runs 7:00-23:00).

Trad on the Prom—This fine traditional-music and dance troupe was started by Galway-born performers who returned home after years of touring with *Riverdance* and *The Chieftains*. It's a great way to enjoy live step dancing and accomplished musicians in a fairly intimate venue.

Cost and Hours: €30, mid-May-Sept only, shows generally at 19:00 and 21:00 Tue, Thu, and Sun—call to confirm; in Salthill Hotel, 30-minute walk west of town along the Salthill promenade or short ride on bus #1 from Eyre Square; tel. 091/582-860, mobile 087-2388-489, www.tradontheprom.com.

Dog Racing—Join the locals and cheer on the greyhounds. The stadium is a 10-minute walk from Eyre Square and barking distance from my recommended B&Bs.

Cost and Hours: €10, Thu-Sat evenings from 20:00 to 22:30, tel. 091/562-273, www.igb.ie.

Nightlife in Galway

▲**Traditional Irish Music**—Galway, like Dingle and Doolin, is a mecca for good Irish music (nightly 21:30-23:30). But unlike Dingle and Doolin, this is a university town (enrollment: 12,000), and many pubs are often overrun with noisy students. Still, your chances of landing a seat close to a churning band surrounded by new Irish friends are good any evening of the year. Touristy and student pubs are found and filled along the main drag down from Eyre Square to the Spanish Arch, and across Wolfe Tone Bridge, along William Street West and Dominick Street. If it happens to be Tuesday, cross the bridge and start at **Monroe's,** with its vast, music-filled interior (trad music and set-dancing Tue at 21:00, a mixed bag of folk/rock music other nights, Dominick Street, tel. 091/583-397, www.monroes.ie). Several other pubs within earshot frequently feature traditional music.

Pubs known for Irish music along the main drag include **Tig Coili,** featuring Galway's best trad sessions (Mon-Sat at 18:00 and 21:00, Sun at 14:00 and 21:00, intersection of Main Guard Street and High Street, tel. 091/561-294, www.tigcoili. com); **Taaffe's** (nightly music sessions at 17:30 and 21:30, Shop Street, across from St. Nicholas Church, tel. 091/564-066); and **The Quays** (traditional music Mon-Tue at 21:30, Fri and Sun at 17:00, young scene, Quay Street, tel. 091/568-347).

An Pucán Pub, a cauldron of music and beer drinking with an older crowd—including lots of tourists—is worth a look. An Irish dance troupe called Mystic Force performs Monday through Thursday at 20:00 (music nightly at 22:00, usually traditional, just off Eyre Square on Forster Street, tel. 091/561-528, www.anpucan. com).

The **Collegiate Church of St. Nicholas** is the mellow medieval venue for "Tunes in the Church," with a rotating line-up of accomplished trad musicians. The 1.5-hour concerts are fun for early-birds who don't want to stay up to catch the same great players in a local pub later that night (€15; Mon, Wed, and Fri at 20:00; where High Street and Shop Street intersect, tel. 087/962-5425, www. tunesinthechurch.com).

Sleeping in Galway

There are three price tiers for most beds in Galway: off-season, high season (Easter-Oct), and charge-what-you-like festivals and race weekends (see "Crowd Control" on page 295). I've listed high-season rates. B&Bs simply play the market. If you're on a tight budget, call around and see where the best prices are. All B&Bs include a full "Irish fry" breakfast.

Hotels

For a fancy place, Park House Hotel offers the best value. For a budget hotel, go to Jurys Inn. For cheap beds, hit the hostel.

$$$ Park House Hotel, a plush, business-class hotel, is ide-

Sleep Code

(€1 = about $1.30, country code: 353, area code: 091)
S = Single, **D** = Double/Twin, **T** = Triple, **Q** = Quad, **b** = bath-room, **s** = shower only. All of these places accept credit cards.
　　To help you easily sort through these listings, I've divided the rooms into three categories, based on the price for a standard double room with bath:

$$$ **Higher Priced**—Most rooms €120 or more.
　$$ **Moderately Priced**—Most rooms between €60-120.
　　$ **Lower Priced**—Most rooms €60 or less.

　　Prices can change without notice; verify the hotel's current rates online or by email.

---

ally located a block from the train station and Eyre Square. Its 84 spacious rooms come with all the comforts you'd expect (Db-€99-169, online discounts, expensive full Irish breakfast-€22.50, elevator, great restaurant, free garage, helpful staff, Forster Street, tel. 091/564-924, www.parkhousehotel.ie, parkhousehotel@eircom. net).

　　$$$ Skeffington Arms Hotel, which feels more Irish than the Park House or Jurys Inn, escapes most of the tour-group scene because it has only 24 rooms. Centrally located on Eyre Square, it's renovated and furnished in a modern style (Sb-€65-110, Db-€80-165, Tb-€125-200, Qb-€170-225, online discounts, Wi-Fi, pub next door, Eyre Square, tel. 091/563-173, fax 091/561-679, www. skeffington.ie, reception@skeffington.ie).

　　$$$ Hotel Meyrick, filled with palatial Old World elegance and 97 rooms, marks the end of the Dublin-Galway train line and the beginning of Galway. Since 1845, it has been Galway's landmark hotel...JFK stayed here in 1963 when it was the Great Southern (Db-€165-199, some discounts during slow times, best rates when you book online, at the head of Eyre Square, tel. 091/564-041, fax 091/566-704, www.hotelmeyrick.ie, reshm@monogram hotels.ie).

　　$$$ Jurys Inn Galway has 130 American-style rooms in a modern hotel, centrally located where the old town hits the river. The big, bright rooms have two double beds and huge modern bathrooms. You'll pay the same per room whether it's for a single, a couple, three adults, or a family of four (€79-119 Sun-Thu, €109-155 Fri-Sat, prices depend on season, breakfast-€10, elevator, lots of tour groups, parking-€10, Quay Street, tel. 091/566-444, fax 091/568-415, US tel. 800-423-6953, www.jurysinns.com, jurysinngalway@jurysinns.com).

Hostel: **$ Kinlay Hostel** is a no-nonsense place just 100 yards from the train station, with 224 beds (1-8 beds per room) in bare, clean, and simple rooms, including 15 doubles/twins. Easygoing people of any age feel welcome here, but if you want a double, book well ahead—several months in advance for weekends (dorm bed-€16-25, Sb-€48-60, Db-€60-70, Internet access and Wi-Fi, elevator, self-service kitchen, baggage storage, on Merchants Road just off Eyre Square, tel. 091/565-244, fax 091/565-245, www.kinlay galway.ie, info@kinlaygalway.ie).

B&Bs

Drivers who follow city-center signs into Galway will pass a string of B&Bs just after the greyhound-racing stadium. On foot, the B&Bs are about a 10-minute walk from Eyre Square (from the station, walk up Forster Street, which turns into College Road). The following places are lined up like battleships on College Road. All have free parking. Although there are other B&Bs on this road, my favorites are the ones where the owner lives on-site (and whose pride of ownership shows).

$$ Petra House, a peaceful-feeling brick building, rents nine great rooms, including a family room. The owners, Joan and Frank Maher, keep everything lovingly maintained. Breakfasts are a highlight (Sb-€50-65, Db-€70-100, Tb-€100-120, Qb-€120-140, elegant sitting room, free Internet access, Wi-Fi, 29 College Road, tel. 091/566-580, www.galway.net/pages/petra-house, petra house@eircom.net).

$$ Ardawn House is a welcoming B&B with nine fresh and comfortable rooms. The Guilfoyles—friendly Breda and Arctic explorer Mike—are great sources for local tips (Sb-€55-75, Db-€70-120, Tb-€110-150, Qb-€120-160, Wi-Fi, 31 College Road, near stadium on right, tel. 091/568-833, fax 091/563-454, www. ardawnhouse.com, ardawn@iol.ie).

$$ Four Seasons B&B is well-kept, with seven inviting rooms hosted by Eddie and Helen Fitzgerald (Sb-€45-55, Db-€70-90, Tb-€90-120, Qb-€120-140, Wi-Fi, 23 College Road, tel. 091/564-078, www.fourseasonsgalway.com, info@fourseasons galway.com).

$$ Balcony House B&B rents eight pleasant rooms (Sb-€45-60, Db-€80-120, Tb-€105-140, Qb-€140-160, Wi-Fi, 27 College Road, tel. 091/563-438, www.aaabalconyhouse.com, info@aaa balconyhouse.com). Teresa Coyne provides treats in your room on arrival.

$$ Asgard Guest House offers eight restful rooms and an appealing glass-atrium breakfast room (Sb-€45-60, Db-€70-

90, Tb-€90-120, Qb-€140-160, Wi-Fi, 21 College Road, tel. 091/566-855, www.galwaycityguesthouse.com, info@galwaycity guesthouse.com, Mary O'Flynn).

Near Galway, in Salthill

Salthill is Galway's equivalent of a beach town, with a fine sandy promenade for summer evening walks. (For more on Salthill, see page 303.)

$$ Clarevilla B&B, a good, quiet choice 200 yards from the beach in a mellow residential area, has six serenely decorated, white rooms (Sb-€45-50, Db-€70-75, Tb-€90, cash only, Wi-Fi, closed Nov-Feb, 38 Threadneedle Road, tel. 091/522-520, clarevilla@ yahoo.com, Christina Connolly). By car, it's a seven-minute drive from Galway. Follow the beach past Salthill, and take a right on Threadneedle Road just before the beach's high diving board—it's on your left, 200 yards up, next to the Tennis Club. By bus, take #402 (3/hour, €1.65) from Eyre Square (picks up on the opposite side of square from the Skeffington Arms pub). Get off at the Threadneedle stop and walk up Threadneedle Road.

Eating in Galway

This college town is filled with colorful, inexpensive eateries. People everywhere seem to be enjoying their food.

At the Bottom of the Old Town

Each of these places is within a block or two of Jurys Inn.

Kirwan's Lane Restaurant & Seafood Bar is considered Galway's best dining experience. The seafood bar downstairs and the restaurant up top have the same hours. Both are dressy places where reservations are required (€16-22 lunches, €24-30 dinners, daily 12:30-14:30 & 18:00-22:00, no lunch on Sun, on Kirwan's Lane a block from Jurys Inn, tel. 091/568-266).

Busker Brownes has three eateries in a sprawling spot popular for its good, cheap food. Enter on Cross Street for the restaurant and walk to the back for better seating, or enter on Kirwan's Lane for the ground-floor pub; the third section is upstairs from the pub (€11-22 meals, daily 10:30-21:30, cleanse your palate with jazz sessions Sun at 12:00 and Mon at 21:30, Cross Street and Kirwan's Lane, tel. 091/563-377).

McDonagh's Fish-and-Chips is a favorite among residents. It has a fast, cheap, all-day section and a classier dinner-only restaurant. If you're determined to try Galway oysters, remember that they're in season from September through April only. At other times, you'll eat Pacific oysters—go figure (€10 lunch, €15-25 in restaurant, €20 two-course early-bird special served 17:00-18:45;

chipper open Mon-Sat 12:00-22:00, Sun 16:00-22:00; restaurant open Mon-Sat 17:00-22:00, closed Sun; 22 Quay Street, tel. 091/565-001).

Nimmo's Wine Bar Bistro and **Ard Bia Café** peacefully co-exist in an old stone warehouse behind the Spanish Arch. The upstairs is a mellow hangout with great cheese platters and wine. The candlelit ambience is great any night, even for a cup of coffee (€15-24 meals, café lunches Tue-Sat 10:30-15:30, wine-bar dinners Tue-Sun 18:00-21:30, closed Mon, Long Walk Street, tel. 091/561-114 or 091/539-897).

Near Eyre Square

Elwood's Grill, conveniently located next door to the TI, is closest to my College Road B&B listings. Its friendly modern pub (up front) serves better than average pub fare, while the fine restaurant out back offers romantic dinners (€11-16 lunches, €18-24 dinners, daily 12:00-22:30, Forster Street, tel. 091/564-111).

McSwiggan's, with a downstairs pub and upstairs restaurant, is a maze of wooden stairways, brick walls, and hidden alcoves, serving hearty traditional Irish meals (€12-18 lunches, €17-22 dinners, daily 12:00-22:30, Eyre Street, tel. 091/568-917).

The **Galway Bakery Company (GBC)** is a popular, basic place for a quick Irish meal (€12-17 meals in ground-floor cafeteria, pricier restaurant upstairs, daily 12:00-21:00, 7 Williams Gate, near Eyre Square, tel. 091/563-087).

Supermarket: You can get to **Dunnes** through the Eyre Square Shopping Centre or around the corner at tiny Castle Street, off the pedestrian Williams Gate (Mon-Sat 9:00-19:00, Thu-Fri until 20:00, Sun 11:00-19:00, supermarket in basement). Lots of smaller grocery shops are scattered throughout town.

Near Galway, in Salthill

Lohan's Restaurant is right on the seafront promenade in Salthill (just west of the aquarium) and offers traditional Irish favorites at reasonable prices (€11-16 meals, daily 12:00-22:00, 232 Upper Salthill, tel. 091/522-696).

Outside Galway

If you have a car, consider a **Dunguaire Castle medieval banquet** in Kinvarra, a 30-minute drive south of Galway (for details, see page 292). You can fit in the banquet very efficiently when you're driving into or out of Galway (B&Bs can accommodate late arrivals if you call).

Galway Connections

From Galway by Train to: Dublin (8/day, 2.5-3 hours), **Limerick** (5/day, 2 hours), **Ennis** (5/day, 1.25 hours). For **Belfast, Tralee,** and **Rosslare,** you'll change in or near Dublin. Train info: Tel. 091/561-444, www.irishrail.ie.

By Bus to: Dublin (hourly, 3.25 hours; also see Citylink, below), **Kilkenny** (3/day, 5 hours), **Cork** (hourly, 4.25 hours), **Ennis** (hourly, 1.25 hours), **Shannon Airport** (hourly, 1.75 hours), **Cliffs of Moher** (2/day in summer, some with change in Ennis, 2 hours), **Doolin** (1/day, 1.5-2 hours), **Limerick** (8/day, 2.25 hours), **Dingle** (5/day, 6.5 hours), **Tralee** (8/day, 4.5 hours), **Westport** (5-7/ day, 1.5-2.75 hours), **Rosslare** (hourly, 7.5 hours), **Belfast** (hourly, 7 hours, change in Dublin), **Derry** (5/day, 6 hours). Bus info: Tel. 091/562-000, www.buseireann.ie.

Citylink (tel. 091/564-164, www.citylink.ie) runs cheap and fast bus service from the coach station near the TI to **Dublin** (arriving at Bachelor's Walk, a block from Tara Street DART station; hourly, 2.5 hours), **Dublin Airport** (hourly, 3 hours), and **Cork Airport** (6/day, 3.75 hours).

By Car: For ideas on driving from Galway to Derry or Portrush in Northern Ireland, see "Sights Between Galway and Derry" at the end of the Connemara and County Mayo chapter, which describes sights in the Republic of Ireland. For sights on this route in Northern Ireland, see "Between Derry and Galway" on page 423 of the Derry and County Donegal chapter.

GALWAY

ARAN ISLANDS

Inishmore • Inisheer

Strewn like limestone chips hammered off the jagged west coast, the three Aran Islands—Inishmore, Inishmaan, and Inisheer—confront the wild Atlantic with stubborn grit. The largest, Inishmore (9 miles by 2 miles), is by far the most populated, interesting, and visited (try to spend a night here). Inisheer, the smallest (1.5 miles square), and best reached from Doolin, is worth considering for travelers with less time.

The landscape of all three islands is harsh: steep, rugged cliffs and windswept rocky fields divided by stone walls. During the winter, severe gales sweep through; because of this, most of the settlements on the islands are found on the more sheltered northeastern side. There's a stark beauty about the Aran Islands and the simple lives their inhabitants eke out of a mean sea and less than six inches of topsoil. Precious little of the land is productive. In the past, people made a precarious living here from fishing and farming. The scoured bedrock offered little in the way of soil, so it was created by the islanders—the result of centuries of layering seaweed with limestone sand and animal dung. Fields are small, divided by several thousand miles of "drystone" wall (made without mortar). Most of these are built in the Aran "gap" style, in which spaces between angled upright stones are filled with smaller stones. This allows a farmer who wants to move stock to dismantle and rebuild the wall. It also allows the harsh winter winds to blow through without knocking down the wall. Nowadays, tourism boosts the islands' economy.

The islands are a Gaeltacht area. While the islanders speak Irish amongst themselves, they happily speak English for their visitors. Many of them have direct, personal connections with close relatives in America. Recently, I met a minivan driver who served in the US Navy aboard a destroyer before coming back home to Inishmore. Five of his six children now have American passports.

Today, the 900 people of Inishmore (literally "the big island") greet as many as 2,000 visitors a day. The vast majority of these are day-trippers. They'll hop on a minivan at the dock for a 2.5-hour visit to Dún Aenghus (the must-see Iron Age fort), and then spend an hour or two browsing through the few shops or sitting at a picnic table outside a pub with a pint of Guinness.

The other islands, Inisheer and Inishmaan, are smaller, much less populated, and less touristy. While extremely quiet, they do have B&Bs, daily flights, and ferry service. For most, the big island is quiet enough. But Inisheer is a good alternative if your travel plans take you to Doolin (a 25-minute ferry ride away) and not Galway, which is closer to Inishmore's port.

Inishmore

The largest of the Aran Islands has a blockbuster sight: the striking Dún Aenghus fort, set on a sheer cliff. Everyone arrives at Kilronan, the Aran Islands' biggest town, though it's just a village. Groups of backpackers wash ashore with the docking of each ferry. Minivans, bike shops, and a few men in pony carts sop up the tourists.

Planning Your Time

Most travelers visit Inishmore (Inis Mór) as a day trip by boat from Galway. (Boats from Doolin are too slow and weather-dependent to allow enough time for a same-day round-trip to Inishmore.) Here's a good framework for a day trip: Leave Galway at 9:00 on the shuttle bus to Rossaveel, where you'll catch the 10:30 boat. You'll step off the boat in Kilronan at about 11:15. Arrange minivan transport or rent a bike, visit Dún Aenghus, and grab a bite at a café near the base of the Dún Aenghus fort trail. Explore the island during low tide, and depart on the boat when high tides return between 16:00 and 18:00. You can squeeze an extra hour or two out of your day trip by booking an early flight over and a late flight back from Connemara Regional Airport near Rossaveel. For more details on these options, see "Aran Islands Connections" at the end of this chapter.

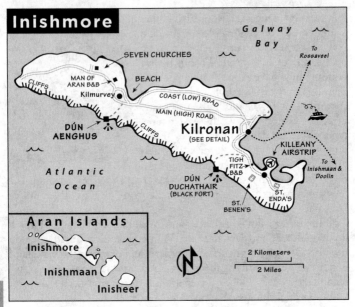

Staying Overnight: Travelers spending the night can savor the quiet time before and after the day-trip crowds. Here's how I'd suggest you spend your arrival day: Since most day-trippers make a beeline straight off the boat to Dún Aenghus, head in the opposite direction to check out the subtle charms of the less-visited eastern end of the island. Grab a quick bite en route at the Óstán Árann hotel, or buy a picnic at the Spar supermarket in Kilronan. Then walk to either the ruins of tiny St. Benen's Church (easy 20-minute hike one way from Tigh Fitz B&B) or the rugged Black Fort ruins (rocky 45-minute scramble one way from Óstán Árann). Save Dún Aenghus for later in the afternoon, after the midday crowds have subsided (allow an hour at Dún Aenghus, closes at 18:00 March-Oct, off-season at 16:00, last entry one hour before closing). Enjoy an evening in the pubs and take a no-rush midmorning boat trip back to the mainland the next day.

Orientation to Inishmore

Your first stop on Inishmore is the town of Kilronan, huddling around the pier. There are about a dozen shops and B&Bs, about half as many restaurants, and a couple of bike-rental huts (bikes cost about €10/day plus €10 deposit).

A few blocks inland up the high road, you'll find the best folk-music pub (Joe Watty's), a post office (Mon-Fri 9:00-13:00 & 14:00-17:30, Sat 9:00-13:00, closed Sun), and a tiny bank across from the roofless Anglican church ruins (open only on Wed 10:00-12:30 & 13:30-15:00, plus Thu June-Aug). A friendly Internet café lurks behind the stony Aran Sweater Market building, across from the high cross (May-Sept daily 10:00-20:00, shorter hours in winter, €1/10 minutes, €5/hour, also shows *Man of Aran* film described later, under "Sights on Inishmore").

The huge Spar supermarket, two blocks inland from the harbor, seems too big for the tiny community and has the island's only ATM. If you don't have plenty of cash on you, get some here—most B&Bs and quite a few other businesses don't accept credit cards.

Tourist Information

Kilronan's TI is helpful, but don't rely on it for accommodations; the B&B owners who work with the TI are out of town and desperate (daily 10:00-17:00, July-Aug until 18:00, shorter hours in winter, faces the harbor, tel. 099/61263). The TI will store bags for day-trippers for €1 per bag and offers free maps of the island (though your ferry operator may have already given you one). This map is all the average day-tripper or leisure biker will need to navigate. But serious hikers who plan on scampering out to the island's craggy fringes will want to invest in the detailed black-and-white *Oileáin Árann* map and companion book by Tim Robinson (€16, sold in Kilronan TI and some bookstores in Galway). Public WCs are 100 yards beyond the TI on the harbor road.

Getting Around Inishmore

Just about anything on wheels functions as a taxi here. A trip from Kilronan to Dún Aenghus to the Seven Churches and back to Kilronan costs €10 per person in a shared minivan. Pony carts cost about €40 for two people (€75 for 4) for a trip to Dún Aenghus and back.

Biking is great, although the terrain is hilly and there are occasional headwinds and unpredictable showers (30-minute ride to start of trailhead up to Dún Aenghus). Cyclists should take the high road over and the low road back—fewer hills, scenic shoreline, and at low tide, a dozen seals basking in the sun. Keep a sharp lookout along the roads for handy, modern stone signposts (with distances in kilometers) that point the way to important sights. They're in Irish, but you'll be clued in by the small metal depictions of the sights embedded within them.

Tours on Inishmore

▲**Island Minivan Tours**—Roughly 100 vehicles roam the island, and most of them seem to be minivans. A line of vans awaits the arrival of each ferry, offering €10, 2.5-hour island tours. Chat with a few drivers to find one who likes to talk. On my tour, I learned that 800 islanders live in 14 villages, with three elementary schools and three churches. Most islanders own a small detached field where they keep a couple of cows (sheep are too much trouble). When pressed for more information, my

guide explained that there are 400 different flowers and 19 different types of bees on the island.

The tour, a convenient time-saver, zips you to the end of the island for a quick stroll in the desolate fields, gives you 10 minutes to wander through the historic but visually unimpressive Seven Churches, and then drops you off for two hours at Dún Aenghus (30 minutes to hike up, 30 minutes at the fort, 20-minute hike back down, 40 minutes in café for lunch or shopping at drop-off point) before running you back to Kilronan. Ask your driver to take you back along the smaller coastal road (scenic beaches and sunbathing seals at low tide).

Sights on Inishmore

In Kilronan

Man of Aran **Film**—This award-winning 1934 movie (1.25 hours) is a documentary about traditional island life with an all-local cast. It's basically a silent movie with the sounds of surf, seagull, and sailor (muttering in barely audible Irish) dubbed in. Yet it's a strangely fascinating glimpse of the past and was groundbreaking in its time. The movie tries to re-create life in the early 1900s—when you couldn't rent bikes—and features *currach*s (canoe-like boats) in a storm, shark fishing with handheld harpoons, and farmers cultivating the fields from bare rock.

Cost and Hours: €5, 3 showings/day—usually on request, plays in Internet café behind Aran Sweater Market—see page 313 for hours.

Beyond the Town

▲▲▲**Dún Aenghus (Dun Aonghasa)**—This is the island's blockbuster sight. The stone fortress hangs spectacularly and precariously on the edge of a cliff 300 feet above the Atlantic. The crashing

waves seem to say, "You've come to the end of the world." Little is known about this 2,000-year-old Celtic fort. Its concentric walls are 13 feet thick and 10 feet high. As an added defense, the fort is ringed with a commotion of spiky stones, sticking up like lances, called a *chevaux-de-frise* (literally, "Frisian horses," named for the Frisian soldiers who used pikes to stop charging cavalry). Slowly, as the cliff erodes, hunks of the fort fall into the sea. Dún Aenghus doesn't get crowded until after 11:00. I enjoyed a half-hour completely alone at 10:00 in the tourist season; if you can, get there early or late. A small museum displays findings from recent digs and tells the story of the fort. Advice from rangers: Wear walking shoes and watch your kids closely; there's no fence between you and a crumbling 300-foot cliff overlooking the sea.

Cost and Hours: €3, daily March-Oct 9:00-18:00, Nov-Feb 10:00-16:00, last entry one hour before closing, from June-Aug guides at the trailhead answer questions and can sometimes give free tours up at the fort if you call ahead, 5.5 miles from Kilronan, tel. 099/61008.

Seven Churches (Na Seacht Teampaill)—Close to the western tip of the island, this gathering of ruined chapels, monastic houses, and fragments of a high cross dates from the 8th to 11th centuries. The island is dotted with reminders that Christianity was brought to the islands in the fifth century by St. Enda, who established a monastery here. Many great monks studied under Enda. Among these "Irish apostles" who started Ireland's "Age of Saints and Scholars" (A.D. 500-900), was Columba (Colmcille in Irish), the founder of a monastery on the island of Iona in Scotland, where the Book of Kells was later written.

Kilmurvey—The island's second village sits below Dún Aenghus. With a gaggle of homes, a B&B, a great sheltered swimming beach, and a pub, this is the place for peaceful solitude (except for the folk music in the pub).

Ancient Sites near Killeany—The quiet eastern end of Inishmore offers ancient sites in evocative settings for overnight visitors with more time, or for those seeking rocky hikes devoid of crowds. First, get a good hiking map from the Kilronan TI. Then consider lunch at the Óstán Árann hotel, or assemble a picnic, to fuel up either before or after you spend a couple of hours exploring these sights on foot. Ask the folks in town for directions (almost always a memorable experience in Ireland).

Closest to the road, amid the dunes one mile past the Tigh Fitz B&B and just south of the airport, is the eighth-century

St. Enda's Church (Teaghlach Einne). Protected from wave erosion by a stubborn breakwater, it sits half-submerged in a sandy graveyard, surrounded by a sea of sawgrass and peppered with tombstones. St. Enda is said to be buried here, along with 125 other saints who flocked to Inishmore in the fifth century to learn from him.

St. Benen's Church (Teampall Bheanáin) perches high on a desolate ridge opposite the Tigh Fitz B&B. Walk up the stone-

walled lane, passing a holy well and the stubby remains of a round tower. Then take another visual fix on the church's silhouette on the horizon, and zigzag up the stone terraces to the top. The 20-minute hike up from the B&B pays off with a great view. Dedicated to St. Benen, a young disciple of St. Patrick himself, this tiny (12 foot by 6 foot) 10th-century oratory is aligned north-south (instead of the usual east-west) to protect the doorway from prevailing winds.

About a five-minute walk past the Tigh Fitz B&B (heading toward the airport), you'll notice an abandoned stone pier and an adjacent, modest medieval ruin. This was **Arkin Fort,** built by Cromwell's soldiers in 1652 using cut stones taken from the round tower and the monastic ruins that once stood below St. Benen's Church. The fort was used as a prison for outlawed priests before they were sent by English authorities to the West Indies to be sold into slavery.

Hidden on a remote, ragged headland an hour's walk from Kilronan to the south side of the island, you'll find the **Black Fort** (Dún Duchathair). After Dún Aenghus, this is Inishmore's most dramatic fortification. Built on a promontory with cliffs on three sides, its defenders would have held out behind drystone ramparts, facing the island's interior attackers. Watch your step on the uneven ground, be ready to course-correct as you go, and chances are you'll have this windswept ruin all to yourself.

Entertainment on Inishmore

Pub Music—Kilronan's pubs offer music sporadically on summer nights. Nothing is regularly scheduled, so ask at your B&B or look for posted notices on the front of the Spar supermarket or post office. **Joe Watty's Pub,** on the high road 100 yards past the post office, has good Irish folk music on Wednesdays and weekends. The more central **Joe Mac's Pub** (next to the hostel) and the **American Bar** (next to the high cross at the base of the high road) are also possibilities.

Sleep Code

(€1 = about $1.30, country code: 353, area code: 099)
S = Single, **D** = Double/Twin, **T** = Triple, **Q** = Quad, **b** = bathroom, **s** = shower only. Breakfast is included and most places are cash-only.

To help you easily sort through these listings, I've divided the accommodations into three categories, based on the price for a standard double room with bath:

$$$ **Higher Priced**—Most rooms €80 or more.
$$ **Moderately Priced**—Most rooms between €50-80.
$ **Lower Priced**—Most rooms €50 or less.

Prices can change without notice; verify the hotel's current rates online or by email.

Dancing—The **Halla Ronain community center** becomes a dance hall on a few Saturday nights, when from midnight to 2:00 in the morning, locals have a *ceilidh* (KAY-lee), the Irish equivalent of a hoedown. Ask at the TI to see if one is scheduled during your stay.

Sleeping on Inishmore

Remember, this is a poor island. Most rooms are plain, with sparse plumbing. Only Óstán Árann and the Pier House take credit cards.

In Kilronan

$$$ Óstán Árann is Inishmore's only modern hotel, with a good restaurant and 22 large, comfortable rooms, five with grand patio views of the harbor (Sb-€59-69, Db-€79-119, Tb-€119-179, Qb-€169-229, Wi-Fi; 10-minute walk from pier, about 100 yards past Halla Ronain community center; tel. 099/61104, fax 099/61225, www.aranislandshotel.com, info@aranislandshotel.com).

$$$ The Pier House stands solidly, 50 yards from the pier, offering 13 decent rooms, a good restaurant downstairs, and sea views from many of its rooms (Db-€70-100, Wi-Fi, tel. 099/61417, fax 099/61122, www.pierhousearan.com, pierhousearan@gmail.com).

$$ Clai Ban, the only really cheery place in town, has six rooms and is worth the 10-minute uphill walk from the pier. The Hernon youngsters are avid traditional musicians. The place is patrolled by their friendly and pudgy Corgi, Guinness (Sb-€50-70, Db-€60-70, Tb-€90-105, cash only, walk past bank out of town and down lane on left, tel. 099/61111, claibanhouse@gmail.com, Marion and Bartley Hernon).

ARAN ISLANDS

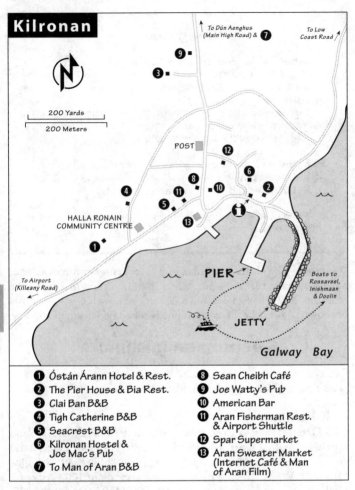

Kilronan

To Dún Aenghus (Main High Road) & ➐

To Low Coast Road

200 Yards

200 Meters

POST

HALLA RONAIN COMMUNITY CENTRE

To Airport (Killeany Road)

PIER

JETTY

Boats to Rossaveel, Inishmaan & Doolin

Galway Bay

ARAN ISLANDS

❶ Óstán Árann Hotel & Rest.
❷ The Pier House & Bia Rest.
❸ Clai Ban B&B
❹ Tigh Catherine B&B
❺ Seacrest B&B
❻ Kilronan Hostel & Joe Mac's Pub
❼ To Man of Aran B&B

❽ Sean Cheibh Café
❾ Joe Watty's Pub
❿ American Bar
⓫ Aran Fisherman Rest. & Airport Shuttle
⓬ Spar Supermarket
⓭ Aran Sweater Market (Internet Café & Man of Aran Film)

$$ Tigh Catherine is a well-kept B&B with four homey rooms overlooking the harbor (Sb-€45-50, Db-€70, cash only, on Church Road up behind the Halla Ronain community center, tel. 099/61464, mobile 087-980-9748, catherineandstiofain@gmail. com, Catherine Mulkerrin).

$$ Seacrest B&B offers six uncluttered rooms in a central location next to the Aran Fisherman restaurant (Sb-€45-50, Db-€70, Tb-€90, cash only, Wi-Fi, tel. 099/61292, mobile 087-161-6507, seacrestaran@gmail.com, Geraldine and Tom Faherty).

$ Kilronan Hostel, overlooking the harbor near the TI, is cheap but noisy above Joe Mac's Pub (€20-25 beds in 4- to 6-bed rooms, cash only, includes breakfast, free Internet access and Wi-

Fi, self-service kitchen, tel. 099/61255, www.kilronanhostel.com, kilronanhostel@ireland.com).

Elsewhere on Inishmore

$$$ Man of Aran B&B, as classy as a thatched cottage can be, is in the peaceful countryside four miles outside of touristy Kilronan, toward the western end of the island. Rooms are quiet and rustic, with fireplaces. The restaurant serves €22-25 meals (with home-grown vegetables and herbs) only to overnight guests. The setting is pristine—this is where the movie of the same name was filmed 80 years ago (S-€55, Sb-€60, D-€80, Db-€90, cash only, reserve well in advance, closed Nov-Feb; 4 miles/6.5 km from Kilronan, bear right 100 yards after passing Kilmurvey Beach before Dún Aenghus turnoff; tel. 099/61301, www.manofarancottage.com, manofaran@eircom.net, Maura and Joe Wolf).

Eating on Inishmore

There are few restaurants in Kilronan. The best is the modern **Óstán Árann** hotel on the south fringe of town (lunch 12:30-18:00 in the Patin Jack Bar, dinner 18:00-21:30, tel. 099/61104).

The Pier House operates the dependable **Bia Restaurant** below its guest house (€12-18 lunches, €18-25 dinners, daily 11:00-22:00, tel. 099/61811).

Otherwise, Kilronan's modest cafés dish up hearty soup, soda bread, sandwiches, and tea.

Sean Cheibh ("Old Pier"), which seems to slam out more meals than the rest of the town combined, is popular for its fish-and-chips and great clam chowder (eat in or take out, April-mid-Oct daily 11:00-19:00, closed mid-Oct-March, tel. 099/61228).

Supermarket: The **Spar** has all the groceries you'll need (June-Aug Mon-Sat 9:00-20:00, Sun 10:00-17:00; Sept-May Mon-Sat 9:00-18:00, closed Sun).

Inisheer

The roughly circular little island of Inisheer (Inis Oir) has only a quarter of the land area and population of Inishmore—my island of choice. But Inisheer's close proximity to the mainland makes it an easy 25-minute boat journey from Doolin and a good option for those with limited time who aren't going north to Galway (closer to Inishmore's port at Rossaveel).

Inisheer offers a vivid glimpse of Aran Island culture and has an engaging smorgasbord of sights. For some reason, this quaint

ARAN ISLANDS

little island seems to attract as many German-speaking visitors as English-speaking ones.

Planning Your Time

Take an early boat from Doolin to maximize your time on Inisheer. For more details, see "Aran Islands Connections" at the end of this chapter.

Orientation to Inisheer

You'll dock on the north side of the island in its only settlement. Facing inland with your back to the pier, you'll be able to see nearly all of the island's landmarks (except for the *An Plassy* shipwreck and the lighthouse on the southern shore). Although a handful of pony carts and minivan drivers meet you at the pier, I'd rely on them only on a rainy day (€10, but prices are soft...negotiate).

For me, the joy of compact Inisheer is seeing it on a bike ride or a long breezy walk. The bike rental outfit is right at the base of the pier (€10/day, no deposit necessary "unless you look suspicious"). Any of the boat operators in Doolin can give you a free map of the island showing Inisheer's primitive road network. That's all you'll need to navigate.

There are three pubs on the island, one small grocery store (see "Eating on Inisheer," later), and no ATMs. All of the sights, with the exception of the lonely lighthouse on the southern coast, are concentrated on the northern half of an already small island.

Inisheer lacks the dramatic (and much higher) coastal cliffs of Inishmore, but has its own unique photogenic charms. Fans of the 1990s British sitcom "Father Ted" may recognize parts of the island, which were featured in the show's intro depicting its fictional Craggy Island location.

Sights on Inisheer

The sights described below are free, open all the time, and marked on your free boat company map. See them in the order listed, from west to east, across the northern half of the island. If you bike rather than hike, be prepared to walk up (or down) short, steep hills.

O'Brien's Castle (Caislean Ui Bhriain)—The ruins of this castle dominate the hilltop and are visible from almost anywhere on the

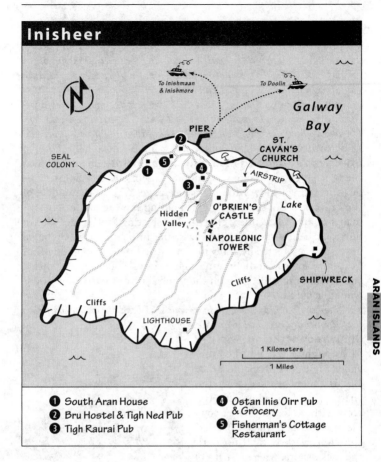

Inisheer

To Inishmaan & Inishmore

To Doolin

PIER

Galway Bay

SEAL COLONY

ST. CAVAN'S CHURCH

AIRSTRIP

O'BRIEN'S CASTLE

Lake

Hidden Valley

NAPOLEONIC TOWER

Cliffs

SHIPWRECK

Cliffs

LIGHTHOUSE

1 Kilometers

1 Miles

ARAN ISLANDS

❶ South Aran House
❷ Bru Hostel & Tigh Ned Pub
❸ Tigh Raurai Pub
❹ Ostan Inis Oirr Pub & Grocery
❺ Fisherman's Cottage Restaurant

northern half of the island. It's a steep 20-minute walk from the pier up to the castle ruins. The small castle was built as a tower house refuge around 1400 by the O'Brien clan from nearby County Clare. It sits inside a low wall of a much older Iron Age ring fort. Cromwell's troops attacked the castle in 1652, leaving the evocative ruins you see today.

If you've huffed your way up to O'Brien's Castle, then go another easy five minutes to the **Napoleonic Tower (An Tur Faire),** which was built in the early 1800s to watch for a feared French invasion that never took place. The views from this highest point on the island are terrific.

• *Consult your map and continue walking (south) on the paved road* *into the heart of the island. Take your first right turn, roughly 100 yards after the Napoleonic Tower, onto a rocky, grassy cow lane that zigzags downhill into a lush **hidden valley**, displaying the prettiest mosaic of ivy tangled rock walls and small green fields I've seen anywhere on the Aran Islands. Unholster your camera and fire away.*

Once you've wound your way back down to the main north-shore road again, turn right and continue east with the airstrip on your left. On your right, you'll soon see a time-passed graveyard up on a sandy hill. Hike the 50 yards up into the graveyard to find...

St. Cavan's Church (Teampall Chaomhain)—St. Cavan was the brother of St. Kevin, who founded the monastery at Glendal-ough in the Wicklow Mountains (see page 132). In the middle of the graveyard is a sunken sandpit holding the rugged roofless remains of an 11th-century church. The shifting sand dunes almost buried it before sawgrass stabilized the hill. St. Cavan's reputed gravesite is protected by a tiny modern structure worth poking your head into for its candlelit atmosphere. Local folklore held that if you spent a night sleeping on the tomb lid, your particular illness would be cured.

• *Walk back down to the north-shore road and head out on the coast road (to the southeast) 30 minutes to the remote...*

Shipwreck of the *An Plassy*—  This freighter was wrecked off-shore on Finn's Rock in 1960. But islanders worked with the coastal patrol to help rescue the crew with no loss of life. A couple of weeks later the unmanned ship was washed high up onto the rocky shore, where it still sits today, a rusty but fairly intact ghost ship with a broken back. Beware of turning an ankle on the rounded cobbles thrown up by the surf near the wreck.

• *With more time, consult your map and seek out the remaining intimate little church ruins and holy wells that the island has to offer. Or head back to town for a beverage while you await the return ferry.*

Sleeping on Inisheer

A scattering of B&Bs dots the northern half of the island. Here are two good options:

$$ South Aran House is a quiet, well-run place with five spic-and-span, black-and-white rooms. Friendly Enda and Maria Con-neely are generous with local tips and also run the nearby Fisher-man's Cottage restaurant, where you'll have breakfast (Sb-€45-55, Db-€70-90, an easy 10-minute walk west of pier on north-shore

ARAN ISLANDS

road, call ahead with your ferry arrival time so they can meet you with keys, tel. 099/75073, mobile 087-340-5687, www.southaran. com, info@southaran.com).

$ Bru Hostel is simple, economical, and just 100 yards west of the pier, next to Tigh Ned Pub (€18 dorm beds, tel. 099/75024, radharcnamara@hotmail.com).

Eating on Inisheer

Inisheer's three main pubs offer decent pub grub (usually 12:30-20:30). **Tigh Raurai Pub** (House of Rory) is the epicenter of island social life (from the pier, head east to the edge of the beach and turn right—inland—up a narrow lane for 100 yards). Just below it, closer to the beach, is **Ostan Inis Oirr Pub** (Hotel Inisheer) with a colorful collage of international flags draping the pub's ceiling. **Tigh Ned Pub** (House of Ned) is right next door to Bru Hostel, near the pier on the north-shore road. Life could be worse than to sit outside at their appealing front tables on a summer evening, enjoying a pint in the salt air.

For a mellow evening meal, try the **Fisherman's Cottage,** a five-minute walk west of the pier on the north-shore road (daily 12:00-15:00 & 19:00-21:00, tel. 099/75073, mobile 087-340-5687).

The island's small **grocery,** Siopa XL, is behind Ostan Inis Oirr Pub and below Tigh Raurai Pub (Mon-Sat 9:00-17:00, Sun 10:00-15:00).

Aran Islands Connections

For an overview map of the region, see page 274.

By Ferry from Rossaveel (near Galway)

Island Ferries sails to Inishmore from Rossaveel, a port 20 miles west of Galway. The company sells tickets at the Galway TI and runs a 45-minute shuttle bus from Galway to the Rossaveel dock (3/day April-Oct, 2/day Nov-March, 45-minute crossing; coming from Galway, allow 2 hours in transit one-way including 45-minute bus ride; €25 round-trip boat crossing plus €7 round-trip for Galway-Rossaveel shuttle bus, 10 percent discount if you book online, WCs on board). Catch shuttle buses from Galway on Queen Street, a block behind the Kinlay Hostel (check-in 1.5 hours before sailing); shuttles return to Galway immediately after each boat arrives. Ferry schedule for April-Oct: from Rossaveel at 10:30, 13:00, and 18:30; from Inishmore at 8:15, 12:00, 16:00, and 17:00 (plus 19:30 June-Aug). Island Ferries has two offices in Galway: on Forster Street across from the TI and across from Kinlay Hostel on

Merchants Road (tel. 091/568-903, after-hours tel. 091/572-273, www.aranislandferries.com).

Beware: The boat you take out to the islands may not be the same as the one you come back on. And sometimes you'll board by walking up the gangplank of one boat and walking across its deck to another boat docked beside or behind it. Make sure to ask.

Drivers should go straight to the ferry landing in Rossaveel, passing several ticket agencies and pay parking lots. At the boat dock, you'll find a convenient €5-per-day lot and a small office that sells tickets for Island Ferries. Check to see what's going when and for how much.

By Ferry from Doolin

Boats from Doolin to the Aran Islands can be handy, but they are often canceled or run late. Even a balmy day can be too windy (or the tide can be too low) to allow for a sailing from Doolin's crude little port. While it's possible to travel from Doolin to Inishmore and back in one day, keep in mind that it's a longer trip to distant Inishmore than the other two Aran Islands (leaving less time ashore to explore before you have to turn around and sail back to Doolin). Instead, consider an overnight stay on Inishmore, or opt for a day trip to nearby, though less spectacular, Inisheer.

Parking is free beside the Doolin pier, even overnight. If you have a car, Doolin is easy to reach; without one, it's better to get to Inishmore from Rossaveel (described earlier).

The scene at the Doolin ferry dock is a confusing mosh pit of competition. Three ferry companies have similar schedules and compete hard for your business (though company names can change from year to year). They often honor the other's return tickets if you decide you want to return at a different time. Note that the wind and tides can cause cancellations on any Aran ferries. Prices can vary with the intensity of the competition. Although they may promise to get you to Inishmore in an hour, every one of my trips in the past few years has included brief stops at Inisheer and Inishmaan en route, making the actual crossing time about 1.5 hours.

Aran Doolin Ferries has been at it longest (to Inishmore: €20 round-trip, 2/day, 1.5 hours, leaves at 10:00 and 13:00, returns at 11:30 and 16:00; to Inisheer: €15 same-day round-trip, does not include Cliffs of Moher, 2/day, 30 minutes, departs 10:00 and 13:00, returns 12:30 and 16:45; tel. 065/707-4455, www.doolinferries.com). **Doolin2Aran Ferries,** run by friendly Donie Garrihy, operates essentially the same service at the same prices. They also offer a fun €25 triangular day trip that takes you from Doolin to Inisheer, drops you off on Inisheer for about four hours, then returns to Doolin along the base of the Cliffs of Moher (departs 9:00, has you back in Doolin by 16:00, runs April-Oct, tel. 065/707-5949, mobile 087-245-3239, www.doolin2aranferries.com). **O'Brien Line** has similar schedules and prices as the other two outfits, and they too offer a cruise along the base of the Cliffs of Moher that includes a stop at Inisheer (€30, tel. 065/707-5555, www.obrienline.com). No matter which company you choose, it's smart to phone a day or two ahead to confirm schedules and prices.

By Plane

Aer Arann Islands, a friendly and flexible little airline, flies daily from Connemara Regional Airport, stopping at all three islands (3/day, up to 11/day in peak season, €23 one-way (when boating back), €45 round-trip, groups of 4 or more pay €40 each, 10-min-

ute flight, tel. 091/593-034, fax 091/593-238, www.aerarannislands.ie, aerarann@iol.ie). These eight-seat planes get booked up—reserve two or three days in advance with a credit card. Connemara Regional Airport is 20 slow miles west of Galway— allow 45 minutes for the drive, plus 30 minutes to check in before the scheduled departure. A minibus shuttle—€3 one-way—runs from Victoria Hotel off Eyre Square in Galway an hour before each flight. Be sure to reserve a space on the shuttle bus at the same time you book your flight. The Kilronan airport on Inishmore is minuscule. A minibus shuttle travels the two miles between the airport and Kilronan (buses stop at Aran Fisherman restaurant) and costs €5 round-trip.

In July and August, a sightseeing-only Aer Arann flight leaves from the same airport at 12:00 each day. You'll fly above all three Aran Islands with an extra swoop past the Cliffs of Moher (€55, 30 minutes, may not go if not enough people sign up).

ARAN ISLANDS

CONNEMARA
and COUNTY MAYO

If you have a car, consider spending a day exploring the wild western Irish fringe known as Connemara and straying into historic County Mayo. Gaze up at the peak of Croagh Patrick, the mountain from which St. Patrick supposedly banished the snakes from Ireland. Pass through the desolate Doo Lough Valley on a road stained with tragic famine history. Bounce on a springy peat bog, and drop in at a Westport pub owned by a member of the Chieftains (a well-known traditional Irish music group). This beautiful area also claims a couple of towns—Cong and Leenane—where classic Irish movies were filmed, as well as the photogenic Kylemore Abbey.

Connemara makes a satisfying day trip by car from Galway. Without a car, you can take a tour from Galway or at least get to Westport by bus. Public transportation in this region is patchy, and some areas are not served at all. Trains connect Galway and Westport to Dublin, but not to each other.

Bus Tours of Connemara

Three Galway-based organizations—**Lally Tours, O'Neachtain Tours,** and **Galway Tour Company**—run all-day tours of nearby regions (€20-25). Tours of Connemara include the *Quiet Man* cottage, Kylemore Abbey, Clifden, and the "Famine Village." Galway Tour Company takes a slightly different route that includes Cong but omits the coast of Connemara. Tours go most days, heading out about 10:00 and returning at 17:30 (departing from in front of Kinlay Hostel on Merchant's Road in Galway, call to confirm exact itinerary: Lally Tours tel. 091/562-905, www.lallytours.com; O'Neachtain Tours tel. 091/553-188, mobile 087-166-5060,

www.ontours.biz; Galway Tour Company tel. 091/566-566, www.
galwaytourcompany.com). All three companies also offer tours of
the Burren and Cliffs of Moher, with discounts if you book two
separate tours. Drivers take cash only; to pay with a credit card,
book at Galway's TI.

Self-Guided Driving Tour

Connemara and Mayo Loop Trip

This tour takes a full day and involves five hours of driving, not
including stops (almost 200 miles/320 km, using Galway as your
base). Start early, so your day will be less rushed. Those wanting
to slow down and linger can sleep in Westport. These country
roads, punctuated by blind curves and surprise bumps, are shared
by trucks, tractors, cyclists, more tractors, and sheep. Drive sanely,
and bring rain gear and your sense of humor. This is rural Ireland
with all the trimmings.

Bring along a good map (Ordnance Survey atlases are widely
sold in Ireland), and before you start, study the loop connecting
these points: Galway, Cong, Westport, Louisburgh, Leenane, Kylemore Abbey, Clifden, and back to Galway.

Route Summary: Take N-84 north out of Galway; the road
changes names to R-334 in Headford. At Cross, take R-346 into
Cong and R-345 back out again. At Neale, go north, putting you
back on R-334. Pick up N-84 again as it winds through Ballinrobe to Partry. Take R-330 from Partry to Westport. After lunch
in Westport, go west on R-335 through Louisburgh and south
through Doo Lough Valley all the way to Leenane. Meet N-59 in
Leenane and take it to Kylemore Abbey, continuing to Letterfrack
and Connemara National Park. Continue south to Clifden, where
you'll turn off onto R-341. Hug the coast through Roundstone before finding the junction with N-59 near Recess. Follow N-59 back
to Galway via Maam Cross and Oughterard.

The Tour Begins

• *From Galway's Eyre Square, drive north out of town on Prospect Hill
Road. Follow the signs at each roundabout in the direction of Castlebar
onto N-84. You'll soon be out of Galway's suburbs and crossing miles of
flat bogland laced with simple rock walls. At Headford, keep straight
through town as the road changes names to R-334. At Cross, take R-346
to Cong. You'll pass the grand, gray gateway of Ashford Castle (on the
left) as you approach the town.*

Cong

Plan to spend an hour in Cong (1.5 hours if you include the Ashford Castle grounds). Cross the small bridge and park in front of

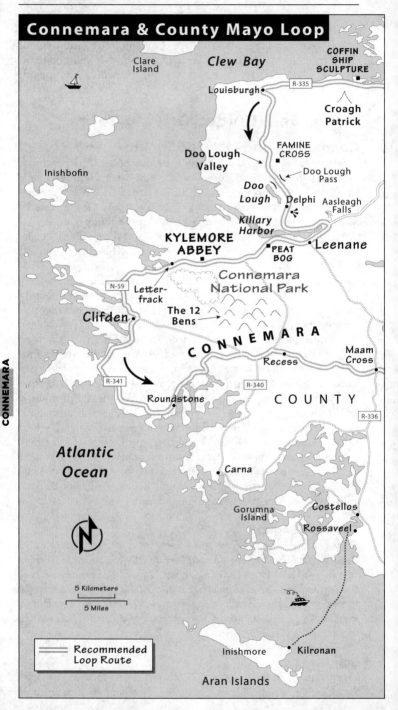

Connemara & County Mayo Loop

COFFIN SHIP SCULPTURE

Clew Bay

Clare Island

R-335

Louisburgh

Croagh Patrick

FAMINE CROSS

Doo Lough Valley

Inishbofin

Doo Lough Pass

Doo Lough

Delphi

Aasleagh Falls

Killary Harbor

Leenane

KYLEMORE ABBEY

PEAT BOG

N-59

Letter-frack

Connemara National Park

Clifden

The 12 Bens

CONNEMARA

Recess

Maam Cross

R-341

R-340

Roundstone

COUNTY

R-336

Atlantic Ocean

Carna

Gorumna Island

Costellos

Rossaveel

N

5 Kilometers

5 Miles

Inishmore

Kilronan

Recommended Loop Route

Aran Islands

CONNEMARA

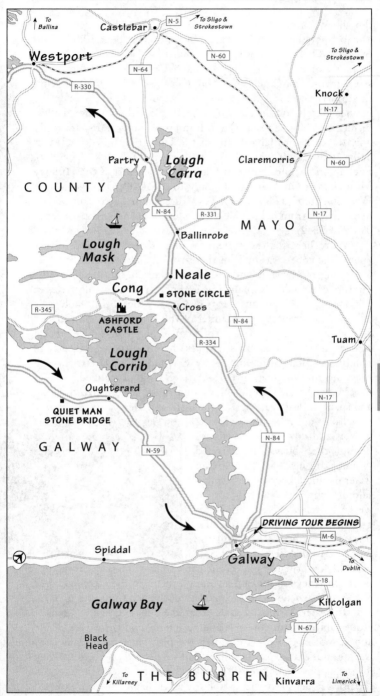

the abbey. Drop into the **TI** across from the abbey entrance for a map (sporadic hours but generally daily May-Sept 10:00-13:00 & 14:00-17:30, closed Oct-April, tel. 094/954-6542). There are no banks or ATMs in Cong. Public WCs are 50 yards down the street across from the *Quiet Man* **cottage.** That's right, pilgrim, this town is where John Wayne and Maureen O'Hara made the famous John Ford film *The Quiet Man* in 1951. The cottage's modest historical exhibits (upstairs) and film props (downstairs) are really only worth it for diehard fans of the Duke (€5, mid-March-Oct daily 10:30-16:00, closed Nov-mid-March, tel. 094/954-6089). Fuel up on a cup of coffee and homemade dessert at the **Hungry Monk Café** (mid-March-Sept daily 10:00-18:00; Oct-mid-March Wed-Sun 10:00-17:30, closed Mon-Tue; Internet access, on Abbey Street across from public WCs and a few doors down from TI, tel. 094/954-5842).

We're here for the ruins of **Cong Abbey** (free and always open). The abbey was built in the early 1100s, when Romanesque was going out of style and Gothic was coming in; you'll see the mixture of rounded Romanesque and pointy Gothic arch styles in the doorway. The famous Cross of Cong, which held a holy relic of what was supposedly a splinter of the True Cross, was hoisted aloft at the front of processions of Augustinian monks during High Masses in this church. This Irish art treasure is now on display in Dublin's National Museum. Rory O'Connor, the last Irish high king, died in this abbey in 1198. After O'Connor realized he could never outfight the superior Norman armies, he retreated to Cong and spent his last years here in monastic isolation.

Take a walk through the cloister and down the gravel path behind the abbey. The forested grounds are lush, and the stream water is incredibly clear. Cong's salmon hatchery contributes to western Ireland's reputation for great fishing. The monks fished for more than sinners. They built the modest **Monks' Fishing Hut,** just over the footbridge, right on the bank so that the river flowed underneath. They lowered a net through the floor and attached a bell to the rope; whenever a fish was netted, the bell would ring.

To reach **Ashford Castle** from the abbey, face the Romanesque/Gothic main entrance and go left around the corner of the abbey, walking 15 minutes down the pleasant forested lane onto the grounds of the castle, which is hidden behind the trees. Garden lovers happily hand over €5 to a kid hired by the castle to patrol the bridge, just so they can stroll the lakeside paradise once owned by the Guinness beer family (entry fee in effect June-Aug, usually free rest of year). The renovated Victorian castle rents some of the finest rooms in all of Ireland, and casual gawkers are discouraged inside. President Reagan stayed here in 1984, and actor Pierce Brosnan chose these gardens for his wedding reception in 2001. Many scenes from *The Quiet Man* were filmed on the castle grounds. As you stroll the grounds, contemplate the fact that "tourism" (the notion of travel solely for enjoyment) didn't exist until the Victorian Age. Before that time, travel was a chore only endured by armies, refugees, traders, emigrants, and religious pilgrims.

Cong (from *conga,* Irish for "isthmus") lies between two large lakes. Departing Cong over the same bridge on which you entered, try to imagine the dry canal that once existed here. Built between 1848 and 1854, this canal was a Great Potato Famine work project that stoked only appetites. The canal, complete with locks, would have linked Lough Mask to the north with Lough Corrib to the south. But the limestone bedrock proved too porous, and the canal wouldn't hold water.

• *Take R-345 out of Cong (left turn opposite the main stone gateway to the grounds of Ashford Castle). Heading north, you'll pass through the tiny hamlet of...*

Neale

About 130 years ago, a retired army captain named Boycott was hired to manage the nearby estate of Lord Erne. But the strict captain treated the tenants who worked his lands harshly, so they united to ostracize him by deserting their jobs and isolating his estate. Over time, the agitation worked, and eventually "boycotting" became a popular tactic in labor conflicts.

• *At Neale, go north on R-334, then take N-84 from Ballinrobe to Partry. At Partry, turn left off N-84 onto R-330 in the direction of Westport (the easy-to-miss turnoff is just after you pass the thatch-roofed Village Inn). In the countryside a few kilometers to your right is the site of the...*

Battle of Castlebar

In 1798, a French invasion force supported by locals dealt the British an embarrassing loss here. The surprised British forces were routed, and their rapid retreat is slyly remembered in Irish rebel lore as the "Castlebar races." Unfortunately for the rebels, this proved to be the last glimmer of hope for Irish victory in that uprising. The

CONNEMARA

Red Coats reorganized and within weeks defeated the small force of 1,300 Frenchmen and the ill-equipped Irish rebels. The captured French soldiers were treated as prisoners of war, while the Irish rebels were executed.

• *Continue on R-330 to...*

Westport

On arrival in Westport, soak up the genteel vibe—lacking in most other Irish towns. Park along the Mall under the trees that line the shallow canal-like river. This is a planned town, built in Georgian style in the late 1700s to support the adjacent estate of Westport House (skip it for better manors at

Mount Stewart House and Muckross House). The town once thrived on the linen industry created by local Irish handlooms. But after the Act of Union with Britain in 1801, Westport was unable to compete with the industrialized British linen-makers and fell into decline. The town is still pretty and a good place for a relaxed lunch and some exploration on foot.

Tourist Information: The TI is on James Street (July-Aug daily 9:00-18:00; Sept-June Mon-Fri 9:00-17:00, Sat 10:00-17:00, closed Sun; tel. 098/25711).

Helpful Hints: For a short visit, free **parking** is allowed on the street for two hours; for longer stays, park at your B&B (if sleeping here), or use the pay-and-display lots (€0.70/first hour, €0.30/hour after that, pay at meter and display ticket on dashboard).

The **post office** is on the North Mall (Mon-Fri 9:00-17:30, Sat 9:00-13:00, closed Sun). **Laundry** can be dropped off early at Gills and picked up late the same day (€10/load, Mon-Fri 9:00-18:30, Sat 9:00-18:00, closed Sun, James Street, tel. 098/25819). Check out **The Bookshop** for rainy-day browsing (Mon-Sat 9:30-18:30, Sun 11:00-18:00, Bridge Street, tel. 098/26816).

Activities in Westport: **Clew Bay Bike Hire and Outdoor Adventures,** run by Dave O'Gorman, rents a selection of mountain bikes (€15/5 hours, €20/24 hours) and electronic assisted bikes (€30/5 hours, €35/24 hours). They can also set up fishing, sailing, kayaking, and horseback riding outings (daily 9:00-18:00, Distillery Road, tel. 098/24818, mobile 086/327-3615, www.clewbayoutdoors.ie).

For a scenic **hike or bike ride,** consider the 26-mile (42 km) route to Achill Island along the Great Western Greenway (www.greenway.ie). From 1895 to 1937, a narrow-gauge railway operated

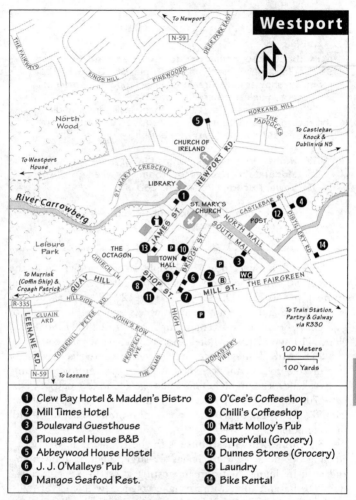

Westport

To Newport
N-59
DEER PARK EAST

THE FAIRWAYS

KINGS HILL

PINEWOODS

North Wood

HORKANS HILL

THE PADDOCKS

To Castlebar, Knock & Dublin via N5

5

CHURCH OF IRELAND

To Westport House

ST. MARY'S CRESCENT

NEWPORT RD.

LIBRARY

1

River Carrowberg

ST. MARY'S CHURCH

CASTLEBAR ST.

4

POST

12

JAMES ST.

NORTH MALL

DISTILLERY RD.

Leisure Park

THE OCTAGON

13

P

10

BRIDGE ST.

SOUTH MALL

14

To Murrisk (Coffin Ship) & Croagh Patrick

QUAY HILL

CHURCH LN.

TOWN HALL

9

P

3

R-335

HILLSIDE RD.

8

SHOP ST.

6

2

B

WC

THE FAIRGREEN

CLUAIN ARD

LEENANE RD.

TOBERHILL PETER

JOHN'S ROW

11

7

MILL ST.

P

To Train Station, Partry & Galway via R330

PROSPECT AVE.

HIGH ST.

MONASTERY VIEW

100 Meters
100 Yards

N-59

To Leenane

THE ELMS

1 Clew Bay Hotel & Madden's Bistro
2 Mill Times Hotel
3 Boulevard Guesthouse
4 Plougastel House B&B
5 Abbeywood House Hostel
6 J. J. O'Malleys' Pub
7 Mangos Seafood Rest.

8 O'Cee's Coffeeshop
9 Chilli's Coffeeshop
10 Matt Molloy's Pub
11 SuperValu (Grocery)
12 Dunnes Stores (Grocery)
13 Laundry
14 Bike Rental

CONNEMARA

from Westport to Achill Island. By 2010, the rails had been replaced by a level, paved path, creating an ideal rural route dedicated to bikers and walkers (no vehicles, dogs, or horses allowed). You'll cross stone bridges, wind through forested sections as well as open bog stretches, and usually have the sea in sight as you hug the flatter coastline. If you only want to bike a section of the route, you can arrange a shuttle-bus pick-up for Newport, Mulranny, or Achill Sound through Clew Bay Bike Hire (listed above).

Sleeping in Westport: For those wanting extra time to explore, Westport is the best place along this route to spend a night. All of the following listings are centrally located. Prices vary quite a bit depending on the season.

Sleep Code

(€1 = about $1.30, country code: 353, area code: 098)
S = Single, **D** = Double/Twin, **T** = Triple, **Q** = Quad, **b** = bathroom, **s** = shower only. Breakfast is included and credit cards are accepted unless otherwise noted.

To help you easily sort through these listings, I've divided the accommodations into three categories, based on the price for a standard double room with bath:

$$$ **Higher Priced**—Most rooms €90 or more.
$$ **Moderately Priced**—Most rooms between €60-90.
$ **Lower Priced**—Most rooms €60 or less.

Prices can change without notice; verify the hotel's current rates online or by email.

$$$ Clew Bay Hotel is a couple of doors down from the TI, with 50 large, modern rooms decked out in cherrywood furniture (Sb-€60-120, Db-€90-170, Tb-€120-190, prices depend on room size and demand, Internet access and Wi-Fi, free use of adjacent pool and fitness center, James Street, tel. 098/28088, fax 098/39110, www.clewbayhotel.com, info@clewbayhotel.com).

$$$ Mill Times Hotel has a fresh, woody feel, with 34 comfortable rooms and convenient, free underground parking. On weekends, the nightclub next door gets loud (Sb-€50-95, Db-€90-170, Tb-€135-255, prices depend on demand, Mill Street, tel. 098/29200, fax 098/29250, www.milltimeshotel.ie, info@milltimeshotel.ie).

$$ Boulevard Guesthouse is the best value in town. Located right on the leafy Mall, it has six large, quiet, tasteful rooms and a cushy lounge with an interesting guest library under the stairs. Sadie and John Moran make you feel welcome (Sb-€45-50, Db-€75-80, Tb-€105, Qb-€120-140, cash only, discount for multiple-night stays, Wi-Fi, parking, tel. 098/25138, mobile 087-284-4018, www.boulevard-guesthouse.com, boulevardguesthouse@gmail.com).

$$ Plougastel House B&B, named after Westport's sister town in Brittany, has six inviting, smartly furnished earth-tone rooms with marble-floored bathrooms (Sb-€40-50, Db-€70-80, cash only, Wi-Fi, Distillery Road, tel. 098/25198, info@plougastel-house.com, www.plougastel-house.com, Sandra Corcoran).

$ Abbeywood House Hostel, hidden uphill behind the Church of Ireland, is a former monastery renting seven rooms with views of Croagh Patrick (dorm beds-€20-24, D-€60, includes continental breakfast, kitchen, Wi-Fi, closed Oct-April except for large groups, Newport Road, tel. 098/25496, mobile 087-241-0641, www.abbeywoodhouse.com, info@abbeywoodhouse.com).

Eating in Westport: Most of your best bets are clustered on Bridge Street. A good choice for dinner is **J. J. O'Malleys'** restaurant (€16-28 meals, daily 17:00-22:00, Bridge Street—upstairs, above their pub, tel. 098/27307). Because **Mangos Seafood Restaurant** serves the town's best fish in a cozy atmosphere, reservations are a good idea (€15-25 meals, daily 17:45-22:30, July-Aug also serves lunch 12:30-15:00, Bridge Street, tel. 098/24999, mobile 087-665-6368). **Madden's Bistro** is on the ground floor of the Clew Bay Hotel, offering contemporary casual dining (daily 12:30-21:00, James Street, tel. 098/28088). For a quick and easy lunch, try **O'Cee's Coffeeshop** (€9 cafeteria-style lunches, Mon-Sat 8:30-18:00, Sun 10:00-16:00, Shop Street, tel. 098/27000) or **Chilli's Coffeeshop** (Mon-Sat 9:00-18:00, Sun 11:00-18:00; Bridge Street, tel. 098/27611). Irish music fans seek out **Matt Molloy's** pub (Bridge Street, tel. 098/26655). Matt Molloy isn't just the owner of the pub—he's also a flutist for the Chieftains, the group credited with much of the worldwide resurgence of interest in Irish music over the past 50 years. The **SuperValu** market has picnic fare (Mon-Sat 8:00-22:00, Sun 9:00-21:00, Shop Street). **Dunnes Stores** has a similar grocery selection (Mon-Wed 8:30-18:00, Thu-Sat until 19:00, closed Sun).

Westport Connections: If you want to visit Westport but lack wheels, here are your options. You can take a bus to/from **Galway** (5-7/day, 1.5-2.75 hours), **Derry** (2-4/day, 4.75-5.5 hours, change in Sligo), or **Dublin** (6-7/day, 4-6 hours). For details, see www.buseireann.ie. You can also reach Dublin by train (3/day, 3.75 hours, www.irishrail.ie).

• *Leave Westport heading west on R-335. After about eight kilometers (5 miles), as you're driving along scenic Clew Bay, you'll reach a wide spot in the road called Murrisk. Stop here. In the field on your right (opposite Campbell's Pub) is the...*

Coffin Ship

This bronze ship sculpture is one of the most powerful famine memorials that you'll see in Ireland. It's a "coffin ship," like those of the late 1840s that carried the sick and starving famine survivors across the ocean in hope of a new life. Unfortunately, many of the ships contracted to take the desperate immigrants were barely seaworthy, no longer fit for dependable commerce. The poor were weak from starvation and vulnerable to "famine fever," which they then spread to others in the putrid, cramped holds of these awful ships. Many who lived through the six- to eight-week journey died shortly after reaching their new country. Pause a moment to look at the silent skeletons swirling around the ship's masts. Now contemplate the fact that famine still exists in the world. And before judging the lack of effective relief intervention by the British government of that time, consider the rich world's ability to ignore similar suffering today.

• *Across the road from the coffin ship is...*

Croagh Patrick

This small mountain rises 2,500 feet above the bay. In the fifth century, St. Patrick is said to have fasted on its summit for the 40 days of Lent. It's from here that he supposedly rang his bell, driving all the snakes out of Ireland. The snakes never existed, of course, but they represent the pagan beliefs that Patrick's newly arrived Christianity replaced. Every year on the last Sunday of July, "Reek Sunday" (a "reek" is a mountain peak), 30,000 pilgrims hike three hours up the rocky trail to the summit in honor of St. Patrick. The most penitent attempt the hike barefoot (more than one comes down on a stretcher). On that Sunday, Mass is celebrated throughout the day in a modest chapel on the top.

Hikers should allow three hours to reach the top and two hours to get back down (bring plenty of water, sunscreen, and rain gear). There is a primitive WC on the summit, 30 yards below the chapel. The trail is easy to follow, but the upper half of the mountain is a steep slope of loose, shifting scree that can bang or turn exposed ankles. Both times I've climbed this, I've been glad I wore boots.

A few years ago, valuable gold deposits were discovered within Croagh Patrick. Luckily, public sentiment has kept the sacred mountain free of any commercial mining activity.

• *Continue west on R-335.*

Stretched out beside you is **Clew Bay,** peppered with more than 300 humpbacked islands of glacial gravel dumped by retreating glaciers at the end of the last Ice Age. A notorious 16th-century local named Grace O'Malley (dubbed the "Pirate Queen") once ruled this bay, even earning the grudging respect of Queen Elizabeth I herself with her clever exploits. John Lennon later chose Dorinish Island to found a short-lived hippie commune. He bought it in 1967 for £1,700; after his death Yoko Ono sold it for £30,000 (which she then donated to an Irish orphanage).

• *Passing through Louisburgh, you'll turn south to enter some of the most rugged and desolate country in Ireland.*

Doo Lough Valley

Signs of human habitation vanish from the bogland, and ghosts begin to appear beside the road. About 13 kilometers (8 miles) south of Louisburgh, stop at the simple gray-stone cross on the left. The lake ahead is Doo Lough (Irish for "Black Lake"). This is the site of one of the saddest famine tales.

In the early 1800s, County Mayo's rural folk depended almost exclusively on the potato for food and were the hardest hit when the Great Potato Famine came in 1845. In the winter of 1849, about 600 starving Irish walked 12 miles from Louisburgh to Delphi Lodge, hoping to get food from their landlord, but they were turned away. On the walk back, almost 200 of them died along the side of this road. Today, the road still seems to echo with the despair of those hungry souls, and it inspires an annual walk that commemorates the tragedy. Archbishop Desmond Tutu made the walk in 1991, shortly before South Africa ended its apartheid system.

• *Continue south on R-335. You'll get a fine view of **Aasleagh Falls** on the left. In late May, the banks below the falls explode with lush, wild, purple rhododendron blossoms. Cross the bridge after the falls, and turn right onto N-59 toward Leenane. You'll drive along Killary Harbor, an Irish example of a fjord. This long, narrow body of water was carved by an advancing glacier.*

Leenane

This "town" (actually just a crossroads) is a good place for a break. The 1990 movie *The Field*, starring Limerick-born Richard Harris, was filmed here. Take a glance at the photos of the making of the movie on the wall of **Hamilton's Pub.** While you're there, find the old photo of the British dreadnought battleships that filled Killary Harbor when King Edward VII visited a century ago. Drop into the **Leenane Sheep and Wool Centre** (on the left as you enter town) to see interesting wool-spinning and weaving demonstrations (€5, April-Oct daily 9:30-18:00, closed Nov-March, tel. 095/42323, www.sheepandwoolcentre.com).

• *As you continue west on N-59, notice the rows of blue floats in Killary Harbor. They're there to mark mussel farms growing on hanging nets in*

Ireland's Misunderstood Nomads

When you see a small cluster of trailers at the side of an Irish road, you're looking at a dying way of life. These are the Travellers, a nomadic throwback to the days when wandering craftsmen, musicians, and evicted unfortunates crowded rural Ireland. Often mislabeled as Gypsies, they have no ethnic ties to those Eastern European nomads, but rather have an Irish heritage going back centuries.

There were once many more Travellers, who lived in tents and used horse-drawn carts as they wandered the countryside in search of work. Before the famine, when Irish hospitality was a given, Travellers filled a niche in Irish society. They would do odd jobs, such as repairing furniture, sweeping chimneys, and selling horses. Skilled tinsmiths, they mended pots, pans, and stills for *poitn*—Irish moonshine. (Travellers used to be called "tinkers," but this label is now considered derogatory.) Settled-down farm folk, who rarely ventured more than 20 miles from home their entire lives, depended on the roaming Travellers for news and gossip from farther-flung regions. But post-famine rural depopulation and the gradual urbanization of the countryside forced this nomadic group to adapt to an almost sedentary existence on the fringes of towns.

Today, the 30,000 remaining Travellers are outsiders, usually treated with suspicion by the traditionally conservative Irish. Locals often complain that petty thefts go up when Travellers set up camp in a nearby "halting site," and that they leave garbage behind when they depart. Although most visible in rural encampments, Travellers still frequent the outdoor horse market at Smithfield Village in Dublin on the first Sunday of each month. They are very religious and often camp near the pilgrimage town of Knock.

Travellers tend to keep to themselves, marry young, have large families, and speak their own Gaelic-based language (called Shelta, Gammon, or Cant). Attempts to settle Travellers in government housing and integrate their children into schools have met with mixed success, as portrayed poignantly in the 1992 movie *Into the West*.

the cold seawater. As you climb out of the fjord valley about 8 kilometers (5 miles) past Leenane, you'll pass (on the left) some areas that offer good, close looks at a turf cut in a peat bog.

A Slog on the Bog

Walk a few yards onto the spongy green carpet. (Watch your step on wet days to avoid squishing into a couple of inches of water.)

Find a dry spot and jump up and down to get a feel for it. Have your companion jump; you'll feel the vibrations 30 feet away.

These bogs once covered almost 20 percent of Ireland. As the climate got warmer at the end of the last Ice Age, plants began growing along the sides of the many shallow lakes and ponds. When the plants died in these waterlogged areas, there wasn't enough oxygen for them to fully decompose. Over the centuries, the moss built up, layer after dead layer, helping to slowly fill in the lakes. During World War I, this sphagnum moss was collected to use in bandages to soak up blood (it absorbs many times its weight in fluids).

It's this wet, oxygen-starved ecosystem that has preserved ancient artifacts so well, many of which can be seen in Dublin's National Museum. Even forgotten containers of butter, churned centuries ago and buried to keep cool, have been discovered. But most bizarre are the wrinkled bog mummies that are occasionally unearthed. These human remains (some of them close to 2,000 years old) are so incredibly intact that their eyelashes, hairstyles, and the last meal in their stomachs can be identified. They were likely sacrificial offerings to the pagan gods of Celtic times.

Since these acidic bogs contain few nutrients, unique species of carnivorous plants have adapted to life here by trapping and digesting insects. The tiny pink sundew (less than an inch tall) has delicate spikes glistening with insect-attracting fluid. Take a moment to find a mossy area and look closely at the variety of tiny plants. In summer, you'll see white tufts of bog cotton growing in marshy areas.

People have been cutting, drying, and burning peat as a fuel source for more than a thousand years. The cutting usually begins in April or May, when drier weather approaches. You'll probably see stacks of "turf" piled up to dry along recent cuts. Pick up a brick and fondle it. Dried peat is surprisingly light and stiff. In central Ireland, there are even industrial peat cuts that were begun after World War II to fuel power stations. But in the past few decades, bogs have been recognized as a rare habitat, and conservation efforts have been encouraged. These days, the sweet, nostalgic smell of burning peat is becoming increasingly rare.

• *Continue west on N-59. The road soon crosses a shallow lake, with a great view of Kylemore Abbey to the right. But don't stop here—you'll get a better photo from the parking lot, a few hundred yards ahead. Pull into the lot and take a few minutes to enjoy the view (gate closes at 18:00).*

Kylemore Abbey

This Neo-Gothic country house was built by the wealthy English businessman Mitchell Henry in the 1860s, after he and his wife had honeymooned in the area. Now they are both buried on the grounds. After World War I, refugee Benedictine nuns from Ypres, Belgium, took it over and ran it as an exclusive girls' boarding school—which peaked at 200 students—until it closed in 2010. The nuns still live upstairs, but you can visit the half-dozen open downstairs rooms that display the Henry family's cushy lifestyle (with a 15-minute audiovisual presentation). For me, the best thing about the abbey is the view of it from the lakeshore. But garden enthusiasts will seek out the extensive walled Victorian gardens. From the abbey, the gardens are a one-mile, level walk or quick shuttle bus ride (runs every 15 minutes). Hourly tours of the abbey and gardens are so-so; it's best just to enjoy the setting.

Cost and Hours: Overpriced €12.50 combo-ticket for abbey and gardens, 10 percent discount if bought online, daily March-Oct 9:00-17:30, shorter hours off-season, WCs in gift shop next to parking lot, cafeteria swims with the chaos of multiple big-bus tour groups, tel. 095/52001, www.kylemoreabbeytourism.ie.

• *Heading west from the abbey, you'll drive less than 8 kilometers (five miles) to the town of Letterfrack. Pass through the town and go left off N-59 to reach...*

Connemara National Park

This park encompasses almost 5,000 acres of wild bog and mountain scenery. The visitors center displays worthwhile exhibits of local flora and fauna, which are well-explained in the 15-minute *Man and the Landscape* film that runs every half-hour (free, daily June-Aug 9:30-18:30, March-May and Sept-Oct 10:00-17:30, last entry 45 minutes before closing, tel. 095/41054, www.heritageireland.ie). Nature lovers may want to reverse the direction of my driving loop (and skimp on sightseeing time at other stops) in order to enjoy a two-hour walking tour with a park naturalist (July-Aug Wed and Fri at 11:00, departs from visitors center). Call ahead to confirm walking tour schedules, and bring rain gear and hiking shoes.

• *If you're running short on time, you could stay on N-59 the whole way back to Galway. But I prefer to turn south off N-59 in Clifden to enjoy a scenic coastal loop on R-341.*

Coastal Connemara

The essence of scenic Connemara—rocky yet seductive—is captured in a neat little 24-mile (38 km) lumpy loop on R-341. The 12 Bens (peaks) of Connemara loom deeper inland. In the foreground, broad shelves of bare bedrock are netted with stone walls, which interlock through the landscape. The ocean slaps the hardscrabble shore. Fishermen cast into their favorite little lakes, and ponies trot in windswept fields. Abandoned roofless stone cottages stand mute, keeping their stories to themselves. The only settlement on this loop to speak of is Roundstone, a perfect place to stop for a cup of coffee before turning home.

• *R-341 links back up with N-59 near Recess. At the junction with N-59, turn right, and follow Galway signs back through Recess, Maam Cross, and Oughterard. Our tour is over.*

Sights Between Galway and Derry

Travelers continuing on to Northern Ireland (or County Donegal) should get an early start. Allow a long day for the drive from Galway to Derry (or Portrush), with these interesting stops along the way. The town of Knock is right on N-17 as you head north out of Galway, while Strokestown is farther east in County Roscommon. Fill up your tank after crossing into Northern Ireland, since gas is a little cheaper there than in the Republic.

Knock—In 1879, locals saw the Virgin Mary, St. Joseph, and St. John appear against the south gable of this tiny town's church. Word of miraculous healings turned the trickle of pilgrims into a flood and put Knock solidly on the pilgrimage

map. Today, you can visit the shrine. At the edge of the site, a small but interesting folk museum shows "evidence" of the healings, photos of a papal visit, and interesting slices of traditional life.

▲▲Strokestown Park National Famine Museum—The Great Potato Famine of 1845-1849 was the bleakest period in Irish history—so traumatic that it halved the Irish population, sent desperate, hungry Irish peasants across the globe, and crystallized Irish-nationalist hatred of British rule. The National Famine Museum fills a mansion on the former estate of the Mahon family in the market town of Strokestown, 60 miles (96.5 km) northeast of Galway. Visitors can absorb the thoughtful exhibits explaining how three million Irish peasants survived on a surprisingly nutritious pre-famine diet of buttermilk and potatoes (12 pounds per day per average male laborer...potatoes are 80 percent water).

Major Mahon, the ill-fated landlord here during the famine, found it cheaper to fill three "coffin ships" bound for America with his evicted, starving tenants than pay the taxes for their upkeep in the local workhouse. When almost half died at sea of "famine fever," he was assassinated.

After visiting the museum, take a tour of the musty "Big House." The tours provide insights into the gulf that divided the Protestant ascendancy and their Catholic house staff. Afterward, find the servants' tunnel—connecting the kitchen to the stable—built to avoid cluttering the Mahon family's views with unsightly common laborers.

Cost and Hours: €13 for museum, house tour, and Georgian gardens; daily mid-March-Oct 10:30-17:30, Nov-mid-March 11:30-16:00; "Big House" tours go daily in high season at 12:00, 14:30, and 16:00, tel. 071/963-3013, www.strokestownpark.ie.

Eating: Drivers connecting Westport or Galway to either Dublin or Northern Ireland can stop here en route and grab lunch in the museum café.

NORTHERN IRELAND

NORTHERN IRELAND

 The island of Ireland was once the longest-held colony of Great Britain. Unlike its Celtic cousins, Scotland and Wales, Ireland has always been distant from London—a distance due more to its Catholicism than the Irish Sea.

Four hundred years ago, Protestant settlers from England and Scotland were strategically "planted" in Catholic Ireland to help assimilate the island into the British economy. These settlers established their own cultural toehold on the island, while the Catholic Irish held strong to their Gaelic culture.

Over the centuries, British rule hasn't been easy. By the beginning of the 20th century, the sparse Protestant population could no longer control the entire island. When Ireland won its independence in 1921 (after a bloody guerrilla war against British rule), 26 of the island's 32 counties became the Irish Free State, ruled from Dublin with dominion status in the British Commonwealth—similar to Canada's level of sovereignty. In 1949, these 26 counties left the Commonwealth and became the Republic of Ireland, severing all political ties with Britain. Meanwhile, the six remaining northeastern counties—the only ones with a Protestant majority—chose not to join the Irish Free State, and remained part of the UK.

But embedded within these six counties—now joined as the political entity called Northern Ireland—was a large, disaffected Catholic minority who felt they'd been sold down the river by the drawing of the new international border. Their political opponents were the "Unionists"—Protestants eager to defend the union with Britain, who were primarily led by two groups: the long-established Orange Order, and the military muscle of the newly mobilized Ulster Volunteer Force (UVF). This was countered on the Catholic side by the Irish Republican Army (IRA), which wanted all 32 of Ireland's counties to be united in one Irish nation—their political goals were "Nationalist."

In World War II, the Republic stayed neutral while the North enthusiastically supported the Allied cause—winning a spot close to London's heart. Derry (a.k.a. Londonderry) became an essential Allied convoy port, while Belfast lost more than 800 civilians dur-

Northern Ireland

Atlantic Ocean

See Antrim Coast map

Antrim Coast / Rathlin Island

Bushmills / GIANT'S CAUSEWAY

Portrush

Coleraine / GLENS OF ANTRIM

Letterkenny

Derry

COUNTY DONEGAL

Ballymena / Larne

Carrickfergus

Antrim

NORTHERN IRELAND

Donegal

■ULSTER-AMERICAN FOLK PARK
● Omagh

Lough Neagh

Belfast / George Best City Airport

Belfast International Airport

To Cairnryan & Troon, Scotland

To Cairnryan, Scotland & Liverpool, England

Bangor

MOUNT STEWART HOUSE

Strangford Lough

Lower Lough Erne

Belleek

● Enniskillen

Upper Lough Erne

To Galway

Armagh

Mourne Mtns.

Downpatrick

Newry

REPUBLIC OF IRELAND

20 Kilometers

20 Miles

Dundalk

Irish Sea

To Dublin

ing four Luftwaffe bombing raids in 1941. After the war, the split between North and South seemed permanent, and Britain invested heavily in Northern Ireland to bring it solidly into the UK fold.

In the Republic of Ireland (the South), where 94 percent of the population was Catholic and only 6 percent Protestant, there was a clearly dominant majority. But in the North, at the time it was formed, Catholics were still a sizable 35 percent of the population—enough to demand attention. To maintain the status quo, Protestants considered certain forms of anti-Catholic discrimination necessary. It was this discrimination that led to the Troubles, the conflict that filled headlines from the late 1960s to the late 1990s.

Four hundred years ago (during the Reformation), this was a fight over Protestant and Catholic religious differences. But over the last century, the conflict has been not about faith, but about politics: Will Northern Ireland stay part of the UK, or become part of the Republic of Ireland? The indigenous Irish of Northern Ireland, who generally want to unite with Ireland, happen to be Catholic. The descendants of the Scottish and English settlers, who generally want to remain part of Britain, happen to be Protestant.

Northern Ireland Almanac

Official Name: Since Northern Ireland is not an independent state, there is no official country name. Some call it Ulster, while others label it the Six Counties. Population-wise, it's the smallest country of the UK (the other three are England, Wales, and Scotland).

Population: Northern Ireland's 1.8 million people are about 45 percent Protestant (mostly Presbyterian and Anglican) and 40 percent Catholic. Another 5 percent profess different religions, and 10 percent claim no religious ties. English is far and away the chief language, though Gaelic (Irish) is also spoken in staunchly Nationalist Catholic communities.

Despite the country's genetic homogeneity, the population is highly segregated along political, religious, and cultural lines. Roughly speaking, the eastern seaboard is more Unionist, Protestant, and of English-Scottish heritage, while the south and west (bordering the Republic of Ireland) are Nationalist, Catholic, and of Irish descent. Cities are often clearly divided between neighborhoods of one group or the other. Early in life, locals learn to identify the highly symbolic (and highly charged) colors, jewelry, music, names, and vocabulary that distinguish the cultural groups.

Latitude and Longitude: 54°N and 5°W. It's as far north as parts of the Alaskan panhandle.

Area: 5,400 square miles (about the size of Connecticut), constituting a sixth of the island. Northern Ireland includes 6 of the island's traditional 32 counties.

Geography: Northern Ireland is shaped roughly like a doughnut, with the UK's largest lake in the middle (Lough Neagh, 150 square miles and a prime eel fishery). The terrain comprises gently rolling hills of green grass, rising to the 2,800-foot Slieve Donard. The weather is temperate, cloudy, moist, windy, and hard to predict.

Biggest Cities: Belfast, the capital, has 300,000 residents. Half a million people—nearly one in three Northern Irish—inhabit the greater Belfast area. Derry (called Londonderry by

Unionists) has 85,000 people.

Economy: Northern Ireland's economy is more closely tied to the UK than to the Republic of Ireland. Sectarian violence has held back growth, and the economy gets subsidies from the UK and the EU. Traditional agriculture (potatoes and grain) is fading fast, though modern techniques and abundant grassland make Northern Ireland a major producer of sheep, cows, and grass seed. Modern software and communications companies are replacing traditional manufacturing. Shipyards are rusty relics, and the linen industry is now threadbare; both are victims of cheaper labor available in Asia.

Currency: Northern Ireland uses not the euro, but the pound (£).

Exchange rate: £1 = about $1.60.

Government: Northern Ireland is not a self-governing nation, but is part of the UK, ruled from London by Queen Elizabeth II and Prime Minister David Cameron, and represented in Parliament by 18 elected Members of Parliament. For 50 years (1922-1972), Northern Ireland was granted a great deal of autonomy and self-governance, known as "Home Rule." The current National Assembly (108-seat Parliament)—after an ineffective decade of political logjams—has recently begun to show signs of rejuvenation.

Politics are dominated, of course, by the ongoing debate between Unionists (who want to preserve the union with the UK) and Nationalists (who want to join the Republic of Ireland). Two high-profile and controversial figures have been at opposite ends of this debate: the elderly firebrand Reverend Ian Paisley for the Unionists (who now serves in the British House of Lords); and assassination-attack survivor Gerry Adams of Sinn Fein, the political arm of the IRA (who now serves in the Republic of Ireland's parliament). In a hopeful development in the spring of 2007, the two allowed themselves to be photographed together across a negotiation table (a moment both had once sworn would never happen) as London returned control of the government to Belfast.

Flag: The official flag of Northern Ireland is the Union flag of the UK. But you'll also see the green, white, and orange Irish tricolor (waved by Nationalists) and the Northern Irish flag (white with a red cross and a red hand at its center), which is used by Unionists (see "The Red Hand of Ulster" sidebar on page 372).

NORTHERN IRELAND

Partly inspired by Martin Luther King Jr. and the civil rights movement in America in the 1960s—beamed into Irish living rooms by the new magic of television news—the Catholic minority in Northern Ireland began a nonviolent struggle to end discrimination, advocating for better jobs and housing. Extremists polarized issues, and demonstrations—also broadcast on TV news—became violent. Unionists were afraid that if the island became one nation, the relatively poor Republic of Ireland would drag down the comparatively affluent North, and that the high percentage of Catholics would spell repression for the Protestants. As Unionist Protestants and Nationalist Catholics clashed in 1969, the British Army entered the fray. Their role, initially a peacekeeping one, gradually evolved into acting as muscle for the Unionist government. In 1972, a watershed year, more than 500 people died as combatants moved from petrol bombs to guns, and a new, more violent IRA emerged. In that 30-year (1968-1998) chapter of the struggle for an independent and united Ireland, more than 3,000 people were killed.

A 1985 agreement granted Dublin a consulting role in the Northern Ireland government. Unionists bucked this idea, and violence escalated. That same year, Belfast City Hall draped a huge, defiant banner under its dome, proclaiming, *Belfast Says No.*

In 1994, the banner came down. In the 1990s—with Ireland's membership in the EU, the growth of its economy, and the weakening of the Catholic Church's influence—the consequences of a united Ireland became slightly less threatening to the Unionists. Also in 1994, the IRA declared a cease-fire, and the Protestant Ulster Volunteer Force (UVF) followed suit.

The Nationalists wanted British troops out of Northern Ireland, while the Unionists demanded that the IRA turn in its arms. Optimists hailed the signing of a breakthrough peace plan in 1998, called the "Good Friday Accord" by Nationalists, or the "Belfast Agreement" by Unionists. This led to the release of prisoners on both sides in 2000—a highly emotional event.

Recently, additional progress has taken place on both fronts. The IRA finally "verifiably put their arms beyond use" in 2005, and backed the political peace process. In 2009, most Loyalist paramilitary groups did the same. Meanwhile, British Army surveillance towers were dismantled in 2006, and the army formally ended its 38-year-long Operation Banner campaign in 2007.

A tiny splinter group of stubborn IRA diehards (calling themselves the "Real IRA") continues to smolder. Their efforts at publicity are roundly condemned not only by hard-line Unionists, but also by former IRA leaders like government minister Martin McGuinness and his Sinn Fein party, who prefer to pursue their Nationalist goals through the democratic process.

In 2010, the peace process was jolted forward by a surprisingly forthright apology offered by British Prime Minister David Cameron, who expressed regret for the British Army's offenses on Bloody Sunday (see sidebar on page 413). The apology was prompted by the Saville Report—the results of an investigation conducted by the UK government as part of the Good Friday Accord. It found that the 1972 shootings of Nationalist civil-rights marchers on Bloody Sunday by British soldiers was "unjustified" and the victims innocent (to the intense relief of the victims' families, who had fought since 1972 to clear their loved ones' names).

Major hurdles to a lasting peace persist, but the downtown checkpoints are history, and the "bomb-damage clearance sales" are over. And today, more tourists than ever are venturing north to Belfast and Derry.

Terminology

Ulster (one of Ireland's four ancient provinces) consists of nine counties in the northern part of the island of Ireland. Six of these make up Northern Ireland (pronounced "Norn Iron" by locals), while three counties remain part of the Republic.

Unionists—and the more hard-line, working-class **Loyalists**—want the North to remain in the UK. The **Ulster Unionist Party (UUP),** the political party representing moderate Unionist views, is currently led by Mike Nesbitt (Nobel Peace Prize co-winner David Trimble led the UUP from 1995 to 2005). The **Democratic Unionist Party (DUP),** led by Peter Robinson (protégé of retired Reverend Ian Paisley), takes a harder stance in defense of Unionism. The **Ulster Volunteer Force (UVF),** the **Ulster Freedom Fighters (UFF),** and the **Ulster Defense Association (UDA)** are the Loyalist paramilitary organizations mentioned most frequently in newspapers and on spray-painted walls.

Nationalists—and the more hard-line, working-class **Republicans**—want a united and independent Ireland ruled by Dublin. The **Social Democratic Labor Party (SDLP),** founded by Nobel Peace Prize co-winner John Hume and currently led by Alasdair McDonnell, is the moderate political party representing Nationalist views. **Sinn Fein** (shin fayn), led by Gerry Adams, takes a harder stance in defense of Nationalism. The **Irish Republican Army (IRA)** is the Nationalist paramilitary organization (linked with Sinn Fein) mentioned most often in the press and in graffiti.

To gain more insight into the complexity of the Troubles, see the University of Ulster's informative and evenhanded Conflict Archive at http://cain.ulst.ac.uk/index.html.

NORTHERN IRELAND

Safety

A generation ago, Northern Ireland was a sadly contorted corner of the world. On my first visit, I remember thinking that even the name of this region sounded painful ("Ulster" sounded to me like a combination of "ulcer" and "blister").

Today tourists in Northern Ireland are no longer considered courageous (or reckless). When locals spot you with a map and a lost look on your face, they're likely to ask, "Wot yer lookin fer?" in their distinctive Northern accent. They're not suspicious of you, but rather trying to help you find your way. You're safer in Belfast than in many other UK cities—and far safer than in most major US cities. You have to look for trouble to find it here. Just don't seek out spit-and-sawdust pubs in working-class neighborhoods and spew simplistic and naive opinions about sensitive local topics.

Tourists notice the tension mainly during the "marching season" (Easter-Aug, peaking in early July). July 12—"the Twelfth"—is traditionally the most confrontational day of the year in the North, when proud Protestant Unionist Orangemen march to celebrate their Britishness and their separate identity from the Republic of Ireland (often through staunchly Nationalist Catholic neighborhoods). Lay low if you stumble onto any big Orange parades.

Northern Ireland Is a Different Country

The border is almost invisible. But when you leave the Republic of Ireland and enter Northern Ireland, you *are* crossing an international border. Although you don't have to flash your passport, you do change stamps, phone cards, and money. Gas is a little more expensive in the Republic of Ireland than in Northern Ireland (so fill up after crossing the border). Groceries are cheaper here, too. These price differences create a lively daily shopping trade for those living near the border.

You won't use euros here; Northern Ireland issues its own Ulster pound, which, like the Scottish pound, is interchangeable with the English pound (€1 = about £0.80; £1 = about $1.60). Some establishments near the border may take your euros, but at a lousy exchange rate. So keep any euros for your return to the Republic, and get pounds from an ATM inside Northern Ireland instead. And if you're heading to Britain next, it's best to change your Ulster pounds into English ones (free at any bank in Northern Ireland, England, Wales, or Scotland).

BELFAST

Seventeenth-century Belfast was just a village. With the influx, or "plantation," of English and (more often) Scottish settlers, the character of the place changed. After the Scots and English were brought in—and the native Irish were subjugated—Belfast boomed, spurred by the success of the local linen, rope-making, and especially shipbuilding industries. The Industrial Revolution took root with a vengeance. While the rest of Ireland remained rural and agricultural, Belfast earned its nickname ("Old Smoke") during the time when many of the brick buildings that you'll see today were built. The year 1888 marked the birth of modern Belfast. After Queen Victoria granted city status to this boomtown of 300,000, its citizens built Belfast's centerpiece, City Hall.

Belfast is the birthplace of the *Titanic* (and many other ships that didn't sink). In 2012—to mark the 100th anniversary of the *Titanic* disaster—a modern new attraction was launched in Belfast's shipyard, telling the ill-fated ship's fascinating and tragic story. Nearby, two huge, mustard-colored cranes (built in the 1970s, and for a time the biggest in the world, nicknamed Samson and Goliath) rise like skyscrapers. They stand idle now, but serve as a reminder of this town's former shipbuilding might...strategic enough to be the target of four Luftwaffe bombing raids in World War II.

At the beginning of the 21st century, investments from south of the border—the Republic of Ireland—injected quiet optimism into the dejected shipyards where the *Titanic* was built. Though funding has declined, Belfast officials hope the historic Titanic Quarter will attract more development in the future—and lots of tourists.

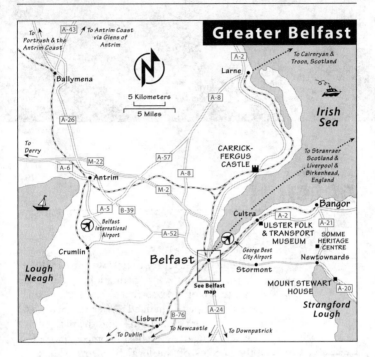

Despite the economic downturn, it feels like a new morning in Belfast. It's hard to believe that the bright and bustling pedestrian center was once a subdued, traffic-free security zone. Now there's no hint of security checks, once a tiresome daily routine. These days, both Catholics and Protestants are rooting for the Belfast Giants ice hockey team, one of many reasons to live together peacefully.

Still, it's a fragile peace and a tenuous hope. Mean-spirited murals, hateful bonfires built a month before they're actually burned, and pubs with security gates are reminders that the island is still split—and 900,000 Protestant Unionists in the North prefer it that way.

Planning Your Time

Big Belfast is thin on sights. For most, one day of sightseeing is plenty.

Day Trip from Dublin: On the handy, two-hour Dublin-Belfast train (cheap €40 "day return" tickets, €20 if booked online; can cost more Fri-Sun), you could make Belfast a day trip:

7:35   Catch the early-morning train from Dublin's Connolly Station (arriving in Belfast's Central Station at 9:45)

11:00   City Hall tour (Mon-Fri; later on Sat, none on Sun),

browse the pedestrian zone, lunch, ride a shared black
taxi up Falls Road

15:00 Visit Titanic Belfast (after midday crowds subside)
or side-trip to the Ulster Folk Park and Transport
Museum in nearby Cultra

Evening Return to Dublin (last train departs Belfast Mon-Sat
at 20:10 and arrives in Dublin at 22:18)

Sunday's trains depart later and return earlier, compressing
your already limited time here (first train departs Dublin at 10:00
and arrives in Belfast at 12:16; last train departs Belfast at 19:00
and pulls into Dublin at 21:05). Confirm train times at local stations. Note that the TI offers the Historic Belfast Walk at 14:00 on
Friday-Sunday (Sat-Sun only Nov-Feb). On Friday and Saturday,
St. George's Market bustles in the morning. On Saturday, the only
tours of City Hall are at 14:00 and 15:00. There are no tours on
Sunday.

Staying Overnight: Belfast makes a pleasant overnight stop,
with plenty of cheap hostels, reasonable B&Bs, weekend hotel
deals (Fri-Sun), and a relaxed neighborhood full of B&Bs 30 minutes away in Bangor.

Two Days in Belfast: On the first day, follow my day-trip itinerary described earlier. For your second day, take the City Sightseeing bus tour in the morning, then visit Carrickfergus Castle in the
afternoon.

Two Days in Small-Town Northern Ireland: From Dublin (via Belfast), take the train to Portrush; allow two nights and
a day to tour the Causeway Coast (castle, whiskey distilleries,
Giant's Causeway, resort fun), then follow the Belfast-in-a-day
plan described earlier. With a third day, add Derry.

Coming from Scotland or England: With good ferry connections (from Troon in Scotland or Liverpool in England; see
"Belfast Connections," later), it's easy to begin your exploration of
the Emerald Isle in Belfast, and then head south to Dublin and the
Republic.

Orientation to Belfast

For the first-time visitor in town for a quick look, Belfast is pretty simple. There are four zones of interest: **northern** (Titanic
Quarter—docklands with Odyssey and Titanic Belfast), **western**
(working-class sectarian neighborhoods west of the freeway), **central** (Donegall Square, City Hall, pedestrian shopping, TI), and
southern (Botanic Gardens, Queen's University, Ulster Museum).

The modern bookends of sightseeing interest are the Titanic
Belfast attraction (in the Titanic Quarter to the north) and the
Lyric Theatre (near the university district to the south). Their

contemporary angularities are hard to miss, as they contrast sharply with the redbrick uniformity of old Belfast. But the core of your city navigating will hinge on four more central landmarks (listed from north to south): Albert Clock Tower, City Hall, Shaftesbury Square, and Queen's University. Find them on your map, and use them to navigate as you stroll the town.

Belfast's "Golden Mile"—stretching from Hotel Europa to the university district—connects the central and southern zones with many of the best dinner and entertainment spots.

Tourist Information

The modern TI (look for *Welcome Centre* signs) has fine, free city maps and an enjoyable bookshop with Internet access. Staff at the *Failte Ireland* desk can answer questions about travel in the Republic of Ireland (June-Sept Mon-Sat 9:00-19:00, Sun 11:00-16:00; Oct-May Mon-Sat 9:00-17:30, Sun 11:00-16:00; one block north of City Hall at 47 Donegall Place, tel. 028/9024-6609, www.gotobelfast.com). City walking tours depart from the TI (see "Tours in Belfast," later). For the latest on evening fun, get a copy of *What About Belfast*, free at the TI.

Arrival in Belfast

By Train: Arriving by fast train, you'll go directly to Belfast's Central Station (with ATMs and free city maps at the ticket counter). From the station, a free Centrelink bus loops to Donegall Square, with stops near Shaftesbury Square (recommended hostels), the bus station (some recommended hotels), and the TI (free with any train or bus ticket, 4/hour, never on Sun; during morning rush hour, bus runs only between station and Donegall Square). Allow about £5 for a taxi from Central Station to Donegall Square, or £7 to my B&B listings in south Belfast.

Slower trains arc through the city, stopping at several downtown stations, including Central Station, Great Victoria Station (most central, near Donegall Square and most hotels), Botanic Station (close to the university, Botanic Gardens, and some recommended hostels), and Adelaide (near several recommended B&Bs). It's easy and cheap to connect stations by train (£1.50).

By Car: Driving in Belfast, although not as bad as in Dublin, is still a pain. Avoid it if possible. Street parking in the city center is geared for short shopping stops (use pay-and-display machines, £.30/15 minutes, one-hour maximum, Mon-Sat 9:00-18:00, free in evenings and on Sun).

BELFAST

Helpful Hints

Market: On Friday, Saturday, and Sunday (roughly until 15:00), the Victorian confines of **St. George's Market** is a commotion of commerce and a people-watching delight. Friday is a variety market, Saturday blooms with food and garden items, and Sunday creaks with crafts and antiques (at corner of Oxford and East Bridge Streets, 5 blocks east of Donegall Square, tel. 028/9043-5704, www.belfastcity.gov.uk/markets).

Shopping Mall: Victoria Square is a glitzy American-style mall. Its huge glass dome reflects Belfast's economic rejuvenation. For fine city views, ride the free elevator to the observation platform high up inside the dome (Mon-Tue 9:00-19:00, Wed-Fri 9:00-21:00, Sat 9:00-18:00, Sun 13:00-18:00; 3 blocks east of City Hall—bordered by Chichester, Victoria, Ann, and Montgomery streets; www.victoriasquare.com).

Phone Tips: To call the Republic of Ireland from Northern Ireland, dial 00-353, then the area code without its initial 0, and finally the local number. To call Northern Ireland from the Republic of Ireland, dial 048, and then the local eight-digit number.

Internet Access: Belfast's Internet cafés are here-today, gone-tomorrow ventures operating on a shoestring. The **TI** offers dependable Internet access at a half-dozen handy terminals (£2/hour). There's Wi-Fi at the Student Union, listed below.

Post Office: The main post office, with lots of fun postcards, is at the intersection of High and Bridge Streets (Mon-Fri 9:00-17:30, Sat 9:00-12:30, closed Sun, 3 long blocks north of Donegall Square). A second branch is located closer to my accommodations listings on University Road, across from the Ulster Museum, and a third location lurks north of City Hall, at the corner of High and North Streets (all same hours).

Laundry: Globe Launderers is at 37-39 Botanic Avenue (£5 self-serve, £8 drop-off service, Mon-Fri 8:00-21:00, Sat 8:00-18:00, Sun 12:00-18:00, tel. 028/9024-3956). For the B&B neighborhood south of town, the closest is **Whistle Cleaners** (£8 drop-off service, Mon-Fri 8:30-18:00, Sat 9:00-17:30, closed Sun, 160 Lisburn Road, at intersection with Eglantine Avenue, tel. 028/9038-1297). For locations, see the map on page 374.

Bike Rental: McConvey Cycles is south of the city center at 183 Ormeau Road (£20/24 hours, Mon-Sat 9:00-18:00, Thu until 20:00, closed Sun, tel. 028/9033-0322, www.mcconveycycles.com).

Queen's University Student Union: Located directly across University Road from the red-brick University building, the Student Union is just as handy for tourists as it is for college

BELFAST

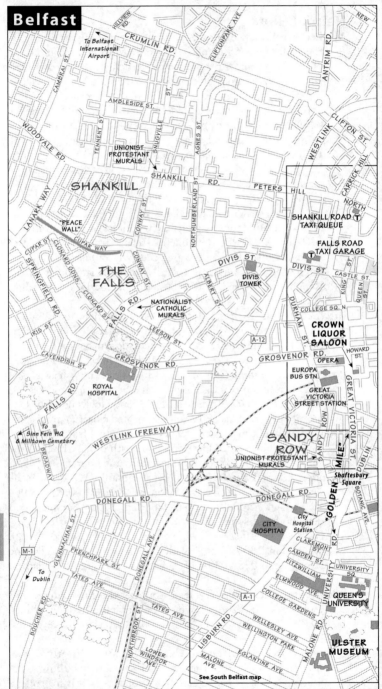

Belfast

To Belfast International Airport

CRUMLIN RD.

HILLVIEW RD.

NEW

CLIFTONPARK AVE.

ANTRIM RD.

WESTLINK

CLIFTON ST.

CARRICK HILL

NORTH

CAMBRAI ST.

WOODVALE RD.

TENNENT ST.

SNUGVILLE ST.

AGNES ST.

AMBLESIDE ST.

UNIONIST PROTESTANT MURALS

SHANKILL ST.

SHANKILL

SHANKILL RD.

PETERS HILL

SHANKILL ROAD TAXI QUEUE Ⓣ

LANARK WAY

"PEACE WALL"

CONWAY ST.

NORTHUMBERLAND ST.

FALLS ROAD TAXI GARAGE Ⓣ

CUPAR ST.

CUPAR WAY

SPRINGFIELD RD.

CLONARD GDNS.

CONWAY ST.

DIVIS ST.

DIVIS ST.

CASTLE ST.

KING ST.

QUEEN ST.

THE FALLS

CLONARD ST.

ALBERT ST.

DIVIS TOWER

DURHAM ST.

COLLEGE SQ. N.

IRIS ST.

FALLS RD.

NATIONALIST CATHOLIC MURALS

LEESON ST.

A-12

COLLEGE SQ.

CROWN LIQUOR SALOON

CAVENDISH ST.

GROSVENOR RD.

GROSVENOR RD.

HOWARD ST.

OPERA

FALLS RD.

ROYAL HOSPITAL

EUROPA BUS STN.

GREAT VICTORIA ST.

To Sinn Fein HQ & Milltown Cemetery

WESTLINK (FREEWAY)

GREAT VICTORIA STREET STATION

SANDY ROW

SANDY ROW

UNIONIST PROTESTANT MURALS

"GOLDEN MILE"

DUBLIN RD.

BOTANIC AVE.

Shaftesbury Square

BROADWAY

DONEGALL RD.

DONEGALL RD.

City Hospital Station

M-1

GLENMACHAN ST.

FRENCHPARK ST.

DONEGALL AVE.

CITY HOSPITAL

CLAREMONT ST.

CAMDEN ST.

To Dublin

TATES AVE.

FITZWILLIAM

UNIVERSITY SQ.

ELMWOOD AVE.

UNIVERSITY RD.

QUEEN'S UNIVERSITY

BOUCHER RD.

NORTHBROOK ST.

TATES AVE.

A-1

COLLEGE GARDENS

LISBURN RD.

WELLESLEY AVE.

MALONE RD.

ULSTER MUSEUM

LOWER WINDSOR AVE.

WELLINGTON PARK

MALONE AVE.

EGLANTINE AVE.

See South Belfast map

BELFAST

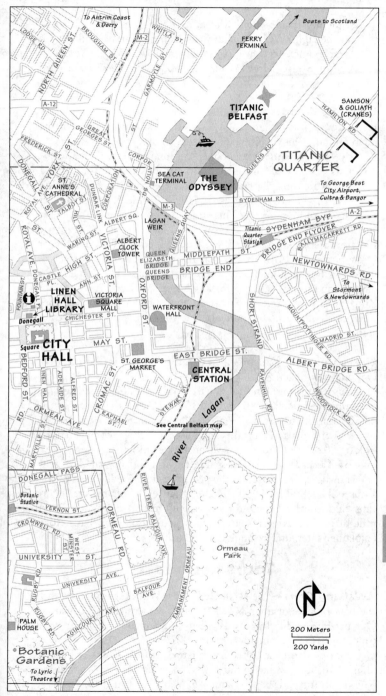

students. Inside you'll find an ATM (at end of main hall, on the right), WCs, a pharmacy, a mini-market, and Wi-Fi. Grab a quick and cheap £4 sandwich and coffee at **Clement's Coffee Shop** (Mon-Fri 8:30-22:30, Sat 9:00-22:00, closed Sun).

Getting Around Belfast

If you line up your sightseeing logically, you can do most of the town on foot. On wheels, you have several options.

By Train or Bus: Ask about iLink smartcards, which give individuals one day of unlimited train and bus travel. The Zone 1 card (£6.50) covers the city center and George Best Belfast City Airport. The handy Zone 2 card (£10.50) includes Cultra (Ulster Folk Park and Transport Museum), Bangor, and Carrickfergus Castle. The Zone 3 card (£14) is really only useful for reaching Belfast's distant airport or the Ulster American Folk Park near Omagh. Zone 4 (£16.50) gets you anywhere in Northern Ireland, including Portrush and Derry. You can purchase additional iLink days to top up your card (£5 for Zone 1, £9 for Zone 2, £12.50 for Zone 3, £15 for Zone 4). For those lingering in the North, one-week cards offer even better deals. Buy your iLink card at any train station in the city.

If you're only traveling to one destination—Carrickfergus Castle, Cultra, or Bangor—a "day return" ticket is cheaper than two one-way tickets.

Buses go from Donegall Square East to Malone Road and my recommended B&Bs (#8B or #8C, 3/hour, £1.60, all-day pass costs £3.50 Mon-Sat before 9:30—after 9:30 and on Sun it's £2.70).

For information on trains and buses in Belfast, contact Translink (tel. 028/9066-6630, www.translink.co.uk).

By Taxi: Taxis are reasonable and a good option. For general transport, as opposed to the taxi tours described later, try **Valu Cabs** (tel. 028/9080-9080). Rather than use their meters, many cabs charge a flat £5 rate for any ride up to two miles. It's £2 per mile after that. Ride a shared cab if you're going up Falls Road (explained later, under "Sights in Belfast").

Tours in Belfast

▲**Walking Tours**—The **Historic Belfast Walk** takes you through the historic core of town (£6, 1.5 hours; departs from TI March-Oct Fri-Sun at 14:00; Nov-Feb Sat and Sun only; confirm tour times with TI, book in advance, tel. 028/9024-6609).

Mixing drinks and history, **Historical Pub Tours of Belfast** offers two-hour walking tours that start at the Crown Dining Room pub and end six pubs later (£6; May-Oct Thu at 19:00, Sat at

BELFAST

16:00; book in advance, meet at pub above Crown Liquor Saloon at 46 Great Victoria Street across from Hotel Europa, tel. 028/9268-3665, www.belfastpubtours.com).

Coiste Irish Political Tours leads extended, three-hour walks along the Falls Road to explain the history of the neighborhood from an intensely Republican perspective. Led by former IRA prisoners, you'll visit murals, gardens of remembrance, peace walls, and community centers in this rejuvenating section of gritty Belfast. Tours meet beside the Divis Tower (the 20-story apartment house at the east end of the Divis Road near the A-12 Westlink motorway overpass) and end at the Milltown Cemetery (£8, Mon-Sat at 11:00, Sun at 14:00, tel. 028/9020-0770, www.coiste.ie, Seamus Kelley).

▲**Big Bus Tours—City Sightseeing** offer the best quick introduction to the city's recent and complicated political and social history. You'll cruise the Catholic and Protestant working-class neighborhoods as well as the dramatically situated Stormont Parliament building, with a commentary explaining the political murals and places of interest—mostly dealing with the Troubles of the last 40 years. You see sights from the bus and get out only for photos (£12.50, 2/hour, daily 10:00-16:30, tickets valid for 48 hours, fewer tours in winter—call first, makes 20 stops over a 1.5-hour loop; departs from Castle Place on High Street, 2 blocks west of Albert Clock Tower; pay cash on bus, or book by phone with credit card, tel. 028/9045-9035, www.city-sightseeing.com).

Their new cousin tour is the **Titanic Explorer** hop-on, hop-off bus, which focuses only on the Titanic Quarter. Stops lace together the Odyssey, S.S. *Nomadic* tender ship, Titanic Belfast, and Harland and Wolff drawing offices, and include a brief guided tour of *Titanic*'s dock and pump-house (£10, hourly, daily 9:45-16:00, ticket valid 24 hours, fewer in winter—call first, makes eight stops over 45-minute loop; departs from Castle Place on High Street, 2 blocks west of Albert Clock Tower, pay cash on bus, or book by phone with credit card, tel. 028/9032-1321, www.titanicexplorer.com).

Bike Tours—Explore the countryside south of town on **Belfast Bike Tours.** Departing from the front gate of Queen's University, you'll spend 2.5 hours peddling along an old canal towpath to the Giant's Ring (ancient dolmen) and back on generally flat terrain (£15, April-Oct Mon-Sat at 10:30 and 14:00; bikes, helmets, and bottle of water provided; must reserve ahead by phone or email, mobile 078-1211-4235, www.belfastbiketours.com).

Minibus Tours—**McComb's** Giant's Causeway Tour visits Carrickfergus Castle, the Giant's Causeway, Dunluce Castle (photo stop only), Carrick-a-Rede Rope Bridge, and Old Bushmills Distillery (£25, doesn't include distillery admission, daily 9:45-18:45 depending on demand, book through and depart from the recommended Belfast International City Hostel). They also have private guides (book in advance, tel. 028/9031-5333, www.minicoachni. co.uk).

Titanic Tours Belfast is run by former TV reporter Susie Millar, who is the great-granddaughter of a crew member on the

fateful cruise. It's operated as a minivan tour (seats five) that picks up and drops off at your hotel. She spends half a day driving you around the major *Titanic* sights in Belfast, explaining them as you go. This is by far Belfast's most intimate glimpse of the *Titanic*'s tragic history (ask her about her great-grandfather's departing two-penny promise). She is also available for longer, customized tours (£30, tel. 028/9065-9971, mobile 078-5271-6655, www.titanictours-belfast.co.uk, info@titanictours-belfast.co.uk).

Boat Tours—The Lagan Boat Company shows you shipyards on a one-hour **Titanic Tour** cruise, narrated by a member of the Belfast Titanic Society. The tour shows off the fruits of the city's £800 million investment in its harbor, including a weir built to control the tides and stabilize the depth of the harbor (it doubles as a free pedestrian bridge over the River Lagan). The heart of the tour is a lazy harbor cruise past rusty dry-dock gates, brought alive by the guide's proud commentary and passed-around historical photos (£10; daily sailings at 12:30, 14:00, and 15:30; fewer off-season, tel. 028/9033-0844, mobile 077-1891-0423, www.laganboatcompany. com). Tours depart from the Lagan Pedestrian Bridge and Weir on Donegall Quay. The quay is located just past the leaning Albert Clock Tower, a five-minute walk from the TI.

Local Guide—**Ken Harper** has a vast knowledge of Belfast and does insightful tours from his taxi, focusing on both Catholic and Protestant neighborhoods, *Titanic*-related sights, and Belfast's favorite sons—author C. S. Lewis, musician Van Morrison, and soccer star/playboy George Best. He's also available for custom tours, which he calls "Pick Ken's Brain" (£30 minimum or £10/person, 1.25 hours, tel. 028/9074-2711, mobile 077-1175-7178, www. harpertaxitours.com, kenharper2004@hotmail.com).

Sights in Belfast

Most sights of interest are located in four areas: the Titanic Quarter to the north of the city center, the sectarian neighborhoods to the west of the city center, central Belfast, and south Belfast (clustered around Queen's University).

Titanic Quarter

Up until the mid-1990s, this district was a barren wasteland of cement slabs and rusting industrial relics. But during the Celtic Tiger boom years (which spilled over into the North), shrewd investors saw the real-estate potential and began building posh, high-rise condos.

The first landmark project to be completed was the Odyssey complex (in 2000). To draw more visitors and commemorate the proud shipbuilding industry of the Victorian and Edwardian Ages, another flagship attraction was needed. The 100th anniversary of the *Titanic* disaster in 2012 provided the perfect opportunity, and the result is a brand-new attraction called Titanic Belfast.

The Odyssey—This huge millennium-project complex offers a food pavilion, bowling alley, and W5 science center with interactive, educational exhibits for youngsters. Where else can a kid play a harp with laser-light strings? The "W5" stands for "who, what, when, where, and why." There's also a 12-screen cinema, laser-tag gaming area, and an 8,000-seat arena where the Belfast Giants professional ice hockey team skates from September to March (£15 game tickets, tel. 028/9073-9074, www.belfastgiants.com).

Cost and Hours: Science center-£7.90, kids-£5.90, Mon-Fri 10:00-17:00, Sat 10:00-18:00, Sun 12:00-18:00, 2 Queen's Quay, 10-minute walk north of Belfast's Central Station, tel. 028/9046-7790, www.w5online.co.uk.

▲▲▲Titanic Belfast—This £97-million attraction opened in 2012, just in time for the 100th anniversary of the *Titanic's* fatal voyage. It sits on the site of the original dry dock where the ship was built. High-tech displays tell the tale of the famous cruise liner, proudly heralded as the largest man-made moving object of its time.

Cost and Hours: £13.50, audioguide for infoholics-£3; April-Sept Mon-Sat 9:00-19:00, Sun 10:00-17:00; Oct-March daily 10:00-17:00; located where the famous ship was built on Queen's Island, tel. 028/9076-6399, www.titanicbelfast.com.

Crowd-Beating Tips: Go early or late; big bus-tour crowds clog the exhibits from 10:00 to 14:00.

Eating: The ground floor includes a sandwich café as well as a carvery-style restaurant.

Getting There: From Donegall Square, take bus #26 or #26B (both stop behind Belfast Metropolitan College, a block away from Donegall Square), or go by taxi (£6 ride). The Titanic Quarter train station is a 10-minute walk to the south of the Titanic Belfast—

Titanic Trio

Most of us already know the sad story of the famous *Titanic*, when the unthinkable happened to the unsinkable: Launched in Belfast in 1911, the *Titanic* was the largest and most cel-  ebrated luxury cruise liner of its time. Locals thought them- selves the best shipbuilders since Noah. The *Titanic*'s sud- den demise in 1912 is the most famous sea disaster of the modern era. Only 716 of the 2,260 aboard were rescued.

But few people know that *Titanic* was the middle sister of three unfortunate ships, each built by the prestigious Harland and Wolff shipyards for the White Star Line.

In 1910, the **Olympic** was the first of the three similar ves- sels to be launched. It soon collided with the naval cruiser HMS *Hawke* and returned to Belfast to be repaired with parts taken from the still-under-construction **Titanic.** When World War I began, the *Olympic* served as a troop transport ship. During the war, it struck and sank a German submarine (the U-103). After the war, it returned to commercial service and later col- lided with the *Nantucket Lightship* (killing seven). The *Olym- pic*'s last voyage was in 1935, and it was demolished in 1937.

The last of the three to be built was the **Gigantic** in 1914. But after the *Titanic* sank, its name was changed (while still under construction) to **Britannic**...which was thought to be a luckier name. It was repainted white and converted to a hos- pital ship at the start of World War I. In 1915, it was serving in the Aegean Sea when it hit a mine—or was struck by a torpedo from a U-boat. Fortunately it had more advanced safety fea- tures than its two older sisters—it had enough lifeboats for all onboard, and was designed to sink more slowly. Luckily, the ship had no patients yet, as it was on its way to Greece to pick up wounded soldiers. Most of those onboard were saved (only 30 of the almost 1,100 crew and medical staff died). In 1976, French underwater explorer Jacques Cousteau found the wreck of the *Britannic* 400 feet down and brought up a few of its artifacts.

Amazingly, a single human thread ties all three ships together. A stewardess and nurse named Violet Jessop was aboard the *Olympic* when it collided with the HMS *Hawke*. She was also one of the lucky few to be rescued from the *Titanic*. And yes, incredibly, she was again among those rescued from the sinking *Britannic*. Talk about a buoyant personality...

easy to navigate as you'll have a clear view of the unique building across a mostly flat and empty industrial landscape.

Visiting the Titanic Belfast: Nine galleries take you from booming 1900s Belfast, through the construction and launch of the *Titanic*, and ultimately to a re-creation of its watery grave. A highlight is the Shipyard Ride, which takes you through a mock-up of the ship while it was being built. You'll learn how workers toughed out months of deafening and dangerous duty, working in five-man teams to hammer in red-hot rivets (they were paid by the rivet, and frequently burned by chips flying off the metal). Left- and right-handers were assigned specific hammering positions for efficiency. Young boys had the hot and hazardous job of quickly catching the glowing rivets and placing them for the hammerers.

Other exhibits cover the wider story of the Harland and Wolff shipyards, including the construction of *Titanic's* lesser known and also ill-fated sister ships: *Olympic* and *Britannic* (see sidebar). An upper floor viewpoint employs innovative electronic windows to project an image of the huge, partially built *Titanic* in dry dock beside you, masking the reality of today's barren shipyard below. Another gallery surrounds you on three sides with animated screens that glide through multiple decks, giving you a realistic feel for the ship in all its full-steam-ahead glory.

The human story of its passengers—from promenade-deck aristocrats to heroic crew members to steerage-class rabble—is also here. You'll see a broad cross-section of relics from the ship's short but opulent existence.

The big-screen "Titanic Beneath" theater shows the now-famous underwater footage of the wreck nearly 12,500 feet down on the bottom. Only 20 percent of the dead were ever recovered. Don't miss the clear floor panels at the foot of the movie screen, which allow you to stand on top of the watery debris field as the virtual wreck slowly passes beneath your feet.

The spacey architecture of Titanic Belfast's new building is already a landmark on the city's skyline. Six stories tall, it's clad in over 3,000 sun-reflecting aluminum panels. Its four corners represent the bows of the many ships that were built in these yards during the golden age of Belfast.

Sectarian Neighborhoods in West Belfast

It will be a happy day when the sectarian neighborhoods of Belfast have nothing to be sectarian about. For a look at three of the original home bases of the Troubles, explore the working-class neighborhoods of Catholic Falls Road and Protestant Shankill Road (west of the Westlink motorway), or Protestant Sandy Row (south of the Westlink motorway).

Murals (found in working-class, sectarian areas) are a memo-

BELFAST

rable part of any visit to Belfast. But with more peaceful times, the character of these murals is slowly changing. The Re-Imaging Communities Program has spent £3 million in government money to replace aggressive murals with positive ones. Paramilitary themes are gradually being covered over with images of pride in each neighborhood's culture. The *Titanic* was built primarily by proud Protestant Ulster stock and is often seen in their neighborhood murals—reflecting their industrious work ethic. Over in the Catholic neighborhoods, you'll see more murals depicting mythological heroes from the days before the English came.

You can get taxi tours of Falls Road or Shankill Road (see next listings), but rarely are both combined well in one tour. Ken Harper is one of a new breed of Belfast taxi drivers who will give you an insightful private tour of both neighborhoods (for contact info, see "Tours in Belfast—Local Guide," earlier).

▲▲**Falls Road (Catholic)**—At  the intersection of Castle and King Streets, you'll find the Castle Junction Car Park. On the ground floor of this nine-story parking garage, a passenger terminal (entrance on King Street) connects travelers with old black cabs—and the only Irish-language signs in downtown Belfast. These shared black cabs efficiently shuttle residents from outlying neighborhoods up and down Falls Road and to the city center. This service originated more than 40 years ago at the beginning of the Troubles, when locals would hijack city buses and use them as barricades in the street fighting. When bus service was discontinued, local paramilitary groups established the shared taxi service. Although the buses are now running again, these cab rides are still a great value for their drivers' commentary.

Any cab goes up Falls Road, past Sinn Fein headquarters and lots of murals, to the Milltown Cemetery (£6, sit in front and talk to the cabbie). Hop in and out. Easy-to-flag-down cabs run every minute or so in each direction on Falls Road.

Forty trained cabbies do one-hour tours (minimum £30, £10/person for 1.5 hours, £20/additional hour, cheap for a small group of up to 6 riders, tel. 028/9031-5777 or mobile 078-9271-6660, www.taxitrax.com).

The Sinn Fein office and bookstore are near the bottom of Falls Road. The **bookstore** is worth a look. Page through books featuring color photos of the political murals that decorated these buildings. Money raised here supports the families of deceased IRA members.

A sad, corrugated struc-
ture called the **Peace Wall**
runs a block or so north of
Falls Road (along Cupar Way),
separating the Catholics from
the Protestants in the Shankill
Road area. The first cement
wall was 20 feet high—it was
later extended another 10 feet
by a solid metal addition, and
then another 15 feet with a metal screen. Seemingly high enough
now to deter a projectile being lobbed over, this is just one of 17
such walls in Belfast.

At the **Milltown Cemetery,**
walk past all the Gaelic crosses down
to the far right-hand corner (closest
to the highway), where the IRA Roll
of Honor is set apart from the thousands of other graves by little green
railings. They are treated like fallen
soldiers. Notice the memorial to
Bobby Sands and nine other hunger
strikers. They starved themselves to
death in the nearby Maze prison in
1981, protesting for political prisoner status as opposed to terrorist
criminal treatment. Maze prison closed in the fall of 2000.

Shankill Road and Sandy Row (Protestant)—You can ride a
shared black cab through the Protestant
Shankill Road area (£30/1-2 people for
one hour, £40/3-6 people, tel. 028/9032-
8775). They depart from North Street
near the intersection with Millfield
Road; it's not well-marked, but watch
where the cabs circle and pick up locals
on the south side of the street.

An easier (and cheaper) way to get a
dose of the Unionist side is to walk Sandy
Row. From Hotel Europa, walk a block
down Glengall Street, then turn left for
a 10-minute walk along a working-class
Protestant street. A stop in a Unionist memorabilia shop, a pub, or
one of the many cheap eateries here may give you an opportunity
to talk to a local. You'll see murals filled with Unionist symbolism.
The mural of William of Orange's victory over the Catholic King
James II (Battle of the Boyne, 1690) thrills Unionist hearts.

1916

This pivotal year means vastly different things to Northern Ireland's two communities. When you say "1776" to most Americans, it means revolution and independence from tyranny (unless, perhaps, you're a Native American). But when you say "1916" to someone in Northern Ireland, the response depends on who's talking.

To Nationalists (who are usually Catholic), "1916" brings to mind the Easter Uprising—which took place in Dublin in April of that year and was the beginning of the end of 750 years of British rule for most of Ireland (see sidebar on page 78). Some Nationalist murals still use images of Dublin's rebel headquarters or martyred leaders like Patrick Pearse and James Connolly. To this community, 1916 emphasizes their proud Gaelic identity, their willingness to fight to preserve it, and their stubborn anti-British attitude.

To Unionists (who are usually Protestant), "1916" means the brutal WWI Battle

Central Belfast

▲▲City Hall—This grand structure's 173-foot-tall copper dome dominates the town center. Built between 1898 and 1906, with its statue of Queen Victoria scowling down Belfast's main drag and the Union Jack flapping behind her, the City Hall is a stirring sight. In the garden, you'll find memorials to the *Titanic* and the landing of the US Expeditionary Force in 1942—the first American troops to arrive in Europe en route to Berlin.

Take the worthwhile and free 45-minute tour, which gives you a rundown on city government and an explanation of the decor that makes this an Ulster political hall of fame. Queen Victoria and King Edward VII look down on city council meetings. The 1613 original charter of Belfast granted by James I is on display. Its Great Hall—bombed by the Germans in 1941—looks as great as it did the day it was made. If you can't manage a tour, at least step inside to admire the marble swirl staircase and the view up into the dome. A handy Bobbin coffee shop is also inside.

Cost and Hours: Free; tours Mon-Fri at 11:00, 14:00, and 15:00; Sat at 14:00 and 15:00, no tours on Sun; entrance on north

of the Somme in France, which began that July. (For more on the Somme, visit the Somme Heritage Centre in Bangor; described on page 383). Although both Catholic and Protestant soldiers died in this long and bloody battle, the first wave of young men who went over the top were the sons of proud Ulster Unionists. The Unionists hoped this sacrifice would prove their loyalty to the crown—and assurance that the British would never let them be gobbled up by an Irish Nationalist state (a possible scenario just before the Great War's outbreak). You'll see Tommies heroically climbing out of their trenches in some of Belfast's Unionist murals. For the Unionists, 1916 is synonymous with devout, almost righteously divine, Britishness.

It will be interesting to see how the people of Northern Ireland choose to celebrate the 100th anniversary of 1916... coming up in the not-so-distant future.

side of building behind Queen Victoria statue, call to check schedule and to reserve a tour, tel. 028/9032-0202, www.belfastcity.gov.uk/cityhall.

Linen Hall Library—Across the street from City Hall, the 200-year-old Linen Hall Library welcomes guests (notice the red hand above the former front door facing Donegall Square North; for more on its meaning, see the sidebar on page 372). Described as "Ulster's attic," the library takes pride in being a neutral space where anyone trying to make sense of the sectarian conflict can view the Troubled Images, a historical collection of engrossing political posters. It has a fine hardbound ambience, a coffee shop, and a royal newspaper reading room.

Cost and Hours: Free, Mon-Fri 9:30-17:30, Sat 9:30-16:00, closed Sun, entrance on Fountain Street, 17 Donegall Square North, tel. 028/9032-1707, www.linenhall.com.

Golden Mile—This is the overstated nickname of Belfast's liveliest dining and entertainment district, which stretches from the Opera House (Great Victoria Street) to the university (University Road).

The **Grand Opera House,** originally built in 1895, bombed and rebuilt in 1991, and bombed and rebuilt again in 1993, is extravagantly Victorian and *the* place to take in a concert, play, or opera (ticket office open Mon-Fri 9:30-17:30, Sat 12:00-17:00, closed Sun; ticket office to right of main front door on Great

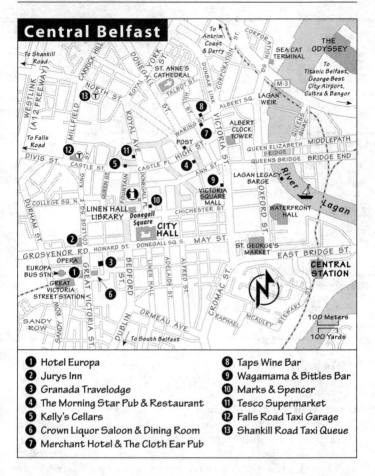

Central Belfast

To Antrim Coast & Derry
To Shankill Road
SEA CAT TERMINAL
THE ODYSSEY
To Titanic Belfast, George Best City Airport, Cultra & Bangor
CARRICK HILL
CORPORATION ST.
ST. ANNE'S CATHEDRAL
DONEGALL ST.
YORK ST.
ROYAL AVE.
NORTH ST.
DUNBAR LINK
TALBOT ST.
CORPORATION ST.
ALBERT SQ.
M-3
LAGAN WEIR
To Falls Road
WESTLINK (A12 FREEWAY)
MILLFIELD
WARING
HIGH ST.
POST
VICTORIA ST.
ALBERT CLOCK TOWER
QUEEN ELIZABETH BRIDGE
QUEENS BRIDGE
BRIDGE END
MIDDLEPATH
River Lagan
QUEENS QUAY
DIVIS ST.
CASTLE ST.
KING ST.
QUEEN ST.
FOUNTAIN
CASTLE PL.
DONEGALL PL.
ANN ST.
CHICHESTER ST.
VICTORIA SQUARE MALL
OXFORD ST.
LAGAN LEGACY BARGE
WATERFRONT HALL
COLLEGE SQ. N.
LINEN HALL LIBRARY
Donegall Square
CITY HALL
COLLEGE SQ. E.
DURHAM ST.
GROSVENOR RD.
HOWARD ST.
DONEGALL SQ. S.
MAY ST.
ST. GEORGE'S MARKET
EAST BRIDGE ST.
CENTRAL STATION
OPERA
EUROPA BUS STN.
GREAT VICTORIA STREET STATION
BEDFORD ST.
LINEN HALL
ADELAIDE ST.
ALFRED ST.
CROMAC ST.
SANDY ROW
SANDY ROW
GREAT VICTORIA ST.
DUBLIN ST.
ORMEAU AVE.
RAPHAEL
MCAULEY
STEWART ST.
To South Belfast
100 Meters
100 Yards

1 Hotel Europa
2 Jurys Inn
3 Granada Travelodge
4 The Morning Star Pub & Restaurant
5 Kelly's Cellars
6 Crown Liquor Saloon & Dining Room
7 Merchant Hotel & The Cloth Ear Pub
8 Taps Wine Bar
9 Wagamama & Bittles Bar
10 Marks & Spencer
11 Tesco Supermarket
12 Falls Road Taxi Garage
13 Shankill Road Taxi Queue

BELFAST

Victoria Street, tel. 028/9024-1919, www.goh.co.uk). The recommended **Hotel Europa,** next door, while considered to be the most-bombed hotel in the world, actually feels pretty casual (but is expensive to stay in).

Across the street is the museum-like **Crown Liquor Saloon.** Built in 1849, it's now a part of the National Trust. A wander through its mahogany, glass, and marble interior is a trip back into the days of Queen Victoria, although the privacy provided by the snugs—booths—allows for un-Victorian behavior (Mon-Sat 11:30-24:00, Sun 12:30-23:00, consider a lunch stop—see listing under "Eating in Belfast," later). Upstairs, the Crown Dining Room serves pub grub, is decorated

with historic photos, and is the starting point for a pub walk (listed earlier, under "Tours in Belfast").

Lagan Legacy—Housed in the barge M.V. Confiance, docked on the west bank of the Lagan River, this museum bridges the gap between the Ulster Museum's eclectic displays and Titanic Belfast's modern pizazz. More of a city museum for Belfast, the exhibits here were donated by locals who valued the preservation of their proud industrial and maritime heritage. A visit starts with an interesting 30-minute film giving a good overview of city history. You're then free to wander the hold of the ship, exploring interactive displays about the lives of average workers as well as models of industrial innovations like the huge Harland and Wolff cranes and Belfast-built oil rigs. The museum proclaims that the story of Belfast is "the greatest story never told."

Cost and Hours: £4, daily 10:00-16:00, coffee shop on main deck, at Lanyon Quay just south of Queen's Bridge, tel. 028/9023-2555, www.belfastbarge.com.

South Belfast

▲**Ulster Museum**—While mediocre by European standards, this is Belfast's most venerable museum. Recently renovated, it offers an earnest and occasionally thought-provoking look at a cross-section of local artifacts.

The four-floor museum is free and pretty painless. Ride the elevator to the top floor and follow the spiraling exhibits downhill through various zones. The top floor is dedicated to rotating art exhibits, the next floor down covers local nature, and the one below that focuses on history. The ground floor covers the modern Troubles, and has a coffee shop and gift shop.

The Art Zone displays a beautifully crafted Belleek vase and a you-gotta-be-kidding-me Victorian silver-gilt toilet seat. In the Nature Zone, audiovisuals trace how the Ice Age affected the local landscape. Kids will enjoy the interactive Discover History room.

The delicately worded History Zone has an interesting British slant (such as the implication that most deaths in the Great Potato Famine of 1845-1849 were caused by typhus and fever epidemics—without mentioning the starvation that made peasants susceptible to these diseases in the first place). But the coverage of the modern-day Troubles is balanced and thought-provoking.

After a peek at a pretty good mummy, top things off with the *Girona* treasure. Soggy bits of gold, silver, leather, and wood were salvaged from the Spanish Armada's shipwrecked *Girona*, lost off the Antrim Coast north of Belfast in 1588.

Cost and Hours: Free, Tue-Sun 10:00-17:00, closed Mon, in Botanic Gardens on Stranmillis Road, south of downtown, tel. 028/9044-0000, www.nmni.com.

▲**Botanic Gardens**—This is the backyard of Queen's University, and on a sunny day, you couldn't imagine a more relaxing park setting. On a cold day, step into the Tropical Ravine for a jungle of heat and humidity. Take a quick walk through the Palm House, reminiscent of the one in London's Kew Gardens but smaller. The Ulster Museum is on the garden's grounds.

Cost and Hours: Free, gardens open daily 8:00 until dusk; Palm House open Mon-Fri 10:00-12:00 & 13:00-17:00, Sat-Sun 13:00-17:00, shorter hours in winter; tel. 028/9031-4762, www.belfastcity.gov.uk/parks.

Lyric Theatre—Rebuilt in 2011, this Belfast institution represents the recent cultural rejuvenation of the city. It's located beside the Lagan River (near Queen's University) in an architecturally innovative building partially funded by donations from famous actors such as Liam Neeson, Kenneth Branagh, and Meryl Streep. While there are no public tours, it's a good place to see quality local productions (tickets-£15-25; box office open Mon-Sat 10:00-17:00, closed Sun; 55 Ridgeway Street, tel. 028/9038-1081, www.lyrictheatre.co.uk).

Near Belfast

▲▲**Ulster Folk Park and Transport Museum**—This sprawling 180-acre, two-museum complex straddles the road and rail line at Cultra, midway between Bangor and Belfast (8 miles east of town). You'll arrive (by rail or car) between the two museums at a point somewhat closer to the Transport Museum. From here, you have a choice of going downhill to the Transport Museum or uphill into the Folk Park. Assess your energy level and plan accordingly. Note that the Transport Museum is all indoors—a good bet if it's rainy. The Folk Park involves more walking between buildings spread across the upper hillside. Most people will spend an hour in the Transport Museum and a couple of hours at the Folk Park.

Cost and Hours: £6.50 for Folk Park, £6.50 for Transport Museum, £8 combo-ticket for both, £21.50 for families; March-Sept Tue-Sun 10:00-17:00; Oct-Feb Tue-Fri 10:00-16:00, Sat-Sun 11:00-16:00; closed Mon year-round; check the schedule for the day's special events, tel. 028/9042-8428, www.nmni.com. Allow three hours for your visit, and expect lots of walking. Those with a car can drive from one section to the next.

Getting There: From Belfast, you can reach Cultra by taxi (£15), bus #502 (2/hour, 30 minutes from Laganside Bus Centre), or train (£5.20 round-trip, 2/hour, 15 minutes, from any Belfast train station or from Bangor). Trains and buses stop right in the park, but train service is more dependable. Public-transport schedules are skimpy on Saturday and Sunday.

Visiting the Museums: The **Transport Museum** (downhill, over the road from the folk section) consists of three buildings.

Start at the bottom and trace the evolution of transportation from 7,500 years ago—when people first decided to load an ox—to the first vertical take-off jet. In 1909, the Belfast-based Shorts Aviation Company partnered with the Wright brothers to manufacture the

first commercially available aircraft. The middle building holds an intriguing section on the sinking of the Belfast-made *Titanic*, expanded for the 100th anniversary. The top building covers the history of bikes, cars, and trains. The car section rumbles from the first car in Ireland (an 1898 Benz) through the "Cortina Culture" of the 1960s, to the local adventures of controversial automobile designer John DeLorean and a 1981 model of his sleek sports car.

The **Folk Park,** an open-air collection of 34 reconstructed buildings from all over the nine counties of Ulster, showcases the region's traditional lifestyles. After wandering through the old-town site (church, print shop, schoolhouse, humble Belfast row house, silent movie theater, and so on), you'll head off into the country to nip into cottages, farmhouses, and mills. Most houses are warmed by a wonderful peat fire and a friendly attendant. It can be dull or vibrant, depending upon when you visit and your ability to chat with the attendants. Drop a peat brick on the fire.

Carrickfergus Castle—Built during the Norman invasion of the late 1100s, this historic castle stands sentry on the shore of Belfast Lough. William of Orange landed here in 1690, when he began his Irish campaign against deposed King James II. In 1778, the American privateer ship *Ranger* (the first ever to fly the Stars-and-

Stripes), under the command of John Paul Jones, defeated the more heavily armed HMS *Drake* just offshore. These days the castle feels a bit sanitized and geared for kids, but it's an easy excursion if you're seeking a castle experience near the city.

BELFAST

Cost and Hours: £5; April-Sept Mon-Sat 10:00-18:00, Sun 12:00-18:00; Oct-March Mon-Sat 10:00-16:00, Sun 14:00-16:00; last entry 30 minutes before closing, tel. 028/9335-1273.

Getting There: It's a 20-minute train ride from Belfast (on the line to Larne, £3.90 round-trip after 9:30, £6 before 9:30). Turn left as you exit the train station and walk straight downhill for five minutes—all the way to the waterfront—passing under the arch of the old town wall en route. You'll find the castle on your right.

The Red Hand of Ulster

All over Belfast, you'll notice a curious symbol: a red hand facing you as if swearing a pledge or telling you to halt. You'll spot it, faded, above the Linen Hall Library door, in the wrought-iron fences of the Merchant Hotel, on old-fashioned clothes wringers (in the Ulster Folk Park and Transport Museum at Cultra), above the front door of a bank in Bangor, in the shape of a flowerbed at Mount Stewart House, in Loyalist paramilitary murals, on shield emblems in the gates of Republican memorials, and even on the flag of Northern Ireland (the white flag with the red cross of St. George). It's known as the Red Hand of Ulster—and it seems to pop up everywhere. Although it's more often associated with Unionist traditions, it's one of the few emblems used by both communities in Northern Ireland.

Nationalists display a red-hand-on-a-yellow-shield as a symbol of the ancient province of Ulster. It was the official crest of the once-dominant O'Neill clan (who fought tooth and nail against English rule) and today signifies resistance to British rule in these communities.

But you'll more often see the red hand in Unionist areas. They see it as a potent symbol of the political entity of Northern Ireland. The Ulster Volunteer Force chose it for their symbol in 1913 and embedded it in the center of the Northern Irish flag upon partition of the island in 1921. You may see the red hand clenched as a fist in Loyalist murals. One Loyalist paramilitary group even named itself the Red Hand Commandos.

The origin of the red hand comes from a mythological tale of two rival clans that raced by boat to claim a far shore. The first clan leader to touch the shore would win it for his people. Everyone aboard both vessels strained mightily at their oars, near exhaustion as they approached the shore. Finally, in desperation, the chieftain leader of the slower boat whipped out his sword and lopped off his right hand...which he then flung onto the shore, thus winning the coveted land. Moral of the story? The fearless folk of Ulster will do *whatever* it takes to get the job done.

Sleeping in Belfast

Belfast is more of a business town than a tourist town, so business-class room rates are lower or soft on weekends (best prices booked from their websites).

In Central Belfast

To locate these hotels, see the map on page 368.

$$$ Hotel Europa is Belfast's landmark hotel—fancy, comfortable, and central—with four stars and good weekend rates. Modern yet elegant, this place was Bill Clinton's choice when he visited (Db-£90-120 plus £16 breakfast, President Clinton's suite-£400, Great Victoria Street, tel. 028/9027-1066, fax 028/9026-6099, www.hastingshotels.com, res@eur.hastingshotels.com).

$$ Jurys Inn, an American-style place that rents 190 identical modern rooms, is perfectly located two blocks from City Hall (up to 3 adults or 2 adults and 2 kids for £65-110, price varies based on season and weekend rates, breakfast-£8.50/person, Fisherwick Place, tel. 028/9053-3500, fax 028/9053-3511, www.jurysinns. com, jurysinnbelfast@jurysinns.com).

$$ Granada Travelodge, quiet and extremely central, is a basic Jurys-style business hotel with 90 cookie-cutter rooms that are high on value but low on character (Db-£59-109, a block from Hotel Europa and City Hall at 15 Brunswick Street, tel. 028/9033-3555, fax 028/9023-2999, www.travelodge.ie, belfast@travelodge. ie).

South of Queen's University

Many of Belfast's best budget beds cluster in a comfortable, leafy neighborhood of row houses just south of Queen's University (near the Ulster Museum). Two train stations (Botanic and Adelaide) are nearby, and buses (£1.60) zip down Malone Road every 20 minutes. Any bus on Malone Road goes to Donegall Square East. Taxis take you downtown for about £6 (your host can call one).

$$$ Malone Lodge Hotel, by far the classiest listing in this neighborhood, provides slick, business-class comfort in 92 spacious rooms on a quiet street (Sb-£79-135, Db-£95-150, superior Db-£115-155, mid-week deals, elevator, Wi-Fi, restaurant, parking, 60 Eglantine Avenue, tel. 028/9038-8000, fax 028/9038-8088, www. malonelodgehotelbelfast.com, info@malonelodgehotel.com).

$$ Wellington Park Hotel is a dependable, if unimaginative, chain-style hotel with 75 rooms. It's predictable but in a good location (Db-£65-99, Wi-Fi, parking-£5/day, 21 Malone Road, tel. 028/9038-1111, fax 028/9066-5410, www.wellingtonparkhotel. com, info@wellingtonparkhotel.com).

$$ Camera Guest House rents nine smoke-free rooms and

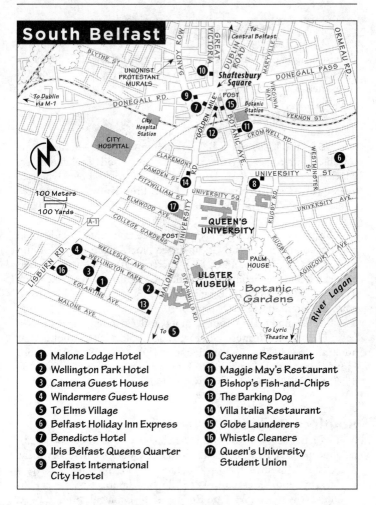

South Belfast

1 Malone Lodge Hotel
2 Wellington Park Hotel
3 Camera Guest House
4 Windermere Guest House
5 To Elms Village
6 Belfast Holiday Inn Express
7 Benedicts Hotel
8 Ibis Belfast Queens Quarter
9 Belfast International
  City Hostel

10 Cayenne Restaurant
11 Maggie May's Restaurant
12 Bishop's Fish-and-Chips
13 The Barking Dog
14 Villa Italia Restaurant
15 Globe Launderers
16 Whistle Cleaners
17 Queen's University
   Student Union

has an airy, hardwood feeling throughout (S-£34, Sb-£48, Db-£62, family room-£78, 44 Wellington Park, tel. 028/9066-0026, mobile 075/4501-7140, www.cameraguesthouse.com, camera_gh@hotmail.com, Miriam and Danny Nash).

$ Windermere Guest House has 11 basic rooms, including several small-but-pleasant singles, in a large Victorian house (S-£34, Sb-£45, D-£58, Db-£65, cash only, 60 Wellington Park, tel. 028/9066-2693, www.windermereguesthouse.co.uk, windermereguesthouse@gmail.com).

$ Elms Village, a huge Queen's University dorm complex, rents 100 basic, institutional rooms (mostly singles, with a few doubles) to travelers during summer break (mid-June-early-Sept only, Sb-£39, Db-£54, includes breakfast, coin-op laundry, self-serve

Sleep Code

(£1 = about $1.60; country code: 44, area code: 028)
To call Belfast from the Republic of Ireland, dial 048 before the local 8-digit number.
S = Single, **D** = Double/Twin, **T** = Triple, **Q** = Quad, **b** = bathroom, **s** = shower only. Unless otherwise noted, breakfast is included and credit cards are accepted.

To help you easily sort through these listings, I've divided the rooms into three categories, based on the price for a double room with bath:

$$$ **Higher Priced**—Most rooms £90 or more.
$$ **Moderately Priced**—Most rooms between £60-90.
$ **Lower Priced**—Most rooms £60 or less.

Prices can change without notice; verify the hotel's current rates online or by email.

kitchen; reception building is 50 yards down entry street, marked *Elms Village* on low brick wall, 78 Malone Road; tel. 028/9097-4525, www.stayatqueens.com, accommodation@qub.ac.uk).

Between Queen's University and Shaftesbury Square

$$ Belfast Holiday Inn Express is a 10-minute walk east of Queen's University. Even though it's not as central as other hotels, its 114 refurbished rooms offer a good value (Db-£69-79, better deals online, kids free, elevator, by Botanic Station at 106A University Street, parking, tel. 028/9031-1909, fax 028/9031-1910, www.exhi-belfast.com, mail@exhi-belfast.com).

$$ Benedicts Hotel has 32 rooms in a good location at the northern fringe of the Queen's University district. Its popular bar is a maze of polished wood and can be loud on weekend nights (Sb-£50-70, Db-£69-80, elevator, 7-21 Bradbury Place, tel. 028/9059-1999, fax 028/9059-1990, www.benedictshotel.co.uk, info@benedictshotel.co.uk).

$$ Ibis Belfast Queens Quarter, part of a major European hotel chain, has 56 practical rooms in a convenient location. It's a great deal if you're not looking for cozy character (Db-£55-70, better deals online, breakfast-£7, elevator, a block north of Queen's University at 75 University Street, tel. 028/9033-3366, fax 028/9033-3399, www.ibishotel.com).

$ Belfast International City Hostel is big, creatively run, and provides the best value among Belfast's hostels. It has 200 beds in single and double rooms along with dorms, and is located near Botanic Station, in the heart of the lively university district. Features include free lockers, elevator, baggage storage, pay Internet access and Wi-Fi, kitchen, self-serve laundry (£4), a cheap breakfast-only cafeteria, 24-hour reception, and no curfew (bed in 6-bed dorm-£10.50, bed in quad-£12, S-£22, Db-£38, 22-32 Donegall Road, tel. 028/9031-5435, fax 028/9043-9699, www.hini.org.uk, info@hini.org.uk). Paul, the manager of the hostel, is a veritable TI, with a passion for his work. The hostel is the starting point for **McComb's** minibus tours (described earlier, under "Tours in Belfast").

Eating in Belfast

Downtown

If it's £12 pub grub you want, consider these drinking holes with varied atmospheres. For locations, see the map on page 368.

The Morning Star is woody and elegant (£9-15 restaurant dinners upstairs, £5.50 buffet Mon-Sat 12:00-16:00; open Mon-Sat 12:00-22:00, closed Sun; down alley just off High Street at 17 Pottinger's Entry, alley entry is roughly opposite the post office, tel. 028/9023-5986).

Kelly's Cellars—once a rebel hangout (see plaque above door)—still has a very gritty Irish feel. It's 300 years old and hard to find, but worth it. The pub grub is basic, but the atmosphere is delicious (Mon-Sat 11:30-24:30, Sun 13:00-23:30; live traditional music Tue-Fri and Sun at 21:30, Sat at 16:30; 32 Bank Street, 100 yards behind Tesco supermarket, access via alley on left side when facing Tesco, tel. 028/9024-6058).

Crown Liquor Saloon, a recommended stop along the Golden Mile, is small and antique. Its mesmerizing mishmash of mosaics and shareable snugs—booths—are topped with a smoky tin ceiling (Mon-Sat lunch only 11:30-15:00, Sun 12:30-16:00, 46 Great Victoria Street, across from Hotel Europa, tel. 028/9024-3187). The **Crown Dining Room** upstairs offers dependable £9-13 meals (daily 12:00-21:00, tel. 028/9024-3187, use entry on Amelia Street when the Crown Liquor Saloon is closed).

Supermarkets: **Marks & Spencer** has a coffee shop serving skinny lattes and a supermarket in its basement (Mon-Fri 9:00-19:00, Thu until 21:00, Sat 8:30-18:00, Sun 13:00-18:00, WCs on

second floor, Donegall Place, a block north of Donegall Square).
Tesco, another supermarket, is a block north of Marks & Spencer
and two blocks north of Donegall Square (Mon-Sat 8:00-19:00,
Thu until 21:00, Sun 13:00-18:00, Royal Avenue and Bank Street).
Picnic on the City Hall lawn.

On Waring Street, in the Cathedral Quarter

I like the cluster of culture surrounding the Cotton Court section
of Waring Street. It's about a 10-minute walk northeast of the City
Hall. For locations, see the map on page 368.

Check out the lobby of **Merchant Hotel** (a grand former
bank) for a glimpse of crushed-velvet Victorian splendor under an
opulent dome, and consider indulging Belfast's best afternoon tea
splurge. Don't show up in shorts and sneakers (£19.50 tea, Mon-
Fri 12:00-16:30, Sat-Sun reserve ahead for two seatings: 12:30 or
15:00, 35-39 Waring Street, tel. 028/9023-4888).

Taps Wine Bar is a whiff of Mediterranean warmth in this
cold brick city. Try a cheerful tapas or paella meal washed down
with sangria (May-Sept daily 12:00-22:00, Oct-April closed Sun-
Mon, 42 Waring Street, tel. 028/9031-1414).

The Cloth Ear is a friendly, modern bar serving better-than-
average pub grub from the kitchen of the posh Merchant Hotel
next door (Mon-Sat 12:30-21:00, Sun 13:00-19:00, 33 Waring
Street, tel. 028/9026-2719).

Victoria Square Area

Although Victoria Square is a big glitzy mall, a couple of eating
options are worth considering—one inside the mall and one next
door. For locations, see the map on page 368.

Wagamama is a Japanese noodle bar, located on the first floor
of the Victoria Square Mall. Hearty portions of chicken ramen,
yakisoba, and cumin beef salad are menu highlights (daily 12:00-
21:00, Victoria Square, tel. 028/9023-6098).

Bittles Bar is a tiny, wedge-shaped throwback to Victorian
days, hidden in the shadows on the east side of the mall. The
minuscule interior is decorated with caricatures of literary figures, with good pub grub served in a friendly atmosphere (daily
12:00-22:00, 70 Upper Church Lane just off Victoria Street, tel.
028/9031-1088).

Near Shaftesbury Square and Botanic Station

Nearby Queen's University gives this neighborhood an energetic
feel, with a mixed bag of dining options ranging from cosmopolitan to deep-fried. For locations, see the map on page 374.

Cayenne is a trendy-yet-friendly restaurant refuge hiding
behind Belfast's most understated exterior. It's your best bet for

gourmet food—innovative global cuisine—without a snobby attitude. Owner Paul Rankin stars in the *Ready Steady Cook* TV show on the BBC (£15-22 meals, £17 three-course lunch; great £19.50 three-course early-bird dinner special before 18:45; open daily for dinner 17:00-late, also open for lunch Thu-Fri 12:00-14:15 and Sun 12:00-16:00; reservations a good idea on weekends; Shaftesbury Square at 7 Ascot House—look for plain, gray, blocky slab front; tel. 028/9033-1532).

Maggie May's serves hearty, simple, cheap £8-12 meals (Mon-Sat 8:00-22:30, Sun 10:00-22:30, one block south of Botanic Station at 50 Botanic Avenue, tel. 028/9032-2662).

Bishop's is the locals' choice for fish-and-chips (daily 12:00-23:30, pasta and veggie options, classier side has table service, just south of Shaftesbury Square at Bradbury Place, tel. 028/9043-9070).

South of Queen's University

For locations, see the map on page 374.

The Barking Dog is closest to my cluster of B&B listings in this area. It's a hip grill serving tasty, beefy burgers, duck, scallops, and other filling fare. If the weather's fine, the outdoor tree-shaded front tables are ideal for people-watching (£6-9 lunches, £10-15 dinners, Mon-Sat 12:00-15:30 & 17:30-22:00, Sun 12:00-21:00, near corner of Eglantine Avenue at 33-35 Malone Road, tel. 028/9066-1885).

Villa Italia packs in crowds hungry for linguini and *bistecca*. With its checkered tablecloths and a wood-beamed ceiling draped with grape leaves, it's a little bit of Italy in Belfast (£9-15 meals, Mon-Fri 17:00-23:00, Sat-Sun 16:00-23:00, 3 long blocks south of Shaftesbury Square, at intersection with University Street, 39 University Road, tel. 028/9032-8356).

Belfast Connections

For updated schedules and prices for both trains and buses in Northern Ireland, check with Translink (tel. 028/9066-6630, www.translink.co.uk). Consider a Zone 4 iLink smartcard, good for all-day train and bus use in Northern Ireland (see page 358). Service is less frequent on Sundays.

From Belfast by Train to: Dublin (8/day Mon-Sat, 5/day Sun, 2 hours), **Derry** (9/day, 2.5 hours), **Larne** (hourly, 1 hour), **Portrush** (11/day, 5/day Sun, 2 hours, transfer in Coleraine), **Bangor** (2/hour, 30 minutes).

By Bus to: Portrush (12/day, 2 hours, £8; scenic-coast route, 2.5 hours), **Derry** (hourly, 1.75 hours), **Dublin** (hourly, most via Dublin Airport, 2.75-3 hours), **Galway** (hourly, 7 hours, change in

Dublin), **Glasgow** (3/day, 5.75 hours), **Edinburgh** (3/day, 7 hours). The Europa Bus Centre is behind Hotel Europa (Ulsterbus tel. 028/9033-7003 for destinations in Scotland and England).

By Plane: Belfast has two airports. **George Best Belfast City Airport** (airport code: BHD, tel. 028/9093-9093, www.belfast cityairport.com) is a five-minute taxi ride from town (near the docks), while **Belfast International Airport** (airport code: BFS, tel. 028/9448-4848, www.belfastairport.com) is 18 miles west of town, connected by buses from the Europa Bus Centre behind the Europa Hotel. There are cheap flights to **Glasgow,** Scotland, on easyJet (www.easyjet.com) and Flybe (www.flybe.com).

By Ferry to Scotland: There are a number of options, ports, and companies. You can sail between Belfast and **Stranraer** on the Stena Line ferry (4-6/day, 2-3.25 hours, £28, tel. 028/9074-7747, www.stenaline.co.uk). The P&O Ferry (toll tel. 0870-2424-777, www.poferries.com) goes from **Larne** (20 miles north of Belfast, hourly trains, 1-hour trip, TI tel. 028/2826-0088) to **Cairnryan** (10/day, 1 hour) or to **Troon** (2/day, 2 hours).

By Ferry to England: You can sail from Belfast to **Liverpool** (generally 2/day, 8 hours, prices vary widely, arrives in port of Birkenhead—10 minutes from Liverpool, tel. 028/9074-7747, www.stenaline.co.uk).

Bangor

To stay in a laid-back seaside hometown—with more comfort per pound—sleep 12 miles east of Belfast in Bangor (BANG-grr). It's a handy alternative for travelers who find Belfast booked up by oc-

casional conventions and conferences. Formerly a Victorian resort and seaside escape from the big city nearby, Bangor now has a sleepy residential feeling. With elegant old homes facing its spruced-up harbor and not even a hint of big-city Belfast, Bangor has appeal. The harbor is a 10-minute walk from the train station.

To visit two worthwhile sights near Bangor—the Somme Heritage Centre and Mount Stewart House—consider renting a car for the day from Enterprise in Bangor (10 Enterprise Road, tel. 028/9146-1616, www.enterprise.co.uk). You can also rent cars from nearby George Best Belfast City Airport, a 15-minute train trip from Bangor.

BELFAST

Getting There

Catch the train to Bangor from either Belfast's Central or Great Victoria Street stations; both on the same line (2/hour, 30 minutes, go to the end of the line—don't get off at Bangor West). Before 9:30, it costs £8.10 round-trip (but after 9:30, it's only £5.40 round-trip). Consider stopping en route at Cultra (Ulster Folk Park and Transport Museum; see page 370). The journey gives you a good close-up look at the giant Belfast harbor cranes.

If day-tripping into Belfast from Bangor, get off at Central Station (free shuttle bus to the town center, 4/hour, none on Sun; some trains may also stop at the more convenient Great Victoria Street Station), or stay on until Botanic Station for the Ulster Museum, the Golden Mile, and Sandy Row.

Orientation to Bangor

Bangor's **TI** is on the harborfront at 34 Quay Street (Mon-Fri 9:00-17:00, Sat 10:00-17:00, Sun 13:00-17:00 except closed Sun Sept-April, tel. 028/9127-0069, www.northdowntourism.com). You'll find **Speediwash Launderette** at 96 Abbey Street, a couple of blocks south of the train station (Mon-Fri 9:00-18:00, Sat 9:00-17:00, closed Sun, tel. 028/9127-0074). You can get free Internet access at the **library** on Hamilton Road (30-minute limit). **Bangor Cabs** provides local taxi service (tel. 028/9145-6456).

Sights in Bangor

For sightseeing, your time is better spent in Belfast. But if you have time to burn in Bangor, enjoy a walk next to the water on the **Coastal Path,** which leads west out of town from the marina. A couple of miles walk along the water leads you to Crawfordsburn Country Park. Here you'll find Grey Point Fort, with its WWI artillery bunkers guarding the shore.

For a shorter walk with views of the marina, head to the end of the **North Pier,** where you'll find a mosaic honoring the D-Day fleet that rendezvoused offshore in 1944, far from Nazi reconnaissance aircraft. Keep an eye out in the marina for Rose the seal. Little kids may enjoy the **Pickie Fun Park** next to the marina, with paddle-boat swan rides and miniature golf.

The **North Down Museum** covers local history, from monastic days to Viking raids to Victorian splendor. It's hidden on the grassy grounds behind the City Hall, uphill and opposite from the train station (free, Tue-Sat 10:00-16:30, Sun 14:00-16:30, closed Mon, tel. 028/9127-1200).

BELFAST

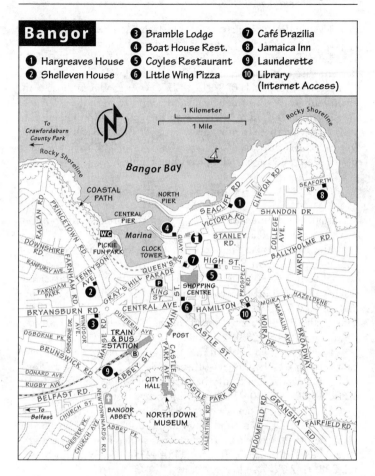

Bangor	❸ Bramble Lodge	❼ Café Brazilia
	❹ Boat House Rest.	❽ Jamaica Inn
❶ Hargreaves House	❺ Coyles Restaurant	❾ Launderette
❷ Shelleven House	❻ Little Wing Pizza	❿ Library (Internet Access)

Sleeping in Bangor

(£1 = about $1.60, country code: 44, area code: 028)

Visitors arriving in Bangor (by train) come down Main Street to reach the harbor marina. You'll find my first listing to the right, along the waterfront east of the marina on Seacliff Road. The other two listings are to the left, just uphill and west of the marina.

$$ Hargreaves House, a homey Victorian waterfront refuge, is Bangor's best value and has three cozy rooms (S-£45, Sb-£50, Db-£65, large Db-£85, 10 percent discount with cash and 2-night stay—only with 2013 edition of this book in hand upon arrival, on-line discounts, Wi-Fi, 15-minute walk from train station but worth it, 78 Seacliff Road, tel. 028/9146-4071, mobile 079-8058-5047, www.hargreaveshouse.com, info@hargreaveshouse.com, Pauline Mendez).

$$ Shelleven House is an old-fashioned, well-kept, stately place with 11 prim rooms on the quiet corner of Princetown Road and Tennyson Avenue (Sb-£40-45, Db-£70-85, Tb-£95, 10 percent discount with cash and 2-night stay, Wi-Fi, parking, 61 Princetown Road, tel. 028/9127-1777, www.shellevenhouse.com, shellevenhouse@aol.com, Mary and Philip Weston).

$ Bramble Lodge is closest to the train station (10-minute walk), offering three inviting and spotless rooms (Sb-£40, Db-£65, Wi-Fi, 1 Bryansburn Road, tel. 028/9145-7924, jacquihanna_bramblelodge@yahoo.co.uk, Jacquiline Hanna).

Eating in Bangor

Habitually late diners should be aware that most restaurants in town close at 21:00 and stop seating at about 20:30.

The **Boat House** is a stout stone structure hiding the finest dining experience in Bangor. It's run by two Dutch brothers who specialize in some of the freshest fish dishes in Northern Ireland. Their £18 early-bird two-course meal or £21.50 three-course special, offered before 19:30, are great values (Mon-Sat 12:00-21:00, Sun 12:00-20:00, reserve ahead, on Sea Cliff Road opposite the TI, tel. 028/9146-9253).

Coyles has two floors of fun. Upstairs is a classy, jazzy restaurant serving £11-17 dinners (Tue-Sun 17:00-21:00, closed Mon), while downstairs is a comfy bar with dependable pub grub (daily 12:00-15:00 & 17:00-21:00, 44 High Street, tel. 028/9127-0362).

Little Wing Pizza is a friendly joint serving tasty pizza, pasta, and salads. Grab your food to go and munch by the marina. It's also one of the few places in town that serves food later at night (Sun-Wed 11:00-22:00, Thu-Sat 11:00-23:00, 37-39 Main Street, tel. 028/9147-2777).

Café Brazilia, a popular locals' hangout at lunch, is across from the stubby clock tower (Mon-Fri 8:30-20:30, Sat 8:30-16:30, closed Sun, 13 Bridge Street, tel. 028/9127-2763).

The **Jamaica Inn** offers pleasant pub grub with a breezy waterfront porch (food served from about 12:00-21:00, 10-minute walk east of the TI on Seacliff Road, 188 Seacliff Road, tel. 028/9147-1610).

Near Bangor

The eastern fringe of Northern Ireland is populated mostly by people who consider themselves true-blue British citizens with a history of loyalty to the crown that goes back more than 400 years. Two sights within reach by car from Bangor highlight this area's firm roots in British culture: the Somme Heritage Centre and Mount Stewart House.

Getting There

Patchy bus service (bus #6) can be used to reach these sights from Bangor (check schedule with Bangor TI first). I'd rent a car instead. Enterprise Rent-A-Car has a handy outlet in Bangor (10 Enterprise Road, tel. 028/9146-1616, www.enterprise.co.uk). You can also rent cars from nearby George Best Belfast City Airport (described on page 379), which is only 15 minutes by train from Bangor or 10 minutes from Central Station. Because the airport is east of Belfast, your drive to these rural sights skips the headache of urban Belfast. Call ahead to confirm sight opening hours.

Sights near Bangor

Somme Heritage Centre

World War I's trench warfare was a meat grinder. More British soldiers died in the last year of the war than in all of World War II. Northern Ireland's men were not spared—especially during the bloody Battle of the Somme in France, starting in July 1916 (see the "1916" sidebar, earlier). Among the Allied forces was the British Army's 36th Ulster Division, which drew heavily from this loyal heartland of Northern Ireland. The 36th Ulster Division suffered brutal losses at the Battle of the Somme—of the 760 men recruited from the Shankill Road area in Belfast, only 10 percent survived.

Exhibits portray the battle experience through a mix of military artifacts, photos, historical newsreels, and life-size figures posed in trench warfare re-creations. To access the majority of the exhibits, it's essential to take the one-hour guided tour (leaving hourly, on the hour). Visiting this place is a moving experience, but it can only hint at the horrific conditions endured by these soldiers.

Cost and Hours: £5; July-Aug Mon-Fri 10:00-17:00, Sat-Sun 12:00-17:00; April-June and Sept Mon-Thu 10:00-16:00, Sat 12:00-16:00, closed Fri and Sun; Oct-March Mon-Thu 10:00-16:00, closed Fri-Sun; 3 miles south of Bangor just off A-21 at 233 Bangor Road, tel. 028/9182-3202, www.irishsoldier.org. A coffee shop is located at the center.

Mount Stewart House

No manor house in Ireland better illuminates the affluent lifestyle of the Protestant ascendancy than this lush estate. After the defeat of James II (the last Catholic king of England) at the Battle of the Boyne in 1690, the Protestant monarchy was in

BELFAST

control—and the privileged status of landowners of the same faith was assured. In the 1700s, Ireland's many Catholic rebellions seemed finally to be squashed, so Anglican landlords felt safe flaunting their wealth in manor houses surrounded by utterly perfect gardens. The Mount Stewart House in particular was designed to dazzle.

Cost and Hours: £7.40 for house and gardens, £5.60 for gardens only; July-Aug daily 12:00-18:00; May-June and Sept Wed-Mon 13:00-18:00, closed Tue; April and Oct Thu-Sun 12:00-18:00, closed Mon-Wed; March Sat-Sun 12:00-18:00, closed weekdays; closed Nov-Feb; 8 miles south of Bangor, just off A-20 beside Strangford Lough, tel. 028/4278-8387, www.nationaltrust.org.uk.

Visiting the House: Hourly tours give you a glimpse of the cushy life led by the Marquess of Londonderry and his heirs over the past three centuries. The main entry hall is a stunner, with a black-and-white checkerboard tile floor, marble columns, classical statues, and pink walls supporting a balcony with a domed ceiling and a fine chandelier. In the dining room, you'll see the original seats occupied by the rears of European heads of state, brought back from the Congress of Vienna after Napoleon's 1815 defeat. A huge painting of Hambletonian, a prize-winning racehorse, hangs above the grand staircase, dwarfing a portrait of the Duke of Wellington in a hall nearby. The heroic duke (worried that his Irish birth would be seen as lower class by British blue-bloods) once quipped in Parliament, "Just because one is born in a stable does not make him a horse." Irish emancipator Daniel O'Connell retorted, "Yes, but it could make you an ass."

Afterwards, wander the expansive manicured gardens. The fantasy life of parasol-toting, upper-crust Victorian society seems to ooze from every viewpoint. Fanciful sculptures of extinct dodo birds and monkeys holding vases on their heads set off predictably classic Italian and Spanish sections. An Irish harp has been trimmed out of a hedge a few feet from a flowerbed shaped like the Red Hand of Ulster. Swans glide serenely among the lily pads on a small lake.

PORTRUSH and the ANTRIM COAST

The Antrim Coast—the north of Northern Ireland—is one of the most interesting and scenic coastlines in Ireland. Portrush, at the end of the train line, is an ideal base for exploring the highlights of the Antrim Coast. Within a few miles of the train terminal, you can visit evocative castle ruins, tour the world's oldest whiskey distillery, catch a thrill on a bouncy rope bridge, and hike along the famous Giant's Causeway.

Planning Your Time

You need a full day to explore the Antrim Coast, so allow two nights in Portrush. An ideal day could lace together Dunluce Castle, Old Bushmills Distillery, and the Giant's Causeway, followed by nine holes on the Portrush pitch-and-putt course. In summer months, the long days this far north extend your sightseeing time (and most golf courses stay open until dusk).

Getting Around the Antrim Coast

By Car: A car is the best way to explore the charms of the Antrim coast. Distances are short and parking is easy. If time allows, don't miss the slower-but-scenic coastal route down to the Glens of Antrim.

By Bus: From June through September, an all-day bus pass helps you get around the region economically. The £6 **Causeway Rambler** links Portrush to Old Bushmills Distillery, the Giant's Causeway, and the Carrick-a-Rede Rope Bridge hourly (operates roughly 10:00-17:30). The bus journey from Portrush to Carrick-a-Rede takes 45 minutes. Pick up a Rambler bus schedule at the TI, and buy the ticket from the driver (in Portrush, the Rambler stops at Dunluce Avenue, next to public WC, a 2-minute walk from TI). For more info, call Translink (tel. 028/9066-6630, www.translink. co.uk).

By Bus Tour: If you're based in Belfast, you can visit most of the sights on the Antrim Coast with a **McComb's** tour (see page 359). Those based in Derry can get to the Giant's Causeway on a **Top Tours** tour (see page 408).

By Taxi: Groups (up to four) can reasonably visit most sights (except the more distant Carrick-a-Rede) by taxi. One-way from Portrush, it's roughly £6 to Dunluce Castle, about £8 to Old Bushmills Distillery, and about £10 to the Giant's Causeway. Try Andy Brown's Taxi (tel. 028/7082-2223), Hugh's Taxi (mobile 077-0298-6110), or North West Taxi (tel. 028/7082-4446).

Portrush

Homey Portrush used to be known as "the Brighton of the North." It first became a resort in the late 1800s, as railroads expanded to offer the new middle class a weekend by the shore. Victorian society believed that swimming in salt water would cure many common ailments.

This is County Antrim, the Bible Belt of Northern Ireland. When a large supermarket chain decided to stay open on Sundays, a local reverend called for a boycott of the store for not honoring the Sabbath. His words were taken seriously enough to rate an article in the newspaper.

While it's seen its best days, Portrush retains the atmosphere and architecture of a genteel seaside resort. Its peninsula is filled with lowbrow, family-oriented amusements, fun eateries, and B&Bs. Summertime fun-seekers promenade along the tiny harbor and tumble down to the sandy beaches, which extend in sweeping white crescents on either side.

Superficially, Portrush has the appearance of any small British seaside resort, but its history and large population of young people (students from the University of Ulster at Coleraine) give the town a little more personality. Along with the usual arcade amusements, there are nightclubs, restaurants, summer theater productions (July-Aug) in the town hall, and convivial pubs that attract customers all the way from Belfast.

Orientation to Portrush

Portrush's pleasant and easily walkable town center features sea views in every direction. On one side are the harbor and most of the restaurants, and on the other are Victorian townhouses and vast, salty vistas. The tip of the peninsula is filled with tennis courts, lawn-bowling greens, putting greens, and a park.

The town is busy with students during the school year. July and August are beach-resort boom time. June and September are laid-back and lazy. Families pack Portrush on Saturdays, and revelers from Belfast crowd its hotels on Saturday nights.

Tourist Information

The TI, more generous and helpful than those in the Republic, is in the modern Dunluce Centre, with a fake lighthouse sprouting from its roof (July-Aug daily 9:00-19:00; April-June and Sept Mon-Fri 9:00-17:00, Sat-Sun 12:00-17:00; March and Oct Sat-Sun 12:00-17:00, closed Mon-Fri; closed Nov-Feb; tel. 028/7082-3333). Get the Collins Northern Ireland road map (£4), the free *Visitor Attractions* brochure, and a free Belfast map if you're Belfast-bound.

Arrival in Portrush

The train tracks stop at the base of the tiny peninsula that Portrush fills (no baggage storage at station). The TI is three long blocks from the train station (follow signs down Eglinton Street and turn left at the fire station). All of my listed B&Bs are within a 10-minute walk of the train station. The bus stop is two blocks from the train station.

Helpful Hints

Crowds: Over a four-day weekend in late May, thousands of die-hard motorcycle fans converge on Portrush, Port Stewart, and Coleraine to watch the **Northwest 200 Race.** Fearless racers scorch the roads at 200 miles per hour on the longest straightaway in motorsports. Accommodations fill up a year ahead, and traffic is the pits (dates and details at www.northwest200.org).

Phone Tips: To call the Republic of Ireland from Northern Ireland, dial 00-353, then the area code without its initial 0, and finally the local number. To call Northern Ireland from the Republic of Ireland, dial 048, and then the local eight-digit number.

Internet Access: Ground Espresso Bar has coin-op machines with fast connections (£1/20 minutes, daily June-Aug 8:30-22:00, Sept-May 8:30-18:00, 52 Main Street, tel. 028/7082-5979).

Laundry: Viking Launderette charges £9/load for full service

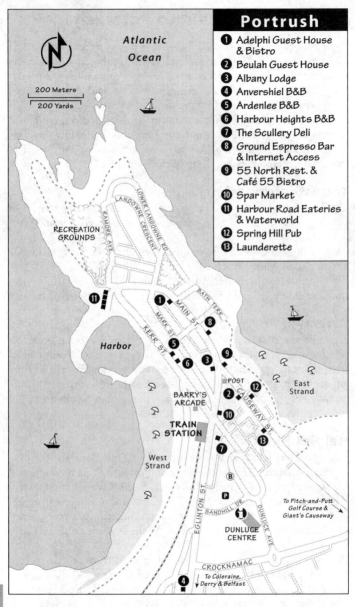

Portrush

1. Adelphi Guest House & Bistro
2. Beulah Guest House
3. Albany Lodge
4. Anvershiel B&B
5. Ardenlee B&B
6. Harbour Heights B&B
7. The Scullery Deli
8. Ground Espresso Bar & Internet Access
9. 55 North Rest. & Café 55 Bistro
10. Spar Market
11. Harbour Road Eateries & Waterworld
12. Spring Hill Pub
13. Launderette

Atlantic Ocean

200 Meters
200 Yards

RECREATION GROUNDS

LANDOWNE RD.
RAMORE AVE.
LOWER LANDOWNE CRESCENT
BATH TERR.
MAIN ST.
MARK ST.
KERR ST.

Harbor

POST

BARRY'S ARCADE

TRAIN STATION

CAUSEWAY ST.

East Strand

West Strand

EGLINTON ST.

B

P

i

SANDHILL DR.

DUNLUCE AVE.

DUNLUCE CENTRE

To Pitch-and-Putt Golf Course & Giant's Causeway

CROCKNAMAC

To Coleraine, Derry & Belfast

PORTRUSH

(Mon-Tue and Thu-Fri 9:00-13:00 & 14:00-17:30, Sat 9:00-13:00, closed Sun and Wed, 68 Causeway Street, tel. 028/7082-2060).

Bike Rental: The recommended **Harbour Heights B&B** rents sturdy new mountain bikes for £12/day, a great way to experience the gorgeous Antrim Coast (see listing under "Sleeping in Portrush," later).

Sights in Portrush

Barry's Old Time Amusement Arcade—This is a fine chance to see Northern Ireland at play (open weekends and summer only). Located just below the train station on the harbor, it's filled with "candy floss" (cotton candy) stands and little kids learning the art of one-armed bandits, 10p at a time. Get £1 worth of 10p coins from the machine and go wild, or brave the roller coaster and bumper cars (July-mid-Sept daily 12:30-22:30; May-June Mon-Fri 10:00-18:00, Sat 12:30-22:30, Sun 12:30-21:30; closed mid-Sept-April, tel. 028/7082-2340).

Pitch-and-Putt at the Royal Portrush Golf Course—Irish courses, like those in Scotland, are highly sought after for their lush but dry greens in glorious settings. Serious golfers can get a tee time at the Royal Portrush, occasional home of the Senior British Open (greens fees Mon-Fri-£140, Sat-Sun-£160). Those on a budget can play the adjacent, slightly shorter Valley Course (greens fees Mon-Fri-£37.50, Sat-Sun-£45). Meanwhile, rookies can get a wee dose of this wonderful golf setting at the neighboring Skerry 9 Hole Links pitch-and-putt range. You get two clubs and balls for £6, and they don't care if you go around twice (daily 8:30-19:00, 10-minute walk from station, tel. 028/7082-2311).

Portrush Recreation Grounds—For some easygoing exercise right in town, this well-organized park offers lawn-bowling greens (£4.70/hour with gear), putting greens, tennis courts, a great kids' play park, and a snack bar. You can rent tennis shoes, balls, and rackets all for £9.30/hour (mid-May-mid-Sept Mon-Sat 10:00-dusk, Sun 13:00-19:00, closed mid-Sept-mid-May, tel. 028/7082-4441).

More Fun—Consider **Dunluce Centre** (kid-oriented fun zone, in same building with TI) and **Waterworld** (£4.50, pool, waterslides, bowling; June-Aug daily 10:00-19:00; closed Sept-May; wedged between the Harbour Bistro and Ramore Wine Bar, tel. 028/7082-2001).

Sleeping in Portrush

Portrush has a range of hotels, from decent to ritzy. Some B&Bs can be well-worn. August and Saturday nights can be tight (and loud) with young party groups. Otherwise, it's a "you take half a loaf when you can get it" town. Rates vary with the view and season—probe for softness. Many listings face the sea, though sea views are worth paying for only if you get a bay window. Ask for a big room (some doubles can be very small; twins are bigger). Lounges are invariably grand and have bay-window views. All places listed have lots of stairs, but most are perfectly central and within a few minutes' walk of the train station. Parking is easy.

$$ Adelphi Guest House is a breath of fresh air, with 28 tastefully furnished modern rooms, friendly staff, and a hearty bistro downstairs (Sb-£55-105, Db-£65-115, Tb-£75-135, Qb-£105-165, 67-71 Main Street, Wi-Fi, tel. 028/7082-5544, www.adelphi portrush.com, stay@adelphiportrush.com).

$ Beulah Guest House is a traditional, good-value place. It's centrally located and run by cheerful Rachel and Jimmy Anderson, with 11 prim and smoke-free rooms (Ss-£33, Sb-£45-60, Db-£60-75, Tb-£85-95, Wi-Fi, parking at rear, 16 Causeway Street, tel. 028/7082-2413, www.beulahguesthouse.com, stay@beulahguest house.com).

$ Albany Lodge is a rejuvenated 85-year-old guest house smack dab in the center of town. Kate and Gwynne Fletcher create an upbeat vibe with their nine bright rooms, many with scenic sea views (Sb-£49-79, Db-£50-95, Tb-£80-95, ask about 2-night deals including fine dinner at 55 North, Wi-Fi, 2 Eglinton Street, tel. 028/7082-3492, www.albanylodge.net, albanylodge@hotmail. co.uk).

$ Anvershiel B&B, with six rooms, is a 10-minute walk south of the train station. Jovial Victor Bow, who runs the show with his wife Erna, is in the know about local golf (Sb-£45, Db-£65, Tb-£95, Qb-£125, cash only, 5 percent discount on Db with 2-night stay except July-Aug, Wi-Fi, parking, 16 Coleraine Road, tel. 028/7082-3861, www.anvershiel.com, enquiries@anvershiel. com).

$ Ardenlee B&B offers six smartly refurbished rooms, some with fine views of the ocean (Sb-£35-50, Db-£60-90, Tb-£100, Wi-Fi, 19 Kerr Street, tel. 028/7082-2639, mobile 078-0725-9460, www.ardenleehouse.com, russell.rafferty@btconnect.com).

$ Harbour Heights B&B rents nine homey rooms, each named after a different town in County Antrim. It has an inviting guest lounge overlooking the harbor, and friendly South African hosts Sam and Tim Swart (Sb-£40, Db-£70-80, family rooms, Wi-Fi, bike rentals, 17 Kerr Street, tel. 028/7082-2765, mobile

Sleep Code

(£1 = about $1.60, country code: 44, area code: 028)
To call Portrush from the Republic of Ireland, dial 048 before the local 8-digit number.

S = Single, **D** = Double/Twin, **T** = Triple, **Q** = Quad, **b** = bathroom, **s** = shower only. Breakfast is included and credit cards are accepted unless otherwise noted.

To help you easily sort through these listings, I've divided the accommodations into two categories, based on the price for a standard double room with bath:

$$ Higher Priced—Most rooms £80 or more.
$ Lower Priced—Most rooms less than £80.

Prices can change without notice; verify the hotel's current rates online or by email.

078-9586-6534, www.harbourheightsportrush.com, info@harbour heightsportrush.com).

Eating in Portrush

Being a get-away-from-Belfast town and close to a university town (Coleraine), Portrush has more than enough chips joints. Eglinton Street is lined with cheap-and-cheery eateries.

Lunch Spots

The Scullery is a tiny hole-in-the-wall, making sandwiches and healthy wraps to take away and enjoy by the beach—or on an Antrim Coast picnic (Mon-Sat 9:00-17:00, Sun 10:00-16:00, close to the train station at 4 Eglinton Lane, tel. 028/7082-1000).

Ground Espresso Bar makes fresh £4 sandwiches or paninis, soup, and excellent coffee (daily June-Aug 9:00-22:00, Sept-May 9:00-17:00, 52 Main Street, tel. 028/7082-5979). They also offer coin-op Internet access (see "Helpful Hints," earlier).

Café 55 Bistro serves basic sandwiches with a great patio view (Mon-Fri 9:00-17:00, Sat-Sun 9:00-21:30, shorter hours off-season, 1 Causeway Street, beneath fancier 55 North restaurant run by same owners—listed below, tel. 028/7082-2811).

The **Spar Market** has what you'll need for your Antrim Coast picnic (Mon-Sat 7:00-20:00, Sun 7:00-19:00, across from Barry's Arcade on Main Street, tel. 028/7082-5447).

PORTRUSH

Fine Dining

55 North (named for the local latitude) has the best sea views in town, with windows on all sides. The classy pasta-and-fish plates are a joy (£9-17 plates, daily 12:30-14:00 & 17:00-21:00 except closed Mon Sept-June, 1 Causeway Street, tel. 028/7082-2811).

Adelphi Bistro is a good bet for its relaxed family-friendly atmosphere and hearty meals (daily 12:00-15:00 & 17:00-21:00, 67-71 Main Street, tel. 028/7082-5544).

Harbour Road Eateries

The following four restaurants are located within 50 yards of each other (all under the same ownership and overlooking the harbor on Harbour Road), offering some of the best food values in town.

Ramore Wine Bar—salty, modern, and much-loved—bursts with happy eaters. They have the most inviting menu that I've seen in Ireland, featuring huge meals ranging from steaks to vegetarian food. Share a piece of the decadent banoffee (banana toffee) pie with a friend (£9-15 plates, daily 12:15-14:15 & 17:00-21:30, Sun until 21:00, tel. 028/7082-4313).

Downstairs, sharing the same building as the Ramore Wine Bar, is the energetic **Coast Pizzeria,** with great Italian dishes. Come early for a table or sit at the bar (Mon-Fri 17:00-21:30, Sat 16:30-22:00, Sun 15:00-21:00; Sept-June closed Mon-Tue; tel. 028/7082-3311).

The **Harbour Bistro** offers a more subdued, darker bistro ambience than the previous two eateries, with meals for a few pounds more (£9-16 dinners, daily 17:00-21:30, tel. 028/7082-2430).

Ramore Oriental sits at the high end of the bunch, farthest from the water, and serves the best Asian cuisine in town (£10-15 dinners, Wed-Sat 17:30-22:00, Sun 17:30-21:00, closed Mon-Tue, tel. 028/7082-4313).

Pubs

The **Harbour Bar** (next to the Harbour Bistro) has an old-fashioned pub downstairs and a plush, overstuffed, dark lounge upstairs. Or try the **Spring Hill Pub** (Causeway Street), with a friendly vibe and occasional music session nights.

Portrush Connections

PORTRUSH

Consider a £16.50 Zone 4 iLink smartcard, good for all-day train and bus use in Northern Ireland year-round (£15 top-up for each additional day; for more on iLink cards, see page 358). Translink has useful updated schedules and prices for both trains and buses in Northern Ireland (tel. 028/9066-6630, www.translink.co.uk).

From Portrush by Train to: Coleraine (hourly, 12 minutes, sparse on Sun morning), **Belfast** (11/day, 5/day Sun, 2 hours, transfer in Coleraine), **Dublin** (7/day, 2/day Sun, 5 hours, transfer in Coleraine or Belfast).

By Bus to: **Belfast** (12/day, 2 hours; scenic coastal route, 2.5 hours), **Dublin** (4/day, 5.5 hours).

Antrim Coast

The craggy 20-mile stretch of the Antrim Coast, extending eastward from Portrush to Ballycastle, rates second only to the tip of the Dingle Peninsula as the prettiest chunk of coastal Ireland. From your base in Portrush, you have a varied grab bag of sightseeing choices: the Giant's Causeway, Old Bushmills Distillery, Dunluce Castle, Carrick-a-Rede Rope Bridge, and Rathlin Island.

It's easy to weave these sights together by car, but connections are patchy by public transportation. Bus service is viable only in summer, and taxi fares are reasonable only for the sights closest to Portrush (Dunluce Castle and the Old Bushmills Distillery). For more on your transportation options, see "Getting Around the Antrim Coast," earlier.

Planning Your Time

With a car, you can visit the Giant's Causeway, Old Bushmills Distillery, Carrick-a-Rede Rope Bridge, and Dunluce Castle in one busy day. Call ahead to reserve the Old Bushmills Distillery tour, and get an early start. Arrive at the Giant's Causeway by 9:00 when crowds are sparse. Park your car in the causeway lot and pay as you exit (after the visitors center opens). Although the Causeway's visitors center doesn't open until 9:30 (and the shuttle bus doesn't run until 10:00), the trails are free and always open. Spend an hour and a half scrambling over Ireland's most unique alligator-skin geology.

Then catch a late-morning tour of the Old Bushmills Distillery, a 400-year-old whiskey distillery. Grab a cheap lunch in the hospitality room afterwards. A 20-minute drive east brings you to Carrick-a-Rede, where you can enjoy a scenic cliff-top trail hike all the way to the lofty rope bridge (one hour round-trip, 1.5 hours if you cross the rope bridge and explore the sea stack). Hop in your car and double back west all the way to dramatically cliff-perched

The Scottish Connection

The Romans called the Irish the "Scoti" (meaning pirates). When the Scoti crossed the narrow Irish Sea and invaded the land of the Picts 1,500 years ago, that region became known as Scotiland. Ireland and Scotland were never conquered by the Romans, and they retained similar clannish Celtic traits. Both share the same Gaelic branch of the linguistic tree.

On clear summer days from Carrick-a-Rede, the island of Mull in Scotland—only 17 miles away—is visible. Much closer on the horizon is the boomerang-shaped Rathlin Island, part of Northern Ireland. Rathlin is where Scottish leader Robert the Bruce (a compatriot of William "Braveheart" Wallace) retreated in 1307 after defeat at the hands of the English. Legend has it that he hid in a cave on the island, where he observed a spider patiently rebuilding its web each time a breeze knocked it down. Inspired by the spider's perseverance, Robert gathered his Scottish forces once more and finally defeated the English at the decisive battle of Bannockburn.

Flush with confidence from his victory, Robert the Bruce decided to open a second front against the English...in Ireland. In 1315, he sent his brother Edward over to enlist their Celtic Irish cousins in an effort to thwart the English. After securing Ireland, Edward hoped to move on and enlist the Welsh, thus cornering England with their pan-Celtic nation. But Edward's timing was bad—Ireland was in the midst of famine. His Scottish troops had to live off the land and began to take food and supplies from the starving Irish. He might also have been trying to destroy Ireland's crops to keep them from being used as a colonial "breadbasket" to feed English troops. The Scots quickly wore out their welcome, and Edward the Bruce was eventually killed in battle near Dundalk in 1318.

This was the first time in history that Ireland was used as a pawn by England's enemies. Spain and France saw Ireland as the English Achilles' heel, and both countries later attempted invasions of the island. The English Tudor and Stuart royalty countered these threats in the 16th and 17th centuries by starting the "plantation" of loyal subjects in Ireland. The only successful long-term settlement by the English was here in Northern Ireland, which remains part of the United Kingdom today.

It's interesting to speculate how things would be different today if Ireland and Scotland had been permanently welded together as a nation 700 years ago. You'll notice the strong Scottish influence in this part of Ireland when you ask a local a question and he answers, "Aye, a wee bit." The Irish joke that the Scots are just Irish people who couldn't swim home.

Dunluce Castle for a late-afternoon tour. From here, you're only a five-minute drive from Portrush.

Those with extra time, a car, and a hankering to seek out dramatic coastal cliff scenery may want to spend a half-day boating out to Rathlin Island, Northern Ireland's only inhabited island.

Sights on the Antrim Coast

▲▲Giant's Causeway

This five-mile-long stretch of coastline, a World Heritage Site, is famous for its bizarre basalt columns. The shore is covered with largely hexagonal pillars that stick up at various heights. It's as if the earth were offering God his choice of 37,000 six-sided cigarettes.

Geologists claim the Giant's Causeway was formed by volcanic eruptions more than 60 million years ago. As the surface of the lava flow quickly cooled, it contracted and crystallized into hexagonal columns. As the rock (looking like geologic alligator skin) later settled and eroded, the columns broke off into many stair-like steps.

Of course, in actuality, the Giant's Causeway was made by a giant Ulster warrior named Finn MacCool who knew of a rival giant living on the Scottish island of Staffa. Finn built a stone bridge over to Staffa to spy on his rival, and found out that the Scottish giant was much bigger than him. Finn retreated back to Ireland and had his wife dress him as a sleeping infant, just in time for the rival giant to come across the causeway to spy on Finn. The rival, shocked at the infant's size, fled back to Scotland in terror of whomever had sired this giant baby. Breathing a sigh of relief, Finn tore off the baby clothes and prudently knocked down the bridge. Today, proof of this encounter exists in the geologic formation that still extends undersea: It surfaces at Staffa.

Giant's Causeway Visitors Centre—For cute variations on the Finn story, as well as details on the ridiculous theories of modern geologists, start out in the visitors center. It's filled with interactive exhibits giving a worthwhile history of the Giant's Causeway, with a regional overview. Check out the interesting short film (just inside the entrance) showing the evolution of the causeway from molten lava to the geometric, geologic wonderland of today. The large 3-D model of the causeway offers a bird's-eye view of the region. Some of the exhibits are geared to kids who get a kick out of all things giant-related. A gift shop and cafe are standing by.

PORTRUSH

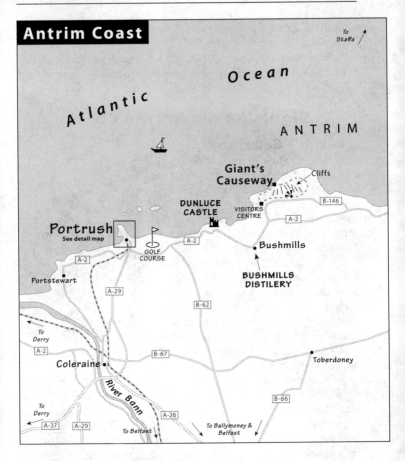

Cost and Hours: Visitors center—£8.50 plus £6 to park, open daily 9:00-18:00; hiking trails free and open from dawn to dusk; tel. 028/2073-1855, www.nationaltrust.org.uk.

Visiting the Causeway—The causeway itself—the highlight of the entire coast—is free and always open. From the visitors center, you have several options for visiting the causeway:

By Minibus: A minibus (4/hour from 10:00, £1 each way) zips tired tourists a half-mile directly from the visitors center to the causeway.

By Foot: For a better dose of the causeway, check the trail map at the visitors center. Then take the easy-to-follow, cliff-top trail uphill from the visitors center 10 minutes to a great precipice viewpoint. It's level from here and only 15 minutes farther to reach the Shepherd's Stairway. Then grab the banister on the steep stairs and zigzag down the switchbacks to the coast; at the T-junction, go 100 yards right, to the towering rock pipes of "the Organ." Then retrace

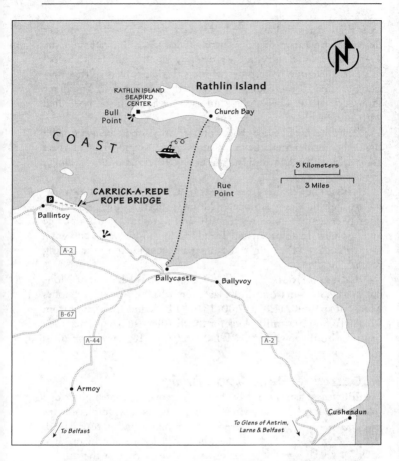

your steps and continue down to the tidal zone, where the "Giant's Boot" (six feet tall, on the right) provides some photo fun. Another 100 yards farther is the dramatic point where the causeway meets the sea. Just beyond that, at the asphalt turnaround, is the bus stop where you can catch a lift back to the visitors center.

You could also walk the trail that runs along the entire five-mile-long Causeway Coast, though rock falls and slides occasionally close the trail. The £1 hiking guide points out the highlights named by 18th-century guides (Camel's Back, Giant's Eye, and so on).

▲▲Old Bushmills Distillery

Bushmills claims to be the world's oldest distillery. Though King James I (of Bible fame) only granted Bushmills its license to distill "Aqua Vitae" in 1608, whiskey has been made here since the 13th century. Distillery tours waft you through the process, making it clear that Irish whiskey is triple distilled—and therefore smoother than Scotch whisky (distilled merely twice and minus the "e"). The 45-minute tour starts with the mash pit, which is filled with a porridge that eventually becomes whiskey. (The leftovers of that porridge are fed to the county's particularly happy cows.) You'll see thousands of oak casks—the kind used for Spanish sherry—filled with aging whiskey.

The finale, of course, is the opportunity for a sip in the 1608 Bar—the former malt barn. Visitors get a single glass of their choice. Hot-drink enthusiasts might enjoy a cinnamon-and-cloves hot toddy.

To see the distillery at its lively best, visit when the 100 workers are staffing the machinery—Monday morning through Friday noon (weekend tours see a still still). Tours are limited to 35 people and book up. In summer, call ahead to put in your name and get a tour time. After the tour, you can get a decent lunch in the tasting room.

Cost and Hours: £7; April-Oct tours on the half-hour Mon-Sat from 9:30, Sun from 12:00, last tour at 16:00; Nov-March tours Mon-Sat at 10:00, 11:00, 12:00, 13:30, 14:30, and 15:30, Sun from 12:00. To find Bushmills, look for the distillery sign a quarter-mile from Bushmills town center. Tel. 028/2073-3218, www.bushmills.com.

▲▲Carrick-a-Rede Rope Bridge

For 200 years, fishermen have hung a narrow, 90-foot-high bridge (planks strung between wires) across a 65-foot-wide chasm be-

tween the mainland and a tiny island. Today, the bridge (while not the original version) still gives access to the salmon nets that are set during the summer months to catch the fish turning the coast's corner. (The complicated system is described at the gateway.) A pleasant, 30-minute one-mile walk from the parking lot takes you to the rope bridge. Cross over to the island for fine views and great seabird-watching, especially during nesting season.

Cost and Hours: £5.60 trail and bridge fee, pay at hut beside parking lot, coffee shop and WCs near parking lot; March-Oct daily 10:00-18:00, July-Aug until 19:00; closed Nov-Feb; tel. 028/2076-9839, www.nationaltrust.org.uk.

Nearby: If you have a car and a picnic lunch, don't miss the terrific coastal **viewpoint** rest area one mile steeply uphill and east of Carrick-a-Rede (on B-15 to Ballycastle). This grassy area offers one of the best picnic views in Northern Ireland (picnic tables but no WCs). Feast on bird's-eye views of the rope bridge, nearby Rathlin Island, and the not-so-distant Island of Mull in Scotland.

▲Dunluce Castle

These romantic ruins, perched dramatically on the edge of a rocky head-land, are a testimony to this region's turbulent past. During the Middle Ages, the castle resisted several sieges. But on a stormy night in 1639, dinner was interrupted as half of the kitchen fell into the sea and took the servants with it (Ireland's first fast-food?). That was the last straw for the lady of the castle. The countess of Antrim packed up and moved inland, and the castle "began its slow submission to the forces of nature." While it's one of the largest castles in Northern Ireland and is beautifully situated, there's precious little left to see among its broken walls.

The 16th-century expansion of the castle was financed by the salvaging of a shipwreck. In 1588, the Spanish Armada's *Girona*—overloaded with sailors and the valuables of three abandoned sister ships—sank on her way home after the aborted mission against England. More than 1,300 drowned, and only 5 survivors washed ashore. The shipwreck was excavated in 1967, and a bounty of golden odds and silver ends wound up in Belfast's Ulster Museum.

Castle admission includes an impromptu guided tour of the ruins given by a small stable of dedicated guides. Before entering, catch the great seven-minute film about the history of the castle (across from the ticket desk).

Cost and Hours: £5, free audioguide requires £10 refundable deposit, daily April-Sept 10:00-17:30, Oct-March 10:00-16:30, last entry 30 minutes before closing, tel. 028/2073-1938.

Rathlin Island

The only inhabited island off the coast of Northern Ireland, Rathlin is a quiet haven for hikers, bird-watchers, and seal spotters. Less than seven miles from end to end, this "L"-shaped island is reachable by ferry from the town of Ballycastle.

Getting There: The Rathlin Island ferry departs from Ballycastle, just east of Carrick-a-Rede. It does 10 crossings per day in summer. Six are fast 20-minute trips on passenger boats, and

four are slower 45-minute trips on car ferries (£11.20 round-trip per passenger on either type of boat, reserve ahead, tel. 028/2076-9299, www.rathlin ballycastleferry.com).

Travelers with rental cars will have no problem reaching Ballycastle. A taxi from Portrush to Ballycastle runs £25 one-way. Bus service from Portrush to Ballycastle is spotty (check with the TI in Portrush, or contact Translink—tel. 028/9066-6630, www.translink.co.uk).

Visiting Rathlin Island: Rathlin's population of 75 islanders clusters around the ferry dock at Church Bay. Here you'll find the Rathlin Manor House, offering the island's most convenient lodging, a restaurant, and a pub (tel. 028/2076-3964, www.rathlinmanorhouse.co.uk). The **Rathlin Boathouse Visitor Centre** operates as the island's TI (May-Aug daily 10:30-13:30 & 14:00-16:00, on the bay 100 yards east of the ferry dock, tel. 028/2076-2225).

In summer, the Puffin shuttle bus (£5 round-trip, seats 25) meets arriving ferries and drives visitors to the **Rathlin Island Seabird Centre** at the west end of the island. Here a lighthouse extends down the cliff with its beacon at the bottom. It's upside down because the coast guard wants the light visible only from a certain distance out to sea. The bird observation terrace at the center (next to the lighthouse) overlooks one of the most dramatic coastal views in Ireland—a sheer drop of more than 300 feet to craggy sea stacks just offshore that are draped in thousands of sea birds. Photographers will want to bring their most powerful zoom lens.

For such a snoozy island, Rathlin has seen its fair share of history. Flint axe-heads were quarried here in Neolithic times. The island was one of the first in Ireland to be raided by Vikings, in 795. Robert the Bruce hid out from English pursuers on Rathlin in the early 1300s (see "The Scottish Connection" sidebar, earlier). In the late 1500s, local warlord Sorely Boy MacDonnell stashed his extended family on Rathlin and waited on the mainland at Dunluce Castle to face his English enemies...only to watch in horror as they headed for the island instead to massacre his loved ones. And in 1917, a WWI U-boat sank the British cruiser HMS *Drake* in Church Bay. The wreck is now a popular scuba-dive destination.

PORTRUSH

▲Antrim Mountains and Glens

Not particularly high (never more than 1,500 feet), the Antrim Mountains are cut by a series of large glens running northeast to the sea. Glenariff, with its waterfalls (especially the Mare's Tail), is the most beautiful of the nine glens. Travelers going by car can take a pleasant drive from Portrush to Belfast, sticking to the A-2 road that takes in parts of all of the Glens of Antrim. The two best stops en route are Cushendall (nice beach for a picnic) and the castle at Carrickfergus (see page 371).

DERRY
and COUNTY DONEGAL

The town of Derry (or Londonderry to Unionists) is the mecca of Ulster Unionism. When Ireland was being divvied up, the River Foyle was the logical border between the North and the Republic. But, for sentimental and economic reasons, the North kept Derry, which is on the Republic's side of the river. Consequently, this predominantly Catholic city has been much contested throughout the Troubles.

Even its name is disputed. While most of its population and its city council call it "Derry," some maps, road signs, and all train schedules in the UK use "Londonderry," the name on its 1662 royal charter and the one favored by Unionists. I once asked a Northern Ireland rail employee for a ticket to "Derry"; he replied that there was no such place, but he would sell me one to "Londonderry."

Still, the conflict is only one dimension of Derry; this pivotal city has a more diverse history and a prettier setting than Belfast. Derry was a vibrant city back when Belfast was just a mudflat. With a quarter of the population (85,000), Derry feels more welcoming and manageable to visitors. And in 2013, Derry will be in the spotlight as it proudly celebrates being the UK City of Culture.

County Donegal, to the west of Derry, is about as far-flung as Ireland gets. A forgotten economic backwater (part of the Republic but riding piggyback on the North), it lacks blockbuster museums or sights. But a visit here is more about the journey, and adventurous drivers—a car is a must—will be rewarded with a time-capsule peek into old Irish ways and starkly beautiful scenery.

Planning Your Time

Travelers heading north from Westport or Galway should get an early start. Donegal town makes a good lunch stop, with lots of choices surrounding its triangular town square, and then it's on to Derry, where you can spend a couple of hours seeing the essentials. Visit the Tower Museum and catch some views from the town wall before continuing on to Portrush for the night.

With more time, spend a night in Derry, so you can see the powerful Bogside murals (illuminated after dark) and take a walking tour around the town walls—you'll appreciate this underrated city. With two nights in Derry, consider crossing the border into the Republic for a scenic driving loop through part of remote County Donegal.

Derry

No city in Ireland connects the kaleidoscope of historical dots more colorfully than Derry. From a leafy monastic hamlet to a Viking-pillaged port, from a cannonball-battered siege survivor to an Industrial Revolution sweatshop, from an essential WWII naval base to a wrenching flashpoint of sectarian Troubles...Derry has seen it all.

But the past few years have brought some refreshing changes. Manned British Army surveillance towers were taken down in 2006, and most British troops finally departed in mid-2007, after 38 years in Northern Ireland. In June of 2011, a new, curvy pedestrian bridge across the River Foyle was completed. Locals have dubbed it the "Peace Bridge" because it links the predominantly Protestant Waterside (east bank) with the predominantly Catholic Cityside (west bank). Today, you can feel comfortable wandering the streets and enjoying this unique Irish city.

Orientation to Derry

The River Foyle flows north, slicing Derry into eastern and western chunks. The old town walls and worthwhile sights are all on the west side. Waterloo Place and the adjacent Guildhall Square, just outside the north corner of the old city walls, are the pedestrian hubs of city activity. The Strand Road area extending north from Waterloo Place makes a comfortable home base, with the majority of lodging and restaurant suggestions within a block or two on either side. The Diamond and its War Memorial statue mark the heart of the old city within the walls.

DERRY

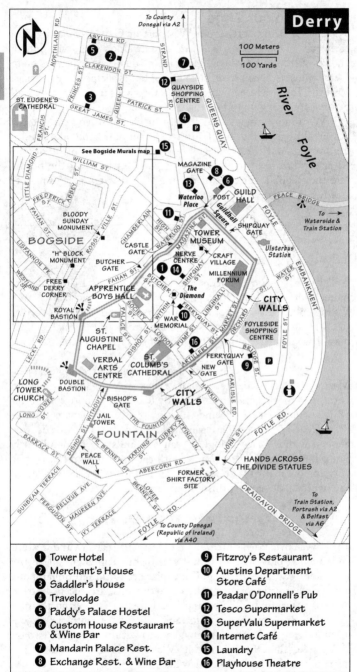

Derry

To County
Donegal via A2

100 Meters
100 Yards

River
Foyle

PEACE BRIDGE

To →
Waterside &
Train Station

To County Donegal (Republic of Ireland)
via A40

To
Train Station,
Portrush via A2
& Belfast
via A6

NORTHLAND RD.
ASYLUM RD.
CLARENDON ST.
PRINCES ST.
QUEEN ST.
GREAT JAMES ST.
PATRICK ST.
FRANCIS ST.
STRAND RD.
QUEENS QUAY

ST. EUGENE'S CATHEDRAL

QUAYSIDE SHOPPING CENTRE

See Bogside Murals map

LITTLE DIAMOND
FREDERICK ST.
WILLIAM ST.
ABBEY ST.
VILLE ST.

BOGSIDE

BLOODY SUNDAY MONUMENT
"H" BLOCK MONUMENT
BUTCHER GATE
FREE DERRY CORNER
LECKY RD.
FAHAN ST.
CHAMBERLAIN
CASTLE GATE

MAGAZINE GATE
POST
GUILD HALL
Guildhall Square
SHIPQUAY GATE

Waterloo Place

TOWER MUSEUM
NERVE CENTRE
CRAFT VILLAGE
MILLENNIUM FORUM

Ulsterbus Station

WATER ST.
EMBANKMENT
CITY WALLS
FOYLESIDE SHOPPING CENTRE

APPRENTICE BOYS HALL
The Diamond
WAR MEMORIAL
ST. AUGUSTINE CHAPEL
ROYAL BASTION
DOUBLE BASTION
VERBAL ARTS CENTRE
ST. COLUMB'S CATHEDRAL

FERRYQUAY GATE
NEW GATE
CITY WALLS
BISHOP'S GATE
JAIL TOWER
PEACE WALL

LONG TOWER CHURCH

FOUNTAIN

FORMER SHIRT FACTORY SITE

HANDS ACROSS THE DIVIDE STATUES

CRAIGAVON BRIDGE

❶ Tower Hotel	❾ Fitzroy's Restaurant
❷ Merchant's House	❿ Austins Department Store Café
❸ Saddler's House	⓫ Peadar O'Donnell's Pub
❹ Travelodge	⓬ Tesco Supermarket
❺ Paddy's Palace Hostel	⓭ SuperValu Supermarket
❻ Custom House Restaurant & Wine Bar	⓮ Internet Café
❼ Mandarin Palace Rest.	⓯ Laundry
❽ Exchange Rest. & Wine Bar	⓰ Playhouse Theatre

Tourist Information

The TI sits on the riverfront and offers a room-finding service, rents bikes, books bus and walking tours (see "Tours in Derry," later), and gives out free city maps (July-Sept Mon-Fri 9:00-19:00, Sat 10:00-18:00, Sun 10:00-16:00; Oct-June Mon-Fri 9:00-18:00, Sat 10:00-17:00, closed Sun; 44 Foyle Street, tel. 028/7126-7284, www.derryvisitor.com).

Arrival in Derry

Next to the river on the east side of town, Derry's little end-of-the-line train station (no storage lockers) has service to Portrush, Belfast, and Dublin. Free shuttle buses to Ulsterbus station (on the west side of town, a couple of minutes' walk south of Guildhall Square on Foyle Street) await each arriving train. Otherwise, it's a £5 taxi ride to Guildhall Square. The same free shuttle service leaves Ulsterbus station 15 minutes before each departing train. Unfortunately, there's not yet a footpath from the train station to the pedestrian Peace Bridge.

Derry is compact enough to see on foot; drivers stopping for a few hours can park at the Foyleside parking garage across from the TI (£1/hour, £3/4 hours, Mon-Tue 8:00-19:00, Wed-Fri 8:00-22:00, Sat 8:00-20:00, Sun 12:00-19:00, tel. 028/7137-7575). Drivers staying overnight can ask about parking at their B&B or try the Quayside parking garage behind the Travelodge (£0.80/hour, £3.20/4 hours, Mon-Fri 7:30-21:00, Sat 7:30-20:00, Sun 10:30-18:00).

Helpful Hints

Phone Tips: To call the Republic of Ireland from Northern Ireland, dial 00-353, then the area code without its initial 0, and finally the local number. To call Northern Ireland from the Republic of Ireland, dial 048, and then the local eight-digit number.

Money: Northern Bank is on Guildhall Square, and the **Bank of Ireland** is on Strand Road (both open Mon-Fri 9:30-16:30, Sat 9:30-12:30, closed Sun).

Internet Access: Located inside the walls, **Claudes Café** is just north of the Diamond on Shipquay Street (£3/30 minutes, daily 9:00-17:30, tel. 028/7127-9379).

Bookstore: Foyle Books is a dusty little pleasure for random browsing (Mon-Sat 11:00-17:00, closed Sun, 12 Magazine Street at entrance to Craft Village, tel. 028/7137-2530).

Post Office: The main post office is just off Waterloo Place (Mon-Fri 9:00-17:30, Sat 9:00-12:30, closed Sun, Custom House Street).

Derry's History

Once an island in the River Foyle, Derry (from *daire,* Irish for "oak grove") was chosen by St. Colmcille (St. Columba in English) circa A.D. 546 for a monastic settlement. He later banished himself to the island of Iona in Scotland out of remorse for sparking a bloody battle over the rights to a holy manuscript that he had secretly copied.

A thousand years later, the English defeated the last Ulster-based Gaelic chieftains in the battle of Kinsale (1601). With victory at hand, the English took advantage of the power vacuum. They began the "plantation" of Ulster with loyal Protestant subjects imported from Scotland and England. The native Irish were displaced to less desirable rocky or boggy lands, sowing the seeds of resentment that fueled the modern-day Troubles.

A dozen wealthy London guilds (grocers, haberdashers, tailors, and others) took on Derry as an investment and changed its name to "Londonderry." They built the last great walled city in Ireland to protect their investment from the surrounding—and hostile—Irish locals. The walls proved their worth in 1688-1689, when the town's Protestant defenders, loyal to King William of Orange, withstood a prolonged siege by the forces of Catholic King James II. "No surrender" is still a passionate rallying cry among Ulster Unionists determined to remain part of the United Kingdom.

The town became a major port of emigration to the New World in the early 1800s. Then, when the Industrial Revolution provided a steam-powered sewing factory, the city developed a thriving shirt-making industry. The factories here employed mostly Catholic women who had honed their skills in rural

Laundry: Smooth Operators can do a load of laundry for about £8.50 (drop off in morning to pick up later that day, Mon-Fri 8:30-18:00, Sat 8:30-17:30, closed Sun, 8 Sackville Street, tel. 028/7136-0529).

Taxi: Try **The Taxi Company** (tel. 028/7126-2626) or **Foyle Taxis** (tel. 028/7126-3905).

Car Rental: Enterprise is a handy place to rent a car (tel. 028/7186-1699, 70 Clooney Road, www.enterprise.co.uk).

County Donegal. Although Belfast grew larger and wealthier, Unionists tightened their grip on "Londonderry" and the walls that they regarded with almost holy reverence. In 1921, they insisted that the city be included in Northern Ireland when the province was partitioned from the new Irish Free State (later to become the Republic of Ireland). A bit of gerrymandering (with three lightly populated Unionist districts outvoting two densely populated Nationalist districts) ensured that the Protestant minority maintained control of the city, despite its Catholic majority.

Derry was a key escort base for US convoys headed for Britain during World War II, and 60 surviving German U-boats were instructed to surrender here at the end of the war. After the war, poor Catholics—unable to find housing—took over the abandoned military barracks, with multiple families living in each dwelling. Only homeowners were allowed to vote, and the Unionist minority, which controlled city government, was not eager to build more housing that would tip the voting balance away from them. Over the years, sectarian pressures gradually built—until they reached the boiling point. The ugly events of Bloody Sunday on January 30, 1972, brought worldwide attention to the Troubles (for more details, see "Bloody Sunday" sidebar on page 413).

Today, life has stabilized in Derry, and the population has increased by 25 percent in the last 30 years, to about 85,000. The modern Foyleside Shopping Centre, bankrolled by investors from Boston, opened in 1995. The 1998 Good Friday Peace Accord has provided significant progress toward peace, and the British Army withdrew 90 percent of its troops in mid-2007. With a population that is 70 percent Catholic, the city has agreed to alternate Nationalist and Unionist mayors. There is a feeling of cautious optimism as Derry—the epicenter of bombs and bloody conflicts in the 1960s and 1970s—now boasts a history museum that airs all viewpoints.

Tours in Derry

Walking Tours—**Martin McCrossan** and his staff lead insightful hour-long tours of the city, departing from 11 Carlisle Road just below Ferryquay Gate (£4; daily at 10:00, 12:00, and 14:00; call to confirm schedule; they also offer private tours—one-hour city tour-£25, four-hour Giant's Causeway or County Donegal tour-£100; tel. 028/7127-1996, mobile 077-1293-7997, www.irishtourguides.com).

Stephen McPhilemy leads private tours of Derry (his hometown), Belfast, and the North Coast—when he's not on the road guiding Rick Steves tours several months a year (tel. 028/7130-9051, mobile 078-0101-1027, www.irishexperience.ie, steve@irish experience.ie). Stephen also runs the recommended Paddy's Palace Hostel.

Bus Tours—**Top Tours'** double-decker buses are a good option on a rainy day. You'll be driven around the city in a one-hour loop that covers both sides of the river, including the Guild Hall, the old city walls, political wall murals (Nationalist as well as Unionist), cathedrals, and former shirt factories. Your ticket is good for one lap around the loop, and you stay on the bus for the duration (£8, pay driver, April-Sept daily on the hour 10:00-16:00, departs from in front of TI and Guildhall Square, tel. 028/7137-0067, mobile 077-9116-4431, www.toptoursireland.com, info@toptoursireland.com).

Top Tours also offers trips from Derry to the Giant's Causeway and Carrick-a-Rede Rope Bridge in County Antrim (£20, runs daily May-Sept, depart TI at 11:00, return by 18:00). In addition, they offer tours to Glenveagh National Park in County Donegal (depart TI at 9:00, return by 15:00). You can book any of their tours through the Derry TI.

Self-Guided Walks

Though calm today, Derry is marked by years of tumultuous conflict. These two walks (each taking less than an hour) will increase your understanding of the town's history. The first walk, starting on the old city walls and ending at the Anglican Cathedral, focuses on Derry's early days. The second walking tour helps you easily find the city's compelling murals, which document the time of the Troubles. These tours can be done separately or linked, depending on your time.

▲▲Walk the Walls

Squatting determinedly in the city center, the old city walls of Derry (built 1613-1618 and still intact, except for wider gates to handle modern vehicles) hold an almost mythic place in Irish history.

It was here in 1688 that a group of brave apprentice boys, many of whom had been shipped to Derry as orphans after the great fire of London in 1666, made their stand. They slammed the city gates shut in the face of the approaching Catholic forces of deposed King James II. With this act, the boys galvanized the city's indecisive Protestant defenders inside the walls.

Months of negotiations and a grinding 105-day siege followed, during which a third of the 20,000 refugees and defenders crammed into the city perished. The siege was finally broken in 1689, when supply ships broke through a boom stretched across the

River Foyle. The sacrifice and defiant survival of the city turned the tide in favor of newly crowned Protestant King William of Orange, who arrived in Ireland soon after and defeated James at the pivotal Battle of the Boyne.

To fully appreciate the walls, take a walk on top of them (free and open from dawn to dusk). Almost 20 feet high and at least as thick, the walls form a mile-long oval loop that you can cover in less than an hour. But the most interesting section is the half-circuit facing the Bogside, starting at Magazine Gate (stairs face the Tower Museum Derry inside the walls) and finishing at Bishop's Gate.

• *Enter the walls at Magazine Gate and find the stairs opposite the Tower Museum. Once atop the walls, head left.*

Walk the wall as it heads uphill, snaking along the earth's contours like a mini-Great Wall of China. In the row of buildings on the left (just before crossing over Castle Gate), you'll see an arch entry into the **Craft Village,** an alley lined with a cluster of cute shops and cafés that showcase the economic rejuvenation of Derry (Mon-Sat 9:30-17:30, closed Sun).

• *After crossing over Butcher Gate, stop in front of the grand building with the four columns to view the...*

First Derry Presbyterian Church: This impressive-looking building is the second church to occupy this site. The first was built by Queen Mary in the 1690s to thank the Presbyterian community for standing by their Anglican brethren during the dark days of the famous siege. That church was later torn down to make room for this stately Neoclassical, red-sandstone church finished in 1780. Over the next 200 years, time took its toll on the structure, which was eventually closed due to dry rot and Republican firebombings. But in 2011, the renovated church reopened to a chorus of cross-community approval (yet one more sign of the slow reconciliation taking place in Derry). The **Blue Coat School** exhibit behind the church highlights the important role of Presbyterians in local history (free but donation expected, May-Sept Wed-Fri 11:00-16:00, closed Sat-Tue, closed Oct-April, tel. 028/7126-1550).

• *Just up the block is the...*

Apprentice Boys Memorial Hall: Built in 1873, this houses the private lodge and meeting rooms of an all-male Protestant organization. The group is dedicated to the memory of the original 13 apprentice boys who saved the day during the 1688 siege. Each year, on the Saturday closest to the August 12 anniversary date, the modern-day Apprentice Boys Society celebrates the end of the siege with a controversial march atop the walls. These walls are considered sacred ground for devout Unionists, who claim that many who died during the famous siege were buried within the battered walls because of lack of space.

Next, you'll pass a large, square pedestal on the right atop Royal Bastion. It once supported a column in honor of Governor George Walker, the commander of the defenders during the famous siege. In 1972, the IRA blew up the column, which had 105 steps to the top (one for each day of the siege).

• *Opposite the empty pedestal is the small Anglican...*

St. Augustine Chapel: Set in a pretty graveyard, this Anglican chapel is where some believe the original sixth-century monastery of St. Columba (St. Colmcille in Irish) stood. In Victorian times, this stretch of the walls was a fashionable promenade walk.

As you walk, you'll pass a long wall (on the left)—all that's left of a **British Army base** that stood here until 2006. A 50-foot tower used to loom out of it, bristling with cameras and listening devices. Soldiers built it here for its bird's-eye view of the once-turbulent Catholic Bogside district below. The tower's dismantlement—as well as the removal of most of the British Army from Northern Ireland—is another positive sign in cautiously optimistic Derry. The walls of this former army base now contain a parking lot.

Stop at the Double Bastion **fortified platform** that occupies this corner of the city walls. The old cannon is nicknamed "Roaring Meg" for the fury of its firing during the siege.

From here, you can see across the Bogside to the not-so-far-away hills of County Donegal in the Republic. Derry was once an island, but as the River Foyle gradually changed its course, the area you see below the wall began to drain. Over time, and especially after the Great Potato Famine (1845-1849), Catholic peasants from rural Donegal began to move into Derry to find work during the Industrial Revolution. They settled on this least desirable land...on the soggy bog side of the city.

Directly below and to the right are Free Derry Corner and Rossville Street, where the tragic events of Bloody Sunday took place in 1972 (see page 413). Down on the left is the 18th-century Long Tower Catholic church, named after the monk-built round tower that once stood in the area (see page 420).

• *Head to the grand brick building behind you. This is the...*

Verbal Arts Centre: A former Presbyterian school, this center promotes the development of local literary arts in the form of poetry, drama, writing, and storytelling. You can drop in for a cup of coffee in their café and see what performances might be on during your visit (Mon-Thu 9:00-17:30, Fri 9:00-16:00, closed Sat-Sun, tel. 028/7126-6946, www.verbalartscentre.co.uk).

• *Go left another 50 yards around the corner to reach...*

Bishop's Gate: From here, look up Bishop Street Within (inside the walls). This was the site of another British Army surveillance tower. Placed just inside the town walls, it overlooked the neighborhood until 2006. Now look in the other direction to see Bishop Street Without (outside the walls). You'll spot a modern wall topped by a high mesh fence, running along the left side of Bishop Street Without. This is a so-called **"peace wall,"** built to ensure the security of the Protestant enclave living behind it in Derry's Fountain neighborhood. When the Troubles reignited more than 40 years ago, 20,000 Protestants lived on this side of the river. Sadly, this small housing development of 1,000 people is all that remains of that proud community today. The rest have chosen to move across the river to the mostly Protestant Waterside district. The stone tower halfway down the "peace wall" is all that remains of the old jail that briefly held doomed rebel Wolfe Tone after the 1798 revolt against the British.

• *From Bishop's Gate, those short on time can descend from the walls and walk 15 minutes directly back through the heart of the old city, along Bishop Street Within and Shipquay Street to Guildhall Square. With more time, consider visiting St. Columb's Cathedral, the Long Tower Church, and the murals of the Bogside.*

▲▲Bogside Murals Walk

The Catholic Bogside area was the tinderbox of the modern Troubles in Northern Ireland. Bloody Sunday, a terrible confrontation during a march that occurred more than 40 years ago, sparked a sectarian inferno, and the ashes have not yet fully cooled. Today, the murals of the Bogside give visitors an accessible glimpse of this community's passionate perception of those events.

The events are memorialized in 12 **murals** painted on the ends of residential flats along a 300-yard stretch of Rossville Street and Lecky Road, where the march took place. You can reach them from Waterloo Place via William Street, from the old city walls at Butcher Gate via the long set of stairs extending below Fahan Street on the grassy hillside, or by the stairs leading down from the Long Tower Church. These days, this neighborhood is gritty but quiet and safe, and the murals are even lit up at night.

Two brothers, Tom and William Kelly, and their childhood friend Kevin Hasson are known as the Bogside Artists. They grew up in the Bogside and witnessed the tragic events that took place there, which led them to begin painting the murals in 1994. One of the brothers, Tom, gained a reputation as a "heritage mural"

DERRY

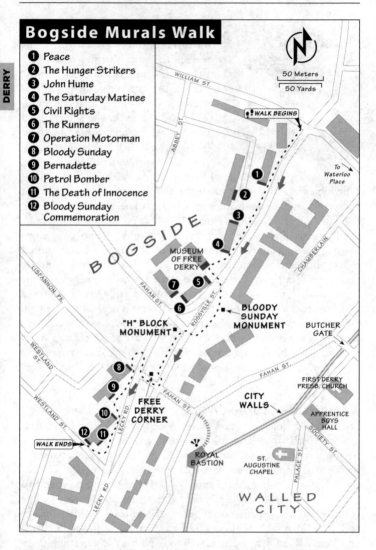

Bogside Murals Walk

1. Peace
2. The Hunger Strikers
3. John Hume
4. The Saturday Matinee
5. Civil Rights
6. The Runners
7. Operation Motorman
8. Bloody Sunday
9. Bernadette
10. Petrol Bomber
11. The Death of Innocence
12. Bloody Sunday Commemoration

N

50 Meters
50 Yards

WILLIAM ST.

WALK BEGINS

To Waterloo Place

ABBEY ST.

CHAMBERLAIN

BOGSIDE

LISPANNON PK.

FAHAN ST.

MUSEUM OF FREE DERRY

ROSSVILLE ST.

BLOODY SUNDAY MONUMENT

BUTCHER GATE

"H" BLOCK MONUMENT

WESTLAND ST.

WESTLAND ST.

FAHAN ST.

FIRST DERRY PRESB. CHURCH

LECKY RD.

FAHAN ST.

CITY WALLS

FREE DERRY CORNER

APPRENTICE BOYS HALL

SOCIETY ST.

WALK ENDS

LECKY RD.

ROYAL BASTION

ST. AUGUSTINE CHAPEL

PALACE ST.

WALLED CITY

painter, specializing in scenes of life in the old days. In a surprising and hopeful development, Tom was later invited into Derry's Protestant Fountain neighborhood to work with a youth club there on three proud heritage murals that were painted over paramilitary graffiti. For more about this unique trio, visit their website—www.bogsideartists.com.

The Walk: Start out at the corner of Rossville and William Streets.

The Bogside murals face different directions (and some are partially hidden by buildings), so they're not all visible from a sin-

Bloody Sunday

Inspired by civil rights marches in America in the mid-1960s, and the Prague Spring uprising and Paris student strikes of 1968, civil rights groups began to protest in Northern Ireland. Initially, their goals were to gain better housing, secure fair voting rights, and end employment discrimination for Catholics in the North. Tensions mounted, and clashes with the predominantly Protestant Royal Ulster Constabulary police force became frequent. Eventually, the British Army was called in to keep the peace.

On January 30, 1972, about 10,000 people protesting internment without trial held an illegal march sponsored by the Northern Ireland Civil Rights Association. British Army barricades kept them from the center of Derry, so they marched through the Bogside neighborhood.

That afternoon, some youths rioted on the fringe of the march. An elite parachute regiment had orders to move in and make arrests in the Rossville Street area. Shooting broke out and after 25 minutes, 13 marchers were dead and 13 were wounded (one of the wounded later died). The soldiers claimed they came under attack from gunfire and nail-bombs. The marchers said the army shot indiscriminately at unarmed civilians.

The tragic clash, called "Bloody Sunday," led to a dramatic increase in Nationalism and a flood of fresh IRA volunteers. An investigation at the time exonerated the soldiers, but the relatives of the victims insisted on their innocence.

In 1998, then-British Prime Minister Tony Blair promised a new inquiry—which became the longest and most expensive in British legal history. In 2010, a 12-year investigation—the Saville Report—determined that the Bloody Sunday civil rights protesters were innocent and called the deaths of 14 protesters unjustified.

In a dramatic 2010 speech in the House of Commons, British Prime Minister David Cameron apologized to the people of Derry. "What happened on Bloody Sunday was both unjustified and unjustifiable. It was wrong," he declared. Cheers rang out in Derry's Guildhall Square, where thousands had gathered to watch the speech on a video screen. After 38 years of struggle, Northern Ireland's bloodiest wound started healing.

gle viewpoint. Plan on walking three long blocks along Rossville Street (which becomes Lecky Road) to see them all. Residents are used to visitors and don't mind if you photograph the murals.

From William Street, walk south along the right side of Rossville Street toward Free Derry Corner. The murals will all be on your right.

The first mural you'll walk past is the colorful ❶ *Peace*, showing the silhouette of a dove in flight (left side of mural) and an oak leaf (right side of mural), both created from a single ribbon. A peace campaign asked Derry city schoolchildren to write suggestions for positive peacetime images; their words inspired this artwork. The dove is a traditional symbol of peace, and the oak leaf is a traditional symbol of Derry—recognized by both communities. The dove flies from the sad blue of the past toward the warm yellow of the future.

Next, ❷ *The Hunger Strikers* features two long-haired figures wearing blankets. This mural represents the IRA prisoners who refused to wear the uniforms of common criminal inmates—an attempt to force the British to treat them instead as legitimate political prisoners (who were allowed to wear their own clothes). The giant red letter *H* looms behind them, a symbol of the H-block layout of Maze Prison near Belfast.

Smaller and easy to miss (above a ramp with banisters) is ❸ *John Hume.* It's actually a collection of four faces (clockwise from upper left): Nationalist leader John Hume, Martin Luther King Jr., Nelson Mandela, and Mother Teresa. The Brooklyn Bridge in the middle symbolizes the long-term bridges of understanding that the work of these four Nobel Peace Prize-winning activists created. Born in the Bogside, Hume still maintains a home here.

Now look for ❹ *The Saturday Matinee,* which depicts an outgunned but undaunted local youth behind a screen shield. He holds a stone, ready to throw, while a British armored vehicle approaches (echoing the famous Tiananmen Square photo of the lone Chinese man facing the tank). Why *Saturday Matinee?* It's because the weekend was the best time for locals to "have a go at" the army; people were off work and youths were out of school.

Nearby is ❺ *Civil Rights,* showing a marching Derry crowd carrying an antisectarian banner. It dates from the days when Martin Luther King Jr.'s successful nonviolent marches were being seen worldwide on TV, creating a dramatic, global ripple effect. Civil rights marches, inspired by King and using the same methods to combat a similar set of grievances, gave this long-suffering community a powerful new voice.

In the building behind this mural, you'll find the small but

Political Murals

The dramatic and emotional murals you'll encounter in Northern Ireland will likely be one of the enduring travel memories that you'll take home with you. During the 19th century, Protestant neighborhoods hung flags and streamers each July to commemorate the victory of King William of Orange at the Battle of the Boyne in 1690. Modern murals evolved from these colorful annual displays. With the advent of industrial paints, temporary seasonal displays became permanent territorial statements.

Unionist murals were created during the extended political debate that eventually led to the partitioning of the island in 1921 and the creation of Northern Ireland. Murals that expressed opposing views in Nationalist Catholic neighborhoods were outlawed. The ban remained until the eruption of the modern Troubles, when staunchly Nationalist Catholic communities isolated themselves behind barricades, eluding state control and gaining freedom to express their pent-up passions. In Derry, this form of symbolic, cultural, and ideological resistance first appeared in 1969 with the simple "You are now entering Free Derry" message that you'll still see painted on the surviving gable wall at Free Derry Corner.

Found mostly in working-class neighborhoods of Belfast and Derry, today's political murals have become a dynamic form of popular culture. They blur the line between art and propaganda, giving visitors a striking glimpse of each community's history, identity, and values.

intense **Museum of Free Derry** (£3, Mon-Fri 9:30-16:30 year-round, April-Sept Sat 13:00-16:00, July-Sept Sun 13:00-16:00, 55 Glenfada Park, tel. 028/7136-0880, www.museumoffreederry.org). Photos, shirts with bullet holes, and a 45-minute video documentary convey the painful experience of the people of the Bogside during the worst of the Troubles.

Cross over to the other side of Rossville Street to see the **Bloody Sunday Monument.** This small, fenced-off stone obelisk lists the names of those who died that day, most within 50 yards of this spot. Take a look at the map pedestal by the monument, which shows how a rubble barricade was erected to block the street. A 10-story housing project called Rossville Flats stood here in those days. After peaceful protests failed (with Bloody Sunday being the watershed event), Nationalist youths became more aggressive. British troops were wary of being hit by Molotov cocktails thrown from the rooftop of the housing project.

Cross back again, this time over to the grassy median strip that runs down the middle of Rossville Street. At this end stands a granite letter *H* inscribed with the names of the 10 IRA hunger strikers who died in the H-block of Maze Prison in 1981. The prison was closed after the release of all prisoners (both Unionist and Nationalist) in 2000.

From here, as you look across at the corner of Fahan Street, you get a good view of two murals. In ❻ *The Runners* (right), three rioting youths flee tear gas from canisters used by the British Army to disperse hostile crowds. More than 1,000 canisters were used during the Battle of the Bogside; "nonlethal" rubber bullets killed 17 people over the course of the Troubles. Meanwhile, in ❼ *Operation Motorman* (left), a soldier wields a sledgehammer to break through a house door, depicting the massive push by the British Army to open up the Bogside's barricaded "no-go" areas that the IRA had controlled for three years (1969-1972).

Walk down to the other end of the median strip where the white wall of **Free Derry Corner** announces "You are now entering Free Derry" (imitating a similarly defiant slogan of the time in once-isolated West Berlin). This was the gabled end of a string of houses that stood here over 40 years ago. During the Troubles, it became a traditional meeting place for speakers to address crowds.

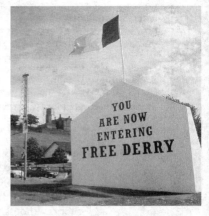

Cross back to the right side of the street (now Lecky Road) to see ❽ *Bloody Sunday,* in which a small group of men carry a body from that ill-fated march. It's based on a famous photo of Father Edward Daly that was taken that terrible day. Hunched over, he waves a white handkerchief to request safe passage in order to evacuate a mortally wounded protester. The blood-stained civil rights banner was inserted under the soldier's feet for extra emphasis. After Bloody Sunday, the previously marginal IRA suddenly found itself swamped with bitterly determined young recruits.

Near it is a mural called ❾ *Bernadette.* The woman with the megaphone is Bernadette Devlin McAliskey, an outspoken civil rights leader, who at age 21 became the youngest elected member of British Parliament. Behind her kneels a female supporter, banging a trash-can lid against the street in a traditional expression of protest in Nationalist neighborhoods. Trash-can lids were also used to warn neighbors of the approach of British patrols.

❿ *Petrol Bomber,* showing a teen wearing an army-surplus gas mask, captures the Battle of the Bogside, when locals barricaded their community, effectively shutting out British rule. Though the main figure's face is obscured by the mask, his body clearly communicates the resolve of an oppressed people. In the background, the long-gone Rossville Flats housing project still looms, with an Irish tricolor flag flying from its top.

In ⓫ *The Death of Innocence,* a young girl stands in front of bomb wreckage. She is Annette McGavigan, a 14-year-old who was killed on this corner by crossfire in 1971. She was the 100th

fatality of the Troubles, which eventually took more than 3,000 lives (and she was also a cousin of one of the artists). The broken gun beside her points to the ground, signifying that it's no longer being wielded. The large butterfly above her shoulder symbolizes the hope for peace. For years, the artists left the butterfly an empty silhouette until they felt confident that the peace process had succeeded. They finally filled in the butterfly with optimistic colors in the summer of 2006.

Finally, around the corner, you'll see a circle of male faces. This mural, painted in 1997 to observe the 25th anniversary of the tragedy, is called ⓬ *Bloody Sunday Commemoration* and shows the 14 victims. They are surrounded by a ring of 14 oak leaves—the symbol of Derry. When relatives of the dead learned that the three Bogside Artists were beginning to paint this mural, many came forward to loan the artists precious photos of their loved ones, so they could be more accurately depicted.

While these murals preserve the struggles of the late 20th century, today sectarian violence has given way to negotiations and a settlement that seems to be working. The British apology for the Bloody Sunday shootings was a huge step forward. Nationalist leader John Hume (who shared the

1998 Nobel Peace Prize with Unionist leader David Trimble) once borrowed a quote from Gandhi to explain his nonviolent approach to the peace process: "An eye for an eye leaves everyone blind."

Sights in Derry

▲▲**Tower Museum Derry**—Housed in a modern reconstruction of a fortified medieval tower house that belonged to the local O'Doherty clan, this well-organized museum provides an excellent introduction to the city. Combining modern audiovisuals with historical artifacts, the displays tell the story of the city from a skillfully unbiased viewpoint, sorting out some of the tangled historical roots of Northern Ireland's Troubles. The museum is divided into two sections: the Story of Derry (on the ground floor) and the Spanish Armada (on the four floors of the tower).

Start with the Story of Derry, which explains the city's monastic origins 1,500 years ago. It moves through pivotal events, such as the 1688-1689 siege, as well as unexpected blips, like Amelia Earhart's emergency landing. Catch the thought-provoking 15-minute film in the small theater—it offers an evenhanded local perspective on the tragic events of the modern sectarian conflict, giving you a better handle on what makes this unique city tick. Scan the displays of paramilitary paraphernalia in the hallway lined with colored curbstones—red, white, and blue Union Jack colors for Unionists; and green, white, and orange Irish tricolor for Nationalists.

The tower section holds the Spanish Armada exhibits, filled with items taken from the wreck of *La Trinidad Valencera*. It sank in fierce storms nicknamed the "Protestant Winds" off the coast of Donegal in 1588.

Cost and Hours: £4.20; June-Aug Mon-Sat 10:00-16:30, closed Sun; Sept-May Tue-Sat 10:00-16:30, closed Sun-Mon; Union Hall Place, tel. 028/7137-2411.

Guild Hall—This Neo-Gothic building, complete with clock tower, is the ceremonial seat of city government. It first opened in 1890 on reclaimed lands that were once the mudflats of the River Foyle. Destroyed by fire and rebuilt in 1913, it was massively damaged by IRA bombs in 1972. In an ironic twist, Gerry Doherty, one of those convicted of the bombings, was elected as a member of the Derry City Council a dozen years later. In November of 1995, US President Bill Clinton spoke to thousands who packed into Guildhall Square. Inside the hall are the Council Chamber, party offices, and

an assembly hall featuring stained-glass windows showing scenes from Derry history. Take an informational pamphlet from the front window and explore, if civic and cultural events are not taking place inside.

Cost and Hours: Free, Mon-Fri 9:00-17:30, closed Sat-Sun, tel. 028/7137-7335, www.derrycity.gov.uk/guildhall.

Peace Bridge Stroll—A stroll across the architecturally fetching Peace Bridge rewards you with great views as you look back west across the river toward the city center. The €14-million pedestrian Peace Bridge opened in 2011, linking neighborhoods long divided by the river. On the far side, the former Ebrington Barracks British Army base (1841-2003) sits on prime real estate and surrounds a huge square that was once the military parade ground. This area will eventually be developed with a hotel, restaurant, and museum complex. The slope down to the river has been dubbed "Mute Meadows," where 40 pillars will be lit up at night with shifting colors. Eventually the site will become an outdoor concert venue and gathering place for the whole community. Events will be staged here during the UK City of Culture year in 2013...another hopeful sign of healing.

Hands Across the Divide—Designed by local teacher Maurice Harron after the fall of the Iron Curtain, this powerful metal sculpture of two figures extending their hands to each other was inspired by the growing hope for peace and reconciliation in Northern Ireland (located in a roundabout at the west end of Craigavon Bridge).

Until recently, the Tillie and Henderson's shirt factory (opened in 1857 and burned down in 2003) stood on the banks of the river beside the bridge, looming over the figures. In its heyday, Derry's shirt industry employed more than 15,000 workers (90 percent of whom were women) in sweathouses typical of the human toll of the Industrial Revolution. Karl Marx mentioned this factory in *Das Kapital* as an example of women's transition from domestic to industrial work lives.

St. Columb's Cathedral—Marked by the tall spire inside the walls, this Anglican cathedral was built from 1628 to 1633 in a style called "Planter's Gothic." Its construction was financed by the same London companies that backed the Protestant plantation of Londonderry. It was the first Protestant cathedral built in Britain after the Reformation, and the cathedral played an important part in the defense of the city during the siege. During that time, cannons were mounted on its roof, and the original spire was scavenged for lead to melt into cannon shot. Before you enter, walk over to the "Heroes' Mound" at the end of the churchyard closest to the town wall. Underneath this grassy dome is a mass grave of some of those who died during the 1689 siege.

In the cathedral entryway, you'll find a hollow cannonball that was lobbed into the city—it contained the besiegers' surrender terms. Inside, along the nave, hangs a musty collection of battle flags and Union Jacks that once inspired troops during the siege, the Crimean War, and World War II. The American flag hangs among them, from the time when the first GIs to enter the European theater in World War II were based in Northern Ireland. Check out the small chapter-house museum in the back of the church to see the original locks of the gates of Derry and more relics of the siege.

Cost and Hours: £2 donation, Mon-Sat 9:00-17:00, closed Sun, tel. 028/7126-7313, www.stcolumbscathedral.org.

Long Tower Church—Built below the walls on the hillside above the Bogside, this modest-looking church is worth a visit for its stunning high altar. The name comes from a stone monastic round tower that stood here for centuries but was dismantled and used for building materials in the 1600s. Long Tower Church is the oldest Catholic church in Derry. It was finished in 1786, during a time of enlightened relations between the city's two religious communities. Protestant Bishop Hervey gave a generous-for-the-time £200 donation and had the four Corinthian columns shipped in from Naples to frame the Neo-Renaissance altar.

Hidden outside, behind the church and facing the Bogside, is a simple shrine beneath a hawthorn tree. It marks the spot where outlawed Masses were secretly held before this church was built, during the infamous Penal Law period of the early 1700s. Through the Penal Laws, the English attempted to weaken Catholicism's influence by banishing priests and forbidding Catholics from buying land, attending school, voting, and holding office.

Cost and Hours: Free, generally open Mon-Sat 7:30-20:30, Sun 7:30-19:00—depending on available staff and church functions, tel. 028/7126-2301, www.longtowerchurch.org.

Nightlife in Derry

The **Millennium Forum** is a modern venue that reflects the city's revived investment in local culture, concerts, and plays (box office open Mon-Sat 9:30-17:30, inside city walls on Newmarket Street near Ferryquay Gate, tel. 028/7126-4455, www.millenniumforum. co.uk, boxoffice@millenniumforum.co.uk).

The **Nerve Centre** shows a wide variety of art-house films and live concerts (inside city walls at 7-8 Magazine Street, near Butcher Gate, tel. 028/7126-0562, www.nerve-centre.org.uk).

The **Playhouse Theatre** is an intimate venue for plays (inside

---

Sleep Code

(£1 = about $1.60, country code: 44, area code: 028)
S = Single, **D** = Double/Twin, **T** = Triple, **Q** = Quad, **b** = bathroom, **s** = shower only. Breakfast is included and credit cards are accepted unless otherwise noted.

To help you easily sort through these listings, I've divided the accommodations into three categories, based on the price for a standard double room with bath:

$$$ **Higher Priced**—Most rooms £80 or more.
$$ **Moderately Priced**—Most rooms between £40-80.
$ **Lower Priced**—Most rooms £40 or less.

Prices can change without notice; verify the hotel's current rates online or by email.

---

the walls on Artillery Street, between New Gate and Ferryquay Gate, tel. 028/7126-8027, www.derryplayhouse.co.uk).

If you want to get away from tourists and mingle with Derry residents, try **Peadar O'Donnell's** pub on Waterloo Street for Derry's best nightly traditional-music sessions (53 Waterloo Street, tel. 028/7137-2318).

Sleeping in Derry

$$$ Tower Hotel is the only hotel actually inside Derry's historic walls. It's a real splurge, with 93 modern and immaculate rooms, a classy bistro restaurant, and private basement parking (Sb-£57-99, Db-£64-110, online deals, Butcher Street, tel. 028/7137-1000, fax 028/7137-1234, www.towerhotelderry.com, reservations@thd.ie).

$$ Merchant's House, on a quiet street a 10-minute stroll from Waterloo Place, is a fine Georgian townhouse with a grand, colorful drawing room and nine rooms sporting marble fireplaces and ornate plasterwork (S-£35, Sb-£45-55, Db-£60-65, Tb-£75, Qb-£80-100, Wi-Fi, 16 Queen Street, tel. 028/7126-9691, www.thesaddlershouse.com, saddlershouse@btinternet.com, Joan and Peter Pyne also run the Saddler's House, next). Ask the Pynes about their appealing self-catering townhouse rentals inside the walls (great for families or anyone needing extra space).

$$ Saddler's House, run by the owners of Merchant's House, is a charming Victorian townhouse with seven rooms located a couple of blocks closer to the old town walls (S-£35, Sb-£40-50, Db-£60-65, Wi-Fi, 36 Great James Street, tel. 028/7126-9691, www.thesaddlershouse.com, saddlershouse@btinternet.com).

$$ Travelodge has 44 comfortable rooms, a great location, and a handy adjacent parking garage—but beware of large, loud party groups on weekends (Db-£55 Sun-Thu, Db-£65-80 Fri-Sat, significant online discounts if you book ahead, continental breakfast-£7, 22-24 Strand Road, tel. 028/7127-1271, www.travelodge. ie).

$ Paddy's Palace Hostel, located in the city center, rents 40 decent beds for £12-15 a night with breakfast. Look for the green-and-yellow building, and pause to read the great Mark Twain quote above the front door (4-6 beds/room, family rooms with private bathroom for up to four-£50, Internet access, laundry facilities, kitchen, 1 Woodleigh Terrace, Asylum Road, tel. 028/7130-9051, www.paddyspalace.com, steve@irishexperience.ie, Stephen Mc-Philemy). Ask about their adjacent self-catering apartments. Stephen also offers walking tours (see "Tours in Derry," earlier).

Eating in Derry

The **Custom House Restaurant & Wine Bar** is the classiest place in town, serving great £14-19 meals and a selection of fine wines in a posh, calm space. It faces the river half a block from the Guild Hall (Mon-Sat 12:00-14:30 & 17:30-21:30, Sun 15:00-21:00, Queens Quay, tel. 028/7137-3366).

The hip, trendy **Exchange Restaurant and Wine Bar** offers £7-10 lunches and quality £12-16 dinners with flair, in a central location near the river behind Waterloo Place (Mon-Sat 12:00-14:30 & 17:30-22:00, Sun 16:00-21:00, Queen's Quay, tel. 028/7127-3990).

The **Mandarin Palace** dishes up good £10-15 Chinese dinners in a crisp dining room facing the river (Mon-Fri 12:00-14:30 & 16:30-23:00, Sat 16:30-23:00, Sun 13:00-22:00, weekday buffet lunch, £10 two-course early-bird deals 16:30-19:00, Queens Quay at Lower Clarendon Street, tel. 028/7137-3656).

Easygoing **Fitzroy's,** tucked below Ferryquay Gate, serves good £8-12 lunches and £9-15 dinners (Mon-Sat 12:00-22:00, Sun 13:00-20:00, 2-4 Bridge Street, tel. 028/7126-6211).

Austins Department Store, right on the Diamond in the center of the old city, is Ireland's oldest department store (1830). It predates Harrods in London by 15 years and Macy's in New York by 25 years. Its basic top-floor café comes with lofty views and £5 lunch specials (Mon-Sat 9:30-17:30, Sun 13:00-17:00, 2-6 The Diamond, tel. 028/7126-1817).

Supermarkets: **Tesco** has everything for picnics and road munchies (Mon-Fri 8:00-21:00, Sat 8:00-20:00, Sun 13:00-18:00, corner of Strand Road and Clarendon Street). **SuperValu** meets the same needs (Mon-Wed and Sat 8:30-19:00, Thu-Fri 8:30-20:00, Sun 12:30-17:30, Waterloo Place).

Derry Connections

From Derry, it's an hour's drive to Portrush. If you're using public transportation, consider spending £16.50 for a Zone 4 iLink smartcard (£15 top-up for each additional day), good for all-day train and bus use in Northern Ireland (see page 358). Translink has useful updated schedules and prices for both trains and buses in Northern Ireland (tel. 028/9066-6630, www.translink.co.uk). Keep in mind that some bus and train schedules, road signs, and maps may say "Londonderry" or "L'Derry" instead of "Derry."

From Derry by Train to: Portrush (9/day, 1.5 hours, change in Coleraine), **Belfast** (9/day, 2.5 hours), **Dublin** (7/day, 5 hours).

By Bus to: Galway (4/day, 5 hours), **Portrush** (5/day, 1.25 hours, change in Coleraine), **Belfast** (hourly, 1.75 hours), **Dublin** (5/day, 4.5 hours).

Between Derry and Galway

If you're driving into Northern Ireland from Galway, Westport, or Strokestown and don't have time to explore Donegal, consider these two interesting stops in the interior.

Belleek Pottery Visitors Centre— Just over the Northern Ireland border (30 miles/48 km northeast of Sligo) is the cute town of Belleek, famous for its pottery. The Belleek Parian China factory welcomes visitors with a small gallery and museum, a 20-minute video, a cheery cafeteria, and fascinating 30-minute guided tours of its working factory. Crazed shoppers who forget to fill out a VAT refund form will find their finances looking Belleek.

Cost and Hours: Free, £4 tours, visitors center open March-Sept Mon-Fri 9:00-17:30, Sat 10:00-17:30, Sun 14:00-17:30; longer hours July-Sept, shorter hours Oct-Feb; closed Sat Jan-Feb; closed Sun Nov-Feb; no tours Sat-Sun; call to confirm tour schedule and reserve a spot, tel. 028/6865-8501, www.belleek.ie.

▲**Ulster American Folk Park**—North of Omagh (five miles/8 km on A-5), this combination museum and folk park commemorates the many Irish who left their homeland during the hard times of the 19th century. Exhibits show life before emigration, on the boat, and in America. You'll gain insight into the origins of the tough Scots-Irish stock—think Davy Crockett (his people were from Derry) and Andrew Jackson (Carrickfergus roots)—who later

DERRY

shaped America's westward migration. You'll also find good coverage of the *Titanic* tragedy, and its effect on the Ulster folk who built the ship and the loved ones it left behind.

Cost and Hours: £6.50; March-Sept Tue-Sun 10:00-17:00; Oct-Feb Tue-Fri 10:00-16:00, Sat-Sun 11:00-16:00; closed Mon year-round; cafeteria, 2 Mellon Road, tel. 028/8224-3292, www.nmni.com.

Nearby: The adjacent **Mellon Centre for Migration Studies** is handy for genealogy searches (Mon-Fri 10:30-17:00, closed Sat-Sun, tel. 028/8225-6315, www.qub.ac.uk/cms).

County Donegal

Donegal is the most remote (and perhaps the most ruggedly beautiful) county in Ireland. It's not on the way to anywhere, and it wears its isolation well. With more native Irish speakers than in any other county, the old ways are better preserved here. The northernmost part of Ireland, Donegal remains connected to the Republic by a slim, five-mile-wide umbilical cord of land on its southern coast. It's also Ireland's second-biggest county, with a wide-open "big sky" interior and a shattered-glass, 200-mile, jagged coastline of islands and inlets.

This is the home turf of St. Colmcille (St. Columba in English; means "dove of the church" in Irish), who was born here in 521. In the hierarchy of revered Irish saints, he's second only to St. Patrick. A proud Gaelic culture held out in Donegal to the bitter end, when the O'Donnells and the O'Dohertys, the two most famous local clans, were finally defeated by the English in the early 1600s. After their defeat, the region became known as Dun na nGall ("the fort of the foreigner"), which was eventually anglicized to Donegal.

As the English moved in, four Donegal-dwelling friars (certain that Gaelic ways would be lost forever) painstakingly wrote down Irish history from Noah's Ark to their present. This labor of love became known as the Annals of the Four Masters, and without it, much of our knowledge of early Irish history and myth would have been lost. An obelisk stands in their honor in the main square of Donegal town.

The hardy people of County Donegal have come out on the short end of the modern technology stick. They were famous for their quality tweed weaving, a cottage industry that has gradually given way to modern industrial production in far-off cities. A small but energetic Irish fishing fleet still churns offshore—in the wake of larger EU factory ships poaching traditionally Irish waters.

But culturally, the county shines. The traditional Irish musicians of Donegal play a driving style of music with a distinctively fast and forceful rhythm. Meanwhile, Enya (local Gweedore gal made good) has crafted languid, ethereal tunes that glide from mood to mood. Both *Dancing at Lughnasa* and *The Secret of Roan Inish* were filmed in County Donegal. Today, emigration has taken its toll, and the region relies on a trickle of tourism spilling over from Northern Ireland.

Orientation to County Donegal

Remember, you are leaving the UK for the Republic of Ireland. Once you cross into the Republic, all currency is in euros, not pounds. For B&B rates, entry fees, and all other costs in Donegal, keep this exchange rate in mind: €1 = about $1.30. Long-distance dialing is different too. To call Northern Ireland from the Republic of Ireland, dial 048 and then the local eight-digit number. To call the Republic of Ireland from Northern Ireland, dial 00-353, then the area code without its initial 0, and finally the local number.

Self-Guided Driving Tour

Donegal Loop Trip

Here's my choice for a scenic mix of Donegal highlands and coastal views, organized as a daylong circuit (240 km/150 miles) for drivers based across the border in Derry. If you're coming north from Galway or Westport, you could incorporate parts of this drive into your itinerary.

Route Summary: Drive west out of Derry (direction: Letterkenny) on Buncrana Road, which becomes A-2 (and then N-13 across the border in the Republic). Follow the signs into Letterkenny, and take R-250 out the other (west) end of town. Veer right (north) onto R-251, and stay on it through Church Hill, all the way across the highlands, until you link up with N-56 approaching Bunbeg. After a couple of kilometers on N-56, take R-258 from Gweedore; it's another six kilometers (four miles) into Bunbeg. Depart Bunbeg going north on R-257, around Bloody Foreland, and rejoin N-56 near Gortahork. Take N-56 through Dunfanaghy (possible Horn Head mini-loop option here) and then south, back into Letterkenny. Retrace your route from Letterkenny via N-13 and A-2 back into Derry.

Driving Tips: An early start and an Ordnance Survey atlas are essential. It's cheapest to top off your gas tank in Letterkenny. Consider bringing along a picnic lunch to enjoy from a scenic roadside pullout along the Bloody Foreland R-257 road, or out on the

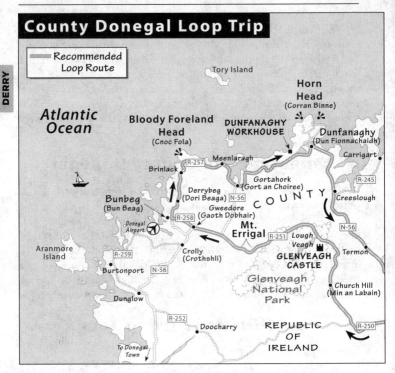

County Donegal Loop Trip

Recommended Loop Route

Atlantic Ocean

Tory Island

Horn Head (Corran Binne)

Bloody Foreland Head (Cnoc Fola)

DUNFANAGHY WORKHOUSE

Dunfanaghy (Dun Fionnachaidh)

Carrigart

Meenlaragh

Brinlack   R-257

Gortahork (Gort an Choiree)

R-245

Derrybeg (Dori Beaga)   N-56

COUNTY

Creeslough

Bunbeg (Bun Beag)

Gweedore (Gaoth Dobhair)

R-258

Donegal Airport

Mt. Errigal   R-251   Lough Veagh   N-56

GLENVEAGH CASTLE

Termon

Aranmore Island

R-259

Crolly (Crothshli)

Burtonport   N-56

Glenveagh National Park

Church Hill (Min an Labain)

Dunglow

R-252   Doocharry

REPUBLIC OF IRELAND   R-250

To Donegal Town

Horn Head loop. Bring your camera and remember—not all who wander are lost.

The sights along this route are well-marked. Don't underestimate the time it takes to get around here, as the narrow roads are full of curves and bumps. Dogs, bred to herd sheep, dart from side lanes to practice their bluffing techniques on their reflections in your hubcaps. If you average 65 kilometers per hour (about 40 mph) over the course of the day, you've got a very good suspension system. Folks wanting to linger at more than a couple of sights will need to slow down and consider an overnight stop in Bunbeg or Dunfanaghy.

The Tour Begins
• *Leave Derry on A-2, which becomes N-13 near the town of Bridge End. You'll see a sign for the Grianan Aileach Ring Fort posted on N-13, not far from the junction with R-239. Turn up the steep hill at the modern church with the round roof, and follow signs three kilometers (2 miles) to find...*

▲Grianan Aileach Ring Fort
This dramatic, ancient ring fort perches on an 800-foot hill just inside the Republic, a stone's throw from Derry. It's an Iron Age

fortification, built about the time of Christ, and was once the royal stronghold of the O'Neill clan, which dominated Ulster for centuries. Its stout, drystone walls (no mortar) are 12 feet thick and 18 feet high, creating an interior sanctuary 80 feet in diameter (entry is free and unattended).

Once inside, you can scramble up the stairs, which are built into the walls, to enjoy panoramic views in all directions. Murtagh O'Brien, King of Desmond (roughly, today's Limerick, Clare, and Tipperary counties), destroyed the fort in 1101...the same power-play year in which he gave the Rock of Cashel to the Church. He had each of his soldiers carry away one stone, attempting to make it tougher for the O'Neill clan to find the raw materials to rebuild. What you see today is mostly a reconstruction from the 1870s.

• *Return to N-13 and head to and through Letterkenny, continuing out the other (west) end of town on R-250. Eight kilometers (5 miles) west of Letterkenny on this road, you'll reach the...*

DERRY

Newmills Corn and Flax Mills

Come here for a glimpse of the 175-year-old Industrial Revolution, shown high-tech Ulster style. Linen, which comes from flax, was

king in this region. The 15-minute film does a nifty job of explaining the process, showing how the common flax plant ends up as cloth. Working in a mill sounds like a mellow job, but conditions were noisy, unhealthy, and exhausting. Veteran mill workers often braved respiratory disease, deafness, lost fingers, and extreme fire danger. For their trouble, they usually got to keep about 10 percent of what they milled.

The corn mill is still in working condition but requires a skilled miller to operate it. This mill ground oats—"corn" means oats in Ireland. (What we call corn, they call maize.) The huge waterwheel, powered by the River Swilly, made five revolutions per minute and generated eight horsepower.

The entire operation could be handled by one miller, who knew every cog, lever, and flume in the joint. Call ahead to see when working mill demonstrations are scheduled; otherwise, tours last 20 minutes and are available on request.

Cost and Hours: Free, mid-May–mid-Aug daily 10:00–18:00, last entry 45 minutes before closing, closed off-season, Churchill Road, Letterkenny, tel. 074/912-5115.

• *Continue on R-250, staying right at Driminaught as the road becomes R-251. Watch for* Glenveagh Castle and National Park *signs, and park in the visitors center lot.*

▲▲Glenveagh Castle and National Park

One of Ireland's six national parks, Glenveagh's jewel is pristine Lough Veagh (Loch Ghleann Bheatha in Gaelic). The lake is three miles long, occupying a U-shaped valley scoured out of the Derryveagh mountains by powerful glaciers during the last Ice Age.

In the 1850s, this scenic area attracted the wealthy land speculator John George Adair, who bought the valley in 1857. Right away, Adair clashed with local tenants, whom he accused of stealing his sheep. After his managing agent was found murdered, he evicted all 244 of his bitter tenants to great controversy, and set about to create a hunting estate in grand Victorian style.

His pride and joy was his country mansion, Glenveagh Castle,

Donegal or Bust

Part of western County Donegal is in the Gaeltacht, where locals speak the Irish (Gaelic) language. In the spring of 2005, a controversial law was passed that erased all English place names from local road signs in Gaeltacht areas. Signs now only have the Irish-language equivalent, an attempt to protect the region from the further (and inevitable) encroachment of the English language.

Here's a cheat sheet to help you decipher the signs as you drive the Donegal loop (parts of which are in the Gaeltacht). There's also a complete translation of all Irish place names in the recommended *Complete Road Atlas of Ireland* by Ordnance Survey (€10), in the Gazetteer section in the back.

Gaelic Name	Pronounced	English Name
Leitir Ceanainn	*LET-ir CAN-ning*	Letterkenny
Min an Labain	*MEEN on law-BAWN*	Churchill
Loch Ghleann	*LOCKH thown*	Lough (Lake)
Bheatha	*eh-VEH-heh*	Veagh
An Earagail	*on AIR-i-gul*	Mt. Errigal
Gaoth Dobhair	*GWEE door*	Gweedore
Crothshli	*CROTH-lee*	Crolly
Bun Beag	*bun bee-OWG*	Bunbeg
Dori Beaga	*DOR-uh bee-OWG-uh*	Derrybeg
Cnoc Fola	*NOK FAW-luh*	Bloody Foreland
Gort an Choirce	*gurt on HER-kuh*	Gortahork
Dun Fionnachaidh	*doon on-AH-keh*	Dunfanaghy
Corran Binne	*COR-on BIN-eh*	Horn Head

finished in 1873 on the shore of Lough Veagh. After his death, his widow added to the castle and introduced rhododendrons and rare red deer to the estate. After her death, Harvard art professor Kingsley Porter bought the estate and promptly disappeared on the Donegal coast. (He's thought to have drowned.) The last owner was Philadelphia millionaire Henry McIlhenny, who filled the mansion with fine art and furniture while perfecting the lush surrounding gardens. He donated the castle to the Irish nation in 1981.

Cost and Hours: Park entry-free, guided castle tour-€5, daily mid-March-Oct 9:30-18:00, Nov-mid-March 9:00-17:00, last entry one hour before closing, tel. 074/913-7090, www.glenveagh nationalpark.ie. Without a car, you can reach Glenveagh Castle and National Park by bus tour from Derry (see "Tours in Derry," earlier).

Visting the Castle and National Park: The **Glenveagh National Park Visitors Centre** explains the region's natural history. Hiking trails in the park are scenic and tempting, but beware of the tiny midges that seem to want to nest in your nostrils.

The **castle** is only accessible by a 30-minute hike or a 10-minute shuttle-bus ride (€3 round-trip, 4/hour, depart from visitors center, last shuttle at 17:00). Take the 45-minute castle tour, letting your Jane Austen and Agatha Christie fantasies go wild. Antlers abound on walls, in chandeliers, and in paintings by Victorian hunting artists. A table crafted from rare bog oak (from ancient trees hundreds of years old, found buried in the muck) stands at attention in one room, while Venetian glass chandeliers illuminate a bathroom. A round pink bedroom at the top of a tower is decorated in Oriental style, with inlaid mother-of-pearl furnishings. The library, which displays paintings by George Russell, has the castle's best lake views.

Afterward, stroll through the gardens and enjoy the lovely setting. A lakeside swimming pool had boilers underneath it to keep it heated. It's no wonder that Greta Garbo was an occasional guest, coming to visit whenever she "vanted" to be alone.

• *Leave the national park and follow R-251 west, watching for the Mount Errigal trailhead. It's southeast of the mountain, and starts at the small parking lot beside R-251 on the mountain's lower slope (easy to spot, with a low surrounding stone wall in the middle of open bog land).*

Mount Errigal (An Earagail)

The mountain (2,400 feet) dominates the horizon for miles around. Rising from the relatively flat interior bog land, it looks taller from a distance than it is. Beautifully cone-shaped (but not a volcano), it offers a hearty, non-technical climb with panoramic views (four  hours round-trip, covering five miles). Hikers should get a weather report before setting out (frequent mists squat on the summit).

• *Continue on R-251 as it merges into N-56 headed west; at Gweedore, stay west on R-258. After six kilometers (4 miles), you'll reach R-257 and...*

Bunbeg (Bun Beag)

This modest town offers a fine sandy beach. Otherwise, it's a strip of scattered pubs, shops, markets, gas stations, and vacation homes. Take the trouble to seek out the quaint, hidden fishing harbor at the rocky south end of town. The harbor-access road is directly in front of you as you approach the town from the east on R-258 and pull up to the stop sign where R-258 meets R-257. At the dead end of the half-mile access road is a cute, watercolor-worthy harbor, with an old stone warehouse and a good guesthouse.

There's an ATM at the AIB bank (on the left, going north on R-257, 100 yards past Seaview Hotel). The post office is at the R-258/R-257 junction, next to the DVD rental shop (Mon-Fri 9:00-17:30, Sat 9:00-13:00, closed Sun).

Turasmara operates a limited ferry service from Bunbeg harbor. It's a 1.5-hour voyage to the ultra-remote and rugged Tory Island (€20-25 round-trip, runs daily June-Sept—weather permitting, departs at 9:00 and returns at 18:00, call to confirm schedule, tel. 074/953-1340).

Sleeping in Bunbeg: **$$ Bunbeg House,** overlooking the snug and charming Bunbeg fishing harbor, has 12 simple, spacious rooms and a tiny, inviting pub downstairs (Sb-€40-45, Db-€70-80, Tb-€90-110, parking, tel. 074/953-1305, fax 074/953-1420, www.bunbeghouse.com, bunbeghouse@eircom.net, Andy and Jean Carr).

$$ Teach Anraoi B&B is a comfortable traditional home with five clean, economical, unpretentious rooms (Sb-€30, Db-€55, cash only; on R-257 in the middle of Bunbeg, 100 yards past the bank, down a steep driveway; tel. 074/953-1092, Sean and Roisin Gallagher).

Eating in Bunbeg: Try the **Seaview Hotel Bistro,** which specializes in fish dishes (€20-25 meals, June-Sept daily 18:30-21:00, Oct-May Fri-Sat only 18:30-21:00, on R-257, tel. 074/953-1159). You'll find a fine pub dinner, plus late-evening traditional-music sessions nightly, at **Leo's Tavern,** run by the father of famed Irish singer, Enya. To get there from Bunbeg, leave town on R-257 going south, hop on N-56, and continue south through the nearby hamlet of Crolly. Take a right onto R-259 (sign says *Aerphort*), and go a half-mile, following signs to Leo's, which will bring you to an uphill right turn. The pub is 100 yards up on the left (food served Mon-Sat 16:00-21:00, Sun 12:00-15:30, tel. 074/954-8143). Groceries are sold at the **Spar Market** in nearby Derrybeg (Mon-Sat 9:00-19:30, Sun 9:00-13:30).

• *The eight kilometers (5 miles) of road heading north—as Bunbeg blends into Derrybeg (Dori Beage) and a bit beyond—are some of the most densely populated sections of this loop tour. Modern holiday cottages pepper the landscape in what the Irish have come to call "Bungalow Bliss" (or "Bungalow Blight" to nature-lovers). Next you'll come to the...*

Bloody Foreland (Cnoc Fola)

Named for the shade of red that backlit heather turns at sunset, this scenic headland is laced with rock walls and forgotten cottage ruins. Pull off at one of the lofty roadside viewpoints and savor a picnic lunch and rugged coastal views.

• *Continue on R-257, meeting N-56 near Gortahork. Stay on N-56 to the Dunfanaghy Workhouse, about a kilometer south of Dunfanaghy town.*

Dunfanaghy Workhouse

Opened in 1845, this structure was part of an extensive workhouse compound (separating families by gender and age)—a dreaded last resort for the utterly destitute of coastal Donegal. There were once many identical compounds built across Ireland, a rigid Victorian solution to the spiraling problem of Ireland's rapidly multiplying poor. Authorities at the time thought that poverty stemmed from laziness and should be punished. So, to motivate those lodging at the workhouse to pull themselves up by their bootstraps, conditions were made hard. But the system was unable to cope with the starving, homeless multitudes who were victims of the famine.

The harsh workhouse experience is told through the true-life narrative of Wee Hannah Herrity, a wandering orphan and former resident of this workhouse. She survived the famine by taking refuge here, dying at age 90 in 1926. With the audioguide, you'll visit three upstairs rooms where stiff papier-mâché figures relate the powerful episodes in her life.

Cost and Hours: €4.50, includes audioguide; June-Sept daily 9:30-17:30, shorter hours off-season, call to confirm winter hours, good bookstore and coffee shop, tel. 074/913-6540, www.dunfa naghyworkhouse.ie.

• *Now continue into the town of...*

Dunfanaghy (Dun Fionnachaidh)

This planned town, founded by the English in the early 1600s for local markets and fairs, has a prim and proper appearance. In Dunfanaghy (dun-FAN-ah-hee), you can grab a pub lunch or some picnic fixings from the town market. Enjoy them from a scenic viewpoint on the nearby Horn Head loop drive (described later).

The modest town square, mostly a parking lot, marks the center of town. The post office is at the southern end of the village (Mon-Fri 9:00-17:30, Sat 9:00-13:00, closed Sun). Groceries are sold in the **Centra Market** (Mon-Thu 7:30-21:00, Fri-Sun 7:30-22:00) on the main road opposite the town square.

Sleeping in Dunfanaghy: **$$$ The Mill Restaurant and Accommodation** is a diamond in the Donegal rough. Susan Alcorn nurtures six wonderful rooms with classy decor, while her husband Derek is the chef in their fine restaurant downstairs (Sb-€60-70, Db-€100-105, Tb-€135, Wi-Fi, parking, tel. 074/913-6985, www. themillrestaurant.com, info@themillrestaurant.com).

Irish Fishermen Feel the Squeeze

The biggest fishing port in Ireland is Killybegs, about 30 kilometers (19 miles) west of Donegal town. But today, fishing is a sadly withering lifestyle. When Ireland joined the EU in 1973, Irish farmers and infrastructure benefited most from generous subsidies that helped transform the country a generation later into the "Celtic Tiger." But as the country reaped over €35 billion from the EU in its first 25 years of membership, the Irish fishing industry suffered. With the Mediterranean overfished, other EU nations set sail for rich Irish waters that were newly opened to them. It's now estimated that 40 percent of the fish caught in Europe come from Irish territorial seas—€175 billion in fish have been caught. Huge factory ships from Spain are far more efficient at hauling in a catch than the 1,500 remaining Irish boats (most of which are under 40 feet long). Irish fishermen lament that for every €1 accepted in EU subsidies, €5 have gone out in foreign nets. And the irony is that much of the fish sold in Irish grocery stores and restaurants is now imported from other EU nations...who caught the fish off the Irish coast. Today, the biggest Irish fishing port may be the airport.

$$ The Whins B&B has three inviting rooms with tasteful furnishings, which range from exotic African accents to a sturdy four-poster bed (Sb-€35-45, Db-€70, Tb-€90-105, Wi-Fi, parking, 10-minute walk north of town, tel. 074/913-6481, mobile 086/162-3948, www.thewhins.com, annemarie@thewhins.com, Anne Marie Moore).

Eating in Dunfanaghy: **The Mill Restaurant and Accommodation** is gourmet all the way, specializing in memorable lamb or lobster dinners, worth booking days ahead of time (€45, Tue-Sun 19:00-21:00, closed Mon, tel. 074/913-6985). **Muck & Muffin** is a simple sandwich café, great for quick, cheap lunches. It's above the pottery shop in the stone warehouse on the town square (Mon-Sat 9:30-17:00, until 21:00 mid-June-mid-Sept; Sun 10:30-17:00; tel. 074/913-6780). **The Great Wall** is a hole-in-the-wall Chinese takeaway place (daily 16:30-23:00, tel. 074/910-0111, next door to Centra Market). A few doors down, **The Oyster Bar** does pub grub and live music on Friday and Saturday nights.

• *From Dunfanaghy, you can head back to Derry via Letterkenny, but first consider a detour to Horn Head.*

Horn Head Loop (Corran Binne)

If you have extra time, take an hour to embark on a lost-world plateau drive. This heaving headland with few trees has coastal views that will have you gripping your steering wheel in amazement. Consult your map and get off N-56, following the Horn Head signs all the way around the eastern lobe of the peninsula. There are fewer than eight kilometers (5 miles) of narrow, single-lane road out here, with very little traffic. But be alert and willing to pull over at wide spots to cooperate with other cars.

This stone-studded peninsula was once an island. Then, shortly after the last Ice Age ended, ocean currents deposited a sandy spit in the calm water behind the island. A hundred years ago, locals harvested its stabilizing dune grass, using it for roof thatching and sending it abroad to Flanders, where soldiers used it to create beds for horses during World War I. However, with the grass gone, the sandy spit was free to migrate again. It promptly silted up the harbor, created a true peninsula, and ruined Dunfanaghy as a port town.

A short spur road leads to the summit of the headland, where you can park your car and walk another 50 yards up to the abandoned WWII lookout shelter. The views from here are dramatic, looking west toward Tory Island and south to Mount Errigal. Some may choose to hike an additional 30 minutes across the heather, to the ruins of the distant signal tower (not a castle, but instead a lookout for a feared Napoleonic invasion), clearly visible near the cliffs. The trails are not maintained, but it's easy to bushwhack your way through (in sturdy footwear) to the rewarding cliff views. Navigate back to your car, using the lookout shelter on the summit as a landmark.

IRELAND: PAST and PRESENT

Ireland is rich with history, art, and language. And the country continues to transform and grow today, learning from its experience with the Celtic Tiger economy (a bittersweet memory), making progress toward peace, and reexamining some of its long-held social customs.

Irish History

Hunters, Farmers, and Mysterious Mounds (Prehistory)

Ireland became an island when rising seas covered the last land bridge (7000 B.C.), a separation from Britain that the Irish would fight to maintain for the next 9,000 years. By 6000 B.C., Stone Age hunter-fishers had settled on the east coast, followed by Neolithic farmers (from the island of Britain). These early inhabitants left behind impressive but mysterious funeral mounds (passage graves) and large Stonehenge-type stone circles.

The Celts: Language and Legends (500 B.C.-A.D. 450)

Perhaps more an invasion of ideas than of armies, the Celtic culture from Central Europe (particularly that of the most influential tribe, called the **Gaels**) settled in Ireland, where it would dominate for a thousand years. A warrior people with more than a hundred petty kings, they feuded constantly with rival clans and gathered in ring forts for protection. There were more than 300 *tuatha* (clans) in Ireland, each with its own *rí* (king), who would've happily chopped the legs off anyone who called him "petty." The island was nominally ruled by a single *Ard Rí* (high king) at the **Hill of Tara** (north of Dublin), though there was no centralized nation.

What's a Celt?

The Irish are a Celtic people. The Celts, who came from Central Europe, began migrating west in about 1500 B.C. Over time, many settled in the British Isles and in western France. When the Angles and Saxons came later, grabbing the best land in the British Isles (which became Angle-land...or England), the Celts survived in Brittany, Cornwall, Wales, Scotland, and Ireland. Today, this "Celtic Crescent" still nearly encircles England. The word "Celtic" (pronounced with a hard *C*) comes from the Greek "Keltoi," meaning barbarian.

From about 700 B.C. on, various Celtic tribes mixed, mingled, and fought in Ireland. The last and most powerful of the Celtic tribes to enter the fray were the Gaels, who probably came to Ireland from Scotland. The Irish and Scottish language, Gaelic, is named for them.

Celtic society revolved around warrior kings, who gathered groups of families into regional kingdoms. These small kingdoms combined to make the five large provincial kingdoms of ancient Ireland (whose names survive on maps today): Leinster, Munster, Connacht, Ulster, and the Middle Kingdom (now County Meath).

For defensive purposes, these early Irish peoples lived in small thatched huts built on manmade islands or on high ground surrounded by ditches and a stone or earthen wall. A strictly observed hierarchy governed Celtic societies: the king on top, followed by poets, druids (priests), legal men, skilled craftsmen, freemen, and slaves. Rarely did a high king rule the entire island. Loyalty to one's clan came first, and alliances between clans were often temporary, lasting only until a more advantageous alliance could be struck with a rival clan. This fluid system of alliances ebbing and flowing across the Celtic-warrior cultural landscape meant that the Celts would never unite as a single nation. It also meant that an invading army could not destroy one main capital or kill one king to bring the entire island to its knees. Celtic culture was a multi-headed monster...tough to slay.

Unlike the Celtic tribes living in Western Europe and England, the Celts in Ireland were never conquered by the Romans. This gives Ireland a cultural continuity and uniqueness rare in Europe. Their culture—which evolved apart from Europe—remained strong and independent for centuries. Then, in the 12th century, English dominance led to suppression of the Gaelic language and Celtic traditions. But with Irish independence—won only in the 20th century—Irish ways are no longer threatened. The most traditional areas (generally along the west coast, such as the Dingle Peninsula) are protected as a Gaeltacht. The Gaeltacht (literally, places where the Gaelic language is spoken) is a kind of national park for the traditional culture. If much of Ireland's charm can be credited to its Celtic roots, that charm is most vivid in the Gaeltacht.

Druid priests conducted pagan, solar-calendar rituals among the megalithic stones erected by earlier inhabitants. The Celtic people peppered the countryside with thousands of Iron Age monuments. While most of the sights are little more than rock piles that take a vigorous imagination to reconstruct (ring forts, wedge tombs, standing stones, and so on), just standing next to a megalith that predates the pharaohs is stirring.

The Celtic world lives on today in the Gaelic language and in legends of Celtic warriors such as **Finn McCool,** who led a merry band of heroes in battle and in play. Tourists marvel at large ritual stones decorated with ogham (rhymes with "poem") script, the peculiar Celtic-Latin alphabet that used lines as letters. The **Tara Brooch** and elaborately inscribed, jewel-encrusted daggers in Dublin's National Museum attest to the sophistication of this warrior society.

In 55 B.C., the Romans conquered the Celts in England, but Ireland and Scotland remained independent, their history forever skewed in a different direction—Gaelic, not Latin. The Romans called Ireland **Hibernia,** meaning Land of Winter; it was apparently too cold and bleak to merit an attempt at colonization. The biggest nonevent in Irish history is that the Romans never invaded. While the mix of Celtic and Roman is part of what makes the French French and the English English, the Irish are purely Celtic. Hurling, the wild Irish national pastime, goes back more than 2,000 years to Celtic days, when it was played almost as a substitute for warfare. Perhaps best described as something like airborne hockey with no injury time-outs, hurling is as central to the Irish culture as cricket is to the English, or *boules* to the French.

Christianity: The Age of Saints and Scholars (A.D. 450-800)

When Ancient Rome fell and took the Continent with it, Gaelic Ireland remained. There was no Dark Age here, and the island was a beacon of culture for the rest of Europe. Ireland (population c. 750,000) was still a land of many feuding kings, but the culture was stable.

Christianity and Latin culture arrived first as a trickle from trading contacts with Christian Gaul (France), then more emphatically in A.D. 432 with **St. Patrick,** who persuasively converted the sun-and-nature-worshipping Celts. (Perhaps St. Patrick had an easy time converting the locals because they had so little sun to worship.) Patrick (c. 389-461), a Latin-speaking Christian from Roman Britain, was kidnapped as a teenager and carried off into slavery for six years in Ireland. He escaped back to Britain, then traveled to Gaul to study for a life in the clergy. Inspired by a dream, he eventually returned to Ireland, determined to convert the pagan, often hostile, Celtic inhabitants. Legends say he drove Ireland's snakes (symbolic of pagan beliefs) into the sea and explained the Trinity with a shamrock—three leaves on one stem.

Later monks (such as **St. Columba,** 521-597) continued Christianizing the island, and foreign monks flocked to isolated Ireland. They withdrew to scattered, isolated monasteries, living in stone igloo beehive huts, translating and illustrating (illuminating) manuscripts. Perhaps the greatest works of art of Dark Age Europe are these manuscripts, particularly the ninth-century **Book of Kells,** which you'll see at Dublin's Trinity College. Irish monks—heads shaved cross-wise from ear to ear, like the former Druids—were known throughout Europe as ascetic scholars.

St. Columbanus (c. 600; different from St. Columba) was one of several traveling missionary monks who helped to bring Christianity back to Western Europe, which had reverted to paganism and barbarism after the fall of the Roman Empire. The monks established monastic centers of learning that produced great Christian teachers and community builders. One of the monks, **St. Brendan,** may have sailed to America.

By 800, **Charlemagne** was importing Irish monks to help run his Frankish kingdom. Meanwhile, Ireland remained a relatively cohesive society based on monastic settlements rather than cities. Impressive round towers from those settlements still dot the Irish landscape—silent reminders of this exalted age.

Viking Invasion and Defeat (800-1100)

In 795, Viking pirates from Norway invaded, first testing isolated island monasteries, then boldly sailing up Irish rivers into the interior. The many raids immediately wreaked havoc on the monasteries and continued to shake Irish civilization for two chaotic centuries. The Vikings raped, pillaged, and burned Christian churches, making off with prized monastic booty such as gold chalices, silver candlestick holders, and the jeweled book covers of sacred illuminated manuscripts. Monks stood guard from their round towers to spy approaching marauders, ring the warning bells, and protect the citizens. In 841, a conquering Viking band decided to winter in Ireland, eventually building the island's first permanent walled cities, Dublin and Waterford. Viking raiders slowly evolved into Viking traders. They were the first to introduce urban life and commerce to Ireland.

Finally, **High King Brian Boru** led a Gaelic revival, briefly controlling the entire island in the late 900s. His rule ended at the Battle of Clontarf (1014), near Dublin. Though he defeated a mercenary Viking army, which had allied with rebellious clans, Boru and most of his sons died in the battle, and his unified kingdom quickly fell apart. Over the centuries, Viking settlers married Gaelic gals and slowly blended in.

Anglo-Norman Arrival (1100-1500)

The Normans were Ireland's next aggressive guests. In 1169, a small army of well-armed and fearless soldiers of fortune invaded Ireland under the pretense of helping a deposed Irish king regain

his lands. With the blessing of the only English pope in history (Adrian IV and his papal bull), a Welsh conquistador named **Strongbow** (c. 1130-1176) took Dublin and Waterford, married the local king's daughter, then succeeded his father-in-law as king of Leinster. This was the spearhead of a century-long invasion by the so-called Anglo-Normans—the French-speaking rulers of England, descended from William the Conqueror and his troops, who had invaded and conquered England a hundred years earlier at the Battle of Hastings (1066).

King Henry II of England soon followed (1171) to remind Strongbow who was boss, proclaiming the entire island under English (Anglo-Norman) rule. By 1250, the Anglo-Normans occupied two-thirds of the island, controlling the best land while clustered in walled cities surrounded by hostile Gaels. These invaders, who were big-time administrators, ushered in a new age in which society (government, cities, and religious organizations) was organized on a grander scale. They imposed feudalism and scoffed at the old Gaelic clan system that they intended to replace. Riding on the coattails of the Normans, monastic orders (Franciscans, Augustinians, Benedictines, and Cistercians) came over from the Continent and eclipsed Ireland's individual monastic settlements, once the foundation of Irish society, back in the Age of Saints and Scholars.

Normans lived in tightly packed settlements surrounded by their superior fortifications. But when the **Black Death** came in 1348, it spread more rapidly and fatally in these tight quarters than it did in rural, far-flung Gaelic clan settlements. The plague, along

Stone Circles: The Riddle of the Rocks

Ireland is home to more than 200 evocative stone circles. These jaggedly sparse boulder rings are rudimentary in comparison to Britain's more famous Stonehenge. But their misty, mossy settings provide curious travelers with an intimate and accessible glimpse of the mysterious people who lived in Ireland before the arrival of the Celts.

Bronze Age Ireland (2000-600 B.C.) was populated by farming folk who had mastered the craft of smelting heated tin and copper together to produce bronze, which was used to produce more durable tools and weapons. Late in the Bronze Age, many of these primitive, clannish communities also put considerable time and effort into gathering huge rocks and arranging them into ceremonial circles for use in rituals with long-forgotten  meanings. Scholars believe that these circles may have been used as solar observatories, to calculate solstices and equinoxes as they planned life-sustaining seasonal crop-planting cycles. Archaeologists have discovered a few ancient remains in the center of some circles, but their primary use seems to have been ceremonial rather than as burial sites. And without any written records, we can only make educated guesses as to their exact purpose.

In the Middle Ages, superstitious people believed that the stones had been arranged by an earlier race of giants. Later, some thought that at least one circle was made up of petrified partiers who had dared to dance on the Sabbath. A nearby

with Normans intermarrying with Gaels, eventually diluted Norman identity and shrank English control.

England, preoccupied with the Hundred Years' War with France and its own internal Wars of the Roses, "ruled" through deputized locals such as the earls of Kildare. Many Irish landowners actually resided in England, a pattern of absentee-landlordism that would persist for centuries. England's laws were fully enforced only in a 50-mile foothold around Dublin (**the Pale**—from the Norman-French word for a defensive ditch). A couple of centuries after invading, the Anglo-Normans saw their area of control shrink to only the Pale (perhaps 20 percent of the island)—with the rest of the island "beyond the Pale."

Even as their power eroded, the English kings considered Ireland theirs. To keep their small islands of English culture undiluted by Irish heathen ways, they passed the **Statutes of Kilkenny**

standing stone was supposed to be the frozen figure of the piper who had been playing the dance tunes.

Irish stone circles are concentrated in two main regional clusters consisting of more than a hundred circles each: central Ulster, in the North (radiocarbon-dated 1500-700 B.C.); and County Cork and County Kerry, in the south (radiocarbon-dated 1000-700 B.C.). The remaining dozen circles are scattered across central Ireland. Some circles have only recently been rediscovered, having been buried over the centuries by rapidly accumulating bog growth.

Dedicated travelers seeking stone circles will find them marked in the Ordnance Survey atlas and signposted along rural Irish roads. Ask a local farmer for directions—and savor the experience (wear shoes impervious to grass dew and sheep doo).

Here are my five favorite Irish stone circles, all within a druid's dance of other destinations mentioned in this book:

Kenmare's is in County Kerry, on the western fringe of Kenmare town. It's the most easily accessible of the circles listed here.

Dromberg is in County Cork, 35 miles (56 km) southwest of Kinsale, up a narrow winding lane just south of the R-597 coastal road.

Glebe is in County Mayo, two miles (3 km) east of Cong and 100 yards south of the R-345 road to Neale (across a minefield of sheep droppings).

Beltany is in County Donegal, 10 miles (16 km) southeast of Letterkenny, straight south of Raphoe.

Beaghmore is in County Tyrone, 20 miles (32 km) east of Omagh, north off A-505 (Cookstown Road).

(1366). These laws prohibited the settlers from going native and being seduced by Gaelic ways...or people. Intermarriage between Irish locals and English settlers, adoption of Irish dress, and the speaking of the Gaelic language were all outlawed. In practice, the statutes were rarely enforced.

The End of Gaelic Rule (1500s)

As European powers raced west to establish profitable colonies in North and South America, Ireland's location on the western edge of Europe took on more strategic importance. England's naval power grew to threaten Spain's monopoly on New World riches. Meanwhile, Spain viewed Ireland as England's vulnerable back door—the best place to attack. (Think of how the USSR used Cuba to threaten the US in the early 1960s.) Martin Luther's **Reformation** split the Christian churches into Catholic and Protestant,

Typical Castle Architecture

Castles were fortified residences for medieval nobles. In Ireland, they were introduced by Norman (evolving into English) warlords in the late 1100s. Castles come in all shapes and sizes, but knowing a few general terms will help you understand them.

The Keep (or Donjon): A high, strong stone tower in the center of the castle complex that was the lord's home and refuge of last resort.

Great Hall: The largest room in the castle, serving as throne room, conference center, and dining hall.

The Yard (or Bailey or Ward): An open courtyard inside the castle walls.

Loopholes: Narrow slits in the walls (also called embrasures, arrow slits, or arrow loops) through which soldiers could shoot arrows at the enemy.

Towers: Tall structures serving as lookouts, chapels, living quarters, or the dungeon. Towers could be square or round, with either crenellated tops or conical roofs.

Turret: A small lookout tower projecting up from the top of the wall.

Moat: A ditch encircling the wall, often filled with water.

Wall Walk (or Allure): A pathway atop the wall where guards could patrol and where soldiers stood to fire at the enemy.

Parapet: Outer railing of the wall walk.

Crenellation: A gap-toothed pattern of stones atop the parapet.

Hoardings (or Gallery or Brattice): Wooden huts built onto the upper parts of the stone walls. They served as watch towers, living quarters, and fighting platforms.

making Catholic Ireland an even hotter potato for newly Protestant England to handle. Catholic Spain and, later, France would use their shared Catholicism with Ireland as divine justification for alliances against heretic England.

In 1534, angered by **Henry VIII** and his break with Catholicism (and taking advantage of England's Reformation chaos), the **Earls of Kildare** (father, then son) led a rebellion. Henry crushed the revolt, executed the earls, and confiscated their land. Henry's daughter, **Queen Elizabeth I,** gave the land to colonists ("planters"), mainly English Protestants. The next four centuries would see a series of rebellions by Catholic, Gaelic-speaking Irish farmers fighting to free themselves from rule by Protestant, English-speaking landowners.

Hugh O'Neill (1540-1616), a Gaelic chieftain educated in Queen Elizabeth's court, was angered by planters and English

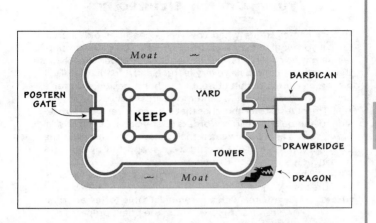

Machicolation: A stone ledge jutting out from the wall, fitted with holes in the bottom. If the enemy was scaling the walls, soldiers could drop rocks or boiling oil down through the holes and onto the enemy below.

Barbican: A fortified gatehouse, sometimes a stand-alone building located outside the main walls.

Drawbridge: A bridge that could be raised or lowered, using counterweights or a chain-and-winch.

Portcullis: A heavy iron grille that could be lowered across the entrance.

Postern Gate: A small, unfortified side or rear entrance used during peacetime. In wartime, it could become a "sally-port" used to launch surprise attacks, or as an escape route.

abuses. He soon led a Gaelic revolt, in 1595. The rebels were supported by the Spanish, who were fellow Catholics and England's archrival on the high seas. At the Battle of Yellow Ford (1598), guerrilla tactics brought about an initial Irish victory.

But the **Battle of Kinsale** (1601) ended the revolt. The exhausted Irish, who had marched the length of Ireland in winter, arrived to help Spanish troops, who were pinned down inside the town. Though the Irish were skilled at guerrilla warfare on their own turf, they were no match for the English on open and unfamiliar ground, and were quickly crushed before they could join the Spanish. The Spanish soon surrendered, and O'Neill knelt before the conquering general, ceding half a million acres to England. Then he and other proud, Gaelic, Ulster-based nobles unexpectedly abandoned their remaining land and sailed to the Continent (the Flight of the Earls, 1607). They searched for further support

Typical Church Architecture

History comes to life when you visit a centuries-old church. Even if you wouldn't know your apse from a hole in the ground, learning a few simple terms will enrich your experience. Note that not every church has every feature, and a "cathedral" isn't a type of church architecture, but rather a designation for a church that's a governing center for a local bishop.

The oldest stone churches that survive in Ireland were designed and built by religious orders (Cistercians, Benedictines, Franciscans, and Dominicans) that came to Ireland from the Continent in the mid-1100s, and were supported by the Norman invaders who soon followed.

Aisles: The long, generally low-ceilinged arcades that flank the nave.

Altar: The raised area with a ceremonial table (often adorned with candles or a crucifix), where the priest prepares and serves the bread and wine for Communion.

Apse: The space beyond the altar, often bordered with small chapels.

Barrel Vault: A continuous round-arched ceiling that resembles an extended upside-down U.

Choir: A cozy area, often screened off, located within the church nave and near the high altar where services are sung in a more intimate setting.

Cloister: Covered hallways bordering a (usually square-shaped) open-air courtyard, traditionally where monks and nuns got fresh air.

on the Continent, but died before they could enlist additional armies to bring back to Ireland. Their flight signaled the end of Gaelic Irish rule.

English Colonization and Irish Rebellions (1600s)

King James I took advantage of the Gaelic power vacuum and sent 25,000 Protestant English and Scottish planters into the confiscated land (1610-1641), making Ulster (in the northeast) the most English area of the island. The Irish responded with two major rebellions.

In 1642, while England was embroiled in a civil war between a divine-right monarch (who answered only to God) and a power-hungry Parliament, Irish rebels capitalized on the instability. Tensions were already high, as tenant farmers had recently taken up pitchforks against their English landlords, slaughtering 4,000 in the **Massacre of the Planters** (1641). The landless, Irish-speaking

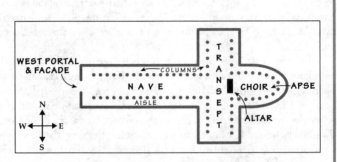

Facade: The exterior surface of the church's main (west) entrance, generally highly decorated.

Groin Vault: An arched ceiling formed where two equal barrel vaults meet at right angles. Less common usage: term for a medieval jock strap.

Narthex: The area (portico or foyer) between the main entry and the nave.

Nave: The long, central section of the church (running west to east, from the entrance to the altar) where the congregation sits or stands through the service.

Transept: In a traditional cross-shaped floor plan, the transept is one of the two parts forming the "arms" of the cross. The transepts run north-south, perpendicularly crossing the east-west nave.

West Portal: The main entry to the church (on the west end, opposite the main altar).

rebels hadn't attacked the middle tier of Irish society—the English-speaking, but still Irish, landed gentry (descendants of the first Anglo-Norman invaders, they were called, rather confusingly, "Old English"). Like the peasant rebels, the "Old English" were Catholic, and they wanted more autonomy for Ireland. Both groups feared the rise of Protestant power in England, and together they formed a pro-Royalist confederation in opposition to the new Protestant Parliament of **Oliver Cromwell.** (This meant, oddly enough, that the Irish now found themselves on the side of the English monarchy.)

Once Cromwell had pulled off his *coup d'état* and executed King Charles I, he invaded Ireland with 12,000 men (1649-1650). Out to obliterate the last Royalist forces and to exact retaliation for the Massacre of the Planters, and armed with Puritanical, anti-Catholic religious zeal, he conquered the country—brutally. Thousands were slaughtered, priests were tortured, villages were pillaged, and rebels were sold into slavery. Cromwell confiscated

PAST & PRESENT

11 million acres of land from Catholic Irish landowners to give to English Protestants. Cromwell's scorched-earth invasion was so harsh, it became known as the "curse of Cromwell"—and it still raises hackles in Ireland (for more on Cromwell, see the sidebar on page 167).

In 1688-1689, rebels again took advantage of England's political chaos. They rallied around Catholic **King James II,** who had been deposed by the English Parliament in the "Glorious Revolution" of 1688 and then had fled to France. He wound up in Ireland, where he formed an army to retake the crown. In the **Siege of Londonderry,** James' Catholic army surrounded the city, the last loyal Protestant power base. But some local apprentice boys locked them out, and after months of negotiations and a 105-day siege, James went away empty-handed.

The showdown came at the massive **Battle of the Boyne** (1690), north of Dublin. Catholic James II and his 25,000 men were defeated by the 36,000 troops of Protestant **King William III** of Orange. From this point on, the color orange became a symbol in Ireland for pro-English, pro-Protestant forces.

As the 17th century came to a close, Protestant England had successfully put down every rebellion. To counter Irish feistiness, the ruling English out-and-out attacked the indigenous Gaelic culture through legislation called the **Penal Laws.** Catholics couldn't vote, hold office, buy land, join the army, play the harp, or even own a horse worth more than £5. Catholic education was banned and priests were outlawed. But the Penal Laws were difficult to enforce, and many Catholics were taught at hidden outdoor "hedge schools," and worshipped in private or at secluded "Mass rocks" in the countryside.

Protestant Rule (1700s)

During the 18th century, urban Ireland thrived economically, and even culturally, under the English. Dublin in the 1700s (pop. 50,000) was Britain's second city, one of Europe's wealthiest and most sophisticated. It's still decorated in Georgian (Neoclassical) style, named for the English kings of the time (consecutive kings George I, II, III, and IV, who ruled for more than a century).

But beyond the Pale surrounding Dublin, rebellion continued to brew. Over time, greed on the top and dissent on the bottom led to more repressive colonial policies. The Enlightenment provided ideas of freedom, and the Revolutionary Age emboldened the Irish masses. Irish nationalists were inspired by budding democratic revolutions in America (1776) and France (1789). The Irish say, "The Tree of Liberty sprouted in America, blossomed in France, and dropped seeds in Ireland." Increasingly, the issue of Irish independence was less a religious question than a political one, as poor, disenfranchised colonists demanded a political voice.

In Dublin, **Jonathan Swift** (1667-1745), the dean of St. Patrick's Cathedral, published his satirical *Gulliver's Travels* with veiled references to English colonialism. He anonymously wrote pamphlets advising, "Burn all that's British, except its coal."

The **Irish Parliament** was an exclusive club, and only Protestant male landowners could be elected to a seat (1 percent of the population qualified). In 1782, led by **Henry Grattan** (1746-1820), the Parliament negotiated limited autonomy from England (while remaining loyal to the king) and fairer treatment of the Catholics. England, chastened by the American Revolution (and soon preoccupied with the French Revolution), tolerated a more-or-less independent Irish Parliament for two decades.

Then, in 1798, came the bloodiest Irish Rebellion. Inspired by the American and French revolutionary successes and buoyed by an "if they can do it, so can we" attitude, a band of Irish idealists rose up and rebelled. The **United Irishmen** (whose goals included introducing the term "Irishman" for all Irish, rather than labeling people as either Protestant or Catholic) revolted against Britain, led by **Wolfe Tone** (1763-1798), a Protestant Dublin lawyer. Tone, trained in the French Revolution, had gained French aid for the Irish cause (though a French naval invasion in 1796 already had failed after a freakish "Protestant wind" blew the ships away from Ireland's shores). The Rebellion was marked by bitter fighting—30,000 died over six weeks—before British troops crushed the revolt.

England tried to solve the Irish problem politically by forcing Ireland into a "Union" with England as part of a "United Kingdom" (**Act of Union,** 1801). The 500-year-old Irish Parliament was dissolved, with its members becoming part of England's Parliament in London. Catholics were not allowed in Parliament. From then on, "Unionists" have been  those who oppose Irish independence, wanting to preserve the country's union with England.

Votes, Violence, and the Famine (1800s)

Irish politicians lobbied in the British Parliament for Catholic rights, reform of absentee-landlordism, and for **Home Rule**—i.e., independence. Meanwhile, secret societies of revolutionaries pursued justice through violence.

Daniel O'Connell (1775-1847), known as The Liberator, campaigned for Catholic equality and for the repeal of the Act of Union (independence). Having personally witnessed the violence of the French Revolution in 1789 and the 1798 United Irishman Rebellion, O'Connell chose peaceful, legal means to achieve his ends. He was a charismatic speaker, drawing half a million people to one of his "monster meeting" demonstrations at the Hill of Tara (1843). But any hope of an Irish revival was soon snuffed out by the biggest catastrophe in Irish history: the Great Potato Famine.

The **Great Potato Famine** (1845-1849) was caused by a fungus *(Phytophthora infestans)* that destroyed Ireland's main food crop.

Legions of people starved to death or died of related diseases (estimates range between 500,000 and 1.1 million). Another one to two million emigrated—most to America and others to Canada and Australia.

The poorest were hardest hit. Potatoes were their main food source, because other crops—grown by tenant farmers on their landlords' land—went to pay the rent and were destined for export.

Britain—then the richest nation on earth, with an empire stretching around the globe— could seemingly do nothing to help its starving citizens. A toxic combination of laissez-faire economic policies, racial bigotry, and religious self-righteousness conspired to blind the English to the plight of the Irish. While the English tend to blame the famine on overpopulation (Ireland's population had doubled in the 40 years leading up to this period), many Irish say there actually was no famine, per se—just a calculated attempt to starve down the local population. For this reason, devout Irish Nationalists do not refer to this period as "the famine" (implying a lack of food) but rather as "An Gort Mór" (The Great Hunger...imposed by British colonial policies). Over the course of five long years, Ireland was ruined. To this day, Irish weather reports include mention of potential potato-blight conditions.

The island's population was suddenly cut by almost a third (from 8.4 million to 6 million). Many of their best and brightest had fled, and the island's economy—and spirit—took generations to recover. The Irish language, spoken by the majority of the population before the famine, became a badge of ignorance and was considered

useless to those hoping to emigrate. By 1900, emigration had further cut the island's population to just over 4 million (half of what it
had been just before the famine).

Ireland, which remained one of Europe's poorest countries
for more than a century, was slow to forget England's indifference.
Ireland's population has only recently begun to grow again; Irish
Nationalists point out that Britain's population, on the other hand,
has grown from 12 million in 1845 to about 60 million today.

Before the famine, land was subdivided—each son got a piece
of the family estate (which grew smaller with each generation).
After the famine, the oldest son got the estate, and the younger sib-
lings—with fewer options for making a living in Ireland (primarily
joining the priesthood)—emigrated to Britain, Australia, Canada,
or the US. Because of the huge emigration to the US (today there
are 50 million Irish Americans), US influence increased. (During
the negotiations between Northern Ireland and the Irish Republic,
US involvement in the talks was welcomed and considered essential
by nearly all parties.)

Occasional violence demonstrated the fury of Irish nationalism, with the tragedy of the famine inflaming the movement. In
1848, the **Young Irelander** armed uprising was easily squelched.
In 1858, the **Irish Republican Brotherhood** was formed (the
forerunner of the IRA). Also called the **Fenians,** they launched
a campaign for independence by planting terrorist bombs. Irish
Americans sent money to help finance these revolutionaries. Uprising after uprising made it clear that Ireland was ready to close this
800-year chapter of invasions and colonialism.

Home Rule Party leader **Charles Stuart Parnell** (1846-1891),
an Irishman educated in England, made "the Irish problem" the
focus of London's Parliament. Parnell lobbied for independence
and for the rights of poor tenant farmers living under absentee
landlords, pioneering the first boycott tactics. Then, in 1890, at the
peak of his power and about to achieve Home Rule for Ireland, he
was drummed out of politics by a scandal involving his mistress,
scuttling the Home Rule issue for another 20 years (for more on
Parnell, see page 76).

Culturally, the old Gaelic, rural Ireland was being crushed
under the Industrial Revolution and the political control wielded
by Protestant England. The **Gaelic Athletic Association** was
founded in 1884 to resurrect pride in ancient Irish sports such as
hurling (see sidebar on page 88). Soon after, in 1893, writers and
educators formed the **Gaelic League** to preserve the traditional
language, music, and poetry. Building on the tradition of old Celtic bards, Ireland turned out a series of influential writers: **W. B.
Yeats, Oscar Wilde, George Bernard Shaw,** and **James Joyce** (see
"Irish Literature," later).

Easter Uprising, War of Independence, Partition, and Civil War (1900-1950)

As the century turned, Ireland prepared for the inevitable showdown with Britain.

The **Sinn Fein** party (meaning "Ourselves") lobbied politically for independence. The **Irish Volunteers** were more Catholic and more militant. Also on the scene was the **Irish Citizens Army,** with a socialist agenda to protect labor unions and clean up Dublin's hideous tenements, where 15 percent of children died before the age of one.

Of course, many Irish were Protestant and pro-British. The **Ulster Volunteers** (Unionists, and mostly Orangemen) feared that Home Rule would result in a Catholic-dominated state that would oppress the Protestant minority.

Meanwhile, Britain was preoccupied with World War I, where it was "fighting to protect the rights of small nations" (except Ireland's), and so it delayed granting Irish independence. The increasingly militant Irish rebels, believing that England's misfortune was Ireland's opportunity, decided to rise up and take independence while the time was ripe.

On Easter Monday, April 24, 1916, 1,500 Irish Volunteers, along with members of the Irish Citizens Army, marched on Dublin, occupied the General Post Office (and six other key buildings across town), and raised a green, white, and orange flag. The teacher and poet **Patrick Pearse** stood in front of the post office and proclaimed Ireland an independent republic.

British troops struck back—in a week of street fighting and intense shelling, some 300 died. By Saturday, the greatly outnumbered rebels had been killed or arrested. The small-scale uprising—which failed to go national and was never popular even in Dublin—was apparently over.

However, the British government overreacted by swiftly ex-

ecuting the 16 ringleaders, including Pearse. Ireland was outraged, no longer seeing the rebels as troublemakers but as martyrs. From this point on, Ireland was resolved to win its independence at all costs. A poem by W. B. Yeats, "Easter, 1916," captured the struggle with his words: "All changed, changed utterly: A terrible beauty is born."

In the 1918 elections, the Sinn Fein party won big, but the new members of Parliament refused to go to London, instead forming their own independent Irish Parliament in Dublin. Then Irish rebels began ambushing policemen—seen as the eyes and ears of British control—sparking two years of confrontations called the **War of Independence.** The fledgling Irish Republican Army faced 40,000 British troops, including the notorious Black and Tans (named for the color of their clothes: black for police and tan for army-surplus uniforms). A thousand people died in this war of street fighting, sniper fire, jailhouse beatings, terrorist bombs, and reprisals (for a more detailed timeline of the war and events leading up to it, see the sidebar on page 78).

Finally, Britain, tired of extended war after the slaughterhouse of World War I, agreed to Irish independence. But Ireland itself was a divided nation—the southern three-quarters of the island was mostly Catholic, Gaelic, rural, and for Home Rule; the northern quarter was Protestant, English, industrial, and Unionist. The solution? In 1920, in the **Government of Ireland Act,** the British Parliament partitioned the island into two independent, self-governing countries within the British Commonwealth: **Northern Ireland** and the **Irish Free State.** While the northern six counties (the only ones without a Catholic majority) chose to stay with Britain as Northern Ireland, the remaining 26 counties became the Irish Free State. (For a review of the ongoing issues between the North and the Republic, see the Northern Ireland chapter.)

Ireland's various political factions wrestled with this compromise solution, and the island plunged into a yearlong **Civil War** (1922-1923). The hard-line IRA opposed the partition, unwilling to accept a divided island, an oath of loyalty to the crown, or the remaining British Navy bases on Irish soil. They waged a street war on the armies of the Irish Free State, whose leaders supported the political settlement. Dublin and the southeast were ravaged in a year of bitter fighting before the Irish Free State, led by the charismatic young Nationalist **Michael Collins,** emerged victorious. The IRA went underground, moving its fight north and trying for the rest of the century to topple the government of Northern Ireland.

Out of the ashes of the Civil War came the two parties that still dominate Ireland's politics today. **Fine Gael** spawned from those who approved the treaty and the creation of the Irish Free State. **Fianna Fáil** was founded by **Eamon de Valera,** the figurehead of the anti-treaty side. Interestingly, Fianna Fáil, which developed from the losing side of the Civil War, has been in power 70 percent of the time since its inception.

In 1937, the Irish Free State severed more ties with the British

Commonwealth, writing up a new national constitution and taking an old name—**Éire** (pronounced AIR-uh). This new constitution reflected De Valera's conservative views, giving the Catholic Church "special status" and decreeing that a woman's place was in the home. Ireland called World War II "The Emergency" and remained neutral. In 1949, the separation from Britain was completed, as the Irish Free State left the Commonwealth and officially became the **Republic of Ireland.**

Celtic Tiger in the South, Troubles in the North (1950-2000)

Beginning in the 1960s, the Republic of Ireland—formerly a poor, rural region—was transformed into a modern, economic nation. The dropping of trade-strangling tariffs lured foreign investors. In 1973, membership in the European Union opened new Continental markets to Irish trade. No longer would Britain be the dominant trade partner. At the same time, reforms to Ireland's antiquated education system created a new generation of young people prepared for more than life on the farm.

The big social changes in the Republic were reflected in the 1990 election of Mary Robinson (a feminist lawyer who was outspoken on issues of divorce, contraception, and abortion) as the first female president of a once ultraconservative Ireland. Her much-respected seven-year tenure was followed by the equally graceful presidency of Mary McAleese (1997-2011). Born in the North, McAleese is another example of the shrinking divide between the two political states that occupy the island.

Through the late 1990s, the Republic's booming, globalized economy grew a whopping 40 percent, and Dublin's property values tripled (between 1995 and 2007), earning the Republic's economy the nickname "The Celtic Tiger." (Like elsewhere, the global recession hit hard here in 2008—bursting the property bubble, sending home values plummeting and driving up unemployment.)

Meanwhile, as the Republic moved toward prosperity, Northern Ireland—with a slight Protestant majority and a large, disaffected Catholic minority—was plagued by the **Troubles.** In 1967, the Northern Ireland Civil Rights Movement, inspired by the African American rights movement in the US, organized marches and demonstrations demanding equal treatment for Catholics (better housing, job opportunities, and voting rights). But they didn't have a Martin Luther King or a Bishop Desmond Tutu to advocate for them from a position of moral authority. Protestant **Unionist Orangemen** countered by continuing their marches through Catholic neighborhoods, flaunting their politically dominant position in the name of tradition, and thus provoking riots. In 1969, Britain sent troops to help Northern Ireland keep the peace and met resistance from the IRA, which saw them as an occupying army supporting the Protestant pro-British majority.

From the 1970s to the 1990s, the North was a low-level battle-field, with the IRA using ter-rorist tactics to achieve their political ends. The Troubles, which claimed some 3,000 lives, continued with bomb-ings, marches, hunger strikes, rock-throwing, and riots (no-tably Derry's **Bloody Sunday** in 1972—see sidebar on page 413). These were interrupted

by periods of cease-fires, broken cease-fires, and a string of failed peace agreements.

Then came the watershed 1998 settlement known as the **Good Friday Peace Accord** (to pro-Irish Nationalists) or the **Belfast Agreement** (to pro-British Unionists).

Global Nations (2000 and Beyond)

After years of negotiation, in 2005 the IRA formally announced an end to its armed campaign, promising to pursue peaceful, demo-cratic means to achieve its goals. In 2006, I was stunned to dis-cover that the British Army surveillance towers in Derry—disturb-ing fixtures since my very first visit—had been torn down. In the spring of 2007, the unthinkable happened when **Gerry Adams,** leader of the ultra-Nationalist Sinn Fein party, sat down across a table from **Reverend Ian Paisley,** head of the ultra-Unionist DUP party. It was their first face-to-face meeting. Also in 2007, Lon-don returned control of Northern Ireland to the popularly elected Northern Ireland Assembly. Perhaps most important of all, after almost 40 years, the British Army withdrew 90 percent of its forces from Northern Ireland that summer. In 2010, the long-awaited Saville Report—the result of a 12-year investigation by the British government—found that the Bloody Sunday shootings were unjus-tified, and the victims legally innocent.

Now it's up to Northern Ireland to keep the peace. The 1998 peace accord gives Northern Ireland the freedom to leave the UK if ever the majority of the population approves a referendum to do so. At the same time, the Republic of Ireland withdrew its consti-tutional claim to the entire island of Ireland. Northern Ireland now has limited autonomy from London, with its own democratically elected, power-sharing government. It will be up to this body to untie this stubborn Gordian knot.

Great Britain is also trying to mend its relationship with the Republic. In 2011, Queen Elizabeth II became the first British monarch to visit the Republic of Ireland since it broke away in 1921 (she has been to the North numerous times). The Queen took the gutsy step of visiting Dublin's Croke Park stadium, where British Black and Tan troops massacred 14 people at a 1921 Gaelic football match—see sidebar on page 88. She also visited Dublin's Garden of Remembrance, a quiet urban plot devoted to the 1916 Easter Uprising. In 2012, she took it a step further by shaking hands with ex-IRA leader and current Deputy First Minister of Northern Ireland, Martin McGuinness. These acts of reconciliation, though controversial and dramatic, were another step toward building an amicable relationship between the two countries.

Today, both Northern Ireland and the Republic of Ireland have reason to be optimistic about the future. In spite of the current recession, their economic growth through the 1990s and 2000s was impressive, and political and cultural problems have trailed off.

The formerly isolated island is welcoming tourists with open arms and reaching out to the rest of the globe. In 1999, the number of tourists visiting Ireland topped the 6 million mark, exceeding for the first time the native population of the island. And visitors returning to Ireland are amazed at the country's transformation (although there can still be some tense areas in the North—as in all big cities).

During its Celtic Tiger economic boom, the Irish imported labor and surpassed the English in per-capita income—both for the first time ever. Starting in 1980, when Apple set up its European headquarters here, streams of multinational and US corporations opened offices in Ireland. Ireland has one of the youngest populations in Europe. And those young Irish, beneficiaries of one of Europe's best education systems, provide these corporations with a highly skilled workforce. Ireland's pharmaceutical, chemical, and software industries are well-established—this little country is second only to the US in the exportation of software. The island's close business ties to its American partners mean its economy is highly reactive to US market fluctuations. The Irish say, "When America sneezes, we get pneumonia."

By 2003, the rising economic tide had lifted Ireland to float beside Finland as one of the two most expensive countries in the European Union. But by 2011 that tide had receded: The global recession has been a cold shower on Ireland's long period of economic good times, and the Irish economy fell farther, by percentage, than any other EU country during this period.

This century's rapid growth and then decline has caused other problems. Urban sprawl, big-city traffic snarls, water and air pollution, and the homogenizing effects of globalization have left their mark. Per-capita consumption of alcohol has tripled since 1970. And in 2008, the irrationally exuberant Irish housing bubble burst, wiping out retirement nest eggs and littering the Irish landscape with empty "ghost estates" (built on spec during the boom, these snazzy housing developments remain mostly unsold). The average value of Irish homes dropped 45 percent between 2007 and 2011. The final stage of this humbling financial buzzkill came in the fall of 2010, when the EU bailed out Ireland's teetering banks (an event wedged painfully between similar bailouts of Greece and Portugal).

Today's Irish parents (who remember 20 percent unemployment in the early 1980s) worry how their affluent young adult children will adjust to the new economic realities. Still, the Celtic Tiger economy, although tamed by the recession, taught the formerly downtrodden Irish that their luck can change for the better. The Irish—now skilled and business-savvy—are primed and ready for the next recovery. It can't come soon enough.

Meanwhile, the challenges of immigration (new arrivals into Ireland) have replaced problems associated with the generations of emigration (young people leaving Ireland). Until a few years ago, Ireland had the most liberal citizenship laws in the European Union, granting Irish citizenship to anyone born on Irish soil (even if neither parent had an Irish passport). This led to a flood of pregnant immigrant women arriving from Eastern Europe and Africa to give birth in Ireland so their children would gain EU citizenship. Families with a child born in an EU country faced fewer border restrictions, increasing their chances of moving into one of the EU nations. In 2004, the Irish people closed that legal loophole in a referendum vote.

While the Irish are embracing the new economies and industries of the 21st century, many still see their island as an oasis of morality and traditional values when it comes to sex and marriage (homosexuality was decriminalized only 25 years ago). The Catholic Church continues to exert influence on Irish society. But since the Church no longer controls the legislature, the Irish government—driven by the popular demands of the youngest population in Europe—will undoubtedly push for some changes on the following issues.

Birth Control: People in the US take for granted that birth control is readily available. But Ireland only began allowing the widespread sale of condoms in 1993.

Abortion: Abortion is still illegal in Ireland. Women who choose to terminate their pregnancies must go to England for help—and counseling Irish women to go to England for abortions has only been legal since 1993. This was a big issue in 2001, when the Dutch anchored their "abortion ship" in Dublin's harbor, and again in 2002, when a referendum legalizing abortion was nar-

PAST & PRESENT

Irish Brogue with a Polish Accent

As you walk down the street in an Irish city these days, you might be perplexed when you overhear an unfamiliar language being spoken by groups of enthusiastic young adults. It's Polish, and it may soon be to Ireland what Spanish is to the US: a good language to know if you want to communicate with a huge immigrant population. Polish food sections are popping up in grocery stores. Bilingual Eng-

lish-Polish menus have made an appearance in some restaurants. And ask that chambermaid or waiter with the unusual accent where they're from. Chances are good that they'll say Warsaw or Kraków.

When 10 mostly Eastern European nations joined the EU in 2004, Sweden, Britain, and Ireland immediately removed major barriers for employment of these new EU nationals. Ireland's booming economy at that time needed a cheap labor force to fill the growing number of minimum-wage jobs. Hardworking, ambitious young Poles headed west to the land of opportunity. Ireland was their first choice because of its Catholicism, stronger economy, and opportunity to learn English (the international language of business). Now many of my favorite Irish B&B owners purr about their Polish chambermaids as if they were the latest innovation in household appliances, saying, "I don't know how I got along before without one!"

Granted, the Poles are not the only Eastern Europeans learning about capitalism, Irish-style. But the numbers of arriving Poles dwarf the number of Slovaks, Latvians, Estonians, and other Eastern Europeans headed to the Emerald Isle. Many Irish have taken to calling them all "Poles," just as many Americans might mistake a Guatemalan or Venezuelan for a "Mexican."

The healthy influx of new blood has added ethnic diversity to Ireland not seen since Spanish Armada sailors washed ashore 400 years ago. The Catholic Church has been re-energized with Poles attending Mass. Intermarriage is creating fun new combinations of names like Bridgit Jaruzelski or Colleen Kraszewski. And in the most recent Irish census, Polish has replaced Irish Gaelic as Ireland's second most-spoken language, with 120,000 people speaking it in their homes.

However, the recession has some Polish immigrants thinking twice. As the recession hit Ireland in 2008, Dell computer decided to close its big plant in Limerick. Where to move this facility? Production is now being handled by cheaper labor in a Dell factory in Łódź, Poland. And now many Polish immigrants are headed east, looking to apply their Irish business skills back home.

rowly defeated. Watch for more referendums proposing the legalization of abortion. Many Irish refer to this as their next civil war.

Divorce: Ireland voted to legalize divorce in 1995—but only on very strict conditions. After the divorce papers are signed, it takes a four-year waiting period before the divorce is considered official, and little compensation is offered to Irish women who work as homemakers.

Irish Art

Megalithic tombs, ancient gold- and metalwork, illuminated manuscripts, high crosses carved in stone, paintings of rural Ireland, and provocative political murals—Ireland comes with some fascinating art. To best appreciate this art in your travels, kick off your tour in Ireland's two top museums, both in Dublin—the **National Museum: Archaeology and History** and the **National Gallery.** Each provides a good context to help you enjoy Irish art and architecture—from ancient to modern and both rural and urban. Here's a quick survey.

Megalithic Period: During the Stone Age, 5,000 years ago, farmers living in the **Valley of the Boyne,** north of Dublin, built a "cemetery" of approximately 40 **burial mounds.** The most famous of these mound tombs is the passage tomb at Newgrange (part of Brú na Bóinne). More than 300 feet in diameter and composed of 200,000 tons of loose stone, Newgrange was constructed so that the light from the winter solstice sunrise (Dec 21) would pass through the eastern entrance to the tomb, travel down a 60-foot passage, and illuminate the inner burial chamber (not bad engineering for Stone Age architects). The effect is now re-created daily, so visitors can experience this ancient ritual of renewal and rebirth any time of year (see the Near Dublin chapter).

Some of Europe's best examples of megalithic (big rock) art are also at Newgrange. Carved on the tomb's stones are zigzags, chevrons, parallel arcs, and concentric spirals. Scholars think these designs symbolize a belief in the eternal cycle of life and the continuation of the life force, or that they pay homage to the elements in nature on which these ancient peoples depended for their existence.

Exploring these burial mounds (only Newgrange and Knowth are open to the public), you begin to understand the reverence that these ancient people had for nature, and the need they felt to bury their dead in these great mound tombs, returning their kin to the womb of Mother Earth.

Bronze Age: As ancient Irish cultures developed from 2000 B.C., so did their metalworking skills. Gold and bronze were used to create **tools, jewelry,** and **religious objects.** (The National Museum: Archaeology and History in Dublin houses the most dazzling of these works.) Gold neck rings worn by both men and women, cufflink-like dress fasteners, bracelets, and lock rings (to hold hair in place) are just a few of the personal adornments fashioned by the ancient Irish.

Most of these objects were deliberately buried, often in bogs, as votive offerings to their gods or to prevent warring tribes from stealing them. Like the earlier megaliths, they're decorated with geometric and organic motifs.

Iron Age: The Celts, a warrior society from Central Europe, arrived in Ireland perhaps as early as the seventh century B.C. With their metalworking skills and superior iron weaponry, they soon overwhelmed the native population. And, though the Celts may have been fierce warriors, they wreaked havoc with a flair for the aesthetic. **Shields, swords,** and **scabbards** were embellished with delicate patterns, often enhanced with vivid colors. The dynamic energy of these decorations must have reflected the ferocious power of the Celts.

The Age of Saints and Scholars: Christianity grew in Ireland from St. Patrick's first efforts in the fifth century A.D. In the sixth and seventh centuries, its many great saints (such as St. Columba) established monastic settlements throughout Ireland, Britain, and the Continent, where learning, literature, and the arts flourished. During this "Golden Age" of Irish civilization, monks, along with metalworkers and stonemasons, created imaginative designs and distinctive stylistic motifs for **manuscripts, metal objects,** and **crosses.**

Monks wrote out and richly decorated manuscripts of the Gospels. These manuscripts—which preserved the written word in Latin, Greek, and Irish—eventually had more power than the oral tales of the ancient pagan heroes.

The most beautiful and imaginative of these illuminated manuscripts is the **Book of Kells** (c. A.D. 800), on display in the Old Library at Trinity College in Dublin. Crafted by Irish monks at a monastery on the Scottish island of Iona, the book was brought to Ireland for safekeeping from rampaging Vikings. The skins of 150 calves were used to make the vellum, which is painted with rich pigments from plants and minerals. The entire manuscript is colorfully decorated with flat, stylized human or angelic forms and intricate, interlacing animal and knot patterns. Full-page illustrations depict the life of Christ, and many pages are given over to highly complex yet symmetrical designs that resemble an Eastern carpet. Many consider this book the finest piece of art from Europe's Dark Ages.

The most renowned metalwork of this period is the **Ardagh Chalice,** made sometime in the eighth century. Now on display at the National Museum in Dublin, the silver and bronze gilt chalice is as impressive as the Book of Kells. Ribbons of gold wrap around the chalice stem, while intricate knot patterns ring the cup. A magnificent gold ring and a large glass stone on the chalice bottom reflect the desire to please God. (He would see this side of the chalice when the priest drank during the Mass.)

The monks used Irish high crosses to celebrate the triumph of Christianity and to provide a means of educating the illiterate masses through simple stone carvings. The **Cross of Murdock** (Muiredach's Cross, A.D. 923) is 18 feet tall, towering over the remains of the monastic settlement at Monasterboice. It is but one of many monumental crosses that you'll come across throughout Ireland. Typically, stone carvers depicted Bible stories and surrounded these with the same intricate patterns seen in the Book of Kells and the Ardagh Chalice.

Early Irish art focused on organic, geometric, and linear designs. Unlike Mediterranean art, Irish art of this early period was not preoccupied with a naturalistic representation of people, animals, or the landscape. Instead, it reflects Irish society's rituals and the elements and rhythms of nature.

The Suppression of Native Irish Art: After invading Ireland in 1169, the English suppressed Celtic Irish culture. English traditions in architecture, painting, and literature replaced native styles until the late 19th century, when revivals in Irish language, folklore, music, and art began to surface.

Painters in the late 19th and early 20th centuries went to the west of Ireland, which was untouched by English dominance and influence, in search of traditional Irish subject matter. **Jack B. Yeats** (1871-1957, brother of the poet W. B. Yeats), Belfast-born painter **Paul Henry** (1876-1958), and **Sean Keating** (1889-1977) were among those who looked to the west for inspiration. The National Gallery in Dublin holds many of these artists' greatest works, with an entire gallery dedicated to Jack Yeats. Many of his early paintings illustrate scenes of his beloved Sligo. His later paintings are more expressionistic in style and patriotic in subject matter.

Henry's paintings depict the rugged beauty of the Connemara

region and its people, with scenes of rustic cottages, mountains, and boglands. Keating, the most political of the three painters, featured stirring scenes from Ireland's struggle against the English for independence.

Contemporary Irish art is often linked to the social, political, and environmental issues that face Ireland today. Themes include the position of the Church in the daily lives of the modern Irish, the effects of development on the countryside, the changing roles of women in Ireland, and the Troubles. Look for this provocative art at the Irish Museum of Modern Art in Dublin (on Military Road, www.imma. ie) and at city galleries.

Today's Irish respect the artistic process, so much so that a provision in the tax system in the Republic of Ireland allows income from art sales to go untaxed. This is one reason many artists immigrate to Ireland.

In Northern Ireland, murals in sectarian neighborhoods (such as the Shankill and Falls Roads in Belfast and the Bogside in Derry) are stirring public testaments to the martyrs and heroes of the Troubles.

Irish Literature

Since the Book of Kells, Ireland's greatest contributions to the world of art have been through words. As there was no Irish Gaelic written language, the inhabitants of Ireland were illiterate until Christianity came in the fourth century. Far from ignorant, Celtic society maintained a complex set of laws and historical records and legends...verbally. The druidic priests and bards who passed down this rich oral tradition from generation to generation were the most respected members of the clan, next to the king. After Christianity transformed Ireland into a refuge of literacy (while the rest of Europe crumbled into the Dark Ages), Charlemagne's imported Irish monks invented "minuscule," which became the basis of the lower-case letters we use in our alphabet today. The cultural importance placed on the word (spoken, and for the past 1,500 years, written) is today reflected in the rich output of modern Irish writers.

Three hundred years ago, Dublin native **Jonathan Swift** created his masterpiece, *Gulliver's Travels,* as an acidic satire of British colonialism. It pokes fun at religious hard-liners and the pompous bureaucrats in London who shaped England's misguided Irish policies, and ironically has survived as a children's classic.

William Butler Yeats, also born and raised in Dublin, dedi-

SENATOR
WILLIAM
BUTLER YEATS
1865 – 1939

POET & PLAYWRIGHT

LIVED HERE 1922 – 1928

cated his early writings in the 1880s to the "Celtic Twilight" rebirth of pride in mythic Irish heroes and heroines. His early poems and plays are filled with fairies and idyllic rural innocence, while his later poems reflect Ireland's painful transition to independence. Yeats' Nobel Prize for literature (1923) was eventually matched by three later, Nobel-winning Irish authors: **George Bernard Shaw** (1925), **Samuel Beckett** (1969), and **Seamus Heaney** (1995).

Oscar Wilde, born in Dublin and a graduate of Trinity College, wowed London with his quick wit, outrageous clothes, and flamboyant personality. Wilde wrote the darkly fascinating novel *The Picture of Dorian Gray* (1890) and skewered upper-class Victorian society in witty comedic plays (such as *The Importance of Being Earnest,* 1895), with characters who speak very elegantly about the trivial concerns of the idle rich. He was

the toast of London in the 1890s—before the scandal of his homosexuality turned Victorian society against him. Meanwhile, **Bram Stoker** was conjuring up a Gothic thriller called *Dracula* (1897).

Most inventive of all, perhaps, was **James Joyce,** who broke new ground and captured literary lightning in a bottle when he focused on Dublin's seedier side in a modern, stream-of-consciousness style. His famous novel *Ulysses,* set on a single day (June 16, 1904), follows Dubliners on an odyssey through the city's pubs, hospitals, libraries, churches, and brothels.

The **Abbey Theatre** (championed by W. B. Yeats) was the world's first national theater, built to house plays intended to give a voice to Ireland's flowering playwrights. When **J. M. Synge** staged *The Playboy of the Western World* there in 1907, his unflattering comic portrayal of Irish peasant life (and mention of women's underwear) caused riots. Twenty years later, **Sean O'Casey** provoked more riots at the Abbey when his *Plough and the Stars* production depicted the 1916 Uprising in a way that was at odds with the audience's cherished views of their heroes.

In recent decades, the bittersweet Irish literary parade has been inhabited by tragically volcanic characters like **Brendan Behan,** who exclaimed, "I'm not a writer with a drinking problem...I'm a drinker with a writing problem." Bleak poverty experienced in childhood was the catalyst for **Frank McCourt**'s memorable *Angela's Ashes*. Among the most celebrated of today's Irish writers is **Roddy Doyle,** whose feel for working-class Dublin resonates in his novels of contemporary life (such as *The Commitments*) as well as in historical slices of life (such as *A Star Called Henry*). **Seamus Heaney,** a poet who has won the Nobel and Pulitzer prizes, published a new translation in 1999 of the Old English epic *Beowulf*—wedding the old with the new.

Irish Language

The Irish have a rich oral tradition that goes back to their ancient fireside storytelling days. Part of the fun of traveling here is getting an ear for the way locals express themselves.

Irish Gaelic is one of four surviving Celtic languages, along with Scottish Gaelic, Welsh, and Breton (spoken in parts of French Brittany). A couple of centuries ago, there were seven surviving Celtic languages. But Cornish (spoken in Cornwall) is on life support, and two others—Manx (from the Isle of Man) and Gallaic (spoken in Northern Spain)—have died out. Some proud Irish choose to call their native tongue "Irish" instead of "Gaelic" to ensure that there is no confusion with what is spoken in parts of Scotland.

Only 165 years ago, the majority of the Irish population spoke Irish Gaelic. But most of the speakers were of the poor laborer class that either died or emigrated during the famine. After the famine, Irish Gaelic was seen as a badge of backwardness. Parents and teachers understood that English was the language that would serve children best when they emigrated to better lives in the US, Canada, Australia, or England. Children in schools wore a tally stick around their necks, and a notch was cut by teachers each time a child was caught speaking Irish. At the end of the day, the child received a whack for each notch in the stick. It wasn't until the resurgence of cultural pride, brought on by the Gaelic League in 1884, that an attempt was made to promote use of the language again.

These days, less than 5 percent of the Irish population is fluent in their native tongue. However, it's taken seriously enough that all national laws passed must first be written in Irish, then translated into English. Irish Gaelic can be heard most often in the

Gaeltacht Regions

N. IRE. BELFAST

GALWAY

REP. OF IRELAND DUBLIN

DINGLE (AN DAINGEAN)

CORK

AREAS SHOWN IN BLACK ARE PART OF THE GAELTACHT

western counties of Kerry, Galway, Mayo, and Donegal. Each of these counties has a slightly different dialect. You'll know you're entering an Irish Gaelic-speaking area when you see a sign saying *Gaeltacht* (GAIL-tekt).

Irish Gaelic doesn't use the letters *j, k, q, x,* or *z*. And there's no "th" sound—which you can hear today when an Irish person says something like "turdy-tree" (33). There is also no equivalent of the simple words "yes" or "no." Instead, answers are given in the affirmative or negative rephrasing of the question. For example, a question like "Did you mail the letter today?" would be answered with "I did (mail the letter)," rather than a simple "yes." Or "It's a nice day today, isn't it?" would be answered with "It is," or "'Tis."

Irish Place Names

Here are a few words that appear in Irish place names. You'll see these on road signs or at tourist sights.

Irish	Phonetics	English
Alt	ahlt	cliff
An Lár	ahn lar	city center
Ard	ard	high, height, hillock
Baile	BALL-yah	town, town land
Beag	beg	little
Bearna	bar-na	gap
Boireann	burr-en	large rock, rocky area
Bóthar	boh-er	road
Bun	bun	end, bottom
Caiseal	CASH-el	circular stone fort
Caislean	cash-LOIN	castle
Cathair	caht-HAR	circular stone fort, city
Cill	kill	church
Cloch	clockh	stone
Doire	dih-ruh	oak
Droichead	DROCKH-ed	bridge
Drumlin	DRUM-lin	small hill
Dun	doon	fort
Fionn	fin	white, fair-haired person
Gaeltacht	GAIL-tekt	Irish language district

Gall	gaul	foreigner
Garda	gar-dah	police
Gort	gort	field
Inis	in-ish	island
Mileac	mee-luch	low marshy ground
Mór	mor	large
Muck	muck	pig
Oifig an Phoist	UFF-ig un fwisht	post office
Poll	poll	hole, cave
Rath	rath	ancient earthen fort
Ross	ross	peninsula
Sí	shee	fairy mound, bewitching
Slí	slee	route, way
Sliabh	sleeve	mountain
Sraid	shrawd	street
Teach	chockh	house
Trá	traw	beach, strand
Tur	toor	tower

Irish Pleasantries

When you reach the more remote western fringe of Ireland, you're likely to hear folks speaking Irish. Although locals in these areas can readily converse with you in English, it's fascinating to hear their ancient Celtic language spoken. Here are some basic Irish phrases:

Irish	Phonetics	English
Fáilte	FAHLT-shuh	Welcome
Conas ta tu?	CONN-us A-thaw too	How are you?
Go raibh maith agat	guh rov mah UG-ut	Thank you
Slán	slawn	Bye

Irish Pub and Music Words

The Irish love to socialize. Pubs are like public living rooms, where friends gather in a corner to play tunes and anyone is a welcome guest. Here are some useful pub and music words:

Irish	Phonetics	English
Poitín	po-CHEEN	moonshine, homemade liquor
Craic	crack	fun atmosphere, good conversation
Bodhrán	BO-run	traditional drum
Uilleann	ILL-in	elbow (uilleann pipes are elbow bagpipes)
Trad	trad	traditional Irish music

Ceilidh	KAY-lee	Irish dance gathering
Fleadh	flah	music festival
Slainte	SLAWN-chuh	cheers, to your health
Táim súgach!	taw im SOO-gakh	I'm tipsy!
Lei thras	LEH-hrass	toilets
Mná	min-AW	women's room
Fír	fear	men's room

Irish Politics

Politics is a popular topic of conversation in Ireland. Whether you pick up a local newspaper or turn on your car radio, you're likely to encounter these Irish political terms in the media:

Irish	Phonetics	English
Taoiseach	TEE-shock	Prime minister of Irish Republic
Seanad	SHAN-ud	Irish Senate
Dáil	DOY-ill	Irish House of Representatives
Teachta Dála (TD)	TALK-tah DOLL-ah	Member of Irish Parliament
Is féidir linn.	ess FAY-dur lin	Yes we can.

Irish-Yankee Vocabulary

If some of these words seem more British than Irish, those are ones you're likely to hear more often in Northern Ireland (part of the UK).

advert—advertisement
anticlockwise—counterclockwise
aubergine—eggplant
banger—sausage
bang on—correct
banjaxed—messed up
bank holiday—legal holiday
beer mat—coaster
bespoke—custom
billion—a thousand of our billions (a trillion)
biro—ballpoint pen
biscuit—cookie
Black Mariah—police van
black pudding—sausage made from pig's blood
black stuff—Guinness
blather—rambling, empty talk
bloody—damn (from medieval blasphemy: "Christ's blood")
blow off—fart
boffin—nerd
bog—slang for toilet
bolshy—argumentative
bonnet—car hood
boot—car trunk
braces—suspenders
bridle way—path for walkers, bikers, and horse riders
brilliant—cool
bum—bottom or "backside"
busker—street musician
cacks—trousers, underpants
candy floss—cotton candy
caravan—trailer
car boot sale—temporary flea market, often for charity
car park—parking lot
carry on—nonsense
casualty—emergency room
cat's eyes—road reflectors
ceilidh—dance, party
champ—mashed potatoes and onions
chemist—pharmacist
chicory—endive

chippy—fish-and-chips shop
chips—french fries
chock-a-block—jam-packed
chuffed—pleased
cider—alcoholic apple cider
clearway—road where you can't stop
coach—long-distance bus
concession—discounted admission
cos—romaine lettuce
cotton buds—cotton swabs
courgette—zucchini
craic (pronounced "crack")—fun, good conversation
crisps—potato chips
crusties—New Age hippies
culchie—hick, country yokel
cuppa—cup of tea
Da—father
deadly—really good
dear—expensive
digestives—round graham crackers
dinner—lunch or dinner
diversion—detour
dodgy—iffy, risky
dole—welfare
done and dusted—completed
donkey's years—until the cows come home, forever
draughts (pronounced "drafts")—checkers
draw—marijuana
dual carriageway—divided highway (four lanes)
Dubs—people from Dublin
eejit—moron
Emergency, The—World War II
en suite—bathroom attached to room
face flannel—washcloth
fair play (to you)—well done, good job
fanny—vagina
fiddler's fart—worthless thing
first floor—second floor (one floor above ground)
fiver—five-euro note
flat—apartment
fluthered—drunk
flutter—a bet
football—Gaelic football
fortnight—two weeks
full monty—the whole shebang, everything
GAA—Gaelic Athletic Association

gallery—balcony
gammon—ham
gangway—aisle
gaol—jail (same pronunciation)
Garda—police
gargle—to have an alcoholic drink
gasman—the life of the party
give way—yield
giving out—chewing out, yelling at
glen—valley
gob—mouth
gobsmacked—astounded
grand—good, well ("How are you?" "I'm grand, thanks")
guards—police *(Garda)*
gurrier—hooligan
half eight—8:30 (not 7:30)
hen night—bachelorette party
holiday—vacation
homely—likable or cozy
hooley—party or informal shindig
hoover—vacuum cleaner
hurling—Irish field hockey
iced lolly—popsicle
interval—intermission
ironmonger—hardware store
jacket potato—baked potato
jacks—toilet
jars—drinks (alcohol)
jelly—Jell-O
jumble—sale, rummage sale
jumper—sweater
just a tick—just a second
kipper—smoked herring
knackered—exhausted
knickers—ladies' panties
knocked—torn down (buildings)
knocking shop—brothel
knock up—wake up or visit
ladybird—ladybug
lash—a try ("give it a lash")
left luggage—baggage check
let—rent
lift—elevator
listed—protected historic building
lorry—truck
Ma, Mam, Mammy—mother

mac—mackintosh (trench) coat
mangetout—snow peas
mate—buddy (boy or girl)
mean—stingy
mental—crazy
minced meat—hamburger
minerals—soft drinks
mobile (MOH-bile)—cellphone
mod cons—modern conveniences (not convicts in bell-bottoms)
naff—dorky, tacky
nappy—diaper
natter—talk and talk
"Norn Iron" (pronounced)—Northern Ireland
nought—zero
noughties—the decade from 2000-2009
noughts & crosses—tic-tac-toe
OAP—old-age pensioner (qualified for senior discounts)
off-license—liquor store
Oirish—exaggerated Irish accent
on offer—for sale
paddywhackery—exaggerated Irish accent
paralytic—passed-out drunk
pasty—(PASS-tee) crusted savory (usually meat) pie
pavement—sidewalk
pear-shaped—messed up, gone wrong
petrol—gas
pissed (rude), paralytic, bevvied, wellied, popped up, ratted, pissed as a newt—drunk
pitch—playing field
plaster—Band-Aid
publican—pub manager
pull—to attract romantic attention
punter—partygoer, customer
put a sock in it—shut up
quay (pronounced "key")—waterside street, ship offloading area
queue—line
queue up—line up
quick smart—immediately
quid—pound (money in Northern Ireland, worth about $1.60)
ramps—speed bumps
randy—horny
redundant, made—laid off
return ticket—round-trip
ride—have sex with
ring up—call (telephone)
ROI—Republic of Ireland

roundabout—traffic circle
RTE—Irish Republic's broadcast network
rubber—eraser
sanitary towel—sanitary pad
sausage roll—sausage wrapped in a flaky pastry (like a pig in a blanket)
scarlet—embarrassed
Scotch egg—hard-boiled egg wrapped in sausage meat
self-catering—apartment with kitchen
sellotape—Scotch tape
serviette—napkin
session—musical evening
shag—have sex with
shag all—hardly any
shebeen—illegal drinking hole
single ticket—one-way ticket
skint—broke, poor
skip—Dumpster
slag—to ridicule, tease
smalls—underwear
snogging—kissing, making out
solicitor—lawyer
sort out—figure out, organize
spanner—wrench
spend a penny—urinate
splash out—splurge
stag night—bachelor party
starkers—buck naked
starters—appetizers
stick—criticism
stone—14 pounds (weight)
strand—beach
stroppy—bad-tempered
subway—underground pedestrian passageway
sultanas—golden raisins
surgical spirit—rubbing alcohol
swede—rutabaga
take the mickey—tease
tatty—worn out or tacky
taxi rank—taxi stand
tenner—10-euro note
theatre—live stage
tick—a check mark
tight as a Scotsman (derogatory)—cheapskate
tights—panty hose
Tipp—County Tipperary

tipper lorry—dump truck
tin—can
to let—for rent
top up—refill a drink or your mobile-phone credit
torch—flashlight
towpath—path along a river
trad—traditional music
Travellers—itinerants, once known as Tinkers
turf accountant—bookie
twee—corny, too cute
twitcher—bird-watcher
verge—grassy edge of road
victualler—butcher
wain—small child
way out—exit
wee (v.)—urinate
wee (n.)—tiny (in the North)
Wellingtons, wellies—rubber boots
whacked—exhausted
whinge (rhymes with hinge)—whine
witter on—gab and gab
woolies—warm clothes
your man—that guy, this guy
zebra crossing—crosswalk
zed—the letter Z

APPENDIX

Contents

Tourist Information

Tourist Offices

Ireland's national tourist office **in the US**—called **Tourism Ireland**—offers a wealth of information on both the Republic of Ireland and Northern Ireland. Before your trip, scan their website (www.discoverireland.com) and download brochures and maps. You can ask questions and request that information be mailed to you (such as the free vacation planning packet, regional and city maps, walking routes, and festival schedules) by emailing info.us@tourismireland.com, or calling 800-SHAMROC (US tel. 800-742-6762).

    In Ireland, your best first stop in every town is generally the tourist information office—abbreviated **TI** in this book. TIs are good places to get a city map and information on public transit (including bus and train schedules), walking tours, special events, and nightlife. Many TIs have information on the entire country or at least the region, so try to pick up maps for destinations you'll be visiting later in your trip. If you're arriving in town after the TI closes, call ahead or pick up a map in a neighboring town.

In **Dublin,** try to get everything you'll need for Ireland in one stop at the TI in the old church on Suffolk Street (see page 48). The general nationwide tourist-information phone number for travelers calling from within Ireland is 1-850-230-330 (and their nation-wide room-booking phone number is 1-800-363-626; office open Mon-Sat 9:00-20:00, closed Sun).

Despite all the help TIs offer, steer clear of their room-finding services (bloated prices, booking fee up to €5, no opinions, and they take a 10 percent cut from your B&B host).

Communicating

Telephones

Smart travelers use the telephone to reserve or reconfirm rooms, get tourist information, reserve restaurants, confirm tour times, or phone home. This section covers dialing instructions, phone cards, and types of phones (for more in-depth information, see www.rick-steves.com/phoning).

How to Dial

Calling from the US to Ireland, or vice versa, is simple—once you break the code. The European calling chart in this chapter will walk you through it.

Dialing Domestically Within Ireland

Ireland, like much of the US, uses an area-code dialing system. To make domestic calls, if you're dialing from within an area code, you just dial the local number to be connected; but if you're calling from outside an area code, you have to dial both the area code (which starts with a 0) and the local number.

Area codes are listed in this book, and are available from directory assistance (dial 11811 in the Republic, 192 in Northern Ireland).

The Republic of Ireland has a special way to call Northern Ireland: dial 048, and then the local number without the area code. For instructions on how to call the Republic of Ireland from Northern Ireland, see below.

These instructions apply to dialing from a landline (such as a pay phone or your hotel-room phone) or an Irish mobile phone.

If you're dialing within Ireland using your US mobile phone, you may need to dial as if you're making a domestic call, or you may need to dial as if you're calling from the US (see "Dialing Internationally," next). Try it one way, and if that doesn't work, try it the other way.

Dialing Internationally to or from Ireland

To make an international call, follow these steps:

• Dial the international access code (00 if you're calling from Europe, 011 from the US or Canada). If you're dialing from a mobile phone, you can replace the international access code with +, which works regardless of where you're calling from. (On many mobile phones, you can insert a + by pressing and holding the 0 key.)

• Dial the country code of the country you're calling (353 for the Republic of Ireland, 44 for Northern Ireland, or 1 for the US or Canada).

• Dial the area code (Dublin's area code is 01) and the local number, keeping in mind that if you're calling Ireland, drop the initial zero of the area code (the European calling chart lists specifics per country).

Calling from the US to the Republic of Ireland: To call a recommended Dublin hotel from the US, dial 011 (the US international access code), 353 (the Republic of Ireland's country code), 1 (Dublin's area code without its initial 0), and then 679-6500 (the hotel's number).

Calling from any European country—including Northern Ireland—to the Republic of Ireland: Dial 00-353, then the area code without its initial 0, and then the local number.

From the US or Canada to Northern Ireland: Dial 011-44-28 (44 is the country code for the United Kingdom; 28 is Northern Ireland's area code without its initial 0), and then the local number.

From the Republic of Ireland to Northern Ireland: Dial 048, and then the local number. (In this case, you omit Northern Ireland's area code, 028, entirely.)

From any European Country (except the Republic of Ireland) to Northern Ireland: Dial 00-44-28 (Northern Ireland's area code without its initial 0), and then the local number.

From anywhere in Ireland (Republic and Northern Ireland) to the US: To call from Ireland to my office in Edmonds, Washington, I dial 00 (Ireland's international access code), 1 (the US country code), 425 (Edmonds' area code), and 771-8303.

Mobile Phones

Traveling with a mobile phone is handy and practical. Whether you're using a smartphone or a conventional cellphone, the basics for how to make calls and send texts are the same. For specifics on using your smartphone to get online, see the sidebar.

Roaming with Your Mobile Phone: Your US mobile phone works in Europe if it's GSM-enabled, tri-band or quad-band, and on a calling plan that includes international calls. Phones from AT&T and T-Mobile, which use the same GSM technology as

European Calling Chart

Just smile and dial, using this key:
AC = Area Code, LN = Local Number.

European Country	Calling long distance within ...	Calling from the US or Canada to ...	Calling from a European country to ...
Austria	AC + LN	011 + 43 + AC (without the initial zero) + LN	00 + 43 + AC (without the initial zero) + LN
Belgium	LN	011 + 32 + LN (without initial zero)	00 + 32 + LN (without initial zero)
Bosnia-Herzegovina	AC + LN	011 + 387 + AC (without initial zero) + LN	00 + 387 + AC (without initial zero) + LN
Britain	AC + LN	011 + 44 + AC (without initial zero) + LN	00 + 44 + AC (without initial zero) + LN
Croatia	AC + LN	011 + 385 + AC (without initial zero) + LN	00 + 385 + AC (without initial zero) + LN
Czech Republic	LN	011 + 420 + LN	00 + 420 + LN
Denmark	LN	011 + 45 + LN	00 + 45 + LN
Estonia	LN	011 + 372 + LN	00 + 372 + LN
Finland	AC + LN	011 + 358 + AC (without initial zero) + LN	999 (or other 900 number) + 358 + AC (without initial zero) + LN
France	LN	011 + 33 + LN (without initial zero)	00 + 33 + LN (without initial zero)
Germany	AC + LN	011 + 49 + AC (without initial zero) + LN	00 + 49 + AC (without initial zero) + LN
Gibraltar	LN	011 + 350 + LN	00 + 350 + LN
Greece	LN	011 + 30 + LN	00 + 30 + LN
Hungary	06 + AC + LN	011 + 36 + AC + LN	00 + 36 + AC + LN
Ireland	AC + LN	011 + 353 + AC (without initial zero) + LN	00 + 353 + AC (without initial zero) + LN

European Country	Calling long distance within ...	Calling from the US or Canada to ...	Calling from a European country to ...
Italy	LN	011 + 39 + LN	00 + 39 + LN
Montenegro	AC + LN	011 + 382 + AC (without initial zero) + LN	00 + 382 + AC (without initial zero) + LN
Morocco	LN	011 + 212 + LN (without initial zero)	00 + 212 + LN (without initial zero)
Netherlands	AC + LN	011 + 31 + AC (without initial zero) + LN	00 + 31 + AC (without initial zero) + LN
Norway	LN	011 + 47 + LN	00 + 47 + LN
Poland	LN	011 + 48 + LN	00 + 48 + LN
Portugal	LN	011 + 351 + LN	00 + 351 + LN
Slovakia	AC + LN	011 + 421 + AC (without initial zero) + LN	00 + 421 + AC (without initial zero) + LN
Slovenia	AC + LN	011 + 386 + AC (without initial zero) + LN	00 + 386 + AC (without initial zero) + LN
Spain	LN	011 + 34 + LN	00 + 34 + LN
Sweden	AC + LN	011 + 46 + AC (without initial zero) + LN	00 + 46 + AC (without initial zero) + LN
Switzerland	LN	011 + 41 + LN (without initial zero)	00 + 41 + LN (without initial zero)
Turkey	AC (if there's no initial zero, add one) + LN	011 + 90 + AC (without initial zero) + LN	00 + 90 + AC (without initial zero) + LN

APPENDIX

- The instructions above apply whether you're calling to or from a European landline or mobile phone.
- If calling from any mobile phone, you can replace the international access code with "+" (press and hold 0 to insert it).
- The international access code is 011 if you're calling from the US or Canada.
- To call the US or Canada from Europe, dial 00, then 1 (country code for US and Canada), then the area code and number. In short, 00 + 1 + AC + LN = Hi, Mom!

Europe, are more likely to work overseas than Verizon or Sprint phones (if you're not sure, ask your service provider). Most US providers will charge you $1.29-1.99 per minute to make or receive calls while roaming internationally, and 20-50 cents to send or receive text messages. If you bother to sign up for an international calling plan with your provider, you'll save a few dimes per minute. Though pricey, roaming on your own phone is easy and can be a cost-effective way to keep in touch—especially on a short trip or if you won't be making many calls.

Buying and Using SIM Cards in Europe: You'll pay much cheaper rates if you put a European SIM card in your mobile phone; to do this, your phone must be electronically "unlocked" (ask your provider for the details, buy an unlocked phone before you leave, or get one in Europe—see "Other Mobile-Phone Options," next). Then, in Europe, you can buy a fingernail-size **SIM card,** which gives you a European phone number. SIM cards are sold at mobile-phone stores and some newsstand kiosks for $5-10, and often include at least that much prepaid domestic calling time (making the card itself almost free). When you buy a SIM card, you may need to show ID, such as your passport.

Insert the SIM card in your phone (usually in a slot behind the battery or on the side) and it will work like a European mobile phone. Before purchasing a SIM card, always ask about fees for domestic and international calls, roaming charges, and how to check your credit balance and buy more time. When you're in the SIM card's home country, domestic calls average 10-20 cents per minute, and incoming calls are free. Rates are higher if you're roaming in another country, and you may pay more to call a toll number than you would if you were dialing from a fixed line.

Other Mobile-Phone Options: Many travelers like to carry two phones: both their own US mobile phone (allowing them to stay reachable on their own phone number) and a second, unlocked European phone (which lets them do all their local calling at far cheaper rates). You could either bring two phones from home, or get one in Europe. If you have an old mobile phone sitting around, ask your provider for the "unlock code" so you can use the phone with European SIM cards. Or buy a cheap, basic phone before you go (search your favorite online shopping site for "unlocked quad-band GSM phone").

In Europe, basic phones are sold at hole-in-the-wall vendors at many airports and train stations, and at phone desks within larger department stores. Phones that are "locked" to work with a single provider start around $40; "unlocked" phones (which work with any SIM card) start around $60. Regardless of how you get your phone, remember that you'll need a SIM card to make it work.

On my last visit to Ireland, I bought a cheap and durable

"locked" €30 phone from Vodafone (www.vodafone.ie) as soon as I arrived. These basic phones can only make and receive calls, and send and receive text messages. They usually come pre-loaded with €10 of phone time. When necessary, I could "top up" (add more phone time) at mini-markets, magazine shops, or other Vodafone stores in Ireland.

Car-rental companies and mobile-phone companies offer the option to rent a mobile phone with a European number. While this seems convenient, hidden fees (such as high per-minute charges or expensive shipping costs) can really add up—which usually makes it a bad value. One exception is Verizon's Global Travel Program, available only to Verizon customers.

Calling over the Internet

Some things that seem too good to be true...actually are true. If you're traveling with a laptop, tablet, or smartphone, you can make free calls over the Internet to another wireless device, anywhere in the world, for free. (Or you can pay a few cents to call from your computer to a telephone.) The major providers are Skype, Google Talk, and (on Apple devices) FaceTime. You can get online at a Wi-Fi hotspot and use these apps to make calls without ringing up expensive roaming charges (though call quality can be spotty on slow connections). You can make Internet calls even if you're traveling without your own mobile device: Many European Internet cafés have Skype, as well as microphones and webcams, on their terminals—just log on and chat away.

Landline Telephones

As in the US, these days most Europeans do the majority of their phoning on mobile phones. But you'll still encounter landlines in hotel rooms and at pay phones.

Hotel-Room Phones: Calling from your hotel room (in-room phones are rare in B&Bs) can be great for local calls and for international calls if you have an international phone card (described later). Otherwise, hotel-room phones can be an almost criminal rip-off for long-distance or international calls. Many hotels charge a fee for local and sometimes even "toll-free" numbers—always ask for the rates before you dial. Incoming calls are free, making this a cheap way for friends and family to stay in touch (provided they have a long-distance plan with good international rates—and a list of your hotels' phone numbers).

Public Pay Phones: Coin-op phones are virtually extinct in Europe. To make calls from public phones, you'll need a prepaid phone card, described next.

Smartphones and Data Roaming

I take my smartphone to Europe, using it to make phone calls (sparingly) and send texts, but also to check email, listen to audiotours, and browse the Internet. If you're clever, you can do all this without incurring huge data-roaming fees. Here's how.

Many smartphones, such as the iPhone, Android, and BlackBerry, work in Europe (though some older Verizon iPhones don't). For voice calls and text messaging, smartphones work like any mobile phone (as described under "Roaming with Your Mobile Phone," earlier)—unless you're connected to free Wi-Fi, in which case you can use Skype, Google Talk, or FaceTime to call for free (or at least very cheaply; see "Calling over the Internet," previous page).

The (potentially) *really* expensive aspect of using smartphones in Europe is not voice calls or text messages, but sky-high rates for using data: checking email, browsing the Internet, streaming videos, using certain apps, and so on. If you don't proactively adjust your settings, these charges can mount up even if you're not actually using your phone—because the phone is constantly "roaming" to update your email and such. (One tip is to switch your email settings from "push" to "fetch," so you can choose when to download your emails rather than having them automatically "pushed" over the Internet to your device.)

The best solution: Disable data roaming entirely, and use your device to access the Internet only when you find free Wi-Fi (at your hotel, for example). Then you can surf the net to your heart's content, or make free (or extremely cheap) phone calls via Skype. You can manually turn off data roaming on your phone's menu (check under the "Network" settings). For added security, you can call and ask your service provider to temporarily suspend your data account entirely for the length of your trip.

Some travelers enjoy the flexibility of getting online even when they're not on free Wi-Fi. But be careful: If you simply switch on data roaming, you'll pay exorbitant rates of about $20 per megabyte (figure around 40 cents per email downloaded, or about $3 to view a typical Web page)—much more expensive than it is back home. If you know you'll be doing some data roaming, it's far more affordable to sign up for a limited international data-roaming plan through your carrier (but be very clear on your megabyte limit to avoid inflated overage charges). In general, ask your provider in advance how to avoid unwittingly roaming your way to a huge bill.

Types of Telephone Cards

There are two types of phone cards: insertable (for pay phones) and international (cheap for overseas calls and usable from any type of phone). Both types of phone card work only within the country of purchase, with the exception of some brands of cards that are usable in both the Republic of Ireland and the UK—confirm before buying a card by checking for both an 1800 access number (used in the Republic of Ireland) and an 0800 access number (for the UK—don't use the 0845, 0870, or 0871 numbers, which cost about 10p per minute). If you have a live card at the end of your trip, give it to another traveler to use—most cards expire 3-6 months after the first use.

Insertable Phone Cards: This type of card can be used only at Irish pay phones. It's handy and affordable for local and domestic calls, but more expensive for international calls. Telecom Éireann phone cards are sold for €5, €10, or €20 at newsstands, TIs, and post offices. To use the card, physically insert it into a slot in the pay phone.

International Phone Cards: With these cards, phone calls from Ireland to the US can cost less than a nickel a minute. The cards can also be used to make local calls, and they work from any type of phone, including your hotel-room phone or a mobile phone with a European SIM card. To use the card, dial a toll-free access number, and then enter your scratch-to-reveal PIN code.

You can buy the cards at many post offices, newsstands, minimarts, and exchange bureaus. Ask the clerk which of the various brands has the best rates for calls to America. Buy a lower denomination in case the card is a dud. Since you don't need the actual card or receipt to use the account, you can write down the access number and code and share it with friends.

US Calling Cards: These cards—such as the ones offered by AT&T, Verizon, and Sprint—are a rotten value and are being phased out. Try any of the options outlined earlier.

Useful Phone Numbers

Note that calls beginning with 1800 are free throughout Ireland, but 1850 calls cost the same as local calls.

Emergency Needs
In the Republic of Ireland
Emergency (police and ambulance): Tel. 999

In Northern Ireland
Emergency (police and ambulance): Tel. 999

US Embassies and Consulates

In the Republic of Ireland: 42 Elgin Road, Dublin, Mon-Tue and Thu-Fri 8:30-11:30, closed Wed and Sat-Sun, tel. 01/668-7122 or 01/668-8777, http://dublin.usembassy.gov

In Northern Ireland: Danesfort House, 223 Stranmillis Road, Belfast, Mon-Fri 8:30-17:00, closed Sat-Sun, tel. 028/9038-6100, after-hours emergency mobile 075-4550-7738, http://belfast.us-consulate.gov

Canadian Embassies

In the Republic of Ireland: 7-8 Wilton Terrace, Dublin, Mon-Fri 9:00-13:00 & 14:00-16:30, consular and passport services open Mon-Fri 9:00-12:00, closed Sat-Sun, tel. 01/234-4000, www.canada.ie

In Northern Ireland: 9 Cromac Avenue, Belfast, tel. 028/9127-2060

Travel Advisories

US Department of State: Tel. 888-407-4747, from outside US tel. 1-202-501-4444, www.travel.state.gov

Canadian Department of Foreign Affairs: Canadian tel. 800-267-8376, from outside Canada tel. 1-613-996-8885, www.voyage.gc.ca

US Centers for Disease Control and Prevention: Tel. 800-CDC-INFO (800-232-4636), www.cdc.gov/travel

Directory Assistance
In the Republic of Ireland

Operator Assistance: Tel. 10 for Ireland, tel. 114 to call outside Ireland

Directory Assistance Within Ireland: Tel. 11811 (free from phone booth)

International Info: Tel. 11818 (free from phone booth)

In Northern Ireland

Operator Assistance: Tel. 100 for Britain, tel. 155 to call outside Britain

Directory Assistance Within Britain: Tel. 192 (20p from phone booth, otherwise £1.50)

International Info: Tel. 153 (20p from phone booth, otherwise £1.50)

Airlines

These are phone numbers for the Republic of Ireland.

Aer Arann: Tel. 0818-365-044, www.aerarann.com

Aer Lingus: Tel. 0818-365-000, www.aerlingus.com

APPENDIX

Air Canada: Tel. 180-070-9900, www.aircanada.com
Air France: Tel. 0818-776-057, www.airfrance.com
American: Tel. 0818-286-597, www.aa.com
Delta: Tel. 0818-904-872, www.delta.com
Iberia: Tel. 0818-462-000, www.iberia.com
Lufthansa: Tel. 01/844-5544, www.lufthansa.com
Ryanair (cheap fares): Tel. 081-830-3030, www.ryanair.com
Scandinavian Airlines System (SAS): Tel. 01/844-5440, www.flysas.com
Swiss Air: Tel. 1890-200-515, www.swiss.com
United: Tel. 1890-925-252, www.united.com
US Airways: Tel. 1890-925-065, www.usairways.com

Airports

Dublin: Tel. 01/814-1111 (airport code: DUB, www.dublinairport.ie)
Shannon: Tel. 061/712-000 (airport code: SNN, www.shannonairport.ie)
Cork: Tel. 021/431-3131 (airport code: ORK, www.corkairport.com)
Belfast: Belfast International Airport—tel. 028/9448-4848 (airport code: BFS, www.belfastairport.com); George Best Belfast City Airport—tel. 028/9093-9093 (airport code: BHD, www.belfastcityairport.com)

Dublin Car-Rental Agencies

Avis: 35-39 Old Kilmainham Road, tel. 021/428-1111, airport tel. 01/605-7500, www.avis.ie
Hertz: 151 South Circular Road, tel. 01/676-7476, airport tel. 01/844-5466, www.hertz.ie
Budget: 151 Lower Drumcondra Road, tel. 01/837-9611, central reservations tel. 09066/27711, airport tel. 01/844-5150, www.budget.ie
Europcar: 2 Haddington Road, tel. 01/614-2888, airport tel. 01/812-0410, www.europcar.ie

Internet Access

It's useful to get online periodically as you travel—to confirm trip plans, check train or bus schedules, get weather forecasts, catch up on email, blog or post photos from your trip, or call folks back home (explained earlier, under "Calling over the Internet").

Your Mobile Device: The majority of accommodations in Ireland offer Wi-Fi, as do many cafés, making it easy for you to get online with your laptop, tablet, or smartphone. Access is often free, but sometimes there's a fee.

Some hotel rooms and Internet cafés have high-speed Internet jacks that you can plug into with an Ethernet cable. A cellular modem—which lets your device access the Internet over a mobile network—provides more extensive coverage, but is much more expensive than Wi-Fi.

Public Internet Terminals: Many accommodations offer a computer in the lobby with Internet access for guests. If you ask politely, smaller places may let you sit at their desk for a few minutes just to check your email. If your hotelier doesn't have access, ask to be directed to the nearest place to get online.

Security: Whether you're accessing the Internet with your own device or at a public terminal, using a shared network or computer comes with the potential for increased security risks. Be careful about storing personal information online, such as passport and credit-card numbers. If you're not convinced a connection is secure, avoid accessing any sites that could be vulnerable to fraud (such as online banking).

Mail

You can mail one package per day to yourself worth up to $200 duty-free from Europe to the US (mark it "personal purchases"). If you're sending a gift to someone, mark it "unsolicited gift." For details, visit www.cbp.gov and search for "Know Before You Go."

The Irish postal service works fine, but for quick transatlantic delivery (in either direction), consider services such as DHL (www.dhl.com). Get stamps at the neighborhood post office, newsstands within fancy hotels, and some mini-marts and card shops. Don't use stamps from the Republic of Ireland on postcards mailed in Northern Ireland (part of the UK), and vice versa.

Transportation

By Car or Public Transportation?

To see all of Ireland, especially the sights with far-flung rural charm, I prefer the freedom of a rental car. Connemara, the Ring of Kerry, the Antrim Coast, County Donegal, County Wexford, and the Valley of the Boyne are really only worth it if you have wheels.

Cars are best for three or more traveling together (especially families with small kids), those packing heavy, and those scouring the countryside. Trains and buses are best for solo travelers, blitz tourists, and city-to-city travelers; and those who don't want to drive in Ireland. Ireland has a good train-and-bus system, though departures are not as frequent as the European norm. Most rail lines spoke outward from Dublin, so you'll need to mix in bus transportation to bridge the gaps. Buses pick you up when the trains let you down.

I've included a sample itinerary for drivers (with tips and tweaks for those using public transportation) to help you explore Ireland smoothly; you'll find it on page 10.

Public Transportation

The best overall source of schedules for public transportation in the Republic of Ireland as well as Northern Ireland—including rail, cross-country and city buses, and Dublin's DART and LUAS transit—is the Tourism Ireland website: www.discoverireland.com (select "Plan Your Visit," and then "Getting Around").

Trains

Ireland's various passes offer a marginally better value than BritRail's pricey "BritRail plus Ireland" pass (see chart on page 489). It's easy to purchase Irish railpasses in Ireland at major stations (Dublin info tel. 01/836-6222). For a free summary of rail-pass deals and the latest prices, check my Guide to Eurail passes at www.ricksteves.com/rail. To research your rail options online, check www.bahn.com (Germany's excellent Europe-wide time-table).

Most tourists don't travel enough in Ireland to make a rail or bus pass pay off. Chances are that you'll save money by buying point-to-point tickets as you go. Fares are often higher for peak travel on Fridays and Sundays. To avoid long station lines in Dublin, you can book train tickets in advance online (often with a hefty discount on the fare). Otherwise, you can book by phone with your credit card or in person at the Iarnrod Éireann Travel Centre (Mon-Fri 9:00-17:00, closed Sat-Sun, 35 Lower Abbey Street, tel. 01/703-4070).

Students are eligible for an **Irish Rail Student Travelcard** (which offers varying discounts per ride and is good for 16 months), but you have to plan a couple of months ahead: Go to www.studenttravelcard.ie, print the application form, get it stamped at your university student-travel office, and mail it to Ireland (include two passport photos and €12, payable by credit card; they'll mail you the card in 4-6 weeks).

Buses

If you opt for public transportation, you'll probably spend more time on Irish buses than Irish trains. But be aware: Public transportation (especially cross-country Irish buses) will likely put your travels into slow motion.

Ireland Public Transportation

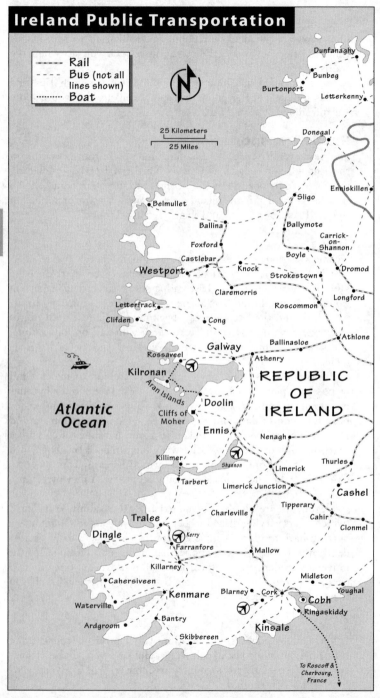

Rail
Bus (not all
lines shown)
Boat

25 Kilometers
25 Miles

Dunfanaghy
Bunbeg
Burtonport
Letterkenny
Donegal
Enniskillen
Belmullet
Sligo
Ballina
Ballymote
Foxford
Carrick-on-Shannon
Castlebar
Boyle
Dromod
Westport
Knock
Strokestown
Claremorris
Longford
Roscommon
Letterfrack
Cong
Clifden
Athlone
Galway
Ballinasloe
Rossaveel
Athenry
Kilronan
Aran Islands
Doolin
Cliffs of Moher
Ennis
Nenagh
Thurles
Killimer
Shannon
Tarbert
Limerick
Limerick Junction
Cashel
Charleville
Tipperary
Cahir
Tralee
Mallow
Clonmel
Dingle
Kerry
Farranfore
Killarney
Midleton
Cahersiveen
Blarney
Cork
Youghal
Kenmare
Cobh
Waterville
Ringaskiddy
Ardgroom
Bantry
Kinsale
Skibbereen

REPUBLIC
OF
IRELAND

Atlantic
Ocean

To Roscoff &
Cherbourg,
France

APPENDIX

For example, driving across County Kerry from Kenmare to Dingle takes two hours. If you go by bus, the same trip takes four hours—twice as long. The trip by bus necessitates two transfers (in Killarney and Tralee, each involving a wait for the next bus), and the buses often take a rural milk-run route, making multiple stops along the way. Not every Irish coach trip will involve this kind of delay. But if you opt to go by coach, be realistic about your itinerary and study the schedules ahead of time. The Bus Éireann Expressway Bus Timetable comes in handy (free, available at some bus stations or online at www.buseireann.ie, bus info tel. 01/836-6111).

Even though buses are slower than trains (by about a third), they're also much cheaper. Round-trip bus tickets usually cost less than two one-way fares (for example, Tralee to Dingle is €12.30 one-way and €20 round-trip). The Irish distinguish between "buses" (for in-city travel with lots of stops) and "coaches" (long-distance cross-country runs).

You may need to do some trips partly by train. For instance, if you're going from Dublin to Dingle without a car, you'll need to take a train to Tralee and catch a bus from there. Similarly, to go from Dublin to Kinsale without a car, take a train to Cork and then a bus; and from Dublin to Doolin, take a train to Galway or Ennis and then a bus.

If you're traveling up and down Ireland's west coast, buses are best (or a combination of buses and trains); relying on rail-only here is too time-consuming. Note that some rural coach stops are by "request only." This means the coach will drive right on by unless you flag it down by extending your arm straight out, with your palm open.

Bus stations are normally at or near train stations. Before you board the coach, you'll be asked to stow your bag in the large compartment beneath the passenger cabin. Try to get a window seat on the side of the coach where the luggage is unloaded, and be alert whenever the bus stops to take on or let off passengers. Otherwise, someone may—likely accidentally—take your bag. Many bags look alike; decorate yours distinctively. On some Irish buses, sports games are piped throughout the bus; have earplugs handy if you prefer a quieter ride.

Some companies offer **backpacker's bus circuits.** These hop-on, hop-off bus circuits take mostly youth hostelers around the country cheaply and easily, with the assumption that they'll be sleeping in hostels along the way. For example, Paddy Wagon cuts Ireland in half and offers three- to six-day "tours" of each half (north and south) that can be combined into one whole tour connecting Dublin, Cork, Killarney, Dingle, Galway, Westport, Donegal, Derry, and Belfast (May-Oct, 5 Beresford Palace, Dublin, tel. 01/823-0822, toll-free from UK tel. 0800-783-4191,

Railpasses

Prices listed are for 2012 and are subject to change. For the latest prices, details, and train schedules (and easy online ordering), see my comprehensive *Guide to Eurail Passes* at www.ricksteves.com/rail.

BRITRAIL PLUS IRELAND PASS

	1st Class	2nd Class
5 days in 1 month	$725	$489
10 days in 1 month	$1,299	$875

Covers trains in the entire British Isles (England, Wales, Scotland, Northern Ireland, and the Republic of Ireland). Does not cover ferries or buses. Consider the BritRail passes (online) over this 10-day version. The fare for kiddies 5–15 is half the fare. Kids under age 5 travel free.

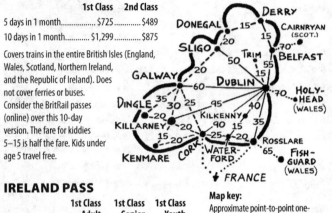

IRELAND PASS

	1st Class Adult	1st Class Senior	1st Class Youth
5 days in 1 month	$361	$272	$307

	2nd Class Adult	2nd Class Senior	2nd Class Youth
5 days in 1 month	$289	$218	$247

Covers trains (not buses) on the whole island; plus some ferry discounts.

Map key:
Approximate point-to-point one-way second-class fares in US dollars by rail (solid line), bus (dashed line), and ferry (dotted line). First class trains cost 50 percent more. Add up fares for your itinerary to see whether a rail and/or bus pass will save you money.

DEALS ONCE YOU GET TO IRELAND:

These local specials are sold at major train stations in Ireland. €1 = about $1.30 US.

Pass Name	Version	Area	Duration	Price
Irish Explorer	Rail & Bus	Republic only	8 out of 15 days	€245
	Rail only	Republic only	5 out of 15 days	€160
Irish Rover	Bus only	Republic & North	3 out of 8 days	€84
			8 out of 15 days	€190
			15 out of 30 days	€280

Open Road Pass
This pass covers buses in the Republic of Ireland.

Duration	Price
3 out of 6 days	€54
4 out of 8 days	€69
5 out of 10 days	€84
6 out of 12 days	€99
7 out of 14 days	€114
8 out of 16 days	€129
9 out of 18 days	€144

Duration	Price
10 out of 20 days	€159
11 out of 22 days	€174
12 out of 24 days	€189
13 out of 26 days	€204
14 out of 28 days	€219
15 out of 30 days	€234

Ferry Information

INTERNATIONAL FERRY CONNECTIONS

Ireland has good ferry connections with Britain and France. Check the websites listed per route below for specifics on price, frequency, and length of journey.

Republic of Ireland

Irish Port	To...	Web Site
Dublin	Liverpool (England)	www.poirishsea.com and www.steam-packet.com
Dublin	Birkenhead (near Liverpool)	www.norfolkline-ferries.co.uk
Dublin	Holyhead (Wales)	www.irishferries.com
Dun Laoghaire (nr Dublin)	Holyhead (Wales)	www.stenaline.com
Rosslare	Fishguard (Wales)	www.stenaline.com
Rosslare	Pembroke (Wales)	www.irishferries.com
Rosslare	Cherbourg (France)	www.irishferries.com and www.aferry.co.uk/celtic-link-ferries.htm
Rosslare	Roscoff (France)	www.irishferries.com
Ringaskiddy (near Cork)	Roscoff (France)	www.brittanyferries.ie

Northern Ireland

Belfast	Liverpool (England)	www.steam-packet.com
Belfast	Birkenhead (near Liverpool)	www.norfolkline-ferries.co.uk
Belfast	Cairnryan (Scotland)	www.stenaline.com
Larne (near Belfast)	Troon (Scotland)	www.poirishsea.com
Larne	Cairnryan (Scotland)	www.poirishsea.com
Larne	Fleetwood (near Blackpool, England)	www.stenaline.com

www.paddywagontours.com). They also offer day tours to the Giant's Causeway, Belfast, Cliffs of Moher, Glendalough, or Kilkenny.

Students can use their ISIC (student card, www.isic.org) to get discounts on cross-country coaches (up to 50 percent). Children 5-15 pay half-price on trains, and wee ones under age 5 go free.

Renting a Car

Travelers from North America are understandably hesitant when they consider driving in Ireland. But careful drivers—with the patient support of an alert navigator—usually get the hang of it by the end of the first day.

If you're renting a car in Ireland, bring your driver's license. It's recommended, but not required, that you also have an International Driving Permit if your driver's license has been renewed within the last year (sold at your local AAA office for $15 plus the cost of two passport-type photos, www.aaa.com); I've frequently rented cars in Ireland and traveled problem-free with just my US license.

Rental companies generally require you to be at least 21 years old and to have held your license for two years. Drivers under 25 may incur a young-driver surcharge (if that describes you, try STA Travel, which seeks young renters; www.statravel.com, tel. 800-781-4040). In the Republic of Ireland, you generally can't rent a car if you're 75 or over, and you'll pay extra if you're 70-74. Some companies in Northern Ireland won't rent to anyone over 69. (Note that you can't lease a car in Ireland; you can only rent.)

Research car rentals before you go. It's cheaper to arrange most car rentals from the US. Call several companies and look online to compare rates, or arrange a rental through your hometown travel agent. Most of the major US rental agencies (including National, Avis, Budget, Hertz, and Thrifty) have offices throughout Europe. Also consider the two major Europe-based agencies, Europcar and Sixt. It can be cheaper to use a consolidator, such as Auto Europe (www.autoeurope.com) or Europe by Car (www.ebctravel.com), which compares rates at several companies to get you the best deal. However, my readers have reported problems with consolidators, ranging from misinformation to unexpected fees; because you're going through a middleman, it can be more challenging to resolve disputes that arise with the rental agency.

Regardless of the car-rental company you choose, always read the contract carefully. The fine print can conceal a host of common add-on charges—such as one-way drop-off fees, airport surcharges, or mandatory insurance policies—that aren't included in the "total price," but can be tacked on when you pick up your car. You may need to query rental agents pointedly to find out your actual cost.

For the best deal, rent by the week with unlimited mileage. To save money on gas, ask for a diesel car. In mid-summer expect to pay about $260 per week ($500 for an automatic), including gas and minimum insurance, for a basic compact-size car (like a Ford Escort 1.3-liter). With full insurance, the price of the same car goes up to about $480 per week ($575 for an automatic). Smaller economy-size cars cost about $75 less per week, but they don't feel as smooth on the motorways or as safe on small roads. Minibuses are a great, budget way to go for larger groups (five to nine people). But don't forget to factor in the space for everyone's luggage.

Almost all rentals are manual by default, so if you need an automatic, you must request one in advance. Be aware that an automatic transmission costs more and is usually more available in larger models (which are not as maneuverable on narrow, winding roads). Weigh these considerations against the fact that in Ireland you'll be sitting on the right side of the car and shifting with your left hand...while driving on the left side of the road. The floor pedals are in the same locations as in the US, and the gears are still found in the same basic "H" pattern as at home (i.e., first gear, second, etc.).

You can sometimes get a GPS unit with your rental car for an additional fee (around $15/day; be sure it has all the maps you need before you drive off). Or, if you have a portable GPS device at home, consider taking it with you to Europe (buy and upload European maps before your trip). GPS apps are also available for smartphones, but roaming charges in Europe could lead to an exorbitant data-roaming bill (for more details, see the sidebar on page 480).

Big companies have offices in most cities; ask to be picked up at your hotel. Small local rental companies can be cheaper but aren't as flexible. Some companies, such as Auto Europe (www.autoeurope.com) or Dan Dooley (www.dan-dooley.ie), will do longer-term rentals at a slight discount.

Compare pickup costs (downtown can be less expensive than the airport), and explore drop-off options. When selecting a location, don't trust the agency's description of "downtown" or "city center." In some cases, a "downtown" branch can be on the outskirts of the city—a long, costly taxi ride from the center. Before choosing, plug the addresses into a mapping website. You may find that the "train station" location is handier. Returning a car at a big-city train station or downtown agency can be tricky; get precise details on the car drop-off location and hours and allow ample time to find it. Note that rental offices usually close from midday Saturday until Monday morning.

When you pick up the rental car, check it thoroughly and make sure any damage is noted on your rental agreement. Find out how your car's lights, turn signals, wipers, and fuel cap function, and know what kind of fuel the car takes. When you return the car, make sure the agent verifies its condition with you.

If your trip covers both Ireland and Great Britain (Scotland, England, and Wales), you're better off with two separate car rentals, rather than paying for your car to ride the ferry between the two islands. On an all-Ireland trip, you can drive your rental car from the Republic of Ireland into Northern Ireland, but be aware of drop-off charges ($75-150) if you return it in the North. You'll pay a smaller drop-off charge ($25-50) for picking up the car at one place and dropping it off at another within the same country (even picking up in downtown Dublin and dropping off at Dublin Airport). If you pick up the car in a smaller city, you'll more likely survive your first day on the Irish roads. If you drop the car off early or keep it longer, you'll be credited or charged at a fair, prorated price.

Car Insurance Options

When you rent a car, you're liable for a very high deductible, sometimes equal to the entire value of the car. Limit your financial risk by choosing one of these two options: Buy Collision Damage Waiver (CDW) coverage from the car-rental company, or get coverage through your credit card (more complicated, and few credit cards now offer free coverage in Ireland).

CDW includes a very high deductible (typically $1,000-1,500). Though each rental company has its own variation, basic **CDW** costs $15-35 a day (figure roughly 30 percent extra) and reduces your liability, but does not eliminate it. When you pick up the car, you'll be offered the chance to "buy down" the basic deductible to zero (for an additional $10-30/day; this is sometimes called "super CDW").

If you opt for **credit-card coverage** (and your credit card is one of the few accepted for this type of coverage in Ireland), there's a catch. You'll technically have to decline all coverage offered by the car-rental company, which means they can place a hold on your card (which can be up to the full value of the car). In case of damage, it can be time-consuming to resolve the charges with your credit-card company. Before you decide on this option, quiz your credit-card company about how it works.

For more on car-rental insurance, see www.ricksteves.com/cdw.

Driving

Ireland's new motorways have vastly improved the cross-country driving experience and now link most major cities (Dublin, Belfast, Cork, Waterford, Limerick, and Galway). But the best intimate sites still require you to drive on narrow country lanes.

Note that your US credit and debit cards are unlikely to work at self-service gas pumps and automated parking garages. Luckily, the vast majority of Irish gas stations have a live attendant inside who can process your gas purchase (as long as it's not too late at night). The easiest solution is carrying sufficient cash in euros (pounds in the North).

Road Rules: Driving in Ireland is basically wonderful—once you remember to stay on the left and after you've mastered the roundabouts. Don't let a roundabout spook you. After all, you routinely merge into much faster traffic with cars slipping into your blind spot on American highways back home. The traffic in a roundabout has the right-of-way; entering traffic yields (look to

Driving in Ireland

Kilronan
Aran Islands
Doolin
7m .25h
25m .75h
Cliffs of Moher
31m 1h
Ennis
Kilrush
Killimer
Tarbert
30m .75h
Tralee

Bunbeg
Loop: 7.5m 4h
40m .75h
Portrush
Giant's Causeway
Derry
10m .25h
60m 1.25h
Bangor
35m .75h
45m 1.25h
60m 1.75h
Donegal
40m 1h
Omagh
Sligo
NORTHERN IRELAND
100m 2.5h
15m .25h
Belfast
65m 1.5h
130m 3.25h
105m 2.5h
Westport
30m 1h
Cong
IRELAND
Brú na Bóinne (Newgrange)
Letterfrack
45m 1.75h
50m 1.25h
Rossaveel
30m 1h
Galway
30m 1h
125m 2.5h
20m .5h
Trim
35m .75h
30m .5h
Aran Islands
See detail map above
45m 1.25h
Dublin
Doolin
50m 1.25h
40m 1h
125m 2.75h
30m 1h
Shannon
15m .25h
75m 1.5h
95m 2.25h
Glendalough
Dingle
Loop: 30m 2h
30m 1.25h
60m 1.5h
Limerick
Kilkenny
Tralee
Cashel 40m 1h
30m .75h
65m 1.25h
m = miles
h = hours
...... = ferry
130m 3h
45m 1.25h
40m 1.5h
20m .5h
60m 1.25h
60m 1.25h
75m 2h
35m 1h
Wexford
Rosslare
Killarney
Blarney
Waterford
20m 1h
Cork
10m .25h
Loop: 100m 4.5h
Kenmare
90m 2.5h
Cobh
Kinsale
15m .5h
Note: Your times may vary based on traffic, construction, and sheep on road.

your right as you merge). It helps to remember that the driver is always in the center of the road.

Seat belts are mandatory for all, and kids under 12 or under 1.5 meters tall (about 4 feet, 9 inches) must ride in a child-safety seat. An Irish Automobile Association membership comes with most rentals (www.aaireland.ie). Understand its towing and emergency road-service benefits.

But be warned: Every year I get a few emails from traveling readers advising me that, for them, trying to drive in Ireland was a nerve-racking and regrettable mistake. If you want to get a little slack on the roads, drop by a gas station or auto shop and buy a red *L* (new driver with license) sign to put in your back

window. Wait to use it until you get away from Dublin, as Irish "Learners" are not allowed to drive on the motorways that cluster around the city.

Be aware of other road rules: You may not use a mobile phone while driving (unless you have a hands-free headset), and head-lights must be on in poor day lighting. For more information, ask your car-rental company or check the US State Department web-site (www.travel.state.gov, click on "International Travel," specify your country of choice, and then click "Traffic Safety and Road Conditions").

Speed Limits: Speed limits are 50 kilometers per hour (rough-ly 30 miles per hour) in towns, 80 kph (approximately 50 mph) on rural roads (such as R-257, R-600, etc.), 100 kph (about 60 mph) on national roads (N-8, N-30, etc.), and 120 kph (roughly 75 mph) on motorways (M-1, M-50, etc.). Note that road-surveillance cameras strictly enforce speed limits. Any driver (including foreigners rent-ing cars) photographed speeding will get a nasty bill in the mail. (Cameras—you'll see the foreboding gray boxes—flash on your rear license plate in order not to invade the privacy of anyone shar-ing the front seat with someone they shouldn't be with.)

Tolls: The M-50 ring road surrounding Dublin carries a €3 toll, paid electronically with an eFlow pass. Get details from your rental-car company at Dublin Airport (see page 51; more details at www.eflow.ie).

Parking: Parking is confusing. One yellow line marked on the pave-ment means no parking Monday through Sat-urday during business hours. Double yellow lines mean no parking at any time. Broken yellow lines mean short stops are OK, but you should always look for explicit signs or ask a passerby.

Even in small towns, rather than fight it, I just pull into the most central parking lot I can find. As for street parking, signs along the street will state whether pay-and-display

or parking disk laws are in effect for that area. The modern pay-and-display machines are solar-powered and placed regularly along

Tips on Driving

Driving gives you access to the most rural sights and is my favorite mode of transportation in Ireland. Here's what I've learned in the school of hard brakes and adrenaline rushes:

- *The Complete Road Atlas of Ireland* by Ordnance Survey (€10, handy ring-binder style, 1:210,000 scale) is the  best Irish road map, and includes translations of Irish place names on the last pages. It covers every road your car can wedge onto. Flipping to the next page of an atlas is easier to manage in a cramped front seat than wrestling with a large, ungainly folding map. Buy the atlas at the first TI or gas station you come to.

- Study your map before taking off. Get a sense of the areas you'll be visiting, as road numbers are inconsistent.

- Road signs can be confusing, too little, and too late. There are three main kinds of signs: (1) Those with white lettering on a green background are found on major routes and give distances in kilometers. (2) Signs with black lettering on a white background are older and trickier: Distances shown with a "km" following the numbers are in kilometers, while distances with nothing following the numbers are in miles (and are slowly being phased out). (3) Brown signs with white lettering alert drivers to sights, lodging, and tourist offices.

- Figure out your lights, wipers, and radio before you're on the road.

- Adjust your side-view mirrors and get in the habit of using them. Many are spring-loaded to snap back into place (a pragmatic solution on narrow roads). Get comfortable with the sound of vegetation whisking the side of your car (it rarely scratches).

- Drive with your lights on to make your vehicle more visible.

- Get used to shifting with your left hand. Find reverse... before you need it. (I love the smell of burnt clutch in the morning.)

- The most common mistake is getting a late start, which causes you to rush, which makes you miss turns, which causes you stress, which decreases your enjoyment, which makes your trip feel less like a vacation.

- Car travel in Ireland isn't fast (although more motorways are being built). Plan your itinerary estimating an average speed of 40 mph (1 km per minute). Give your itinerary a reality check by finding distances and driving times between towns on the driving map (see the chart in this chapter) or online (www.viamichelin.com).

- The shortest distance between any two points is usually the motorway (highway). Miss a motorway exit and you can lose 30 minutes.

- Avoid driving in big cities if possible; use ring roads to skirt the congestion. Dublin is clogged with traffic—you'll find sightseeing easier on foot, by bus (particularly the hop-on, hop-off tours), or by taxi. Spare yourself the traffic stress and parking expense (€3/hour) of trying to drive in Dublin.

- When it comes to narrow rural roads, adjust your perceptions of personal space. It's not "my side of the road" or "your side of the road." It's just "the road"—and it's shared as a cooperative adventure. Locals are usually courteous, pulling over against a hedgerow and blinking their headlights for you to pass while they wait. Return the favor when you are closer to a wide spot in the road than they are. Pull over frequently—to let faster drivers pass and to check the map.

- Watch the road ahead and expect a slow tractor, a flock of sheep, a one-lane bridge, and a baby stroller to lurk around the next turn. Honk when approaching blind corners to alert approaching drivers.

- On narrow rural roads, buses always have the right of way, so you'll need to back up to give way.

- Tune in to RTE One, the national radio station (89 FM), for long drives. Its interviews and music are an education in Irish culture. The same goes for BBC Ulster (94.5 FM) in Northern Ireland.

- Make your road trip fun. Establish a cardboard-box pantry of munchies. Keep a rack of liter boxes of juice in the trunk. Buy some Windex and a roll of paper towels for cleaner sightseeing. A bottle of sparkling mineral water makes a dandy windshield cleaner in a pinch.

- Don't drink and drive. The Gardí (police) set up random checkpoints. If you've had more than one pint, you're legally drunk in Ireland.

- If you're driving between the Republic and Northern Ireland, keep these basic differences in mind: In the Republic, the speed limit is in kilometers per hour, unleaded costs about €1.65 per liter ($8.12 per gallon), and the roads can be bumpy, narrow, and winding. In Northern Ireland, the speed limit is in miles per hour, unleaded costs about £1.35 per liter ($8 per gallon), and roads are better maintained.

- Travelers who want to use designated disabled parking spaces in Ireland can bring their Disabled Persons Parking Card from the US (even though the Irish have a different card that they set on their dashboard). For more information, call the Irish Wheelchair Association at tel. 045/893-094 (from the US, dial 011-353-45-893-094).

the street (about six feet tall, look for blue circle with white letter *P*). I keep some extra coins in the ashtray for these machines (no change given for large coins). The use of parking disks is less common these days, but if you need disks, they're sold at nearby shops. You buy one disk for each hour you want to stay. Scratch off the time you arrived on the disk and put it on your dashboard.

Cheap Flights

If you're considering a train ride that's more than five hours long, a flight may save you both time and money. When comparing your options, factor in the time it takes to get to the airport and how early you'll need to arrive to check in.

The best comparison search engine for both international and intra-European flights is www. kayak.com. For inexpensive flights within Europe, try www.sky-scanner.com or www.hipmunk.com. If you're not sure who flies to your destination, check its airport's website for a list of carriers.

Well-known cheapo airlines include Ryanair (Irish tel. 081-830-3030, www.ryanair.com), Aer Lingus (Irish tel. 081-836-5000, www.aerlingus.com), Flybe (British tel. 0139-226-8529, www.flybe.com), and easyJet (flies in and out of Belfast only, Irish tel. 1-890-923-922, British tel. 0871-244-2366, www.easyjet.com). For flights within Ireland, try Aer Arann (Irish tel. 0818-365-044, British tel. 0800-587-2324, www.aerarann.com).

Be aware of the potential drawbacks of flying on the cheap: nonrefundable and nonchangeable tickets, minimal or nonexistent customer service, treks to airports far outside town, and pricey baggage fees. If you're traveling with lots of luggage, a cheap flight can quickly become a bad deal. To avoid unpleasant surprises, read the small print before you book.

Airports

All direct flights from the US land in either Dublin, Shannon, or Belfast. Cork has become a handy arrival point as well (via connecting flights from London). If you're offered a choice and have no interest in sightseeing in busy, congested Dublin, you'll find Shannon Airport to be a far less stressful entry or exit point into or out of Ireland. Drivers will especially appreciate getting used to the "other side of the road" around rural Shannon, as compared to urban Dublin. Be aware that smaller regional airports may have fewer car-rental offices.

Resources

Resources from Rick Steves

Rick Steves' Ireland 2013 is one of many books in my series on European travel, which includes country guidebooks (such as *Rick Steves' Great Britain*, covering nearby Wales, Scotland, and England), city and regional guidebooks (London, Rome, Florence, Paris, etc.), Snapshot guides (excerpted chapters from my country guides), Pocket Guides (full-color little books on big cities), and my budget-travel skills handbook, *Rick Steves' Europe Through the Back Door*. Most of my titles are

available as ebooks. My phrase books—for French, Italian, German, Spanish, and Portuguese—are practical and budget-oriented. My other books include *Europe 101* (a crash course on art and history), *Mediterranean Cruise Ports* (how to make the most of your time in port), and *Travel as a Political Act* (a travelogue sprinkled with tips for bringing home a global perspective). A more complete list of my titles appears near the end of this book.

Video: My public television series, *Rick Steves' Europe,* covers European destinations in 100 shows, with four episodes on Ireland. To watch episodes, visit www.hulu.com/rick-steves-europe; for scripts and local airtimes, see www.ricksteves.com/tv.

Audio: My weekly public radio show, *Travel with Rick Steves,*

features interviews with travel experts from around the world. All of this audio content is available for free at Rick Steves Audio Europe, an extensive online library organized by destination. Choose whatever interests you, and download it for free via the Rick Steves Audio Europe smartphone app, www.ricksteves.com/audioeurope, iTunes, or Google Play.

Maps

The black-and-white maps in this book are concise and simple, designed to help you locate recommended places and get to local TIs, where you can pick up more in-depth maps of towns or regions (usually free). Better maps are sold at newsstands and bookstores. Before you buy a map, check that it has the level of detail you want.

Train travelers do fine with a simple rail map (available as part of the free Intercity Timetable found at Irish train stations) and city

Begin Your Trip at www.ricksteves.com

At ricksteves.com, you'll discover a wealth of free informa-tion on European destinations, including fresh monthly news and helpful tips from thousands of fellow travelers. You'll find my latest guidebook updates (www.ricksteves.com/update), a monthly travel e-newsletter (easy and free to sign up), my personal travel blog, and my free Rick Steves Audio Europe smartphone app (if you don't have a smartphone, you can ac-cess the same content via podcasts). You can even follow me on Facebook and Twitter.

Our **online Travel Store** offers travel bags and accesso-ries that I've designed specifically to help you travel smarter and lighter. These include my popular carry-on bags (roll-aboard and backpack versions), money belts, totes, toilet-ries kits, adapters, other accessories, and a wide selection of guidebooks, planning maps, and DVDs.

Choosing the right **railpass** for your trip—amid hundreds of options—can drive you nutty. We'll help you choose the best pass for your needs and ship it to you for free.

Want to travel with greater efficiency and less stress? We organize **tours** with more than three dozen itineraries and more than 500 departures reaching the best destinations in this book...and beyond. We offer a 14-day Ireland tour, as well as multiple tours in nearby England, Wales, and Scotland. You'll enjoy great guides, a bunch of travel partners (with small groups of generally around 24-28 travelers), and plenty of room to spread out in a big, comfy bus. You'll find European adventures to fit every vacation length. For all the details, and to get our Tour Catalog and a free Rick Steves Tour Experience DVD (filmed on location during an actual tour), visit www.rick steves.com or call the Tour Department at 425/608-4217.

maps from the TI offices. (You can get free maps of Dublin and Ireland from Tourism Ireland before you go; see "Tourist Offices" at the beginning of this chapter.) If you're driving, get a road atlas that covers all of Ireland. Ordnance Survey atlases are best and available only once you reach Ireland (€10 in TIs, gas stations, and bookstores). Drivers, hikers, and cyclists may want more detailed maps for Dingle, Connemara, Donegal, Wexford, the Antrim Coast, the Ring of Kerry, and the Valley of the Boyne (easy to buy locally at TIs).

Other Guidebooks

If you're like most travelers, this book is all you need. But if you're heading beyond my recommended destinations, $40 for extra maps and books can be money well spent.

Racks of fine guidebooks are sold at bookstores throughout Ireland and in the US, and each place you will visit has plenty of great little guidebooks to fill you in on local history. Especially for several people traveling by car, the extra weight and expense are negligible. Note that most of the following guidebooks are not updated annually; check the publication date before you buy.

For cultural and sightseeing background in bigger chunks, Michelin and Cadogan guides to Ireland are good. The Lonely Planet and Let's Go books on Ireland are fine budget-travel guides—Lonely Planet's guidebook is more thorough and informative; *Let's Go Ireland* is youth-oriented, with good coverage of nightlife, hostels, and cheap transportation deals. Also consider *Culture Shock: Ireland* and *Living Abroad in Ireland*, especially if you'll be in the Emerald Isle for an extended stay.

Recommended Books and Movies

To learn more about Ireland past and present, check out a few of these books or films:

Nonfiction

For a quick overview, Richard Killeen's *A Short History of Ireland* is a well-illustrated walk through key events. *Ireland: A Concise History* (Máire and Conor Cruise O'Brien) is just that, while *How the Irish Saved Civilization* (Thomas Cahill) shows how this "island of saints and scholars" changed the course of world history. In *Traveller's History of Ireland,* Peter Neville leads readers on a tour through Ireland's complicated history.

Frank McCourt's autobiography, *Angela's Ashes,* recounts his impoverished childhood in 1930s Limerick. *Are You Somebody? The Accidental Memoir of a Dublin Woman* (Nuala O'Faolain) and *To School Through the Fields* (Alice Taylor) are well-written memoirs. Two New Yorkers move to a tiny Irish village in *O Come Ye Back to*

502 Rick Steves' Ireland

Ireland (first in a series of four books by Niall Williams and Christine Breen). For a humorous jaunt through the Irish countryside, read *Round Ireland with a Fridge* (Tony Hawks) or *The Back of Beyond: A Search for the Soul of Ireland* (James Charles Roy).

Fiction

Ireland is the home to its share of great writers, among them masters such as James Joyce (try his *Dubliners* for a look at Irish life in the 1900s), Oscar Wilde, Jonathan Swift, W. B. Yeats, George Bernard Shaw, and Samuel Beckett. Other classic Irish authors include Brendan Behan, Oliver Goldsmith, Thomas Kinsella, and Seamus Heaney (for more on Irish literature, see page 460).

Edward Rutherfurd's thick, two-part *Dublin Saga* traces key events in Irish history from A.D. 430 to the fight for independence. Other historical epics include *Trinity* (Leon Uris), *The Last Prince of Ireland* (Morgan Llywelyn), and *Ireland* (Frank Delaney).

The Bódhran Makers (John B. Keane) is a heartwarming look at poor families in 1950s Ireland. Roddy Doyle's gritty novels, such as *The Barrytown Trilogy* and *A Star Called Henry,* capture the day-to-day life of working-class Dubliners. Also set in Dublin, *Finbar's Hotel* and *Ladies' Night at Finbar's Hotel* (Dermot Bolger) were written collaboratively, with each chapter penned by a different modern Irish author. Consider also any of Maeve Binchy's soapy novels such as *Circle of Friends.*

Films

The Quiet Man (1952), starring John Wayne as a disgraced boxer, remains a sentimental favorite. David Lean's epic WWI love story *Ryan's Daughter* (1970) was filmed near Dingle. If you're visiting the Aran Islands, *Man of Aran* (1934) is a classic documentary about the life of the island's people in the early 20th century (see page 314 for more details). For hard-hitting drama, see *The Field* (1991, an Irish farmer fights to keep his land) or *Angela's Ashes* (1999, based on the Frank McCourt memoir). In *Evelyn* (2002), single-dad Pierce Brosnan goes to court to keep his kids. Unwed mothers struggle to survive an abusive 1960s nunnery in *The Magdalene Sisters* (2003).

For insight into the struggle for independence from Britain, see *Michael Collins* (1996, Liam Neeson), a biopic about the Irish Free State revolutionary, and *The Wind That Shakes the Barley* (2006), told through the story of two brothers. *Odd Man Out* (1947) is a film noir about the early IRA, with a great scene filmed in Belfast's Crown Bar. The Troubles haunt a widow and her lover in *Cal* (1984). In *In the Name of the Father* (1993, Daniel Day-Lewis) is a biopic of accused bomber Gerry Conlon. The families of IRA hunger strikers are the focus of *Some Mother's Son* (1996), while the documentary-like *Omagh* (2004) recounts a deadly 1998 IRA bombing. In *Fifty Dead Men Walking* (2008), an IRA informer navigates the brutal world of the Troubles.

Equally bleak but worthwhile films include *My Left Foot* (1989), which garnered an Academy Award for Daniel Day-Lewis, and *Veronica Guerin* (2003), in which Cate Blanchett exposes drug lords as a journalist.

For a fun, throwaway romance, try *Far and Away* (1992), with Tom Cruise and Nicole Kidman as penniless Irish immigrants. For a comedic break, watch at least one of the films adapted from books by Roddy Doyle: *The Commitments* (1991), *The Snapper* (1993), or *The Van* (1996). In *Waking Ned Devine* (1998), a deceased villager wins the lottery (it's funnier than it sounds). Children bring Irish folk tales to life in *Into the West* (1993) and *The Secret of Roan Inish* (1995). *Leap Year* (2009), with Amy Adams, was filmed on Inishmore (which was confusingly called Dingle in the film).

Holidays and Festivals

This list includes selected festivals in major cities, plus national holidays observed throughout Ireland in 2013. Many sights and banks close down on national holidays—keep this in mind when planning your itinerary. Before planning a trip around a festival, make sure you verify its dates by checking the festival's website or TI site (www.discoverireland.com). For sports events, see www.sportsevents365.com for schedules and ticket information.

Jan 1	New Year's Day (banks closed)
Jan 23-27	Temple Bar Trad, Dublin (Irish music and culture festival, http://templebartrad.com)
March 15-18	St. Patrick's Day celebration throughout Ireland (parades, drunkenness, 4-day festival in Dublin, www.stpatricksday.ie)
March 29	Good Friday (banks closed)
March 31-April 1	Easter Sunday and Monday
Early April	Pan Celtic International Festival (festival rotates locations every year, www.panceltic.ie)
May 6	Early May Bank Holiday, Ireland and UK (banks closed)
June 3	Spring Bank Holiday, UK (banks closed); also June Holiday, Ireland (banks closed)
June 16	Bloomsday, Dublin (James Joyce festival, www.jamesjoyce.ie)

APPENDIX

2013

JANUARY
S	M	T	W	T	F	S
		1	2	3	4	5
6	7	8	9	10	11	12
13	14	15	16	17	18	19
20	21	22	23	24	25	26
27	28	29	30	31		

FEBRUARY
S	M	T	W	T	F	S
					1	2
3	4	5	6	7	8	9
10	11	12	13	14	15	16
17	18	19	20	21	22	23
24	25	26	27	28		

MARCH
S	M	T	W	T	F	S
					1	2
3	4	5	6	7	8	9
10	11	12	13	14	15	16
17	18	19	20	21	22	23
24/31	25	26	27	28	29	30

APRIL
S	M	T	W	T	F	S
	1	2	3	4	5	6
7	8	9	10	11	12	13
14	15	16	17	18	19	20
21	22	23	24	25	26	27
28	29	30				

MAY
S	M	T	W	T	F	S
			1	2	3	4
5	6	7	8	9	10	11
12	13	14	15	16	17	18
19	20	21	22	23	24	25
26	27	28	29	30	31	

JUNE
S	M	T	W	T	F	S
						1
2	3	4	5	6	7	8
9	10	11	12	13	14	15
16	17	18	19	20	21	22
23/30	24	25	26	27	28	29

JULY
S	M	T	W	T	F	S
	1	2	3	4	5	6
7	8	9	10	11	12	13
14	15	16	17	18	19	20
21	22	23	24	25	26	27
28	29	30	31			

AUGUST
S	M	T	W	T	F	S
				1	2	3
4	5	6	7	8	9	10
11	12	13	14	15	16	17
18	19	20	21	22	23	24
25	26	27	28	29	30	31

SEPTEMBER
S	M	T	W	T	F	S
1	2	3	4	5	6	7
8	9	10	11	12	13	14
15	16	17	18	19	20	21
22	23	24	25	26	27	28
29	30					

OCTOBER
S	M	T	W	T	F	S
		1	2	3	4	5
6	7	8	9	10	11	12
13	14	15	16	17	18	19
20	21	22	23	24	25	26
27	28	29	30	31		

NOVEMBER
S	M	T	W	T	F	S
					1	2
3	4	5	6	7	8	9
10	11	12	13	14	15	16
17	18	19	20	21	22	23
24	25	26	27	28	29	30

DECEMBER
S	M	T	W	T	F	S
1	2	3	4	5	6	7
8	9	10	11	12	13	14
15	16	17	18	19	20	21
22	23	24	25	26	27	28
29	30	31				

July 12	Battle of the Boyne anniversary, Northern Ireland (Protestant marches, protests)
Mid- to late July	Galway Arts Festival (www.galwayartsfestival.com)
Late July-early Aug	Galway Races (www.galwayraces.com)
Aug 5	August Bank Holiday, Ireland (banks closed)
Early Aug	Dingle Races (horse races, www.dingleraces.ie)
Early-Mid-Aug	Dingle Regatta (boat races)
Aug 10-12	Puck Fair, Killorglin, Kerry ("Ireland's Oldest Fair" and drink-fest, www.puckfair.ie)
Mid-Aug	Kenmare Fair (www.kenmare.com)

Mid-Aug	Féile an Phobail, West Belfast (Irish cultural festival, www.feilebelfast.com)
Aug 26	Late Summer Bank Holiday, UK only (banks closed)
Late Aug	Rose of Tralee International Festival (http://roseoftralee.ie)
Late Aug-Early Sept	Blessing of the Boats, Dingle (maritime festival)
Mid-Sept	Galway Races (www.galwayraces.com)
Late Sept	Galway Oyster Festival (4 days, www.galwayoysterfest.com)
Late Oct-Early Nov	Belfast Festival at Queen's (www.belfastfestival.com)
Late Oct	Galway Races (www.galwayraces.com)
Oct 28	October Bank Holiday, Ireland (banks closed)
Dec 25	Christmas holiday, Ireland and UK
Dec 26	St. Stephen's Day, Ireland (religious festival); Boxing Day, UK
Dec 31	New Year's Eve

Conversions and Climate

Numbers and Stumblers

• In Europe, dates appear as day/month/year, so Christmas is 25/12/13.

• What Americans call the second floor of a building is the first floor in Europe.

• On escalators and moving sidewalks, Europeans keep the left "lane" open for passing. Keep to the right.

Metric Conversions (Approximate)

Both the Republic of Ireland and Northern Ireland use the metric system for nearly everything but driving measurements. Weight and volume are typically calculated in metric: A kilogram is 2.2 pounds, and a liter is about a quart. The weight of a person is measured by "stone" (one stone equals 14 pounds). Temperatures are generally given in both Celsius and Fahrenheit.

On the road, the Republic of Ireland is still converting from miles to kilometers, and you'll likely see signs in both (especially in rural destinations). Northern Ireland uses miles and posts speed limits in miles per hour.

1 foot = 0.3 meter	1 square yard = 0.8 square meter
1 yard = 0.9 meter	1 square mile = 2.6 square kilometers
1 mile = 1.6 kilometers	1 ounce = 28 grams
1 centimeter = 0.4 inch	1 quart = 0.95 liter

1 meter = 39.4 inches   1 kilogram = 2.2 pounds
1 kilometer = 0.62 mile   32°F = 0°C

Clothing Sizes

When shopping for clothing, use these US-to-Ireland comparisons as general guidelines (but note that no conversion is perfect).

- Women's dresses and blouses: Add 4 (US women's size 10 = Ireland size 14)
- Men's suits and jackets: US and Ireland use the same sizing
- Men's shirts: US and Ireland use the same sizing
- Women's shoes: Subtract 2½ (US size 8 = Ireland size 5½)
- Men's shoes: Subtract about ½ (US size 9 = Ireland size 8½)

Ireland's Climate

First line, average daily high; second line, average daily low; third line, average days without rain. For more detailed weather statistics for destinations in this book (as well as the rest of the world), check www.worldclimate.com.

J	F	M	A	M	J	J	A	S	O	N	D
Dublin											
46°	47°	51°	55°	60°	65°	67°	67°	63°	57°	51°	47°
34°	35°	37°	39°	43°	48°	52°	51°	48°	43°	39°	37°
18	18	21	19	21	19	18	19	18	20	18	17

Temperature Conversion: Fahrenheit and Celsius

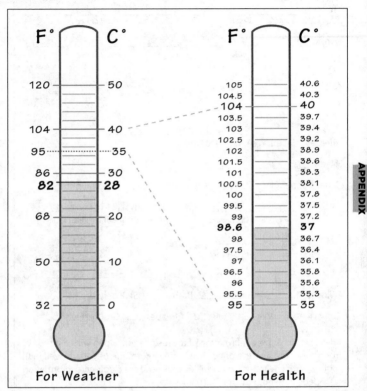

For Weather　　　　　For Health

Ireland uses both Celsius and Fahrenheit to take its temperature. For a rough conversion from Celsius to Fahrenheit, double the number and add 30. For weather, remember that 28°C is 82°F—perfect. For health, 37°C is just right.

Hotel Reservation

To: _____   _____
         hotel   **email or fax**

From: _____   _____
         name   **email or fax**

Today's date: _____ /_____ /_____
                day   **month**   **year**

Dear Hotel _____ ,
Please make this reservation for me:

Name: _____

Total # of people: _____   # of rooms: _____   # of nights: _____

Arriving: ____ /____ /____   My time of arrival (24-hr clock): _____
         day month year   (I will telephone if I will be late)

Departing: ____ /____ /____
            day month year

Room(s): Single___   Double ___   Twin___   Triple ___   Quad___

With: Toilet ___   Shower ___   Bath ___   Sink only___

Special needs: View___   Quiet___   Cheapest ___   Ground Floor___

Please email or fax confirmation of my reservation, along with the type of room reserved and the price. Please also inform me of your cancellation policy. After I hear from you, I will quickly send my credit-card information as a deposit to hold the room. Thank you.

_____
Name

_____
Address

_____
City   **State**   **Zip Code**   **Country**

Before hoteliers can make your reservation, they want to know the information listed above. You can use this form as the basis for your email, or you can photocopy this page, fill in the information, and send it as a fax (also available online at www.ricksteves.com/reservation).

Packing Checklist

Whether you're traveling for five days or five weeks, here's what you'll need to bring. Pack light to enjoy the sweet freedom of true mobility. Happy travels!

- ❑ 5 shirts: long- and short-sleeve
- ❑ 1 sweater or lightweight fleece
- ❑ 2 pairs pants
- ❑ 1 pair shorts
- ❑ 1 swimsuit
- ❑ 5 pairs underwear and socks
- ❑ 1 pair shoes
- ❑ 1 rainproof jacket with hood
- ❑ Tie or scarf
- ❑ Money belt
- ❑ Money—your mix of:
  - ❑ Debit card (for ATM withdrawals)
  - ❑ Credit card
  - ❑ Hard cash (in easy-to-exchange $20 bills)
- ❑ Documents plus photocopies:
  - ❑ Passport
  - ❑ Printout of airline eticket
  - ❑ Driver's license
  - ❑ Student ID and hostel card
  - ❑ Railpass/car rental voucher
  - ❑ Insurance details
- ❑ Daypack
- ❑ Electronics—your choice of:
  - ❑ Camera (and related gear)
  - ❑ Computer/mobile devices (phone, MP3 player, ereader, etc.)
  - ❑ Chargers for each of the above
  - ❑ Plug adapter
- ❑ Empty water bottle

- ❑ Wristwatch and alarm clock
- ❑ Earplugs
- ❑ Toiletries kit
  - ❑ Toiletries
  - ❑ Medicines and vitamins
  - ❑ First-aid kit
  - ❑ Glasses/contacts/sunglasses (with prescriptions)
- ❑ Sealable plastic baggies
- ❑ Laundry soap
- ❑ Clothesline
- ❑ Small towel
- ❑ Sewing kit
- ❑ Travel information (guidebooks and maps)
- ❑ Address list (for sending postcards)
- ❑ Postcards and photos from home
- ❑ Notepad and pen
- ❑ Journal

If you plan to carry on your luggage, note that all liquids must be in 3.4-ounce or smaller containers and fit within a single quart-size sealable baggie. For details, see www.tsa.gov/travelers.

INDEX

MAP INDEX

Rick's Free Travel App

Get your FREE **Rick Steves Audio Europe**™ app to enjoy...

- Dozens of self-guided tours of Europe's top museums, sights and historic walks
- Hundreds of tracks filled with cultural insights and sightseeing tips from Rick's radio interviews
- All organized into handy geographic playlists
- For iPhone, iPad, iPod Touch, Android

With Rick whispering in your ear, Europe gets even better.

Find out more at ricksteves.com

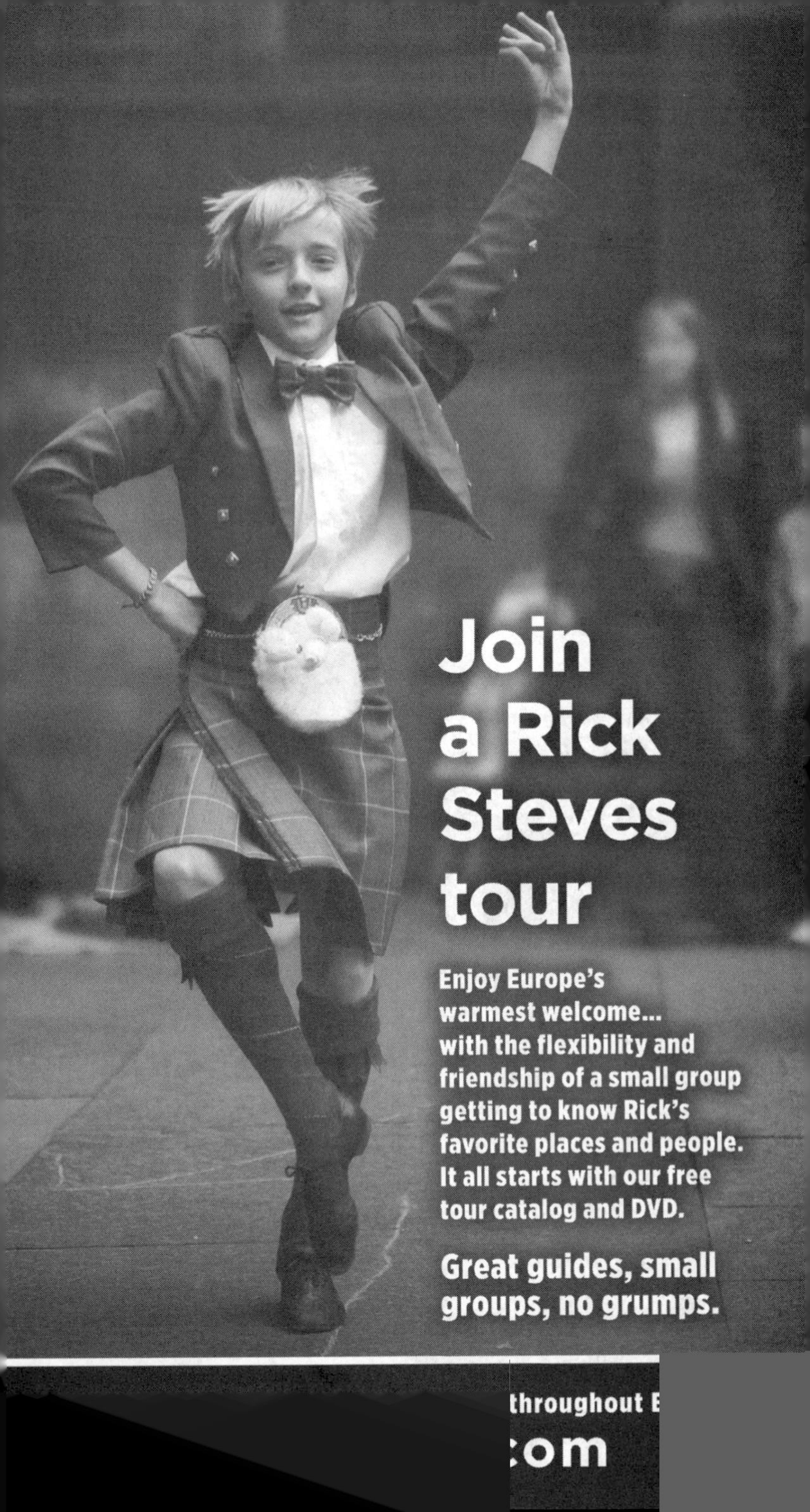

Join a Rick Steves tour

Enjoy Europe's warmest welcome... with the flexibility and friendship of a small group getting to know Rick's favorite places and people. It all starts with our free tour catalog and DVD.

Great guides, small groups, no grumps.

throughout E

:om

▶ Plan Your Trip

Browse thousands of articles and a wealth of money-saving tips for planning your dream trip. You'll find up-to-date information on Europe's best destinations, packing smart, getting around, finding rooms, staying healthy, avoiding scams and more.

▶ Eurail Passes

Find out, step-by-step, if a railpass makes sense for your trip—and how to avoid buying more than you need. Get free shipping on online orders

▶ Graffiti Wall & Travelers Helpline

Learn, ask, share—our online community of savvy travelers is a great resource for first-time travelers to Europe, as well as seasoned pros.

Rick Steves' Europe Through the Back Door, Inc.

turn your travel dreams into affordable reality

▸ Free Audio Tours & Travel Newsletter

Get your nose out of this guide book and focus on what you'll be seeing with Rick's free audio tours of the greatest sights in Athens, Austria, Florence, Germany, London, Paris, Rome, Turkey and Venice.

Subscribe to our free Travel News e-newsletter, and get monthly articles from Rick on what's happening in Europe.

▸ Great Gear from Rick's Travel Store

Pack light and right—on a budget—with Rick's custom-designed carry-on bags, wheeled bags, day packs, travel accessories, guidebooks, journals, maps and DVDs of his TV shows.

130 Fourth Avenue North, PO Box 2009 • Edmonds, WA 98020 USA
Phone: (425) 771-8303 • Fax: (425) 771-0833 • ricksteves.com

Rick Steves®

www.ricksteves.com

EUROPE GUIDES

Best of Europe
Eastern Europe
Europe Through the Back Door
Mediterranean Cruise Ports
Northern European Cruise Ports

COUNTRY GUIDES

Croatia & Slovenia
England
France
Germany
Great Britain
Ireland
Italy
Portugal
Scandinavia
Spain
Switzerland

CITY & REGIONAL GUIDES

Amsterdam, Bruges & Brussels
Barcelona
Budapest
Florence & Tuscany
Greece: Athens & the Peloponnese
Istanbul
London
Paris
Prague & the Czech Republic
Provence & the French Riviera
Rome
Venice
Vienna, Salzburg & Tirol

SNAPSHOT GUIDES

Berlin
Bruges & Brussels
Copenhagen & the Best of Denmark
Dublin
Dubrovnik
Hill Towns of Central Italy
Italy's Cinque Terre
Krakow, Warsaw & Gdansk
Lisbon
Madrid & Toledo
Milan & the Italian Lakes District
Munich, Bavaria & Salzburg
Naples & the Amalfi Coast
Northern Ireland
Norway
Scotland
Sevilla, Granada & Southern Spain
Stockholm

POCKET GUIDES

Athens
Barcelona
Florence
London
Paris
Rome
Venice

Rick Steves guidebooks are published by Avalon Travel,
a member of the Perseus Books Group.

NOW AVAILABLE:
eBOOKS, DVD & BLU-RAY

TRAVEL CULTURE

Europe 101
European Christmas
Postcards from Europe
Travel as a Political Act

eBOOKS

*Nearly all Rick Steves guides
are available as eBooks. Check
with your favorite bookseller.*

RICK STEVES' EUROPE DVDs

11 New Shows 2013–2014
Austria & the Alps
Eastern Europe
England & Wales
European Christmas
European Travel Skills & Specials
France
Germany, BeNeLux & More
Greece, Turkey & Portugal
Iran
Ireland & Scotland
Italy's Cities
Italy's Countryside
Scandinavia
Spain
Travel Extras

BLU-RAY

Celtic Charms
Eastern Europe Favorites
European Christmas
Italy Through the Back Door
Mediterranean Mosaic
Surprising Cities of Europe

PHRASE BOOKS & DICTIONARIES

French
French, Italian & German
German
Italian
Portuguese
Spanish

JOURNALS

Rick Steves' Pocket Travel Journal
Rick Steves' Travel Journal

PLANNING MAPS

Britain, Ireland & London
Europe
France & Paris
Germany, Austria & Switzerland
Ireland
Italy
Spain & Portugal

Rick Steves books and DVDs are available at bookstores
and through online booksellers.

Credits

Contributor
Gene Openshaw

Gene is the co-author of 10 Rick Steves books. For this book, he wrote material on Ireland's art, history, and contemporary culture. When not traveling, Gene enjoys composing music, recovering from his 1973 trip to Europe with Rick, and living every-day life with his daughter.

Acknowledgments
Thanks to Rozanne Stringer for her writing on the Celts, the Celtic Tiger, St. Brendan, and Irish art. Thanks also to Mike Kelly for his help.

Images

Location	Photographer
Republic of Ireland (full page): Cliffs of Moher, near Galway	Pat O'Connor
Dublin: Ha' Penny Bridge	Pat O'Connor
Near Dublin: Newgrange, in Valley of the Boyne	Pat O'Connor
Kilkenny and Cashel: Rock of Cashel	Pat O'Connor
Waterford and County Wexford: Waterford's Waterfront	Pat O'Connor
Kinsale and Cobh: Kinsale's Summer Cove Area	Pat O'Connor
Kenmare and Ring of Kerry: Ring of Kerry	Pat O'Connor
Dingle Peninsula: Great Blasket Island	Pat O'Connor
County Clare and the Burren: Poulnabrone Dolmen, The Burren	Pat O'Connor
Galway: High Street	Pat O'Connor
The Aran Islands: The Aran Islands	Pat O'Connor
Connemara and County Mayo: Lough Corrib, Connemara	Pat O'Connor
Northern Ireland (full page): Giant's Causeway, Antrim Coast	Pat O'Connor
Belfast: Donegall Square and City Hall	Pat O'Connor
Portrush and Antrim Coast: Portrush Harbor	Pat O'Connor
Derry and County Donegal: Derry's Walls	David C. Hoerlein